THE
Norton Anthology of Poetry

SHORTER EDITION

THE
Norton Anthology
of Poetry

SHORTER EDITION

ARTHUR M. EASTMAN, *Coordinating Editor*
CARNEGIE-MELLON UNIVERSITY

ALEXANDER W. ALLISON
UNIVERSITY OF MICHIGAN

HERBERT BARROWS
UNIVERSITY OF MICHIGAN

CAESAR R. BLAKE
UNIVERSITY OF TORONTO

ARTHUR J. CARR
WILLIAMS COLLEGE

HUBERT M. ENGLISH, JR.
UNIVERSITY OF MICHIGAN

W · W · NORTON & COMPANY · INC ·
NEW YORK

Contents

Preface

꘎꘎꘎

The Shorter Edition of *The Norton Anthology of Poetry*, like the larger book of English and American poetry from which it is compacted, is particularly ample at both ends of the chronological spectrum, the medieval being lyrically richer than is sometimes recognized and the contemporary, denied the endorsement of tradition, meriting a generous if tentative acceptance. All along, the book attempts a discriminating selection of the poets it contains. Long-familiar selections have been re-examined, though without animus, and have sometimes been displaced by works less familiar. Manifestly this edition contains fewer of the long works of the larger edition, but since the goal has been to represent the whole range of verse in English, the long as well as the lyric and epigrammatic, space has still been found for *The Nun's Priest's Tale* and *The Rape of the Lock,* and for whole and self-contained segments from *The Prelude* and *In Memoriam.*

The order is chronological, poets appearing according to the dates of their births (American poets conflated with the British), and their poems according to the dates of their publication in volume form. These dates follow the poems on the right; when two appear together, they point to significantly different published versions. Dates toward the left, when given, are those of composition.

Texts derive from authoritative editions but have been normalized in spelling and capitalization according to modern American usage—except in the many instances in which changes would significantly obscure meter or meaning. The works of Spenser and Burns, contrivedly archaic or dialectic in spelling, have been left untouched, as have the oldest of the medieval poems, which would remain to modern eyes almost as opaque after normalizing and modernizing as before. The metrically idiosyncratic Hopkins also remains unchanged. For the normalized text of Chaucer selections (except for "Against Women Unconstant"), as well as for the notes to them, the editors particularly wish to thank Professor E. T. Donaldson.

Notes, as Dr. Johnson observed, are necessary, but necessary evils. They have been provided for information, not criticism; they gloss words and allusions but refrain, as much as possible, from interpretive comment. A terminal glossary, with a prefatory commentary, identifies the technical terms of prosody.

The editors are pleased to acknowledge the critical assistance they have received from Professors John E. Booty of The Episcopal Theological School, David Brewster of the University of Washington, Robert Dana of Cornell College, Lawrence Dembo of The University of Wisconsin, Donald Finkel of Bennington College, Charles Fuqua of Williams College, Cecil M. McCulley of the College of William and Mary, Robert Pack of Middlebury College, Richard Poirier of Rutgers University, and William C. Pratt of Miami University. And, most especially, they wish to recognize the saving sanity with which M. H. Abrams guided them at certain perilous junctures, and the sharp eyes, tolerance, and immense helpfulness on which they came regularly to rely from John Benedict and his co-workers at W. W. Norton, Mrs. Elissa Epel and Mrs. Carol Paradis.

Note on the Modernizing of Medieval Texts

Changes that have taken place in pronunciation obscure for the modern reader the regular metrical character of some Middle English verse. The most important of these changes is the loss of an unstressed syllable in many word endings. We still pronounce some endings as separate syllables (*roses, wedded*), but for Chaucer the full syllabic value of an ending was available generally, even though its pronunciation was not always mandatory. Moreover, a great many final *—e's*, vestiges of fuller endings at an earlier stage of the language, were still often pronounced (ə) in the ordinary speech of the day, so that the poet could treat them as syllables or not, according to the requirements of his meter, as *boughte* (pronounced either *bought* or *boughtë*) and *ofte* (pronounced either *oft* or *oftë*).

In modernizing, the editors have tried wherever possible to preserve or devise spellings that do not cut the reader off from the possibility of recovering the original rhythms. A non-modern spelling, especially at the end of a word, means that in the original text there is warrant for supposing that an "extra" syllable might have been pronounced at this point to justify metrical expectation. At the same time the editors have tried to avoid imposing a non-modern reading in those cases where a clear metrical pattern is not manifest.

THE
Norton Anthology of Poetry

SHORTER EDITION

ANONYMOUS LYRICS OF THE
THIRTEENTH AND FOURTEENTH CENTURIES

The Cuckoo Song[1]

Sing, cuccu, nu. Sing, cuccu.
Sing, cuccu. Sing, cuccu, nu.

Sumer is i-cumen in—
   Lhude sing, cuccu!
Groweth sed and bloweth med
   And springth the wude nu.
     Sing, cuccu!

Awe bleteth after lomb,
   Lhouth after calve cu,
Bulluc sterteth, bucke verteth—
   Murie sing, cuccu!
     Cuccu, cuccu.
Wel singes thu, cuccu.
Ne swik thu naver nu!

Ubi Sunt Qui Ante Nos Fuerunt?

Were beth they biforen us weren,[2]
Houndes ladden and hauekes beren
   And hadden feld and wode?
   The riche levedies in hoere bour,
     That wereden gold in hoere tressour,
With hoere brightte rode,

Eten and drounken and maden hem glad;
Hoere lif was al with gamen i-lad;
   Men keneleden hem biforen;
     They beren hem wel swithe heye—
     And in a twincling of an eye
Hoere soules weren forloren.

1. *Translation:* Sing, cuckoo, now. Sing, cuckoo. / Sing, cuckoo. Sing, cuckoo, now.
Spring is come in— / Sing loud, cuckoo! / The seed grows, the meadow blooms / And buck breaks wind— / Sing merrily cuckoo!
The ewe bleats after the lamb, / The cow lows after the calf, / The bullock leaps, the buck breaks wind— / Sing merrily, cuckoo! / Cuckoo, cuckoo. / Well singest thou, cuckoo. / Cease thou never now!
2. The poem's first line translates the title. *Translation:* Where be they who before us were, / Who led hounds and bore hawks / And owned fields and woods? / The rich ladies in their bowers, / That wore gold in their coiffures, / and had fair faces,
[That] ate and drank and rejoiced; / Their life was all a game; / Men knelt before them; / They bore themselves exceeding high— / And in the twinkling of an eye / Their souls were lost.
Where is that laughing and that song, / That trailing [of garments] and that proud gait, / Those hawks and those hounds? / All that joy is gone away; / That well has come to wellaway, / To many hard times.
Their paradise they took here, / And now they lie in hell together— / The fire it burns ever. / Long is their "ay" and long their "oh," / Long their "alas" and long their "woe"— / Thence shall they come never.

Suffer here, man, then if thou wilt, / The little pain thou art asked to bear. / Withdraw thine eyes oft [from the things of this world]. / Though thy pain be severe, / If thou think on thy reward, / It shall seem soft to thee.
If that fiend, that foul thing, / Through wicked counsel, through false tempting, / Has cast thee down, / Up and be a good champion! / Stand, and fall no more / For a little blast [for a mere puff of wind].
Take thou the cross for thy staff / And think on him that thereon gave / His life that was so dear. / He gave it for thee; repay him for it / Against his foe. Take thou that staff / And avenge him on that thief.
Of right belief [true faith] take thou the shield / While thou art in the field. / Seek to strengthen thy hand / And keep thy foe at staff's end / And make that traitor say the word [of surrender]. Gain that merry land
Wherein is day without night, / Without end strength and might, / And vengeance on every foe, / With God himself eternal life, / And peace and rest without strife, / Weal without woe.
Maiden mother, heaven's queen, / Thou might and can and ought to be / Our shield against the fiend. / Help us to flee from sins / That we may see thy son / In joy without end. / Amen.

Were is that lawing and that song,
That trayling and that proude yong,
15   Tho hauekes and tho houndes?
      Al that joye is went away;
      That wele is comen to welaway,
    To manie harde stoundes.

Hoere paradis hy nomen here,
20   And nou they lien in helle i-fere—
    The fuir hit brennes hevere.
      Long is ay and long is ho,
      Long is wy and long is wo—
    Thennes ne cometh they nevere.

25   Dreghy here, man, thenne if thou wilt,
A luitel pine, that me the bit.
    Withdrau thine eyses ofte.
      They thi pine be ounrede,
      And thou thenke on thi mede,
30   Hit sal the thinken softe.

If that fend, that foule thing,
Thorou wikke roun, thorou fals egging,
    Nethere the haveth i-cast,
      Oup, and be god chaunpioun!
35   Stond, ne fal namore adoun
    For a luytel blast.

Thou tak the rode to thi staf
And thenk on him that thereonne yaf
    His lif that wes so lef.
40   He hit yaf for the; thou yelde hit him
      Ayein his fo. That staf thou nim
    And wrek him of that thef.

Of rightte bileve thou nim that sheld
The wiles that thou best in that feld.
45   Thin hond to strenkthen fonde
      And kep thy fo with staves ord
      And do that traytre seien that word.
    Biget that murie londe

Thereinne is day withouten night,
50   Withouten ende strenkthe and might,
    And wreche of everich fo,
      Mid god himselwen eche lif
      And pes and rest withoute strif,
    Wele withouten wo.

55   Mayden moder, hevene quene,
Thou might and const and owest to bene
    Oure sheld ayein the fende.
      Help ous sunne for to flen
      That we moten thi sone i-seen
60   In joye withouten hende.
                 Amen.

Steadfast Cross

Stedefast crosse, among all other
  Thou art a tree mickle of price;[3]
In branch and flower swilk° another
  I ne wot° none in wood no rys,°   *such / know / nor thicket*
5 Sweete be the nailes and sweete be the tree,
  And sweeter be the burden that hanges upon thee.

such
know / nor thicket

Bishop Loreless

Bishop loreless,°   *without learning*
King redeless,°   *without counsel*
Young men reckless,°   *heedless*
Old man witless,
5 Woman shameless—
  I swear by heaven's king,
  Those be five lither thing!°   *evil things*

All Night by the Rose

All night by the rose, rose—
  All night by the rose I lay;
Dared I not the rose steal,
  And yet I bore the flower away.

At a Spring-Well

At a spring-well° under a thorn   *spring*
There was bote of bale[4] a little here a-forn;°   *before*
  There beside stands a maid
Full of love i-bound.°   *bound*
5   Whoso will seek true love,
In her it shall be found.

GEOFFREY CHAUCER
(ca. 1343–1400)

The Nun's Priest's Tale

A poore widwe somdeel stape° in age   *advanced*
Was whilom° dwelling in a narwe° cotage,   *once upon a time / small*
Biside a grove, stonding in a dale:
This widwe of which I telle you my tale,
5 Sin thilke° day that she was last a wif,   *that same*
In pacience ladde° a ful simple lif.   *led*
For litel was hir catel° and hir rente,°   *property / income*
By housbondrye° of swich as God hire sente   *economy*
She foond° hirself and eek hir doughtren two.   *provided for*
10 Three large sowes hadde she and namo,
Three kin,° and eek a sheep that highte Malle.   *cows*
Ful sooty was hir bowr° and eek hir halle,   *bedroom*
In which she eet ful many a sclendre° meel;   *scanty*
Of poinant° sauce hire needed neveradeel: *pungent*

3. Great of worth.   4. Remedy for evil.

15 No daintee morsel passed thurgh hir throte—
    Hir diete was accordant to hir cote.° — *cottage*
    Repleccioun° ne made hire nevere sik: — *overeating*
    Attempre° diete was al hir physik,° — *moderate / medicine*
    And exercise and hertes suffisaunce.° — *contentment*
20 The goute lette hire nothing for to daunce,[1]
    N'apoplexye shente° nat hir heed.° — *hurt / head*
    No win ne drank she, neither whit ne reed:° — *red*
    Hir boord° was served most with whit and blak,[2] — *table*
    Milk and brown breed, in which she foond no lak;[3]
25 Seind bacon, and somtime an ey° or twaye, — *egg*
    For she was as it were a manere daye.[4]
    A yeerd° she hadde, enclosed al withoute — *yard*
    With stikkes, and a drye dich aboute,
    In which she hadde a cok heet° Chauntecleer: — *named*
30 In al the land of crowing nas° his peer. — *was not*
    His vois was merier than the merye orgon
    On massedayes that in the chirche goon;[5]
    Wel sikerer[6] was his crowing in his logge° — *dwelling*
    Than is a clok or an abbeye orlogge;° — *timepiece*
35 By nature he knew eech ascensioun
    Of th'equinoxial[7] in thilke town:
    For whan degrees fifteene were ascended,
    Thanne crew° he that it mighte nat been amended.° — *crowed / improved*
    His comb was redder than the fin coral,
40 And batailed° as it were a castel wal; — *battlemented*
    His bile° was blak, and as the jeet° it shoon; — *bill / jet*
    Like asure° were his legges and his toon;° — *lapis lazuli / toes*
    His nailes whitter° than the lilye flowr, — *whiter*
    And lik the burned° gold was his colour. — *burnished*
45 This gentil cok hadde in his governaunce
    Sevene hennes for to doon al his plesaunce,° — *pleasure*
    Whiche were his sustres and his paramours,[8]
    And wonder like to him as of colours;
    Of whiche the faireste hewed° on hir throte — *colored*
50 Was cleped faire damoisele Pertelote:
    Curteis she was, discreet, and debonaire,° — *meek*
    And compaignable,° and bar° hirself so faire, — *companionable / bore*
    Sin thilke day that she was seven night old,
    That trewely she hath the herte in hold
55 Of Chauntecleer, loken° in every lith.° — *locked / limb*
    He loved hire so that wel was him therwith.[9]
    But swich a joye was it to heere hem singe,
    Whan that the brighte sonne gan to springe,
    In sweete accord *My Lief is Faren in Londe*[1]—
60 For thilke time, as I have understonde,
    Beestes and briddes couden speke and singe.
        And so bifel that in a daweninge,
    As Chauntecleer among his wives alle
    Sat on his perche that was in the halle,
65 And next him sat this faire Pertelote,
    This Chauntecleer gan gronen in his throte,
    As man that in his dreem is drecched° sore. — *troubled*
        And whan that Pertelote thus herde him rore,
    She was agast, and saide, "Herte dere,

---

1. The gout didn't hinder her at all from dancing.
2. I.e., milk and bread.
3. Found no fault. "Seind": scorched (i.e., broiled).
4. I.e., a kind of dairymaid.
5. I.e., is played.
6. More reliable.
7. I.e., he knew by instinct each step in the progression of the celestial equator. The celestial equator was thought to make a 360-degree rotation around the earth every 24 hours; therefore a progression of 15 degrees would be equal to the passage of an hour (line 37).
8. His sisters and his mistresses.
9. That he was well contented.
1. A popular song of the time.

70 What aileth you to grone in this manere?
    Ye been a verray slepere,[2] fy, for shame!"
        And he answerde and said thus, "Madame,
    I praye you that ye take it nat agrief.°   *amiss*
    By God, me mette I was in swich meschief[3]
75 Right now, that yit myn herte is sore afright.
    Now God," quod he, "my swevene recche aright.[4]
    And keepe my body out of foul prisoun!
    Me mette how that I romed up and down
    Within oure yeerd, wher as I sawgh a beest,
80 Was lik an hound and wolde han maad arrest[5]
    Upon my body, and han had me deed.[6]
    His colour was bitwixe yelow and reed,
    And tipped was his tail and bothe his eres
    With blak, unlik the remenant° of his heres;°   *rest / hairs*
85 His snoute smal, with glowing yën twaye.
    Yit of his look for fere almost I deye:°   *die*
    This caused me my groning, doutelees."
        "Avoi,"° quod she, "fy on you, hertelees!°   *fie / coward*
    Allas," quod she, "for by that God above,
90 Now han ye lost myn herte and al my love!
    I can nat love a coward, by my faith.
    For certes, what so any womman saith,
    We alle desiren, if it mighte be,
    To han housbondes hardy, wise, and free,°   *generous*
95 And secree,° and no nigard, ne no fool,   *discreet*
    Ne him that is agast of every tool,°   *weapon*
    Ne noon avauntour.° By that God above,   *boaster*
    How dorste ye sayn for shame unto youre love
    That any thing mighte make you aferd?
100 Have ye no mannes herte and han a beerd?
    Allas, and conne° ye been agast of swevenes?°   *can / dreams*
    No thing, God woot, but vanitee[7] in swevene is!
    Swevenes engendren of replexiouns,[8]
    And ofte of fume° and of complexiouns,°   *gas / bodily humors*
105 Whan humours been too habundant in a wight.[9]
    Certes, this dreem which ye han met° tonight   *dreamed*
    Comth of the grete superfluitee
    Of youre rede colera,[1] pardee,
    Which causeth folk to dreden° in hir dremes   *fear*
110 Of arwes,° and of fir with rede lemes,°   *arrows / flames*
    Of rede beestes, that they wol hem bite,
    Of contek,° and of whelpes grete and lite[2]—   *strife*
    Right° as the humour of malencolye[3]   *just*
    Causeth ful many a man in sleep to crye
115 For fere of blake beres° or boles° blake,   *hears / bulls*
    Or elles blake develes wol hem take.
    Of othere humours coude I tell also
    That werken many a man in sleep ful wo,
    But I wol passe as lightly° as I can.   *quickly*
120 Lo, Caton,[4] which that was so wis a man,
    Saide he nat thus? 'Ne do no fors of[5] dremes.'
    Now, sire," quod she, "whan we flee fro the bemes,[6]
    For Goddes love, as take som laxatif.

2. I.e., sound sleeper.
3. I dreamed that I was in such misfortune.
4. Interpret my dream correctly (i.e., in an auspicious manner).
5. Would have laid hold.
6. I.e., killed me.
7. I.e., empty illusion.
8. Dreams have their origin in overeating.
9. I.e., when humors are too abundant in a person. Pertelote's diagnosis is based on the familiar concept that an overabundance of one of the bodily humors in a person affected his temperament.
1. Red bile.
2. And of big and little dogs.
3. I.e., black bile.
4. Dionysius Cato, supposed author of a book of maxims used in elementary education.
5. Pay no attention to.
6. Fly down from the rafters.

Up° peril of my soule and of my lif,   *upon*
125   I conseile you the beste, I wol nat lie,
That bothe of colere and of malencolye
Ye purge you; and for° ye shal nat tarye,   *in order that*
Though in this town is noon apothecarye,
I shal myself to herbes techen you,
130   That shal been for youre hele[7] and for youre prow,
And in oure yeerd tho herbes shal I finde,
The whiche han of hir propretee by kinde°   *nature*
To purge you binethe and eek above;
Foryet° nat this, for Goddes owene love.   *forget*
135   Ye been ful colerik° of complexioun;   *bilious*
Ware° the sonne in his ascencioun   *beware that*
Ne finde you nat repleet° of humours hote;°   *filled / hot*
And if it do, I dar wel laye° a grote   *bet*
That ye shul have a fevere terciane,[8]
140   Or an agu that may be youre bane.°   *death*
A day or two ye shul han digestives
Of wormes, er ye take youre laxatives
Of lauriol, centaure, and fumetere,[9]
Or elles of ellebor° that groweth there,   *hellebore*
145   Of catapuce,° or of gaitres beries,°   *caper berry / gaiter berry*
Of herbe-ive° growing in oure yeerd ther merye is.[1]   *herb ivy*
Pekke hem right up as they growe and ete hem in.
Be merye, housbonde, for youre fader kin!
Dredeth no dreem: I can saye you namore."
150   "Madame," quod he, "graunt mercy of youre lore.[2]
But nathelees, as touching daun° Catoun,   *master*
That hath of wisdom swich a greet renown,
Though that he bad no dremes for to drede,
By God, men may in olde bookes rede
155   Of many a man more of auctoritee°   *authority*
Than evere Caton was, so mote I thee,°   *thrive*
That al the revers sayn of his sentence,°   *opinion*
And han wel founden by experience
That dremes been significaciouns
160   As wel of joye as tribulaciouns
That folk enduren in this lif present.
Ther needeth make of this noon argument:
The verray preve[3] sheweth it in deede.
"Oon of the gretteste auctour[4] that men rede
165   Saith thus, that whilom two felawes wente
On pilgrimage in a ful good entente,
And happed so they comen in a town,
Wher as ther was swich congregacioun
Of peple, and eek so strait of herbergage,[5]
170   That they ne founde as muche as oo cotage
In which they bothe mighte ylogged° be;   *lodged*
Wherfore they mosten° of necessitee   *must*
As for that night departe° compaignye.   *part*
And eech of hem gooth to his hostelrye,
175   And took his logging as it wolde falle.°   *befall*
That oon of hem was logged in a stalle,
Fer° in a yeerd, with oxen of the plough;   *far away*
That other man was logged wel ynough,
As was his aventure° or his fortune,   *lot*
180   That us governeth alle as in commune.

---

7. Health; "prow": benefit.
8. Tertian (recurring every other day).
9. Of laureole, centaury, and fumitory. These, and the herbs mentioned in the next lines, were all common medieval medicines used as cathartics.

1. Where it is pleasant.
2. Many thanks for your instruction.
3. Actual experience.
4. I.e., one of the greatest authors (perhaps Cicero).
5. And also such a shortage of lodging.

And so bifel that longe er it were day,
This man mette° in his bed, ther as he lay,　　　　　　　　*dreamed*
How that his felawe gan upon him calle,
And saide, 'Allas, for in an oxes stalle
185　This night I shal be mordred° ther I lie!　　　　　　　*murdered*
Now help me, dere brother, or I die!
In alle haste com to me,' he saide.
　　　"This man out of his sleep for fere abraide,°　　　*started up*
But whan that he was wakened of his sleep,
190　He turned him and took of this no keep:°　　　　　　*heed*
Him thoughte his dreem nas but a vanitee.
Thus twies in his sleeping dremed he,
And atte thridde time yit his felawe
Cam, as him thoughte, and saide, 'I am now slawe:°　　*slain*
195　Bihold my bloody woundes deepe and wide.
Aris up erly in the morwe tide⁶
And atte west gate of the town,' quod he,
'A carte ful of dong° ther shaltou see,　　　　　　　　*dung*
In which my body is hid ful prively:
200　Do thilke carte arresten boldely.⁷
My gold caused my mordre, sooth to sayn'—
And tolde him every point how he was slain,
With a ful pitous face, pale of hewe.
And truste wel, his dreem he foond° ful trewe,　　　　*found*
205　For on the morwe° as soone as it was day,　　　　　*morning*
To his felawes in° he took the way,　　　　　　　　　*lodging*
And whan that he cam to this oxes stalle,
After his felawe he bigan to calle.
　　　"The hostiler° answerde him anoon,　　　　　　*innkeeper*
210　And saide, 'Sire, youre felawe is agoon:°　　　　　*gone away*
As soone as day he wente out of the town.'
　　　"This man gan fallen in suspecioun,
Remembring on his dremes that he mette;°　　　　　　*dreamed*
And forth he gooth, no lenger wolde he lette,°　　　　*tarry*
215　Unto the west gate of the town, and foond
A dong carte, wente as it were to donge° lond,　　　*put manure on*
That was arrayed in that same wise
As ye han herd the dede° man devise;　　　　　　　　*dead*
And with an hardy herte he gan to crye,
220　'Vengeance and justice of this felonye!
My felawe mordred is this same night,
And in this carte he lith° gaping upright!'°　　　　*lies / supine*
I crye out on the ministres,' quod he,
'That sholde keepe and rulen this citee.
225　Harrow,° allas, here lith my felawe slain!'　　　　*help*
What sholde I more unto this tale sayn?
The peple up sterte° and caste the carte to grounde,　*started*
And in the middel of the dong they founde
The dede man that mordred was al newe.⁸
230　"O blisful God that art so just and trewe,
Lo, how that thou biwrayest° mordre alway!　　　　　*disclose*
Mordre wol out, that see we day by day:
Mordre is so wlatsom° and abhominable　　　　　　　*loathsome*
To God that is so just and resonable,
235　That he ne wol nat suffre it heled° be,　　　　　　*concealed*
Though it abide a yeer or two or three.
Mordre wol out: this my conclusioun.
And right anoon ministres of that town
Han hent° the cartere and so sore him pined,°　　　*seized / tortured*
240　And eek the hostiler so sore engined,°　　　　　　*racked*

6. In the morning.　　　　　　　　　8. Recently.
7. Boldly have this same cart stopped.

That they biknewe° hir wikkednesse anoon,   *confessed*
And were anhanged° by the nekke boon.   *hanged*
Here may men seen that dremes been to drede.[9]
      "And certes, in the same book I rede—
245 Right in the nexte chapitre after this—
I gabbe° nat, so have I joye or blis—   *lie*
Two men that wolde han passed over see
For certain cause into a fer contree,
If that the wind ne hadde been contrarye
250 That made hem in a citee for to tarye,
That stood ful merye upon an haven° side—   *harbor's*
But on a day again° the even tide   *toward*
The wind gan chaunge, and blewe right as hem leste:[1]
Jolif° and glad they wenten unto reste,   *merry*
255 And casten hem[2] ful erly for to saile.
      "But to that oo man fil° a greet mervaile;   *befell*
That oon of hem, in sleeping as he lay,
Him mette[3] a wonder dreem again the day:
Him thoughte a man stood by his beddes side,
260 And him comanded that he sholde abide,
And saide him thus, 'If thou tomorwe wende,
Thou shalt be dreint:° my tale is at an ende.'   *drowned*
      "He wook and tolde his felawe what he mette,
And prayed him his viage° to lette;°   *voyage / delay*
265 As for that day he prayed him to bide.
      "His felawe that lay by his beddes side
Gan for to laughe, and scorned him ful faste.°   *hard*
'No dreem,' quod he, 'may so myn herte agaste°   *terrify*
That I wol lette° for to do my thinges.°   *delay / business*
270 I sette nat a straw by thy dreminges,[4]
For swevenes been but vanitees and japes:[5]
Men dreme alday° of owles or of apes,[6]   *constantly*
And of many a maze° therwithal—   *delusion*
Men dreme of thing that nevere was ne shal.[7]
275 But sith I see that thou wolt here abide,
And thus forsleuthen° wilfully thy tide,°   *waste / time*
Good woot, it reweth me;[8] and have good day.'
And thus he took his leve and wente his way.
But er that he hadde half his cours ysailed—
280 Noot I nat why ne what meschaunce it ailed—
But casuelly the shippes botme rente,[9]
And ship and man under the water wente,
In sighte of othere shippes it biside,
That with hem sailed at the same tide.
285 And therfore, faire Pertelote so dere,
By swiche ensamples olde maistou lere°   *learn*
That no man sholde been too recchelees°   *careless*
Of dremes, for I saye thee doutelees
That many a dreem ful sore is for to drede.
290   "Lo, in the lif of Saint Kenelm[1] I rede—
That was Kenulphus sone, the noble king
Of Mercenrike°—how Kenelm mette a thing   *Mercia*
A lite° er he was mordred on a day.   *little*
His mordre in his avision° he sey.°   *dream / saw*
295 His norice° him expounded everydeel°   *nurse / entirely*

9. Worthy of being feared.
1. Just as they wished.
2. Determined.
3. He dreamed.
4. I don't care a straw for your dreamings.
5. Dreams are but illusions and frauds.
6. I.e., of absurdities.
7. I.e., shall be.

8. I'm sorry.
9. I don't know why nor what was the trouble with it—but accidentally the ship's bottom split.
1. Kenelm succeeded his father as king of Mercia at the age of 7 but was slain by his aunt (in 821).

His swevene, and bad him for to keepe him[2] weel
For traison, but he nas but seven yeer old,
And therfore litel tale hath he told
Of any dreem,[3] so holy was his herte.
300 By God, I hadde levere than my sherte[4]
That ye hadde rad° his legende as have I.   *read*
    "Dame Pertelote, I saye you trewely,
Macrobeus,[5] that writ the *Avisioun*
In Affrike of the worthy Scipioun,
305 Affermeth° dremes, and saith that they been   *confirms*
Warning of thinges that men after seen.
    "And ferthermore, I praye you looketh wel
In the Olde Testament of Daniel,
If he heeld° dremes any vanitee;[6]   *considered*
310 "Rede eek of Joseph[7] and ther shul ye see
Wher° dremes be somtime—I saye nat alle—   *whether*
Warning of thinges that shul after falle.
    "Looke of Egypte the king daun Pharao,
His bakere and his botelere° also,   *butler*
315 Wher they ne felte noon effect in dremes.[8]
Whoso wol seeke actes of sondry remes°   *realms*
May rede of dremes many a wonder thing.
    "Lo Cresus, which that was of Lyde° king,   *Lydia*
Mette° he nat that he sat upon a tree,   *dreamed*
320 Which signified he sholde anhanged° be?   *hanged*
    "Lo here Andromacha, Ectores° wif,   *Hector's*
That day that Ector sholde lese° his lif,   *lose*
She dremed on the same night biforn
How that the lif of Ector sholde be lorn,°   *lost*
325 If thilke° day he wente into bataile;   *that same*
She warned him, but it mighte nat availe:°   *do any good*
He wente for to fighte nathelees,
But he was slain anoon° of Achilles.   *right away*
But thilke tale is al too long to telle,
330 And eek it is neigh day, I may nat dwelle.
Shortly I saye, as for conclusioun,
That I shal han of this avisioun[9]
Adversitee, and I saye ferthermoor
That I ne telle of[1] laxatives no stoor,
335 For they been venimes,° I woot it weel: *poisons*
I hem defye, I love hem neveradeel.°   *not a bit*
    "Now lat us speke of mirthe and stinte° al this.   *stop*
Madame Pertelote, so have I blis,
Of oo thing God hath sente me large grace:
340 For whan I see the beautee of youre face—
Ye been so scarlet reed° aboute youre yën—   *red*
It maketh al my drede for to dien.
For also siker° as *In principio*,[2]   *certain*
Mulier est hominis confusio.[3]
345 Madame, the sentence° of this Latin is,   *meaning*
'Womman is mannes joye and al his blis.'
For whan I feele anight youre softe side—
Al be it that I may nat on you ride,
For that oure perche is maad so narwe, allas—

2. Guard himself.
3. Therefore he has set little store by any dream.
4. I.e., I'd give my shirt.
5. Macrobius wrote a famous commentary on Cicero's account in *De Republica* of the dream of Scipio Africanus Minor; the commentary came to be regarded as a standard authority on dream lore.
6. See Daniel vii.
7. See Genesis xxxvii.
8. See Genesis xxxix–xli.
9. Divinely inspired dream (as opposed to the more ordinary "swevene" or "dreem").
1. Set by.
2. A tag from the Gospel of St. John which gives the essential premises of Christianity: "In the beginning was the Word."
3. Woman is man's ruination.

350 I am so ful of joye and of solas°   *delight*
    That I defye bothe swevene and dreem."
    And with that word he fleigh° down fro the beem,   *flew*
    For it was day, and eek his hennes alle,
    And with a "chuk" he gan hem for to calle,
355 For he hadde founde a corn lay in the yeerd.
    Real° he was, he was namore aferd:°   *regal / afraid*
    He fethered⁴ Pertelote twenty time,
    And trad⁵ hire as ofte er it was prime.
    He looketh as it were a grim leoun,
360 And on his toes he rometh up and down:
    Him deined⁶ nat to sette his foot to grounde.
    He chukketh whan he hath a corn yfounde,
    And to him rennen° thanne his wives alle.   *run*
    Thus royal, as a prince is in his halle,
365 Leve I this Chauntecleer in his pasture,
    And after wol I telle his aventure.
        Whan that the month in which the world bigan,
    That highte March, whan God first maked man,
    Was compleet, and passed were also,
370 Sin March bigan, thritty days and two,⁷
    Bifel that Chauntecleer in al his pride,
    His sevene wives walking him biside,
    Caste up his yën to the brighte sonne,
    That in the signe of Taurus hadde yronne
375 Twenty degrees and oon and somwhat more,
    And knew by kinde,° and by noon other lore,   *nature*
    That it was prime, and crew with blisful stevene.°   *voice*
    "The sonne," he saide, "is clomben⁸ up on hevene
    Fourty degrees and oon and more, ywis.
380 Madame Pertelote, my worldes blis,
    Herkneth thise blisful briddes° how they singe,   *birds*
    And see the fresshe flowres how they springe:
    Ful is myn herte of revel and solas."
    But sodeinly him fil° a sorweful cas,°   *befell / chance*
385 For evere the latter ende of joye is wo—
    God woot that worldly joye is soone ago,
    And if a rethor° coude faire endite,   *rhetorician*
    He in a cronicle saufly° mighte it write,   *safely*
    As for a soverein notabilitee.⁹
390 Now every wis man lat him herkne me:
    This storye is also° trewe, I undertake,   *as*
    As is the book of *Launcelot de Lake*,¹
    That wommen holde in ful greet reverence.
    Now wol I turne again to my sentence.°   *main point*
395   A colfox² ful of sly iniquitee,
    That in the grove hadde woned° yeres three,   *dwelled*
    By heigh imaginacion forncast,³
    The same night thurghout the hegges° brast°   *hedges / burst*
    Into the yeerd ther Chauntecleer the faire
400 Was wont, and eek his wives, to repaire;
    And in a bed of wortes° stille he lay   *cabbages*
    Til it was passed undren° of the day,   *midmorning*
    Waiting his time on Chauntecleer to falle,
    As gladly doon thise homicides alle,

4. I.e., embraced.
5. Trod, copulated with; "prime": 9 A.M.
6. He deigned.
7. The rhetorical time-telling is perhaps burlesque; it can be read as yielding the date April 3, though May 3 seems intended from lines 374–75: on May 3 the sun would have passed some twenty degrees through Taurus (the Bull), the second sign of the zodiac; the sun would be forty degrees from the horizon at 9 o'clock in the morning.
8. Has climbed.
9. Indisputable fact.
1. Romances of the courteous knight Lancelot of the Lake were very popular.
2. Fox with black markings.
3. Predestined by divine planning.

405 That in await liggen to mordre[4] men.
O false mordrour, lurking in thy den!
O newe Scariot![5] Newe Geniloun!
False dissimilour!° O Greek Sinoun,[6]   *dissembler*
That broughtest Troye al outrely° to sorwe!   *utterly*
410 O Chauntecleer, accursed be that morwe°   *morning*
That thou into the yeerd flaugh° fro the bemes!   *flew*
Thou were ful wel ywarned by thy dremes
That thilke day was perilous to thee;
But what that God forwoot° moot° needes be,   *foreknows / must*
415 After° the opinion of certain clerkes: *according to*
Witnesse on him that any parfit° clerk is   *perfect*
That in scole is greet altercacioun
In this matere, and greet disputisoun,°   *disputation*
And hath been of an hundred thousand men.
420 But I ne can nat bulte° it to the bren,°   *sift / husks*
As can the holy doctour Augustin,
Or Boece, or the bisshop Bradwardin[7]—
Wheither that Goddes worthy forwiting°   *foreknowledge*
Straineth me nedely[8] for to doon a thing
425 ("Nedely" clepe I simple necessitee),
Or elles if free chois be graunted me
To do that same thing or do it nought,
Though God forwoot° it er that I was wrought;   *foreknew*
Or if his witing° straineth neveradeel,   *knowledge*
430 But by necessitee condicionel[9]—
I wol nat han to do of swich matere:
My tale is of a cok, as ye may heere,
That took his conseil of his wif with sorwe,
To walken in the yeerd upon that morwe
435 That he hadde met° the dreem that I you tolde.   *dreamed*
Wommenes conseils been ful ofte colde,[1]
Wommanes conseil broughte us first to wo,
And made Adam fro Paradis to go,
Ther as he was ful merye and wel at ese.
440 But for I noot° to whom it mighte displese   *don't know*
If I conseil of wommen wolde blame,
Passe over, for I saide it in my game°—   *sport*
Rede auctours where they trete of swich matere,
And what they sayn of wommen ye may heere—
445 Thise been the cokkes wordes and nat mine:
I can noon harm of no womman divine.°   *guess*
    Faire in the sond° to bathe hire merily   *sand*
Lith° Pertelote, and alle hir sustres by,   *lies*
Again° the sonne, and Chauntecleer so free°   *in / noble*
450 Soong° merier than the mermaide in the see—   *sang*
For Physiologus[2] saith sikerly
How that they singen wel and merily.
    And so bifel that as he caste his yë
Among the wortes on a boterflye,°   *butterfly*
455 He was war of this fox that lay ful lowe.
No thing ne liste him[3] thanne for to crowe,
But cride anoon "Cok cok!" and up he sterte,°   *started*

4. That lie in ambush to murder.
5. Judas Iscariot. "Geniloun" is Ganelon, who betrayed Roland to the Saracens (in the medieval French epic *The Song of Roland*).
6. Sinon, who persuaded the Trojans to take the Greeks' wooden horse into their city—with, of course, the result that the city was destroyed.
7. St. Augustine, Boethius (6th-century Roman philosopher, whose *Consolation of Philosophy* was translated by Chaucer), and Thomas Bradwardine (Archbishop of Canterbury, died 1349) were all concerned with the interrelationship between man's free will and God's foreknowledge.
8. Constrains me necessarily.
9. Boethius' "conditional necessity" permitted a large measure of free will.
1. I.e., baneful.
2. Supposed author of a bestiary, a book of moralized zoology describing both natural and supernatural animals (including mermaids).
3. He wished.

As man that[4] was affrayed in his herte—
For naturelly a beest desireth flee
460   Fro his contrarye[5] if he may it see,
Though he nevere erst° hadde seen it with his yë.   *before*
This Chauntecleer, whan he gan him espye,
He wolde han fled, but that the fox anoon
Saide, "Gentil sire, allas, wher wol ye goon?
465   Be ye afraid of me that am youre freend?
Now certes, I were worse than a feend
If I to you wolde° harm or vilainye.   *meant*
I am nat come youre conseil° for t'espye,   *secrets*
But trewely the cause of my cominge
470   Was only for to herkne how that ye singe:
For trewely, ye han as merye a stevene°   *voice*
As any angel hath that is in hevene.
Therwith ye han in musik more feelinge
Than hadde Boece,[6] or any that can singe.
475   My lord your fader—God his soule blesse!—
And eek youre moder, of hir gentilesse,°   *gentility*
Han in myn hous ybeen, to my grete ese.
And certes sire, ful fain° wolde I you plese.   *gladly*
"But for men speke of singing, I wol saye,
480   So mote I brouke[7] wel mine yën twaye,
Save ye, I herde nevere man so singe
As dide youre fader in the morweninge.
Certes, it was of herte[8] al that he soong.°   *sang*
And for to make his vois the more strong,
485   He wolde so paine him[9] that with bothe his yën
He moste winke,[1] so loude wolde he cryen;
And stonden on his tiptoon therwithal,
And strecche forth his nekke long and smal;
And eek he was of swich discrecioun
490   That ther nas no man in no regioun
That him in song or wisdom mighte passe.
I have wel rad° in *Daun Burnel the Asse*[2]   *read*
Among his vers how that ther was a cok,
For a preestes sone yaf him a knok[3]
495   Upon his leg whil he was yong and nice,°   *foolish*
He made him for to lese° his benefice.[4]   *lose*
But certain, ther nis no comparisoun
Bitwixe the wisdom and discrecioun
Of youre fader and of his subtiltee.
500   Now singeth, sire, for sainte° charitee!   *holy*
Lat see, conne° ye youre fader countrefete?"°   *can / imitate*
This Chauntecleer his winges gan to bete,
As man that coude his traison nat espye,
So was he ravisshed with his flaterye.
505   Allas, ye lordes, many a fals flatour°   *flatterer*
Is in youre court, and many a losengeour,°   *deceiver*
That plesen you wel more, by my faith,
Than he that soothfastnesse° unto you saith!   *truth*
Redeth Ecclesiaste[5] of flaterye.
510   Beeth war, ye lordes, of hir trecherye.
This Chauntecleer stood hye upon his toos,
Strecching his nekke, and heeld his yën cloos,
And gan to crowe loude for the nones;°   *occasion*

---

4. Like one who.
5. I.e., his natural enemy.
6. Boethius also wrote a treatise on music.
7. So might I enjoy the use of.
8. Heartfelt.
9. Take pains.
1. He had to shut his eyes.
2. Master Brunellus, a discontented donkey,

was the hero of a 12th-century satirical poem by Nigel Wireker.
3. Because a priest's son gave him a knock.
4. The offended cock neglected to crow so that his master, now grown to manhood, overslept, missing his ordination and losing his benefice.
5. The Book of Ecclesiasticus, in the Apocrypha.

And daun Russel the fox sterte° up atones,	*jumped*
515 And by the gargat° hente° Chauntecleer,	*throat / seized*
And on his bak toward the wode him beer,°	*bore*
For yit ne was ther no man that him sued.°	*followed*
O destinee that maist nat been eschued!°	*eschewed*
Allas that Chauntecleer fleigh° fro the bemes!	*flew*
520 Allas his wif ne roughte nat of⁶ dremes!	
And on a Friday fil° al this meschaunce!	*befell*
O Venus that art goddesse of plesaunce,	
Sin that thy servant was this Chauntecleer,	
And in thy service dide al his power—	
525 More for delit than world⁷ to multiplye—	
Why woldestou suffre him on thy day⁸ to die?	
O Gaufred,⁹ dere maister soverein,	
That, whan thy worthy king Richard was slain	
With shot,¹ complainedest his deeth so sore,	
530 Why ne hadde I now thy sentence and thy lore,²	
The Friday for to chide as diden ye?	
For on a Friday soothly slain was he.	
Thanne wolde I shewe you how that I coulde plaine°	*lament*
For Chauntecleres drede and for his paine.	
535 Certes, swich cry ne lamentacioun	
Was nevere of ladies maad whan Ilioun°	*Ilium, Troy*
Was wonne, and Pyrrus³ with his straite swerd,	
Whan he hadde hent° King Priam by the beerd	*seized*
And slain him, as saith us *Eneidos*,⁴	
540 As maden alle the hennes in the cloos,°	*yard*
Whan they hadde seen of Chauntecleer the sighte.	
But sovereinly° Dame Pertelote shrighte°	*splendidly / shrieked*
Ful louder than dide Hasdrubales⁵ wif	
Whan that hir housbonde hadde lost his lif,	
545 And that the Romains hadden brend° Cartage:	*burned*
She was so ful of torment and of rage°	*madness*
That wilfully unto the fir she sterte,°	*jumped*
And brende hirselven with a stedefast herte.	
O woful hennes, right so criden ye	
550 As, whan that Nero brende the citee	
Of Rome, criden senatoures wives	
For that hir housbondes losten alle hir lives:⁶	
Withouten gilt this Nero hath hem slain.	
Now wol I turne to my tale again.	
555 The sely° widwe and eek hir doughtres two	*innocent*
Herden thise hennes crye and maken wo,	
And out at dores sterten° they anoon,	*leaped*
And sien° the fox toward the grove goon,	*saw*
And bar upon his bak the cok away,	
560 And criden, "Out, harrow,° and wailaway,	*help*
Ha, ha, the fox," and after him they ran,	
And eek with staves many another man;	
Ran Colle oure dogge, and Talbot and Gerland,⁷	
And Malkin with a distaf in hir hand,	
565 Ran cow and calf, and eek the verray hogges,	
Sore aferd° for berking of the dogges	*frightened*
And shouting of the men and wommen eke.	
They ronne° so hem thoughte hir herte breke;⁸	*ran*

6. Didn't care for.
7. I.e., population.
8. Friday is Venus' day.
9. Geoffrey of Vinsauf, a famous medieval rhetorician, who wrote a lament on the death of Richard I in which he scolded Friday, the day on which the king died.
1. I.e., a missile.
2. Thy wisdom and thy learning.
3. Pyrrhus was the Greek who slew Priam,

king of Troy. "Straite": rigorous, unsparing.
4. As the *Aeneid* tells us.
5. Hasdrubal was king of Carthage when it was destroyed by the Romans.
6. According to the legend, Nero not only set fire to Rome (in A.D. 64) but also put many senators to death.
7. Two other dogs.
8. Would break.

They yelleden as feendes doon in helle;
570 The dokes° criden as men wolde hem quelle;°   *ducks / kill*
The gees for fere flowen° over the trees;   *flew*
Out of the hive cam the swarm of bees;
So hidous was the noise, a, benedicite,°   *bless me*
Certes, he Jakke Straw[9] and him meinee°   *company*
575 Ne made nevere shoutes half so shrille
Whan that they wolden any Fleming kille,
As thilke day was maad upon the fox:
Of bras they broughten bemes° and of box,°   *trumpets / boxwood*
Of horn, of boon,° in whiche they blewe and pouped,[1] *bone*
580 And therwithal they skriked° and they houped°—   *shrieked / whooped*
It seemed as that hevene sholde falle.
    Now goode men, I praye you herkneth alle:
Lo, how Fortune turneth° sodeinly   *reverses, overturns*
The hope and pride eek of hir enemy.
585 This cok that lay upon the foxes bak,
In al his drede unto the fox he spak,
And saide, "Sire, if that I were as ye,
Yit sholde I sayn, as wis° God helpe me,   *surely*
'Turneth ayain, ye proude cherles alle!
590 A verray pestilence upon you falle!
Now am I come unto this wodes side,
Maugree your heed,[2] the cok shal here abide.
I wol him ete, in faith, and that anoon.'"
    The fox answerde, "In faith, it shal be doon."
595 And as he spak that word, al sodeinly
The cok brak from his mouth deliverly,°   *nimbly*
And hye upon a tree he fleigh° anoon.   *flew*
    And whan the fox sawgh that he was agoon,
"Allas," quod he, "O Chauntecleer, allas!
600 I have to you," quod he, "ydoon trespas,
In as muche as I maked you aferd
Whan I you hente° and broghte out of the yeerd.   *seized*
But sire, I dide it in no wikke° entente: *wicked*
Come down, and I shal telle you what I mente.
605 I shal saye sooth to you, God help me so."
    "Nay thanne," quod he, "I shrewe° us bothe two: *curse*
But first I shrewe myself, bothe blood and bones,
If thou bigile me ofter than ones;
Thou shalt namore thurgh thy flaterye
610 Do° me to singe and winken with myn yë.   *cause*
For he that winketh whan he sholde see,
Al wilfully, God lat him nevere thee."°   *thrive*
    "Nay," quod the fox, "but God yive him meschaunce
That is so undiscreet of governaunce°   *self-control*
615 That jangleth° whan he sholde holde his pees."   *chatters*
    Lo, swich it is for to be recchelees°   *careless*
And necligent and truste on flaterye.
But ye that holden this tale a folye
As of a fox, or of a cok and hen,
620 Taketh the moralitee, goode men.
For Saint Paul saith that al that writen is
To oure doctrine it is ywrit, ywis:[3]
Taketh the fruit, and lat the chaf be stille.
Now goode God, if that it be thy wille,
625 As saith my lord, so make us alle goode men,
And bringe us to his hye blisse. Amen.

---

9. One of the leaders of the Peasant's Revolt in 1381, which was partially directed against the Flemings living in London.
1. Tooted.
2. Despite your head—i.e., despite anything you can do.
3. See Romans xv.4.

To Rosamond

Madame, ye been of alle beautee shrine
As fer as cercled is the mapemounde:[4]
For as the crystal glorious ye shine,
And like ruby been youre cheekes rounde.
5 Therwith ye been so merye and so jocounde
That at a revel whan that I see you daunce
It is an oinement unto my wounde,
Though ye to me ne do no daliaunce.[5]

For though I weepe of teres ful a tine,°   *tub*
10 Yit may that wo myn herte nat confounde;
Youre semy° vois, that ye so smale outtwine,[6]   *small*
Maketh my thought in joye and blis habounde:°   *abound*
So curteisly I go with love bounde
That to myselfe I saye in my penaunce,[7]
15 "Suffiseth me to love you, Rosemounde,
Though ye to me ne do no daliaunce."

Was nevere pik walwed in galauntine[8]
As I in love am walwed and ywounde,
For which ful ofte I of myself divine
20 That I am trewe Tristam[9] the secounde;
My love may not refreide nor affounde;[1]
I brenne° ay in amorous plesaunce: *burn*
Do what you list, I wol youre thral° be founde,   *slave*
Though ye to me ne do no daliaunce.

Truth

Flee fro the prees° and dwelle with soothfastnesse;   *crowd*
Suffise° thyn owene thing, though it be smal;   *let suffice*
For hoord hath[2] hate, and climbing tikelnesse;°   *insecurity*
Prees hath envye, and wele° blent° overal.   *prosperity / blinds*
5 Savoure° no more than thee bihoove shal;   *relish*
Rule wel thyself that other folk canst rede:°   *advise*
And Trouthe shal delivere,[3] it is no drede.°   *doubt*

Tempest thee nought al crooked to redresse[4]
In trust of hire[5] that turneth as a bal;
10 Muche wele stant in litel bisinesse;[6]
Be war therfore to spurne ayains an al.[7]
Strive nat as dooth the crokke° with the wal.   *pot*
Daunte° thyself that dauntest otheres deede: *master*
And Trouthe shal delivere, it is no drede.

15 That thee is sent, receive in buxomnesse;°   *obedience*
The wrastling for the world axeth° a fal;   *asks for*
Here is noon hoom, here nis but wildernesse:
Forth, pilgrim, forth! Forth, beest, out of thy stal!
Know thy countree, looke up, thank God of al.
20 Hold the heigh way and lat thy gost° thee lede: *spirit*
And Trouthe shal delivere, it is no drede.

4. I.e., to the farthest circumference of the map of the world.
5. I.e., show me no encouragement.
6. That you so delicately spin out.
7. I.e., pangs of unrequited love.
8. Pike rolled in galantine sauce.
9. The famous lover of Isolt (Iseult, Isolde) in medieval legend, renowned for his constancy.

1. Cool nor chill.
2. Hoarding causes.
3. I.e., truth shall make you free.
4. Do not disturb yourself to straighten all that's crooked.
5. Fortune, who turns like a ball in that she is always presenting a different aspect to men.
6. Peace of mind stands in little anxiety.
7. I.e., to kick against the pricks.

Therfore, thou Vache,[8] leve thyn olde wrecchednesse
Unto the world; leve[9] now to be thral.
Crye him mercy that of his heigh goodnesse
25 Made thee of nought, and in especial
Draw unto him, and pray in general,
For thee and eek for othere, hevenelich meede:°   *reward*
And Trouthe shal delivere, it is no drede.

Gentilesse

The firste fader and findere° of gentilesse,   *founder*
What° man desireth gentil for to be   *whatever*
Moste folwe his traas,° and alle his wittes dresse[1]   *path*
Vertu to sue,° and vices for to flee: *follow*
5   For unto vertu longeth° dignitee,   *belongs*
And nought the revers, saufly° dar I deeme,   *safely*
Al were he[2] mitre, crowne, or diademe.

This firste stok was ground of rightwisnesse,°   *righteousness*
Trewe of his word, sobre, pietous,° and free,°   *merciful / generous*
10 Clene of his gost,° and loved bisinesse   *spirit*
Against the vice of slouthe,° in honestee;   *sloth*
And but his heir love vertu as dide he,
He is nat gentil, though he riche° seeme,   *noble*
Al were he mitre, crowne, or diademe.

15 Vice may wel be heir to old richesse,
But ther may no man, as ye may wel see,
Biquethe his heir his vertuous noblesse:
That is appropred° unto no degree   *exclusively assigned*
But to the firste fader in majestee,
20 That maketh his heir him that wol him queme,°   *please*
Al were he mitre, crowne, or diademe.

Complaint to His Purse

To you, my purs, and to noon other wight,
Complaine I, for ye be my lady dere.
I am so sory, now that ye be light,
For certes, but if[3] ye make me hevy cheere,
5   Me were as lief[4] be laid upon my beere;°   *bier*
For which unto youre mercy thus I crye:
Beeth hevy again, or elles moot° I die.   *must*

Now voucheth sauf this day er it be night
That I of you the blisful soun may heere,
10 Or see youre colour, lik the sonne bright,
That of yelownesse hadde nevere peere.
Ye be my life, ye be myn hertes steere,°   *rudder, guide*
Queene of confort and of good compaignye:
Beeth hevy again, or elles moot I die.

15 Ye purs, that been to me my lives light
And saviour, as in this world down here,
Out of this tonne[5] helpe me thurgh your might,
Sith that ye wol nat be my tresorere;°   *disburser*
For I am shave as neigh° as any frere.°   *close / friar*
20 But yit I praye unto youre curteisye:
Beeth hevy again, or elles moot I die.

8. Probably Sir Philip de la Vache, with a
pun on the French for "cow."
9. I.e., cease.
1. I.e., must follow his (the first father's)
path and dispose all his (own) wits.

2. Even if he wear.
3. Unless.
4. I'd just as soon.
5. Tun, meaning "predicament."

Envoy to Henry IV

O conquerour of Brutus Albioun,[6]
Which that by line and free eleccioun
Been verray king, this song to you I sende:
25 And ye, that mowen° alle oure harmes amende,   *may*
Have minde upon my supplicacioun.

Against Women Unconstant

Madame, for youre newefangelnesse,[7]
Many a servant have ye put out of grace.
I take my leve of your unstedefastnesse,
For wel I woot,° whil ye have lives space,   *know*
5 Ye can not love ful half yeer in a place,
To newe thing youre lust° is ay° so keene;   *appetite / always*
In stede of blew, thus may ye were al greene.[8]

Right as a mirour nothing may enpresse,
But, lightly as it cometh, so mote° it pace,°   *must / pass*
10 So fareth youre love, youre werkes bereth witnesse.
Ther is no faith that may your herte enbrace;
But, as a wedercok, that turneth his face
With every wind, ye fare, and this is seene;
In stede of blew, thus may ye were al greene.

15 Ye might be shrined, for youre brotelnesse,[9]
Bet than Dalida, Criseide or Candace;[1]
For ever in chaunging stant youre sikernesse;°   *constancy*
That tache° may no wight fro your herte arace.° *blemish / uproot*
If ye lese oon, ye can wel twain purchace;
20 Al light for somer,[2] ye woot wel what I mene,
In stede of blew, thus may ye were al greene.

Merciless Beauty

1

Youre yën two wol slee° me sodeinly: *slay*
I may the beautee of hem nat sustene,°   *withstand*
So woundeth it thurghout myn herte keene.°   *keenly*

And but° youre word wol helen hastily   *unless*
5 Myn hertes wounde, whil that it is greene,[3]
    Youre yën two wol slee me sodeinly:
    I may the beautee of hem nat sustene.

Upon my trouthe, I saye you faithfully
That ye been of my lif and deeth the queene,
10 For with my deeth the trouthe shal be seene.
    Youre yën two wol slee me sodeinly:
    I may the beautee of hem nat sustene,
    So woundeth it thurghout myn herte keene.

2

So hath youre beautee fro youre herte chaced
15 Pitee, that me ne availeth nought to plaine:°   *complain*
For Daunger halt[4] youre mercy in his chaine.

6. Britain (Albion) was supposed to have been founded by Brutus, the grandson of Aeneas, the founder of Rome.
7. Fondness for novelty.
8. Blue stands for constancy, green for change.
9. Brittleness, fickleness.
1. Respectively, Samson's betrayer (Delilah), Troilus's faithless mistress, and Alexander's temptress to sloth.
2. To travel "light for summer" as opposed to heavy for winter suggests ease of movement, readiness for change.
3. I.e., fresh.
4. Haughtiness holds.

Giltelees my deeth thus han ye me purchaced;°   *procured*
I saye you sooth, me needeth nought to feine:°   *dissemble*
   So hath youre beautee fro youre herte chaced
20   Pitee, that me ne availeth nought to plaine.

Allas, that nature hath in you compaced°   *enclosed*
So greet beautee that no man may attaine
To mercy, though he sterve° for the paine.   *die*
   So hath youre beautee fro youre herte chaced
25   Pitee, that me ne availeth nought to plaine:
   For Daunger halt youre mercy in his chaine.

              3
Sin I fro Love escaped am so fat,
I nevere thenke° to been in his prison lene: *intend*
Sin I am free, I counte him nat a bene.[5]

30   He may answere and saye right this and that;
I do no fors,[6] I speke right as I mene:
   Sin I fro Love escaped am so fat,
   I nevere thenke to been in his prison lene.

Love hath my name ystrike° out of his sclat,°   *struck / slate*
35   And he is strike out of my bookes clene
For everemo; ther is noon other mene.°   *solution*
   Sin I fro Love escaped am so fat,
   I nevere thenke to been in his prison lene:
   Sin I am free, I counte him nat a bene.

CHARLES D'ORLÉANS
(1391–1465)

My Ghostly Father

My ghostly° father, I me confess,   *spiritual*
   First to God and then to you,
   That at a window (wot° ye how)   *know*
I stole a kiss of great sweetness,
5   Which done was out° advisedness,   *without*
   But it is done, not undone, now,
My ghostly father, I me confess,
   First to God and then to you.
But I restore it shall doubtless
10   Again, if so be that I mow,°   *may*
   And that, God, I make a vow,
And else I ask forgiveness—
My ghostly father, I me confess,
   First to God and then to you.

The Smiling Mouth

The smiling mouth and laughing eyen gray,
The breastes round and long small armes twain,
   The handes smooth, the sides straight and plain,
Your feetes lit°—what should I further say?   *little*
5   It is my craft° when ye are far away   *practice*
   To muse thereon in stinting° of my pain—   *soothing*
The smiling mouth and laughing eyen gray,
   The breastes round and long small armes twain.
So would I pray you, if I durst or may,

5. I don't consider him worth a bean.   6. I don't care.

10   The sight to see as I have seen,
      Forwhy° that craft me is most fain,°   *because / pleasing*
    And will be to the hour in which I day°—   *die*
    The smiling mouth and laughing eyen gray,
      The breastes round and long small armes twain.

Oft in My Thought

    Oft in my thought full busily have I sought,
      Against the beginning of this fresh new year,
    What pretty thing that I best given ought
      To her that was mine hearte's lady dear;
5   But all that thought bitane° is fro° me clear   *taken / from*
      Since death, alas, hath closed her under clay
    And hath this world fornaked° with her here—   *stripped bare*
      God have her soul, I can no better say.

    But for to keep in custom, lo, my thought,
10   And of my seely° service the manere,   *simple*
    In showing als° that I forget her not   *also*
      Unto each wight I shall to my powere
      This dead[7] her serve with masses and prayere;
      For all too foul a shame were me, mafay,°   *by my faith*
15   Her to forget this time that nigheth near—
      God have her soul, I can no better say.

    To her profit now nis° there to be bought   *is not*
      None other thing all° will I buy it dear;   *although*
    Wherefore, thou Lord that lordest all aloft,
20   My deedes take, such as goodness steer,
      And crown her, Lord, within thine heavenly sphere
      As for most truest lady, may I say,
      Most good, most fair, and most benign of cheer°—   *countenance*
      God have her soul, I can no better say.

25   When I her praise, or praising of her hear,
    Although it whilom° were to me pleasere,   *formerly*
      It fill onough it doth mine heart today,
    And doth° me wish I clothed had my bier—   *makes*
      God have her soul, I can no better say.

ANONYMOUS LYRICS OF THE FIFTEENTH CENTURY

Adam Lay I-bounden

Adam lay i-bounden, bounden in a bond;
Foure thousand winter thought he not too long.
And all was for an apple, an apple that he took,
As clerkes finden written in theire book.

5 Ne hadde the apple take been,[1] the apple taken been,
Ne hadde never our Lady aye been Heaven's queen.
Blessed be the time that apple taken was,
Therefore we may singen, "*Deo gracias!*"[2]

---

7. Dead person, the deceased. *Her* is redundant, as is one of the *it*s in line 27.

1. I.e., if the apple had not been taken.
2. Thanks be to God.

I Sing of a Maiden

I sing of a maiden
    That is makeless:°   *mateless, matchless*
King of alle kinges
    To° her son she ches.°   *for / chose*

5   He came also° stille   *as*
    Where his mother was
As dew in Aprille
    That falleth on the grass.

He came also stille
10   To his mother's bower
As dew in Aprille
    That falleth on the flower.

He came also stille
    Where his mother lay
15 As dew in Aprille
    That falleth on the spray.

Mother and maiden
    Was never none but she—
Well may such a lady
20   Godes mother be.

Out of Your Sleep Arise and Wake

    Noel, noel, noel,
    Noel, noel, noel!

Out of your sleep arise and wake,
For God mankind° now hath i-take,°   *human nature / taken*
5 All of° a maid without any make:°   *from / match, mate*
    Of all women she beareth the bell.[3]
    Noel!

And through a maide fair and wise
Now man is made of full great price;°   *worth*
10 Now angels kneel to man's service,
    And at this time all this befell.
    Noel!

Now man is brighter than the sun;
Now man in heaven on high shall wone;°   *dwell*
15 Blessed be God this game is begun,
    And his mother empress of hell.
    Noel!

That° ever was thrall,° now is he free;   *who / captive*
That ever was small, now great is she;
20 Now shall God deem° both thee and me   *judge*
    Unto his bliss if we do well.
    Noel!

Now man may to heaven wend;
Now heaven and earth to him they bend;
25 He that was foe now is our friend.
    This is no nay that I you tell.
    Noel!

3. "Beareth the bell": takes the prize.

Now, blesséd brother, grant us grace
At doomesday to see thy face
30   And in thy court to have a place,
    That we may there sing noel.
    Noel!

This Endris Night

This endris[4] night
I saw a sight,
    A star as bright as day,
And ever among[5]
5   A maiden sung,
    "Lullay, by, by, lullay."

That lovely lady sat and sung,
    And to her child said,
"My Son, my Brother, my Father dear,
10   Why liest thou thus in hay?
    My sweete brid,°   *bird*
    Thus it is betid,°   *happened*
        Though thou be king verray;°   *in truth*
    But nevertheless
15   I will not cesse°   *cease*
        To sing 'By, by, lullay.' "

The child then spake in his talking,
    And to his mother said,
"I am kenned° for Heaven's King   *known*
20   In crib though I be laid,
    For angels bright
    Done° to me light,   *gave*
        Thou knowest it is no nay;
    And of[6] that sight
25   Thou mayst be light[7]
        To sing 'By, by, lullay.' "

"Now, sweet Son, since thou art king,
    Why art thou laid in stall?
Why ne thou ordained thy bedding
30   In some great kinge's hall?
    Methinketh it is right
    That king or knight
        Should lie in good array,
    And then among°   *in that circumstance*
35   It were no wrong
        To sing 'By, by, lullay.' "

"Mary mother, I am thy child,
    Though I be laid in stall;
Lords and dukes shall worship me,
40   And so shall kinges all.
    Ye shall well see
    That kinges three
        Shall come the Twelfth Day.
    For this behest°   *promise*
45   Give me thy breast
        And sing 'By, by, lullay.' "

4. "This endris": the other.   6. I.e., because of.
5. "Ever among": every now and then. 7. "Thou mayst be light": feel free.

"Now tell me, sweet Son, I thee pray,
        Thou are me lief° and dear,   *beloved*
    How should I keep thee to thy pay°   *liking*
50   And make thee glad of cheer?°   *face*
            For all thy will
            I would fulfill,
                Thou wottest full well in fay,°   *faith*
            And for all this
55   I will thee kiss
                And sing 'By, by, lullay.' "

"My dear mother, when time it be,
        Thou take me up on loft,
    And set me upon thy knee,
60   And handle me full soft,
            And in thy arm
            Thou hill° me warm,   *cover*
                And keepe night and day;
            If I weep
65   And may not sleep,
                Then sing 'By, by, lullay.' "

"Now, sweet Son, since it is so,
        That all thing is at thy will,
    I pray thee, grante me a boon,
70   If it be both right and skill:°   *reason*
            That child or man
            That will or can
                Be merry upon my day,
            To bliss them bring,
75   And I shall sing
                'Lullay, by, by, lullay.' "

O! Mankind

O! Mankind,
Have in thy mind
My passion° smart,°   *suffering / bitter*
And thou shalt find
5   Me full kind—
Lo! here my heart.

I Have Labored Sore

I have labored sore and suffered death,
And now I rest and draw my breath;
But I shall come and call right soon
Heaven and earth and hell to doom;°   *judgment*
5   And then shall know both devil and man
What I was and what I am.

Jesus' Wounds So Wide

Jesus' wounds so wide
Be wells of life to the good,
Namely° the stround° of° his side   *particularly / stream / from*
That ran full breme° on the rood.°   *fiercely / cross*

5   If thee list to drink,
To flee from the fiends of hell,
Bow thou down to the brink
And meekly taste of the well.

I Have a Gentle Cock

I have a gentle° cock,   *noble*
   Croweth me day;
He doth me risen[8] early
   My matins for to say.

5 I have a gentle cock,
   Comen he is of great;°   *lofty lineage*
His comb is of red coral,
   His tail is of jet.

I have a gentle cock,
10   Comen he is of kind;°   *good stock*
His comb is of red coral,
   His tail is of inde.°   *indigo*

His legges be of azure,
   So gentle and so small;
15 His spurres are of silver white
   Into the wortewale.[9]

His eyen are of crystal,
   Locked° all in amber;   *set*
And every night he percheth him
20   In my lady's chamber.

Jolly Jankin

"Kyrie, so kyrie,"
Jankin singeth murie,°   *merrily*
   With "Aleison."[1]

As I went on Yule Day
5 In our procession,
Knew I jolly Jankin
   By his merry tone.
   Kyrieleison.

Jankin began the office
10 On the Yule Day,
And yet methinketh it does me good,
So merry gan he say,
   "Kyrieleison."

Jankin read the 'Pistle
15 Full fair and full well,
And yet methinketh it does me good,
As ever have I sel.[2]
   Kyrieleison.

Jankin at the Sanctus
20 Cracketh a merry note,
And yet methinketh it does me good—
I payed for his coat.
   Kyrieleison.

8. "Doth me risen": makes me rise.
9. Up to the root.
1. *Kyrie eleison,* a prayer, "Lord have mercy"; the Epistle (line 13), a reading from Paul or one of the Prophets; the *Sanctus* (line 19), a prayer of rejoicing, "Holy, Holy, Holy"; and the *Agnus* (line 29), an invocation of the Lamb of God are early, middle, and late parts of the divine office (line 9) or Mass.
2. I.e., as ever I (hope to) have good luck.

25	Jankin cracketh notes	
	An hundred on a knot,°	*at a time*
	And yet he hacketh° them smaller	*chops up*
	Than wortes° to the pot.	*herbs*
	Kyrieleison.	

Jankin at the Agnus
30 Beareth the pax-bred;[3]
He twinkled but said nought,
And on my foot he tread.
 Kyrieleison.

Benedicamus Domino,[4]
35 Christ from shame me shield;
Deo gracias thereto—[5]
Alas! I go with child.
 Kyrieleison.

The Blind Eateth Many a Fly

Look well about, ye that lovers be;
 Let not your lustes lead you to dotage.[6]
Be not enamored on all things that ye see—
 Samson the fort° and Solomon the sage   *strong*
5 Deceived were, for all their great corage.°   *confidence*
  Men deem it right, that they see with eye—
  Beware, therefore: the blind eateth many a fly.

I mean, of women, for all their cheeres quaint,[7]
 Trust them not too much—their troth is but geason.°   *barren*
10 The fairest outward° well can they paint;   *exterior*
 Their steadfastness endureth but a season,
 For they feign friendliness and worken treason.
  And for they are changeable naturally,
  Beware, therefore: the blind eateth many a fly.

15 What wight° alive trusteth on their cheers   *man*
 Shall have at last his guerdon° and his meed,° *reward / recompense*
For women can shave nearer than razors or shears.
 All is not gold that shineth—men, take heed.
 Their gall is hid under a sugared° weed.°   *alluring / garment*
20 It is full quaint[8] their fantasy° to espy.°   *pretense / discover*
  Beware, therefore: the blind eateth many a fly.

Though all the world do its busy cure[9]
 To make women stand in stableness,
It will not be, it is against nature:
25 The world is done when they lack doubleness,
 For they can laugh and love not—this is express.°   *definite*
  To trust on them, it is but fantasy.
  Beware, therefore: the blind eateth many a fly.

3. A tablet ("bred": board) bearing a representation of the Crucifixion, kissed by the priests celebrating the Mass, then by the congregation. "Pax": (the kiss of) peace.
4. Let us bless the Lord.
5. Thanks be to God, as well.
6. The *-age* terminations in this stanza, the *-ture* of *nature* at line 24, the *-able* of *scrib-* *-able* at line 37, and the *-cean* of *ocean* at line 38 should receive stress and be pronounced in the French fashion: i.e., *-age* sounds as in *garage*, *-ture* rhymes with *cure*, *-able* sounds like *obble*, and *ocean* is *oh-see-on*.
7. "Cheeres quaint": fine looks.
8. Very ingenious; i.e., very difficult.
9. Should work diligently.

Women of kinde[1] have conditions three:
30   The first is they be full of deceit;
To spin also is theire property;
    And women have a wonderful conceit.°   *trick*
For they can weep oft, and all is a sleight,
    And ever when they list,° the tear is in the eye. *wish*
35   Beware, therefore: the blind eateth many a fly.

In sooth to say, though all the earth so wan°   *dark*
    Were parchment smooth, white, and scribable,[2]
And the great sea that called is the ocean
    Were turned into ink blacker than sable,
40   Every stick a pen, each man a scrivener able,
    Not could they then write woman's treachery.
Beware, therefore: the blind eateth many a fly.

God, That Madest All Things

God, that madest all things of nought[3]
And with thy precious blood us bought,
    Mercy, help, and grace.
As thou art very god and man,
5   And of thy side thy blood ran,
    Forgive us our trespass.
The world, our flesh, the fiend our foe
Maketh us mis-think, mis-speak, mis-do—
    All thus we fall in blame.
10   Of all our sinnes, less and more,
Sweete Jesu, us rueth sore.
    Mercy, for thine holy name.

I Wend to Death

I wend to death, knight stith in stour;[4]
Through fight in field I won the flower;
No fights me taught the death to quell—
I wend to death, sooth I you tell.

5   I wend to death, a king iwis;°   *indeed*
What helpes honor or worlde's bliss?
Death is to man the kinde° way—   *natural*
I wende to be clad in clay.

I wend to death, clerk full of skill,
10   That could with words men mar and dill.[5]
Soon has me made the death an end.
Be ware with[6] me! To death I wend.

Timor Mortis

In what estate° so ever I be   *condition*
Timor mortis conturbat me.[7]

As I went on a merry morning,
I heard a bird both weep and sing.
5   This was the tenor of her talking:
    "*Timor mortis conturbat me.*"

1. "Of kinde": by nature.
2. Susceptible of being written on.
3. I.e., from nothing.
4. "Stith in stour": stout in battle.
5. Mar and keep secret; i.e., expose or conceal.
6. "Be ware with": take warning from.
7. The title phrase comes from the Office of the Dead: "*Peccantem me quotidie et non poenitentem* timor mortis conturbat me. *Quia in inferno nulla est redemptio misere mei Deus et salva me.*" (Since I have been sinning daily and repenting not, *the fear of death distresses me.* Since in hell there is no redemption, have pity on me, God, and save me.)

I asked that bird what she meant.
"I am a musket° both fair and gent;°   *male sparrowhawk / gentle*
For dread of death I am all shent.:°   *ruined*
10   *Timor mortis conturbat me.*

"When I shall die, I know no day;
What country or place I cannot say;
Wherefore this song sing I may:
    Timor mortis conturbat me.

15   "Jesu Christ, when he should die,
To his Father he gan say,
'Father,' he said, 'in Trinity,
    Timor mortis conturbat me.'

"All Christian people, behold and see:
20   This world is but a vanity
And replete with necessity.
    Timor mortis conturbat me.

"Wake I or sleep, eate or drink,
When I on my last end do think,
25   For greate fear my soul do shrink:
    Timor mortis conturbat me.

"God grant us grace him for to serve,
And be at our end when we sterve,°   *die*
And from the fiend he us preserve.
30   *Timor mortis conturbat me.*

A God and Yet a Man?

A god and yet a man?
    A maid and yet a mother?
Wit wonders what wit can
    Conceive this or the other.

5   A god and can he die?
    A dead man, can he live?
What wit can well reply?
    What reason reason give?

God, truth itself, doth teach it.
10   Man's wit sinks too far under
By reason's power to reach it.
    Believe and leave° to wonder.   *cease*

The Corpus Christi[8] Carol

Lully, lullay, lully, lullay,
    The falcon hath born my make° away.   *mate*

He bore him up, he bore him down,
He bore him into an orchard brown.

5   In that orchard there was a hall
That was hanged with purple and pall.°   *black velvet*

And in that hall there was a bed,
It was hanged with gold so red.

8. "Corpus Christi": the body of Christ.

And in that bed there lieth a knight,
His woundes bleeding day and night.

By that bed's side there kneeleth a may°   *maiden*
And she weepeth both night and day.

And by that bed's side there standeth a stone,
Corpus Christi written thereon.

Western Wind

Western wind, when will thou blow,
    The small rain down can rain?
Christ, if my love were in my arms
    And I in my bed again!

A Lyke-Wake⁹ Dirge

This ae° night, this ae night,   *one*
    Every night and all,
Fire and sleet¹ and candle-light,
    And Christ receive thy saul.°   *soul*

5   When thou from hence away are past,
To Whinny-muir² thou comest at last:

If ever thou gavest hosen and shoon,
Sit thee down and put them on:

If hosen and shoon thou ne'er gavest nane,
10   The whins shall prick thee to the bare bane:

From Whinny-muir when thou mayst pass,
To Brig° o' Dread thou comest at last: *bridge*

From Brig o' Dread when thou mayst pass,
To purgatory fire thou comest at last:

15   If ever thou gavest meat or drink,
The fire shall never make thee shrink:

If meat or drink thou ne'er gavest nane,
The fire will burn thee to the bare bane:

This ae night, this ae night,
20   Fire and sleet and candle-light,

Jolly Good Ale and Old

Back and side go bare, go bare,
    Both foot and hand go cold;
But, belly, God send thee good ale enough,
    Whether it be new or old.

5   I cannot eat but little meat,
    My stomach is not good;
But sure I think that I can drink
    With him that wears a hood.³

9. The night watch (*wake*) kept over a corpse (*lyke*).
1. Salt, sometimes placed with earth on the breast of the dead as emblematic of soul and body.

2. Prickly-moor. *Whin* is a name given to various prickly shrubs: furze, heather, buckthorn.
3. I.e., as much as any friar.

Though I go bare, take ye no care,
10   I am nothing a-cold;
I stuff my skin so full within
     Of jolly good ale and old.

I love no roast but a nut-brown toast,[4]
     And a crab° laid in the fire;   *crab apple*
15   A little bread shall do me stead,°   *service*
     Much bread I not desire.
No frost nor snow, no wind, I trow,°   *trust*
     Can hurt me if it would,
I am so wrapped and throughly° lapped°   *thoroughly / swathed*
20   Of° jolly good ale and old.   *in*

And Tib, my wife, that as her life
     Loveth well good ale to seek,
Full oft drinks she till ye may see
     The tears run down her cheek.
25   Then doth she troll° to me the bowl,   *pass*
     Even as a maltworm° should,   *toper*
And saith, "Sweetheart, I took my part
     Of this jolly good ale and old."

Now let them drink till they nod and wink,
30   Even as good fellows should do;
They shall not miss to have the bliss
     Good ale doth bring men to.
And all poor souls that have scoured bowls
     Or have them lustily trolled—
35   God save the lives of them and their wives,
     Whether they be young or old.

JOHN SKELTON
(1460–1529)

My Darling Dear, My Daisy Flower

With lullay, lullay, like a child,
Thou sleepest too long, thou art beguiled.

My darling dear, my daisy flower,
     Let me, quod° he, lie in your lap.   *quoth*
5   Lie still, quod she, my paramour,
     Lie still hardely,° and take a nap.   *indeed*
     His head was heavy, such was his hap,°   *luck*
All drowsy dreaming, drowned in sleep,
That of his love he took no keep.

10   With ba, ba, ba!¹ and bas,° bas, bas!   *kiss*
     She cherished him both cheek and chin,
That he wist° never where he was: *knew*
     He had forgotten all deadly sin.
     He wanted wit her love to win:
15   He trusted her payment and lost all his pay;
She left him sleeping and stole away.

---

4. Used as a sop with ale or wine.   1. The "by" of *lullaby*.

The rivers rough, the waters wan,
   She sparéd not to wet her feet;
She waded over, she found a man
20   That halséd° her heartily and kissed her sweet: *embraced*
   Thus after her cold she caught a heat.
My love, she said, routeth° in his bed;   *roots*
Ywis° he hath an heavy head.   *for certain*

What dreamest thou, drunkard, drowsy pate?
25   Thy lust° and liking is from thee gone;   *desire*
Thou blinkard blowbowl,[2] thou wakest too late,
   Behold thou liest, luggard,° alone.   *sluggard*
Well may thou sigh, well may thou groan,
To deal with her so cowardly:
30 Ywis, pole hatchet,° she bleared thine eye.   *blockhead*

To Mistress Margaret Hussey

Merry Margaret,
   As midsummer flower,
Gentle as falcon
Or hawk of the tower:[3]
5 With solace and gladness,
Much mirth and no madness,
All good and no badness;
   So joyously,
   So maidenly,
10   So womanly
   Her demeaning
   In every thing,
   Far, far passing
   That I can indite,
15   Or suffice to write
Of Merry Margaret
   As midsummer flower,
Gentle as falcon
Or hawk of the tower.
20   As patient and still
And as full of good will
As fair Isaphill,[4]
Coriander,[5]
Sweet pomander,[6]
25 Good Cassander,[7]
Steadfast of thought,
Well made, well wrought,
Far may be sought
Ere that ye can find
30 So courteous, so kind
As Merry Margaret,
   This midsummer flower,
Gentle as falcon
Or hawk of the tower.

2. Blinking sot.
3. Hawk trained to fly high (*tower*).
4. Hypsipyle, princess of Lemnos, savior of her father's life, comforter of the Argives, mother of twins by Jason.
5. An aromatic herb.
6. A mixture of perfumed or aromatic substances made into a ball.
7. Cassandra, daughter of Priam and Hecuba; according to myth her beauty bedazzled Apollo himself, who conferred on her the gift of prophecy.

KING HENRY VIII
(1491–1547)

Green Groweth the Holly

Green groweth the holly,
So doth the ivy.
Though winter blasts blow never so high,
Green groweth the holly.

5   As the holly groweth green,
    And never changeth hue,
So I am, ever hath been,
    Unto my lady true.

As the holly groweth green
10   With ivy all alone
When flowers cannot be seen
    And greenwood leaves be gone,

Now unto my lady,
    Promise to her I make
15 From all other only
    To her I me betake.

Adieu, mine owne lady,
    Adieu, my specïall,
Who hath my heart truely,
20   Be sure, and ever shall.

POPULAR BALLADS

Riddles Wisely Expounded[1]

1
There was a knicht riding frae° the east,   *from*
    Sing the cather banks, the bonnie brume[2]
Wha had been wooing at monie a place.
    And ye may beguile a young thing soon.
2
5   He came unto a widow's door,
And speird° where her three dochters were.   *asked*
3
"The auldest ane's to a washing gane,
The second's to a baking gane.
4
The youngest ane's to a wedding gane,
10 And it will be nicht or° she be hame."   *ere*
5
He sat him doun upon a stane,
Till thir° three lasses came tripping hame.   *these*

1. Ballad versions are conventionally identified by the number and letter assigned them in the monumental collection, *The English and Scottish Popular Ballads*, 1892–98, edited by Francis James Child. "Riddles Wisely Expounded" is No. 1.C.
2. Cather and broom are wildflowers to which folklore attributed properties pertinent to young love. Hempseed, sown on Hallowe'en, permitted a sight, over the left shoulder, of one's true love; broom, associated with witchcraft, provided oracular revelation in matters of the heart.

6

The auldest ane's to the bed making,
And the second ane's to the sheet spreading.

7

15   The youngest ane was bauld and bricht,
And she was to lie wi' this unco° knicht.   *stranger*

8

"Gin° ye will answer me questions ten,   *if*
The morn ye sall° be made my ain.   *shall*

9

"O what is higher nor the tree?
20   And what is deeper nor the sea?

10

"Or what is heavier nor the lead?
And what is better nor the bread?

11

"O what is whiter nor the milk?
Or what is safter nor the silk?

12

25   "Or what is sharper nor a thorn?
Or what is louder nor a horn?

13

"Or what is greener nor the grass?
Or what is waur° nor a woman was?"   *worse*

14

"O heaven is higher nor the tree,
30   And hell is deeper nor the sea.

15

"O sin is heavier nor the lead,
The blessing's better nor the bread.

16

"The snaw is whiter nor the milk,
And the down is safter nor the silk.

17

35   "Hunger is sharper nor a thorn,
And shame is louder nor a horn.

18

"The pies[3] are greener nor the grass,
And Clootie's[4] waur nor a woman was."

19

As soon as she the fiend did name,
40   He flew awa' in a blazing flame.

Lord Randal[5]

1

"O where ha' you been, Lord Randal, my son?
And where ha' you been, my handsome young man?"
"I ha' been at the greenwood; mother, mak my bed soon,
For I'm wearied wi' huntin', and fain wad° lie down."   *would*

2

5   "And wha met ye there, Lord Randal, my son?
And wha met you there, my handsome young man?"
"O I met wi' my true-love; mother, mak my bed soon,
For I'm wearied wi' huntin', and fain wad lie down."

---

3. A name given to various species of wood-
pecker.

4. Like "Hornie" and "Old Nick," a familiar
name for the devil.

5. Child, No. 12.A.

3

"And what did she give you, Lord Randal, my son?
10   And what did she give you, my handsome young man?"
"Eels fried in a pan; mother, mak my bed soon,
For I'm wearied wi' huntin', and fain wad lie down."

4

"And wha gat your leavin's, Lord Randal, my son?
And wha gat your leavin's, my handsome young man?"
15   "My hawks and my hounds; mother, mak my bed soon,
For I'm wearied wi' huntin', and fain wad lie down."

5

"And what becam of them, Lord Randal, my son?
And what becam of them, my handsome young man?"
"They stretched their legs out and died; mother, mak my bed soon,
20   For I'm wearied wi' huntin', and fain wad lie down."

6

"O I fear you are poisoned, Lord Randal, my son!
I fear you are poisoned, my handsome young man!"
"O yes, I am poisoned; mother, mak my bed soon,
For I'm sick at the heart, and I fain wad lie down."

7

25   "What d' ye leave to your mother, Lord Randal, my son?
What d'ye leave to your mother, my handsome young man?"
"Four and twenty milk kye°; mother, mak my bed soon,   *kine, cattle*
For I'm sick at the heart, and I fain wad lie down."

8

"What d' ye leave to your sister, Lord Randal, my son?
30   What d' ye leave to your sister, my handsome young man?"
"My gold and my silver; mother, mak my bed soon,
For I'm sick at the heart, and I fain wad lie down."

9

"What d' ye leave to your brother, Lord Randal, my son?
What d' ye leave to your brother, my handsome young man?"
35   "My houses and my lands; mother, mak my bed soon,
For I'm sick at the heart, and I fain wad lie down."

10

"What d' ye leave to your true-love, Lord Randal, my son?
What d' ye leave to your true-love, my handsome young man?"
"I leave her hell and fire; mother, mak my bed soon,
40   For I'm sick at the heart, and I fain wad lie down."

Edward[6]

1

"Why does your brand° sae° drap wi' bluid,   *sword / so*
      Edward, Edward,
Why does your brand sae drap wi' bluid,
      And why sae sad gang° ye, O?"   *go*
5   "O I ha'e killed my hawk sae guid,
      Mither, mither,
O I ha'e killed my hawk sae guid,
      And I had nae mair but he, O."

2

"Your hawke's bluid was never sae reid,°   *red*
10   Edward, Edward,
Your hawke's bluid was never sae reid,
      My dear son I tell thee, O."
"O I ha'e killed my reid-roan steed,
      Mither, mither,
15   O I ha'e killed my reid-roan steed,
      That erst was sae fair and free, O."

6. Child, No. 13.B.

3

"Your steed was auld, and ye ha'e gat mair,
      Edward, Edward,
Your steed was auld, and ye ha'e gat mair,
20   Some other dule° ye drie,° O."   *grief / suffer*
"O I ha'e killed my fader dear,
      Mither, mither,
O I ha'e killed my fader dear,
      Alas, and wae° is me, O!"   *woe*

4

25 "And whatten° penance wul ye drie for that,   *what sort of*
      Edward, Edward?
And whatten penance wul ye dree for that,
      My dear son, now tell me O?"
"I'll set my feet in yonder boat,
30   Mither, mither,
I'll set my feet in yonder boat,
      And I'll fare over the sea, O."

5

"And what wul ye do wi' your towers and your ha',
      Edward, Edward?
35 And what wul ye do wi' your towers and your ha',
      That were sae fair to see, O?"
"I'll let them stand tul they down fa',
      Mither, mither,
I'll let them stand tul they down fa',
40   For here never mair maun° I be, O."   *must*

6

"And what wul ye leave to your bairns° and your wife,   *children*
      Edward, Edward?
And what wul ye leave to your bairns and your wife,
      Whan ye gang over the sea, O?"
45 "The warlde's room,⁷ let them beg thrae° life,   *through*
      Mither, mither,
The warlde's room, let them beg thrae life,
      For them never mair wul I see, O."

7

"And what wul yo leave to your ain mither dear,
50   Edward, Edward?
And what wul ye leave to your ain mither dear,
      My dear son, now tell me, O?"
"The curse of hell frae° me sall° ye bear,   *from / shall*
      Mither, mither,
55 The curse of hell frae me sall ye bear,
      Sic° counsels ye gave to me, O."   *such*

Hind Horn⁸

1

In Scotland there was a baby born,
   Lill lal, etc.
And his name it was called young Hind Horn.
   With a fal lal, etc.

2

5 He sent a letter to our king.
That he was in love with his daughter Jean.

3

He's gi'en to her a silver wand,
With seven living lavrocks° sitting thereon.   *larks*

---

7. I.e., the wide world.   8. Child, No. 17.A.

4

She's gi'en to him a diamond ring,
10 With seven bright diamonds set therein.

5

"When this ring grows pale and wan,
You may know by it my love is gane."

6

One day as he looked his ring upon,
He saw the diamonds pale and wan.

7

15 He left the sea and came to land,
And the first that he met was an old beggar man.

8

"What news, what news?" said young Hind Horn;
"No news, no news," said the old beggar man.

9

"No news," said the beggar, "no news at a',
20 But there is a wedding in the king's ha'.

10

"But there is a wedding in the king's ha',
That has halden these forty days and twa."

11

"Will ye lend me your begging coat?
And I'll lend you my scarlet cloak.

12

25 "Will you lend me your beggar's rung?°   staff
And I'll gi'e you my steed to ride upon.

13

"Will you lend me your wig o' hair,
To cover mine, because it is fair?"

14

The auld beggar man was bound for the mill,
30 But young Hind Horn for the king's hall.

15

The auld beggar man was bound for to ride,
But young Hind Horn was bound for the bride.

16

When he came to the king's gate,
He sought a drink for Hind Horn's sake.

17

35 The bride came down with a glass of wine,
When he drank out the glass, and dropped in the ring.

18

"O got ye this by sea or land?
Or got ye it off a dead man's hand?"

19

I got not it by sea, I got it by land,
40 And I got it, madam, out of your own hand."

20

"O I'll cast off my gowns of brown,
And beg wi' you frae° town to town.   from

21

"O I'll cast off my gowns of red,
And I'll beg wi' you to win my bread."

22

45 "Ye needna cast off your gowns of brown,
For I'll make you lady o' many a town.

23

"Ye needna cast off your gowns of red,
It's only a sham, the begging o' my bread."

24

The bridegroom he had wedded the bride,
50 But young Hind Horn he took her to bed.

St. Stephen and Herod[9]

1

Saint Stephene was a clerk
  In King Herodes' hall,
And served him of° bread and cloth   *for*
  As every king befall.[1]

2

5 Stephen out of kitchen came
  With boare's head in hand;
He saw a star was fair and bright
  Over Bedlem° stand.   *Bethlehem*

3

He cast adown the boare's head
10   And went into the hall:
"I forsake thee, King Herodes,
  And thy workes all.

4

"I forsake thee, King Herodes,
  And thy workes all:
15 There is a child in Bedlem born
  Is better than we all."

5

"What aileth thee, Stephene?
  What is thee befall?
Lacketh thee either meat or drink
20   In King Herodes' hall?"

6

"Lacketh me neither meat ne drink
  In King Herodes' hall:
There is a child in Bedlem born
  Is better than we all."

7

25 "What aileth thee, Stephen? Art thou wode,°   *mad*
  Or thou 'ginnest to breed?[2]
Lacketh thee either gold or fee°   *property*
  Or any riche weed?"°   *clothing*

8

"Lacketh me neither gold ne fee
30   Ne none riche weed:
There is a child in Bedlem born
  Shall help us at our need."

9

"That is also sooth,[3] Stephen,
  Also sooth, iwis,°   *certainly*
35 As this capon crowe shall
  That li'th° here in my dish."

10

That word was not so soone said,
  That word in that hall,
The capon crew *Christus natus est*[4]
40   Among the lordes all.

11

"Riseth up, my tormentors,
  By two and all be one,
And leadeth Stephen out of this town,
  And stoneth him with stone."

---

9. Child, No. 22.
1. "As is appropriate to every king"
[Donaldson's note].

2. I.e., getting strange notions as pregnant
women do.
3. "Also sooth": as true.
4. Christ is born.

12

45 Tooken they Stephene,
 And stoned him in the way;°   *road*
And therefore is his even° on   *eve*
 Christe's owen day.

The Three Ravens[5]

1

There were three ravens sat on a tree,
 Down a down, hay down, hay down
There were three ravens sat on a tree,
 With a down
5 There were three ravens sat on a tree,
They were as black as they might be.
 With a down derry, derry, derry, down, down.

2

The one of them said to his mate,
"Where shall we our breakfast take?"

3

10 "Down in yonder greene field,
There lies a knight slain under his shield.

4

"His hounds they lie down at his feet,
So well they can their master keep.

5

"His hawks they fly so eagerly,°   *fiercely*
15 There's no fowl dare him come nigh."

6

Down there comes a fallow[6] doe,
As great with young as she might go.

7

She lift up his bloody head
And kissed his wounds that were so red.

8

20 She got him up upon her back
And carried him to earthen lake.°   *pit*

9

She buried him before the prime;[7]
She was dead herself ere even-song time.

10

God send every gentleman
25 Such hawks, such hounds, and such a leman. *lover, sweetheart*

The Twa Corbies[8]

1

As I was walking all alane,
I heard twa corbies making a mane;°   *moan*
The tane° unto the t'other say,   *one*
"Where sall° we gang° and dine to-day?"   *shall / go*

2

5 "In behint you auld fail° dike,   *turf*
I wot there lies a new slain knight;
And naebody kens° that he lies there,   *knows*
But his hawk, his hound, and lady fair.

---

5. Child, No. 26.
6. A species of deer distinguished by color
(fallow: pale brownish or reddish yellow)
from the red deer.

7. The first hour of the day, sunrise.
8. Child, No. 26. "Corbies" are ravens.

3

"His hound is to the hunting gane,
10 His hawk to fetch the wild-fowl hame,
His lady's ta'en another mate,
So we may mak our dinner sweet.

4

"Ye'll sit on his white hause-bane,°   neck-bone
And I'll pike° out his bonny blue een;°   pick / eyes
15 Wi' ae° lock o' his gowden° hair   one / golden
We'll theck° our nest when it grows bare.   thatch

5

"Mony a one for him makes mane,
But nane sall ken where he is gane;
O'er his white banes, when they are bare,
20 The wind sall blaw for evermair."

Thomas Rymer[9]

1

True Thomas lay o'er yond grassy bank,
    And he beheld a lady gay,
A lady that was brisk and bold,
    Come riding o'er the ferny brae.°   slope

2

5 Her skirt was of the grass-green silk,
    Her mantel of the velvet fine,
At ilka tett[1] of her horse's mane
    Hung fifty silver bells and nine.

3

True Thomas he took off his hat,
10   And bowed him low down till his knee:
"All hail, thou mighty Queen of Heaven!
    For your peer on earth I never did see."

4

"O no, O no, True Thomas," she says,
    "That name does not belong to me;
15 I am but the queen of fair Elfland,
    And I'm come here for to visit thee.

5

"But ye maun° go wi' me now, Thomas,   must
    True Thomas, ye maun go wi' me,
For ye maun serve me seven years,
20   Through weal or wae° as may chance to be."   woe

6

She turned about her milk-white steed,
    And took True Thomas up behind,
And aye whene'er her bridle rang,
    The steed flew swifter than the wind.

7

25 For forty days and forty nights
    He wade through red blude to the knee,
And he saw neither sun nor moon,
    But heard the roaring of the sea.

8

O they rade on, and further on,
30   Until they came to a garden green:
"Light down, light down, ye lady free,°   fine, gracious
    Some of that fruit let me pull to thee."

---

9. Child, No. 37.A.   1. "Ilka tett": each lock.

9

"O no, O no, True Thomas," she says,
    "That fruit maun not be touched by thee,
35 For a' the plagues that are in hell
    Light on the fruit of this country.

10

"But I have a loaf here in my lap,
    Likewise a bottle of claret wine,
And now ere we go farther on,
40   We'll rest a while, and ye may dine."

11

When he had eaten and drunk his fill,
    "Lay down your head upon my knee,"
The lady said, "ere we climb yon hill,
    And I will show you fairlies° three.   *wonders*

12

45 "O see not ye you narrow road,
    So thick beset wi' thorns and briars?
That is the path of righteousness,
    Though after it but few enquires.

13

"And see not ye that braid, braid road,
50   That lies across yon lilly leven?[2]
That is the path of wickedness,
    Though some call it the road to heaven.

14

"And see not ye that bonny road,
    Which winds about the ferny brae?
55 That is the road to fair Elfland,
    Where you and I this night maun gae.°   *go*

15

"But Thomas, ye maun hold your tongue,
    Whatever you may hear or see,
For gin° ae° word you should chance to speak,   *if / one*
60   You will ne'er get back to your ain country.

16

He has gotten a coat of the even° cloth,   *smooth*
    And a pair of shoes of velvet green,
And till seven years were past and gone
    True Thomas on earth was never seen.

The Cherry-Tree Carol[3]

1

Joseph was an old man,
    And an old man was he,
When he wedded Mary
    In the land of Galilee.

2

5   Joseph and Mary walked
    Through an orchard good,
Where was cherries and berries
    So red as any blood.

3

Joseph and Mary walked
10   Through an orchard green,
Where was berries and cherries
    As thick as might be seen.

---

2. "Lilly leven": lovely glade.   3. Child, No. 54.A.

4

O then bespoke Mary,
  So meek and so mild:
15 "Pluck me one cherry, Joseph,
  For I am with child."

5

O then bespoke Joseph,
  With words most unkind:
"Let him pluck thee a cherry
20   That brought thee with child."

6

O then bespoke the babe,
  Within his mother's womb:
"Bow down then the tallest tree
  For my mother to have some."

7

25 Then bowed down the highest tree
  Unto his mother's hand;
Then she cried, "See, Joseph,
  I have cherries at command."

8

O then bespake Joseph:
30   "I have done Mary wrong;
But cheer up, my dearest,
  And be not cast down."

9

Then Mary plucked a cherry
  As red as the blood,
35 Then Mary went home
  With her heavy load.

10

Then Mary took her babe
  And sat him on her knee,
Saying, "My dear son, tell me
40   What this world will be."

11

"O I shall be as dead, mother,
  As the stones in the wall;
O the stones in the streets, mother,
  Shall mourn for me all.

12

45 "Upon Easter-day, mother,
  My uprising shall be;
O the sun and the moon, mother,
  Shall both rise with me."

Dives and Lazarus[4]

1

As it fell out upon a day,
  Rich Dives he made a feast,
And he invited all his friends,
  And gentry of the best.

2

5 Then Lazarus laid him down and down,
  And down at Dives' door:
"Some meat, some drink, brother Dives,
  Bestow upon the poor."

4. Child, No. 56.A. See Luke xvi.19–31.

3

"Thou art none of my brother, Lazarus,
    That lies begging at my door;
No meat nor drink will I give thee,
    Nor bestow upon the poor."

4

Then Lazarus laid him down and down,
    And down at Dives' wall:
"Some meat, some drink, brother Dives,
    Or with hunger starve I shall."

5

"Thou art none of my brother, Lazarus,
    That lies begging at my wall;
No meat nor drink will I give thee,
    But with hunger starve you shall."

6

Then Lazarus laid him down and down,
    And down at Dives' gate:
"Some meat, some drink, brother Dives,
    For Jesus Christ his sake."

7

"Thou art none of my brother, Lazarus,
    That lies begging at my gate;
No meat nor drink will I give thee,
    For Jesus Christ his sake."

8

Then Dives sent out his merry men,
    To whip poor Lazarus away;
They had no power to strike a stroke,
    But flung their whips away.

9

Then Dives sent out his hungry dogs,
    To bite him as he lay;
They had no power to bite at all,
    But licked his sores away.

10

As it fell out upon a day,
    Poor Lazarus sickened and died;
Then came two angels out of heaven
    His soul therein to guide.

11

"Rise up, rise up, brother Lazarus,
    And go along with me;
For you've a place prepared in heaven,
    To sit on an angel's knee."

12

As it fell out upon a day,
    Rich Dives sickened and died;
Then came two serpents out of hell,
    His soul therein to guide.

13

"Rise up, rise up, brother Dives,
    And go with us to see
A dismal place, prepared in hell,
    From which thou canst not flee."

14

Then Dives looked up with his eyes,
    And saw poor Lazarus blest:
"Give me one drop of water, brother Lazarus,
    To quench my flaming thirst.

15

"Oh had I as many years to abide
   As there are blades of grass,
Then there would be an end, but now
60   Hell's pains will ne'er be past.
16

"Oh was I now but alive again,
   The space of one half hour!
Oh that I had my peace secure!
   Then the devil should have no power."

Sir Patrick Spens[5]

1

The king sits in Dumferling town,
   Drinking the blude-reid° wine: *blood-red*
"O whar will I get guid sailor,
   To sail this ship of mine?"
2

5 Up and spak an eldern knicht,
   Sat at the king's richt knee:
"Sir Patrick Spens is the best sailor
   That sails upon the sea."
3

The king has written a braid° letter   *broad*
10   And signed it wi' his hand,
And sent it to Sir Patrick Spens,
   Was walking on the sand.
4

The first line that Sir Patrick read,
   A loud lauch° lauched he;   *laugh*
15 The next line that Sir Patrick read,
   The tear blinded his ee.°   *eye*
5

"O wha is this has done this deed,
   This ill deed done to me,
To send me out this time o' the year,
20   To sail upon the sea?
6

"Mak haste, mak haste, my mirry men all,
   Our guid ship sails the morn."
"O say na sae,° my master dear,   *so*
   For I fear a deadly storm.
7

25 "Late, late yestre'en I saw the new moon
   Wi' the auld moon in hir arm,
And I fear, I fear, my dear master,
   That we will come to harm."
8

O our Scots nobles were richt laith°   *loath*
30   To weet° their cork-heeled shoon,°   *wet / shoes*
But lang or° a' the play were played   *before*
   Their hats they swam aboon.[6]
9

O lang, lang may their ladies sit,
   Wi' their fans into their hand,
35 Or ere they see Sir Patrick Spens
   Come sailing to the land.

---

5. Child, No. 58.A.   6. I.e., their hats swam above (them).

10

O lang, lang may the ladies stand
  Wi' their gold kems° in their hair,   *combs*
Waiting for their ain dear lords,
40   For they'll see them na mair.

11

Half o'er, half o'er to Aberdour
  It's fifty fadom deep,
And there lies guid Sir Patrick Spens
  Wi' the Scots lords at his feet.

The Unquiet Grave[7]

1

"The wind doth blow today, my love,
  And a few small drops of rain;
I never had but one true-love,
  In cold grave she was lain.

2

5 "I'll do as much for my true-love
  As any young man may;
I'll sit and mourn all at her grave
  For a twelvemonth and a day."

3

The twelvemonth and a day being up,
10   The dead began to speak:
"Oh who sits weeping on my grave,
  And will not let me sleep?"

4

" 'T is I, my love, sits on your grave,
  And will not let you sleep;
15 For I crave one kiss of your clay-cold lips,
  And that is all I seek."

5

"You crave one kiss of my clay-cold lips,
  But my breath smells earthy strong;
If you have one kiss of my clay-cold lips,
20   Your time will not be long.

6

" 'T is down in yonder garden green,
  Love, where we used to walk,
The finest flower that e'er was seen
  Is withered to a stalk.

7

25 "The stalk is withered dry, my love,
  So will our hearts decay;
So make yourself content, my love,
  Till God calls you away."

The Wife of Usher's Well[8]

1

There lived a wife at Usher's Well,
  And a wealthy wife was she;
She had three stout and stalwart sons,
  And sent them o'er the sea.

7. Child, No. 78.A.   8. Child, No. 79.A.

2

5 They hadna been a week from her,
    A week but barely ane,
  Whan word came to the carlin° wife   *peasant*
    That her three sons were gane.

3

  They hadna been a week from her,
10   A week but barely three,
  Whan word came to the carlin wife
    That her sons she'd never see.

4

  "I wish the wind may never cease,
    Nor fashes° in the flood,   *troubles*
15 Till my three sons come hame to me,
    In earthly flesh and blood."

5

  It fell about the Martinmass,[9]
    When nights are lang and mirk,
  The carlin wife's three sons came hame,
20   And their hats were o' the birk.°   *birch*

6

  It neither grew in syke° nor ditch,   *trench*
    Nor yet in any sheugh;°   *furrow*
  But at the gates o' Paradise,
    That birk grew fair eneugh.

7

25 "Blow up the fire, my maidens,
    Bring water from the well;
  For a' my house shall feast this night,
    Since my three sons are well."

8

  And she has made to them a bed,
30   She's made it large and wide,
  And she's ta'en her mantle her about,
    Sat down at the bed-side.

9

  Up then crew the red, red cock,
    And up and crew the gray;
35 The eldest to the youngest said,
    " 'T is time we were away."

10

  The cock he hadna crawed but once,
    And clapped his wings at a',
  When the youngest to the eldest said,
40   "Brother, we must awa'.

11

  "The cock doth craw, the day doth daw,
    The channerin'° worm doth chide;   *fretting*
  Gin° we be missed out o' our place,   *if*
    A sair° pain we maun° bide.   *sore / must*

12

45 "Fare ye weel, my mother dear!
    Fareweel to barn and byre!°   *cowhouse*
  And fare ye weel, the bonny lass,
    That kindles my mother's fire!"

---

9. The feast of St. Martin (the martyred Pope Martin I, died 655), November 11.

Bonny Barbara Allan[1]

1

It was in and about the Martinmas[2] time,
   When the green leaves were a falling,
That Sir John Græme, in the West Country,
   Fell in love with Barbara Allan.

2

5 He sent his man down through the town,
   To the place where she was dwelling:
"O haste and come to my master dear,
   Gin° ye be Barbara Allan."   *if*

3

O hooly,° hooly rose she up,   *slowly, gently*
10   To the place where he was lying,
And when she drew the curtain by:
   "Young man, I think you're dying."

4

"O it's I'm sick, and very, very sick,
   And 'tis a' for Barbara Allan."
15 "O the better for me ye s'° never be,   *ye shall*
   Though your heart's blood were a-spilling.

5

"O dinna° ye mind, young man," said she,   *don't*
   "When ye was in the tavern a drinking,
That ye made the healths gae° round and round, *go*
20   And slighted Barbara Allan?"

6

He turned his face unto the wall,
   And death was with him dealing:
"Adieu, adieu, my dear friends all,
   And be kind to Barbara Allan."

7

25 And slowly, slowly raise she up,
   And slowly, slowly left him,
And sighing said, she could not stay,
   Since death of life had reft him.

8

She had not gane a mile but twa,
30   When she heard the dead-bell ringing,
And every jow° that the dead-bell geid,°   *stroke / gave*
   It cried, "Woe to Barbara Allan!"

9

"O mother, mother, make my bed!
   O make it saft and narrow!
35 Since my love died for me to-day,
   I'll die for him to-morrow."

The Baffled Knight[3]

1

There was a knight, and he was young,
   A-riding along the way, sir,
And there he met a lady fair,
   Among the cocks of hay, sir.

---

1. Child, No. 84.A.
2. The feast of St. Martin (the martyred   Pope Martin I, died 655), November 11.
                                        3. Child, No. 112.B.

2

5 Quoth he, "Shall you and I, lady,
  Among the grass lie down a?
 And I will have a special care
  Of rumpling of your gown a."

3

 "If you will go along with me
10 Unto my father's hall, sir,
 You shall enjoy my maidenhead,
  And my estate and all, sir."

4

 So he mounted her on a milk-white steed,
  Himself upon another,
15 And then they rid upon the road,
  Like sister and like brother.

5

 And when she came to her father's house,
  Which was moated round about, sir,
 She stepped straight within the gate,
20 And shut this young knight out, sir.

6

 "Here is a purse of gold," she said,
  "Take it for your pains, sir;
 And I will send my father's man
  To go home with you again, sir.

7

25 "And if you meet a lady fair,
  As you go through the next town, sir,
 You must not fear the dew of the grass,
  Nor the rumpling of her gown, sir.

8

 "And if you meet a lady gay,
30 As you go by the hill, sir,
 If you will not when you may,
  You shall not when you will, sir."

Johnie Armstrong[4]

1

There dwelt a man in fair Westmoreland,
 Johnie Armstrong men did him call,
He had neither lands nor rents coming in,
 Yet he kept eight score men in his hall.

2

5 He had horse and harness for them all,
 Goodly steeds were all milk-white;
O the golden bands an about their necks,
 And their weapons, they were all alike.

3

News then was brought unto the king
10 That there was sic° a one as he,   *such*
That livéd lyke a bold outlaw,
 And robbéd all the north country.

4

The king he writ an a letter then,
 A letter which was large and long;
15 He signéd it with his owne hand,
 And he promised to do him no wrong.

---

4. Child, No. 169.A.

5
When this letter came Johnie untill,
  His heart it was as blythe as birds on the tree:
"Never was I sent for before any king,
  My father, my grandfather, nor none but me.
6
"And if we go the king before,
  I would we went most orderly;
Every man of you shall have his scarlet cloak,
  Laced with silver laces three.
7
"Every one of you shall have his velvet coat,
  Laced with silver lace so white;
O the golden bands an about your necks,
  Black hats, white feathers, all alike."
8
By the morrow morning at ten of the clock,
  Towards Edinburgh gone was he,
And with him all his eight score men;
  Good Lord, it was a goodly sight for to see!
9
When Johnie came before the king,
  He fell down on his knee;
"O pardon, my sovereign leige," he said,
  "O pardon my eight score men and me!"
10
"Thou shalt have no pardon, thou traitor strong,
  For thy eight score men nor thee;
For tomorrow morning by ten of the clock,
  Both thou and them shall hang on the gallow-tree."
11
But Johnie looked over his left shoulder,
  Good Lord, what a grevious look looked he!
Saying, "Asking grace of a graceless face—
  Why there is none for you nor me."
12
But Johnie had a bright sword by his side,
  And it was made of the metal so free,[5]
That had not the king stepped his foot aside,
  He had smitten his head from his fair body.
13
Saying, "Fight on, my merry men all,
  And see that none of you be ta'en;
For rather than men shall say we were hanged,
  Let them report how we were slain."
14
Then, God wot, fair Edinburgh rose,
  And so beset poor Johnie round,
That fourscore and ten of Johnie's best men
  Lay gasping all upon the ground.
15
Then like a mad man Johnie laid about,
  And like a mad man then fought he,
Until a false Scot came Johnie behind,
  And run him through the fair body.
16
Saying, "Fight on, my merry men all,
  And see that none of you be ta'en;
For I will stand by and bleed but awhile,
  And then will I come and fight again."

5. "Free" has a range of meanings: noble, ready, workable.

17

65 News then was brought to young Johnie Armstrong,
　　As he stood by his nurse's knee,
Who vowed if e'er he lived for to be a man,
　　O' the treacherous Scots revenged he'd be.

Mary Hamilton[6]

1

Word's gane to the kitchen,
　　And word's gane to the ha',
That Marie Hamilton gangs° wi' bairn°　　　　　　*goes / child*
　　To the hichest° Stewart of a'.　　　　　　　　　*highest*

2

5 He's courted her in the kitchen,
　　He's courted her in the ha',
He's courted her in the laigh cellar,[7]
　　And that was warst of a'.

3

She's tied it in her apron
10　　And she's thrown it in the sea;
Says, "Sink ye, swim ye, bonny wee babe!
　　You'll ne'er get mair o' me."

4

Down then cam the auld queen,
　　Goud° tassels tying her hair:　　　　　　　　　*gold*
15 "O Marie, where's the bonny wee babe
　　That I heard greet sae sair?"[8]

5

"There was never a babe intill° my room,　　　　　*in*
　　As little designs to be;
It was but a touch o' my sair side,
20　　Come o'er my fair body."

6

"O Marie, put on your robes o' black,
　　Or else your robes o' brown,
For ye maun° gang wi' me the night,　　　　　　*must*
　　To see fair Edinbro' town."

7

25 "I winna° put on my robes o' black,　　　　　　*won't*
　　Nor yet my robes o' brown;
But I'll put on my robes o' white,
　　To shine through Edinbro' town."

8

When she gaed° up the Cannogate,[9]　　　　　　*went*
30　　She laughed loud laughters three;
But when she cam down the Cannogate
　　The tear blinded her ee.°　　　　　　　　　　*eye*

9

When she gaed up the Parliament stair,
　　The heel cam aff her shee;
35 And lang or° she cam down again　　　　　　　*before*
　　She was condemned to dee.

10

When she cam down the Cannogate,
　　The Cannogate sae free,
Many a lady looked o'er her window,
40　　Weeping for this lady.

6. Child, No. 173.A.
7. "Laigh cellar": low cellar, basement.
8. "Greet sae sair": cry so sorely.
9. The Cannogate is the Edinburgh street leading uphill from Holyrood House (where the queen and the "four Maries" of line 69 lived) to the Tolbooth, which was both jail and judicial chamber and, on occasion, the place where Parliament (line 33) sat.

11

"Ye need nae weep for me," she says,
  "Ye need nae weep for me;
For had I not slain mine own sweet babe,
  This death I wadna dee.

12

45 "Bring me a bottle of wine," she says,
  "The best that e'er ye ha'e,
That I may drink to my weil-wishers,
  And they may drink to me.

13

"Here's a health to the jolly sailors,
50   That sail upon the main;
Let them never let on to my father and mother
  But what I'm coming hame.

14

"Here's a health to the jolly sailors,
  That sail upon the sea;
55 Let them never let on to my father and mother
  That I cam here to dee.

15

"Oh little did my mother think,
  The day she cradled me,
What lands I was to travel through,
60   What death I was to dee.

16

"Oh little did my father think,
  The day he held up me,
What lands I was to travel through,
  What death I was to dee.

17

65 "Last night I washed the queen's feet,
  And gently laid her down;
And a' the thanks I've gotten the night[1]
  To be hanged in Edinbro' town!

18

"Last night there was four Maries,
70   The night there'll be but three;
There was Marie Seton, and Marie Beton,
  And Marie Carmichael, and me."

Bonnie George Campbell[2]

1

High upon Highlands,
  And laigh° upon Tay,[3]   *low*
Bonnie George Campbell
  Rode out on a day.

2

5 He saddled, he bridled,
  And gallant rode he,
And hame cam his guid horse,
  But never cam he.

3

Out cam his mother dear,
10   Greeting° fu' sair,°   *weeping / sore[ly]*
And out cam his bonnie bride,
  Riving° her hair.   *tearing*

---

1. I.e., tonight.
2. Child, No. 210.C.
3. The longest river in Scotland, coming down from the Highlands into the Lowlands and entering the North Sea at Perth.

4
"The meadow lies green,
  The corn is unshorn,
15 But bonnie George Campbell
  Will never return."

5
Saddled and bridled
  And booted rode he,
A plume in his helmet,
20   A sword at his knee.

6
But toom° cam his saddle,   *empty*
  All bloody to see,
Oh, hame cam his guid horse,
  But never cam he!

Get Up and Bar the Door[4]

1
It fell about the Martinmas[5] time,
  And a gay time it was then,
When our goodwife got puddings to make,
  And she's boiled them in the pan.

2
5 The wind sae° cauld blew south and north,   *so*
  And blew into the floor;
Quoth our goodman to our goodwife,
  "Gae° out and bar the door."   *go*

3
"My hand is in my hussyfskap.°   *housewifery*
10   Goodman, as ye may see;
An° it should nae be barred this hundred year, *if*
  It s'° no be barred for me."   *shall*

4
They made a paction 'tween them twa,
  They made it firm and sure,
15 That the first word whae'er should speak,
  Should rise and bar the door.

5
Then by there came two gentlemen,
  At twelve o'clock at night,
And they could neither see house nor hall,
20   Nor coal nor candle-light.

6
"Now whether is this a rich man's house,
  Or whether is it a poor?"
But ne'er a word wad° ane o' them speak,   *would*
  For barring of the door.

7
25 And first they ate the white puddings,
  And then they ate the black;
Though muckle° thought the goodwife to hersel, *much, a lot*
  Yet ne'er a word she spak.

8
Then said the one unto the other,
30   "Here, man, tak ye my knife;
Do ye tak aff° the auld man's beard,   *off*
  And I'll kiss the goodwife."

---

4. Child, No. 275.A.
5. The feast of St. Martin (the martyred Pope Martin I, died 655), November 11.

9

"But there's nae water in the house,
  And what shall we do then?"
35 "What ails ye at[6] the pudding-broo,°   -broth
  That boils into the pan?"

10

O up then started our goodman,
  An angry man was he:
"Will ye kiss my wife before my een,°   eyes
40 And scad° me wi' pudding-bree?"°   scald / -broth

11

Then up and started our goodwife,
  Gied° three skips on the floor: gave
"Goodman, you've spoken the foremost word,
  Get up and bar the door."

The Bitter Withy

1

As it fell out on a holy day,
  The drops of rain did fall, did fall,
Our Saviour asked leave of his mother Mary
  If he might go play at ball.

2

5 "To play at ball, my own dear son,
  It's time you was going or gone,
But be sure let me hear no complain of you,
  At night when you do come home."

3

It was upling scorn and downling scorn,[7]
10   Oh, there he met three jolly jerdins;°   boys?
Oh, there he asked the jolly jerdins
  If they would go play at ball.

4

"Oh, we are lords' and ladies' sons,
  Born in bower or in hall,
15 And you are some poor maid's child
  Borned in an ox's stall."

5

"If you are lords' and ladies' sons,
  Borned in bower or in hall,
Then at last I'll make it appear
20   That I am above you all."

6

Our Saviour built a bridge with the beams of the sun,
  And over it he gone, he gone he.
And after followed the three jolly jerdins,
  And drownded they were all three.

7

25 It was upling scorn and downling scorn,
  The mothers of them did whoop and call,
Crying out, "Mary mild, call home your child,
  For ours are drownded all."

8

Mary mild, Mary mild, called home her child,
30   And laid our Saviour across her knee,
And with a whole handful of bitter withy°   willow
  She gave him slashes three.

---

6. I.e., what's the matter with.
7. There was scorn everywhere (*upling, downling*).

9

Then he says to his mother, "Oh! the withy, oh! the withy,
  The bitter withy that causes me to smart, to smart,
35 Oh! the withy, it shall be the very first tree
  That perishes at the heart."

THOMAS WYATT
(1503–1542)

The Long Love That in My Thought Doth Harbor[1]

The long love that in my thought doth harbor,
And in my heart doth keep his residence,
Into my face presseth with bold pretense
And there encampeth, spreading his banner.
5 She that me learns° to love and suffer   *teaches*
And wills that my trust and lust's negligence
Be reined by reason, shame, and reverence
With his hardiness takes displeasure.
Wherewithal unto the heart's forest he fleeth,
10 Leaving his enterprise with pain and cry,
And there him hideth, and not appeareth.
What may I do, when my master feareth,
But in the field with him to live and die?
For good is the life ending faithfully.

                                     1557

Whoso List To Hunt[2]

Whoso list to hunt, I know where is an hind,
  But as for me, alas, I may no more;
  The vain travail hath wearied me so sore,
  I am of them that furthest come behind.
5 Yet may I by no means my wearied mind
  Draw from the deer, but as she fleeth afore
  Fainting I follow; I leave off therefore,
  Since in a net I seek to hold the wind.
Who list her hunt, I put him out of doubt,
10   As well as I, may spend his time in vain.
  And graven with diamonds in letters plain,
There is written her fair neck round about,
  "*Noli me tangere*,[3] for Caesar's I am,
  And wild for to hold, though I seem tame."

                                 Egerton Ms.

My Galley Charged with Forgetfulness

My galley charged[4] with forgetfulness
  Thorough sharp seas in winter nights doth pass
  'Tween rock and rock; and eke° mine enemy, alas,   *also*
  That is my lord, steereth with cruelness;

1. Translated from Petrarch. Compare the translation by the Earl of Surrey, *Love That Doth Reign and Live Within My Thought*.
2. This poem, like many of Wyatt's, existed only in manuscript form until comparatively recently. In place of a date of publication, the manuscript source is given for all such poems in this selection.
3. Touch me not.
4. Wyatt's meter is so often irregular that it is difficult to say with certainty when he intended an *-ed* ending to be pronounced as a second syllable and when not. Hence no attempt has been made to mark syllabic endings with an accent in any of Wyatt's poems, although in this particular poem such endings appear to be intended in lines 1, 8, 11, and 13.

5   And every oar a thought in readiness,
  As though that death were light in such a case.
  An endless wind doth tear the sail apace
  Of forced sighs, and trusty fearfulness.
 A rain of tears, a cloud of dark disdain,
10   Hath done the wearied cords great hinderance;
  Wreathed with error and eke with ignorance,
 The stars be hid that led me to this pain;
  Drowned is reason that should me consort,
  And I remain despairing of the port.

1557

They Flee from Me

They flee from me, that sometime did me seek,
With naked foot stalking in my chamber.
I have seen them, gentle, tame, and meek,
That now are wild, and do not remember
5   That sometime they put themselves in danger
To take bread at my hand; and now they range,
Busily seeking with a continual change.

Thanked be Fortune it hath been otherwise,
Twenty times better; but once in special,
10   In thin array, after a pleasant guise,
When her loose gown from her shoulders did fall,
And she me caught in her arms long and small,°   *slender*
And therewith all sweetly did me kiss
And softly said, "Dear heart, how like you this?"

15   It was no dream, I lay broad waking.
But all is turned, thorough my gentleness,
Into a strange fashion of forsaking;
And I have leave to go, of her goodness,
And she also to use newfangleness.
20   But since that I so kindely[5] am served,
I fain would know what she hath deserved.

1557

My Lute, Awake!

My lute, awake! Perform the last
Labor that thou and I shall waste,
And end that I have now begun;
For when this song is sung and past,
5   My lute, be still, for I have done.

As to be heard where ear is none,
As lead to grave° in marble stone,   *engrave*
My song may pierce her heart as soon.
Should we then sigh or sing or moan?
10   No, no, my lute, for I have done.

The rocks do not so cruelly
Repulse the waves continually
As she my suit and affection.
So that I am past remedy,
15   Whereby my lute and I have done.

---

5. I.e., in the normal way of womankind, an older meaning that does not exclude the modern meaning of "kindly."

Proud of the spoil that thou hast got
Of simple hearts, thorough love's shot;
By whom, unkind, thou hast them won,
Think not he hath his bow forgot,
20   Although my lute and I have done.

Vengeance shall fall on thy disdain
That makest but game on earnest pain.
Think not alone under the sun
Unquit° to cause thy lovers plain,   *unrequited*
25   Although my lute and I have done.

Perchance thee lie withered and old
The winter nights that are so cold,
Plaining in vain unto the moon.
Thy wishes then dare not be told.
30   Care then who list,° for I have done.   *likes*

And then may chance thee to repent
The time that thou hast lost and spent
To cause thy lovers sigh and swoon.
Then shalt thou know beauty but lent,
35   And wish and want as I have done.

Now cease, my lute. This is the last
Labor that thou and I shall waste,
And ended is that we begun.
Now is this song both sung and past;
40   My lute, be still, for I have done.

1557

Forget Not Yet

Forget not yet the tried intent
Of such a truth as I have meant;
My great travail so gladly spent
            Forget not yet.

5   Forget not yet when first began
The weary life ye know, since whan°   *when*
The suit, the service none tell can;
            Forget not yet.

Forget not yet the great assays,°   *trials*
10   The cruel wrong, the scornful ways,
The painful patience in denays,°   *denials*
            Forget not yet.

Forget not yet, forget not this,
How long ago hath been and is
15   The mind that never meant amiss;
            Forget not yet.

Forget not then thine own approved,
The which so long hath thee so loved,
Whose steadfast faith yet never moved;
20   Forget not this.

Devonshire Ms.

HENRY HOWARD, EARL OF SURREY
(ca. 1517–1547)

The Soote Season

The soote° season, that bud and bloom forth brings,	*sweet*
With green hath clad the hill and eke° the vale;	*also*
The nightingale with feathers new she sings;	
The turtle° to her make° hath told her tale.	*turtledove / mate*
5 Summer is come, for every spray now springs;	
The hart hath hung his old head on the pale;	
The buck in brake his winter coat he flings,	
The fishes float with new repairéd scale;	
The adder all her slough away she slings,	
10 The swift swallow pursueth the flies small;	
The busy bee her honey now she mings.°	*remembers*
Winter is worn, that was the flowers' bale.°	*harm*
And thus I see among these pleasant things,	
Each care decays, and yet my sorrow springs.	

1557

Love, That Doth Reign and Live Within My Thought[1]

Love, that doth reign and live within my thought,	
And built his seat within my captive breast,	
Clad in the arms wherein with me he fought,	
Oft in my face he doth his banner rest.	
5 But she that taught me love and suffer pain,	
My doubtful hope and eke my hot desire	
With shamefast° look to shadow and refrain,	*shamefaced*
Her smiling grace converteth straight to ire.	
And coward Love, then, to the heart apace	
10 Taketh his flight, where he doth lurk and plain,°	*complain*
His purpose lost, and dare not show his face.	
For my lord's guilt thus faultless bide I pain,	
Yet from my lord shall not my foot remove:	
Sweet is the death that taketh end by love.	

1557

Wyatt Resteth Here

Wyatt resteth here, that quick° could never rest;	*living*
Whose heavenly gifts increaséd by disdain,	
And virtue sank the deeper in his breast;	
Such profit he of envy could obtain.	
5 A head where wisdom mysteries did frame,	
Whose hammers beat still in that lively brain	
As on a stithy,° where some work of fame	*anvil*
Was daily wrought, to turn to Britain's gain.	
A visage stern and mild, where both did grow,	
10 Vice to contemn, in virtues to rejoice,	
Amid great storms, whom grace assuréd so,	
To live upright, and smile at fortune's choice.	
A hand that taught what might be said in rhyme;	
That reft Chaucer the glory of his wit;	

1. Translated from Petrarch. Compare the translation by Sir Thomas Wyatt, *The Long Love That in My Thought Doth Harbor.*

15 A mark, the which—unperfited,° for time—   *uncompleted*
    Some may approach, but never none shall hit.
    A tongue that served in foreign realms his king;
    Whose courteous talk to virtue did enflame
    Each noble heart; a worthy guide to bring
20 Our English youth, by travail, unto fame.
    An eye whose judgment no affect° could blind,   *passion*
    Friends to allure, and foes to reconcile;
    Whose piercing look did represent a mind
    With virtue fraught, reposéd, void of guile.
25 A heart where dread yet never so impressed
    To hide the thought that might the truth advance;
    In neither fortune lost, nor so repressed,
    To swell in wealth, nor yield unto mischance.
    A valiant corps,° where force and beauty met,   *body*
30 Happy, alas! too happy, but for foes,
    Livéd, and ran the race that nature set;
    Of manhood's shape, where she the mold did lose.
    But to the heavens that simple soul is fled,
    Which left with such as covet Christ to know
35 Witness of faith that never shall be dead,
    Sent for our health, but not receivéd so.
    Thus, for our guilt, this jewel have we lost;
    The earth his bones, the heavens possess his ghost.

                                                                 1557

Although I Had a Check

    Although I had a check,
        To give the mate is hard;
    For I have found a neck,°   *nook*
        To keep my men in guard.
5   And you that hardy are
        To give so great assay°   *assault*
    Unto a man of war
        To drive his men away,

    I rede° you take good heed,   *advise*
10   And mark this foolish verse;
    For I will so provide
        That I will have your fers.°   *queen*
    And when your fers is had
        And all your war is done,
15 Then shall yourself be glad
        To end that you begun.

    For if by chance I win
        Your person in the field,
    Too late then come you in,
20   Yourself to me to yield.
    For I will use my power
        As captain full of might,
    And such I will devour
        As use to show me spite.

25 And for because you gave
        Me check in such degree
    This vantage, lo, I have:
        Now check, and guard to thee.
    Defend it if thou may,
30   Stand stiff in thine estate;
    For sure I will assay,°   *try*
        If I can give thee mate.

                                                                 1557

SIR WALTER RALEGH
(ca. 1552–1618)

The Nymph's Reply to the Shepherd[1]

If all the world and love were young,
And truth in every shepherd's tongue,
These pretty pleasures might me move
To live with thee and be thy love.

5 Time drives the flocks from field to fold
When rivers rage and rocks grow cold,
And Philomel° becometh dumb;   *the nightingale*
The rest complains of cares to come.

The flowers do fade, and wanton fields
10 To wayward winter reckoning yields;
A honey tongue, a heart of gall,
Is fancy's spring, but sorrow's fall.

Thy gowns, thy shoes, thy beds of roses,
Thy cap, thy kirtle,[2] and thy posies
15 Soon break, soon wither, soon forgotten—
In folly ripe, in reason rotten.

Thy belt of straw and ivy buds,
Thy coral clasps and amber studs,
All these in me no means can move
20 To come to thee and be thy love.

But could youth last and love still breed,
Had joys no date[3] nor age no need,
Then these delights my mind might move
To live with thee and be thy love.

                                                1600

The Passionate Man's Pilgrimage

Give me my scallop-shell[4] of quiet,
My staff of faith to walk upon,
My scrip[5] of joy, immortal diet,
My bottle of salvation,
5 My gown of glory, hope's true gage,°   *pledge*
And thus I'll take my pilgrimage.

Blood must be my body's balmer,
No other balm will there be given,
Whilst my soul like a white palmer[6]
10 Travels to the land of heaven,
Over the silver mountains,
Where spring the nectar fountains;
And there I'll kiss
The bowl of bliss,
15 And drink my eternal fill
On every milken hill.

1. Written in reply to Christopher Marlowe's *The Passionate Shepherd to His Love.*
2. A long dress, often worn under an outer garment.
3. I.e., terminal date.
4. A scallop shell or something resembling it was worn as the sign of a pilgrim.
5. Pilgrim's knapsack or bag.
6. A person wearing a palm leaf as a sign that he had made a pilgrimage to the Holy Land.

My soul will be a-dry before,
But after it will ne'er thirst more;
And by the happy blissful way
20 More peaceful pilgrims I shall see
That have shook off their gowns of clay
And go appareled fresh like me.
I'll bring them first
To slake their thirst,
25 And then to taste those nectar suckets,°   *confections*
At the clear wells
Where sweetness dwells,
Drawn up by saints in crystal buckets.

And when our bottles and all we
30 Are filled with immortality,
Then the holy paths we'll travel,
Strewed with rubies thick as gravel,
Ceilings of diamonds, sapphire floors,
High walls of coral, and pearl bowers,
35 From thence to heaven's bribeless hall
Where no corrupted voices brawl,
No conscience molten into gold,
Nor forged accusers bought and sold,
No cause deferred, nor vain-spent journey,
40 For there Christ is the king's attorney,
Who pleads for all, without degrees,
And he hath angels,[7] but no fees.
When the grand twelve million jury
Of our sins and sinful fury,
45 'Gainst our souls black verdicts give,
Christ pleads his death, and then we live.
Be thou my speaker, taintless pleader,
Unblotted lawyer, true proceeder;
Thou movest salvation even for alms,
50 Not with a bribed lawyer's palms.
And this is my eternal plea
To him that made heaven, earth, and sea,
Seeing my flesh must die so soon,
And want a head to dine next noon,
55 Just at the stroke when my veins start and spread,
Set on my soul an everlasting head.
Then am I ready, like a palmer fit,
To tread those blest paths which before I writ.

1604

Nature, That Washed Her Hands in Milk

Nature, that washed her hands in milk,
And had forgot to dry them,
Instead of earth took snow and silk,
At love's request to try them,
5 If she a mistress could compose
To please love's fancy out of those.

Her eyes he would should be of light,
A violet breath, and lips of jelly;
Her hair not black, nor overbright,
10 And of the softest down her belly;
As for her inside he'd have it
Only of wantonness and wit.

---

7. A punning reference to the gold coin of that name, ten shillings in value.

At love's entreaty such a one
Nature made, but with her beauty
15   She hath framed a heart of stone;
So as love, by ill destiny,
Must die for her whom nature gave him,
Because her darling would not save him.

But time (which nature doth despise,
20   And rudely gives her love the lie,
Makes hope a fool, and sorrow wise)
His hands do neither wash nor dry;
But being made of steel and rust,
Turns snow and silk and milk to dust.

25   The light, the belly, lips, and breath,
He dims, discolors, and destroys;
With those he feeds but fills not death,
Which sometimes were the food of joys.
Yea, time doth dull each lively wit,
30   And dries all wantonness with it.

Oh, cruel time! which takes in trust
Our youth, our joys, and all we have,
And pays us but with age and dust;
Who in the dark and silent grave
35   When we have wandered all our ways
Shuts up the story of our days.[8]

ca. 1610

EDMUND SPENSER
(ca. 1552–1599)

From Amoretti

Sonnet 67

Lyke as a huntsman after weary chace,
Seeing the game from him escapt away,
Sits downe to rest him in some shady place,
With panting hounds beguiléd of their pray:
5   So after long pursuit and vaine assay,
When I all weary had the chace forsooke,
The gentle deare returnd the selfe-same way,
Thinking to quench her thirst at the next brooke.
There she beholding me with mylder looke,
10   Sought not to fly, but fearelesse still did bide:
Till I in hand her yet halfe trembling tooke,
And with her owne goodwill hir fyrmely tyde.
Strange thing me seemd to see a beast so wyld,
So goodly wonne with her owne will beguyld.

8. Another version of this stanza, traditionally supposed to have been written by Ralegh on the night before his execution, was published in 1628. In it the first three words are changed to "Even such is time," and the following couplet is added: "And from which earth, and grave, and dust/The Lord shall raise me up, I trust." The poem as a whole existed only in manuscript form until 1902.

Sonnet 68

Most glorious Lord of lyfe, that on this day,[1]
Didst make thy triumph over death and sin:
And having harrowd hell,[2] didst bring away
Captivity thence captive us to win:[3]
5 This joyous day, deare Lord, with joy begin,
And grant that we for whom thou diddest dye
Being with thy deare blood clene washt from sin,
May live for ever in felicity.
And that thy love we weighing worthily,
10 May likewise love thee for the same againe:
And for thy sake that all lyke deare didst buy,
With love may one another entertayne.
So let us love, deare love, lyke as we ought,
Love is the lesson which the Lord us taught.[4]

Sonnet 70

Fresh spring the herald of loves mighty king,
In whose cote armour° richly are displayd   *coat of arms*
All sorts of flowers the which on earth do spring
In goodly colours gloriously arrayd.
5 Goe to my love, where she is carelesse layd,
Yet in her winters bowre not well awake:
Tell her the joyous time wil not be staid
Unless she doe him by the forelock take.[5]
Bid her therefore her selfe soone ready make,
10 To wayt on love amongst his lovely crew:
Where every one that misseth then her make,°   *mate*
Shall be by him amearst° with penance dew.   *punished*
Make hast therefore sweet love, whilest it is prime,°   *spring*
For none can call againe the passéd time.

Sonnet 75

One day I wrote her name upon the strand,
But came the waves and washéd it away:
Agayne I wrote it with a second hand,°   *a second time*
But came the tyde, and made my paynes his pray.
5 "Vayne man," sayd she, "that doest in vaine assay,
A mortall thing so to immortalize,
For I my selve shall lyke to this decay,
And eek° my name bee wypéd out lykewize."   *also*
"Not so," quod° I, "let baser things devize°   *quoth / plan*
10 To dy in dust, but you shall live by fame:
My verse your vertues rare shall eternize,
And in the hevens wryte your glorious name.
Where whenas death shall all the world subdew,
Our love shall live, and later life renew."

Epithalamion[6]

Ye learned sisters[7] which have oftentimes
Beene to me ayding, others to adorne:
Whom ye thought worthy of your gracefull rymes,
That even the greatest did not greatly scorne

---

1. Easter.
2. A reference to the apocryphal account of Christ's descent into hell, after his crucifixion, in order to rescue the captive souls of the just.
3. "When he ascended up on high, he led captivity captive" (Ephesians iv.8).
4. "This is my commandment, That ye love one another, as I have loved you" (John xv.12).

5. "To take time by the forelock" is to act promptly.
6. The title (literally "at the bridal chamber") is the Greek word for "wedding song." Spenser's poem was published with the *Amoretti.*
7. The Muses, sources of inspiration.

5 To heare theyr names sung in your simple layes,
  But joyéd in theyr prayse.
  And when ye list your owne mishaps to mourne,
  Which death, or love, or fortunes wreck did rayse,
  Your string could soone to sadder tenor° turne,   *strain*
10 And teach the woods and waters to lament
  Your dolefull dreriment.
  Now lay those sorrowfull complaints aside,
  And having all your heads with girland crownd,
  Helpe me mine owne loves prayses to resound,
15 Ne let the same of any be envíde:
  So Orpheus[8] did for his owne bride,
  So I unto my selfe alone will sing,
  The woods shall to me answer and my Eccho ring.

  Early before the worlds light giving lampe,
20 His golden beame upon the hils doth spred,
  Having disperst the nights unchearefull dampe,
  Doe ye awake, and with fresh lustyhed
  Go to the bowre° of my belovéd love,   *bedchamber*
  My truest turtle dove,
25 Bid her awake; for Hymen[9] is awake,
  And long since ready forth his maske to move,
  With his bright Tead that flames with many a flake,°   *spark*
  And many a bachelor to waite on him,
  In theyr fresh garments trim.
30 Bid her awake therefore and soone her dight,°   *dress*
  For lo the wishéd day is come at last,
  That shall for al the paynes and sorrowes past,
  Pay to her usury of long delight:
  And whylest she doth her dight,
35 Doe ye to her of joy and solace° sing,   *pleasure*
  That all the woods may answer and your eccho ring.

  Bring with you all the Nymphes that you can heare[1]
  Both of the rivers and the forrests greene:
  And of the sea that neighbours to her neare,
40 Al with gay girlands goodly wel beseene.
  And let them also with them bring in hand,
  Another gay girland
  For my fayre love of lillyes and of roses,
  Bound truelove wize with a blew silke riband.
45 And let them make great store of bridale poses,°   *posies*
  And let them eeke bring store of other flowers
  To deck the bridale bowers.
  And let the ground whereas her foot shall tread,
  For feare the stones her tender foot should wrong
50 Be strewed with fragrant flowers all along,
  And diapred lyke the discolored mead.[2]
  Which done, doe at her chamber dore awayt,
  For she will waken strayt,°   *straightway*
  The whiles doe ye this song unto her sing,
55 The woods shall to you answer and your Eccho ring.

  Ye Nymphes of Mulla[3] which with carefull heed,
  The silver scaly trouts doe tend full well,
  And greedy pikes which use therein to feed,

8. Whose music was said to move even inanimate objects and to change foul weather to fair.
9. The Greek god of the wedding feast, represented as a young man bearing a torch ("Tead") and leading a "maske" or procession.
1. I.e., that can hear you.
2. And variegated like the many-colored meadow.
3. The Awbeg River in Ireland, near Spenser's home.

(Those trouts and pikes all others doo excell)
60 And ye likewise which keepe the rushy lake,
Where none doo fishes take,
Bynd up the locks the which hang scatterd light,
And in his waters which your mirror make,
Behold your faces as the christall bright,
65 That when you come whereas my love doth lie,
No blemish she may spie.
And eke ye lightfoot mayds which keepe the deere,
That on the hoary mountayne use to towre,[4]
And the wylde wolves which seeke them to devoure,
70 With your steele darts doo chace from comming neer
Be also present heere,
To helpe to decke her and to help to sing,
That all the woods may answer and your eccho ring.

Wake, now my love, awake; for it is time,
75 The Rosy Morne long since left Tithones bed,[5]
All ready to her silver coche to clyme,
And Phoebus gins to shew his glorious hed.
Hark how the cheerefull birds do chaunt theyr laies
And carroll of loves praise.
80 The merry Larke hir mattins sings aloft.
The thrush replyes, the Mavis descant[6] playes,
The Ouzell shrills, the Ruddock warbles soft,
So goodly all agree with sweet consent,
To this dayes merriment.
85 Ah my deere love why doe ye sleepe thus long,
When meeter were that ye should now awake,
T' awayt the comming of your joyous make,°   mate
And hearken to the birds lovelearnéd song,
The deawy leaves among.
90 For they of joy and pleasance to you sing,
That all the woods them answer and theyr eccho ring.

My love is now awake out of her dreame,
And her fayre eyes like stars that dimméd were
With darksome cloud, now shew theyr goodly beams
95 More bright then Hesperus° his head doth rere.   *evening star*
Come now ye damzels, daughters of delight,
Helpe quickly her to dight,
But first come ye fayre houres which were begot
In Joves sweet paradice, of Day and Night,
100 Which doe the seasons of the yeare allot,
And al that ever in this world is fayre
Doe make and still° repayre.   *continually*
And ye three handmayds of the Cyprian Queene,[7]
The which doe still adorne her beauties pride,
105 Helpe to addorne my beautifullest bride:
And as ye her array, still throw betweene°   *at intervals*
Some graces to be seene,
And as ye use to Venus, to her sing,
The whiles the woods shal answer and your eccho ring.

110 Now is my love all ready forth to come,
Let all the virgins therefore well awayt,
And ye fresh boyes that tend upon her groome

4. A hawking term meaning "to climb high."
5. The dawn, personified in mythology as the goddess Eos or Aurora, was the wife of Tithonus.
6. Melodic counterpart. The mavis, ouzell (or European blackbird), and ruddock (or robin) are all varieties of thrush.

7. Venus, whose handmaids were the three Graces: Aglaia, Thalia, and Euphrosyne. Their names mean "the brilliant one," "she who brings flowers," and "she who rejoices the heart."

Prepare your selves; for he is comming strayt.
Set all your things in seemely good aray
115 Fit for so joyfull day,
The joyfulst day that ever sunne did see.
Faire Sun, shew forth thy favourable ray,
And let thy lifull° heat not fervent be   *lifegiving*
For feare of burning her sunshyny face,
120 Her beauty to disgrace.°   *spoil*
O fayrest Phoebus, father of the Muse,
If ever I did honour thee aright,
Or sing the thing, that mote° thy mind delight,   *might*
Doe not thy servants simple boone° refuse,   *request*
125 But let this day let this one day be myne,
Let all the rest be thine.
Then I thy soverayne prayses loud wil sing,
That all the woods shal answer and theyr eccho ring.

Harke how the Minstrels gin to shrill aloud
130 Their merry Musick that resounds from far
The pipe, the tabor,° and the trembling Croud,°   *drum / viol*
That well agree withouten breach or jar.°   *discord*
But most of all the Damzels doe delite,
When they their tymbrels° smyte,   *tambourines*
135 And thereunto doe daunce and carrol sweet,
That all the sences they doe ravish quite,
The whyles the boyes run up and downe the street,
Crying aloud with strong confuséd noyce,
As if it were one voyce.
140 *Hymen iô*[8] *Hymen, Hymen* they do shout,
That even to the heavens theyr shouting shrill
Doth reach, and all the firmament doth fill,
To which the people standing all about,
As in approvance doe thereto applaud
145 And loud advaunce her laud,
And evermore they *Hymen Hymen* sing,
That al the woods them answer and theyr eccho ring.

Loe where she comes along with portly° pace   *stately*
Lyke Phoebe[9] from her chamber of the East,
150 Arysing forth to run her mighty race,
Clad all in white, that seemes° a virgin best.   *befits*
So well it her beseemes that ye would weene
Some angell she had beene.
Her long loose yellow locks lyke golden wyre,
155 Sprinckled with perle, and perling° flowres a tweene,   *intermingling*
Doe lyke a golden mantle her attyre,
And being crownéd with a girland greene,
Seeme lyke some mayden Queene.
Her modest eyes abashéd to behold
160 So many gazers, as on her do stare,
Upon the lowly ground affixéd are.
Ne dare lift up her countenance too bold,
But blush to heare her prayses sung so loud,
So farre from being proud.
165 Nathlesse° doe ye still loud her prayses sing.   *nevertheless*
That all the woods may answer and your eccho ring.

Tell me ye merchants daughters did ye see
So fayre a creature in your towne before,
So sweet, so lovely, and so mild as she,

8.· A shout of joy or triumph (Greek).   9. Another name for the moon goddess Diana.

170 Adornd with beautyes grace and vertues store,°   *wealth*
    Her goodly eyes lyke Saphyres shining bright,
    Her forehead yvory white,
    Her cheekes lyke apples which the sun hath rudded,
    Her lips lyke cherryes charming men to byte,
175 Her brest like to a bowle of creame uncrudded,°   *uncurdled*
    Her paps lyke lyllies budded,
    Her snowie necke lyke to a marble towre,
    And all her body lyke a pallace fayre,
    Ascending uppe with many a stately stayre,
180 To honors seat and chastities sweet bowre.
    Why stand ye still ye virgins in amaze,
    Upon her so to gaze,
    Whiles ye forget your former lay to sing,
    To which the woods did answer and your eccho ring.

185 But if ye saw that which no eyes can see,
    The inward beauty of her lively spright,°   *spirit*
    Garnisht with heavenly guifts of high degree,
    Much more then would ye wonder at that sight,
    And stand astonisht lyke to those which red°   *saw*
190 Medusaes mazeful hed.[1]
    There dwels sweet love and constant chastity,
    Unspotted fayth and comely womanhood,
    Regard of honour and mild modesty,
    There vertue raynes as Queene in royal throne,
195 And giveth lawes alone.
    The which the base affections° doe obay,   *lowly emotions*
    And yeeld theyr services unto her will,
    Ne thought of thing uncomely ever may
    Thereto approch to tempt her mind to ill.
200 Had ye once seene these her celestial threasures,
    And unrevealéd pleasures,
    Then would ye wonder and her prayses sing,
    That al the woods should answer and your eccho ring.

    Open the temple gates unto my love,
205 Open them wide that she may enter in,
    And all the postes adorne as doth behove,[2]
    And all the pillours deck with girlands trim,
    For to recyve this Saynt with honour dew,
    That commeth in to you.
210 With trembling steps and humble reverence,
    She commeth in, before th' almighties vew,
    Of her ye virgins learne obedience,
    When so ye come into those holy places,
    To humble your proud faces:
215 Bring her up to th' high altar, that she may
    The sacred ceremonies there partake,
    The which do endlesse matrimony make,
    And let the roring Organs loudly play
    The praises of the Lord in lively notes,
220 The whiles with hollow throates
    The Choristers the joyous Antheme sing,
    That al the woods may answere and their eccho ring.

    Behold whiles she before the altar stands
    Hearing the holy priest that to her speakes
225 And blesseth her with his two happy hands,
    How the red roses flush up in her cheekes,

---

1. The Gorgon Medusa had serpents for hair;   2. I.e., as is fitting.
whoever looked upon her was turned to stone.

And the pure snow with goodly vermill° stayne,   *vermilion*
Like crimsin dyde in grayne,[3]
That even th' Angels which continually,
230 About the sacred Altare doe remaine,
Forget their service and about her fly,
Ofte peeping in her face that seemes more fayre,
The more they on it stare.
But her sad° eyes still fastened on the ground,   *sober*
235 Are governéd with goodly modesty,
That suffers not one looke to glaunce awry,
Which may let in a little thought unsownd.
Why blush ye love to give to me your hand,
The pledge of all our band?°   *bond*
240 Sing ye sweet Angels, Alleluya sing,
That all the woods may answere and your eccho ring.

Now al is done; bring home the bride againe,
Bring home the triumph of our victory,
Bring home with you the glory of her gaine,[4]
245 With joyance bring her and with jollity.
Never had man more joyfull day then this,
Whom heaven would heape with blis.
Make feast therefore now all this live long day,
This day for ever to me holy is,
250 Poure out the wine without restraint or stay,
Poure not by cups, but by the belly full,
Poure out to all that wull,°   *will*
And sprinkle all the postes and wals with wine,
That they may sweat, and drunken be withall.
255 Crowne ye God Bacchus with a coronall,°   *garland*
And Hymen also crowne with wreathes of vine,
And let the Graces daunce unto the rest;
For they can doo it best:
The whiles the maydens doe theyr carroll sing,
260 To which the woods shal answer and theyr eccho ring.

Ring ye the bels, ye yong men of the towne,
And leave your wonted labors for this day:
This day is holy; doe ye write it downe,
That ye for ever it remember may.
265 This day the sunne is in his chiefest hight,
With Barnaby the bright,[5]
From whence declining daily by degrees,
He somewhat loseth of his heat and light,
When once the Crab[6] behind his back he sees.
270 But for this time it ill ordainéd was,
To chose the longest day in all the yeare,
And shortest night, when longest fitter weare:
Yet never day so long, but late° would passe.   *finally*
Ring ye the bels, to make it weare away,
275 And bonefiers make all day,
And daunce about them, and about them sing:
That all the woods may answer, and your eccho ring.

Ah when will this long weary day have end,
And lende me leave to come unto my love?
280 How slowly do the houres theyr numbers spend?
How slowly does sad Time his feathers move?

3. I.e., dyed with colorfast dye.
4. I.e., of gaining her.
5. St. Barnabas's day (July 11) was also the
day of the summer solstice in the calendar in
use during Spenser's time.

6. Cancer the Crab, the fourth constellation
in the zodiac, through which the sun passes
in July.

Hast thee O fayrest Planet to thy home[7]
Within the Westerne fome:
Thy tyred steedes long since have need of rest.
285 Long though it be, at last I see it gloome,
And the bright evening star with golden creast
Appeare out of the East.
Fayre childe of beauty, glorious lampe of love
That all the host of heaven in rankes doost lead,
290 And guydest lovers through the nightés dread,
How chearefully thou lookest from above,
And seemst to laugh atweene thy twinkling light
As joying in the sight
Of these glad many which for joy doe sing,
295 That all the woods them answer and their eccho ring.

Now ceasse ye damsels your delights forepast;
Enough is it, that all the day was youres:
Now day is doen, and night is nighing fast:
Now bring the Bryde into the brydall boures.
300 Now night is come, now soone her disaray,
And in her bed her lay;
Lay her in lillies and in violets,
And silken courteins over her display,
And odourd sheetes, and Arras° coverlets.   *tapestry*
305 Behold how goodly my faire love does ly
In proud humility;
Like unto Maia,[8] when as Jove her tooke,
In Tempe, lying on the flowry gras,
Twixt sleepe and wake, after she weary was,
310 With bathing in the Acidalian brooke.
Now it is night, ye damsels may be gon,
And leave my love alone,
And leave likewise your former lay to sing:
The woods no more shal answere, nor your eccho ring.

315 Now welcome night, thou night so long expected,°   *awaited*
That long daies labour doest at last defray,°   *requite*
And all my cares, which cruell love collected,
Hast sumd in one, and cancelléd for aye:
Spread thy broad wing over my love and me,
320 That no man may us see,
And in thy sable mantle us enwrap,
From feare of perrill and foule horror free.
Let no false treason seeke us to entrap,
Nor any dread disquiet once annoy
325 The safety of our joy:
But let the night be calme and quietsome,
Without tempestuous storms or sad afray:°   *dark terror*
Lyke as when Jove with fayre Alcmena[9] lay,
When he begot the great Tirynthian groome:
330 Or lyke as when he with thy selfe did lie,
And begot Majesty.
And let the mayds and yongmen cease to sing:
Ne let the woods them answer, nor theyr eccho ring.

Let no lamenting cryes, nor dolefull teares,
335 Be heard all night within nor yet without:
Ne let false whispers, breeding hidden feares,
Breake gentle sleepe with misconceivéd dout.°   *fear*

7. In Ptolemaic astronomy, still often accepted
in Spenser's time, the sun was one of the
planets, which revolved about the earth.
8. The most beautiful of the Pleiades, who

by Jove became the mother of the god Hermes.
9. The mother of Hercules, who as groom or
servant to the king of Tiryns performed
twelve prodigious labors.

Let no deluding dreames, nor dreadful sights
Make sudden sad affrights;
340 Ne let housefyres, nor lightnings helpelesse harmes,
Ne let the Pouke,[1] nor other evill sprights,
Ne let mischívous witches with theyr charmes,
Ne let hob Goblins, names whose sence we see not,
Fray us with things that be not.
345 Let not the shriech Oule, nor the Storke be heard:
Nor the night Raven that still° deadly yels,   *continually*
Nor damnéd ghosts cald up with mighty spels,
Nor griesly vultures make us once affeard:
Ne let th' unpleasant Quyre of Frogs still croking
350 Make us to wish theyr choking.
Let none of these theyr drery accents sing;
Ne let the woods them answer, nor theyr eccho ring.

But let stil Silence trew night watches keepe,
That sacred peace may in assurance rayne,
355 And tymely sleep, when it is tyme to sleepe,
May poure his limbs forth on your pleasant playne,
The whiles an hundred little wingéd loves,°   *cupids*
Like divers fethered doves,
Shall fly and flutter round about your bed,
360 And in the secret darke, that none reproves,
Their prety stealthes shal worke, and snares shal spread
To filch away sweet snatches of delight,
Conceald through covert night.
Ye sonnes of Venus, play your sports at will,
365 For greedy pleasure, carelesse of your toyes,°   *amorous sports*
Thinks more upon her paradise of joyes,
Then what ye do, albe it good or ill.
All night therefore attend your merry play,
For it will soone be day:
370 Now none doth hinder you, that say or sing,
Ne will the woods now answer, nor your Eccho ring.

Who is the same, which at my window peepes?
Or whose is that faire face, that shines so bright,
Is it not Cinthia,[2] she that never sleepes,
375 But walkes about high heaven al the night?
O fayrest goddesse, do thou not envý
My love with me to spy:
For thou likewise didst love, though now unthought,[3]
And for a fleece of woll,° which privily,   *wool*
380 The Latmian shephard once unto thee brought,
His pleasures with thee wrought.
Therefore to us be favorable now;
And sith of wemens labours thou hast charge,[4]
And generation goodly dost enlarge,
385 Encline thy will t' effect our wishfull vow,
And the chast wombe informe with timely seed,
That may our comfort breed:
Till which we cease our hopefull hap to sing,
Ne let the woods us answere, nor our Eccho ring.

1. Puck, also called Hobgoblin. The same Puck appears as the merely mischievous Robin Goodfellow in Shakespeare's *A Midsummer Night's Dream*.
2. Yet another name for the moon goddess Diana.
3. The moon was often regarded as a symbol of virginity, in spite of several myths recounting her amours. In the next three lines Spenser, perhaps mistakenly, blends the story about Pan, who loved Diana disguised in the fleece of a white ram, with the story of Endymion ("The Latmian shephard"), whom Diana visited nightly in his sleep.
4. Lucina, the goddess of childbirth, is often identified with both Diana and Juno (see lines 394–95).

390 And thou great Juno, which with awful° might   *awe-inspiring*
The lawes of wedlock still dost patronize,
And the religion° of the faith first plight   *sanctity*
With sacred rites hast taught to solemnize:
And eeke for comfort often calléd art
395 Of women in their smart,°   *pains of childbirth*
Eternally bind thou this lovely band,
And all thy blessings unto us impart.
And thou glad Genius,⁵ in whose gentle hand,
The bridale bowre and geniall° bed remaine,   *marriage*
400 Without blemish or staine,
And the sweet pleasures of theyr loves delight
With secret ayde doest succour and supply,
Till they bring forth the fruitfull progeny,
Send us the timely fruit of this same night.
405 And thou fayre Hebe,⁶ and thou Hymen free,
Grant that it may so be.
Til which we cease your further prayse to sing,
Ne any woods shal answer, nor your Eccho ring.

And ye high heavens, the temple of the gods,
410 In which a thousand torches flaming bright
Doe burne, that to us wretched earthly clods,
In dreadful darknesse lend desiréd light;
And all ye powers which in the same remayne,
More then we men can fayne,°   *imagine*
415 Poure out your blessing on us plentiously,
And happy influence upon us raine,
That we may raise a large posterity,
Which from the earth, which they may long possesse,
With lasting happinesse,
420 Up to your haughty pallaces may mount,
And for the guerdon° of theyr glorious merit   *reward*
May heavenly tabernacles there inherit,
Of blessed Saints for to increase the count.
So let us rest, sweet love, in hope of this,
425 And cease till then our tymely joyes to sing,
The woods no more us answer, nor our eccho ring.

Song made in lieu of many ornaments,
With which my love should duly have bene dect,
Which cutting off through hasty accidents,
430 Ye would not stay your dew time to expect,
But promist both to recompens,
Be unto her a goodly ornament,
And for short time an endlesse moniment.

1595

Prothalamion⁷

Calme was the day, and through the trembling ayre,
Sweete breathing Zephyrus⁸ did softly play
A gentle spirit, that lightly did delay
Hot Titans⁹ beames, which then did glyster fayre:
5 When I whom sullein care,
Through discontent of my long fruitlesse stay

---

5. The universal god of generation. By in-
voking both Juno and Genius as patrons of
the marriage bed, Spenser draws also on the
belief that each individual is watched over
from birth by a tutelary spirit called "a
Genius" (for boys) or "a Juno" (for girls).
6. Daughter of Juno and goddess of youth.

7. Literally, "before the bridal chamber." A
nuptial song celebrating the double marriage
of Elizabeth and Katherine Somerset, daugh-
ters of the Earl of Worcester.
8. The west wind.
9. The sun's.

In Princes Court, and expectation vayne
Of idle hopes, which still doe fly away,
Like empty shaddowes, did aflict my brayne,
10   Walkt forth to ease my payne
Along the shoare of silver streaming Themmes,
Whose rutty Bancke, the which his River hemmes,
Was paynted all with variable flowers,
And all the meades adornd with daintie gemmes,
15   Fit to decke maydens bowres,
And crowne their Paramours,
Against the Brydale day, which is not long:
    Sweete Themmes runne softly, till I end my Song.

There, in a Meadow, by the Rivers side,
20   A flocke of Nymphes I chauncéd to espy,
All lovely Daughters of the Flood thereby,
With goodly greenish locks all loose untyde,
As each had bene a Bryde,
And each one had a little wicker basket,
25   Made of fine twigs entrayléd curiously,
In which they gathered flowers to fill their flasket:[1]
And with fine Fingers, cropt full feateously°   *dexterously*
The tender stalkes on hye.
Of every sort, which in that Meadow grew,
30   They gathered some; the Violet pallid blew,
The little Dazie, that at evening closes,
The virgin Lillie, and the Primrose trew,
With store of vermeil° Roses,   *vermilion*
To decke their Bridegromes posies,
35   Against the Brydale day, which was not long:
    Sweete Themmes runne softly, till I end my Song.

With that, I saw two Swannes of goodly hewe,
Come softly swimming downe along the Lee;[2]
Two fairer Birds I yet did never see:
40   The snow which doth the top of Pindus[3] strew,
Did never whiter shew,
Nor Jove himselfe when he a Swan would be
For love of Leda, whiter did appeare:
Yet Leda was they say as white as he,
45   Yet not so white as these, nor nothing neare;
So purely white they were,
That even the gentle streame, the which them bare,
Seemed foule to them, and bad his billowes spare
To wet their silken feathers, least they might
50   Soyle their fayre plumes with water not so fayre,
And marre their beauties bright,
That shone as heavens light,
Against their Brydale day, which was not long:
    Sweete Themmes runne softly, till I end my Song.

55   Eftsoones° the Nymphes, which now had Flowers their fill,   *forthwith*
Ran all in haste, to see that silver brood,
As they came floating on the Christal Flood.
Whom when they sawe, they stood amazéd still,
Their wondring eyes to fill,
60   Them seemed they never saw a sight so fayre,
Of Fowles so lovely, that they sure did deeme
Them heavenly borne, or to be that same payre

---

1. A long, shallow basket.   3. A mountain range in central Greece, the
2. Then a tributary of the Thames.   highest peak of which is Parnassus.

Which through the Skie draw Venus silver Teeme,
For sure they did not seeme
65 To be begot of any earthly Seede,
But rather Angels or of Angels breede:
Yet were they bred of Somers-heat[4] they say,
In sweetest Season, when each Flower and weede
The earth did fresh aray,
70 So fresh they seemed as day,
Even as their Brydale day, which was not long:
    Sweete Themmes runne softly, till I end my Song.

Then forth they all out of their baskets drew,
Great store of Flowers, the honour of the field,
75 That to the sense did fragrant odours yeild,
All which upon those goodly Birds they threw,
And all the Waves did strew,
That like old Peneus[5] Waters they did seeme,
When downe along by pleasant Tempes shore
80 Scattred with Flowres, through Thessaly they streeme,
That they appeare through Lillies plenteous store,
Like a Brydes Chamber flore:
Two of those Nymphes, meane while, two Garlands bound,
Of freshest Flowres which in that Mead° they found,   *meadow*
85 The which presenting all in trim Array,
Their snowie Foreheads therewithall they crownd,
Whil'st one did sing this Lay,
Prepared against that Day,
Against their Brydale day, which was not long:
90   Sweete Themmes runne softly, till I end my Song.

Ye gentle Birdes, the worlds faire ornament,
And heavens glorie, whom this happie hower
Doth leade unto your lovers blisfull bower,
Joy may you have and gentle hearts content
95 Of your loves couplement:
And let faire Venus, that is Queene of love,
With her heart-quelling Sonne upon you smile,
Whose smile they say, hath vertue to remove
All Loves dislike, and friendships faultie guile
100 For ever to assoile.°   *absolve*
Let endlesse Peace your steadfast hearts accord,
And blessed Plentie wait upon your bord,
And let your bed with pleasures chast abound,
That fruitfull issue may to you afford,
105 Which may your foes confound,
And make your joyes redound,
Upon your Brydale day, which is not long:
    Sweete Themmes run softlie, till I end my Song.

So ended she; and all the rest around
110 To her redoubled that her undersong,[6]
Which said, their bridale daye should not be long.
And gentle Eccho from the neighbour ground,
Their accents did resound.
So forth those joyous Birdes did passe along,
115 Adowne the Lee, that to them murmurde low,
As he would speake, but that he lackt a tong
Yeat did by signes his glad affection show,

---

4. A play on the maiden name of the brides.
See note on title.
5. A river in Thessaly that flows through the
Vale of Tempe.

6. "Redoubled that her undersong": repeated
her refrain.

Making his streame run slow.
And all the foule which in his flood did dwell
120   Gan flock about these twaine, that did excell
The rest, so far, as Cynthia doth shend[7]
The lesser starres. So they enrangéd well,
Did on those two attend,
And their best service lend,
125   Against their wedding day, which was not long:
    Sweete Themmes run softly, till I end my Song.

At length they all to mery London came,
To mery London, my most kyndly Nurse,
That to me gave this Lifes first native sourse:
130   Though from another place I take my name,
An house of auncient fame.[8]
There when they came, whereas those bricky towres,[9]
The which on Themmes brode agéd backe doe ryde,
Where now the studious Lawyers have their bowers
135   There whylome wont the Templer Knights to byde,
Till they decayd through pride:
Next whereunto there standes a stately place,[1]
Where oft I gaynéd giftes and goodly grace
Of that great Lord, which therein wont to dwell,
140   Whose want too well now feeles my freendles case:
But Ah here fits not well
Olde woes but joyes to tell
Against the bridale daye, which is not long:
    Sweete Themmes runne softly, till I end my Song.

145   Yet therein now doth lodge a noble Peer,
Great Englands glory and the Worlds wide wonder,
Whose dreadfull name, late through all Spaine did thunder,[2]
And Hercules two pillors standing neere,
Did make to quake and feare:
150   Faire branch of Honor, flower of Chevalrie,
That fillest England with thy triumphs fame,
Joy have thou of thy noble victorie,
And endlesse happinesse of thine owne name
That promiseth the same:
155   That through thy prowesse and victorious armes,
Thy country may be freed from forraine harmes:
And great Elisaes° glorious name may ring   *Elizabeth's*
Through al the world, fild with thy wide Alarmes,
Which some brave muse may sing
160   To ages following,
Upon the Brydale day, which is not long:
    Sweete Themmes runne softly, till I end my Song.

From those high Towers, this noble Lord issuing,
Like Radiant Hesper° when his golden hayre   *evening star*
165   In th'Ocean billowes he hath Bathéd fayre,
Descended to the Rivers open vewing,
With a great traine ensuing.
Above the rest were goodly to bee seene
Two gentle Knights of lovely face and feature
170   Beseeming well the bower of anie Queene,
With gifts of wit and ornaments of nature,

---

7. I.e., as the moon doth surpass.
8. The Spencers of Althorpe, Northampton, to whom Spenser was related.
9. The Temple, residence of law students in London, formerly occupied by the Knights Templars, whose military and religious order was dissolved on suspicion of heretical practices.

1. Leicester House, palace of Spenser's patron, the Earl of Leicester; called Essex House after its occupation by the Earl of Essex in 1596.
2. The Earl of Essex had sacked the city of Cadiz in Spain in August, 1596.

Fit for so goodly stature:
That like the twins of Jove[3] they seemed in sight,
Which decke the Bauldricke of the Heavens bright.
175 They two forth pacing to the Rivers side,
Received those two faire Brides, their Loves delight,
Which at th'appointed tyde,
Each one did make his Bryde,
Against their Brydale day, which is not long:
180   Sweete Themmes runne softly, till I end my Song.

1596

SIR PHILIP SIDNEY
(1554–1586)

Ye Goatherd Gods[1]

STREPHON.[2] Ye goatherd gods, that love the grassy mountains,
       Ye nymphs which haunt the springs in pleasant valleys,
       Ye satyrs joyed with free and quiet forests,
       Vouchsafe your silent ears to plaining music,
5   Which to my woes gives still an early morning,
       And draws the dolor on till weary evening.

KLAIUS. O Mercury,[3] foregoer to the evening,
       O heavenly huntress of the savage mountains,
       O lovely star, entitled of the morning,
10   While that my voice doth fill these woeful valleys,
       Vouchsafe your silent ears to plaining music,
       Which oft hath Echo tired in secret forests.

STREPHON. I, that was once free burgess° of the forests,   *citizen*
       Where shade from sun, and sport I sought in evening,
15   I, that was once esteemed for pleasant music,
       Am banished now among the monstrous mountains
       Of huge despair, and foul affliction's valleys,
       Am grown a screech owl to myself each morning.

KLAIUS. I, that was once delighted every morning,
20   Hunting the wild inhabiters of forests,
       I, that was once the music of these valleys,
       So darkened am that all my day is evening,
       Heartbroken so, that molehills seem high mountains
       And fill the vales with cries instead of music.

25 STREPHON. Long since, alas, my deadly swannish[4] music
       Hath made itself a crier of the morning,
       And hath with wailing strength climbed highest mountains;
       Long since my thoughts more desert be than forests,
       Long since I see my joys come to their evening,
30   And state° thrown down to overtrodden valleys.   *high position*

3. Castor and Pollux, who as the Gemini for the third constellation in the "baldric of the heavens," the zodiac.
1. The poem is in the form of a double sestina, two sets of six six-line stanzas, with a triplet concluding the whole. The same six key words end the lines of each stanza; their order is always a permutation of the order in the stanza just preceding: the pattern is 6 1 5 2 4 3, i.e., the last word of line 1 of any stanza is always the same as the last word of line 6 in the preceding stanza. Line 2 always ends like the preceding stanza's line 1; line 3 like line 5; line 4 like line 2; line 5 like line 4; and line 6 like line 3. All six key words appear in the triplet in the same order as that of the first and seventh stanzas.
2. Strephon and Klaius are shepherds in Sidney's heroic romance *Arcadia*, in which this poem appears.
3. The evening star. The "heavenly huntress" is the goddess Diana, the moon.
4. The swan was supposed to sing only just before it died.

KLAIUS.   Long since the happy dwellers of these valleys
Have prayed me leave my strange exclaiming music,
Which troubles their day's work and joys of evening;
Long since I hate the night, more hate the morning;

35   Long since my thoughts chase me like beasts in forests
And make me wish myself laid under mountains.

STREPHON.   Meseems° I see the high and stately mountains   *it seems to me*
Transform themselves to low dejected valleys;
Meseems I hear in these ill-changéd forests

40   The nightingales do learn of owls their music;
Meseems I feel the comfort of the morning
Turned to the mortal serene[5] of an evening.

KLAIUS.   Meseems I see a filthy cloudy evening
As soon as sun begins to climb the mountains;

45   Meseems I feel a noisome° scent, the morning   *offensive*
When I do smell the flowers of these valleys;
Meseems I hear, when I do hear sweet music,
The dreadful cries of murdered men in forests.

STREPHON.   I wish to fire the trees of all these forests;

50   I give the sun a last farewell each evening;
I curse the fiddling finders-out of music;
With envy I do hate the lofty mountains
And with despite despise the humble valleys;
I do detest night, evening, day, and morning.

55 KLAIUS.   Curse to myself my prayer is, the morning;
My fire is more than can be made with forests,
My state more base than are the basest valleys.
I wish no evenings more to see, each evening;
Shaméd, I hate myself in sight of mountains

60   And stop mine ears, lest I grow mad with music.

STREPHON.   For she whose parts maintained a perfect music,
Whose beauties shined more than the blushing morning,
Who much did pass° in state the stately mountains,   *surpass*
In straightness passed the cedars of the forests,

65   Hath cast me, wretch, into eternal evening
By taking her two suns from these dark valleys.

KLAIUS.   For she, with whom compared, the Alps are valleys,
She, whose least word brings from the spheres their music,
At whose approach the sun rose in the evening,

70   Who where she went bare° in her forehead morning,   *bore*
Is gone, is gone, from these our spoiléd forests,
Turning to deserts our best pastured mountains.

STREPHON.   These mountains witness shall, so shall these valleys,

KLAIUS.   These forests eke,° made wretched by our music,   *also*

75   Our morning hymn this is, and song at evening.

                                 1577–80   1593

The Nightingale

The nightingale, as soon as April bringeth
Unto her rested sense a perfect waking,
While late bare earth, proud of new clothing, springeth,
Sings out her woes, a thorn her song-book making,

5. Damp evening air, thought to produce sickness ("mortal": deadly). The stress is on the first syllable.

5 And mournfully bewailing,
Her throat in tunes expresseth
What grief her breast oppresseth
For Tereus' force on her chaste will prevailing.[6]
Oh Philomela fair, Oh take some gladness,
10 That here is juster cause of plaintful sadness:
Thine earth now springs, mine fadeth;
Thy thorn without, my thorn my heart invadeth.

Alas, she hath no other cause of anguish
But Tereus' love, on her by strong hand wroken,[7]
15 Wherein she suffering, all her spirits languish;
Full womanlike complains her will was broken.
But I, who daily craving,
Cannot have to content me,
Have more cause to lament me,
20 Since wanting is more woe than too much having.
O Philomela fair, O take some gladness,
That here is juster cause of plaintful sadness:
Thine earth now springs, mine fadeth;
Thy thorn without, my thorn my heart invadeth.

                                    1581   1598

Ring Out Your Bells

Ring out your bells, let mourning shows be spread,
For Love is dead.
All Love is dead, infected
With plague of deep disdain;
5 Worth as naught worth rejected,
And Faith fair scorn[8] doth gain.
From so ungrateful fancy,
From such a female franzy,°   *frenzy*
From them that use men thus,
10 Good Lord, deliver us!

Weep, neighbors, weep; do you not hear it said
That Love is dead?
His deathbed peacock's folly,
His winding sheet is shame,
15 His will false-seeming holy,
His sole exec'tor blame.
From so ungrateful, . . .

Let dirge be sung and trentals[9] rightly read,
For Love is dead.
20 Sir Wrong his tomb ordaineth
My mistress, marble heart,
Which epitaph containeth,
"Her eyes were once his dart."
From so ungrateful, . . .

25 Alas, I lie, rage hath this error bred;
Love is not dead.
Love is not dead, but sleepeth
In her unmatchéd mind,
Where she his counsel keepeth,

6. Tereus, the ravisher of Philomela, cut out her tongue to keep her from accusing him. Transformed into a nightingale, she expressed her grief in song.
7. Old past participle of *wreak*, "to urge or force upon."
8. Scorn from the fair.
9. A series of thirty masses for the dead.

30   Till due desert she find.
      Therefore from so vile fancy,
      To call such wit a franzy,
      Who Love can temper thus,
      Good Lord, deliver us!

                                              1581   1598

Thou Blind Man's Mark

      Thou blind man's mark,° thou fool's self-chosen snare,   *target*
      Fond fancy's scum, and dregs of scattered thought,
      Band of all evils, cradle of causeless care,
      Thou web of will, whose end is never wrought;
5   Desire, desire, I have too dearly bought,
      With price of mangled mind, thy worthless ware;
      Too long, too long asleep thou hast me brought,
      Who should my mind to higher things prepare.
      But yet in vain thou hast my ruin sought;
10   In vain thou madest me to vain things aspire;
      In vain thou kindlest all thy smoky fire;
      For virtue hath this better lesson taught:
      Within myself to seek my only hire,°   *payment*
      Desiring naught but how to kill desire.

                                              1581   1598

From Astrophel and Stella

                    1
      Loving in truth, and fain° in verse my love to show,   *eager*
      That the dear she might take some pleasure of my pain,
      Pleasure might cause her read, reading might make her know,
      Knowledge might pity win, and pity grace obtain,
5   I sought fit words to paint the blackest face of woe:
      Studying inventions fine, her wits to entertain,
      Oft turning others' leaves, to see if thence would flow
      Some fresh and fruitful showers upon my sunburned brain.
      But words came halting forth, wanting Invention's stay;
10   Invention, Nature's child, fled stepdame Study's blows;
      And others' feet still seemed but strangers in my way.
      Thus, great with child to speak, and helpless in my throes,
      Biting my truant pen, beating myself for spite:
      "Fool," said my Muse to me, "look in thy heart, and write."

                    25
      The wisest scholar of the wight most wise
      By Phoebus' doom,[1] with sugared sentence says
      That Virtue, if it once met with our eyes,
      Strange flames of love it in our souls would raise;
5   But, for that° man with pain this truth descries,   *because*
      While he each thing in sense's balance weighs,
      And so nor will nor can behold those skies
      Which inward sun to heroic mind displays,
      Virtue of late, with virtuous care to stir
10   Love of herself, takes Stella's shape, that she
      To mortal eyes might sweetly shine in her.
      It is most true, for since I her did see,
      Virtue's great beauty in that face I prove,°   *experience*
      And find th'effect, for I do burn in love.

---

1. Judgment. The "wight most wise" was   pupil, was Plato, who (in *Phaedrus* 250D) pro-
Socrates, so called by the oracle of Apollo   vides the basis for lines 3–8.
(Phoebus) at Delphi. His "wisest scholar," or

31

With how sad steps, Oh Moon, thou climb'st the skies,
How silently, and with how wan a face!
What, may it be that even in heav'nly place
That busy archer[2] his sharp arrows tries?
5   Sure, if that long-with-love-acquainted eyes
Can judge of love, thou feel'st a lover's case;
I read it in thy looks: thy languished grace,
To me that feel the like, thy state descries.
Then even of fellowship, Oh Moon, tell me,
10   Is constant love deemed there but want of wit?
Are beauties there as proud as here they be?
Do they above love to be loved, and yet
Those lovers scorn whom that love doth possess?
Do they call virtue there ungratefulness?

41

Having this day my horse, my hand, my lance
Guided so well that I obtained the prize,
Both by the judgment of the English eyes
And of some sent from that sweet enemy, France,
5   Horsemen my skill in horsemanship advance,
Town-folks my strength; a daintier° judge applies   *more discriminating*
His praise to sleight which from good use° doth rise;   *practice*
Some lucky wits impute it but to chance;
Others, because of both sides I do take
10   My blood from them who did excel in this,
Think nature me a man of arms did make.
How far they shoot awry! The true cause is,
Stella looked on, and from her heavenly face
Sent forth the beams which made so fair my race.

48

Soul's joy, bend not those morning stars from me,
Where virtue is made strong by beauty's might,
Where love is chasteness, pain doth learn delight,
And humbleness grows one with majesty.
5   Whatever may ensue, O let me be
Co-partner of the riches of that sight;
Let not mine eyes be hell driv'n from that light;
O look, O shine, O let me die and see.
For though I oft my self of them bemoan,
10   That through my heart their beamy darts be gone,
Whose cureless wounds even now most freshly bleed,
Yet since my death wound is already got,
Dear killer, spare not thy sweet cruel shot;
A kind of grace it is to slay with speed.

MICHAEL DRAYTON
(1563–1631)

From Idea

To the Reader of these Sonnets

Into these loves who but for passion looks,
At this first sight here let him lay them by
And seek elsewhere, in turning other books,
Which better may his labor satisfy.
5   No far-fetched sigh shall ever wound my breast,
Love from mine eye a tear shall never wring,

---

2. I.e., Cupid.

Nor in *Ah me*'s my whining sonnets dressed,
A libertine, fantastically I sing.
My verse is the true image of my mind,
10   Ever in motion, still desiring change;
And as thus to variety inclined,
So in all humors sportively I range:
   My muse is rightly of the English strain,
   That cannot long one fashion entertain.

14

If he from heaven that filched that living fire[1]
Condemned by Jove to endless torment be,
I greatly marvel how you still go free,
That far beyond Prometheus did aspire.
5   The fire he stole, although of heavenly kind,
Which from above he craftily did take,
Of liveless clods, us living men to make,
He did bestow in temper of the mind.
But you broke into heaven's immortal store,
10   Where virtue, honor, wit, and beauty lay;
Which taking thence you have escaped away,
Yet stand as free as ere you did before;
   Yet old Prometheus punished for his rape.
   Thus poor thieves suffer when the greater 'scape.

61

Since there's no help, come let us kiss and part;
Nay, I have done, you get no more of me,
And I am glad, yea glad with all my heart
That thus so cleanly I myself can free;
5   Shake hands forever, cancel all our vows,
And when we meet at any time again,
Be it not seen in either of our brows
That we one jot of former love retain.
Now at the last gasp of love's latest breath,
10   When, his pulse failing, passion speechless lies,
When faith is kneeling by his bed of death,
And innocence is closing up his eyes,
   Now if thou wouldst, when all have given him over,
   From death to life thou mightst him yet recover.

63

Truce, gentle love, a parley now I crave,
Methinks 'tis long since first these wars begun;
Nor thou nor I the better yet can have;
Bad is the match where neither party won.
5   I offer free conditions of fair peace,
My heart for hostage that it shall remain;
Discharge our forces, here let malice cease,
So for my pledge thou give me pledge again.
Or if no thing but death will serve thy turn,
10   Still thirsting for subversion of my state,
Do what thou canst, raze, massacre, and burn,
Let the world see the utmost of thy hate;
   I send defiance, since if overthrown,
   Thou vanquishing, the conquest is mine own.

                 1619

1. Prometheus, having stolen fire for mankind, was chained to a rock and preyed upon daily by a vulture that tore at his vitals. The gift of fire is sometimes interpreted to mean that Prometheus created mankind.

CHRISTOPHER MARLOWE
(1564–1593)

The Passionate Shepherd to His Love[2]

Come live with me and be my love,
And we will all the pleasures prove°   *try*
That valleys, groves, hills, and fields,
Woods, or steepy mountain yields.

5   And we will sit upon the rocks,
Seeing the shepherds feed their flocks,
By shallow rivers to whose falls
Melodious birds sing madrigals.

And I will make thee beds of roses
10   And a thousand fragrant posies,
A cap of flowers, and a kirtle
Embroidered all with leaves of myrtle;

A gown made of the finest wool
Which from our pretty lambs we pull;
15   Fair lined slippers for the cold,
With buckles of the purest gold;

A belt of straw and ivy buds,
With coral clasps and amber studs:
And if these pleasures may thee move,
20   Come live with me, and be my love.

The shepherds' swains shall dance and sing
For thy delight each May morning:
If these delights thy mind may move,
Then live with me and be my love.

                                                            1599, 1600

WILLIAM SHAKESPEARE
(1564–1616)

From Sonnets

18
Shall I compare thee to a summer's day?
Thou art more lovely and more temperate:
Rough winds do shake the darling buds of May,
And summer's lease hath all too short a date:
5   Sometimes too hot the eye of heaven shines,
And often is his gold complexion dimmed;
And every fair from fair sometimes declines,
By chance or nature's changing course untrimmed;[1]
But thy eternal summer shall not fade,
10   Nor lose possession of that fair thou ow'st;°   *ownest*
Nor shall death brag thou wander'st in his shade,

2. See the response by Sir Walter Ralegh,   1. Divested of its beauty.
The Nymph's Reply to the Shepherd.

When in eternal lines to time thou grow'st:
So long as men can breathe, or eyes can see,
So long lives this, and this gives life to thee.

30

When to the sessions² of sweet silent thought
I summon up remembrance of things past,
I sigh the lack of many a thing I sought,
And with old woes new wail my dear time's waste:
5   Then can I drown an eye, unused to flow,
For precious friends hid in death's dateless° night,   *endless*
And weep afresh love's long since canceled woe,
And moan the expense° of many a vanished sight: *loss*
Then can I grieve at grievances foregone,
10   And heavily from woe to woe tell o'er
The sad account of fore-bemoanéd moan,
Which I new pay as if not paid before.
But if the while I think on thee, dear friend,
All losses are restored and sorrows end.

64

When I have seen by time's fell° hand defaced   *destroying*
The rich-proud cost of outworn buried age;
When sometime° lofty towers I see down-razed,   *formerly*
And brass eternal slave to mortal rage;
5   When I have seen the hungry ocean gain
Advantage on the kingdom of the shore,
And the firm soil win of the watery main,
Increasing store with loss, and loss with store;
When I have seen such interchange of state,
10   Or state itself confounded to decay,
Ruin hath taught me thus to ruminate,
That time will come and take my love away.
This thought is as a death, which cannot choose
But weep to have that which it fears to lose.

65

Since brass, nor³ stone, nor earth, nor boundless sea
But sad mortality o'er-sways their power,
How with this rage shall beauty hold a plea,
Whose action is no stronger than a flower?
5   O, how shall summer's honey breath hold out
Against the wreckful siege of battering days,
When rocks impregnable are not so stout,
Nor gates of steel so strong, but Time decays?
O fearful meditation! where, alack,
10   Shall Time's best jewel from Time's chest lie hid?
Or what strong hand can hold his swift foot back?
Or who his spoil of beauty can forbid?
O, none, unless this miracle have might,
That in black ink my love may still shine bright.

73

That time of year thou mayst in me behold
When yellow leaves, or none, or few, do hang
Upon those boughs which shake against the cold,
Bare ruined choirs, where late the sweet birds sang.
5   In me thou see'st the twilight of such day
As after sunset fadeth in the west;
Which by and by black night doth take away,
Death's second self, that seals up all in rest.
In me thou see'st the glowing of such fire,
10   That on the ashes of his youth doth lie,
As the deathbed whereon it must expire,

---

2. Sittings of a court.   3. I.e., since there is neither brass nor.

Consumed with that which it was nourished by.
This thou perceiv'st, which makes thy love more strong,
To love that well which thou must leave ere long.

107

Not mine own fears, nor the prophetic soul
Of the wide world dreaming on things to come,
Can yet the lease of my true love control,
Supposed as forfeit to a cónfined doom.
5　The mortal moon[4] hath her eclipse endured,
And the sad augurs mock their own presage;
Incertainties now crown themselves assured,
And peace proclaims olives of endless age.
Now with the drops of this most balmy time
10　My love looks fresh, and death to me subscribes,°　　　*submits*
Since, spite of him, I'll live in this poor rhyme,
While he insults o'er dull and speechless tribes:
And thou in this shalt find thy monument,
When tyrants' crests and tombs of brass are spent.

116

Let me not to the marriage of true minds
Admit impediments. Love is not love
Which alters when it alteration finds,
Or bends with the remover to remove:
5　Oh, no! it is an ever-fixéd mark,
That looks on tempests and is never shaken;
It is the star to every wandering bark,
Whose worth's unknown, although his height be taken.[5]
Love's not Time's fool, though rosy lips and cheeks
10　Within his bending sickle's compass come;
Love alters not with his brief hours and weeks.
But bears it out even to the edge of doom.[6]
If this be error and upon me proved,
I never writ, nor no man ever loved.

129

Th' expense of spirit in a waste of shame
Is lust in action; and till action, lust
Is perjured, murderous, bloody, full of blame,
Savage, extreme, rude, cruel, not to trust;
5　Enjoyed no sooner but despiséd straight:
Past reason hunted; and no sooner had,
Past reason hated, as a swallowed bait,
On purpose laid to make the taker mad:
Mad in pursuit, and in possession so;
10　Had, having, and in quest to have, extreme;
A bliss in proof,[7] and proved, a very woe;
Before, a joy proposed; behind, a dream.
All this the world well knows; yet none knows well
To shun the heaven that leads men to this hell.

130

My mistress' eyes are nothing like the sun;
Coral is far more red than her lips' red;
If snow be white, why then her breasts are dun;
If hairs be wires, black wires grow on her head.
5　I have seen roses damasked,° red and white,　　　*variegated*
But no such roses see I in her cheeks;
And in some perfumes is there more delight
Than in the breath that from my mistress reeks.
I love to hear her speak, yet well I know
10　That music hath a far more pleasing sound;

---

4. Queen Elizabeth, whose sixty-third year had been anticipated by astrologers ("augurs") as a time of disaster.
5. I.e., although its elevation may be measured.
6. Judgment Day, the end of the world.
7. I.e., in the experience.

I grant I never saw a goddess go;°   *walk*
My mistress, when she walks, treads on the ground.
And yet, by heaven, I think my love as rare
As any she belied with false compare.

146

Poor soul, the center of my sinful earth,
Lord of[8] these rebel powers that thee array,°   *dress, deck out*
Why dost thou pine within and suffer dearth,
Painting thy outward walls so costly gay?
5   Why so large cost, having so short a lease,
Dost thou upon thy fading mansion spend?
Shall worms, inheritors of this excess,
Eat up thy charge? Is this thy body's end?
Then, soul, live thou upon thy servant's loss,
10 And let that pine to aggravate° thy store;   *increase*
Buy terms divine in selling hours of dross;
Within be fed, without be rich no more.
So shalt thou feed on death, that feeds on men,
And death once dead, there's no more dying then.

When Daisies Pied[9]

Spring

When daisies pied and violets blue
    And ladysmocks all silver-white
And cuckoobuds of yellow hue
    Do paint the meadows with delight,
5   The cuckoo then, on every tree,
Mocks married men;[1] for thus sings he,
                Cuckoo;
Cuckoo, cuckoo: Oh word of fear.
Unpleasing to a married ear!

10 When shepherds pipe on oaten straws,
    And merry larks are plowmen's clocks,
When turtles tread,[2] and rooks, and daws,
    And maidens bleach their summer smocks,
The cuckoo then, on every tree,
15 Mocks married men; for thus sings he,
                Cuckoo;
Cuckoo, cuckoo: Oh word of fear,
Unpleasing to a married ear!

Winter

When icicles hang by the wall
20 And Dick the shepherd blows his nail[3]
And Tom bears logs into the hall,
    And milk comes frozen home in pail.
When blood is nipped and ways be foul,
Then nightly sings the staring owl,
25   Tu-who;
Tu-whit, tu-who: a merry note,
While greasy Joan doth keel[4] the pot.

When all aloud the wind doth blow,
    And coughing drowns the parson's saw,°   *wise saying*
30 And birds sit brooding in the snow,

---

8. The original text repeats "My sinful earth," apparently a mistake, in place of "Lord of" at the beginning of this line. Other possibilities have been suggested, e.g., "Rebuke," "Thrall to," "Pressed by."
9. From *Love's Labour's Lost.*

1. The cuckoo's song was often taken fancifully as "Cuckold!"
2. I.e., when turtledoves mate.
3. I.e., breathes on his fingers to warm them.
4. Keep from boiling over by stirring.

And Marian's nose looks red and raw,
When roasted crabs° hiss in the bowl,   *crab apples*
Then nightly sings the staring owl,
            Tu-who;
35   Tu-whit, tu-who: a merry note
While greasy Joan doth keel the pot.

                                              1595?   1598

Under the Greenwood Tree[5]

Under the greenwood tree
Who loves to lie with me,
And turn his merry note
Unto the sweet bird's throat,
5   Come hither, come hither, come hither:
        Here shall he see
        No enemy
But winter and rough weather.

Who doth ambition shun
10   And loves to live i' the sun,
Seeking the food he eats,
And pleased with what he gets,
Come hither, come hither, come hither:
        Here shall he see
        No enemy
But winter and rough weather.

                                              1599?   1623

Fear No More the Heat o' the Sun[6]

Fear no more the heat o' the sun,
    Nor the furious winter's rages;
Thou thy worldly task hast done,
    Home art gone, and ta'en thy wages:
5   Golden lads and girls all must,
As chimney-sweepers, come to dust.

Fear no more the frown o' the great;
    Thou art past the tyrant's stroke;
Care no more to clothe and eat;
10   To thee the reed is as the oak:
The scepter, learning, physic, must
All follow this, and come to dust.

Fear no more the lightning flash,
    Nor the all-dreaded thunder stone;[7]
15   Fear not slander, censure rash;
    Thou hast finished joy and moan:
All lovers young, all lovers must
Consign to thee, and come to dust.

No exorciser harm thee!
20   Nor no witchcraft charm thee!
Ghost unlaid forbear thee!
Nothing ill come near thee!
Quiet consummation have;
And renownéd be thy grave!

                                              1610?   1623

5. From *As You Like It.*   7. Thunder was thought to be caused by mete-
6. From *Cymbeline.*   orites falling from the sky.

When Daffodils Begin to Peer[8]

When daffodils begin to peer,
    With heigh! the doxy° over the dale,   *trollop, mistress*
Why, then comes in the sweet o' the year;
    For the red blood reigns in the winter's pale.[9]

5   The white sheet bleaching on the hedge,
    With heigh! the sweet birds, Oh, how they sing!
Doth set my pugging° tooth on edge;   *thieving*
    For a quart of ale is a dish for a king.

The lark, that tirra-lirra chants,
10   With heigh! with heigh! the thrush and the jay,
Are summer songs for me and my aunts,°   *sweethearts*
    While we lie tumbling in the hay.

                            1611   1623

Full Fathom Five[10]

Full fathom five thy father lies;
    Of his bones are coral made;
Those are pearls that were his eyes:
    Nothing of him that doth fade,
5   But doth suffer a sea change
Into something rich and strange.
Sea nymphs hourly ring his knell:
    Ding-dong.
Hark! now I hear them—Ding-dong, bell.

                            1611   1623

SONGS FROM PLAYS AND OTHER WORKS

JOHN LYLY
(1554–1606)

Cupid and My Campaspe

Cupid and my Campaspe played
At cards for kisses; Cupid paid.
He stakes his quiver, bow, and arrows,
His mother's[1] doves and team of sparrows,
5   Loses them too; then down he throws
The coral of his lip, the rose
Growing on 's cheek (but none knows how),
With these the crystal of his brow,
And then the dimple of his chin:
10 All these did my Campaspe win.
At last he set her both his eyes;
She won, and Cupid blind did rise.
    Oh Love! has she done this to thee?
    What shall, alas, become of me?

                              1632

---

8. From *The Winter's Tale.*   10. From *The Tempest.*
9. Territory, as well as lack of color.   1. I.e., Venus'.

Oh, For a Bowl of Fat Canary

Oh, for a bowl of fat Canary,
Rich Palermo, sparkling Sherry,
Some nectar else, from Juno's dairy;[2]
Oh, these draughts would make us merry!

5   Oh, for a wench (I deal in faces,
And in other daintier things);
Tickled am I with her embraces,
Fine dancing in such fairy rings.

Oh, for a plump fat leg of mutton,
10 Veal, lamb, capon, pig, and coney;°   *rabbit*
None is happy but a glutton,
None an ass but who wants money.

Wines indeed and girls are good,
But brave victuals feast the blood;
15 For wenches, wine, and lusty cheer,
Jove would leap down to surfeit here.

                                       1640

GEORGE PEELE
(1557–1596)

His Golden Locks Time Hath to Silver Turned[3]

His golden locks time hath to silver turned;
   Oh, time too swift, oh, swiftness never ceasing!
His youth 'gainst time and age hath ever spurned,°   *kicked*
   But spurned in vain; youth waneth by increasing.
5 Beauty, strength, youth, are flowers but fading seen;
Duty, faith, love, are roots, and ever green.

His helmet now shall make a hive for bees,
   And lover's sonnets turned to holy psalms,
A man-at-arms must now serve on his knees,
10   And feed on prayers, which are age his[4] alms;
But though from court to cottage he depart,
His saint is sure of his unspotted heart.

And when he saddest sits in homely cell,
   He'll teach his swains this carol for a song:
15 Blest be the hearts that wish my sovereign well,
   Cursed be the souls that think her any wrong!
Goddess, allow this aged man his right,
To be your beadsman[5] now, that was your knight.

                                       1590

2. Nectar, the drink of the gods, was sometimes thought to resemble mead, a drink made from milk and honey; hence it might be regarded figuratively as coming from the "dairy" of Juno, the queen of the gods.
3. This poem refers to Sir Henry Lee, for years Queen Elizabeth's champion in courtly jousts or contests of arms. At the age of sixty, too old to take part in the queen's birthday tournament of 1590, he retired in favor of a younger man.
4. "Age his": age's.
5. One who offers prayers for the soul of another.

When As the Rye Reach to the Chin

When as the rye reach to the chin,
And chopcherry, chopcherry ripe within,
Strawberries swimming in the cream,
And schoolboys playing in the stream;
5   Then O, then O, then O my truelove said,
Till that time come again
She could not live a maid.

1595

Hot Sun, Cool Fire

Hot sun, cool fire, tempered with sweet air,
Black shade, fair nurse, shadow my white hair.
Shine, sun; burn, fire; breathe, air, and ease me;
Black shade, fair nurse, shroud me and please me.
5   Shadow, my sweet nurse, keep me from burning;
Make not my glad cause cause of mourning.
    Let not my beauty's fire
    Inflame unstaid desire,
    Nor pierce any bright eye
10   That wandereth lightly.

1599

THOMAS LODGE
(1558–1625)

Rosalind's Madrigal

Love in my bosom like a bee
   Doth suck his sweet;
Now with his wings he plays with me,
   Now with his feet.
5   Within mine eyes he makes his nest,
His bed amidst my tender breast;
My kisses are his daily feast,
And yet he robs me of my rest.
    Ah, wanton, will ye?

10   And if I sleep, then percheth he
   With pretty flight,
And makes his pillow of my knee
   The livelong night.
Strike I my lute, he tunes the string;
15   He music plays if so I sing;
He lends me every lovely thing;
Yet cruel he my heart doth sting.
    Whist,° wanton, still ye!   *be silent*

Else I with roses every day
20   Will whip you hence,
And bind you, when you long to play,
   For your offense.
I'll shut mine eyes to keep you in,
I'll make you fast it for your sin,
25   I'll count your power not worth a pin.
    Alas! what hereby shall I win
     If he gainsay me?

What if I beat the wanton boy
   With many a rod?
30 He will repay me with annoy,
   Because a god.
Then sit thou safely on my knee,
And let thy bower my bosom be;
Lurk in mine eyes, I like of thee.
35 O Cupid, so thou pity me,
   Spare not, but play thee!

1590

Thomas Nashe
(1567–1601)

Spring, the Sweet Spring

Spring, the sweet spring, is the year's pleasant king,
Then blooms each thing, then maids dance in a ring,
Cold doth not sting, the pretty birds do sing:
   Cuckoo, jug-jug, pu-we, to-witta-woo![6]

5 The palm and may make country houses gay,
Lambs frisk and play, the shepherds pipe all day,
And we hear aye birds tune this merry lay:
   Cuckoo, jug-jug, pu-we, to-witta-woo!

The fields breathe sweet, the daisies kiss our feet,
10 Young lovers meet, old wives a-sunning sit,
In every street these tunes our ears do greet:
   Cuckoo, jug-jug, pu-we, to-witta-woo!
      Spring, the sweet spring!

1600

A Litany in Time of Plague

Adieu, farewell, earth's bliss;
This world uncertain is;
Fond° are life's lustful joys;   *foolish*
Death proves them all but toys;°   *trifles*
5 None from his darts can fly;
I am sick, I must die.
   Lord, have mercy on us!

Rich men, trust not in wealth,
Gold cannot buy you health;
10 Physic himself must fade.
All things to end are made,
The plague full swift goes by;
I am sick, I must die.
   Lord, have mercy on us!

15 Beauty is but a flower
Which wrinkles will devour;
Brightness falls from the air;
Queens have died young and fair;
Dust hath closed Helen's eye.
20 I am sick, I must die.
   Lord, have mercy on us!

---

6. Bird songs of the cuckoo, nightingale, lapwing, owl.

Strength stoops unto the grave,
Worms feed on Hector brave;
Swords may not fight with fate,
25 Earth still holds ope her gate.
"Come, come!" the bells do cry.
I am sick, I must die.
    Lord, have mercy on us.

Wit with his wantonness
30 Tasteth death's bitterness;
Hell's executioner
Hath no ears for to hear
What vain art can reply.
I am sick, I must die.
35   Lord, have mercy on us.

Haste, therefore, each degree,
To welcome destiny;
Heaven is our heritage,
Earth but a player's stage;
40 Mount we unto the sky.
I am sick, I must die.
    Lord, have mercy on us.

                                1592   1600

John Webster
(ca. 1580–1625)

Call for the Robin Redbreast and the Wren

Call for the robin redbreast and the wren,
Since o'er shady groves they hover,
And with leaves and flowers do cover
The friendless bodies of unburied men.
5 Call unto his funeral dole°   *sorrow*
The ant, the field mouse, and the mole,
To rear him hillocks that shall keep him warm,
And, when gay tombs are robbed, sustain no harm;
But keep the wolf far thence, that's foe to men,
10 For with his nails he'll dig them up again.

                                                1612

Hark, Now Everything Is Still

Hark, now everything is still;
The screech owl and the whistler shrill
Call upon our dame aloud,
And bid her quickly don her shroud.
5 Much you had of land and rent;
Your length in clay's now competent.
A long war disturbed your mind;
Here your perfect peace is signed.
Of what is 't fools make such vain keeping?
10 Sin their conception, their birth weeping,
Their life a general mist of error,
Their death a hideous storm of terror.
Strew your hair with powders sweet,
Don clean linen, bathe your feet,

15 And, the foul fiend more to check,
A crucifix let bless your neck.
'Tis now full tide, 'tween night and day,
End your groan and come away.

1623

JOHN FLETCHER
(1579–1625)

Take, Oh, Take Those Lips Away[7]

Take, oh, take those lips away
That so sweetly were forsworn
And those eyes, like break of day,
Lights that do mislead the morn;
5 But my kisses bring again,
Seals of love, though sealed in vain.

Hide, oh, hide those hills of snow,·
Which thy frozen bosom bears,
On whose tops the pinks that grow
10 Are of those that April wears;
But first set my poor heart free,
Bound in those icy chains by thee.

1639

JAMES SHIRLEY
(1596–1666)

The Glories of Our Blood and State

The glories of our blood and state
Are shadows, not substantial things;
There is no armor against fate;
Death lays his icy hand on kings.
5   Scepter and crown
Must tumble down
And in the dust be equal made
With the poor crooked scythe and spade.

Some men with swords may reap the field
10 And plant fresh laurels where they kill,
But their strong nerves at last must yield;
They tame but one another still.
Early or late
They stoop to fate
15 And must give up their murmuring breath,
When they, pale captives, creep to death.

The garlands wither on your brow,
Then boast no more your mighty deeds;
Upon death's purple altar now
20 See where the victor-victim bleeds.
Your heads must come
To the cold tomb;
Only the actions of the just
Smell sweet and blossom in their dust.

1659

7. The first stanza of this song appears as a complete poem in Shakespeare's play *Measure for Measure*. It is likely that Fletcher simply appropriated it.

THOMAS CAMPION
(1567–1620)

My Sweetest Lesbia[1]

My sweetest Lesbia, let us live and love,
And though the sager sort our deeds reprove,
Let us not weigh them. Heaven's great lamps do dive
Into their west, and straight again revive,
5 But soon as once set is our little light,
Then must we sleep one ever-during night.

If all would lead their lives in love like me,
Then bloody swords and armor should not be;
No drum nor trumpet peaceful sleeps should move,
10 Unless alarm came from the camp of love.
But fools do live, and waste their little light,
And seek with pain their ever-during night.

When timely death my life and fortune ends,
Let not my hearse be vexed with mourning friends,
15 But let all lovers, rich in triumph, come
And with sweet pastimes grace my happy tomb;
And Lesbia, close up thou my little light,
And crown with love my ever-during night.

1601

Follow Thy Fair Sun

Follow thy fair sun, unhappy shadow;
Though thou be black as night,
And she made all of light,
Yet follow thy fair sun, unhappy shadow.

5 Follow her whose light thy light depriveth;
Though here thou liv'st disgraced,
And she in heaven is placed,
Yet follow her whose light the world reviveth!

Follow those pure beams whose beauty burneth,
10 That so have scorched thee,
As thou still black must be,
Till her kind beams thy black to brightness turneth.

Follow her while yet her glory shineth;
There comes a luckless night,
15 That will dim all her light;
And this the black unhappy shade divineth.

Follow still since so thy fates ordained;
The sun must have his shade,
Till both at once do fade;
20 The sun still proved,° the shadow still disdained.

approved
1601

---

1. The Roman poet Catullus sang the praises of his Lesbia in a poem here imitated and partly translated by Campion. Compare Ben Jonson's adaptation of the same poem in *Song: To Celia.*

When Thou Must Home

When thou must home to shades of underground,
And there arrived, a new admiréd guest,
The beauteous spirits do engirt thee round,
White Iope, blithe Helen,[2] and the rest,
5   To hear the stories of thy finished love
From that smooth tongue whose music hell can move,

Then wilt thou speak of banqueting delights,
Of masques and revels which sweet youth did make,
Of tourneys and great challenges of knights,
10   And all these triumphs for thy beauty's sake;
When thou hast told these honors done to thee,
Then tell, Oh tell, how thou didst murther me.

                                          1601

Rose-cheeked Laura

Rose-cheeked Laura, come,
Sing thou smoothly with thy beauty's
Silent music, either other
    Sweetly gracing.

5   Lovely forms do flow
From concent° divinely framed;   *sounds in harmony*
Heav'n is music, and thy beauty's
    Birth is heavenly.

These dull notes we sing
10   Discords need for helps to grace them;
Only beauty purely loving
    Knows no discord,

But still moves delight,
Like clear springs renewed by flowing,
15   Ever perfect, ever in them-
    Selves eternal.

                                            1602

Now Winter Nights Enlarge

Now winter nights enlarge
    The number of their hours;
And clouds their storms discharge
    Upon the airy towers.
5   Let now the chimneys blaze
    And cups o'erflow with wine,
Let well-tuned words amaze
    With harmony divine.
Now yellow waxen lights
10   Shall wait on honey love
While youthful revels, masques, and courtly sights
    Sleep's leaden spells remove.

This time doth well dispense
    With[3] lovers' long discourse;
15   Much speech hath some defense,

---

2. Iope or Cassiopeia and Helen of Troy, the first renowned for beauty and vanity, the second for beauty and fickleness.

3. Put up with, deal indulgently with.

Though beauty no remorse.
All do not all things well;
   Some measures comely tread,
Some knotted riddles tell,
20   Some poems smoothly read.
The summer hath his joys,
   And winter his delights;
Though love and all his pleasures are but toys,
   They shorten tedious nights.

1617

Thrice Toss These Oaken Ashes

Thrice toss these oaken ashes in the air,
Thrice sit thou mute in this enchanted chair;
Then thrice three times tie up this truelove's knot,
And murmur soft "She will, or she will not."

5   Go burn these poisonous weeds in yon blue fire,
These screech-owl's feathers and this prickling briar,
This cypress gathered at a dead man's grave,
That all thy fears and cares an end may have.

Then come, you fairies, dance with me a round;
10 Melt her hard heart with your melodious sound.
In vain are all the charms I can devise:
She hath an art to break them with her eyes.

1617

There Is a Garden in Her Face

There is a garden in her face,
Where roses and white lilies grow,
A heavenly paradise is that place,
Wherein all pleasant fruits do flow.
5   There cherries grow, which none may buy
Till "Cherry ripe!"[4] themselves do cry.

Those cherries fairly do enclose
Of orient pearl a double row,
Which when her lovely laughter shows,
10 They look like rosebuds filled with snow.
Yet them nor peer nor prince can buy,
Till "Cherry ripe!" themselves do cry.

Her eyes like angels watch them still;
Her brows like bended bows do stand,
15 Threatening with piercing frowns to kill
All that attempt with eye or hand
Those sacred cherries to come nigh,
Till "Cherry ripe!" themselves do cry.

1617

4. A London street vendor's cry.

JOHN DONNE
(1572–1631)

Song

Go and catch a falling star,
   Get with child a mandrake root,[1]
Tell me where all past years are,
   Or who cleft the Devil's foot,
5 Teach me to hear mermaids singing,
Or to keep off envy's stinging,
       And find
       What wind
Serves to advance an honest mind.

10 If thou beest born to strange sights,
   Things invisible to see,
Ride ten thousand days and nights,
   Till age snow white hairs on thee.
Thou, when thou return'st, wilt tell me
15 All strange wonders that befell thee,
       And swear
       Nowhere
Lives a woman true, and fair.

If thou find'st one, let me know,
20   Such a pilgrimage were sweet;
Yet do not, I would not go,
   Though at next door we might meet;
Though she were true when you met her,
And last till you write your letter,
25   Yet she
       Will be
False, ere I come, to two, or three.

                       1633

Woman's Constancy

Now thou hast loved me one whole day,
Tomorrow when thou leav'st, what wilt thou say?
Wilt thou then antedate some new-made vow?
    Or say that now
5 We are not just those persons which we were?
Or, that oaths made in reverential fear
Of love, and his wrath, any may forswear?
Or, as true deaths true marriages untie,
So lovers' contracts, images of those,
10 Bind but till sleep, death's image, them unloose?
      Or, your own end to justify,
For having purposed change, and falsehood, you
Can have no way but falsehood to be true?
Vain lunatic,[2] against these 'scapes I could
15   Dispute, and conquer, if I would,
      Which I abstain to do,
For by tomorrow, I may think so too.

                       1633

1. The large, forked root of the mandrake, roughly resembling a human body, was often credited with human attributes. As a medicine, it was supposed to promote conception.

2. The word has for Donne the additional meaning of *inconstant* or *fickle,* since lunacy (from *luna,* moon) was supposed to be affected by the changing phases of the moon.

The Sun Rising

Busy old fool, unruly sun,
  Why dost thou thus,
Through windows and through curtains call on us?
Must to thy motions lovers' seasons run?
5   Saucy pedantic wretch, go chide
    Late school boys and sour prentices,
  Go tell court huntsmen that the king will ride,
  Call country ants to harvest offices;
Love, all alike, no season knows nor clime,
10 Nor hours, days, months, which are the rags of time.

    Thy beams, so reverend and strong
      Why shouldst thou think?
I could eclipse and cloud them with a wink,
But that I would not lose her sight so long;
15   If her eyes have not blinded thine,
    Look, and tomorrow late tell me,
  Whether both th' Indias³ of spice and mine
  Be where thou leftst them, or lie here with me.
Ask for those kings whom thou saw'st yesterday,
20 And thou shalt hear, All here in one bed lay.

    She's all states, and all princes, I,
      Nothing else is.
Princes do but play us; compared to this,
All honor's mimic, all wealth alchemy.⁴
25   Thou, sun, art half as happy as we,
    In that the world's contracted thus;
  Thine age asks ease, and since thy duties be
  To warm the world, that's done in warming us.
Shine here to us, and thou art everywhere;
30 This bed thy center is, these walls, thy sphere.

                                                1633

The Canonization

For God's sake hold your tongue, and let me love,
  Or chide my palsy, or my gout,
My five gray hairs, or ruined fortune, flout,
  With wealth your state, your mind with arts improve,
5   Take you a course, get you a place,
      Observe His Honor, or His Grace,
Or the King's real, or his stampéd face⁵
  Contémplate; what you will, approve,°   *try*
  So you will let me love.

10 Alas, alas, who's injured by my love?
    What merchant's ships have my sighs drowned?
Who says my tears have overflowed his ground?
    When did my colds a forward spring remove?
      When did the heats which my veins fill
15   Add one more to the plaguy bill?⁶
Soldiers find wars, and lawyers find out still
    Litigious men, which quarrels move,
    Though she and I do love.

---

3. India and the West Indies, whence came
spices and gold, respectively.
4. I.e., a fraud.

5. I.e., on coins.
6. Weekly list of plague victims.

Call us what you will, we're made such by love;
20   Call her one, me another fly,
We're tapers too, and at our own cost die,[7]
        And we in us find th' eagle and the dove.[8]
            The phoenix[9] riddle hath more wit°   sense
            By us: we two being one, are it.
25 So, to one neutral thing both sexes fit.
        We die and rise the same, and prove
        Mysterious by this love.

We can die by it, if not live by love,
    And if unfit for tombs and hearse
30 Our legend be, it will be fit for verse;
    And if no piece of chronicle we prove,
        We'll build in sonnets pretty rooms;
        As well a well-wrought urn becomes
The greatest ashes, as half-acre tombs;
35   And by these hymns, all shall approve
        Us canonized for love:

And thus invoke us: You whom reverend love
    Made one another's hermitage;
You, to whom love was peace, that now is rage;
40 Who did the whole world's soul contract, and drove
        Into the glasses of your eyes
        (So made such mirrors, and such spies,
That they did all to you epitomize)
    Countries, towns, courts: Beg from above
45 A pattern of your love!

1633

Song

Sweetest love, I do not go
    For weariness of thee,
Nor in hope the world can show
    A fitter love for me;
5   But since that I
Must die at last, 'tis best
To use myself in jest,
    Thus by feigned deaths to die.

Yesternight the sun went hence,
10   And yet is here today;
He hath no desire nor sense,
    Nor half so short a way:
        Then fear not me,
But believe that I shall make
15 Speedier journeys, since I take
    More wings and spurs than he.

O how feeble is man's power,
    That if good fortune fall,
Cannot add another hour,
20   Nor a lost hour recall!
        But come bad chance,
And we join to'it our strength,
And we teach it art and length,
    Itself o'er us to'advance.

7. Death was a popular metaphor for sexual intercourse in the 17th century. "At our own cost" reflects the common superstition that each act of lovemaking shortened one's life by a day.

8. Common symbols of strength and peace.
9. A legendary bird, the only one of its kind, represented as living five hundred years in the Arabian desert, being consumed in fire, then rising anew from its own ashes.

25 When thou sigh'st, thou sigh'st not wind,
    But sigh'st my soul away;
When thou weep'st, unkindly kind,
    My life's blood doth decay.
        It cannot be
30 That thou lov'st me, as thou say'st,
If in thine my life thou waste;
    Thou art the best of me.

Let not thy divining heart
    Forethink me any ill;
35 Destiny may take thy part,
    And may thy fears fulfill;
        But think that we
Are but turned aside to sleep;
They who one another keep
40   Alive, ne'er parted be.

                                                    1633

A Valediction: Of Weeping

            Let me pour forth
My tears before thy face whilst I stay here,
For thy face coins them, and thy stamp they bear,
And by this mintage they are something worth,
5   For thus they be
            Pregnant of thee;
Fruits of much grief they are, emblems of more;
When a tear falls, that Thou falls which it bore,
So thou and I are nothing then, when on a diverse shore.

10   On a round ball
A workman that hath copies by, can lay
An Europe, Afric, and an Asïa,
And quickly make that, which was nothing, all,
            So doth each tear
15   Which thee doth wear,[1]
A globe, yea world, by that impression grow,
Till thy tears mixed with mine do overflow
This world; by waters sent from thee, my heaven dissolvéd so.

            O more than moon,
20 Draw not up seas to drown me in thy sphere;
Weep me not dead, in thine arms, but forbear
To teach the sea what it may do too soon.
            Let not the wind
            Example find
25 To do me more harm than it purposeth;
Since thou and I sigh one another's breath,
Whoe'er sighs most is cruelest, and hastes the other's death.

                                                    1633

A Valediction: Forbidding Mourning

As virtuous men pass mildly'away,
    And whisper to their souls to go,
Whilst some of their sad friends do say
    The breath goes now, and some say, No;

---

1. I.e., doth wear thee.

5   So let us melt, and make no noise,
      No tear-floods, nor sigh-tempests move,
'Twere profanation of our joys
      To tell the laity our love.

Moving of th' earth brings harms and fears,
10   Men reckon what it did and meant;
But trepidation of the spheres,[2]
      Though greater far, is innocent.

Dull sublunary[3] lovers' love
      (Whose soul is sense) cannot admit
15 Absence, because it doth remove
      Those things which elemented it.

But we by'a love so much refined
      That our selves know not what it is,
Inter-assuréd of the mind,
20   Care less, eyes, lips, and hands to miss.

Our two souls therefore, which are one,
      Though I must go, endure not yet
A breach, but an expansion,
      Like gold to airy thinness beat.

25 If they be two, they are two so
      As stiff twin compasses are two;
Thy soul, the fixed foot, makes no show
      To move, but doth, if th' other do.

And though it in the center sit,
30   Yet when the other far doth roam,
It leans and hearkens after it,
      And grows erect, as that comes home.

Such wilt thou be to me, who must
      Like th' other foot, obliquely run;
35 Thy firmness makes my circle[4] just,
      And makes me end where I begun.

                              1633

The Ecstasy[5]

Where, like a pillow on a bed,
      A pregnant bank swelled up to rest
The violet's reclining head,
      Sat we two, one another's best.
5   Our hands were firmly cémented
      With a fast balm, which thence did spring.
Our eye-beams twisted, and did thread
      Our eyes upon one double string;
So to'intergraft our hands, as yet
10   Was all the means to make us one;
And pictures in our eyes to get°   *beget*
      Was all our propagation.
As 'twixt two equal armies, Fate
      Suspends uncertain victory,

2. A trembling of the celestial spheres, hypothesized by Ptolemaic astronomers to account for unpredicted variations in the paths of the heavenly bodies.
3. Beneath the moon; earthly—hence, changeable.
4. The circle was a symbol of perfection; with a dot in the middle, it was also the alchemist's symbol for gold.
5. Literally, "a standing out." The term was used by religious mystics to describe the experience in which the soul seemed to leave the body and rise superior to it in a state of heightened awareness.

15 Our souls (which to advance their state,
    Were gone out) hung 'twixt her and me.
And whilst our souls negotiate there,
    We like sepulchral statues lay;
All day the same our postures were,
20   And we said nothing all the day.
If any, so by love refined
    That he soul's language understood,
And by good love were grown all mind,
    Within convenient distance stood,
25 He (though he knew not which soul spake,
    Because both meant, both spake the same)
Might thence a new concoction[6] take,
    And part far purer than he came.
This ecstasy doth unperplex,
30   We said, and tell us what we love;
We see by this it was not sex;
    We see we saw not what did move;
But as all several° souls contain   *separate*
    Mixture of things, they know not what,
35 Love these mixed souls doth mix again,
    And makes both one, each this and that.
A single violet transplant,
    The strength, the colour, and the size
(All which before was poor, and scant)
40   Redoubles still, and multiplies.
When love, with one another so
    Interinanimates two souls,
That abler soul, which thence doth flow,
    Defects of loneliness controls.
45 We then, who are this new soul, know,
    Of what we are composed, and made,
For, th' atomies° of which we grow,   *atoms*
    Are souls, whom no change can invade.
But O alas, so long, so far
50   Our bodies why do we forbear?
They're ours, though they're not we; we are
    Th' intelligences, they the spheres.[7]
We owe them thanks because they thus,
    Did us to us at first convey,
55 Yielded their forces, sense, to us,
    Nor are dross to us, but allay.°   *alloy*
On man heaven's influence works not so
    But that it first imprints the air,[8]
So soul into the soul may flow,
60   Though it to body first repair.
As our blood labors to beget
    Spirits as like souls as it can,[9]
Because such fingers need to knit
    That subtle knot which makes us man:
65 So must pure lovers' souls descend
    To' affections, and to faculties
Which sense may reach and apprehend;
    Else a great Prince in prison lies.
To'our bodies turn we then, that so
70   Weak men on love revealed may look;

6. Mixture of diverse elements refined by heat (alchemical term).
7. The nine orders of angels ("intelligences") were believed to govern the nine spheres of Ptolemaic astronomy.
8. Influences from the heavenly bodies were conceived of as being transmitted through the medium of the air; also, angels were thought to assume bodies of air in their dealings with men.
9. "Spirits" were vapors believed to permeate the blood and to mediate between the body and the soul.

Love's mysteries in souls do grow,
   But yet the body is his book.
And if some lover, such as we,
   Have heard this dialogue of one,
75 Let him still mark us; he shall see
   Small change when we're to bodies gone.

1633

The Funeral

Whoever comes to shroud me, do not harm
   Nor question much
That subtle wreath of hair which crowns my arm;
The mystery, the sign you must not touch,
5   For 'tis my outward soul,
Viceroy to that, which then to heaven being gone,
   Will leave this to control,
And keep these limbs, her provinces, from dissolution.

For if the sinewy thread my brain lets fall
10   Through every part
Can tie those parts and make me one of all;
These hairs, which upward grew, and strength and art
   Have from a better brain,
Can better do'it; except she meant that I
15   By this should know my pain,
As prisoners then are manacled, when they're condemned to die.

Whate'er she meant by 'it, bury it with me,
   For since I am
Love's martyr, it might breed idolatry,
20 If into other's hands these relics came;
   As 'twas humility
To'afford to it all that a soul can do,
   So 'tis some bravery,
That since you would save none of me, I bury some of you.

1633

The Relic

When my grave is broke up again
   Some second guest to entertain[1]
   (For graves have learned that woman-head°   *womanhood*
   To be to more than one a bed),
5   And he that digs it, spies
A bracelet of bright hair about the bone,
   Will he not let'us alone,
And think that there a loving couple lies,
Who thought that this device might be some way
10 To make their souls, at the last busy day,[2]
Meet at this grave, and make a little stay?

   If this fall in a time, or land,
   Where mis-devotion doth command,
   Then he that digs us up, will bring
15   Us to the Bishop and the King,
     To make us relics; then

---

1. Re-use of a grave, after an interval of years, was a common 17th-century practice.
2. Judgment Day, when all parts of the body would be reassembled and reunited with the soul in the resurrection.

Thou shalt be'a Mary Magdalen,[3] and I
    A something else thereby;
All women shall adore us, and some men;
20 And since at such time, miracles are sought,
I would have that age by this paper taught
What miracles we harmless lovers wrought.

    First, we loved well and faithfully,
    Yet knew not what we loved, nor why,
25   Difference of sex no more we knew,
    Than our guardian angels do;
      Coming and going, we
Perchance might kiss, but not between those meals;
    Our hands ne'er touched the seals,
Which nature, injured by late law, sets free:
30 These miracles we did; but now, alas,
All measure and all language I should pass,
Should I tell what a miracle she was.

                  1633

Satire III. Religion

Kind pity chokes my spleen; brave scorn forbids
Those tears to issue which swell my eyelids;
I must not laugh, nor weep sins, and be wise,
Can railing then cure these worn maladies?
5 Is not our mistress, fair Religion,
As worthy'of all our souls' devotion,
As virtue was to the first blinded age?[4]
Are not heaven's joys as valiant to assuage
Lusts, as earth's honor was to them? Alas,
10 As we do them in means, shall they surpass
Us in the end, and shall thy father's spirit
Meet blind philosophers in heaven, whose merit
Of strict life may be'imputed faith, and hear
Thee, whom he taught so easy ways and near
15 To follow, damned? O, if thou dar'st, fear this;
This fear great courage and high valor is.
Dar'st thou aid mutinous Dutch,[5] and dar'st thou lay
Thee in ships, wooden sepulchers, a prey
To leaders' rage, to storms, to shot, to dearth?
20 Dar'st thou dive seas and dungeons of the earth?
Hast thou courageous fire to thaw the ice
Of frozen North discoveries? and thrice
Colder than salamanders,[6] like divine
Children in the oven, fires of Spain, and the line,°   *equator*
25 Whose countries limbecks° to our bodies be,   *retorts*
Canst thou for gain bear? And must every he
Which cries not, "Goddess!" to thy mistress, draw,
Or eat thy poisonous words? Courage of straw!
O desperate coward, wilt thou seem bold, and
30 To thy foes and his (who made thee to stand
Sentinel in his world's garrison) thus yield,
And for forbidden wars, leave th' appointed field?
Know thy foes: The foul Devil he'is, whom thou
Strivest to please: for hate, not love, would allow

3. The woman out of whom Christ had cast seven devils (Luke viii.2), traditionally identified with the repentant prostitute of Luke vii.37–50.
4. I.e., before the Christian revelation.
5. In 1582 the English had aided the Dutch in their revolt against rule by Spain.

6. Salamanders were thought to be able to endure fire. The "divine children" were Shadrach, Meshach, and Abednego, who survived the fiery furnace unharmed (Daniel iii.20–30). "Fires of Spain" refers to the Inquisition, in which heretics were burned at the stake.

35   Thee fain his whole realm to be quit;[7] and as
      The world's all parts wither away and pass,
      So the world's self, thy other loved foe, is
      In her decrepit wane, and thou, loving this,
      Dost love a withered and worn strumpet; last,
40   Flesh (itself's death) and joys which flesh can taste,
      Thou lovest; and thy fair goodly soul, which doth
      Give this flesh power to taste joy, thou dost loathe.
      Seek true religion. O, where? Mirreus,
      Thinking her unhoused here, and fled from us,
45   Seeks her at Rome; there, because he doth know
      That she was there a thousand years ago.
      He loves her rags so, as we here obey
      The statecloth where the Prince sat yesterday.
      Crantz to such brave loves will not be enthralled,
50   But loves her only, who'at Geneva's[8] is called
      Religion—plain, simple, sullen, young,
      Contemptuous, yet unhandsome; as among
      Lecherous humors,° there is one that judges   *dispositions*
      No wenches wholesome but coarse country drudges.
55   Graius stays still at home here, and because
      Some preachers, vile ambitious bawds, and laws
      Still new, like fashions, bid him think that she
      Which dwells with us, is only perfect, he
      Embraceth her whom his Godfathers will
60   Tender to him, being tender, as wards still
      Take such wives as their guardians offer, or
      Pay values.° Careless Phrygius doth abhor   *fines*
      All, because all cannot be good, as one
      Knowing some women whores, dares marry none.
65   Graccus loves all as one, and thinks that so
      As women do in divers countries go
      In divers habits, yet are still one kind,
      So doth, so is religion; and this blind-
      ness too much light breeds; but unmovéd thou
70   Of force must one, and forced but one allow;
      And the right, ask thy father which is she,
      Let him ask his; though truth and falsehood be
      Near twins, yet truth a little older is;
      Be busy to seek her, believe me this,
75   He's not of none, nor worst, that seeks the best.
      To'adore, or scorn an image, or protest,
      May all be bad; doubt wisely; in strange way
      To stand inquiring right, is not to stray;
      To sleep, or run wrong, is. On a huge hill,
80   Craggéd and steep, Truth stands, and he that will
      Reach her, about must, and about must go,
      And what th' hill's suddenness resists, win so;
      Yet strive so, that before age, death's twilight,
      Thy soul rest, for none can work in that night.
85   To will implies delay, therefore now do.
      Hard deeds, the body's pains; hard knowledge too
      The mind's endeavors reach, and mysteries
      Are like the sun, dazzling, yet plain to'all eyes.
      Keep th' truth which thou hast found; men do not stand
90   In so ill case that God hath with his hand
      Signed kings' blank charters[9] to kill whom they hate,
      Nor are they vicars, but hangmen to fate.
      Fool and wretch, wilt thou let thy soul be tied
      To man's laws, by which she shall not be tried

---

7. To have concluded a bargain.
8. The center of Calvinism.

9. *Carte blanche,* i.e., unconditional authority.

95   At the last day? O, will it then boot° thee   *profit*
       To say a Philip, or a Gregory,
       A Harry, or a Martin[1] taught thee this?
       Is not this excuse for mere contraries
       Equally strong? Cannot both sides say so?
100   That thou mayest rightly'obey power, her bounds know;
       Those passed, her nature'and name is changed; to be
       Then humble to her is idolatry.
       As streams are, power is; those blest flowers that dwell
       At the rough stream's calm head, thrive and do well,
105   But having left their roots, and themselves given
       To the stream's tyrannous rage, alas, are driven
       Through mills, and rocks, and woods, and at last, almost
       Consumed in going, in the sea are lost.
       So perish souls, which more choose men's unjust
110   Power from God claimed, than God himself to trust.

                                                                                      1633

Good Friday, 1613. Riding Westward

       Let man's soul be a sphere, and then, in this,
       Th' intelligence that moves,[2] devotion is,
       And as the other spheres, by being grown
       Subject to foreign motions, lose their own,
5   And being by others hurried every day,
       Scarce in a year their natural form obey;
       Pleasure or business, so, our souls admit
       For their first mover, and are whirled by it.
       Hence is 't, that I am carried towards the West
10   This day, when my soul's form bends towards the East.
       There I should see a Sun, by rising, set,
       And by that setting endless day beget:
       But that Christ on this cross did rise and fall,
       Sin had eternally benighted all.
15   Yet dare I'almost be glad I do not see
       That spectacle, of too much weight for me.
       Who sees God's face, that is self-life, must die;
       What a death were it then to see God die?
       It made his own lieutenant, Nature, shrink;
20   It made his footstool crack, and the sun wink.[3]
       Could I behold those hands which span the poles,
       And tune all spheres at once, pierced with those holes?
       Could I behold that endless height which is
       Zenith to us, and to'our antipodes,[4]
25   Humbled below us? Or that blood which is
       The seat of all our souls, if not of His,
       Make dirt of dust, or that flesh which was worn
       By God, for his apparel, ragg'd and torn?
       If on these things I durst not look, durst I
30   Upon his miserable mother cast mine eye,
       Who was God's partner here, and furnished thus
       Half of that sacrifice which ransomed us?
       Though these things, as I ride, be from mine eye,
       They're present yet unto my memory,

1. Philip II of Spain, Pope Gregory XIII, Henry VIII of England, and Martin Luther.
2. An angel was believed to govern the movements of each of the nine celestial spheres in Ptolemaic astronomy. Each sphere, in addition to its own motion, was influenced by the motions of those outside it ("foreign motions," line 4), the outermost being known as the *primum mobile*, "first mover" (line 8).
3. "Thus saith the Lord * * * the earth is my footstool" (Isaiah lxvi.1). An earthquake and an eclipse accompanied the crucifixion of Jesus (Matthew xxvii.45, 51).
4. The zenith is that part of the heavens directly above any point on earth; the antipodes are that part of the earth diametrically opposite such a point.

35   For that looks towards them; and Thou look'st towards me,
      O Saviour, as Thou hang'st upon the tree.
      I turn my back to Thee but to receive
      Corrections, till Thy mercies bid Thee leave.
      O think me worth Thine anger; punish me;
40   Burn off my rusts and my deformity;
      Restore Thine image so much, by Thy grace,
      That Thou may'st know me, and I'll turn my face.

                                                      1633

From Holy Sonnets

1

      Thou hast made me, and shall Thy work decay?
      Repair me now, for now mine end doth haste;
      I run to death, and death meets me as fast,
      And all my pleasures are like yesterday.
5   I dare not move my dim eyes any way,
      Despair behind, and death before doth cast
      Such terror, and my feeble flesh doth waste
      By sin in it, which it towards hell doth weigh.
      Only Thou art above, and when towards Thee
10   By Thy leave I can look, I rise again;
      But our old subtle foe so tempteth me
      That not one hour myself I can sustain.
      Thy grace may wing me to prevent his art,
      And Thou like adamant° draw mine iron heart.   *loadstone*
                                                             1635

7

      At the round earth's imagined corners, blow
      Your trumpets, angels;[5] and arise, arise
      From death, you numberless infinities
      Of souls, and to your scattered bodies go;
5   All whom the flood did, and fire shall,[6] o'erthrow,
      All whom war, dearth, age, agues, tyrannies,
      Despair, law, chance hath slain, and you whose eyes
      Shall behold God, and never taste death's woe.[7]
      But let them sleep, Lord, and me mourn a space,
10   For, if above all these, my sins abound,
      'Tis late to ask abundance of Thy grace
      When we are there. Here on this lowly ground,
      Teach me how to repent; for that's as good
      As if Thou'hadst sealed my pardon with Thy blood.

                                                      1633

9

      If poisonous minerals, and if that tree
      Whose fruit threw death on else immortal us,
      If lecherous goats, if serpents envious
      Cannot be damned, alas, why should I be?
5   Why should intent or reason, born in me,
      Make sins, else equal, in me more heinous?
      And mercy being easy and glorious
      To God, in his stern wrath why threatens he?
      But who am I, that dare dispute with thee,

---

5. "* * * I saw four angels standing on the four corners of the earth, holding the four winds of the earth * * *" (Revelation vii.1).
6. At the end of the world, "* * * the elements shall melt with fervent heat, the earth also and the works that are therein shall be burned up" (II Peter iii.10).

7. "But I tell you of a truth, there be some standing here, which shall not taste of death, till they see the kingdom of God" (Christ's words to his disciples, Luke ix.27).

10 O God? Oh! of thine only worthy blood,
And my tears, make a heavenly Lethean[8] flood,
And drown in it my sins' black memory.
That thou remember them, some claim as debt;
I think it mercy if thou wilt forget.

1633

10

Death, be not proud, though some have calléd thee
Mighty and dreadful, for thou are not so;
For those whom thou think'st thou dost overthrow
Die not, poor Death, nor yet canst thou kill me.
5 From rest and sleep, which but thy pictures be,
Much pleasure; then from thee much more must flow,
And soonest our best men with thee do go,
Rest of their bones, and soul's delivery.
Thou'art slave to fate, chance, kings, and desperate men,
10 And dost with poison, war, and sickness dwell,
And poppy'or charms can make us sleep as well
And better than thy stroke; why swell'st thou then?
One short sleep past, we wake eternally
And death shall be no more; Death, thou shalt die.

1633

14

Batter my heart, three-personed God; for You
As yet but knock, breathe, shine, and seek to mend;
That I may rise and stand, o'erthrow me,'and bend
Your force to break, blow, burn, and make me new.
5 I, like an usurped town, to'another due,
Labor to'admit You, but O, to no end;
Reason, Your viceroy'in me, me should defend,
But is captíved, and proves weak or untrue.
Yet dearly'I love You,'and would be lovéd fain,
10 But am betrothed unto Your enemy.
Divorce me,'untie or break that knot again;
Take me to You, imprison me, for I,
Except You'enthrall me, never shall be free,
Nor ever chaste, except You ravish me.

1633

BEN JONSON
(1573–1637)

To the Reader

Pray thee, take care, that tak'st my book in hand,
To read it well: that is, to understand.

1616

To Doctor Empirick

When men a dangerous disease did 'scape
Of old, they gave a cock to Aesculape;[1]
Let me give two, that doubly am got free
From my disease's danger, and from thee.

1616

---

8. Lethe was a river in the classical under-
world; drinking of its waters caused one to
forget the past.

1. Aesculapius, the Roman god of medicine
and healing.

On My First Daughter

Here lies, to each her parents' ruth,°   sorrow
Mary, the daughter of their youth;
Yet all heaven's gifts being heaven's due,
It makes the father less to rue.
5   At six months' end she parted hence
With safety of her innocence;
Whose soul heaven's queen, whose name she bears,
In comfort of her mother's tears,
Hath placed amongst her virgin-train:
10 Where, while that severed doth remain,
This grave partakes the fleshly birth;
Which cover lightly, gentle earth!

1616

On My First Son

Farewell, thou child of my right hand,[2] and joy;
My sin was too much hope of thee, loved boy:
Seven years thou'wert lent to me, and I thee pay,
Exacted by thy fate, on the just day.[3]
5   O could I lose all father now! for why
Will man lament the state he should envý,
To have so soon 'scaped world's and flesh's rage,
And, if no other misery, yet age?
Rest in soft peace, and asked, say, "Here doth lie
10 Ben Jonson his best piece of poetry."
For whose sake henceforth all his vows be such
As what he loves may never like too much.

1616

To Fool or Knave

Thy praise or dispraise is to me alike:
One doth not stroke me, nor the other strike.

1616

To Fine Lady Would-Be

Fine Madam Would-Be, wherefore should you fear,
That love to make so well, a child to bear?
The world reputes you barren; but I know
Your 'pothecary, and his drug says no.
5   Is it the pain affrights? That's soon forgot.
Or your complexion's loss? You have a pot
That can restore that. Will it hurt your feature?
To make amends, you're thought a wholesome creature.
What should the cause be? Oh, you live at court,
10 And there's both loss of time and loss of sport
In a great belly. Write, then, on thy womb,
Of the not born, yet buried, here's the tomb.

1616

2. A literal translation of the Hebrew *Ben-*
jamin, the boy's name.

3. Jonson's son died on his seventh birthday
in 1603.

On Playwright

Playwright, convict° of public wrongs to men,   *convicted*
Takes private beatings and begins again.
Two kinds of valor he doth show at once:
Active in 's brain, and passive in his bones.

1616

On English Monsieur

Would you believe, when you this mónsieur[4] see,
That his whole body should speak French, not he?
That so much scarf of France, and hat, and feather,
And shoe, and tie, and garter should come hether,°   *hither*
5 And land on one whose face durst never be
Toward the sea farther than Half-Way Tree?[5]
That he, untraveled, should be French so much
As Frenchmen in his company should seem Dutch?
Or had his father, when he did him get,
10 The French disease,[6] with which he labors yet?
Or hung some mónsieur's picture on the wall,
By which his dam conceived him, clothes and all?
Or is it some French statue? No: 'T doth move,
And stoop, and cringe. O then, it needs must prove
15 The new French tailor's motion,° monthly made,   *puppet*
Daily to turn in Paul's,[7] and help the trade.

1616

Inviting a Friend to Supper

Tonight, grave sir, both my poor house, and I
Do equally desire your company;
Not that we think us worthy such a guest,
But that your worth will dignify our feast
5 With those that come, whose grace may make that seem
Something, which else could hope for no esteem.
It is the fair acceptance, sir, creates
The entertainment perfect, not the cates.°   *food*
Yet shall you have, to rectify your palate,
10 An olive, capers, or some better salad
Ushering the mutton; with a short-legged hen,
If we can get her, full of eggs, and then
Lemons, and wine for sauce; to these a cony°   *rabbit*
Is not to be despaired of, for our money;
15 And, though fowl now be scarce, yet there are clerks,
The sky not falling, think we may have larks.[8]
I'll tell you of more, and lie, so you will come:
Of partridge, pheasant, woodcock, of which some
May yet be there, and godwit,[9] if we can;
20 Knot, rail, and ruff too. Howsoe'er, my man
Shall read a piece of Virgil, Tacitus,
Livy, or of some better book to us,
Of which we'll speak our minds, amidst our meat;

---

4. Stress on first syllable; often spelled *monser* in Jonson's time, suggesting an Anglicized pronunciation.
5. Perhaps a landmark between London and Dover, where a traveler would embark for France.
6. I.e., syphilis.
7. St. Paul's Cathedral in London. In the 17th century St. Paul's was a popular gathering place; merchants hired men to walk up and down in the yard advertising their wares.
8. According to an old proverb, "When the sky falls we shall have larks."
9. The godwit, knot, rail, and ruff are all wading birds related to the curlew or sandpiper. They were formerly regarded as delicacies.

And I'll profess no verses to repeat.
25 To this, if aught appear which I not know of,
That will the pastry, not my paper, show of.
Digestive[1] cheese and fruit there sure will be;
But that which most doth take my Muse and me,
Is a pure cup of rich Canary wine,
30 Which is the Mermaid's[2] now, but shall be mine;
Of which had Horace, or Anacreon tasted,
Their lives, as do their lines, till now had lasted.
Tobacco,[3] nectar, or the Thespian spring,
Are all but Luther's beer[4] to this I sing.
35 Of this we will sup free, but moderately,
And we will have no Pooley, or Parrot[5] by,
Nor shall our cups make any guilty men;
But, at our parting we will be as when
We innocently met. No simple word
40 That shall be uttered at our mirthful board,
Shall make us sad next morning or affright
The liberty that we'll enjoy tonight.

1616

On Gut

Gut eats all day and lechers all the night;
So all his meat he tasteth over twice;
And, striving so to double his delight,
He makes himself a thoroughfare of vice.
5 Thus in his belly can he change a sin:
Lust it comes out, that gluttony went in.

1616

Epitaph on Salomon Pavy, a Child of Queen Elizabeth's Chapel[6]

Weep with me, all you that read
  This little story,
And know, for whom a tear you shed,
  Death's self is sorry.
5 'Twas a child, that so did thrive
  In grace and feature,
As Heaven and Nature seemed to strive
  Which owned the creature.
Years he numbered scarce thirteen
10 When Fates turned cruel,
Yet three filled zodiacs[7] had he been
  The stage's jewel,
And did act, what now we moan,
  Old men so duly,
15 As, sooth, the Parcae[8] thought him one,
  He played so truly.
So, by error, to his fate
  They all consented;
But viewing him since (alas, too late)
20 They have repented.

---

1. Promoting or aiding digestion.
2. A famous tavern—a favorite haunt of Jonson's.
3. Smoking was often called "drinking tobacco."
4. German beer, considered inferior.
5. Notorious government informers.

6. The Children of Queen Elizabeth's Chapel were a company of boy actors. Salomon Pavy had acted in Jonson's plays.
7. I.e., three years.
8. The three Fates, who determined men's destinies.

And have sought, to give new birth,
   In baths to steep him;[9]
But, being so much too good for earth,
   Heaven vows to keep him.

                                     1616

To Penshurst[1]

Thou art not, Penshurst, built to envious show,
Of touch° or marble; nor canst boast a row   *touchstone, basanite*
Of polished pillars, or a roof of gold;
Thou hast no lantern,[2] whereof tales are told,
5   Or stair, or courts; but stand'st an ancient pile,
And, these grudged at, art reverenced the while.
Thou joy'st in better marks, of soil, of air,
Of wood, of water; therein thou art fair.
Thou hast thy walks for health, as well as sport;
10   Thy mount, to which the dryads° do resort,   *wood nymphs*
Where Pan and Bacchus their high feasts have made,
Beneath the broad beech and the chestnut shade;
That taller tree, which of a nut was set
At his great birth[3] where all the Muses met.
15   There in the writhéd bark are cut the names
Of many a sylvan,° taken with his flames;   *forest dweller*
And thence the ruddy satyrs oft provoke
The lighter fauns to reach thy Lady's Oak.
Thy copse too, named of Gamage,[4] thou hast there,
20   That never fails to serve thee seasoned deer
When thou wouldst feast or exercise thy friends.
The lower land, that to the river bends,
Thy sheep, thy bullocks, kine, and calves do feed;
The middle grounds thy mares and horses breed.
25   Each bank doth yield thee conies;° and the tops,   *rabbits*
Fertile of wood, Ashore and Sidney's copse,
To crown thy open table, doth provide
The purpled pheasant with the speckled side;
The painted partridge lies in every field,
30   And for thy mess is willing to be killed.
And if the high-swollen Medway[5] fail thy dish,
Thou hast thy ponds, that pay thee tribute fish,
Fat aged carps that run into thy net,
And pikes, now weary their own kind to eat,
35   As loath the second draught or cast to stay,°   *await*
Officiously° at first themselves betray;   *dutifully*
Bright eels that emulate them, and leap on land
Before the fisher, or into his hand.
Then hath thy orchard fruit, thy garden flowers,
40   Fresh as the air, and new as are the hours.
The early cherry, with the later plum,
Fig, grape, and quince, each in his time doth come;
The blushing apricot and woolly peach
Hang on thy walls, that every child may reach.
45   And though thy walls be of the country stone,
They're reared with no man's ruin, no man's groan;
There's none that dwell about them wish them down;
But all come in, the farmer and the clown,°   *countryman*

9. Aeson, the father of Jason, was made young again by a magic bath prepared by Jason's wife Medea.
1. The country estate of the Sidney family, in Kent.
2. A glassed or open structure raised above the roof of a house.
3. Sir Philip Sidney's, November 30, 1554.
4. Barbara Gamage, wife of Sir Robert Sidney, Philip's younger brother and the current owner of Penshurst.
5. The local river.

And no one empty-handed, to salute
50 Thy lord and lady, though they have no suit.
Some bring a capon, some a rural cake,
Some nuts, some apples; some that think they make
The better cheeses bring them, or else send
By their ripe daughters, whom they would commend
55 This way to husbands, and whose baskets bear
An emblem of themselves in plum or pear.
But what can this (more than express their love)
Add to thy free provisions, far above
The need of such? whose liberal board doth flow
60 With all that hospitality doth know;
Where comes no guest but is allowed to eat,
Without his fear, and of thy lord's own meat;
Where the same beer and bread, and selfsame wine,
That is his lordship's shall be also mine,
65 And I not fain° to sit (as some this day   *obliged*
At great men's tables), and yet dine away.
Here no man tells° my cups; nor, standing by,   *counts*
A waiter doth my gluttony envý,
But gives me what I call, and lets me eat;
70 He knows below he shall find plenty of meat.
Thy tables hoard not up for the next day;
Nor, when I take my lodging, need I pray
For fire, or lights, or livery;° all is there,   *provisions*
As if thou then wert mine, or I reigned here:
75 There's nothing I can wish, for which I stay.
That found King James when, hunting late this way
With his brave son, the prince, they saw thy fires
Shine bright on every hearth, as the desires
Of thy Penates⁶ had been set on flame
80 To entertain them; or the country came
With all their zeal to warm their welcome here.
What (great I will not say, but) sudden cheer
Didst thou then make 'em! and what praise was heaped
On thy good lady then, who therein reaped
85 The just reward of her high housewifery;
To have her linen, plate, and all things nigh,
When she was far; and not a room but dressed
As if it had expected such a guest!
These, Penshurst, are thy praise, and yet not all.
90 Thy lady's noble, friutful, chaste withal.
His children thy great lord may call his own,
A fortune in this age but rarely known.
They are, and have been, taught religion; thence
Their gentler spirits have sucked innocence.
95 Each morn and even they are taught to pray,
With the whole household, and may, every day,
Read in their virtuous parents' noble parts
The mysteries of manners, arms, and arts.
Now, Penshurst, they that will proportion° thee   *compare*
100 With other edifices, when they see
Those proud, ambitious heaps, and nothing else,
May say their lords have built, but thy lord dwells.

1616

6. Roman household gods.

Song: To Celia

Drink to me only with thine eyes,
And I will pledge with mine;
Or leave a kiss but in the cup,
And I'll not look for wine.
5   The thirst that from the soul doth rise,
Doth ask a drink divine:
But might I of Jove's nectar sup,
I would not change for thine.

I sent thee late a rosy wreath,
10   Not so much honoring thee,
As giving it a hope, that there
It could not withered be.
But thou thereon did'st only breathe,
And sent'st it back to me;
15   Since when it grows and smells, I swear,
Not of itself, but thee.

                                1616

Slow, Slow, Fresh Fount[7]

Slow, slow, fresh fount, keep time with my salt tears;
Yet slower, yet, O faintly, gentle springs!
List to the heavy part the music bears,
Woe weeps out her division,[8] when she sings.
5   Droop herbs and flowers;
        Fall grief in showers;
Our beauties are not ours. O, I could still,
Like melting snow upon some craggy hill,
       Drop, drop, drop, drop,
10   Since nature's pride is now a withered daffodil.

                                1600

Still to Be Neat[9]

Still to be neat, still to be dressed,
As you were going to a feast;
Still to be powdered, still perfumed;
Lady, it is to be presumed,
5   Though art's hid causes are not found,
All is not sweet, all is not sound.

Give me a look, give me a face
That makes simplicity a grace;
Robes loosely flowing, hair as free;
10   Such sweet neglect more taketh me
Then all th' adulteries of art.
They strike mine eyes, but not my heart.

                                1609

---

7. From *Cynthia's Revels*, sung by Echo for Narcissus, who fell in love with his own reflection and was changed into the flower that bears his name. The daffodil (line 11) is a species of narcissus.
8. Part in a song.
9. From *The Silent Woman*.

Though I Am Young and Cannot Tell[1]

Though I am young, and cannot tell
  Either what Death or Love is well,
Yet I have heard they both bear darts,
  And both do aim at human hearts.
5 And then again, I have been told
  Love wounds with heat, as Death with cold;
So that I fear they do but bring
  Extremes to touch, and mean one thing.

As in a ruin we it call
10 One thing to be blown up, or fall;
Or to our end like way may have
  By a flash of lightning, or a wave;
So Love's inflaméd shaft or brand
  May kill as soon as Death's cold hand;
15 Except Love's fires the virtue have
  To fright the frost out of the grave.

1641

To the Memory of My Beloved, the Author Mr. William Shakespeare

AND WHAT HE HATH LEFT US[2]

To draw no envy, Shakespeare, on thy name,
Am I thus ample to thy book and fame,
While I confess thy writings to be such
As neither man nor Muse can praise too much.
5 'Tis true, and all men's suffrage.° But these ways   *consent*
Were not the paths I meant unto thy praise:
For silliest ignorance on these may light,
Which, when it sounds at best, but echoes right;
Or blind affection,° which doth ne'er advance   *feeling*
10 The truth, but gropes, and urgeth all by chance;
Or crafty malice might pretend this praise,
And think to ruin where it seemed to raise.
These are as some infamous bawd or whore
Should praise a matron. What could hurt her more?
15 But thou art proof against them, and, indeed,
Above th' ill fortune of them, or the need.
I therefore will begin. Soul of the age!
The applause! delight! the wonder of our stage!
My Shakespeare, rise; I will not lodge thee by
20 Chaucer or Spenser, or bid Beaumont lie
A little further to make thee a room:[3]
Thou art a monument without a tomb,
And art alive still while thy book doth live,
And we have wits to read and praise to give.
25 That I not mix thee so, my brain excuses,
I mean with great, but disproportioned° Muses;   *not comparable*
For, if I thought my judgment were of years,
I should commit thee surely with thy peers,
And tell how far thou didst our Lyly outshine,
30 Or sporting Kyd, or Marlowe's mighty line.[4]

---

1. From *The Sad Shepherd.*
2. Prefixed to the first folio edition of Shakespeare's works, 1623.
3. Chaucer, Spenser, and Beaumont are all buried in Westminster Abbey.
4. John Lyly, Thomas Kyd, and Christopher Marlowe, all Elizabethan dramatists.

And though thou hadst small Latin and less Greek,
From thence to honor thee I would not seek
For names, but call forth thund'ring Aeschylus,
Euripides, and Sophocles to us,
35 Pacuvius, Accius, him of Cordova dead,[5]
To life again, to hear thy buskin[6] tread
And shake a stage; or, when thy socks were on,
Leave thee alone for the comparison
Of all that insolent Greece or haughty Rome
40 Sent forth, or since did from their ashes come.
Triumph, my Britain; thou hast one to show
To whom all scenes° of Europe homage owe.   *stages*
He was not of an age, but for all time!
And all the Muses still were in their prime
45 When like Apollo he came forth to warm
Our ears, or like a Mercury to charm.
Nature herself was proud of his designs,
And joyed to wear the dressing of his lines,
Which were so richly spun, and woven so fit,
50 As, since, she will vouchsafe no other wit:
The merry Greek, tart Aristophanes,
Neat Terence, witty Plautus[7] now not please,
But antiquated and deserted lie,
As they were not of Nature's family.
55 Yet must I not give Nature all; thy Art,
My gentle Shakespeare, must enjoy a part.
For though the poet's matter Nature be,
His Art doth give the fashion; and that he
Who casts to write a living line must sweat
60 (Such as thine are) and strike the second heat
Upon the muses' anvil; turn the same,
And himself with it, that he thinks to frame,
Or for the laurel he may gain a scorn;
For a good poet's made as well as born.
65 And such wert thou! Look how the father's face
Lives in his issue, even so the race
Of Shakespeare's mind and manners brightly shines
In his well-turnèd and true-filèd lines,
In each of which he seems to shake a lance,
70 As brandished at the eyes of ignorance.
Sweet swan of Avon, what a sight it were
To see thee in our waters yet appear,
And make those flights upon the banks of Thames
That so did take Eliza and our James![8]
75 But stay; I see thee in the hemisphere
Advanced and made a constellation there!
Shine forth, thou star of poets, and with rage
Or influence[9] chide or cheer the drooping stage,
Which, since thy flight from hence, hath mourned like night,
80 And despairs day, but for thy volume's light.

1623

5. Marcus Pacuvius and Lucius Accius were Roman tragedians of the second century B.C.; "him of Cordova" is the Roman tragedian Seneca of the first century A.D.
6. The high-heeled boot worn by Greek tragic actors; the "sock" or light shoe was worn in comedies.
7. Aristophanes (Greek) and Terence and Plautus (Roman) were comic writers of the fourth to second centuries B.C.
8. Queen Elizabeth and King James.
9. A supposed emanation of power from stars.

ROBERT HERRICK
(1591–1674)

The Argument[1] of His Book

I sing of brooks, of blossoms, birds, and bowers,
Of April, May, of June, and July flowers.
I sing of Maypoles, hock carts, wassails, wakes,[2]
Of bridegrooms, brides, and of their bridal cakes.
5   I write of youth, of love, and have access
By these to sing of cleanly wantonness.
I sing of dews, of rains, and, piece by piece,
Of balm, of oil, of spice, and ambergris.
I sing of times trans-shifting, and I write
10 How roses first came red and lilies white.
I write of groves, of twilights, and I sing
The court of Mab[3] and of the fairy king.
I write of hell; I sing (and ever shall)
Of heaven, and hope to have it after all.

1648

Delight in Disorder

A sweet disorder in the dress
Kindles in clothes a wantonness.
A lawn about the shoulders thrown
Into a fine distraction;
5   An erring lace, which here and there
Enthralls the crimson stomacher;[4]
A cuff neglectful, and thereby
Ribbons to flow confusedly;
A winning wave, deserving note,
10 In the tempestuous petticoat;
A careless shoestring, in whose tie
I see a wild civility;
Do more bewitch me than when art
Is too precise in every part.

1648

Corinna's Going A-Maying

Get up! get up for shame! the blooming morn
Upon her wings presents the god unshorn.[5]
   See how Aurora[6] throws her fair
   Fresh-quilted colors through the air:
5   Get up, sweet slug-a-bed, and see
   The dew bespangling herb and tree.
Each flower has wept and bowéd toward the east
Above an hour since, yet you not dressed;
   Nay, not so much as out of bed?
10 When all the birds have matins said,
   And sung their thankful hymns, 'tis sin,
   Nay, profanation to keep in,
Whenas a thousand virgins on this day
Spring, sooner than the lark, to fetch in May.[7]

1. I.e., subject matter.
2. The hock cart brought in the last load of the harvest. "Wakes": parish festivals as well as watches over the dead.
3. Queen of the fairies.
4. An ornamental piece worn under the open (and often laced) front of a bodice.
5. I.e., Apollo, god of the sun.
6. Goddess of the dawn.
7. Boughs of white hawthorn, traditionally gathered to decorate streets and houses on May Day.

15 Rise, and put on your foliage, and be seen
To come forth, like the springtime, fresh and green,
   And sweet as Flora.[8] Take no care
   For jewels for your gown or hair;
   Fear not; the leaves will strew
20   Gems in abundance upon you;
Besides, the childhood of the day has kept,
Against[9] you come, some orient pearls unwept;
   Come and receive them while the light
   Hangs on the dew-locks of the night,
25   And Titan[1] on the eastern hill
   Retires himself, or else stands still
Till you come forth. Wash, dress, be brief in praying:
Few beads[2] are best when once we go a-Maying.

Come, my Corinna, come; and, coming mark
30 How each field turns a street, each street a park
   Made green and trimmed with trees; see how
   Devotion gives each house a bough
   Or branch: each porch, each door ere this,
   An ark, a tabernacle is,
35 Made up of whitethorn neatly interwove,
As if here were those cooler shades of love.
   Can such delights be in the street
   And open fields, and we not see 't?
   Come, we'll abroad; and let's obey
40   The proclamation made for May,
And sin no more, as we have done, by staying;
But, my Corinna, come, let's go a-Maying.

There's not a budding boy or girl this day
But is got up and gone to bring in May;
45   A deal of youth, ere this, is come
   Back, and with whitethorn laden home.
   Some have dispatched their cakes and cream
   Before that we have left to dream;
And some have wept, and wooed, and plighted troth,
50 And chose their priest, ere we can cast off sloth.
   Many a green-gown has been given,
   Many a kiss, both odd and even,
   Many a glance, too, has been sent
   From out the eye, love's firmament;
55 Many a jest told of the keys betraying
This night, and locks picked; yet we're not a-Maying.

Come, let us go while we are in our prime,
And take the harmless folly of the time.
   We shall grow old apace, and die
60   Before we know our liberty.
   Our life is short, and our days run
   As fast away as does the sun;
And, as a vapor or a drop of rain
Once lost, can ne'er be found again;
65   So when or you or I are made
   A fable, song, or fleeting shade,
   All love, all liking, all delight
   Lies drowned with us in endless night.
Then while time serves, and we are but decaying,
70 Come, my Corinna, come, let's go a-Maying.

1648

---

8. Goddess of flowers.   1. The sun.
9. I.e., in readiness for the time when. "Ori-   2. I.e., prayers.
ent": lustrous, glowing.

To the Virgins, to Make Much of Time

Gather ye rosebuds while ye may,
  Old time is still a-flying;
And this same flower that smiles today
  Tomorrow will be dying.

5 The glorious lamp of heaven, the sun,
  The higher he's a-getting,
The sooner will his race be run,
  And nearer he's to setting.

That age is best which is the first,
10   When youth and blood are warmer;
But being spent, the worse, and worst
  Times still succeed the former.

Then be not coy, but use your time,
  And, while ye may, go marry;
15 For, having lost but once your prime,
  You may forever tarry.

1648

Upon a Child That Died

Here she lies, a pretty bud,
Lately made of flesh and blood,
Who as soon fell fast asleep
As her little eyes did peep.
5 Give her strewings, but not stir
The earth that lightly covers her.

1648

To Daffodils

Fair daffodils, we weep to see
  You haste away so soon:
As yet the early-rising sun
  Has not attained his noon.
5   Stay, stay,
  Until the hasting day
    Has run
  But to the evensong;
And, having prayed together, we
10 Will go with you along.

We have short time to stay as you;
  We have as short a spring;
As quick a growth to meet decay,
  As you or anything.
15   We die,
  As your hours do, and dry
    Away
  Like to the summer's rain;
Or as the pearls of morning's dew,
20 Ne'er to be found again.

1648

His Prayer to Ben Jonson

When I a verse shall make,
      Know I have prayed thee,
For old religion's sake,
      Saint Ben, to aid me.

5   Make the way smooth for me,
      When I, thy Herrick,
Honoring thee, on my knee
      Offer my lyric.

Candles I'll give to thee,
10   And a new altar;
And thou, Saint Ben, shalt be
      Writ in my psalter.

1648

Upon a Child

Here a pretty baby lies
Sung asleep with lullabies:
Pray be silent, and not stir
Th' easy earth that covers her.

1648

Upon Julia's Clothes

Whenas in silks my Julia goes,
Then, then, methinks, how sweetly flows
That liquefaction of her clothes.

Next, when I cast mine eyes, and see
5   That brave vibration, each way free,
O, how that glittering taketh me!

1648

Upon Prue, His Maid

In this little urn is laid
Prudence Baldwin, once my maid,
From whose happy spark here let
Spring the purple violet.

1648

Upon Ben Jonson

Here lies Jonson with the rest
Of the poets; but the best.
Reader, would'st thou more have known?
Ask his story, not this stone.
5   That will speak what this can't tell
Of his glory. So farewell.

1648

An Ode for Him

       Ah, Ben!
     Say how or when
    Shall we, thy guests,
  Meet at those lyric feasts
       Made at the Sun,
The Dog, the Triple Tun,[3]
  Where we such clusters had
As made us nobly wild, not mad;
  And yet each verse of thine
Outdid the meat, outdid the frolic wine.

       My Ben!
    Or come again,
    Or send to us
  Thy wit's great overplus;
       But teach us yet
  Wisely to husband it,
  Lest we that talent spend,
And having once brought to an end
  That precious stock, the store
Of such a wit the world should have no more.

                       1648

The White Island, or Place of the Blest

In this world, the isle of dreams,
While we sit by sorrow's streams,
Tears and terrors are our themes
    Reciting:

But when once from hence we fly,
More and more approaching nigh
Unto young eternity,
    Uniting:

In that whiter island, where
Things are evermore sincere;
Candor° here and luster there   *whiteness*
    Delighting:

There no monstrous fancies shall
Out of hell an horror call,
To create, or cause at all,
    Affrighting.

There, in calm and cooling sleep
We our eyes shall never steep,
But eternal watch shall keep,
    Attending

Pleasures, such as shall pursue
Me immortalized, and you;
And fresh joys, as never too
    Have ending.

                       1648

3. The names of taverns.

HENRY KING
(1592–1669)

The Exequy

Accept, thou shrine of my dead saint,
Instead of dirges, this complaint;
And for sweet flowers to crown thy hearse,
Receive a strew of weeping verse
5   From thy grieved friend, whom thou might'st see
Quite melted into tears for thee.

Dear loss! since thy untimely fate
My task hath been to meditate
On thee, on thee; thou art the book,
10   The library whereon I look,
Though almost blind. For thee, loved clay,
I languish out, not live, the day,
Using no other exercise
But what I practice with mine eyes;
15   By which wet glasses I find out
How lazily time creeps about
To one that mourns: this, only this,
My exercise and business is.
So I compute the weary hours
20   With sighs dissolvéd into showers.

Nor wonder if my time go thus
Backward and most preposterous;
Thou hast benighted me, thy set
This eve of blackness did beget,
25   Who wast my day, though overcast
Before thou hadst thy noontide passed;
And I remember must in tears,
Thou scarce hadst seen so many years
As day tells hours. By thy clear sun
30   My love and fortune first did run;
But thou wilt never more appear
Folded within my hemisphere,
Since both thy light and motiön
Like a fled star is fallen and gone;
35   And 'twixt me and my soul's dear wish
An earth now interposéd is,
Which such a strange eclipse doth make
As ne'er was read in almanac.

I could allow thee for a time
40   To darken me and my sad clime;
Were it a month, a year, or ten,
I would thy exile live till then,
And all that space my mirth adjourn,
So thou wouldst promise to return;
45   And putting off thy ashy shroud,
At length disperse this sorrow's cloud.

But woe is me! the longest date
Too narrow is to calculate
These empty hopes; never shall I
50   Be so much blest as to descry

A glimpse of thee, till that day come
Which shall the earth to cinders doom,
And a fierce fever must calcine[1]
The body of this world—like thine,
55 My little world! That fit of fire
Once off, our bodies shall aspire
To our souls' bliss; then we shall rise
And view ourselves with clearer eyes
In that calm region where no night
60 Can hide us from each other's sight.

Meantime, thou hast her, earth: much good
May my harm do thee. Since it stood
With heaven's will I might not call
Her longer mine, I give thee all
65 My short-lived right and interest
In her whom living I loved best;
With a most free and bounteous grief
I give thee what I could not keep.
Be kind to her, and prithee look
70 Thou write into thy doomsday book
Each parcel of this rarity
Which in thy casket shrined doth lie.
See that thou make thy reckoning straight,
And yield her back again by weight;
75 For thou must audit on thy trust
Each grain and atom of this dust,
As thou wilt answer Him that lent,
Not gave thee, my dear monument.

So close the ground, and 'bout her shade
80 Black curtains draw; my bride is laid.

Sleep on, my love, in thy cold bed,
Never to be disquieted!
My last good-night! Thou wilt not wake
Till I thy fate shall overtake;
85 Till age, or grief, or sickness must
Marry my body to that dust
It so much loves; and fill the room
My heart keeps empty in thy tomb.
Stay for me there; I will not fail
90 To meet thee in that hollow vale.
And think not much of my delay;
I am already on the way,
And follow thee with all the speed
Desire can make, or sorrows breed.
95 Each minute is a short degree,
And every hour a step towards thee.
At night when I betake to rest,
Next morn I rise nearer my west
Of life, almost by eight hours' sail,
100 Than when sleep breathed his drowsy gale.

Thus from the sun my bottom° steers,   vessel
And my day's compass downward bears;
Nor labor I to stem the tide
Through which to thee I swiftly glide.

1. Reduce to dust by heat.

105 'Tis true, with shame and grief I yield,
Thou like the van° first took'st the field,   *vanguard*
And gotten hast the victory
In thus adventuring to die
Before me, whose more years might crave
110 A just precédence in the grave.
But hark! my pulse like a soft drum
Beats my approach, tells thee I come;
And slow howe'er my marches be,
I shall at last sit down by thee.

115 The thought of this bids me go on,
And wait my dissolutiön
With hope and comfort. Dear (forgive
The crime), I am content to live
Divided, with but half a heart,
120 Till we shall meet and never part.

                                        1657

A Contemplation Upon Flowers

Brave flowers, that I could gallant it like you,
And be as little vain;
You come abroad and make a harmless show,
And to your beds of earth again;
5 You are not proud, you know your birth,
For your embroidered garments are from earth.

You do obey your months and times, but I
Would have it ever spring;
My fate would know no winter, never die,
10 Nor think of such a thing;
Oh that I could my bed of earth but view,
And smile and look as cheerfully as you.

Oh teach me to see death and not to fear,
But rather to take truce;
15 How often have I seen you at a bier,
And there look fresh and spruce;
You fragrant flowers then teach me that my breath
Like yours may sweeten and perfume my death.

                                        ca. 1660

GEORGE HERBERT
(1593–1633)

Redemption

Having been tenant long to a rich lord,
        Not thriving, I resolvéd to be bold,
        And make a suit unto him, to afford°   *grant*
A new small-rented lease, and cancel the old.

5   In heaven at his manor I him sought;
        They told me there that he was lately gone
        About some land, which he had dearly bought
Long since on earth, to take possessiön.

I straight returned, and knowing his great birth,
10   Sought him accordingly in great resorts;
      In cities, theaters, gardens, parks, and courts;
At length I heard a ragged noise and mirth
      Of thieves and murderers; there I him espied,
      Who straight, *Your suit is granted,* said, and died.

             1633

Easter Wings

Lord, who createdst man in wealth and store,°   *abundance*
      Though foolishly he lost the same,
          Decaying more and more
             Till he became
5   Most poor:
              With thee
           O let me rise
        As larks, harmoniously,
      And sing this day thy victories:
10 Then shall the fall further the flight in me.

My tender age in sorrow did begin;
      And still with sicknesses and shame
          Thou didst so punish sin,
             That I became
15   Most thin.
             With thee
          Let me combine,
       And feel this day[1] thy victory;
      For, if I imp[2] my wing on thine,
20 Affliction shall advance the flight in me.

             1633

Prayer (I)

Prayer, the church's banquet, angels' age,
  God's breath in man returning to his birth,
  The soul in paraphrase, heart in pilgrimage,
The Christian plummet sounding heaven and earth;

5 Engine against th' Almighty, sinner's tower,
  Reversèd thunder, Christ-side-piercing spear,
  The six-days' world[3] transposing in an hour,
A kind of tune, which all things hear and fear;

Softness, and peace, and joy, and love, and bliss,
10 Exalted manna, gladness of the best,
  Heaven in ordinary,[4] man well dressed,
The Milky Way, the bird of Paradise,

  Church bells beyond the stars heard, the soul's blood,
  The land of spices; something understood.

             1633

1. The words "this day," which are superfluous in the metrical scheme of the poem, were perhaps included in the early editions to emphasize the occasion, Easter. They are omitted, however, in the only surviving manuscript book of Herbert's poems.
2. A term from falconry: additional feathers were "imped" or grafted onto the wing of a hawk to improve its powers of flight.
3. God created the world in six days (Genesis i). Also, of course, the six weekdays might be thought of as a "world" distinct from that of the Sabbath.
4. In the everyday course of things. More specifically, *ordinary* also meant a daily allowance of food or an established order or form, as of the divine service.

Jordan (I)[5]

Who says that fictions only and false hair
Become a verse? Is there in truth no beauty?
Is all good structure in a winding stair?
May no lines pass, except they do their duty
5   Not to a true, but painted chair?[6]

Is it no verse, except enchanted groves
And sudden arbors[7] shadow coarse-spun lines?
Must purling streams refresh a lover's loves?
Must all be veiled while he that reads, divines,
10   Catching the sense at two removes?

Shepherds are honest people; let them sing:
Riddle who list, for me, and pull for prime:[8]
I envy no man's nightingale or spring;
Nor let them punish me with loss of rhyme,
15   Who plainly say, *My God, My King*.

                              1633

Church Monuments

While that my soul repairs to her devotion,
Here I intomb my flesh, that it betimes
May take acquaintance of this heap of dust;
To which the blast of death's incessant motion,
5 Fed with the exhalation of our crimes,
Drives all at last. Therefore I gladly trust

My body to this school, that it may learn
To spell his elements, and find his birth
Written in dusty heraldry and lines;
10 Which dissolution sure doth best discern,
Comparing dust with dust, and earth with earth.
These laugh at jet, and marble put for signs,

To sever the good fellowship of dust,
And spoil the meeting. What shall point out them,
15 When they shall bow, and kneel, and fall down flat
To kiss those heaps, which now they have in trust?
Dear flesh, while I do pray, learn here thy stem
And true descent, that when thou shalt grow fat

And wanton in thy cravings, thou mayst know
20 That flesh is but the glass which holds the dust
That measures all our time; which also shall
Be crumbled into dust. Mark, here below
How tame these ashes are, how free from lust,
That thou mayst fit thyself against thy fall.

                              1633

5. A river in the Holy Land, the cleansing waters of which cured leprosy (II Kings v.10).
6. It was customary to bow or "do one's duty" to the king's chair of state even when unoccupied.

7. One aim of garden design was to incorporate attractive features in such a way that they would be revealed unexpectedly in the course of a walk.
8. Draw for a winning card.

The Windows

Lord, how can man preach thy eternal word?
    He is a brittle crazy° glass;   *flawed*
Yet in thy temple thou dost him afford
    This glorious and transcendent place,
5   To be a window, through thy grace.

But when thou dost anneal in glass thy story,
    Making thy life to shine within
The holy preachers, then the light and glory
    More reverend grows, and more doth win;
10   Which else shows waterish, bleak, and thin.

Doctrine and life, colors and light, in one
    When they combine and mingle, bring
A strong regard and awe; but speech alone
    Doth vanish like a flaring thing,
15   And in the ear, not conscience, ring.

                          1633

Virtue

Sweet day, so cool, so calm, so bright,
    The bridal of the earth and sky:
The dew shall weep thy fall tonight;
    For thou must die.

5 Sweet rose, whose hue, angry and brave,
    Bids the rash gazer wipe his eye:
Thy root is ever in its grave,
    And thou must die.

Sweet spring, full of sweet days and roses,
10 A box where sweets° compacted lie;   *perfumes*
My music shows ye have your closes,⁹
    And all must die.

Only a sweet and virtuous soul,
    Like seasoned timber, never gives;
15 But though the whole world turn to coal,¹
    Then chiefly lives.

                          1633

Artillery

As I one evening sat before my cell,
Methought² a star did shoot into my lap.
I rose and shook my clothes, as knowing well
That from small fires comes oft no small mishap;
5   When suddenly I heard one say,
     "Do as thou usest, disobey,
      Expel good motions from thy breast,
Which have the face of fire, but end in rest."

9. A close is a cadence, the conclusion of a musical strain.

1. An allusion to Judgment Day, when the world will end in a general conflagration.
2. It seemed to me.

I, who had heard of music in the spheres,
10 But not of speech in stars, began to muse;
But turning to my God, whose ministers
The stars and all things are: "If I refuse,
        Dread Lord," said I, "so oft my good,
        Then I refuse not ev'n with blood
15   To wash away my stubborn thought;
For I will do or suffer what I ought.

"But I have also stars and shooters too,
Born where thy servants both artilleries use.
My tears and prayers night and day do woo
20 And work up to thee; yet thou dost refuse.
        Not but I am (I must say still)
        Much more obliged to do thy will
        Than thou to grant mine; but because
Thy promise now hath ev'n set thee thy laws.

25 "Then we are shooters both, and thou dost deign
To enter combat with us, and contest
With thine own clay. But I would parley fain:
Shun not my arrows, and behold my breast.
        Yet if thou shunnest, I am thine:
30   I must be so, if I am mine.
        There is no articling° with thee: *negotiating*
I am but finite, yet thine infinitely."

                                                  1633

The Collar

I struck the board° and cried, "No more;   *table*
        I will abroad!
What? shall I ever sigh and pine?
My lines and life are free, free as the road,
5   Loose as the wind, as large as store.°   *abundance*
        Shall I be still in suit?
Have I no harvest but a thorn
To let me blood, and not restore
What I have lost with cordial° fruit?   *life-giving*
10   Sure there was wine
Before my sighs did dry it; there was corn
        Before my tears did drown it.
Is the year only lost to me?
        Have I no bays[3] to crown it,
15 No flowers, no garlands gay? All blasted?
            All wasted?
Not so, my heart; but there is fruit,
        And thou hast hands.
Recover all thy sigh-blown age
20 On double pleasures: leave thy cold dispute
Of what is fit and not. Forsake thy cage,
        Thy rope of sands,
Which petty thoughts have made, and made to thee
    Good cable, to enforce and draw,
25   And be thy law,
While thou didst wink and wouldst not see.
        Away! take heed;
        I will abroad.
Call in thy death's-head[4] there; tie up thy fears.

---

3. A laurel garland symbolizing honor or
renown.

4. A representation of a human skull intended
to serve as a *memento mori,* a reminder that
all men must die.

30   He that forbears
To suit and serve his need,
Deserves his load."
But as I raved and grew more fierce and wild
At every word,
35 Methought I heard one calling, *Child!*
And I replied, *My Lord.*

1633

The Forerunners

The harbingers[5] are come. See, see their mark:
White is their color, and behold my head.
But must they have my brain? Must they dispark[6]
Those sparkling notions, which therein were bred?
5   Must dullness turn me to a clod?
Yet have they left me, *Thou art still my God.*

Good men ye be, to leave me my best room,
Ev'n all my heart, and what is lodgéd there:
I pass not,° I, what of the rest become,   *I care not*
10 So *Thou art still my God* be out of fear.
He will be pleaséd with that ditty;
And if I please him, I write fine and witty.

Farewell sweet phrases, lovely metaphors.
But will ye leave me thus? When ye before
15 Of stews and brothels only knew the doors,
Then did I wash you with my tears, and more,
Brought you to church well dressed and clad:
My God must have my best, ev'n all I had.

Lovely enchanting language, sugar-cane,
20 Honey of roses, wither wilt thou fly?
Hath some fond lover 'ticed thee to thy bane?
And wilt thou leave the church and love a sty?
Fie, thou wilt soil thy broidered coat,
And hurt thyself, and him that sings the note.

25 Let foolish lovers, if they will love dung,
With canvas, not with arras, clothe their shame:
Let folly speak in her own native tongue.
True beauty dwells on high: ours is a flame
But borrowed thence to light us thither.
30 Beauty and beauteous words should go together.

Yet if you go, I pass not; take your way:
For *Thou art still my God* is all that ye
Perhaps with more embellishment can say.
Go, birds of spring: let winter have his fee;
35   Let a bleak paleness chalk the door,
So all within be livelier than before.

1633

Discipline

Throw away thy rod,
Throw away thy wrath:
O my God,
Take the gentle path.

---

5. The advance agents of the king and his party on a royal progress or tour. They marked with chalk the doors of those dwellings where the court would be accommodated.

6. I.e., *dis-park*, to turn out, as of a park; there may also be a play on *dis-spark* (from "sparkling notions" in the next line).

5   For my heart's desire
    Unto thine is bent:
                    I aspire
    To a full consent.

    Not a word or look
10 I affect to own,
                    But by book,
    And thy book alone.

    Though I fail, I weep:
    Though I halt in pace,
15   Yet I creep
    To the throne of grace.

    Then let wrath remove;
    Love will do the deed:
                    For with love
20 Stony hearts will bleed.

    Love is swift of foot;
    Love's a man of war,[7]
                    And can shoot,
    And can hit from far.

25 Who can 'scape his bow?
    That which wrought on thee,
                    Brought thee low,
    Needs must work on me.

    Throw away thy rod;
30 Though man frailties hath,
                    Thou art God:
    Throw away thy wrath.

                                        1633

Love (III)

    Love bade me welcome: yet my soul drew back,
                Guilty of dust and sin.
    But quick-eyed Love, observing me grow slack
                From my first entrance in,
5   Drew nearer to me, sweetly questioning
                If I lacked anything.

    "A guest," I answered, "worthy to be here":
                Love said, "You shall be he."
    "I, the unkind, ungrateful? Ah, my dear,
10   I cannot look on thee."
    Love took my hand, and smiling did reply,
                "Who made the eyes but I?"

    "Truth, Lord; but I have marred them; let my shame
                Go where it doth deserve."
15 "And know you not," says Love, "who bore the blame?"
                "My dear, then I will serve."
    "You must sit down," says Love, "and taste my meat."
                So I did sit and eat.

                                        1633

---

7. "The Lord is a man of war" (Exodus xv.3).

THOMAS CAREW
(1598?–1639?)

A Song

Ask me no more where Jove bestows,
When June is past, the fading rose;
For in your beauty's orient deep,
These flowers, as in their causes,[1] sleep.

5 Ask me no more whither do stray
The golden atoms of the day;
For in pure love heaven did prepare
Those powders to enrich your hair.

Ask me no more whither doth haste
10 The nightingale when May is past;
For in your sweet dividing[2] throat
She winters, and keeps warm her note.

Ask me no more where those stars light,
That downwards fall in dead of night;
15 For in your eyes they sit, and there
Fixéd become, as in their sphere.

Ask me no more if east or west
The phoenix[3] builds her spicy nest;
For unto you at last she flies,
20 And in your fragrant bosom dies.

1640

Mediocrity in Love Rejected

Give me more love, or more disdain;
    The torrid or the frozen zone
Bring equal ease unto my pain;
    The temperate affords me none:
5 Either extreme, of love or hate,
Is sweeter than a calm estate.

Give me a storm; if it be love,
    Like Danaë in that golden shower,[4]
I swim in pleasure; if it prove
10   Disdain, that torrent will devour
My vulture hopes; and he's possessed
Of heaven that's but from hell released.
    Then crown my joys, or cure my pain;
    Give me more love or more disdain.

1640

1. Aristotelian philosophy regarded that from which a thing is made or comes into being as the "material cause" of the thing.
2. Executing a "division," an embellished musical phrase.
3. A legendary bird, the only one of its kind, represented as living five hundred years in the Arabian desert, being consumed in fire, then rising anew from its own ashes.
4. Danaë, imprisoned by her father in a house of bronze, was visited by Zeus in a shower of gold. The result of their union was the hero Perseus.

An Elegy upon the Death of the Dean of Paul's, Dr. John Donne

Can we not force from widowed poetry,
Now thou art dead, great Donne, one elegy
To crown thy hearse? Why yet did we not trust,
Though with unkneaded dough-baked prose, thy dust,
5 Such as the unscissored[5] lect'rer from the flower
Of fading rhetoric, short-lived as his hour,
Dry as the sand that measures it,[6] should lay
Upon the ashes on the funeral day?
Have we nor tune, nor voice? Didst thou dispense
10 Through all our language both the words and sense?
'Tis a sad truth. The pulpit may her plain
And sober Christian precepts still retain;
Doctrines it may, and wholesome uses, frame,
Grave homilies and lectures; but the flame
15 Of thy brave soul, that shot such heat and light
As burnt our earth and made our darkness bright,
Committed holy rapes upon our will,
Did through the eye the melting heart distil,
And the deep knowledge of dark truths so teach
20 As sense might judge what fancy could not reach,
Must be desired forever. So the fire
That fills with spirit and heat the Delphic choir,[7]
Which, kindled first by thy Promethean[8] breath,
Glowed here a while, lies quenched now in thy death.
25 The Muses' garden, with pedantic weeds
O'erspread, was purged by thee; the lazy seeds
Of servile imitation thrown away,
And fresh invention planted; thou didst pay
The debts of our penurious bankrupt age;
30 Licentious thefts, that make poetic rage
A mimic fury, when our souls must be
Possessed, or with Anacreon's ecstasy,
Or Pindar's,[9] not their own; the subtle cheat
Of sly exchanges, and the juggling feat
35 Of two-edged words, or whatsoever wrong
By ours was done the Greek or Latin tongue,
Thou hast redeemed, and opened us a mine
Of rich and pregnant fancy, drawn a line
Of masculine expression, which had good
40 Old Orpheus[1] seen, or all the ancient brood
Our superstitious fools admire, and hold
Their lead more precious than thy burnished gold,
Thou hadst been their exchequer, and no more
They in each other's dung had searched for ore.
45 Thou shalt yield no precedence, but of time
And the blind fate of language, whose tuned chime
More charms the outward sense; yet thou mayest claim
From so great disadvantage greater fame,
Since to the awe of thy imperious wit
50 Our troublesome language bends, made only fit
With her tough thick-ribbed hoops, to gird about
Thy giant fancy, which had proved too stout

5. I.e., with uncut hair.
6. I.e., the sand in an hourglass.
7. Ie., the choir of poets. Delphi was the site of an oracle of Apollo, the god of poetry.
8. The fire which Prometheus stole from the gods for the benefit of mankind was some-
times interpreted as man's vital spirit.
9. Anacreon and Pindar were famous Greek poets.
1. In Greek mythology, the son of one of the Muses and the greatest of poets and musicians.

For their soft melting phrases. As in time
They had the start, so did they cull the prime
55 Buds of invention many a hundred year,
And left the rifled fields, besides the fear
To touch their harvest; yet from those bare lands
Of what is only thine, thy only hands
(And that their smallest work) have gleanéd more
60 Than all those times and tongues could reap before.
    But thou art gone, and thy strict laws will be
Too hard for libertines in poetry.
They will recall the goodly exiled train
Of gods and goddesses, which in thy just reign
65 Were banished nobler poems; now with these
The silenced tales i' th' *Metamorphoses*[2]
Shall stuff their lines and swell the windy page,
Till verse, refined by thee in this last age,
Turn ballad-rhyme, or those old idols be
70 Adored again with new apostasy.
    O pardon me, that break with untuned verse
The reverend silence that attends thy hearse,
Whose solemn awful murmurs were to thee,
More than these faint lines, a loud elegy,
75 That did proclaim in a dumb eloquence
The death of all the arts, whose influence,
Grown feeble, in these panting numbers lies
Gasping short-winded accents, and so dies:
So doth the swiftly turning wheel not stand
80 In th' instant we withdraw the moving hand,
But some small time retain a faint weak course
By virtue of the first impulsive force;
And so whilst I cast on thy funeral pile
Thy crown of bays,[3] oh, let it crack awhile
85 And spit disdain, till the devouring flashes
Suck all the moisture up; then turn to ashes.
    I will not draw thee envy to engross
All thy perfections, or weep all the loss;
Those are too numerous for one elegy,
90 And this too great to be expressed by me.
Let others carve the rest; it shall suffice
I on thy grave this epitaph incise:

    Here lies a king, that ruled as he thought fit
    The universal monarchy of wit;
95   *Here lie two flamens,° and both those the best:*   priests
    Apollo's first, at last the true God's priest.

1633, 1640

2. Earlier poets had drawn heavily on the stories in Ovid's *Metamorphoses* for the materials of their poetry.

3. In classical times a crown of bays or laurel was the reward of the victor in a poetic competition.

JOHN MILTON
(1608–1674)

Lycidas

IN THIS MONODY[1] THE AUTHOR BEWAILS A LEARNED FRIEND, UNFORTU-
NATELY DROWNED IN HIS PASSAGE FROM CHESTER ON THE IRISH SEAS,
1637. AND BY OCCASION FORETELLS THE RUIN OF OUR CORRUPTED
CLERGY, THEN IN THEIR HEIGHT.

Yet once more, O ye laurels[2] and once more
Ye myrtles brown,° with ivy never sere,°   *dark / withered*
I come to pluck your berries harsh and crude,°   *unripe*
And with forced fingers rude,
5   Shatter your leaves before the mellowing year.
Bitter constraint, and sad occasion dear,°   *severe*
Compels me to disturb your season due;
For Lycidas is dead, dead ere his prime,
Young Lycidas, and hath not left his peer.
10   Who would not sing for Lycidas? He knew
Himself to sing, and build the lofty rhyme.
He must not float upon his watery bier
Unwept, and welter° to the parching wind,   *roll about*
Without the meed° of some melodious tear.   *tribute*
15   Begin then, sisters of the sacred well[3]
That from beneath the seat of Jove doth spring,
Begin, and somewhat loudly sweep the string.
Hence with denial vain, and coy excuse;
So may some gentle Muse°   *poet*
20   With lucky words favor my destined urn,
And as he passes turn,
And bid fair peace be to my sable shroud.
For we were nursed upon the selfsame hill,
Fed the same flock, by fountain, shade, and rill.
25   Together both, ere the high lawns° appeared   *pastures*
Under the opening eyelids of the morn,
We drove afield, and both together heard
What time the grayfly winds her sultry horn,
Battening° our flocks with the fresh dews of night,   *fattening*
30   Oft till the star that rose at evening bright
Toward Heaven's descent had sloped his westering wheel.
Meanwhile the rural ditties were not mute,
Tempered to th' oaten flute,
Rough satyrs danced, and fauns with cloven heel
35   From the glad sound would not be absent long,
And old Damoetas[4] loved to hear our song.
But O the heavy change, now thou art gone,
Now thou art gone, and never must return!
Thee, shepherd, thee the woods and desert caves,
40   With wild thyme and the gadding° vine o'ergrown,   *wandering*
And all their echoes mourn.
The willows and the hazel copses green
Shall now no more be seen,
Fanning their joyous leaves to thy soft lays.

1. An elegy or dirge sung by a single voice.
The "learned friend" was Edward King, Mil-
ton's fellow student at Cambridge.
2. The laurel, myrtle, and ivy were all tra-
ditional materials for poetic garlands.

3. The Muses. The well sacred to them was
Aganippe, at the foot of Mt. Helicon, where
they danced about the altar of Jove.
4. A conventional pastoral name, here perhaps
referring to one of the tutors at Cambridge.

45   As killing as the canker to the rose,
     Or taint-worm to the weanling herds that graze,
     Or frost to flowers that their gay wardrobe wear,
     When first the white thorn blows;°   *blooms*
     Such, Lycidas, thy loss to shepherd's ear.
50   Where were ye, nymphs, when the remorseless deep
     Closed o'er the head of your loved Lycidas?
     For neither were ye playing on the steep,
     Where your old Bards, the famous Druids lie,
     Nor on the shaggy top of Mona high,
55   Nor yet where Deva spreads her wizard stream:[5]
     Ay me! I fondly° dream—   *foolishly*
     Had ye been there—for what could that have done?
     What could the Muse[6] herself that Orpheus bore,
     The Muse herself, for her inchanting son
60   Whom universal Nature did lament,
     When by the rout that made the hideous roar,
     His gory visage down the stream was sent,
     Down the swift Hebrus to the Lesbian shore?
        Alas! What boots° it with uncessant care   *profits*
65   To tend the homely slighted shepherd's trade,
     And strictly meditate the thankless Muse?
     Were it not better done as others use,
     To sport with Amaryllis[7] in the shade,
     Or with the tangles of Neaera's hair?
70   Fame is the spur that the clear spirit doth raise
     (That last infirmity of noble mind)
     To scorn delights, and live laborious days;
     But the fair guerdon° when we hope to find,   *reward*
     And think to burst out into sudden blaze,
75   Comes the blind Fury[8] with th' abhorréd shears,
     And slits the thin spun life. "But not the praise,"
     Phoebus[9] replied, and touched my trembling ears;
     "Fame is no plant that grows on mortal soil,
     Nor in the glistering foil[1]
80   Set off to th' world, nor in broad rumor lies,
     But lives and spreads aloft by those pure eyes,
     And perfect witness of all-judging Jove;
     As he pronounces lastly on each deed,
     Of so much fame in Heaven expect thy meed."
85   O fountain Arethuse,[2] and thou honored flood,
     Smooth-sliding Mincius, crowned with vocal reeds,
     That strain I heard was of a higher mood.
     But now my oat[3] proceeds,
     And listens to the herald of the sea[4]
90   That came in Neptune's plea.
     He asked the waves, and asked the felon winds,
     "What hard mishap hath doomed this gentle swain?"
     And questioned every gust of rugged wings
     That blows from off each beakéd promontory;

5. The "steep" is probably the mountain Kerig-y-Druidion in northern Wales, a Druid burial ground. Mona is the Isle of Anglesey, Deva the River Dee, called "wizard" because its changes of course were supposed to foretell the country's fortune. All three places are just south of that part of the Irish Sea where King was drowned.
6. Calliope, the Muse of epic poetry. Her son Orpheus, the greatest of all poets and musicians, was torn limb from limb by a band of Thracian Maenads, who flung his head into the River Hebrus, whence it drifted across the Aegean to the island of Lesbos.
7. A conventional pastoral name, like "Neaera" in the next line.

8. Atropos, the third of the three Fates, who cut the thread of a man's life after it had been spun and measured by her sisters.
9. Apollo, god of poetic inspiration.
1. The setting for a gem, especially one that enhances the appearance of an inferior or false stone.
2. A fountain in Sicily, associated with the pastoral poems of Theocritus. The Mincius is a river in Italy described in one of Virgil's pastorals.
3. Oaten pipe, song.
4. The merman Triton, who came to plead his master Neptune's innocence of Lycidas' death.

95 They knew not of his story,
    And sage Hippotades⁵ their answer brings,
    That not a blast was from his dungeon strayed,
    The air was calm, and on the level brine,
    Sleek Panope⁶ with all her sisters played.
100 It was that fatal and perfidious bark
    Built in th' eclipse, and rigged with curses dark,
    That sunk so low that sacred head of thine.
        Next Camus,⁷ reverend sire, went footing slow,
    His mantle hairy, and his bonnet sedge,
105 Inwrought with figures dim, and on the edge
    Like to that sanguine flower inscribed with woe.⁸
    "Ah! who hath reft," quoth he, "my dearest pledge?"
    Last came and last did go
    The pilot of the Galilean lake,⁹
110 Two massy keys he bore of metals twain
    (The golden opes, the iron shuts amain).
    He shook his mitered locks, and stern bespake:
    "How well could I have spared for thee, young swain,
    Enow° of such as for their bellies' sake,   *enough*
115 Creep and intrude, and climb into the fold!
    Of other care they little reckoning make,
    Than how to scramble at the shearers' feast,
    And shove away the worthy bidden guest.
    Blind mouths! That scarce themselves know how to hold
120 A sheep-hook, or have learned aught else the least
    That to the faithful herdsman's art belongs!
    What recks it them?¹ What need they? They are sped;
    And when they list, their lean and flashy° songs   *insipid*
    Grate on their scrannel° pipes of wretched straw.   *meager*
125 The hungry sheep look up, and are not fed,
    But swoln with wind, and the rank mist they draw,
    Rot inwardly, and foul contagion spread,
    Besides what the grim wolf with privy paw²
    Daily devours apace, and nothing said.
130 But that two-handed engine at the door
    Stands ready to smite once, and smite no more."³
        Return, Alpheus,⁴ the dread voice is past,
    That shrunk thy streams; return, Sicilian muse,
    And call the vales, and bid them hither cast
135 Their bells and flowerets of a thousand hues.
    Ye valleys low where the mild whispers use,°   *frequent*
    Of shades and wanton winds, and gushing brooks,
    On whose fresh lap the swart star⁵ sparely looks,
    Throw hither all your quaint enameled eyes,
140 That on the green turf suck the honeyed showers,
    And purple all the ground with vernal flowers.
    Bring the rathe° primrose that forsaken dies,   *early*
    The tufted crow-toe, and pale jessamine,

5. Aeolus, son of Hippotas and god of the winds.
6. One of the Nereids, daughters of Nereus, the Old Man of the Sea.
7. The god of the river Cam, representing Cambridge University.
8. The hyacinth, created by Apollo from the blood of the youth Hyacinthus, whom he had killed by accident with a discus. Certain markings on the flower are supposed to be the letters AIAI ("Alas, alas!"), inscribed there by Apollo.
9. St. Peter, the Galilean fisherman, to whom Christ promised the keys of the kingdom of heaven (Matthew xvi.19). He wears the bishop's miter (line 112) as the first head of Christ's church.
1. What does it matter to them?

2. I.e., anti-Protestant forces, either Roman Catholic or Anglican.
3. A satisfactory explanation of these two lines has yet to be made, although many have been attempted. Most have taken the "two-handed engine" as an instrument of retribution against those clergy who neglect their responsibilities (such as the ax of reformation; the two-handed sword of the archangel Michael; the two houses of Parliament; death and damnation).
4. A river god who fell in love with the nymph Arethusa. When she fled to Sicily he pursued her by diving under the sea and coming up in the island. There she was turned into a fountain (see line 85) and their waters mingled.
5. Sirius, the Dog Star, thought to have a swart or malignant influence.

The white pink, and the pansy freaked° with jet,   *mottled*
145   The glowing violet,
The musk-rose, and the well attired woodbine.
With cowslips wan that hang the pensive head,
And every flower that sad embroidery wears:
Bid amaranthus[6] all his beauty shed,
150   And daffadillies fill their cups with tears,
To strew the laureate hearse° where Lycid lies.   *bier*
For so to interpose a little ease,
Let our frail thoughts dally with false surmise.
Ay me! Whilst thee the shores and sounding seas
155   Wash far away, where'er thy bones are hurled,
Whether beyond the stormy Hebrides,
Where thou perhaps under the whelming tide
Visit'st the bottom of the monstrous world;
Or whether thou, to our moist vows denied,
160   Sleep'st by the fable of Bellerus old,[7]
Where the great vision of the guarded mount
Looks toward Namancos and Bayona's hold;
Look homeward angel now, and melt with ruth:°   *pity*
And, O ye dolphins, waft the hapless youth.
165   Weep no more, woeful shepherds, weep no more,
For Lycidas your sorrow is not dead,
Sunk though he be beneath the watery floor,
So sinks the day-star° in the ocean bed,   *sun*
And yet anon repairs his drooping head,
170   And tricks° his beams, and with new-spangled ore,°   *dresses / gold*
Flames in the forehead of the morning sky:
So Lycidas sunk low, but mounted high,
Through the dear might of him that walked the waves,
Where other groves, and other streams along,
175   With nectar pure his oozy locks he laves,
And hears the unexpressive° nuptial song,[8]   *inexpressible*
In the blest kingdoms meek of joy and love.
There entertain him all the saints above,
In solemn troops and sweet societies
180   That sing, and singing in their glory move,
And wipe the tears forever from his eyes.
Now, Lycidas, the shepherds weep no more;
Henceforth thou art the genius° of the shore,   *local divinity*
In thy large recompense, and shalt be good
185   To all that wander in that perilous flood.
   Thus sang the uncouth° swain to th' oaks and rills,   *unlettered*
While the still morn went out with sandals gray;
He touched the tender stops of various quills,[9]
With eager thought warbling his Doric[1] lay:
190   And now the sun had stretched out all the hills,
And now was dropped into the western bay;
At last he rose, and twitched his mantle blue:
Tomorrow to fresh woods, and pastures new.

                                    1637

6. A legendary flower, supposed never to fade.
7. A legendary figure supposedly buried at Land's End in Cornwall. The "mount" of the next line is St. Michael's Mount at the tip of Land's End, "guarded" by the archangel Michael, who gazes southward toward Nemancos and the stronghold of Bayona in northwestern Spain.

8. Milton may have been thinking of the "marriage supper of the Lamb" mentioned in Revelation xix.9.
9. The individual reeds in a set of Panpipes.
1. Pastoral, because Doric was the dialect of the Greek pastoral writers Theocritus, Bion, and Moschus.

On the Morning of Christ's Nativity

1

This is the month, and this the happy morn,
Wherein the Son of Heaven's Eternal King,
Of wedded maid and virgin mother born,
Our great redemption from above did bring;
5   For so the holy sages[2] once did sing,
   That he our deadly forfeit[3] should release,
And with his Father work us a perpetual peace.

2

That glorious form, that light unsufferable,
And that far-beaming blaze of majesty,
10   Wherewith he wont at Heaven's high council-table
To sit the midst of Trinal Unity,
He laid aside, and, here with us to be,
   Forsook the courts of everlasting day,
And chose with us a darksome house of mortal clay.

3

15   Say, Heavenly Muse,[4] shall not thy sacred vein
Afford a present to the Infant God?
Hast thou no verse, no hymn, or solemn strain,
To welcome him to this his new abode,
Now while the heaven, by the Sun's team untrod,
20   Hath took no print of the approaching light,
And all the spangled host keep watch in squadrons
     bright?

4

See how from far upon the eastern road
The star-led wizards[5] haste with odors sweet!
Oh run, prevent° them with thy humble ode,   *go before*
25   And lay it lowly at his blessed feet;
Have thou the honor first thy Lord to greet,
   And join thy voice unto the angel choir
From out his secret altar touched with hallowed fire.

The Hymn

1

It was the winter wild,
30   While the heaven-born child
All meanly wrapt in the rude manger lies;
   Nature, in awe to him,
   Had doffed her gaudy trim,
With her great Master so to sympathize:
35   It was no season then for her
To wanton with the Sun, her lusty paramour.

2

  Only with speeches fair
  She woos the gentle air
To hide her guilty front with innocent snow,
40   And on her naked shame,
  Pollute with sinful blame,
The saintly veil of maiden white to throw;
Confounded, that her Maker's eyes
Should look so near upon her foul deformities.

---

2. I.e., the Hebrew prophets.
3. The penalty of death, occasioned by the sin of Adam.
4. Urania, the Muse of Astronomy, later identified with divine wisdom and treated by Milton as the source of creative inspiration.
5. The "wise men from the east" (Matthew ii.1).

3

45 But he, her fears to cease,
Sent down the meek-eyed Peace:
She, crowned with olive green, came softly sliding
Down through the turning sphere,[6]
His ready harbinger,
50 With turtle wing the amorous clouds dividing;   *dove*
And, waving wide her myrtle wand,
She strikes a universal peace through sea and land.

4

No war, or battle's sound,
Was heard the world around;
55 The idle spear and shield were high uphung;
The hookéd chariot[7] stood,
Unstained with hostile blood;
The trumpet spake not to the arméd throng;
And kings sat still with awful eye,
60 As if they surely knew their sovran Lord was by.

5

But peaceful was the night
Wherein the Prince of Light
His reign of peace upon the earth began.
The winds, with wonder whist,°   *hushed*
65 Smoothly the waters kissed,
Whispering new joys to the mild Ocean,
Who now hath quite forgot to rave,
While birds of calm[8] sit brooding on the charméd wave.

6

The stars, with deep amaze,
70 Stand fixed in steadfast gaze,
Bending one way their precious influence,[9]
And will not take their flight,
For all the morning light,
Or Lucifer[1] that often warned them thence;
75 But in their glimmering orbs[2] did glow,
Until their Lord himself bespake, and bid them go.

7

And, though the shady gloom
Had given day her room,
The Sun himself withheld his wonted speed,
80 And hid his head for shame,
As his inferior flame
The new-enlightened world no more should need:
He saw a greater Sun appear
Than his bright throne or burning axletree could bear.

8

85 The shepherds on the lawn,   *meadow*
Or ere the point of dawn,
Sat simply chatting in a rustic row;
Full little thought they than°   *then*
That the mighty Pan[3]
90 Was kindly come to live with them below:
Perhaps their loves, or else their sheep,
Was all that did their silly° thoughts so busy keep.   *simple*

---

6. The heavens as a whole, which "turn" once daily about the earth because of the earth's rotation.
7. War chariots were sometimes armed with sickle-like hooks projecting from the hubs of the wheels.
8. Halcyons or kingfishers, which in ancient times were believed to build floating nests at sea about the time of the winter solstice, and to calm the waves during the incubation of their young.
9. Medieval astrologers believed that stars emitted an ethereal liquid ("influence") that had the power to nourish or otherwise affect all things on earth.
1. Probably the morning star, although Milton sometimes uses the word for the sun.
2. The concentric crystalline spheres of Ptolemaic astronomy. Each sphere was supposed to contain one or more of the heavenly bodies in its surface and to revolve about the earth.
3. The Greek shepherd god Pan (whose name means "all") was often associated with Christ.

9

When such music sweet
Their hearts and ears did greet
95 As never was by mortal finger strook,°   *struck*
Divinely-warbled voice
Answering the stringéd noise,
As all their souls in blissful rapture took:
The air, such pleasure loth to lose,
100 With thousand echoes still prolongs each heavenly close.°   *cadence*

10

Nature, that heard such sound
Beneath the hollow round
Of Cynthia's seat[4] the airy region thrilling,
Now was almost won
105 To think her part was done,
And that her reign had here its last fulfilling:
She knew such harmony alone
Could hold all Heaven and Earth in happier uniön.

11

At last surrounds their sight
110 A globe of circular light,
That with long beams the shamefaced Night arrayed;
The helméd cherubim
And sworded seraphim[5]
Are seen in glittering ranks with wings displayed,
115 Harping loud and solemn quire,
With unexpressive° notes, to Heaven's new-born Heir.   *inexpressible*

12

Such music (as 'tis said)
Before was never made,
But when of old the sons of morning sung,[6]
120 While the Creator great
His constellations set,
And the well-balanced world on hinges hung,
And cast the dark foundations deep,
And bid the weltering waves their oozy channel keep.

13

125 Ring out, ye crystal spheres,
Once bless our human ears,
If ye have power to touch our senses so;
And let your silver chime
Move in melodious time;
130 And let the bass of heaven's deep organ blow;
And with your ninefold harmony
Make up full consort to th' angelic symphony.

14

For, if such holy song
Enwrap our fancy long,
135 Time will run back and fetch the age of gold;[7]
And speckled vanity
Will sicken soon and die;
And leprous sin will melt from earthly mold;
And Hell itself will pass away,
140 And leave her dolorous mansions to the peering day.

4. I.e., beneath the sphere of the moon.
5. Seraphim and cherubim (both are plural forms) are the two highest of the nine orders of angels in the medieval classification.
6. Job speaks of the creation of the universe as the time "when the morning stars sang together, and all the sons of God shouted for joy" (Job xxxviii.7).
7. The Romans believed that Saturn, after his dethronement by Jupiter, fled to Italy and there brought in the Golden Age, a time of perfect peace and happiness.

15

Yea, Truth and Justice then
Will down return to men,
Orbed in a rainbow; and, like glories wearing,
Mercy will sit between,
145   Throned in celestial sheen,
With radiant feet the tissued clouds down steering;
And Heaven, as at some festival,
Will open wide the gates of her high palace-hall.

16

But wisest Fate says no,
150   This must not yet be so;
The Babe lies yet in smiling infancy
That on the bitter cross
Must redeem our loss,
So both himself and us to glorify:
155 Yet first, to those ychained[8] in sleep,
The wakeful° trump of doom must thunder through the   *awakening*
  deep,

17

With such a horrid clang
As on Mount Sinai rang,[9]
While the red fire and smoldering clouds outbrake:
160   The aged Earth, aghast,
With terror of that blast,
Shall from the surface to the center shake,
When, at the world's last session,
The dreadful Judge in middle air shall spread his throne.

18

165   And then at last our bliss
Full and perfect is,
But now begins; for from this happy day
Th' old Dragon° under ground,   *Satan*
In straiter limits bound,
170 Not half so far casts his usurpéd sway,
And, wroth to see his kingdom fail,
Swinges° the scaly horror of his folded tail.   *lashes*

19

The Oracles are dumb;
No voice or hideous hum
175 Runs through the archéd roof in words deceiving.
Apollo from his shrine
Can no more divine,
With hollow shriek the steep of Delphos leaving.
No nightly trance, or breathéd spell,
180 Inspires the pale-eyed priest from the prophetic cell.

20

The lonely mountains o'er,
And the resounding shore,
A voice of weeping heard and loud lament;
From haunted spring, and dale
185   Edged with poplar pale,
The parting genius° is with sighing sent;   *local spirit*
With flower-inwoven tresses torn
The Nymphs in twilight shade of tangled thickets mourn.

---

8. Milton uses the archaic form of the past participle, common in Chaucer and imitated by Spenser, in which *y-* represents a reduced form of the Old English prefix *ge-*.

9. Moses received the Ten Commandments on Mount Sinai: "* * * there were thunders and lightnings * * * and the voice of the trumpet exceeding loud" (Exodus xix.16).

21

In consecrated earth,
190   And on the holy hearth,
The Lars[1] and Lemures moan with midnight plaint;
In urns and altars round,
A drear and dying sound
Affrights the flamens° at their service quaint;°   *priests / elaborate*
195 And the chill marble seems to sweat,
While each peculiar power forgoes his wonted seat.

22

Peor[2] and Baälim
Forsake their temples dim,
With that twice-battered God of Palestine;[3]
200   And moonéd Ashtaroth,[4]
Heaven's queen and mother both,
Now sits not girt with tapers' holy shine:
The Libyc Hammon[5] shrinks his horn;
In vain the Tyrian maids their wounded Thammuz mourn.[6]

23
205   And sullen Moloch,[7] fled,
Hath left in shadows dread
His burning idol all of blackest hue;
In vain with cymbals' ring
They call the grisly king,
210 In dismal dance about the furnace blue;
The brutish gods of Nile as fast,
Isis, and Orus, and the dog Anubis,[8] haste.

24
Nor is Osiris seen
In Memphian grove or green,
215   Trampling the unshowered grass with lowings loud;
Nor can he be at rest
Within his sacred chest;
Nought but profoundest Hell can be his shroud;
In vain, with timbreled anthems dark,
220 The sable-stoléd sorcerers bear his worshiped ark.

25
He feels from Juda's land
The dreaded Infant's hand;
The rays of Bethlehem blind his dusky eyn;°   *eyes*
Nor all the gods beside
225   Longer dare abide,
Not Typhon[9] huge ending in snaky twine:
Our Babe, to show his Godhead true,
Can in his swaddling bands control the damnéd crew.

26
So, when the sun in bed,
230   Curtained with cloudy red,
Pillows his chin upon an orient° wave,   *eastern*

1. Tutelary gods or spirits of the ancient Romans associated with particular places. Lemures were hostile spirits of the unburied dead.
2. Baal or Baal-Peor, the highest Canaanite god, whose shrine was at Mount Peor. Baalim (the plural form) were lesser gods related to him.
3. Dagon, god of the Philistines, whose statue twice fell to the ground before the ark of the Lord (I Samuel v.1–4).
4. Astarte, a Phoenician goddess identified with the moon.
5. The Egyptian god Ammon, represented as a horned ram. He had a famous temple and oracle at an oasis in the Libyan desert.
6. The death of the god Thammuz, Ashtaroth's lover, symbolized the coming of winter. The Tyrian (Phoenician) women mourned for him in an annual ceremony.
7. A pagan god to whom children were sacrificed. Their cries were drowned out by the clang of cymbals.
8. The Egyptian goddess Isis was represented as a cow, the gods Orus and Anubis as a hawk and a dog (hence "brutish"). Osiris (line 213) the creator, who had a shrine at Memphis, was represented as a bull.
9. A hundred-headed monster destroyed by Zeus.

The flocking shadows pale
      Troop to th' infernal jail;
    Each fettered ghost slips to his several grave,
235 And the yellow-skirted fays
    Fly after the night-steeds, leaving their moon-loved maze.
        27
      But see! the Virgin blest
      Hath laid her Babe to rest.
    Time is our tedious song should here have ending:
240   Heaven's youngest-teeméd star[1]
      Hath fixed her polished car,
    Her sleeping Lord with handmaid lamp attending;
    And all about the courtly stable
    Bright-harnessed angels sit in order serviceable.

                                   1629   1645

How Soon Hath Time

How soon hath Time, the subtle thief of youth,
    Stoln on his wing my three and twentieth year!
    My hasting days fly on with full career,
    But my late spring no bud or blossom shew'th.°   *showeth*
5 Perhaps my semblance might deceive the truth,
    That I to manhood am arrived so near,
    And inward ripeness doth much less appear,
    That some more timely-happy spirits endu'th.°   *endoweth*
  Yet be it less or more, or soon or slow,
10   It shall be still in strictest measure even°   *equal*
    To that same lot, however mean or high,
  Toward which Time leads me, and the will of Heaven;
    All is, if I have grace to use it so,
    As ever in my great Taskmaster's eye.

                                   1631   1645

When the Assault Was Intended to the City[2]

Captain or colonel,[3] or knight in arms,
    Whose chance on these defenseless doors may seize,
    If deed of honor did thee ever please,
    Guard them, and him within protect from harms.
5 He can requite thee; for he knows the charms
    That call fame on such gentle acts as these,
    And he can spread thy name o'er lands and seas,
    Whatever clime the sun's bright circle warms.
  Lift not thy spear against the Muses' bower:
10   The great Emathian conqueror[4] bid spare
    The house of Pindarus, when temple and tower
  Went to the ground; and the repeated air
    Of sad Electra's poet[5] had the power
    To save the Athenian walls from ruin bare.

                                   1642   1645

---

1. I.e., newest-born star, the star that guided the wise men, now imagined as having halted its "car" or chariot over the manger.
2. In November 1642, a Royalist army advanced on London with the hope of capturing it but turned back without a battle when it discovered that it faced a well-trained militia of 20,000 men.
3. Three syllables.
4. Alexander the Great, who in destroying Thebes for its revolt against him is reported by Pliny to have spared the house of the poet Pindar.
5. Euripides. According to Plutarch, Athens was saved from destruction when one of its Spartan conquerors urged clemency on his fellows by quoting from the first chorus of Euripides' *Electra*.

When I Consider How My Light Is Spent[6]

When I consider how my light is spent
 Ere half my days, in this dark world and wide,
 And that one talent which is death to hide[7]
 Lodged with me useless, though my soul more bent
5 To serve therewith my Maker, and present
 My true account, lest he returning chide;
 "Doth God exact day-labor, light denied?"
 I fondly° ask; but Patience to prevent   *foolishly*
That murmur, soon replies, "God doth not need
10 Either man's work or his own gifts; who best
 Bear his mild yoke, they serve him best. His state
Is kingly. Thousands at his bidding speed
 And post o'er land and ocean without rest:
 They also serve who only stand and wait."

          ca. 1652   1673

On the Late Massacre in Piedmont[8]

Avenge, O Lord, thy slaughtered saints, whose bones
 Lie scattered on the Alpine mountains cold,
 Even them who kept thy truth so pure of old
 When all our fathers worshiped stocks° and stones,[9] *idols*
5 Forget not: in thy book record their groans
 Who were thy sheep and in their ancient fold
 Slain by the bloody Piedmontese that rolled
 Mother with infant down the rocks. Their moans
The vales redoubled to the hills, and they
10 To Heaven. Their martyred blood and ashes sow
 O'er all th' Italian fields where still doth sway
The triple tyrant:[1] that from these may grow
 A hundredfold, who having learnt thy way
 Early may fly the Babylonian woe.[2]

          1655   1673

Lawrence[3] of Virtuous Father

Lawrence, of virtuous father virtuous son,
 Now that the fields are dank, and ways are mire,
 Where shall we sometimes meet, and by the fire
 Help waste a sullen day, what may be won
5 From the hard season gaining? Time will run
 On smoother, till Favonius[4] reinspire
 The frozen earth, and clothe in fresh attire
 The lily and rose, that neither sowed nor spun.[5]

6. Milton had become totally blind in 1651.
7. An allusion to the parable of the talents, in which the servant who buried the single talent his lord had given him, instead of investing it, was deprived of all he had and cast "into outer darkness" at the lord's return (Matthew xxv.14–30).
8. Some 1700 members of the Protestant Waldensian sect in the Piedmont in northwestern Italy died as a result of a treacherous attack by the Duke of Savoy's forces on Easter Day, 1655.
9. The Waldenses had existed as a sect, first within the Catholic Church and then as heretics, since the 12th century. They were particularly critical of materialistic tendencies in the Church.

1. The Pope, whose tiara has three crowns.
2. Babylon, as a city of luxury and vice, was often linked with the Papal Court by Protestants, who took the destruction of the city described in Revelation xviii as an allegory of the fate in store for the Roman Church.
3. Edward Lawrence, a friend of Milton's though twenty-five years his junior, was the son of Henry Lawrence, Lord President of the Council of State at the time this sonnet was written.
4. The Latin name of the west wind.
5. "Consider the lilies of the field, how they grow; they toil not, neither do they spin" (Matthew vi.28).

What neat repast shall feast us, light and choice,
10   Of Attic⁶ taste, with wine, whence we may rise
        To hear the lute well touched, or artful voice
Warble immortal notes and Tuscan air?
        He who of those delights can judge, and spare
        To interpose them oft, is not unwise.

                                          ca. 1655   1673

Cyriack,⁷ Whose Grandsire

Cyriack, whose grandsire on the royal bench
        Of British Themis,⁸ with no mean applause,
        Pronounced, and in his volumes taught, our laws,
        Which others at their bar so often wrench,
5 Today deep thoughts resolve with me to drench
        In mirth that after no repenting draws;
        Let Euclid rest, and Archimedes pause,
        And what the Swede intend, and what the French.
To measure life learn thou betimes,° and know   *early*
10   Toward solid good what leads the nearest way;
        For other things mild Heaven a time ordains,
And disapproves that care, though wise in show,
        That with superfluous burden loads the day,
        And, when God sends a cheerful hour, refrains.

                                          ca. 1655   1673

Methought I Saw

Methought I saw my late espoiiséd saint⁹
        Brought to me like Alcestis¹ from the grave,
        Whom Jove's great son to her glad husband gave,
        Rescued from Death by force, though pale and faint.
5 Mine, as whom washed from spot of child-bed taint
        Purification in the Old Law did save,²
        And such, as yet once more I trust to have
        Full sight of her in heaven without restraint,
Came vested all in white, pure as her mind.
10   Her face was veiled; yet to my fancied sight
        Love, sweetness, goodness, in her person shined
So clear as in no face with more delight.
        But O, as to embrace me she inclined,
        I waked, she fled, and day brought back my night.

                                          ca. 1658   1673

6. Athenian; i.e., delicate, discriminating.
7. Cyriack Skinner, a pupil of Milton's and grandson of Sir Edward Coke, the great jurist who had been Chief Justice of the King's Bench under James I.
8. The Greek goddess of justice.
9. The "saint," or soul in heaven, is Milton's second wife, Katherine Woodcock, to whom he had been married less than two years (hence "late espoiiséd") when she died in

1658. Since Milton had become blind in 1651, it is almost certain that he had never seen his wife.
1. The wife who is brought back from the dead to her husband Admetus by Hercules ("Jove's great son") in Euripides' *Alcestis*.
2. Hebrew law (Leviticus xii) prescribed certain sacrificial rituals for the purification of women after childbirth.

SIR JOHN SUCKLING
(1609–1642)

Song

Why so pale and wan, fond lover?
    Prithee, why so pale?
Will, when looking well can't move her,
    Looking ill prevail?
5   Prithee, why so pale?

Why so dull and mute, young sinner?
    Prithee, why so mute?
Will, when speaking well can't win her,
    Saying nothing do 't?
10   Prithee, why so mute?

Quit, quit, for shame; this will not move,
    This cannot take her.
If of herself she will not love,
    Nothing can make her:
15   The devil take her!

                                    1638

Out upon It!

Out upon it! I have loved
    Three whole days together;
And am like to love three more,
    If it prove fair weather.

5 Time shall molt away his wings,
    Ere he shall discover
In the whole wide world again
    Such a constant lover.

But the spite on 't is, no praise
10   Is due at all to me:
Love with me had made no stays
    Had it any been but she.

Had it any been but she,
    And that very face,
15 There had been at least ere this
    A dozen dozen in her place.

                                    1659

RICHARD CRASHAW
(1613–1649)

On the Baptized Ethiopian[1]

Let it no longer be a forlorn hope
        To wash an Ethiope;
He's washed, his gloomy skin a peaceful shade
        For his white soul is made,
5 And now, I doubt not, the Eternal Dove
        A black-faced house will love.

                                        1646

To the Infant Martyrs[2]

Go, smiling souls, your new-built cages break,
In heaven you'll learn to sing, ere here to speak,
Nor let the milky fonts that bathe your thirst
        Be your delay;
5 The place that calls you hence is, at the worst,
        Milk all the way.

                                          1646

Upon the Infant Martyrs

To see both blended in one flood,
The mothers' milk, the children's blood,
Make me doubt° if heaven will gather   *wonder*
Roses hence, or lilies rather.

                                          1646

A Hymn to the Name and Honor of the Admirable Saint Teresa[3]

FOUNDRESS OF THE REFORMATION OF THE DISCALCED[4] CARMELITES, BOTH MEN AND WOMEN. A WOMAN FOR ANGELICAL HEIGHT OF SPECULATION, FOR MASCULINE COURAGE OF PERFORMANCE, MORE THAN A WOMAN; WHO YET A CHILD OUTRAN MATURITY, AND DURST PLOT A MARTYRDOM.

Love, thou art absolute sole lord
Of life and death. To prove the word,
We'll now appeal to none of all
Those thy old soldiers, great and tall,
5 Ripe men of martyrdom, that could reach down
With strong arms their triumphant crown;
Such as could with lusty breath
Speak loud into the face of death
Their great Lord's glorious name; to none
10 Of those whose spacious bosoms spread a throne

---

1. Acts viii.26–39 tells how an Ethiopian eunuch of great authority under Queen Candace was converted and baptized by Philip the Evangelist.
2. The Holy Innocents, all the children of Bethlehem of two years and under, who were slain by Herod in an effort to destroy the one who, according to prophecy, would become the ruler of Israel (Matthew ii.16).
3. The remarkable Spanish mystic (1515–82), canonized in 1622. Her autobiography records how, at the age of six, she ran away from home to convert the Moors. In later visions she saw a seraph with a fire-tipped golden dart who pierced her heart repeatedly, causing simultaneously intense pain and joy. It is these "wounds of love" that constitute the "death more mystical and high" referred to in line 76.
4. Barefoot.

For Love at large to fill. Spare blood and sweat,
And see Him take a private seat;
Making His mansion in the mild
And milky soul of a soft child.
15   Scarce has she learnt to lisp the name
Of Martyr, yet she thinks it shame
Life should so long play with that breath
Which spent can buy so brave a death.
She never undertook to know
20 What death with love should have to do;
Nor has she e'er yet understood
Why to show love she should shed blood;
Yet though she cannot tell you why,
She can love and she can die.
25   Scarce has she blood enough to make
A guilty sword blush for her sake;
Yet has she a heart dares hope to prove
How much less strong is death than love.
Be love but there, let poor six years
30 Be posed with the maturest fears
Man trembles at, you straight shall find
Love knows no nonage, nor the mind.
'Tis love, not years or limbs, that can
Make the martyr or the man.
35   Love touched her heart, and lo it beats
High, and burns with such brave heats,
Such thirsts to die, as dares drink up
A thousand cold deaths in one cup.
Good reason, for she breathes all fire;
40 Her weak breast heaves with strong desire
Of what she may with fruitless wishes
Seek for amongst her mother's kisses.
Since 'tis not to be had at home,
She'll travel to a martyrdom.
45 No home for hers confesses she
But where she may a martyr be.
She'll to the Moors and trade with them
For this unvalued° diadem.   *invaluable*
She'll offer them her dearest breath,
50 With Christ's name in 't, in change for death.
She'll bargain with them, and will give
Them God, teach them how to live
In Him; or, if they this deny,
For Him she'll teach them how to die.
55 So shall she leave amongst them sown
Her Lord's blood, or at least her own.
Farewell then, all the world, adieu!
Teresa is no more for you.
Farewell, all pleasures, sports, and joys,
60 Never till now esteeméd toys;
Farewell, whatever dear may be,
Mother's arms, or father's knee;
Farewell house and farewell home,
She's for the Moors and martyrdom!
65   Sweet, not so fast! lo, thy fair Spouse
Whom thou seek'st with so swift vows
Calls thee back, and bids thee come
T' embrace a milder martyrdom.
Blest powers forbid thy tender life
70 Should bleed upon a barbarous knife;
Or some base hand have power to rase°   *cut*

Thy breast's chaste cabinet, and uncase
A soul kept there so sweet; oh no,
Wise Heav'n will never have it so.
75 Thou art Love's victim, and must die
A death more mystical and high;
Into Love's arms thou shalt let fall
A still surviving funeral.
His is the dart must make the death
80 Whose stroke shall taste thy hallowed breath;
A dart thrice dipped in that rich flame
Which writes thy Spouse's radiant name
Upon the roof of heaven, where aye
It shines, and with a sovereign ray
85 Beats bright upon the burning faces
Of souls which in that name's sweet graces
Find everlasting smiles. So rare,
So spiritual, pure, and fair
Must be th' immortal instrument
90 Upon whose choice point shall be sent
A life so loved; and that there be
Fit executioners for thee,
The fair'st and first-born sons of fire,
Blest seraphim, shall leave their choir
95 And turn Love's soldiers, upon thee
To exercise their archery.
      Oh, how oft shalt thou complain
Of a sweet and subtle pain,
Of intolerable joys,
100 Of a death, in which who dies
Loves his death and dies again,
And would for ever so be slain,
And lives and dies, and knows not why
To live, but that he thus may never leave to die!
105   How kindly will thy gentle heart
Kiss the sweetly killing dart!
And close in his embraces keep
Those delicious wounds, that weep
Balsam to heal themselves with. Thus
110 When these thy deaths, so numerous,
Shall all at last die into one,
And melt thy soul's sweet mansion;
Like a soft lump of incense, hasted
By too hot a fire, and wasted
115 Into perfuming clouds, so fast
Shalt thou exhale to heaven at last
In a resolving sigh; and then,
Oh, what? Ask not the tongues of men;
Angels cannot tell; suffice,
120 Thyself shall feel thine own full joys
And hold them fast for ever. There,
So soon as thou shalt first appear,
The moon of maiden stars, thy white
Mistress, attended by such bright
125 Souls as thy shining self, shall come
And in her first ranks make thee room;
Where 'mongst her snowy family
Immortal welcomes wait for thee.
Oh, what delight when revealed life shall stand
130 And teach thy lips heaven with his hand,
On which thou now mayst to thy wishes
Heap up thy consecrated kisses.

What joys shall seize thy soul when she,
Bending her blessed eyes on thee,
135 Those second smiles of heaven, shall dart
Her mild rays through thy melting heart!
   Angels, thy old friends, there shall greet thee,
Glad at their own home now to meet thee.
   All thy good works which went before
140 And waited for thee at the door
Shall own thee there, and all in one
Weave a constellatïon
Of crowns, with which the King, thy Spouse,
Shall build up thy triumphant brows.
145   All thy old woes shall now smile on thee,
And thy pains sit bright upon thee;
All thy sorrows here shall shine,
All thy sufferings be divine;
Tears shall take comfort and turn gems,
150 And wrongs repent to diadems.
Even thy deaths shall live, and new
Dress the soul that erst they slew;
Thy wounds shall blush to such bright scars
As keep account of the Lamb's wars.
155   Those rare works where thou shalt leave writ
Love's noble history, with wit
Taught thee by none but Him, while here
They feed our souls, shall clothe thine there.
Each heavenly word by whose hid flame
160 Our hard hearts shall strike fire, the same
Shall flourish on thy brows, and be
Both fire to us and flame to thee,
Whose light shall live bright in thy face
By glory, in our hearts by grace.
165   Thou shalt look round about and see
Thousands of crowned souls throng to be
Themselves thy crown; sons of thy vows,
The virgin-births with which thy sovereign Spouse
Made fruitful thy fair soul, go now
170 And with them all about thee, bow
To Him. "Put on," He'll say, "put on,
My rosy love, that, thy rich zone
Sparkling with the sacred flames
Of thousand souls whose happy names
175 Heav'n keeps upon thy score. Thy bright
Life brought them first to kiss the light
That kindled them to stars." And so
Thou with the Lamb, thy Lord, shalt go,
And whereso'er He sets His white
180 Steps, walk with Him those ways of light
Which who in death would live to see
Must learn in life to die like thee.

                                  1652

RICHARD LOVELACE
(1618–1658)

To Althea, from Prison

When Love with unconfinéd wings
Hovers within my gates,
And my divine Althea brings
To whisper at the grates;
5 When I lie tangled in her hair
And fettered to her eye,
The gods[1] that wanton in the air
Know no such liberty.

When flowing cups run swiftly round,
10 With no allaying Thames,[2]
Our careless heads with roses bound,
Our hearts with loyal flames;
When thirsty grief in wine we steep,
When healths and draughts go free,
15 Fishes, that tipple in the deep,
Know no such liberty.

When, like committed° linnets, I   *caged*
With shriller throat shall sing
The sweetness, mercy, majesty,
20 And glories of my King;
When I shall voice aloud how good
He is, how great should be,
Enlargéd winds, that curl the flood,
Know no such liberty.

25 Stone walls do not a prison make,
Nor iron bars a cage;
Minds innocent and quiet take
That for an hermitage.
If I have freedom in my love,
30 And in my soul am free,
Angels alone, that soar above,
Enjoy such liberty.

1649

To Lucasta, Going to the Wars

Tell me not, sweet, I am unkind
That from the nunnery
Of thy chaste breast and quiet mind,
To war and arms I fly.

5 True, a new mistress now I chase,
The first foe in the field;
And with a stronger faith embrace
A sword, a horse, a shield.

Yet this inconstancy is such
10 As you too shall adore;
I could not love thee, dear, so much,
Loved I not honor more.

1649

1. Most 17th-century versions read "birds"
for "gods."

2. I.e., without dilution (the Thames River
flows through London).

To Amarantha, That She Would Dishevel Her Hair

Amarantha sweet and fair,
Ah, braid no more that shining hair!
  As my curious hand or eye,
Hovering round thee, let it fly.

5   Let it fly as unconfined
As its calm ravisher, the wind,
  Who hath left his darling, th' East,
To wanton o'er that spicy nest.

   Every tress must be confessed
10 But neatly tangled at the best,
  Like a clue° of golden thread,   *ball*
Most excellently raveléd.

   Do not then wind up that light
In ribands, and o'ercloud in night;
15 Like the sun in's early ray,
But shake your head and scatter day.

   See, 'tis broke! Within this grove,
The bower and the walks of love,
  Weary lie we down and rest
20 And fan each other's panting breast.

   Here we'll strip and cool our fire
In cream below, in milk-baths higher;
  And when all wells are drawn dry,
I'll drink a tear out of thine eye.

25 Which our very joys shall leave,
That sorrows thus we can deceive;
  Or our very sorrows weep,
That joys so ripe so little keep.

1649

The Grasshopper

TO MY NOBLE FRIEND, MR. CHARLES COTTON

O thou that swing'st upon the waving hair
  Of some well-filléd oaten beard,
Drunk every night with a delicious tear
  Dropped thee from heaven, where now th' art reared;

5 The joys of earth and air are thine entire,
  That with thy feet and wings dost hop and fly;
And, when thy poppy° works, thou dost retire   *sleeping potion*
  To thy carved acorn-bed to lie.

Up with the day, the sun thou welcom'st then,
10 Sport'st in the gilt plats° of his beams,   *hair braids*
And all these merry days mak'st merry men,
  Thyself, and melancholy streams.

But ah, the sickle! Golden ears are cropped;
  Ceres and Bacchus[3] bid good night;
15 Sharp, frosty fingers all your flowers have topped,
  And what scythes spared, winds shave off quite.

3. The grain and the grape, from Ceres, goddess of the harvest, and Bacchus, god of wine.

Poor verdant fool, and now green ice! thy joys,
　Large and as lasting as thy perch of grass,
Bid us lay in 'gainst winter rain, and poise°   *balance*
20　　Their floods with an o'erflowing glass.

Thou best of men and friends! we will create
　A genuine summer in each other's breast,
And spite of this cold time and frozen fate,
　Thaw us a warm seat to our rest.

25　Our sacred hearths shall burn eternally,
　As vestal flames;[4] the North Wind, he
Shall strike his frost-stretched wings, dissolve, and fly
　This Etna[5] in epitome.

Dropping December shall come weeping in,
30　　Bewail th' usurping of his reign:
But when in showers of old Greek[6] we begin,
　Shall cry he hath his crown again!

Night, as clear Hesper,[7] shall our tapers whip
　From the light casements where we play,
35　And the dark hag from her black mantle strip,
　And stick there everlasting day.

Thus richer than untempted kings are we,
　That, asking nothing, nothing need:
Though lord of all what seas embrace, yet he
40　　That wants himself is poor indeed.

1649

ANDREW MARVELL
(1621–1778)

Bermudas

　Where the remote Bermudas ride,
In th' ocean's bosom unespied,
From a small boat that rowed along,
The listening winds received this song:
5　　"What should we do but sing His praise,
That led us through the watery maze
Unto an isle so long unknown,
And yet far kinder than our own?
Where He the huge sea monsters wracks,°   *casts ashore*
10　That lift the deep upon their backs;
He lands us on a grassy stage,
Safe from the storms, and prelate's rage.[1]
He gave us this eternal spring
Which here enamels everything,
15　And sends the fowls to us in care,
On daily visits through the air;
He hangs in shades the orange bright,
Like golden lamps in a green night,

4. The vestal virgins, consecrated to the Roman goddess Vesta, kept a sacred fire burning perpetually on her altar.
5. A Sicilian volcano.
6. Old Greek wine.

7. The morning star.
1. Marvell indicates Puritan sympathies by associating the wrath of prelates with storms at sea.

And does in the pomegranates close
20 Jewels more rich than Ormus[2] shows;
He makes the figs our mouths to meet,
And throws the melons at our feet;
But apples° plants of such a price,   *pineapples*
No tree could ever bear them twice;
25 With cedars, chosen by His hand,
From Lebanon, He stores the land;
And makes the hollow seas, that roar,
Proclaim the ambergris[3] on shore;
He cast (of which we rather boast)
30 The Gospel's pearl upon our coast,
And in these rocks for us did frame
A temple, where to sound His name.
O! let our voice His praise exalt,
Till it arrive at heaven's vault,
35 Which, thence (perhaps) rebounding, may
Echo beyond the Mexique Bay."[4]
    Thus sung they in the English boat,
An holy and a cheerful note;
And all the way, to guide their chime,
40 With falling oars they kept the time.

                                                       1681

The Nymph Complaining for the Death of Her Fawn[5]

The wanton troopers riding by
Have shot my fawn, and it will die.
Ungentle men! they cannot thrive
To kill thee. Thou ne'er didst alive
5 Them any harm, alas! nor could
Thy death yet do them any good.
I'm sure I never wished them ill,
Nor do I for all this, nor will;
But if my simple prayers may yet
10 Prevail with heaven to forget
Thy murder, I will join my tears,
Rather than fail. But, O my fears!
It cannot die so. Heaven's King
Keeps register of everything,
15 And nothing may we use in vain;
Even beasts must be with justice slain,
Else men are made their deodands.[6]
Though they should wash their guilty hands
In this warm life-blood, which doth part
20 From thine, and wound me to the heart,
Yet could they not be clean, their stain
Is dyed in such a purple° grain.°   *brilliant / hue*
There is not such another in
The world to offer for their sin.
25   Unconstant Sylvio, when yet
I had not found him counterfeit,
One morning (I remember well)
Tied in this silver chain and bell,
Gave it to me: nay, and I know
30 What he said then; I'm sure I do:

2. An island off Persia whence gems were exported.
3. A soapy secretion of the sperm whale, gathered on beaches and used in perfumes.
4. I.e., the Gulf of Mexico.
5. "Complaining" means "uttering a poetic lament." Marvell's original spelling "Faun" (for "Fawn") creates an ambiguous expectation, perhaps deliberately.
6. In English law, a deodand was an animal (or object) which, having caused a person's death, was forfeited to the crown to be applied to pious uses.

Said he, "Look how your huntsman here
Hath taught a fawn to hunt his *dear*."
But Sylvio soon had me beguiled;
This waxed tame, while he grew wild,
35   And quite regardless of my smart,
Left me his fawn, but took his heart.
   Thenceforth I set myself to play
My solitary time away
With this, and very well content,
40   Could so mine idle life have spent;
For it was full of sport, and light
Of foot and heart, and did invite
Me to its game: it seemed to bless
Itself in me; how could I less
45   Than love it? Oh, I cannot be
Unkind to a beast that loveth me.
   Had it lived long, I do not know
Whether it too might have done so
As Sylvio did; his gifts might be
50   Perhaps as false, or more, than he;
But I am sure, for aught that I
Could in so short a time espy,
Thy love was far more better than
The love of false and cruel men.
55   With sweetest milk and sugar, first
I it at mine own fingers nursed;
And as it grew, so every day
It waxed more white and sweet than they.
It had so sweet a breath! And oft
60   I blushed to see its foot more soft
And white, shall I say than my hand?
Nay, any lady's of the land.
   It is a wondrous thing how fleet
'Twas on those little silver feet;
65   With what a pretty skipping grace
It oft would challenge me the race;
And when it had left me far away,
'Twould stay, and run again, and stay;
For it was nimbler much than hinds,
70   And trod as if on the four winds.
   I have a garden of my own,
But so with roses overgrown,
And lilies, that you would it guess
To be a little wilderness;
75   And all the springtime of the year
It only loved to be there.
Among the beds of lilies I
Have sought it oft, where it should lie,
Yet could not, till itself would rise,
80   Find it, although before mine eyes;
For, in the flaxen lilies' shade,
It like a bank of lilies laid.
Upon the roses it would feed,
Until its lips e'en seemed to bleed;
85   And then to me 'twould boldly trip,
And print those roses on my lip.
But all its chief delight was still
On roses thus itself to fill,
And its pure virgin limbs to fold
90   In whitest sheets of lilies cold:
Had it lived long, it would have been

Lilies without, roses within.
   O help! O help! I see it faint
And die as calmly as a saint!
95 See how it weeps! the tears do come
Sad, slowly dropping like a gum.
So weeps the wounded balsam; so
The holy frankincense[7] doth flow;
The brotherless Heliades[8]
100 Melt in such amber tears as these.
   I in a golden vial will
Keep these two crystal tears, and fill
It till it do o'erflow with mine;
Then place it in Diana's shrine.
105   Now my sweet fawn is vanished to
Whither the swans and turtles° go,   *turtledoves*
In fair Elysium to endure,
With milk-white lambs and ermines pure.
O do not run too fast; for I
110 Will but bespeak° thy grave, and die.   *address*
   First, my unhappy statue shall
Be cut in marble, and withal,
Let it be weeping too; but there
The engraver sure his art may spare;
115 For I so truly thee bemoan
That I shall weep, though I be stone,
Until my tears, still dropping, wear
My breast, themselves engraving there.
There at my feet shalt thou be laid,
120 Of purest alabaster made;
For I would have thine image be
White as I can, though not as thee.

                         1681

To His Coy Mistress

   Had we but world enough, and time,
This coyness, lady, were no crime.
We would sit down, and think which way
To walk, and pass our long love's day.
5 Thou by the Indian Ganges' side
Shoudst rubies[9] find; I by the tide
Of Humber[1] would complain. I would
Love you ten years before the flood,
And you should, if you please, refuse
10 Till the conversion of the Jews.[2]
My vegetable[3] love should grow
Vaster than empires and more slow;
An hundred years should go to praise
Thine eyes, and on thy forehead gaze;
15 Two hundred to adore each breast,
But thirty thousand to the rest;
An age at least to every part,
And the last age should show your heart.
For, lady, you deserve this state,°   *dignity*

---

7. Frankincense, called holy because it is burned in religious ceremonies, is the aromatic gum of an African tree.
8. A name denoting children of Helios, the sun god. Phaethon, the brother referred to, had ventured to drive his father's chariot (the sun) and had been struck dead by Zeus when his wild career endangered the earth. His sisters wept for him until they were turned into poplar trees and their tears into amber.
9. Rubies are talismans, preserving virginity.
1. The Humber flows through Marvell's native town of Hull.
2. To occur, as tradition had it, at the end of recorded history.
3. A technical term: "possessing, like plants, the power of growth but not of consciousness"; in context, "being magnified without conscious nurture."

20 Nor would I love at lower rate.
    But at my back I always hear
Time's wingéd chariot hurrying near;
And yonder all before us lie
Deserts of vast eternity.
25 Thy beauty shall no more be found;
Nor, in thy marble vault, shall sound
My echoing song; then worms shall try
That long-preserved virginity,
And your quaint° honor turn to dust,   *over-subtle*
30 And into ashes all my lust:
The grave's a fine and private place,
But none, I think, do there embrace.
    Now therefore, while the youthful hue
Sits on thy skin like morning glow,[4]
35 And while thy willing soul transpires°   *breathes out*
At every pore with instant fires,
Now let us sport us while we may,
And now, like amorous birds of prey,
Rather at once our time devour
40 Than languish in his slow-chapped° power.   *slow-jawed*
Let us roll all our strength and all
Our sweetness up into one ball,
And tear our pleasures with rough strife
Thorough the iron gates[5] of life:
45 Thus, though we cannot make our sun
Stand still,[6] yet we will make him run.

                                      1681

The Mower's Song

My mind was once the true survey°   *map*
Of all these meadows fresh and gay,
And in the greenness of the grass
Did see its hopes as in a glass;°   *mirror*
5 When Juliana came, and she,
What I do to the grass, does to my thoughts and me.

    But these, while I with sorrow pine,
Grew more luxuriant still and fine,
That not one blade of grass you spied,
10 But had a flower on either side;
When Juliana came, and she,
What I do to the grass, does to my thoughts and me.

    Unthankful meadows, could you so
A fellowship so true forego,
15 And in your gaudy May-games[7] meet,
While I lay trodden under feet?
When Juliana came, and she,
What I do to the grass, does to my thoughts and me.

    But what you in compassion ought,
20 Shall now by my revenge be wrought;
And flowers, and grass, and I, and all
Will in one common ruin fall;
For Juliana comes, and she,
What I do to the grass, does to my thoughts and me.

---

4. In these rhyme-words (originally spelled *hew* and *glew*) the vowel sounds are probably similar and possibly identical: an *eh* gliding into an *oo*.
5. The obscurity "iron gates" suggests that the "ball" of line 42 has become a missile from a siege gun, battering its way into a citadel.

6. We lack, that is, the power of Zeus, who, to prolong his enjoyment of the mortal Alcmena, arrested the diurnal course and created a week-long night.
7. Wherein boys are interspersed with girls as grasses with flowers in the meadow.

25   And thus, ye meadows, which have been
      Companions of my thoughts more green,
      Shall now the heraldry become
      With which I shall adorn my tomb;
      For Juliana comes, and she,
30   What I do to the grass, does to my thoughts and me.

                                                                    1681

The Garden

      How vainly men themselves amaze°   *perplex*
      To win the palm, the oak, or bays,[8]
      And their incessant° labors see   *unceasing*
      Crowned from some single herb, or tree,
5   Whose short and narrow-vergéd[9] shade
      Does prudently their toils upbraid;
      While all flowers and all trees do close°   *join*
      To weave the garlands of repose!

      Fair Quiet, have I found thee here,
10   And Innocence, thy sister dear?
      Mistaken long, I sought you then
      In busy companies of men.
      Your sacred plants,° if here below,   *cuttings*
      Only among the plants will grow;
15   Society is all but rude[1]
      To this delicious solitude.

      No white nor red was ever seen
      So amorous as this lovely green.
      Fond lovers, cruel as their flame,
20   Cut in these trees their mistress' name:
      Little, alas, they know or heed
      How far these beauties hers exceed!
      Fair trees, wheresoe'er your barks I wound,
      No name shall but your own be found.

25   When we have run our passion's heat,°   *course*
      Love hither makes his best retreat.
      The gods, that mortal beauty chase,
      Still in a tree did end their race:
      Apollo hunted Daphne so,
30   Only that she might laurel grow;
      And Pan did after Syrinx speed,
      Not as a nymph, but for a reed.[2]

      What wondrous life is this I lead!
      Ripe apples drop about my head;
35   The luscious clusters of the vine
      Upon my mouth do crush their wine;
      The nectarine and curious° peach   *exquisite*
      Into by hands themselves do reach;
      Stumbling on melons, as I pass,
40   Insnared with flowers, I fall on grass.

8. The wreaths awarded, respectively, for athletic, civic, and poetic accomplishments.
9. Confined, not spreading luxuriantly like the living branch.
1. I.e., all merely barbarous.

2. In the original myths, as told by Ovid, the nymphs frustrated the pursuing gods by turning into the plants named. In Marvell's version, the gods intended the transformations.

Meanwhile the mind, from pleasure less,
Withdraws into its happiness;[3]
The mind, that ocean where each kind
Does straight its own resemblance find;[4]
45 Yet it creates, transcending these,
Far other worlds and other seas,
Annihilating all that's made
To a green thought in a green shade.

Here at the fountain's sliding foot,
50 Or at some fruit tree's mossy root,
Casting the body's vest° aside,   *garment*
My soul into the boughs does glide:
There, like a bird, it sits and sings,
Then whets[5] and combs its silver wings,
55 And, till prepared for longer flight,
Waves in its plumes the various° light.   *iridescent*

Such was that happy garden-state,
While man there walked without a mate:
After a place so pure and sweet,
60 What other help could yet be meet!
But 'twas beyond a mortal's share
To wander solitary there:
Two paradises 'twere in one
To live in paradise alone.

65 How well the skillful gardener drew
Of flowers and herbs this dial[6] new,
Where, from above, the milder sun
Does through a fragrant zodiac run;
And as it works, th' industrious bee
70 Computes its time as well as we!
How could such sweet and wholesome hours
Be reckoned but with herbs and flowers?

1681

HENRY VAUGHAN
(1622–1695)

The Retreat

Happy those early days! when I
Shined in my angel infancy.
Before I understood this place
Appointed for my second race,
5 Or taught my soul to fancy aught
But a white, celestial thought;
When yet I had not walked above
A mile or two from my first love,
And looking back, at that short space,
10 Could see a glimpse of His bright face;
When on some gilded cloud or flower
My gazing soul would dwell an hour,
And in those weaker glories spy

---

3. I.e., its own intellectual happiness is a greater pleasure than the taste of fruits.
4. Every land creature was thought to have its counterpart sea creature.
5. Sharpens its beak. But birds apparently whetting their beaks are actually cleaning them.
6. A plantation of flowers forming a dial face, perhaps surrounding an actual sundial.

Some shadows of eternity;
15 Before I taught my tongue to wound
My conscience with a sinful sound,
Or had the black art to dispense
A several° sin to every sense,   *separate*
But felt through all this fleshly dress
20 Bright shoots of everlastingness.
    O, how I long to travel back,
And tread again that ancient track!
That I might once more reach that plain
Where first I left my glorious train,
25 From whence th' enlightened spirit sees
That shady city of palm trees.
But, ah! my soul with too much stay
Is drunk, and staggers in the way.
Some men a forward motion love;
30 But I by backward steps would move,
And when this dust falls to the urn,
In that state I came, return.

                                                            1650

They Are All Gone into the World of Light!

They are all gone into the world of light!
    And I alone sit lingering here;
Their very memory is fair and bright,
    And my sad thoughts doth clear.

5 It glows and glitters in my cloudy breast
    Like stars upon some gloomy grove,
Or those faint beams in which this hill is dressed
    After the sun's remove.

I see them walking in an air of glory,
10   Whose light doth trample on my days;
My days, which are at best but dull and hoary,
    Mere glimmering and decays.

O holy hope, and high humility,
    High as the heavens above!
15 These are your walks, and you have showed them me
    To kindle my cold love.

Dear, beauteous death! the jewel of the just,
    Shining nowhere but in the dark;
What mysteries do lie beyond thy dust,
20   Could man outlook that mark!°   *boundary*

He that hath found some fledged bird's nest may know
    At first sight if the bird be flown;
But what fair well or grove he sings in now,
    That is to him unknown.

25 And yet, as angels in some brighter dreams
    Call to the soul when man doth sleep,
So some strange thoughts transcend our wonted themes,
    And into glory peep.

If a star were confined into a tomb,
30   Her captive flames must needs burn there;
But when the hand that locked her up gives room,
    She'll shine through all the sphere.

O Father of eternal life, and all
　　Created glories under Thee!
35 Resume° Thy spirit from this world of thrall   *take back*
　　Into true liberty!

Either disperse these mists, which blot and fill
　　My perspective° still as they pass;   *telescope*
Or else remove me hence unto that hill
40　　Where I shall need no glass.

The Timber

Sure thou didst flourish once! and many springs,
Many bright mornings, much dew, many showers
Passed o'er thy head; many light hearts and wings,
Which now are dead, lodged in thy living bowers.

5　And still a new succession sings and flies;
Fresh groves grow up, and their green branches shoot
Toward the old and still enduring skies,
While the low violet thrives at their root.

But thou beneath the sad and heavy line
10　Of death, doth waste all senseless, cold, and dark;
Where not so much as dreams of light may shine,
Nor any thought of greenness, leaf, or bark.

And yet (as if some deep hate and dissent,
Bred in thy growth betwixt high winds and thee,
15　Were still alive) thou dost great storms resent
Before they come, and know'st how near they be.[1]

Else all at rest thou liest, and the fierce breath
Of tempests can no more disturb thy ease;
But this thy strange resentment after death
20 Means° only those who broke in life thy peace.   *is directed at*

So murdered man, when lovely life is done
And his blood freezed, keeps in the center still
Some secret sense, which makes the dead blood run
At his approach, that did the body kill.

25　And is there any murderer worse than sin?
Or any storms more foul than a lewd life?
Or what resentient[2] can work more within
Than true remorse, when with past sins at strife?

He that hath left life's vain joys and vain care,
30　And truly hates to be detained on earth,
Hath got an house where many mansions are,[3]
And keeps his soul unto eternal mirth.

But though thus dead unto the world, and ceased
From sin, he walks a narrow, private way;
35　Yet grief and old wounds make him sore displeased,
And all his life a rainy, weeping day.

1. An allusion to foxfire, the eerie phosphores-
cent light given off by decaying wood, espe-
cially before a storm.

2. That which causes a change of heart.
3. "In my Father's house are many mansions"
(John xiv.2). "Mansions": rooms.

For though he would forsake the world, and live
As mere° a stranger, as men long since dead;   *total*
Yet joy itself will make a right soul grieve
40   To think he should be so long vainly led.

But as shades set off light, so tears and grief
(Though of themselves but a sad blubbered story)
By showing the sin great, show the relief
Far greater, and so speak my Saviour's glory.

45   If my way lies through deserts and wild woods,
Where all the land with scorching heat is curst,
Better the pools should flow with rain and floods
To fill my bottle, than I die with thirst.

Blest showers they are, and streams sent from above
50   Begetting virgins where they use to flow;
And trees of life no other water love;[4]
These upper springs, and none else make them grow.

But these chaste fountains flow not till we die;
Some drops may fall before, but a clear spring
55   And ever running, till we leave° to fling   *cease*
Dirt in her way, will keep above the sky.

                                                            1655

The Waterfall

With what deep murmurs through time's silent stealth
Doth thy transparent, cool, and watery wealth
          Here flowing fall,
          And chide, and call,
5   As if his liquid, loose retínue stayed
Lingering, and were of this steep place afraid,
          The common pass
          Where, clear as glass,
          All must descend—
10   Not to an end,
But quickened by this deep and rocky grave,
Rise to a longer course more bright and brave.   *sparkling*

          Dear stream! dear bank, where often I
          Have sat and pleased my pensive eye,
15   Why, since each drop of thy quick° store   *living*
          Runs thither whence it flowed before,
          Should poor souls fear a shade or night,
          Who came, sure, from a sea of light?
          Or since those drops are all sent back
20   So sure to thee, that none doth lack,
          Why should frail flesh doubt any more
          That what God takes He'll not restore?

          O useful element and clear!
          My sacred wash and cleanser here,[5]
25   My first consignor unto those
          Fountains of life where the Lamb goes![6]

4. "And he shewed me a pure river of water
of life, clear as crystal, proceeding out of the
throne of God and of the Lamb. In the midst
of the street of it, and on either side of the
river, was there the tree of life * * * " (Rev-
elation xxii.1–2).

5. I.e., through baptism.
6. "For the Lamb which is in the midst of the
throne shall feed them, and shall lead them
unto living fountains of waters: and God shall
wipe away all tears from their eyes" (Revela-
tion vii.17).

What sublime truths and wholesome themes
Lodge in thy mystical deep streams!
Such as dull man can never find
30 Unless that Spirit lead his mind
Which first upon thy face did move,[7]
And hatched all with His quickening love.
As this loud brook's incessant fall
In streaming rings restagnates° all,   *becomes stagnant*
35 Which reach by course the bank, and then
Are no more seen, just so pass men.
O my invisible estate,
My glorious liberty,[8] still late!
Thou art the channel my soul seeks,
40 Not this with cataracts and creeks.

1655

The Night

Through that pure virgin shrine,
That sacred veil drawn o'er Thy glorious noon,
That men might look and live, as glowworms shine,
    And face the moon,
5   Wise Nicodemus saw such light
As made him know his God by night.[9]

Most blest believer he!
Who in that land of darkness and blind eyes
Thy long-expected healing wings[1] could see,
10   When Thou didst rise!
And, what can never more be done,
Did at midnight speak with the Sun!

O who will tell me where
He found Thee at that dead and silent hour?
15 What hallowed solitary ground did bear
    So rare a flower,
Within whose sacred leaves did lie
The fulness of the Deity?

No mercy-seat of gold,
20 No dead and dusty cherub,[2] nor carved stone,
But His own living works did my Lord hold
    And lodge alone;
Where trees and herbs did watch and peep
And wonder, while the Jews did sleep.

25   Dear night! this world's defeat;
The stop to busy fools; care's check and curb;
The day of spirits; my soul's calm retreat
    Which none disturb!
Christ's progress, and His prayer time;[3]
30   The hours to which high heaven doth chime;

7. "And the Spirit of God moved upon the face of the waters" (Genesis i.2).
8. "Because the creature itself also shall be delivered from the bondage of corruption into the glorious liberty of the children of God" (Romans viii.21).
9. Nicodemus, coming to Christ at night, addressed him as "come from God"; in the same account Christ speaks of his coming as "the light" (John iii.1–21).

1. "But unto you that fear my Name shall the Sun of righteousness arise with healing in his wings * * * " (Malachi iv.2).
2. "And thou shalt make a mercy seat of pure gold * * * And thou shalt make two cherubims of gold, of beaten work shalt thou make them, in the two ends of the mercy seat" (Exodus xxv.17–18).
3. "*Mark, chap.* i.35. *S. Luke, chap.* xxi.37" [Vaughan's note]. The cited passages mention Christ's praying at night.

God's silent, searching flight;
When my Lord's head is filled with dew, and all
His locks are wet with the clear drops of night;
  His still, soft call;
35 His knocking time;[4] the soul's dumb watch,
When spirits their fair kindred catch.

  Were all my loud, evil days
Calm and unhaunted as is thy dark tent,
Whose peace but by some angel's wing or voice
40   Is seldom rent,
 Then I in heaven all the long year
Would keep, and never wander here.

  But living where the sun
Doth all things wake, and where all mix and tire
45 Themselves and others, I consent and run
   To every mire,
 And by this world's ill-guiding light,
Err more than I can do by night.

  There is in God, some say,
50 A deep but dazzling darkness, as men here
Say it is late and dusky, because they
   See not all clear.
 O for that night! where I in Him
Might live invisible and dim!

             1655

JOHN DRYDEN
(1631–1700)

Song from *Troilus and Cressida*

1
  Can life be a blessing,
  Or worth the possessing,
Can life be a blessing, if love were away?
 Ah, no! though our love all night keep us waking,
5 And though he torment us with cares all the day,
  Yet he sweetens, he sweetens our pains in the taking;
There's an hour at the last, there's an hour to repay.
  2
  In every possessing
  The ravishing blessing,
10 In every possessing the fruit of our pain,
 Poor lovers forget long ages of anguish,
Whate'er they have suffered and done to obtain;
  'Tis a pleasure, a pleasure to sigh and to languish,
When we hope, when we hope to be happy again.

             1679

---

4. "I sleep, but my heart waketh: it is the voice of my beloved that knocketh, saying, Open to me, my sister, my love, my dove, my undefiled: for my head is filled with dew, and my locks with the drops of the night" (Song of Solomon v.2).

Mac Flecknoe

OR A SATIRE UPON THE
TRUE-BLUE-PROTESTANT POET, T. S.[1]

All human things are subject to decay,
And when fate summons, monarchs must obey.
This Flecknoe found, who, like Augustus,[2] young
Was called to empire, and had governed long;
5 In prose and verse, was owned, without dispute,
Through all the realms of Nonsense, absolute.
This aged prince, now flourishing in peace,
And blest with issue of a large increase,
Worn out with business, did at length debate
10 To settle the succession of the state;
And, pondering which of all his sons was fit
To reign, and wage immortal war with wit,[3]
Cried: " 'Tis resolved; for nature pleads that he
Should only rule, who most resembles me.
15 Sh——[4] alone my perfect image bears,
Mature in dullness from his tender years:
Sh—— alone, of all my sons, is he
Who stands confirmed in full stupidity.
The rest to some faint meaning make pretense,
20 But Sh—— never deviates into sense.
Some beams of wit on other souls may fall,
Strike through, and make a lucid interval;
But Sh——'s genuine night admits no ray,
His rising fogs prevail upon the day.
25 Besides, his goodly fabric fills the eye,
And seems designed for thoughtless majesty:
Thoughtless as monarch oaks that shade the plain,
And, spread in solemn state, supinely reign.
Heywood and Shirley[5] were but types of thee,
30 Thou last great prophet of tautology.
Even I, a dunce of more renown than they,
Was sent before but to prepare thy way;
And, coarsely clad in Norwich drugget,[6] came
To teach the nations in thy greater name.
35 My warbling lute, the lute I whilom° strung,   *formerly*
When to King John of Portugal I sung,[7]
Was but the prelude to that glorious day,
When thou on silver Thames didst cut thy way,
With well-timed oars before the royal barge,
40 Swelled with the pride of thy celestial charge;
And big with hymn, commander of a host,
The like was ne'er in Epsom blankets tossed.[8]

1. Thomas Shadwell (1640–92), a comic playwright of respectable talents, who considered himself the dramatic heir of Ben Jonson. He was vain, corpulent, and probably overbearing in manner. Dryden names him *Mac* (son of) *Flecknoe*, making him heir not of Jonson but of the recently dead Irish priest Richard Flecknoe, a poet at once tiresome and prolific. The subtitle (presumably added when the poem, itself non-political, was published in 1682) acknowledges a political controversy fed by Dryden's poems *Absalom and Achitophel* and *The Medal* (a satire on Shaftesbury's acquittal) and Shadwell's rejoinder *The Medal of John Bayes* (John Dryden). Shadwell belonged to the Whig party, the political haven of dissenting Protestants.
2. Augustus became Roman emperor at thirty-two and reigned for forty years.
3. *Wit*, here as in other poems of the time, variously denotes the intellect, the poetic imagination, and a general sprightliness of mind.
4. A transparent pretense to anonymity, admitting here and there a scatological suggestion.
5. Playwrights of the time of Charles I, now out of fashion. Dryden suggests that they prefigure Shadwell as the Old-Testament prophets and (in lines 31–34) John the Baptist prefigured the ultimate revelation in Jesus Christ.
6. A coarse cloth.
7. Flecknoe claimed the king of Portugal as his patron.
8. A simultaneous reference to two of Shadwell's plays: *The Virtuoso*, in which a character is tossed in a blanket, and *Epsom Wells*.

Methinks I see the new Arion[9] sail,
The lute still trembling underneath thy nail.
45 At thy well-sharpened thumb from shore to shore
The treble squeaks for fear, the basses roar;
Echoes from Pissing Alley Sh—— call,
And Sh—— they resound from Aston Hall.
About thy boat the little fishes throng,
50 As at the morning toast[1] that floats along.
Sometimes, as prince of thy harmonious band,
Thou wield'st thy papers in thy threshing hand.
St. André's[2] feet ne'er kept more equal time,
Not ev'n the feet of thy own *Psyche's* rhyme;
55 Though they in number as in sense excel:
So just, so like tautology, they fell,
That, pale with envy, Singleton[3] foreswore ⎫
The lute and sword, which he in triumph bore, ⎬
And vowed he ne'er would act Villerius[4] more." ⎭
60 Here stopped the good old sire, and wept for joy
In silent raptures of the hopeful boy.
All arguments, but most his plays, persuade,
That for anointed dullness he was made.
    Close to the walls which fair Augusta[5] bind
65 (The fair Augusta much to fears inclined),
An ancient fabric° raised to inform the sight,   *building*
There stood of yore, and Barbican it hight:
A watchtower once; but now, so fate ordains,
Of all the pile an empty name remains.
70 From its old ruins brothel houses rise,
Scenes of lewd loves, and of polluted joys,
Where their vast courts the mother-strumpets keep,
And, undisturbed by watch, in silence sleep.
Near these a Nursery[6] erects its head,
75 Where queens are formed, and future heroes bred;
Where unfledged actors learn to laugh and cry,⎫
Where infant punks° their tender voices try,   ⎬   *prostitutes*
And little Maximins[7] the gods defy.   ⎭
Great Fletcher[8] never treads in buskins here,
80 Nor greater Jonson dares in socks appear;
But gentle Simkin[9] just reception finds
Amidst this monument of vanished minds:
Pure clinches° the suburbian Muse affords,   *puns*
And Panton[1] waging harmless war with words.
85 Here Flecknoe, as a place to fame well known,
Ambitiously designed his Sh——'s throne;
For ancient Dekker[2] prophesied long since, ⎫
That in this pile would reign a mighty prince, ⎬
Born for a scourge of wit, and flail of sense; ⎭
90 To whom true dullness should some *Psyches* owe,
But worlds of *Misers* from his pen should flow;[3]
Humorists and *Hypocrites* it should produce,
Whole Raymond families, and tribes of Bruce.
    Now Empress Fame had published the renown
95 Of Sh——'s coronation through the town.

9. When the Greek poet Arion was cast into
the sea, a dolphin, charmed by his singing,
bore him ashore. Shadwell was proud of his
musical accomplishments.
1. A euphemism for sewage.
2. St. André, a French dancing-master, was
choreographer of Shadwell's opera *Psyche.*
3. John Singleton, a musician of the Theatre
Royal.
4. A role in Sir William Davenant's opera,
The Siege of Rhodes.
5. London. (She "fears" Catholic plots.)

6. A training school for actors.
7. The bombastic emperor in Dryden's own
Tyrannic Love.
8. Early 17th-century playwright; *buskins,* the
high-soled boots worn in Athenian tragedy,
are opposed to *socks,* the low shoes worn in
comedy.
9. A clown.
1. A punster.
2. Elizabethan playwright satirized by Jonson.
3. In these lines Dryden names plays of (and
characters in plays by) Shadwell.

Roused by report of Fame, the nations meet,
From near Bunhill, and distant Watling Street.[4]
No Persian carpets spread the imperial way,
But scattered limbs of mangled poets lay;
100 From dusty shops neglected authors[5] come,
Martyrs of pies, and relics of the bum.
Much Heywood, Shirley, Ogilby[6] there lay,
But loads of Sh—— almost choked the way.
Bilked stationers[7] for yeomen stood prepared,
105 And Herringman was captain of the guard.
The hoary prince in majesty appeared,
High on a throne of his own labors reared.
At his right hand our young Ascanius[8] sate,
Rome's other hope, and pillar of the state.
110 His brows thick fogs, instead of glories, grace,
And lambent dullness played around his face.
As Hannibal did to the altars come,
Sworn by his sire a mortal foe to Rome,[9]
So Sh—— swore, nor should his vow be vain,
115 That he till death true dullness would maintain;
And, in his father's right, and realm's defense,
Ne'er to have peace with wit, nor truce with sense.
The king himself the sacred unction° made,   *ointment*
As king by office, and as priest by trade.
120 In his sinister[1] hand, instead of ball,
He placed a mighty mug of potent ale;
Love's Kingdom[2] to his right he did convey,
At once his scepter, and his rule of sway;
Whose righteous lore the prince had practiced young,
125 And from whose loins recorded *Psyche* sprung.
His temples, last, with poppies[3] were o'erspread,
That nodding seemed to consecrate his head.
Just at that point of time, if fame not lie,
On his left hand twelve reverend owls did fly.
130 So Romulus, 'tis sung, by Tiber's brook,
Presage of sway from twice six vultures took.[4]
The admiring throng loud acclamations make,
And omens of his future empire take.
The sire then shook the honors° of his head,   *locks*
135 And from his brows damps° of oblivion shed   *vapors*
Full on the filial dullness: long he stood, ⎫
Repelling from his breast the raging god; ⎬
At length burst out in this prophetic mood:⎭
    "Heavens bless my son, from Ireland let him reign
140 To far Barbadoes on the western main;[5]
Of his dominion may no end be known,
And greater than his father's be his throne;
Beyond *Love's Kingdom* let his stretch his pen!"
He paused, and all the people cried, "Amen."

4. These locations, both within a half-mile of the scene of the supposed coronation ("the Nursery"), circumscribe Shadwell's fame within an unfashionable bourgeois part of London.
5. I.e., unsold books, the paper of which, in that time of relative scarcity, found various uses.
6. John Ogilby, a translator of Virgil and Homer; the derided competitor of Dryden and (later) of Pope.
7. Booksellers, impoverished because they had stocked the works of Shadwell and others, were the guard of honor ("yoemen of the guard"). Their "captain," Henry Herringman, however, had been Dryden's publisher as well as Shadwell's.
8. Aeneas' son; hence, like Shadwell, the destined heir.
9. Hannibal, the Carthaginian general who invaded Italy, was dedicated to his hatred of Rome (it was said) at the age of nine.
1. In British coronations the monarch holds in his left ("sinister") hand a globe surmounted by a cross.
2. A "pastoral tragicomedy" by Flecknoe, apparently visualized by Dryden as a rolled-up manuscript held like a scepter.
3. Connoting both intellectual heaviness and Shadwell's addiction to opiates.
4. When the site which Romulus had chosen for Rome was visited by twelve vultures, or twice as many as had visited the site picked by his brother Remus, the kingship ("sway") of Romulus was presaged.
5. I.e., a realm of empty ocean.

145 Then thus continued he: "My son, advance
     Still in new imprudence, new ignorance.
     Success let others teach, learn thou from me
     Pangs without birth, and fruitless industry.
     Let *Virtuosos* in five years be writ;
150 Yet not one thought accuse thy toil of wit.
     Let gentle George[6] in triumph tread the stage,
     Make Dorimant betray, and Loveit rage;
     Let Cully, Cockwood, Fopling, charm the pit,
     And in their folly show the writer's wit.
155 Yet still thy fools shall stand in thy defense,
     And justify their author's want of sense.
     Let 'em be all by thy own model made
     Of dullness, and desire no foreign aid;
     That they to future ages may be known,
160 Not copies drawn, but issue of thy own.
     Nay, let thy men of wit too be the same,
     All full of thee, and differing but in name.
     But let no alien S—dl—y[7] interpose,
     To lard with wit thy hungry *Epsom* prose.
165 And when false flowers of rhetoric thou wouldst cull,
     Trust nature, do not labor to be dull;
     But write thy best, and top; and, in each line,
     Sir Formal's[8] oratory will be thine:
     Sir Formal, though unsought, attends thy quill,
170 And does thy northern dedications[9] fill.
     Nor let false friends seduce thy mind to fame,
     By arrogating Jonson's hostile name.
     Let father Flecknoe fire thy mind with praise,
     And uncle Ogilby thy envy raise.
175 Thou art my blood, where Jonson has no part:
     What share have we in nature, or in art?
     Where did his wit on learning fix a brand,
     And rail at arts he did not understand?
     Where made he love in Prince Nicander's vein,
180 Or swept the dust in *Psyche's* humble strain?[1]
     Where sold he bargains,[2] 'whip-stitch, kiss my arse,'
     Promised a play and dwindled to a farce?
     When did his Muse from Fletcher scenes purloin,
     As thou whole Eth'rege dost transfuse to thine?
185 But so transfused, as oil on water's flow,
     His always floats above, thine sinks below.
     This is thy province, this thy wondrous way,
     New humors to invent for each new play:
     This is that boasted bias of thy mind,
190 By which one way, to dullness, 'tis inclined;
     Which makes thy writings lean on one side still,
     And, in all changes, that way bends thy will.
     Nor let thy mountain-belly make pretense
     Of likeness; thine's a tympany[3] of sense.
195 A tun of man in thy large bulk is writ,
     But sure thou'rt but a kilderkin of wit.[4]
     Like mine, thy gentle numbers feebly creep;
     Thy tragic Muse gives smiles, thy comic sleep.

6. George Etherege (ca. 1635–91), playwright who set the tone for stylish Restoration comedy; Dryden proceeds to name five of his characters.
7. Sir Charles Sedley (ca. 1639–1701), Restoration wit who had contributed a prologue and (Dryden suggests) a part of the text to Shadwell's *Epsom Wells*.
8. Sir Formal Trifle was an inflated orator in *The Virtuoso*.

9. I.e., to Shadwell's patron the Duke of Newcastle, whose seat was in northern England.
1. Nicander pays court to the title character Psyche in Shadwell's opera.
2. A "bargain" is a gross rejoinder to an innocent question. The rest of the line, itself a kind of bargain, echoes a farcical character in *The Virtuoso*.
3. A swelling caused by air.
4. Tuns are big casks; kilderkins, little ones.

With whate'er gall thou sett'st thyself to write,
200   Thy inoffensive satires never bite.
In thy felonious heart though venom lies,
It does but touch thy Irish pen, and dies.
Thy genius calls thee not to purchase fame
In keen iambics,[5] but mild anagram.
205   Leave writing plays, and choose for thy command
Some peaceful province in acrostic land.
There thou may'st wings display and altars raise,
And torture one poor word ten thousand ways.[6]
Or, if thou wouldst thy different talent suit,
210   Set thy own songs, and sing them to thy lute."
    He said: but his last words were scarcely heard⎤
For Bruce and Longville had a trap prepared,   ⎬
And down they sent the yet declaiming bard.[7]   ⎦
Sinking he left his drugget robe behind,
215   Borne upwards by a subterranean wind.
The mantle fell to the young prophet's part,[8]
With double portion of his father's art.

                                    ca. 1679   1682

To the Memory of Mr. Oldham[9]

Farewell, too little, and too lately known,
Whom I began to think and call my own:
For sure our souls were near allied, and thine
Cast in the same poetic mold with mine.
5   One common note on either lyre did strike,
And knaves and fools we both abhorred alike.
To the same goal did both our studies° drive;   *endeavors*
The last set out the soonest did arrive.
Thus Nisus[1] fell upon the slippery place,
10   While his young friend performed° and won the race.   *completed*
O early ripe! to thy abundant store
What could advancing age have added more?
It might (what nature never gives the young)
Have taught the numbers° of thy native tongue.   *metrics*
15   But satire needs not those, and wit will shine
Through the harsh cadence of a rugged line:
A noble error, and but seldom made,
When poets are by too much force betrayed.
Thy generous fruits, though gathered ere their prime, ⎤
20   Still showed a quickness,° and maturing time   ⎬   *pungency*
But mellows what we write to the dull sweets of rhyme.⎦
Once more, hail and farewell; farewell, thou young,
But ah too short, Marcellus of our tongue;
Thy brows with ivy, and with laurels bound;
25   But fate and gloomy night encompass thee around.[3]

                                                        1684

---

5. The meter of (Greek) satire; hence satire itself.
6. Ingenuities like those mentioned, frequent in the early century, had been put away as trivial.
7. These characters in *The Virtuoso* so trap Sir Formal Trifle.
8. Like the prophet Elijah's mantle falling on Elisha. See II Kings ii, or Cowley's elegy on Crashaw, line 66n.
9. John Oldham (1653–83), author of *Satires Upon the Jesuits*, was a promising young poet, harsh (partly by calculation) in metrics and manner, but earnest and vigorous.

1. A foot racer in Virgil's *Aeneid;* his young friend Euryalus came from behind to reach the goal before him (V.315 ff.).
2. Augustus Caesar's nephew, who died at twenty after a meteoric military career.
3. The Roman elegiac phrase "Hail and farewell!" in line 22; the mention of Marcellus (line 23) and of the classical poet's wreath (line 24); and the echo of Virgil's lament for Marcellus (see *Aeneid* VI.566) conspire to Romanize Oldham.

Song from *Cleomenes*

1

No, no, poor suffering heart, no change endeavor,
Choose to sustain the smart, rather than leave her;
My ravished eyes behold such charms about her,
I can die with her, but not live without her;
5   One tender sigh of hers to see me languish,
Will more than pay the price of my past anguish:
Beware, O cruel fair, how you smile on me,
'Twas a kind look of yours that has undone me.

2

Love has in store for me one happy minute,
10   And she will end my pain, who did begin it;
Then no day void of bliss, or pleasure, leaving,
Ages shall slide away without perceiving:
Cupid shall guard the door, the more to please us,
And keep out Time and Death, when they would seize us;
15   Time and Death shall depart, and say, in flying,
Love has found out a way to live by dying.

1692

THOMAS TRAHERNE
(1637–1674)

Wonder

How like an angel came I down!
    How bright are all things here!
When first among His works I did appear
Oh, how their glory me did crown!
5   The world resembled His eternity,
    In which my soul did walk;
And everything that I did see
    Did with me talk.

The skies in their magnificence,
10   The lively, lovely air,
Oh, how divine, how soft, how sweet, how fair!
The stars did entertain my sense,
And all the works of God, so bright and pure,
    So rich and great did seem,
15   As if they ever must endure
    In my esteem.

A native health and innocence
    Within my bones did grow;
And while my God did all His glories show,
20   I felt a vigor in my sense
That was all spirit. I within did flow
    With seas of life, like wine;
I nothing in the world did know
    But 'twas divine.

25   Harsh ragged objects were concealed;
    Oppressions, tears, and cries,
Sins, griefs, complaints, dissensions, weeping eyes
Were hid, and only things revealed
Which heavenly spirits and the angels prize.
30   The state of innocence
And bliss, not trades and poverties,
    Did fill my sense.

The streets were paved with golden stones,
            The boys and girls were mine,
35   Oh, how did all their lovely faces shine!
            The sons of men were holy ones,
      In joy and beauty they appeared to me,
                  And everything I found,
            While like an angel I did see,
40   Adorned the ground.

      Rich diamond and pearl and gold
            In every place was seen;
      Rare splendors, yellow, blue, red, white, and green,
            Mine eyes did everywhere behold.
45   Great wonders clothed with glory did appear,
                  Amazement was my bliss,
            That and my wealth met everywhere;
                  No joy to° this!   *compared to*

      Cursed and devised proprieties,[1]
50   With envy, avarice,
      And fraud, those fiends that spoil even paradise,
            Flew from the splendor of mine eyes;
      And so did hedges, ditches, limits, bounds:
            I dreamed not aught of those,
55   But wandered over all men's grounds,
                  And found repose.

      Proprieties themselves were mine,
            And hedges ornaments;
      Walls, boxes, coffers, and their rich contents
60   To make me rich combine.
      Clothes, ribbons, jewels, laces, I esteemed
            My joys by others worn:
      For me they all to wear them seemed
                  When I was born.

                                                    1903

The Rapture

      Sweet infancy!
      O heavenly fire! O sacred light!
            How fair and bright!
            How great am I,
5   Whom the whole world doth magnify!

            O heavenly joy!
      O great and sacred blessedness
            Which I possess!
            So great a joy
10   Who did into my arms convey?

            From God above
      Being sent, the gift doth me inflame
            To praise his name;
            The stars do move,
15   The sun doth shine, to show his love.

            O how divine
      Am I! To all this sacred wealth,
            This life and health,
            Who raised? Who mine
20   Did make the same? What hand divine?

                                                    1903

1. Proprietorships, devised or bequeathed in a will.

Shadows in the Water

In unexperienced infancy
Many a sweet mistake doth lie:
Mistake though false, intending° true;   *directing to*
A seeming somewhat more than view;
5   That doth instruct the mind
In things that lie behind,
And many secrets to us show
Which afterwards we come to know.

Thus did I by the water's brink
10   Another world beneath me think;
And while the lofty spacious skies
Reverséd there, abused mine eyes,
I fancied other feet
Came mine to touch or meet;
15   As by some puddle I did play
Another world within it lay.

Beneath the water people drowned,
Yet with another heaven crowned,
In spacious regions seemed to go
20   As freely moving to and fro:
In bright and open space
I saw their very face;
Eyes, hands, and feet they had like mine;
Another sun did with them shine.

25   'Twas strange that people there should walk,
And yet I could not hear them talk:
That through a little watery chink,
Which one dry ox or horse might drink,
We other worlds should see,
30   Yet not admitted be;
And other confines there behold
Of light and darkness, heat and cold.

I called them oft, but called in vain;
No speeches we could entertain:
35   Yet did I there expect to find
Some other world, to please my mind.
I plainly saw by these
A new antipodes,[2]
Whom, though they were so plainly seen,
40   A film kept off that stood between.

By walking men's reverséd feet
I chanced another world to meet;
Though it did not to view exceed
A phantom, 'tis a world indeed,
45   Where skies beneath us shine,
And earth by art divine
Another face presents below,
Where people's feet against ours go.

---

2. People living at a diametrically opposite point on the globe (literally, "with the feet opposite").

Within the regions of the air,
50 Compassed about with heavens fair,
Great tracts of land there may be found
Enriched with fields and fertile ground;
　　Where many numerous hosts
　　In those far distant coasts,
55 For other great and glorious ends
Inhabit, my yet unknown friends.

O ye that stand upon the brink,
Whom I so near me through the chink
With wonder see: what faces there,
60 Whose feet, whose bodies, do ye wear?
　　I my companions see
　　In you, another me.
They seeméd others, but are we;
Our second selves these shadows be.

1910

EDWARD TAYLOR
(ca. 1642–1729)

Meditation 8[1]

I kenning° through astronomy divine   *discerning, knowing*
　　The world's bright battlement, wherein I spy
A golden path my pencil cannot line,
　　From that bright throne unto my threshold lie.
5 　　And while my puzzled thoughts about it pore
　　I find the bread of life in it at my door.

When that this bird of paradise put in
　　This wicker cage (my corpse)[2] to tweedle° praise   *sing*
Had pecked the fruit forbad, and so did fling
10 　　Away its food, and lost its golden days,
　　It fell into celestial famine sore,
　　And never could attain a morsel more.

Alas! alas! Poor bird, what wilt thou do?
　　The creatures' field no food for souls e'er gave.
15 And if thou knock at angels' doors they show
　　An empty barrel; they no soul bread have.
　　Alas! Poor bird, the world's white loaf is done,
　　And cannot yield thee here the smallest crumb.

In this sad state, God's tender bowels[3] run
20 　　Out streams of grace; and he to end all strife
The purest wheat in heaven, his dear, dear son
　　Grinds, and kneads up into this bread of life.
　　Which bread of life from heaven down came and stands
　　Dished on my table up by angels' hands.

25 Did God mould up this bread in heaven, and bake,
　　Which from his table came, and to thine goeth?
Doth he bespeak thee thus: This soul bread take;
　　Come eat thy fill of this thy God's white loaf?
　　It's food too fine for angels, yet come, take
30 　　And eat thy fill: it's heaven's sugar cake.

1. Based on John vi.51: "I am the living
bread which came down from heaven: if any
man eat of this bread, he shall live for ever:
and the bread that I will give is my flesh,
which I will give for the life of the world."

2. In this context, the living body.
3. I.e., God's powers of mercy and compassion.

What grace is this knead in this loaf? This thing
    Souls are but petty things it to admire.
Ye angels, help. This fill would to the brim
    Heaven's whelmed-down[4] crystal meal bowl, yea and higher,
35   This bread of life dropped in thy mouth, doth cry:
    Eat, eat me, soul, and thou shalt never die.

1684   1937

The Glory of and Grace in the Church Set Out

    Come now behold
Within this knot[5] what flowers do grow,
    Spangled like gold,
Whence wreaths of all perfumes do flow.
5 Most curious° colors of all sorts you shall   *amazing*
With all sweet spirits° scent. Yet that's not all.   *odors*

    Oh! Look, and find
These choicest flowers most richly sweet
    Are disciplined
10   With artificial angels meet.[6]
An heap of pearls is precious; but they shall,
When set by art, excel. Yet that's not all.

    Christ's spirit showers
Down in his word, and sacraments
15   Upon these flowers
The clouds of grace divine contents.
Such things of wealthy blessings on them fall
As make them sweetly thrive. Yet that's not all.

    Yet still behold!
20 All flourish not at once. We see
    While some unfold
Their blushing leaves, some buds there be.
Here's faith, hope, charity in flower, which call
On yonders in the bud. Yet that's not all.

25   But as they stand
Like beauties reeking in° perfume   *giving off*
    A divine hand
Doth hand them up to glory's room,
Where each in sweetened songs all praises shall
30 Sing all o'er heaven for aye. And that's but all.

1937

Upon Wedlock, and Death of Children

A curious knot God made in paradise,
    And drew it out enameled° neatly fresh.   *variously colored*
It was the truelove knot, more sweet than spice
    And set with all the flowers of grace's dress.
5   Its wedding knot, that ne'er can be untied;
    No Alexander's sword[7] can it divide.

---

4. Turned over upon something so as to cover it.
5. Plot of ground, or planting-bed.
6. "Artificial angels meet": i.e., appropriate angel-artificers.

7. Gordius, king of Phrygia, devised a complicated knot to be undone only by him who was to rule Asia. Alexander the Great cut the knot with a blow of his sword.

The slips here planted, gay and glorious grow,
  Unless an hellish breath do singe their plumes.
Here primrose, cowslips, roses, lilies blow
  With violets and pinks that void° perfumes: *give off, exude*
  Whose beauteous leaves o'er laid with honey-dew,
  And chanting birds chirp out sweet music true.

When in this knot I planted was, my stock°   *stem*
  Soon knotted, and a manly flower out brake.
And after it my branch again did knot;
  Brought out another flower its sweet breathed mate.
  One knot gave one t'other the t'other's place;
  Whence chuckling smiles fought in each other's face.

But oh! a glorious hand from glory came
  Guarded with angels, soon did crop this flower
Which almost tore the root up of the same
  At that unlooked for, dolesome, darksome hour.
  In prayer to Christ perfumed it did ascend,
  And angels bright did it to heaven tend.

But pausing on't, this sweet perfumed my thought,
  Christ would in glory have a flower, choice, prime,
And having choice, chose this my branch forth brought.
  Lord take't. I thank thee, thou takest aught of mine,
  It is my pledge in glory; part of me
  Is now in it, Lord, glorified with thee.

But praying o'er my branch, my branch did sprout
  And bore another manly flower, and gay;
And after that another, sweet, brake out,
  The which the former hand soon got away.
  But oh! the tortures, vomit, screechings, groans,
  And six weeks fever would pierce hearts like stones.

Grief o'er doth flow, and nature fault would find
  Were not thy will, my spell charm, joy, and gem;
That as I said, I say, take, Lord, they're thine.
  I piecemeal pass to glory bright in them.
  I joy, may I sweet flowers for glory breed,
  Whether thou getst them green, or let them seed.

                                                                1937

Upon a Spider Catching a Fly

Thou sorrow, venom elf:
  Is this thy play,
To spin a web out of thyself
  To catch a fly?
  For why?

I saw a pettish° wasp   *peevish, petulant*
  Fall foul therein,
Whom yet thy whorl-pins[8] did not clasp
  Lest he should fling
  His sting.

---

8. Technically, the flywheel holding the thread on the spindle of a spinning wheel; here, the spider's legs.

But as afraid, remote
    Didst stand hereat
And with thy little fingers stroke
    And gently tap
15   His back.

Thus gently him didst treat
    Lest he should pet,
And in a froppish,° waspish heat   *fretful*
    Should greatly fret
20   Thy net.

Whereas the silly fly,
    Caught by its leg
Thou by the throat tookst hastily
    And hind the head
25   Bite dead.

This goes to pot,[9] that not
    Nature doth call.
Strive not above what strength hath got
    Lest in the brawl
30   Thou fall.

This fray seems thus to us.
    Hell's spider gets
His entrails spun to whip-cords[10] thus,
    And wove to nets
35   And sets.

To tangle Adam's race
    In's strategems
To their destructions, spoiled, made base
    By venom things,
40   Damned sins.

But mighty, gracious Lord
    Communicate
Thy grace to break the cord, afford
    Us glory's gate
45   And state.

We'll nightingale sing like
    When perched on high
In glory's cage, thy glory, bright,
    And thankfully,
50   For joy.

1939

MATTHEW PRIOR
(1664–1721)

An Epitaph

Interred beneath this marble stone,
Lies sauntering Jack and idle Joan.
While rolling threescore years and one[1]
Did round this globe their courses run.

---

9. As in the modern sense, deteriorates.
10. Strong cord or binding, like that made of hemp or catgut.

1. A curtailment of the traditional life-span, "threescore years and ten" (Psalm xc.10).

5 If human things went ill or well,
   If changing empires rose or fell,
   The morning passed, the evening came,
   And found this couple still the same.
   They walked and eat,° good folks—what then?   *ate*
10 Why then they walked and eat again.
   They soundly slept the night away;
   They did just nothing all the day;
   And having buried children four,
   Would not take pains to try for more.
15 Nor sister either had, nor brother;
   They seemed just tallied° for each other.   *duplicated*
       Their moral° and economy°   *morality / household practice*
   Most perfectly they made agree;
   Each virtue kept its proper bound,
20 Nor trespassed on the other's ground.
   Nor fame nor censure they regarded;
   They neither punished nor rewarded.
   He cared not what the footmen did;
   Her maids she neither praised, nor chid;°   *reproved*
25 So every servant took his course,
   And bad at first, they all grew worse.
   Slothful disorder filled his stable,
   And sluttish plenty decked her table.
   Their beer was strong; their wine was port;
30 Their meal was large; their grace was short.
   They gave the poor the remnant-meat,
   Just when it grew not fit to eat.
       They paid the church and parish rate,[2]
   And took, but read not the receipt;
35 For which they claimed their Sunday's due,
   Of slumbering in an upper pew.
       No man's defects sought they to know;
   So never made themselves a foe.
   No man's good deeds did they commend;
40 So never raised themselves a friend.
   Nor cherished they relations poor,
   That might decrease their present store;
   Nor barn nor house did they repair,
   That might oblige their future heir.
45   They neither added nor confounded;
   They neither wanted° nor abounded.   *lacked*
   Each Christmas they accompts° did clear,   *accounts*
   And wound their bottom° round the year.   *thread*
   Nor tear nor smile did they employ
50 At news of public grief or joy.
   When bells were rung, and bonfires made,
   If asked they ne'er denied their aid:
   Their jug was to the ringers carried,[3]
   Whoever either died or married.
55 Their billet at the fire was found,
   Whoever was deposed, or crowned.[4]
       Nor good, nor bad, nor fools, nor wise;
   They would not learn, nor could advise:°   *take thought*
   Without love, hatred, joy, or fear,
60 They led—a kind of—as it were:
   Nor wished, nor cared, nor laughed, nor cried;
   And so they lived; and so they died.

                                                                  1718

2. Assessments for church-support and poor-relief respectively.
3. Bell-ringers for notable funerals or marriages were regaled with gifts of ale from public-spirited citizens.
4. They threw their sticks of wood (billets) on the public bonfires celebrating despositions (as of James II) and coronations (as of William).

JONATHAN SWIFT
(1667–1745)

Frances Harris's Petition

TO THEIR EXCELLENCIES THE LORDS JUSTICES OF
IRELAND,[1] WRITTEN IN THE YEAR 1701

The humble petition of Frances Harries,
Who must starve and die a maid if it miscarries;
Humbly sheweth, that I went to warm myself in Lady Betty's
    chamber, because I was cold;
And I had in a purse seven pound, four shillings, and sixpence,
    besides farthings, in money and gold;
5 So because I had been buying things for my lady last night,
   I was resolved to tell° my money, to see if it was right.   count
   Now, you must know, because my trunk has a very bad lock,
   Therefore all the money I have, which, God knows, is a very
       small stock,
   I keep in my pocket, tied about my middle, next my smock.
10 So when I went to put up my purse, as God would have it,
       my smock was unripped,
   And instead of putting it into my pocket, down it slipped;
   Then the bell rung, and I went down to put my lady to bed;
   And, God knows, I thought my money was as safe as my
       maidenhead.
   So, when I came up again, I found my pocket feel very light;
15 But when I searched, and missed my purse, Lord! I thought
       I should have sunk outright.
   "Lord! madam," says Mary,[2] "how d'ye do?"—"Indeed," says I,
       "never worse:
   But pray, Mary, can you tell what I have done with my purse?"
   "Lord help me!" says Mary, "I never stirred out of this place!"
   "Nay," said I, "I had it in Lady Betty's chamber, that's a
       plain case."
20 So Mary got me to bed, and covered me up warm:
   However, she stole away my garters, that I might do myself
       no harm.
   So I tumbled and tossed all night, as you may very well think,
   But hardly ever set my eyes together, or slept a wink.
   So I was a-dreamed, methought, that I went and searched the
       folks round,
25 And in a corner of Mrs. Dukes's[3] box, tied in a rag, the
       money was found.
   So next morning we told Whittle,[4] and he fell a-swearing:
   Then my dame Wadgar[5] came, and she, you know, is thick
       of hearing.
   "Dame," said I, as loud as I could bawl, "do you know what
       a loss I have had?"
   "Nay," says she, "my Lord Colway's[6] folks are all very sad:
30 For my Lord Dromedary[7] comes a Tuesday without fail."
   "Pugh!" said I, "but that's not the business that I ail."

1. The Lord Justice chiefly involved was the Earl of Berkeley, whom Swift served in the capacity of chaplain from 1699 to 1701. Berkeley's daughter ("Lady Betty"), Frances Harris's mistress, was then a girl of sixteen. The other domestics in the poem are identifiable members of Berkeley's household.

2. A housemaid.
3. Wife to one of the footmen.
4. The Earl of Berkeley's valet.
5. The old housekeeper.
6. A mispronunciation of "Galway," the Lord Justice whose term coincided with Berkeley's.
7. Drogheda, a newly appointed Lord Justice.

Says Cary,[8] says he, "I have been a servant this five and twenty
    years come spring,
And in all the places I lived I never heard of such a thing."
"Yes," says the steward,[9] "I remember when I was at my
    Lord Shrewsbury's,
35 Such a thing as this happened, just about the time of
    gooseberries."
So I went to the party suspected, and I found her full of grief:
(Now, you must know, of all things in the world I hate a thief.)
However, I was resolved to bring the discourse slily about:
"Mrs. Dukes," said I, "here's an ugly accident has happened out:
40 'Tis not that I value the money three skips of a louse;
But the thing I stand upon is the credit of the house.
'Tis true, seven pound, four shillings, and sixpence, makes a
    great hole in my wages:
Besides, as they say, service is no inheritance in these ages.
Now, Mrs. Dukes, you know, and everybody understands,
45 That though 'tis hard to judge, yet money can't go without
    hands."
"The devil take me!" said she (blessing herself), "if ever
    I saw't!"
So she roared like a bedlam,° as though I had called her   *mad person*
    all to naught.
So, you know, what could I say to her any more?
I e'en left her, and came away as wise as I was before.
50 Well; but then they would have had me gone to the
    cunning man:°   *fortune-teller*
"No," said I, " 'tis the same thing, the Chaplain[1] will be
    here anon."
So the Chaplain came in. Now the servants say he is my
    sweetheart,
Because he's always in my chamber, and I always take his part.
So, as the devil would have it, before I was aware, out I blundered,
55 "Parson," said I, "can you cast a nativity[2] when a body's
    plundered?"
(Now you must know, he hates to be called Parson, like the
    devil!)
"Truly," says he, "Mrs. Nab, it might become you to be
    more civil;
If your money be gone, as a learned Divine[3] says, d'ye see,
You are no text for my handling; so take that from me:
60 I was never taken for a conjurer before, I'd have you to know."
"Lord!" said I, "don't be angry, I am sure I never thought
    you so;
You know I honor the cloth; I design to be a parson's wife;
I never took one in your coat[4] for a conjurer in all my life."
With that he twisted his girdle at me like a rope, as who
    should say,
65 "Now you may go hang yourself for me," and so went away.
Well: I thought I should have swooned. "Lord!" said I, "what
    shall I do?
I have lost my money, and shall lose my true love too."
Then my lord called me: "Harry," said my lord, "don't cry;
I'll give you something toward thy loss." "And," says my lady,
    "so will I."
70 "Oh! but," said I, "what if, after all, the Chaplain won't
    come to?"

8. Clerk of the kitchen.
9. One Ferris, whom Swift elsewhere called "a scoundrel dog."
1. Swift himself.
2. Discover things by astrology.
3. Conjecturally, a Dr. Bolton, who had been advanced in the Church before Swift.
4. I.e., clerical garb.

For that, he said (an't please your Excellencies) I must
   petition you.
The premises tenderly considered, I desire your Excellencies'
   protection,
And that I may have a share in next Sunday's collection;
And, over and above, that I may have your Excellencies' letter,
75 With an order for the Chaplain aforesaid, or, instead of him,
   a better:
And then your poor petitioner, both night and day,
Or the Chaplain (for 'tis his trade) as in duty bound, shall
   ever pray.

                             1701   1709

Baucis and Philemon[5]

In ancient times, as story tells,
The saints would often leave their cells,
And stroll about, but hide their quality,°   *profession*
To try good people's hospitality.
5   It happened on a winter night,
As authors of the legend write,
Two brother hermits, saints by trade,
Taking their tour in masquerade,
Disguised in tattered habits, went
10 To a small village down in Kent;
Where, in the strollers' canting strain,
They begged from door to door in vain;
Tried every tone might pity win,
But not a soul would let them in.
15   Our wandering saints in woeful state,
Treated at this ungodly rate,
Having through all the village passed,
To a small cottage came at last;
Where dwelt a good honest old yeoman,
20 Called in the neighbourhood Philemon,
Who kindly did these saints invite
In his poor hut to pass the night:
And then the hospitable sire
Bid Goody° Baucis mend the fire;   *Dame*
25 While he from out the chimney took
A flitch of bacon off the hook;
And freely from the fattest side
Cut out large slices to be fried:
Then stepped aside to fetch 'em drink,
30 Filled a large jug up to the brink;
And saw it fairly° twice go round: *fully*
Yet (what is wonderful) they found
'Twas still replenished to the top,
As if they ne'er had touched a drop.
35 The good old couple was amazed,
And often on each other gazed:
For both were frighted to the heart,
And just began to cry, "What art!"°   *sorcery*
Then softly turned aside to view.
40 Whether the lights were burning blue.[6]
The gentle Pilgrims, soon aware on't,
Told 'em their calling, and their errant:
"Good folks, you need not be afraid,
We are but saints," the hermits said:

---

5. An Anglicized version of the tale in Ovid's
Metamorphoses VIII. 611–724.

6. This would have been evidence of witch-
craft.

45 "No hurt shall come to you or yours:
    But, for that pack of churlish boors,
    Not fit to live on Christian ground,
    They and their houses shall be drowned:
    Whilst you shall see your cottage rise,
50 And grow a church before your eyes."
        They scarce had spoke, when fair and soft,
    The roof began to mount aloft;
    Aloft rose every beam and rafter,
    The heavy wall climbed slowly after.
55   The chimney widened, and grew higher,
    Became a steeple with a spire.
        The kettle to the top was hoist,
    And there stood fastened to a joist;
    But with the upside down, to show
60 Its inclinations for below:
    In vain; for a superior force
    Applied at bottom, stops its course,
    Doomed ever in suspense to dwell,
    'Tis now no kettle, but a bell.
65   A wooden jack,[7] which had almost
    Lost, by disuse, the art to roast,
    A sudden alteration feels,
    Increased by new intestine° wheels: *internal*
    And, what exalts the wonder more,
70 The number made the motion slower.
    The flyer, though't had leaden feet,[8]
    Turned round so quick, you scarce could see't;
    But slackened by some secret power,
    Now hardly moves an inch an hour.
75 The jack and chimney, near allied,
    Had never left each other's side;
    The chimney to a steeple grown,
    The jack would not be left alone,
    But up against the steeple reared,
80 Became a clock, and still adhered:
    And still its love to household cares
    By a shrill voice at noon declares,
    Warning the cook-maid not to burn
    That roast meat which it cannot turn.
85   The groaning chair began to crawl
    Like an huge snail along the wall;
    There stuck aloft, in public view,
    And with small change a pulpit grew.
        The porringers, that in a row
90 Hung high and made a glittering show,
    To a less noble substance changed,
    Were now but leathern buckets ranged.[9]
        The ballads pasted on the wall,
    Of Joan of France and English Moll,
95 Fair Rosamond and Robin Hood,
    The Little Children in the Wood,
    Now seemed to look abundance better,
    Improved in picture, size, and letter,
    And high in order placed, describe
100 The heraldry of every tribe.
        A bedstead of the antique mode,
    Compact° of timber many a load,   *composed*

7. A machine for turning a spit, standing inside the large chimney.
8. The weighted flywheel.

9. The row of pewter porridge-bowls became a row of leather alms basins (like modern collection plates).

Such as our ancestors did use,
Was metamorphosed into pews;
105   Which still their ancient nature keep,
By lodging folks disposed to sleep.
    The cottage, by such feats as these,
Grown to a church by just degrees,
The hermits then desired their host
110   To ask for what he fancied most.
Philemon, having paused a while,
Returned 'em thanks in homely style;
Then said, "My house is grown so fine,
Methinks I still would call it mine:
115   I'm old, and fain would live at ease;
Make me the parson, if you please."
    He spoke, and presently he feels
His grazier's° coat fall down his heels;   *herdsman's*
He sees, yet hardly can believe,
120   About each arm a pudding-sleeve;
His waistcoat to a cassock[1] grew,
And both assumed a sable hue;
But being old, continued just
As threadbare, and as full of dust.
125   His talk was now of tithes and dues;
He smoked his pipe, and read the news;
Knew how to preach old sermons next,
Vamped° in the preface and the text;   *improvised*
At christenings well could act his part,
130   And had the service all by heart;
Wished women might have children fast,
And thought whose sow had farrowed last:
Against dissenters would repine,
And stood up firm for right divine:[2]
135   Found his head filled with many a system,
But classic authors,—he ne'er missed 'em.
    Thus having furbished up a parson,
Dame Baucis next they played their farce on;
Instead of homespun coifs were seen
140   Good pinners edged with colberteen:[3]
Her petticoat transformed apace,
Became black satin flounced with lace.
Plain Goody would no longer down,°   *be tolerated*
'Twas Madam, in her grogram gown.
145   Philemon was in great surprise,
And hardly could believe his eyes,
Amazed to see her look so prim;
And she admired° as much at him.   *wondered*
    Thus, happy in their change of life,
150   Were several years this man and wife;
When on a day, which proved their last,
Discoursing o'er old stories past,
They went by chance, amidst their talk,
To the churchyard to take a walk;
155   When Baucis hastily cried out,
"My dear, I see your forehead sprout!"
"Sprout," quoth the man, "what's this you tell us?
I hope you don't believe me jealous:[4]
But yet, methinks, I feel it true;
160   And really, yours is budding too—

1. The clerical garment worn inside the gown. "Pudding-sleeves" in the line above are sleeves which, being gathered, billow to the size and shape of puddings.
2. The divine right of kings, denied by most "dissenters" from the established church.
3. Instead of skull-caps of coarse cloth, an ample headdress with folds of fine material.
4. I.e., suspicious of possessing the horns of a cuckold.

Nay, now I cannot stir my foot:
It feels as if 'twere taking root."
    Description would but tire my Muse:
In short, they both were turned to yews.
165   Old Goodman Dobson of the green
Remembers he the trees has seen;
He'll talk of them from noon to night,
And goes with folks to show the sight;
On Sundays, after evening prayer,
170 He gathers all the parish there;
Points out the place of either yew;
Here Baucis, there Philemon grew:
Till once, a parson of our town,
To mend his barn, cut Baucis down;
175 At which, 'tis hard to be believed
How much the other tree was grieved,
Grew scrubby, died a-top, was stunted;
So the next parson stubbed and burnt it.

                                   1706   1709

A Description of a City Shower

    Careful observers may foretell the hour
(By sure prognostics) when to dread a shower:
While rain depends,° the pensive cat gives o'er   *impends*
Her frolics, and pursues her tail no more.
5   Returning home at night, you'll find the sink°   *sewer*
Strike your offended sense with double stink.
If you be wise, then go not far to dine;
You'll spend in coach hire more than save in wine.
A coming shower your shooting corns presage,
10 Old achés throb, your hollow tooth will rage.
Sauntering in coffeehouse is Dulman° seen;   *dull-man*
He damns the climate and complains of spleen.°   *melancholy*
    Meanwhile the South,° rising with dabbled wings, *south wind*
A sable cloud athwart the welkin° flings,   *sky*
15 That swilled more liquor than it could contain,
And, like a drunkard, gives it up again.
Brisk Susan whips her linen from the rope,
While the first drizzling shower is borne aslope:
Such is that sprinkling which some careless quean°   *wench*
20 Flirts on you from her mop, but not so clean:
You fly, invoke the gods; then turning, stop
To rail; she singing, still whirls on her mop.
Not yet the dust had shunned the unequal strife,
But, aided by the wind, fought still for life,
25 And wafted with its foe by violent gust,
'Twas doubtful which was rain and which was dust.
Ah! where must needy poet seek for aid,
When dust and rain at once his coat invade?
Sole coat, where dust cemented by the rain
30 Erects the nap, and leaves a mingled stain.
    Now in contiguous drops the flood comes down,
Threatening with deluge this devoted° town.   *doomed*
To shops in crowds the daggled° females fly,   *spattered*
Pretend to cheapen° goods, but nothing buy.   *price*
35 The Templar° spruce, while every spout's abroach,° *law student / running*
Stays till 'tis fair, yet seems to call a coach.
The tucked-up sempstress walks with hasty strides,
While streams run down her oiled umbrella's sides.
Here various kinds, by various fortunes led,
40 Commence acquaintance underneath a shed.

Triumphant Tories and desponding Whigs[5]
Forget their feuds, and join to save their wigs.
Boxed in a chair° the beau impatient sits,   *sedan chair*
While spouts run clattering o'er the roof by fits,
45   And ever and anon with frightful din
The leather[6] sounds; he trembles from within.
So when Troy chairmen bore the wooden steed,
Pregnant with Greeks impatient to be freed
(Those bully Greeks, who, as the moderns do,
50   Instead of paying chairmen, run them through),
Laocoön struck the outside with his spear,
And each imprisoned hero quaked for fear.[7]
       Now from all parts the swelling kennels° flow,   *gutters*
And bear their trophies with them as they go:
55   Filth of all hues and odors seem to tell
What street they sailed from, by their sight and smell.
They, as each torrent drives with rapid force,
From Smithfield or St. Pulchre's shape their course,
And in huge confluence joined at Snow Hill ridge,
60   Fall from the conduit prone to Holborn Bridge.[8]
Sweepings from butchers' stalls, dung, guts, and blood, ⎫
Drowned puppies, stinking sprats,° all drenched in mud, ⎬ *herring*
Dead cats, and turnip tops, come tumbling down the flood. ⎭

1710

ISAAC WATTS
(1674–1748)

The Day of Judgment

AN ODE ATTEMPTED IN ENGLISH SAPPHIC[1]

When the fierce north wind with his airy forces
Rears up the Baltic to a foaming fury,
And the red lightning with a storm of hail comes
                              Rushing amain down,

5   How the poor sailors stand amazed and tremble,
While the hoarse thunder, like a bloody trumpet,
Roars a loud onset to the gaping waters,
                              Quick to devour them!

Such shall the noise be and the wild disorder,
10   (If things eternal may be like these earthly)
Such the dire terror, when the great Archangel
                              Shakes the creation,

Tears the strong pillars of the vault of heaven,
Breaks up old marble, the repose of princes;
15   See the graves open, and the bones arising,
                              Flames all around 'em!

Hark, the shrill outcries of the guilty wretches!
Lively bright horror and amazing anguish
Stare through their eyelids, while the living worm lies
20   Gnawing within them.

5. The Tories (Swift's party) had recently
assumed power.
6. Leather roof of the sedan chair.
7. In *Aeneid* II, Laocoön so struck the side of
the Trojan horse, frightening the Greeks
within.

8. The sewage system referred to is fed first
by the refuse of the Smithfield cattle market
and drains at last into the open Fleet Ditch at
Holborn Bridge.
1. See Glossary, entry on **Sapphic strophe**,
at the end of this anthology.

Thoughts like old vultures prey upon their heart-strings,
And the smart twinges, when the eye beholds the
Lofty Judge frowning, and a flood of vengeance
    Rolling afore him.

25 Hopeless immortals! how they scream and shiver,
While devils push them to the pit wide-yawning
Hideous and gloomy, to receive them headlong
    Down to the center.

Stop here, my fancy: (all away ye horrid
30 Doleful ideas); come, arise to Jesus;
How He sits God-like! and the saints around him
    Throned, yet adoring!

Oh may I sit there when he comes triumphant
Dooming the nations! then ascend to glory
35 While our hosannas all along the passage
    Shout the Redeemer.

         1706

A Cradle Hymn

Hush, my dear, lie still and slumber;
Holy angels guard thy bed!
Heavenly blessings without number
Gently falling on thy head.

5 Sleep, my babe; thy food and raiment,
House and home thy friends provide;
All without thy care or payment,
All thy wants are well supplied.

How much better thou'rt attended
10 Than the Son of God could be,
When from Heaven he descended,
And became a child like thee!

Soft and easy is thy cradle;
Coarse and hard thy Saviour lay,
15 When his birth-place was a stable,
And his softest bed was hay.

Blessed Babe! what glorious features,
Spotless fair, divinely bright!
Must he dwell with brutal creatures?
20 How could angels bear the sight?

Was there nothing but a manger
Cursèd sinners could afford,
To receive the heavenly Stranger?
Did they thus affront their Lord?

25 Soft, my child; I did not chide thee,
Though my song might sound too hard;
'Tis thy {Mother[2] / Nurse that} sits beside thee
And her arm shall be thy guard.

Yet to read the shameful story,
30 How the Jews abused their King,
How they served the Lord of Glory,
Makes me angry while I sing.

2. "Here you may use the words *Brother, Sister, Neighbor, Friend,* &c" [Watts's note].

See the kinder shepherds round him,
Telling wonders from the sky;
35 There they sought him, there they found him,
With his Virgin-Mother by.

See the lovely Babe a-dressing;
Lovely Infant, how he smiled!
When he wept, the Mother's blessing
40 Soothed and hushed the holy Child.

Lo, he slumbers in his manger,
Where the hornéd oxen fed;
Peace, my darling, here's no danger,
Here's no ox anear thy bed.

45 'Twas to save thee, child, from dying,
Save my dear from burning flame,
Bitter groans, and endless crying,
That my blest Redeemer came.

Mayst thou live to know and fear him,
50 Trust and love him all thy days!
Then go dwell forever near him,
See his face, and sing his praise!

I could give thee thousand kisses,
Hoping what I most desire;
55 Not a mother's fondest wishes
Can to greater joys aspire.

1720

JOHN GAY
(1685–1732)

Sweet William's Farewell to Black-eyed Susan

A BALLAD

All in the Downs[1] the fleet was moored,
  The streamers waving in the wind,
When black-eyed Susan came aboard.
  "Oh! where shall I my true love find?
5 Tell me, ye jovial sailors, tell me true,
If my sweet William sails among the crew."

William, who high upon the yard
  Rocked with the billow to and fro,
Soon as her well-known voice he heard,
10 He sighed and cast his eyes below;
The cord slides swiftly through his glowing hands,
And quick as lightning on the deck he stands.

So the sweet lark, high-poised in air,
  Shuts close his pinions to his breast,
15 (If, chance, his mate's shrill call he hear)
  And drops at once into her nest.
The noblest Captain in the British fleet
Might envy William's lip those kisses sweet.

---

1. An anchorage up the English Channel from Dover.

"O Susan, Susan, lovely dear,
20   My vows shall ever true remain;
Let me kiss off that falling tear;
      We only part to meet again.
Change, as ye list, ye winds! my heart shall be
The faithful compass that still points to thee.

25 "Believe not what the landmen say,
      Who tempt with doubts thy constant mind;
They'll tell thee, sailors, when away,
      In every port a mistress find.
Yes, yes, believe them when they tell thee so,
30 For thou art present wheresoe'er I go.

"If to far India's coast we sail,
      Thy eyes are seen in diamonds bright,
Thy breath is Afric's spicy gale,
      Thy skin is ivory, so white.
35 Thus every beauteous object that I view,
Wakes in my soul some charm of lovely Sue.

"Though battle call me from thy arms,
      Let not my pretty Susan mourn;
Though cannons roar, yet safe from harms.
40   William shall to his dear return.
Love turns aside the balls that round me fly,
Lest precious tears should drop from Susan's eye."

The boatswain gave the dreadful word,
      The sails their swelling bosom spread,
45 No longer must she stay aboard;
      They kissed, she sighed, he hung his head;
Her lessening boat unwilling rows to land;
"Adieu!" she cries, and waved her lily hand.

1720

ALEXANDER POPE
(1688–1744)

The Rape of the Lock

AN HEROI-COMICAL POEM[1]

Nolueram, Belinda, tuos violare capillos;
sed juvat hoc precibus me tribuisse tuis.[2]
         —MARTIAL

Canto I

What dire offense from amorous causes springs,
What mighty contests rise from trivial things,
I sing—This verse to Caryll, Muse! is due:
This, even Belinda may vouchsafe to view:
5 Slight is the subject, but not so the praise,
If she inspire, and he approve my lays.
    Say what strange motive, Goddess! could compel
A well-bred lord to assault a gentle belle?
Oh, say what stranger cause, yet unexplored,
10 Could make a gentle belle reject a lord?

1. Based on an actual incident. A young man, Lord Petre, had sportively cut off a lock of a Miss Arabella Fermor's hair. She and her family were angered by the prank, and Pope's friend John Caryll (line 3), a relative of Lord Petre's, asked the poet to turn the incident into jest, so that good relations (and possibly negotiations toward a marriage between the principals) might be resumed. Pope responded by treating the incident in a mock epic or "heroi-comical poem." The epic conventions first encountered are the immediate statement of the topic, which the poet says he will "sing" as if in oral recitation, and the request to the Muse (line 7) to grant him the necessary insight.
2. "I did not want, Belinda, to violate your locks, but it pleases me to have paid this tribute to your prayers." Miss Fermor did not in fact request the poem.

In tasks so bold can little men engage,
And in soft bosoms dwells such mighty rage?
  Sol through white curtains shot a timorous ray,
And oped those eyes that must eclipse the day.[3]
15 Now lapdogs give themselves the rousing shake,
And sleepless lovers just at twelve awake:
Thrice rung the bell, the slipper knocked the ground,[4]
And the pressed watch returned a silver sound.[5]
Belinda still her downy pillow pressed,
20 Her guardian Sylph[6] prolonged the balmy rest:
'Twas he had summoned to her silent bed
The morning dream that hovered o'er her head.
A youth more glittering than a birthnight beau[7]
(That even in slumber caused her cheek to glow)
25 Seemed to her ear his winning lips to lay,
And thus in whispers said, or seemed to say:
  "Fairest of mortals, thou distinguished care
Of thousand bright inhabitants of air!
If e'er one vision touched thy infant thought,
30 Of all the nurse and all the priest have taught,
Of airy elves by moonlight shadows seen,
The silver token, and the circled green,[8]
Or virgins visited by angel powers,
With golden crowns and wreaths of heavenly flowers,
35 Hear and believe! thy own importance know,
Nor bound thy narrow views to things below.
Some secret truths, from learned pride concealed,
To maids alone and children are revealed:
What though no credit doubting wits may give?
40 The fair and innocent shall still believe.
Know, then, unnumbered spirits round thee fly,
The light militia of the lower sky:
These, though unseen, are ever on the wing,
Hang o'er the box, and hover round the Ring.[9]
45 Think what an equipage thou hast in air,
And view with scorn two pages and a chair.°   *sedan chair*
As now your own, our beings were of old,
And once enclosed in woman's beauteous mold;
Thence, by a soft transition, we repair
50 From earthly vehicles[1] to these of air.
Think not, when woman's transient breath is fled,
That all her vanities at once are dead:
Succeeding vanities she still regards,
And though she plays no more, o'erlooks the cards.
55 Her joy in gilded chariots,° when alive,   *carriages*
And love of ombre,[2] after death survive.
For when the Fair in all their pride expire,
To their first elements their souls retire:[3]

3. The eyes of lovely young women—though Belinda herself is still asleep.
4. These are two ways of summoning servants.
5. In the darkened beds, one discovered the approximate time by a watch which chimed the hour and quarter-hour when the stem was pressed.
6. Air-spirit. He accounts for himself in the lines below.
7. Courtier dressed for a royal birthday celebration.
8. The silver token is the coin left by a fairy or elf, and the circled green is a ring of bright green grass, supposed dancing circle of fairies.
9. The box is a theater box; the Ring, the circular carriage course in Hyde Park.
1. Mediums of existence, with a side glance at the fondness of young women for riding in carriages.

2. A popular card game, pronounced *omber*.
3. Namely, to fire, water, earth, and air, the four elements of the old cosmology and the several habitats (in the Rosicrucian myths upon which Pope embroiders) of four different kinds of "spirit." Envisaging these spirits as the transmigrated souls of different kinds of women, Pope causes termagants (scolds) to become fire-spirits or Salamanders (line 60); irresolute women to become water-spirits or Nymphs (line 62); prudes, or women who delight in rejection and negation, to become earth-spirits or Gnomes (line 64); and coquettes to become air-spirits or Sylphs. Since "nymph" could designate either a water-spirit or (in literary usage) a young lady, Pope permits his water-spirits to claim tea as their native element (line 62) and to keep their former company at tea-parties.

The sprites of fiery termagants in flame
60 Mount up, and take a Salamander's name.
Soft yielding minds to water glide away,
And sip, with Nymphs, their elemental tea.[4]
The graver prude sinks downward to a Gnome,
In search of mischief still on earth to roam.
65 The light coquettes in Sylphs aloft repair,
And sport and flutter in the fields of air.
    "Know further yet; whoever fair and chaste
Rejects mankind, is by some Sylph embraced:
For spirits, freed from mortal laws, with ease
70 Assume what sexes and what shapes they please.[5]
What guards the purity of melting maids,
In courtly balls, and midnight masquerades,
Safe from the treacherous friend, the daring spark,
The glance by day, the whisper in the dark,
75 When kind occasion prompts their warm desires,
When music softens, and when dancing fires?
'Tis but their Sylph, the wise Celestials know,
Though Honor is the word with men below.
    "Some nymphs there are, too conscious of their face,
80 For life predestined to the Gnomes' embrace.
These swell their prospects and exalt their pride,
When offers are disdained, and love denied:
Then gay ideas° crowd the vacant brain,   *imaginings*
While peers, and dukes, and all their sweeping train,
85 And garters, stars, and coronets[6] appear,
And in soft sounds, 'your Grace' salutes their ear.
'Tis these that early taint the female soul,
Instruct the eyes of young coquettes to roll,
Teach infant cheeks a bidden blush to know,
90 And little hearts to flutter at a beau.
    "Oft, when the world imagine women stray,
The Sylphs through mystic mazes guide their way,
Through all the giddy circle they pursue,
And old impertinence expel by new.
95 What tender maid but must a victim fall
To one man's treat, but for another's ball?
When Florio speaks what virgin could withstand,
If gentle Damon did not squeeze her hand?
With varying vanities, from every part,
100 They shift the moving toyshop of their heart;
Where wigs with wigs, with sword-knots sword-knots strive,[7]
Beaux banish beaux, and coaches coaches drive.
This erring mortals levity may call;
Oh, blind to truth! the Sylphs contrive it all.
105   "Of these am I, who thy protection claim,
A watchful sprite, and Ariel is my name.
Late, as I ranged the crystal wilds of air,
In the clear mirror of thy ruling star
I saw, alas! some dread event impend,
110 Ere to the main this morning sun descend,
But Heaven reveals not what, or how, or where:
Warned by the Sylph, O pious maid, beware!
This to disclose is all thy guardian can:
Beware of all, but most beware of Man!"
115   He said; when Shock,[8] who thought she slept too long,

4. Pronounced *tay*.
5. Like Milton's angels (*Paradise Lost* I.423 ff.).
6. Insignia of rank and court status.
7. Sword-Knots are ribbons tied to hilts. The verbal repetition and the tangled syntax recall descriptions of the throng and press of battle appearing in English translations of classical epic.
8. A name for lapdogs (like "Poll" for parrots); they looked like little "shocks" of hair.

Leaped up, and waked his mistress with his tongue.
'Twas then, Belinda, if report say true,
Thy eyes first opened on a billet-doux;[9]
Wounds, charms, and ardors were no sooner read,
120   But all the vision vanished from thy head.
    And now, unveiled, the toilet stands displayed,
Each silver vase in mystic order laid.
First, robed in white, the nymph intent adores,
With head uncovered, the cosmetic powers.
125   A heavenly image in the glass[1] appears;
To that she bends, to that her eyes she rears.
The inferior priestess, at her altar's side,
Trembling begins the sacred rites of pride.
Unnumbered treasures ope at once, and here
130   The various offerings of the world appear;
From each she nicely culls with curious toil,
And decks the goddess with the glittering spoil.
This casket India's glowing gems unlocks,
And all Arabia[2] breathes from yonder box.
135   The tortoise here and elephant unite,
Transformed to combs, the speckled and the white.
Here files of pins extend their shining rows,
Puffs, powders, patches, Bibles, billet-doux.
Now awful Beauty put on all its arms;
140   The fair each moment rises in her charms,
Repairs her smiles, awakens every grace,
And calls forth all the wonders of her face;
Sees by degrees a purer blush arise,
And keener lightnings quicken in her eyes.
145   The busy Sylphs surround their darling care,
These set the head, and those divide the hair,
Some fold the sleeve, whilst others plait the gown;
And Betty's praised for labors not her own.

Canto II

    Not with more glories, in the ethereal plain,
The sun first rises o'er the purpled main,
Than, issuing forth, the rival of his beams[3]
Launched on the bosom of the silver Thames.
5   Fair nymphs and well-dressed youths around her shone,
But every eye was fixed on her alone.
On her white breast a sparkling cross she wore,
Which Jews might kiss, and infidels adore.
Her lively looks a sprightly mind disclose,
10   Quick as her eyes, and as unfixed as those:
Favors to none, to all she smiles extends;
Oft she rejects, but never once offends.
Bright as the sun, her eyes the gazers strike,
And, like the sun, they shine on all alike.
15   Yet graceful ease, and sweetness void of pride,
Might hide her faults, if belles had faults to hide:
If to her share some female errors fall,
Look on her face, and you'll forget 'em all.
    This nymph, to the destruction of mankind,
20   Nourished two locks which graceful hung behind
In equal curls, and well conspired to deck

9. A love letter. The affected language of the fashionable love letter is exhibited in the next line.
1. The mirror. Her image is the object of veneration, the "goddess" named later. Belinda presides over the appropriate rites. **Betty**, her maid, is the "inferior priestess."

2. Source of perfumes.
3. I.e., Belinda. She is en route to Hampton Court, a royal palace some twelve miles up the river Thames from London.

With shining ringlets the smooth ivory neck.
Love in these labyrinths his slaves detains,
And mighty hearts are held in slender chains.
25 With hairy springes° we the birds betray,   *snares*
Slight lines of hair surprise the finny prey,
Fair tresses man's imperial race ensnare,
And beauty draws us with a single hair.
     The adventurous Baron the bright locks admired,
30 He saw, he wished, and to the prize aspired.
Resolved to win, he meditates the way,
By force to ravish, or by fraud betray;
For when success a lover's toil attends,
Few ask if fraud or force attained his ends.
35   For this, ere Phoebus rose, he had implored
Propitious Heaven, and every power adored,
But chiefly Love—to Love an altar built,
Of twelve vast French romances, neatly gilt.
There lay three garters, half a pair of gloves,
40 And all the trophies of his former loves.
With tender billet-doux he lights the pyre,
And breathes three amorous sighs to raise the fire.
Then prostrate falls, and begs with ardent eyes
Soon to obtain, and long possess the prize:
45 The powers gave ear, and granted half his prayer,
The rest the winds dispersed in empty air.
     But now secure the painted vessel glides,
The sunbeams trembling on the floating tides,
While melting music steals upon the sky,
50 And softened sounds along the waters die.
Smooth flow the waves, the zephyrs gently play,
Belinda smiled, and all the world was gay.
All but the Sylph—with careful thoughts oppressed,
The impending woe sat heavy on his breast.
55 He summons straight his denizens° of air;   *inhabitants*
The lucid squadrons round the sails repair:°   *assemble*
Soft o'er the shrouds aërial whispers breathe
That seemed but zephyrs to the train beneath.
Some to the sun their insect-wings unfold,
60 Waft on the breeze, or sink in clouds of gold.
Transparent forms too fine for mortal sight,
Their fluid bodies half dissolved in light,
Loose to the wind their airy garments flew,
Thin glittering textures of the filmy dew,[4]
65 Dipped in the richest tincture of the skies,
Where light disports in ever-mingling dyes,
While every beam new transient colors flings,
Colors that change whene'er they wave their wings.
Amid the circle, on the gilded mast,
70 Superior by the head was Ariel placed;
His purple° pinions opening to the sun,   *brilliant*
He raised his azure wand, and thus begun:
     "Ye Sylphs and Sylphids, to your chief give ear!
Fays, Fairies, Genii, Elves, and Daemons, hear!
75 Ye know the spheres and various tasks assigned
By laws eternal to the aërial kind.
Some in the fields of purest ether play,
And bask and whiten in the blaze of day.
Some guide the course of wandering orbs on high,
80 Or roll the planets through the boundless sky.
Some less refined, beneath the moon's pale light

---

4. The supposed material of spider webs.

Pursue the stars that shoot athwart the night,
Or suck the mists in grosser air below,
Or dip their pinions in the painted bow,°   *rainbow*
85   Or brew fierce tempests on the wintry main,
Or o'er the glebe° distill the kindly rain.   *farmland*
Others on earth o'er human race preside,
Watch all their ways, and all their actions guide:
Of these the chief the care of nations own,
90   And guard with arms divine the British Throne.
      "Our humbler province is to tend the Fair,
Not a less pleasing, though less glorious care:
To save the powder from too rude a gale,
Nor let the imprisoned essences exhale;
95   To draw fresh colors from the vernal flowers;
To steal from rainbows e'er they drop in showers
A brighter wash;° to curl their waving hairs,   *(cosmetic) wash*
Assist their blushes, and inspire their airs;
Nay oft, in dreams invention we bestow,
100   To change a flounce, or add a furbelow.
      "This day black omens threat the brightest fair,
That e'er deserved a watchful spirit's care;
Some dire disaster, or by force or slight,
But what, or where, the Fates have wrapped in night:
105   Whether the nymph shall break Diana's law,[5]
Or some frail china jar receive a flaw,
Or stain her honor or her new brocade,
Forget her prayers, or miss a masquerade,
Or lose her heart, or necklace, at a ball;
110   Or whether Heaven has doomed that Shock must fall.
Haste, then, ye spirits! to your charge repair:
The fluttering fan be Zephyretta's care;
The drops° to thee, Brillante, we consign;   *earrings*
And, Momentilla, let the watch be thine;
115   Do thou, Crispissa,[6] tend her favorite Lock;
Ariel himself shall be the guard of Shock.
      "To fifty chosen Sylphs, of special note,
We trust the important charge, the petticoat;
Oft have we known that sevenfold fence to fail,
120   Though stiff with hoops, and armed with ribs of whale.
Form a strong line about the silver bound,
And guard the wide circumference around.
      "Whatever spirit, careless of his charge,
His post neglects, or leaves the fair at large,
125   Shall feel sharp vengeance soon o'ertake his sins,
Be stopped in vials, or transfixed with pins,
Or plunged in lakes of bitter washes lie,
Or wedged whole ages in a bodkin's° eye;   *large needle's*
Gums and pomatums shall his flight restrain,
130   While clogged he beats his silken wings in vain,
Or alum styptics with contracting power
Shrink his thin essence like a riveled° flower: *shriveled*
Or, as Ixion[7] fixed, the wretch shall feel
The giddy motion of the whirling mill,°   *cocoa-mill*
135   In fumes of burning chocolate shall glow,
And tremble at the sea that froths below!"
      He spoke; the spirits from the sails descend;
Some, orb in orb, around the nymph extend;
Some thread the mazy ringlets of her hair;
140   Some hang upon the pendants of her ear:
With beating hearts the dire event they wait,
Anxious, and trembling for the birth of Fate.

---

5. Of chastity.
6. To "crisp" is to curl (hair).

7. For an affront to Juno, Ixion was bound eternally to a turning wheel.

Canto III

Close by those meads, forever crowned with flowers,
Where Thames with pride surveys his rising towers,
There stands a structure of majestic frame,[8]
Which from the neighboring Hampton takes its name.
5 Here Britain's statesmen oft the fall foredoom
Of foreign tyrants and of nymphs at home;
Here thou, great Anna! whom three realms obey,
Dost sometimes counsel take—and sometimes tea.
  Hither the heroes and the nymphs resort,
10 To taste awhile the pleasures of a court;
In various talk the instructive hours they passed,
Who gave the ball, or paid the visit last;
One speaks the glory of the British Queen,
And one describes a charming Indian screen;
15 A third interprets motions, looks, and eyes;
At every word a reputation dies.
Snuff, or the fan, supply each pause of chat,
With singing, laughing, ogling, and all that.
  Meanwhile, declining from the noon of day,
20 The sun obliquely shoots his burning ray;
The hungry judges soon the sentence sign,
And wretches hang that jurymen may dine;
The merchant from the Exchange° returns in peace,   *stock market*
And the long labors of the toilet cease.
25 Belinda now, whom thirst of fame invites,
Burns to encounter two adventurous knights,
At ombre[9] singly to decide their doom,
And swells her breast with conquests yet to come.
Straight the three bands prepare in arms° to join,   *combat*
30 Each band the number of the sacred nine.
Soon as she spreads her hand, the aërial guard
Descend, and sit on each important card:
First Ariel perched upon a Matadore,
Then each according to the rank they bore;
35 For Sylphs, yet mindful of their ancient race,
Are, as when women, wondrous fond of place.
  Behold, four Kings in majesty revered,
With hoary whiskers and a forky beard;
And four fair Queens whose hands sustain a flower,
40 The expressive emblem of their softer power;
Four Knaves in garbs succinct,[1] a trusty band,
Caps on their heads, and halberts in their hand;
And parti-colored troops, a shining train,
Draw forth to combat on the velvet plain.
45 The skillful nymph reviews her force with care;
"Let Spades be trumps!" she said, and trumps they were.
  Now move to war her sable Matadores,
In show like leaders of the swarthy Moors.

---

8. Hampton Court.
9. This game is like three-handed bridge with some features of poker added. From a deck lacking 8's, 9's and 10's, nine cards are dealt to each player (line 30) and the rest put in a central pool. A declarer called the *Ombre* (Spanish *hombre*, man) commits himself to taking more tricks than either of his opponents individually; hence Belinda would "encounter two knights *singly*." Declarer, followed by the other players, then selects discards and replenishes his hand with cards drawn sight unseen from the pool (line 45). He proceeds to name his trumps (line 46). The three principal trumps, called *Matadors* (line 47), always include the black aces. When spades are declared, the Matadors are, in order of value, the ace of spades (called *Spadille*, line 49), the deuce of spades (called *Manille*, line 51), and the ace of clubs (called *Basto*, line 53). The remaining spades fill out the trump suit. In the game here described, Belinda leads out her high trumps (lines 49–56), but the suit breaks badly (line 54); the Baron retains the queen (line 67), with which he presently trumps her king of clubs (line 69). He then leads high diamonds until she is on the verge of a set (called *Codille*, line 92). But she makes her bid at the last trick (line 94), taking his ace of hearts with her king (line 95), this being, in ombre, the highest card in the heart suit. The game is played on a green velvet cloth (line 44).
1. Hemmed up short, not flowing.

Spadillio first, unconquerable lord!
50 Led off two captive trumps, and swept the board.
As many more Manillio forced to yield,
And marched a victor from the verdant field.
Him Basto followed, but his fate more hard
Gained but one trump and one plebeian card.
55 With his broad saber next, a chief in years,
The hoary Majesty of Spades appears,
Puts forth one manly leg, to sight revealed,
The rest his many-colored robe concealed.
The rebel Knave, who dares his prince engage,
60 Proves the just victim of his royal rage.
Even mighty Pam,[2] that kings and queens o'erthrew
And mowed down armies in the fights of loo,
Sad chance of war! now distitute of aid,
Falls undistinguished by the victor Spade.
65   Thus far both armies to Belinda yield;
Now to the Baron fate inclines the field.
His warlike amazon her host invades,
The imperial consort of the crown of Spades.
The Club's black tyrant first her victim died,
70 Spite of his haughty mien and barbarous pride.
What boots the regal circle on his head,
His giant limbs, in state unwieldy spread?
That long behind he trails his pompous robe,
And of all monarchs only grasps the globe?
75   The Baron now his Diamonds pours apace;
The embroidered King who shows but half his face,
And his refulgent Queen, with powers combined
Of broken troops an easy conquest find.
Clubs, Diamonds, Hearts, in wild disorder seen,
80 With throngs promiscuous strew the level green.
Thus when dispersed a routed army runs,
Of Asia's troops, and Afric's sable sons,
With like confusion different nations fly,
Of various habit,° and of various dye,°   *dress / color*
85 The pierced battalions disunited fall
In heaps on heaps; one fate o'erwhelms them all.
    The Knave of Diamonds tries his wily arts,
And wins (oh, shameful chance!) the Queen of Hearts.
At this, the blood the virgin's cheek forsook,
90 A livid paleness spreads o'er all her look;
She sees, and trembles at the approaching ill,
Just in the jaws of ruin, and Codille,
And now (as oft in some distempered state)
On one nice trick depends the general fate.
95 An Ace of Hearts steps forth: the King unseen
Lurked in her hand, and mourned his captive Queen.
He springs to vengeance with an eager pace,
And falls like thunder on the prostrate Ace.
The nymph exulting fills with shouts the sky,
100 The walls, the woods, and long canals[3] reply.
    O thoughtless mortals! ever blind to fate,
Too soon dejected, and too soon elate:
Sudden these honors shall be snatched away,
And cursed forever this victorious day.
105   For lo! the board with cups and spoons is crowned,
The berries crackle, and the mill turns round;[4]
On shining altars of Japan[5] they raise

2. The jack of clubs, paramount trump in the game of loo.   4. As coffee beans are roasted and ground.
3. Passages between avenues of trees.   5. Lacquered tables.

The silver lamp; the fiery spirits blaze:
From silver spouts the grateful liquors glide,
110   While China's earth[6] receives the smoking tide.
At once they gratify their scent and taste,
And frequent cups prolong the rich repast.
Straight hover round the fair her airy band;
Some, as she sipped, the fuming liquor fanned,
115   Some o'er her lap their careful plumes displayed,
Trembling, and conscious of the rich brocade.
Coffee (which makes the politician wise,
And see through all things with his half-shut eyes)
Sent up in vapors to the Baron's brain
120   New stratagems, the radiant Lock to gain.
Ah, cease, rash youth! desist ere 'tis too late,
Fear the just Gods, and think of Scylla's fate![7]
Changed to a bird, and sent to flit in air,
She dearly pays for Nisus' injured hair!
125   But when to mischief mortals bend their will,
How soon they find fit instruments of ill!
Just then, Clarissa drew with tempting grace
A two-edged weapon from her shining case:
So ladies in romance assist their knight,
130   Present the spear, and arm him for the fight.
He takes the gift with reverence, and extends
The little engine on his fingers' ends;
This just behind Belinda's neck he spread,
As o'er the fragrant steams she bends her head.
135   Swift to the Lock a thousand sprites repair,
A thousand wings, by turns, blow back the hair,
And thrice they twitched the diamond in her ear,
Thrice she looked back, and thrice the foe drew near.
Just in that instant, anxious Ariel sought
140   The close recesses of the virgin's thought;
As on the nosegay in her breast reclined,
He watched the ideas rising in her mind,
Sudden he viewed, in spite of all her art,
An earthly lover lurking at her heart.
145   Amazed, confused, he found his power expired,[8]
Resigned to fate, and with a sigh retired.
      The Peer now spreads the glittering forfex° wide,   scissors
To enclose the Lock; now joins it, to divide.
Even then, before the fatal engine closed,
150   A wretched Sylph too fondly interposed;
Fate urged the shears, and cut the Sylph in twain
(But airy substance soon unites again):[9]
The meeting points the sacred hair dissever
From the fair head, forever, and forever!
155   Then flashed the living lightning from her eyes,
And screams of horror rend the affrighted skies.
Not louder shrieks to pitying heaven are cast,
When husbands, or when lapdogs breathe their last;
Or when rich china vessels fallen from high,
160   In glittering dust and painted fragments lie!
"Let wreaths of triumph now my temples twine,"
The victor cried, "the glorious prize is mine!
While fish in streams, or birds delight in air,
Or in a coach and six the British Fair,

6. Ceramic cups.
7. Scylla cut from the head of her father Nisus the lock of hair on which his life depended and gave it to her lover Minos of Crete, who was Scylla's enemy. For this she was turned into a sea-bird relentlessly pursued by an eagle.
8. Belinda, being strongly attracted to the Baron (line 144), can no longer merely coquette. She hence passes beyond Ariel's control.
9. Again as with Milton's angels (Paradise Lost VI.329–31).

165 As long as *Atalantis*[1] shall be read,
    Or the small pillow grace a lady's bed,
    While visits shall be paid on solemn days,
    When numerous wax-lights in bright order blaze,[2]
    While nymphs take treats, or assignations give,
170 So long my honor, name, and praise shall live!
    What Time would spare, from Steel receives its date,°   *termination*
    And monuments, like men, submit to fate!
    Steel could the labor of the Gods destroy,[3]
    And strike to dust the imperial towers of Troy;
175 Steel could the works of mortal pride confound,
    And hew triumphal arches to the ground.
    What wonder then, fair nymph! thy hairs should feel,
    The conquering force of unresisted Steel?"

Canto IV

     But anxious cares the pensive nymph oppressed,
     And secret passions labored in her breast.
     Not youthful kings in battle seized alive,
     Not scornful virgins who their charms survive,
5   Not ardent lovers robbed of all their bliss,
     Not ancient ladies when refused a kiss,
     Not tyrants fierce that unrepenting die,
     Not Cynthia when her manteau's[4] pinned awry,
     E'er felt such rage, resentment, and despair,
10   As thou, sad virgin! for thy ravished hair.
     For, that sad moment, when the Sylphs withdrew
     And Ariel weeping from Belinda flew,
     Umbriel,[5] a dusky, melancholy sprite
     As ever sullied the fair face of light,
15   Down to the central earth, his proper scene,
     Repaired to search the gloomy Cave of Spleen.[6]
     Swift on his sooty pinions flits the Gnome,
     And in a vapor reached the dismal dome.
     No cheerful breeze this sullen region knows,
20   The dreaded east is all the wind that blows.
     Here in a grotto, sheltered close from air,
     And screened in shades from day's detested glare,
     She sighs forever on her pensive bed,
     Pain at her side, and Megrim° at her head.   *migraine*
25   Two handmaids wait the throne: alike in place,
     But differing far in figure and in face.
     Here stood Ill-Nature like an ancient maid,
     Her wrinkled form in black and white arrayed;
     With store of prayers for mornings, nights, and noons,
30   Her hand is filled; her bosom with lampoons.°   *slanders*
     There Affectation, with a sickly mien,
     Shows in her cheek the roses of eighteen,
     Practiced to lisp, and hang the head aside,
     Faints into airs, and languishes with pride,
35   On the rich quilt sinks with becoming woe,
     Wrapped in a gown, for sickness and for show.
     The fair ones feel such maladies as these,
     When each new nightdress gives a new disease.

1. A set of memoirs which, under thin disguise, recounted actual scandals.
2. Attending the formal evening visits of the previous line.
3. Troy (named in the next line) was built by Apollo and Poseidon.
4. I.e., robe is.
5. Suggesting *umbra*, shadow; and *umber*, brown. The final *el* of this name is a further reminiscence of Milton's angels: Gabriel, Abdiel, Zophiel.

6. This journey is formally equivalent to Odysseus' and Aeneas' visits to the underworld. "Spleen" refers to the human organ, the supposed seat of melancholy; hence to melancholy itself. Believed to be induced by misty weather such as the east wind brings (lines 18–20), the condition was also called the "vapors." In its severer manifestations it tends toward madness; in its milder forms, it issues in peevishness and suspicion.

A constant vapor o'er the palace flies,
40 Strange phantoms rising as the mists arise;
Dreadful as hermit's dreams in haunted shades,
Or bright as visions of expiring maids.
Now glaring fiends, and snakes on rolling spires,°   *coils*
Pale specters, gaping tombs, and purple fires;
45 Now lakes of liquid gold, Elysian scenes,
And crystal domes, and angels in machines.[7]
    Unnumbered throngs on every side are seen
Of bodies changed to various forms by Spleen.
Here living teapots stand, one arm held out,
50 One bent; the handle this, and that the spout:
A pipkin[8] there, like Homer's tripod, walks;
Here sighs a jar, and there a goose pie talks;
Men prove with child, as powerful fancy works,
And maids, turned bottles, call aloud for corks.
55   Safe passed the Gnome through this fantastic band,
A branch of healing spleenwort[9] in his hand.
Then thus addressed the Power: "Hail, wayward Queen!
Who rule the sex to fifty from fifteen:
Parent of vapors and of female wit,
60 Who give the hysteric or poetic fit,
On various tempers act by various ways,
Make some take physic, others scribble plays;
Who cause the proud their visits to delay,
And send the godly in a pet to pray.
65 A nymph there is that all thy power disdains,
And thousands more in equal mirth maintains.
But oh! if e'er thy Gnome could spoil a grace,
Or raise a pimple on a beauteous face,
Like citron-waters° matrons' cheeks inflame,   *orange brandy*
70 Or change complexions at a losing game;
If e'er with airy horns I planted heads,[1]
Or rumpled petticoats, or tumbled beds,
Or caused suspicion when no soul was rude,
Or discomposed the headdress of a prude,
75 Or e'er to costive lapdog gave disease,
Which not the tears of brightest eyes could ease,
Hear me, and touch Belinda with chagrin:°   *annoyance*
That single act gives half the world the spleen."
    The Goddess with a discontented air
80 Seems to reject him though she grants his prayer.
A wondrous bag with both her hands she binds,
Like that where once Ulysses held the winds;[2]
There she collects the force of female lungs,
Sighs, sobs, and passions, and the war of tongues.
85 A vial next she fills with fainting fears,
Soft sorrows, melting griefs, and flowing tears.
The Gnome rejoicing bears her gifts away,
Spreads his black wings, and slowly mounts to day.
    Sunk in Thalestris'[3] arms the nymph he found,
90 Her eyes dejected and her hair unbound.
Full o'er their heads the swelling bag he rent,
And all the Furies issued at the vent.
Belinda burns with more than mortal ire,
And fierce Thalestris fans the rising fire.

7. These images are both 1) the hallucinations of insane melancholy and 2) parodies of stage properties and effects.
8. An earthen pot; it walks like the three-legged stools which Vulcan made for the gods in *Iliad* XVIII.
9. A kind of fern, purgative of spleen; sug- gesting the golden bough which Aeneas bore as a passport to Hades in *Aeneid* VI.
1. I.e., made men imagine they were being cuckolded.
2. Aeolus, the wind god, enabled Odysseus so to contain all adverse winds in *Odyssey* X.
3. The name of an Amazon.

95   "O wretched maid!" she spreads her hands, and cried
      (While Hampton's echoes, "Wretched maid!" replied),
      "Was it for this you took such constant care
      The bodkin,° comb, and essence to prepare?   *hairpin*
      For this your locks in paper durance bound,
100   For this with torturing irons wreathed around?
      For this with fillets° strained your tender head,   *bands*
      And bravely bore the double loads of lead?[4]
      Gods! shall the ravisher display your hair,
      While the fops envy, and the ladies stare!
105   Honor forbid! at whose unrivaled shrine
      Ease, pleasure, virtue, all, our sex resign.
      Methinks already I your tears survey,
      Already hear the horrid things they say,
      Already see you a degraded toast,
110   And all your honor in a whisper lost!
      How shall I, then, your helpless fame defend?
      'Twill then be infamy to seem your friend!
      And shall this prize, the inestimable prize,
      Exposed through crystal to the gazing eyes,
115   And heightened by the diamond's circling rays,
      On that rapacious hand forever blaze?
      Sooner shall grass in Hyde Park Circus[5] grow,
      And wits take lodgings in the sound of Bow;[6]
      Sooner let earth, air, sea, to chaos fall,
120   Men, monkeys, lapdogs, parrots, perish all!"
          She said; then raging to Sir Plume repairs,
      And bids her beau demand the precious hairs
      (Sir Plume of amber snuffbox justly vain,
      And the nice° conduct° of a clouded cane).   *precise / handling*
125   With earnest eyes, and round unthinking face,
      He first the snuffbox opened, then the case,
      And thus broke out—"My Lord, why, what the devil!
      Zounds! damn the lock! 'fore Gad, you must be civil!
      Plague on't! 'tis past a jest—nay prithee, pox!
130   Give her the hair"—he spoke, and rapped his box.
          "It grieves me much," replied the Peer again,
      "Who speaks so well should ever speak in vain.
      But by this Lock, this sacred Lock I swear
      (Which never more shall join its parted hair;
135   Which never more its honors shall renew,
      Clipped from the lovely head where late it grew),
      That while my nostrils draw the vital air,
      This hand, which won it, shall forever wear."
      He spoke, and speaking, in proud triumph spread
140   The long-contended honors° of her head.   *ornaments*
          But Umbriel, hateful Gnome, forbears not so;
      He breaks the vial whence the sorrows flow.
      Then see! the nymph in beauteous grief appears,
      Her eyes half languishing, half drowned in tears;
145   On her heaved bosom hung her drooping head,
      Which with a sigh she raised, and thus she said:
          "Forever cursed be this detested day,
      Which snatched my best, my favorite curl away!
      Happy! ah, ten times happy had I been,
150   If Hampton Court these eyes had never seen!
      Yet am not I the first mistaken maid,
      By love of courts to numerous ills betrayed.

---

4. The means by which Belinda's locks were fashioned into a ringlet: lead strips held her curl papers in place.
5. The fashionable carriage course (the "Ring" of I.44).
6. I.e., the sound of the bells of Bowchurch in the unfashionable commercial-section of London.

Oh, had I rather unadmired remained
In some lone isle, or distant northern land;
155 Where the gilt chariot never marks the way,
Where none learn ombre, none e'er taste bohea!°   *fine tea*
There kept my charms concealed from mortal eye,
Like roses that in deserts bloom and die.
What moved my mind with youthful lords to roam?
160 Oh, had I stayed, and said my prayers at home!
'Twas this the morning omens seemed to tell,
Thrice from my trembling hand the patch box⁷ fell;
The tottering china shook without a wind,
Nay, Poll sat mute, and Shock was most unkind!
165 A Sylph too warned me of the threats of fate,
In mystic visions, now believed too late!
See the poor remnants of these slighted hairs!
My hands shall rend what e'en thy rapine spares.
These in two sable ringlets taught to break,
170 Once gave new beauties to the snowy neck;
The sister lock now sits uncouth, alone,
And in its fellow's fate foresees its own;
Uncurled it hangs, the fatal shears demands,
And tempts once more thy sacrilegious hands.
175 Oh, hadst thou, cruel! been content to seize
Hairs less in sight, or any hairs but these!"

Canto V

She said: the pitying audience melt in tears.
But Fate and Jove had stopped the Baron's ears.
In vain Thalestris with reproach assails,
For who can move when fair Belinda fails?
5 Not half so fixed the Trojan could remain,
While Anna begged and Dido raged in vain.⁸
Then grave Clarissa graceful waved her fan;
Silence ensued, and thus the nymph began:
"Say why are beauties praised and honored most,
10 The wise man's passion, and the vain man's toast?
Why decked with all that land and sea afford,
Why angels called, and angel-like adored?
Why round our coaches crowd the white-gloved beaux,
Why bows the side box from its inmost rows?
15 How vain are all these glories, all our pains,
Unless good sense preserve what beauty gains;
That men may say when we the front box grace,
'Behold the first in virtue as in face!'
Oh! if to dance all night, and dress all day,
20 Charmed the smallpox, or chased old age away,
Who would not scorn what housewife's cares produce,
Or who would learn one earthly thing of use?
To patch, nay ogle, might become a saint,
Nor could it sure be such a sin to paint.
25 But since, alas! frail beauty must decay,
Curled or uncurled, since locks will turn to gray;
Since painted, or not painted, all shall fade,
And she who scorns a man must die a maid;
What then remains but well our power to use,
30 And keep good humor still whate'er we lose?
And trust me, dear, good humor can prevail
When airs, and flights, and screams, and scolding fail.
Beauties in vain their pretty eyes may roll;

7. A box for ornamental patches to accent the face.
8. Aeneas was determined to leave Carthage for Italy, though the enamored queen Dido raved and her sister Anna pleaded with him to stay.

Charms strike the sight, but merit wins the soul."[9]
35   So spoke the dame, but no applause ensued;
Belinda frowned, Thalestris called her prude.
"To arms, to arms!" the fierce virago cries,
And swift as lightning to the combat flies.
All side in parties, and begin the attack;
40   Fans clap, silks rustle, and tough whalebones crack;
Heroes' and heroines' shouts confusedly rise,
And bass and treble voices strike the skies.
No common weapons in their hands are found,
Like Gods they fight, nor dread a mortal wound.
45   So when bold Homer makes the Gods engage,
And heavenly breasts with human passions rage;
'Gainst Pallas, Mars; Latona, Hermes arms;[1]
And all Olympus rings with loud alarms:
Jove's thunder roars, heaven trembles all around,
50   Blue Neptune storms, the bellowing deeps resound:
Earth shakes her nodding towers, the ground gives way,
And the pale ghosts start at the flash of day!
Triumphant Umbriel on a sconce's height
Clapped his glad wings, and sat to view the fight:
55   Propped on the bodkin spears, the sprites survey
The growing combat, or assist the fray.
While through the press enraged Thalestris flies,
And scatters death around from both her eyes,
A beau and witling perished in the throng,
60   One died in metaphor, and one in song.
"O cruel nymph! a living death I bear,"
Cried Dapperwit, and sunk beside his chair.
A mournful glance Sir Fopling upwards cast,
"Those eyes are made so killing"—was his last.
65   Thus on Maeander's flowery margin lies
The expiring swan, and as he sings he dies.
When bold Sir Plume had drawn Clarissa down,
Chloe stepped in, and killed him with a frown;
She smiled to see the doughty hero slain,
70   But, at her smile, the beau revived again.
Now Jove suspends his golden scales in air,[2]
Weighs the men's wits against the lady's hair;
The doubtful beam long nods from side to side;
At length the wits mount up, the hairs subside.
75   See, fierce Belinda on the Baron flies,
With more than usual lightning in her eyes;
Nor feared the chief the unequal fight to try,
Who sought no more than on his foe to die.
But this bold lord with manly strength endued,
80   She with one finger and a thumb subdued:
Just where the breath of life his nostrils drew,
A charge of snuff the wily virgin threw;
The Gnomes direct, to every atom just,
The pungent grains of titillating dust.
85   Sudden, with starting tears each eye o'erflows,
And the high dome re-echoes to his nose.
"Now meet thy fate," incensed Belinda cried,
And drew a deadly bodkin[3] from her side.

9. Clarissa's address parallels a speech in *Iliad* XII, wherein Sarpedon tells Glaucus that, as leaders of the army, they must justify their privilege by extraordinary prowess.
1. Mars arms against Pallas, and Hermes against Latona in *Iliad* XX. The tangled syntax is supposed to mirror the press of battle.
2. He so weighs the fortunes of war in classical epic.
3. Here an ornamental hairpin. Its history suggests that of Agamemnon's scepter in *Iliad* II. "Seal rings" (line 91) are for impressing seals on letters and legal documents.

(The same, his ancient personage to deck,
90 Her great-great-grandsire wore about his neck,
In three seal rings; which after, melted down,
Formed a vast buckle for his widow's gown:
Her infant grandame's whistle next it grew,
The bells she jingled, and the whistle blew;
95 Then in a bodkin graced her mother's hairs,
Which long she wore, and now Belinda wears.)
    "Boast not my fall," he cried, "insulting foe!
Thou by some other shalt be laid as low.
Nor think to die dejects my lofty mind:
100 All that I dread is leaving you behind!
Rather than so, ah, let me still survive,
And burn in Cupid's flames—but burn alive."
    "Restore the Lock!" she cries; and all around
"Restore the Lock!" the vaulted roofs rebound.
105 Not fierce Othello in so loud a strain
Roared for the handkerchief that caused his pain.[4]
But see how oft ambitious aims are crossed,
And chiefs contend till all the prize is lost!
The lock, obtained with guilt, and kept with pain,
110 In every place is sought, but sought in vain:
With such a prize no mortal must be blessed,
So Heaven decrees! with Heaven who can contest?
    Some thought it mounted to the lunar sphere,
Since all things lost on earth are treasured there.
115 There heroes' wits are kept in ponderous vases,
And beaux' in snuffboxes and tweezer cases.
There broken vows and deathbed alms are found,
And lovers' hearts with ends of riband bound,
The courtier's promises, and sick man's prayers,
120 The smiles of harlots, and the tears of heirs,
Cages for gnats, and chains to yoke a flea,
Dried butterflies, and tomes of casuistry.
    But trust the Muse—she saw it upward rise,
Though marked by none but quick, poetic eyes
125 (So Rome's great founder to the heavens withdrew,[5]
To Proculus alone confessed in view);
A sudden star, it shot through liquid° air,   clear
And drew behind a radiant trail of hair.
Not Berenice's locks first rose so bright,[6]
130 The heavens bespangling with disheveled light.
The Sylphs behold it kindling as it flies,
And pleased pursue its progress through the skies.
    This the beau monde shall from the Mall[7] survey,
And hail with music its propitious ray.
135 This the blest lover shall for Venus take,
And send up vows from Rosamonda's Lake.
This Partridge[8] soon shall view in cloudless skies,
When next he looks through Galileo's eyes;
And hence the egregious wizard shall foredoom
140 The fate of Louis, and the fall of Rome.
    Then cease, bright nymph! to mourn thy ravished hair,
Which adds new glory to the shining sphere!
Not all the tresses that fair head can boast,
Shall draw such envy as the Lock you lost.

4. In *Othello* III.iv.
5. Romulus was borne heavenward in a storm-cloud and later deified.
6. The locks which the Egyptian queen Berenice dedicated to her husband's safe return were turned into a constellation.
7. A fashionable walk which (like Rosamonda's Lake [line 136]) was in St. James's Park.
8. A London astrologer who predicted calamities on the enemies of England and Protestantism. "Galileo's eyes": the telescope.

145 For, after all the murders of your eye,
       When, after millions slain, yourself shall die:
       When those fair suns shall set, as set they must,
       And all those tresses shall be laid in dust,
       This Lock the Muse shall consecrate to fame,
150 And 'midst the stars inscribe Belinda's name.

                                              1712   1714

Elegy to the Memory of an Unfortunate Lady

        What beckoning ghost, along the moonlight shade
     Invites my steps, and points to yonder glade?
     'Tis she!—but why that bleeding bosom gored,
     Why dimly gleams the visionary sword?
5   O ever beauteous, every friendly! tell,
     Is it, in Heaven, a crime to love too well?
     To bear too tender, or too firm a heart,
     To act a lover's or a Roman's part?[9]
     Is there no bright reversion° in the sky,   *inheritance*
10   For those who greatly think, or bravely die?
        Why bade ye else, ye Powers! her soul aspire
     Above the vulgar flight of low desire?
     Ambition first sprung from your blest abodes;
     The glorious fault of angels and of gods:
15   Thence to their images on earth it flows,
     And in the breasts of kings and heroes glows.
     Most souls, 'tis true, but peep out once an age,
     Dull sullen prisoners in the body's cage:
     Dim lights of life, that burn a length of years
20   Useless, unseen, as lamps in sepulchers;
     Like Eastern kings a lazy state° they keep,   *sedateness*
     And close confined to their own palace, sleep.
        From these perhaps (ere Nature bade her die)
     Fate snatched her early to the pitying sky.
25   As into air the purer spirits flow,
     And separate from their kindred dregs below;
     So flew the soul to its congenial place,
     Nor left one virtue to redeem her race.°   *family*
        But thou, false guardian of a charge too good,
30   Thou, mean deserter of thy brother's blood!
     See on these ruby lips the trembling breath,
     These cheeks, now fading at the blast of death;
     Cold is that breast which warmed the world before,
     And those love-darting eyes must roll no more.
35   Thus, if Eternal Justice rules the ball,
     Thus shall your wives, and thus your children fall:
     On all the line a sudden vengeance waits,
     And frequent hearses shall besiege your gates.
     There passengers shall stand, and pointing say
40   (While the long funerals blacken all the way),
     Lo these were they, whose souls the Furies steeled,
     And cursed with hearts unknowing how to yield.
     Thus unlamented pass the proud away,
     The gaze of fools, and pageant of a day!
45   So perish all, whose breast ne'er learned to glow
     For others' good, or melt at others' woe.
        What can atone (oh, ever-injured shade!)
     Thy fate unpitied, and thy rites unpaid?[1]
     No friend's complaint, no kind domestic tear

9. To commit suicide, as the Roman Stoics
recommended to persons in irremediable dis-
tress.

1. Suicides were denied certain rites of Chris-
tian burial.

50 Pleased thy pale ghost, or graced thy mournful bier.
   By foreign hands thy dying eyes were closed,
   By foreign hands thy decent limbs composed,
   By foreign hands thy humble grave adorned,
   By strangers honored, and by strangers mourned!
55 What though no friends in sable weeds appear,
   Grieve for an hour, perhaps, then mourn a year,
   And bear about the mockery of woe
   To midnight dances, and the public show?
   What though no weeping Loves thy ashes grace,
60 Nor polished marble emulate thy face?
   What though no sacred earth allow thee room,
   Nor hallowed dirge be muttered o'er thy tomb?
   Yet shall thy grave with rising flowers be dressed,
   And the green turf lie lightly on thy breast:
65 There shall the morn her earliest tears bestow,
   There the first roses of the year shall blow;
   While angels with their silver wings o'ershade
   The ground, now sacred by thy reliques made.
      So peaceful rests, without a stone, a name,
70 What once had beauty, titles, wealth, and fame.
   How loved, how honored once, avails thee not,
   To whom related, or by whom begot;
   A heap of dust alone remains of thee,
   'Tis all thou art, and all the proud shall be!
75 Poets themselves must fall, like those they sung,
   Deaf the praised ear, and mute the tuneful tongue.
   Even he, whose soul now melts in mournful lays,
   Shall shortly want the generous tear he pays;
   Then from his closing eyes thy form shall part,
80 And the last pang shall tear thee from his heart,
   Life's idle business at one gasp be o'er,
   The Muse forgot, and thou beloved no more!

                                        1717

From The Dunciad

[*The Booksellers' Race*]²

   And now the Queen,³ to glad her sons, proclaims,
   By herald hawkers, high heroic games.
   They summon all her race: an endless band
20 Pours forth, and leaves unpeopled half the land.
   A motely mixture! in long wigs, in bags,⁴
   In silks, increpes, in Garters, and in rags,⁵
   From drawing-rooms, from colleges, from garrets,
   On horse, on foot, in hacks, and gilded chariots:
25 All who true dunces in her cause appeared,
   And all who knew those dunces to reward.
      Amid that area wide they took their stand,
   Where the tall maypole once o'er-looked the Strand.
   But now (so ANNE and Piety ordain)
30 A church collects the saints of Drury Lane.⁶
      With authors, stationers° obeyed the call,   *booksellers*
   (The field of glory is a field for all).

2. *Dunciad* (B) ii.17–120.
3. The Goddess of Dullness. Through street-criers, she proclaims games which are the burlesque equivalent of the funeral games in the *Iliad* and the *Aeneid*.
4. Short wigs (contained in snoods or "bags").
5. I.e., in fine clothes and in modest; wearing tokens of the highest place (the Order of the Garter) and of the lowest.
6. St. Mary le Strand, on the former site of a maypole, was one of fifty new churches built or projected under Queen Anne. The phrase "saints of Drury Lane" ironically acknowledges the many prostitutes in the area.

Glory, and gain, the industrious tribe provoke;
And gentle Dullness ever loves a joke.
35 A Poet's form she placed before their eyes,
And bade the nimblest racer seize the prize;
No meagre, muse-rid mope, adust° and thin,   *gloomy*
In a dun night-gown of his own loose skin;
But such a bulk as no twelve bards could raise,
40 Twelve starveling bards of these degenerate days.
All as a partridge plump, full-fed, and fair,
She formed this image of well-bodied air;
With pert flat eyes she windowed well its head:
A brain of feathers, and a heart of lead;
45 And empty words she gave, and sounding strain,
But senseless, lifeless! idol void and vain!
Never was dashed out, at one lucky hit,
A fool, so just a copy of a wit;
So like, that critics said, and courtiers swore,
50 A wit it was, and called the phantom Moore.[7]
    All gaze with ardor: some a poet's name,
Others a sword-knot° and laced suit inflame.   *tassel*
But lofty Lintot[8] in the circle rose:
"This prize is mine; who tempt it are my foes;
55 With me began this genius, and shall end."
He spoke: and who with Lintot shall contend?
    Fear held them mute. Alone, untaught to fear,
Stood dauntless Curll;[9] "Behold that rival here!
The race by vigor, not by vaunts is won;
60 So take the hindmost, Hell," he said, and run.
Swift as a bard the bailiff° leaves behind,   *collector of debts*
He left huge Lintot, and outstripped the wind.
As when a dab-chick waddles through the copse
On feet and wings, and flies, and wades, and hops:
65 So laboring on, with shoulders, hands, and head,
Wide as a windmill all his figure spread,
With arms expanded Bérnard rows his state,
And left-legged Jacob[1] seems to emulate.
Full in the middle way there stood a lake,
70 Which Curll's Corinna[2] chanced that morn to make:
(Such was her wont, at early dawn to drop
Her evening cates° before his neighbour's shop,)   *dainties*
Here fortuned Curll to slide; loud shout the band,
And "Bérnard! Bérnard!" rings through all the Strand.
75 Obscene with filth the miscreant lies bewrayed,
Fallen in the plash his wickedness had laid:
Then first (if poets aught of truth declare)
The caitiff vaticide° conceived a prayer.   *poet-murderer*
    "Hear, Jove! whose name my bards and I adore,
80 As much at least as any God's, or more;
And him and his if more devotion warms,
Down with the Bible, up with the Pope's Arms."[3]
    A place there is, betwixt earth, air, and seas,
Where, from ambrosia,[4] Jove retires for ease,
85 There in his seat two spacious vents appear,
On this he sits, to that he leans his ear,

7. James Moore Smyth; a plagiarist, hence without substance as a poet.
8. Barnaby Bernard Lintot (the "Bérnard" of the next paragraph) was a publisher, "a great sputtering fellow," who quarreled with Pope over Pope's translation of the *Odyssey*.
9. Edmund Curll, "an unscrupulous, persistent and adroit publisher, who realized the commercial value of scandal and impudence" (Sutherland). He pirated some of Pope's works and also published personal attacks on him.

1. Jacob Tonson, the leading publisher of the age. His gait was ungainly.
2. Elizabeth Thomas, a woman of easy virtue ("Corinna" was the Roman poet Ovid's mistress) who stole some of Pope's letters and sold them to Curll.
3. Curll's trademark and Lintot's, respectively.
4. Ambrosia is the food of the gods; ichor (below) is their ethereal "blood."

And hears the various vows of fond mankind;
Some beg an eastern, some a western wind:
All vain petitions, mounting to the sky,
90 With reams abundant this abode supply;
Amused he reads, and then returns the bills
Signed with that ichor which from gods distils.
    In office here fair Cloacina[5] stands,
And ministers to Jove with purest hands.
95 Forth from the heap she picked her votary's prayer,
And placed it next him, a distinction rare!
Oft had the goddess heard her servants call,
From her black grottos[6] near the Temple-wall,
Listening delighted to the jest unclean
100 Of link-boys° vile, and watermen obscene;   *torch-bearers*
Where as he fished her nether realms for wit,
She oft had favored him, and favors yet.
Renewed by ordure's sympathetic force,
As oiled with magic juices for the course,
105 Vigorous he rises; from the effluvia strong
Imbibes new life, and scours and stinks along;
Re-passes Lintot, vindicates the race,
Nor heeds the brown dishonors of his face.
    And now the victor stretched his eager hand,
110 Where the tall nothing stood, or seemed to stand;
A shapeless shade, it melted from his sight,
Like forms in clouds, or visions of the night.
To seize his papers, Curll, was next thy care;
His papers light fly diverse, tost in air;
115 Songs, sonnets, epigrams the winds uplift,
And whisk 'em back to Evans, Young, and Swift.[7]
The embroidered suit at least he deemed his prey;
That suit an unpaid tailor snatched away.
No rag, no scrap, of all the beau, or wit,
120 That once so fluttered, and that once so writ.

                                       1728   1741

[The Grand Tour][8]

275   In flowed at once a gay embroidered race,
And tittering pushed the pedants off the place:[9]
Some would have spoken, but the voice was drowned
By the French horn, or by the opening° hound.   *giving tongue*
The first came forwards, with as easy mien,
280 As if he saw St. James's[1] and the Queen.
When thus the attendant orator begun,
"Receive, great Empress! thy accomplished son:
Thine from the birth, and sacred from the rod,
A dauntless infant! never scared with God.[2]
285 The sire saw, one by one, his virtues wake:
The mother begged the blessing of a rake.[3]
Thou gav'st that ripeness, which so soon began,
And ceased so soon, he ne'er was boy nor man.
Through school and college, thy kind cloud o'ercast,
290 Safe and unseen the young Aeneas passed.[4]
Thence bursting glorious, all at once let down,
Stunned with his giddy larum° half the town.   *alarm*

---

5. The Roman goddess of the common sewers.
6. I.e., the coal-wharves.
7. Curll had owned writings of these men.
8. *Dunciad* (B) iv.275–336.
9. Academicians are displaced by those supposedly educated in "the school of life." Foremost among the latter is a young man returning from an "educational" tour of the Continent. His tutor or governor, acting as the formal academic orator, presents him to the Goddess of Dullness (the "great Empress") for a special degree.
1. I.e., the Court.
2. I.e., never imbued with the fear of God.
3. I.e., that her son would become a rake.
4. Aeneas' mother Venus shrouded him in a mist to preserve him from detection in Carthage (*Aeneid* I.411–14).

Intrepid then, o'er seas and lands he flew:
Europe he saw, and Europe saw him too.
295 There all thy gifts and graces we display,
Thou, only thou, directing all our way!
To where the Seine, obsequious as she runs,
Pours at great Bourbon's[5] feet her silken sons;
Or Tiber, now no longer Roman, rolls,
300 Vain of Italian arts, Italian souls:[6]
To happy convents, bosomed deep in vines,
Where slumber abbots, purple as their wines:
To isles of fragrance, lily-silvered vales,
Diffusing languor in the panting gales:
305 To lands of singing, or of dancing slaves,
Love-whispering woods, and lute-resounding waves.
But chief her shrine where naked Venus keeps,
And cupids ride the lion of the deeps;[7]
Where, eased of fleets, the Adriatic main
310 Wafts the smooth eunuch and enamored swain.
Led by my hand, he sauntered Europe round,
And gathered every vice on Christian ground;
Saw every court, heard every king declare
His royal sense of operas or the fair;
315 The stews° and palace equally explored,   *brothels*
Intrigued with glory, and with spirit whored;
Tried all hors d'oeuvres, all liqueurs defined,
Judicious drank, and greatly-daring dined;
Dropped the dull lumber of the Latin store,
320 Spoiled his own language, and acquired no more;
All classic learning lost on classic ground;
And last turned *air*, the echo of a sound!
See now, half-cured, and perfectly well-bred,
With nothing but a solo in his head;
325 As much estate, and principle, and wit,
As Jansen, Fleetwood, Cibber shall think fit;[8]
Stolen from a duel, followed by a nun,
And, if a borough choose him not,[9] undone;
See, to my country happy I restore
330 This glorious youth, and add one Venus more.
Her too receive (for her my soul adores)
So may the sons of sons of sons of whores,
Prop thine, O Empress! like each neighbour throne,
And make a long posterity thy own."
335 Pleased, she accepts the hero, and the dame
Wraps in her veil, and frees from sense of shame.

1741

Epilogue to the Satires

WRITTEN IN 1738

Dialogue I

FRIEND. Not twice a twelvemonth you appear in print,
And when it comes, the court see nothing in't.
You grow correct, that once with rapture writ,
And are, besides, too *moral* for a wit.

---

5. King Louis XV of France.
6. The Tiber, associated once with the disciplined virtue of old Rome, is now proud of the decadent modern Italy.
7. Cupids (gods of love) are astride the winged lion designating Venice. Venice, that is, has substituted pre-eminence in prostitution for its former pre-eminence in trade and naval might.

8. Sir Henry Jansen was a gambler—as, less professionally, were Colley Cibber and Charles Fleetwood, theater managers at Drury Lane.
9. Unless he is elected to Parliament, that is, and thereby becomes immune from arrest for debt.

5   Decay of parts, alas! we all must feel—
     Why now, this moment, don't I see you steal?
     'Tis all from Horace; Horace long before ye
     Said, "Tories called him Whig and Whigs a Tory;" *
     And taught his Romans, in much better meter,
10   "To laugh at fools who put their trust in Peter."[1]
       But Horace, Sir, was delicate, was nice;
     Bubo observes, he lashed no sort of *vice:*
     Horace would say, Sir Billy *served the crown,*
     Blunt could *do business,* Huggins *knew the town;*
15   In Sappho touch the *failings of the sex,*[2]
     In reverend bishops note some *small neglects,*
     And own, the Spaniard did a *waggish thing,*
     Who cropt our ears, and sent them to the King.[3]
     His sly, polite, insinuating style
20   Could please at court, and make Augustus smile:
     An artful manager, that crept between
     His friend and shame, and was a kind of screen.
     But 'faith your very friends will soon be sore;
     Patriots there are, who wish you'd jest no more—
25   And where's the glory? 'twill be only thought
     The great man never offered you a groat,[4]
     Go see Sir Robert——
       POPE   See Sir Robert!—hum—
     And never laugh—for all my life to come?
     Seen him I have, but in his happier hour
30   Of social pleasure, ill-exchanged for power;
     Seen him, uncumbered with the venal tribe,
     Smile without art, and win without a bribe.
     Would he oblige me? let me only find,
     He does not think me what he thinks mankind.
35   Come, come, at all I laugh he laughs, no doubt;
     The only difference is, I dare laugh out.
       FRIEND. Why yes: with Scripture still you may be free;
     A horse-laugh, if you please, at honesty;
     A joke on Jekyl,[5] or some odd Old Whig
40   Who never changed his principle, or wig:
     A patriot is a fool in every age,
     Whom all Lord Chamberlains allow the stage:[6]
     These nothing hurts; they keep their fashion still,
     And wear their strange old virtue, as they will.
45   If any ask you, "Who's the man, so near
     His Prince, that writes in verse, and has his ear?"
     Why, answer, Lyttelton,[7] and I'll engage
     The worthy youth shall ne'er be in a rage:
     But were his verses vile, his whisper base,
50   You'd quickly find him in Lord Fanny's[8] case.
     Sejanus, Wolsey, hurt not honest Fleury,[9]
     But well may put some statesmen in a fury.

1. Peter Walter, an unscrupulous money-lender and financial agent.
2. Bubo is Bubb Dodington, a personally ostentatious Whig politician. Sir Billy is Sir William Yonge, a loyal, voluble, and somewhat dishonest servant of the Whig ministry. Sir John Blunt was Director of the South Sea Company, a notorious financial swindle. John Huggins was a venal prison warden whose influential connections preserved him from being sent to prison himself. Sappho is again Lady Mary Wortley Montagu.
3. A Spanish sea-captain had so used a British Captain named Jenkins. Pope is proposing that the government is obsequious in its foreign relations.
4. I.e., that the prime minister (Sir Robert Walpole, whose motto was that every man had his price) has offered you no bribe.

5. Sir Joseph Jekyl, an elderly Whig ("Old Whig") of unquestioned probity; a loyal but not slavish partisan whom Walpole's supporters sometimes derided.
6. "Patriot" was the designation claimed by the political opposition; "fool" connotes a stage character, as in Shakespeare. The Lord Chamberlain had for a year licensed all plays.
7. Secretary to the Prince of Wales; a Whig opposed to Walpole.
8. "Fanny" is Hervey, the Sporus of the *Epistle to Dr. Arbuthnot,* lines 305 ff.
9. I.e., to be called "Sejanus" and "Wolsey" (the names of self-seeking ministers of the Roman Emperor Tiberius and the English Henry VIII respectively) did not hurt André de Fleury, the moderate advisor to Louis XV of France.

Laugh then at any, but at fools or foes;
These you but anger, and you mend not those.[1]
55　Laugh at your friends, and, if your friends are sore,
So much the better, you may laugh the more;
To vice and folly to confine the jest,
Sets half the world, God knows, against the rest;
Did not the sneer of more impartial men
60　At sense and virtue, balance all again.
Judicious wits spread wide the ridicule,
And charitably comfort knave and fool.
　　POPE. Dear Sir, forgive the prejudice of youth:
Adieu distinction, satire, warmth, and truth!
65　Come, harmless characters that no one hit;
Come, Henley's oratory, Osborn's wit![2]
The honey dropping from Favonio's tongue,
The flowers of Bubo, and the flow of Yonge!
The gracious dew of pulpit eloquence,
70　And all the well-whipped cream of courtly sense,
That first was Hervey's, Fox's next, and then
The Senate's and then Hervey's once again.[3]
O come, that easy Ciceronian style,
So Latin, yet so English all the while,
75　As though the pride of Middleton and Bland,[4]
All boys may read, and girls may understand!
Then might I sing without the least offense,
And all I sung should be the *Nation's sense;*
Or teach the melancholy muse to mourn,
80　Hang the sad verse on Carolina's urn,
And hail her passage to the realms of rest,
All parts performed, and *all* her children blest![5]
So—Satire is no more—I feel it die—
No gazetteer° more innocent than I—　　　　　　　　　　　*government writer*
85　And let, a-God's name, every fool and knave
Be graced through life, and flattered in his grave.
　　FRIEND. Why so? If Satire knows its time and place,
You still may lash the greatest—in disgrace:
For merit will by turns forsake them all;
90　Would you know when? exactly when they fall.
But let all Satire in all changes spare
Immortal Selkirk, and grave Delaware![6]
Silent and soft, as saints remove to Heaven,
All ties dissolved, and every sin forgiven,
95　These may some gentle ministerial wing
Receive, and place forever near a king!
There, where no passion, pride, or shame transport,
Lulled with the sweet Nepenthe[7] of a court;
There, where no father's, brother's, friend's disgrace
100　Once break their rest, or stir them from their place:
But past the sense of human miseries,
All tears are wiped forever from all eyes;[8]
No cheek is known to blush, no heart to throb,
Save when they lose a question,° or a job.　　　　　　　　*parliamentary vote*

1. "These * * * those": the latter . . . the former.
2. Henley was a popular preacher; Osborn, the pseudonym for a government writer, James Pitt.
3. Pope has in mind an address of condolence on the death of Queen Caroline, which was (1) written, as Pope supposed, by Lord Hervey, (2) delivered in the House of Commons by the Whig parliamentarian Henry Fox, (3) adopted by the Commons ("the Senate"), (4) turned into a Latin epitaph by Hervey.
4. Conyers Middleton, Cambridge University librarian, author of the *Life of Cicero;* and Henry Bland, Provost of Eton. Pope implies that they helped Hervey with his Latin.
5. The Queen, on her deathbed, had declined the last sacrament and had refused to be reconciled to her son the Prince of Wales.
6. The "immortal" Earl of Selkirk had been a court officer under William and the two Georges; Earl De La Warr was a current court favorite.
7. A magic potion banishing sad recollections.
8. A reference to heaven, where "God shall wipe away all tears from their eyes" (Revelation xxi.4).

105 POPE. Good Heaven forbid, that I should blast their glory,
Who know how like Whig ministers to Tory,
And when three sovereigns died, could scarce be vexed,
Considering what a *gracious prince* was next.
Have I in silent wonder, seen such things
110 As pride in slaves, and avarice in kings;
And at a peer, or peeress, shall I fret,
Who starves a sister, or forswears a debt?
Virtue, I grant you, is an empty boast;
But shall the dignity of *Vice* be lost?
115 Ye Gods! shall Cibber's son, without rebuke,
Swear like a Lord, or Rich out-whore a Duke?[9]
A favorite's porter with his master vie,
Be bribed as often, and as often lie?
Shall Ward draw contracts with a stateman's skill?
120 Or Japhet pocket, like his Grace, a will?[1]
Is it for Bond, or Peter,[2] (paltry things)
To pay their debts, or keep their faith, like kings?
If Blunt dispatched himself, he played the man,
And so may'st thou, illustrious Passeran![3]
125 But shall a printer, weary of his life,
Learn from their books, to hang himself and wife?
This, this, my friend, I cannot, must not bear;
Vice thus abused demands a nation's care:
This calls the Church to deprecate our sin,
130 And hurls the thunder of the laws on gin.[4]
  Let modest Foster, if he will, excel
Ten metropolitans° in preaching well;[5]   *bishops*
A simple Quaker, or a Quaker's wife,
Outdo Landaff[6] in doctrine,—yea in life:
135 Let humble Allen,[7] with an awkward shame,
Do good by stealth, and blush to find it fame.
Virtue may choose the high or low degree,
'Tis just alike to virtue, and to me;
Dwell in a monk, or light upon a king,
140 She's still the same, beloved, contented thing.
Vice is undone, if she forgets her birth,
And stoops from angels to the dregs of earth:
But 'tis the fall degrades her to a whore;
Let *Greatness* own her, and she's mean no more,
145 Her birth, her beauty, crowds and courts confess,
Chaste matrons praise her, and grave bishops bless;
In golden chains the willing world she draws,
And hers the Gospel is, and hers the Laws,
Mounts the tribunal, lifts her scarlet head,
150 And see pale Virtue carted[8] in her stead.
Lo! at the wheels of her triumphal car,
Old England's Genius, rough with many a scar,
Dragged in the dust! his arms hang idly round,
His flag inverted[9] trails along the ground!
155 Our youth, all liveried[1] o'er with foreign gold,
Before her dance: behind her, crawl the old!

---

9. Theophilus Cibber and John Rich, actors and theater-managers.
1. John Ward and Japhet Crook were forgers. The satiric reference is to the politic suppression of George I's will.
2. Denis Bond and Peter Walter, embezzlers.
3. Charles Blount, who killed himself for love, and the Count of Passerano, an Italian fugitive who philosophically defended suicide; both were professed free-thinkers. The "printer" who is described as taking Passeran's hint was one Richard Smith.
4. An act of 1736.
5. James Foster, an Anabaptist, and Mrs. Mary Drummond, the "Quaker's wife" of the following line, were noted contemporary preachers.
6. Robert Harris, Bishop of the Welsh see of Landaff, had jibed at Pope and Swift in a foolish pamphlet on French manners.
7. Robert Allen, the prototype of Squire Allworthy of Fielding's *Tom Jones.*
8. Being exhibited in a cart was the punishment of prostitutes. The figure Vice has a "scarlet head" by analogy with the Whore of Babylon of Revelation xvii.1–6.
9. "Struck" as in military surrender.
1. Wearing the (often splendid) garb of servitude.

See thronging millions to the pagod[10] run,
And offer country, parent, wife, or son!
Hear her black trumpet through the land proclaim,
160   That NOT TO BE CORRUPTED IS THE SHAME.
In soldier, churchman, patriot, man in power,
'Tis avarice all, ambition is no more!
See, all our nobles begging to be slaves!
See, all our fools aspiring to be knaves!
165   The wit of cheats, the courage of a whore,
Are what ten thousand envy and adore:
All, all look up, with reverential awe,
At crimes that 'scape, or triumph o'er the law:
While truth, worth, wisdom, daily they decry—
170   "Nothing is sacred now but villainy."
     Yet may this verse (if such a verse remain)
Show there was one who held it in disdain.

1738

SAMUEL JOHNSON
(1709–1784)

On the Death of Dr. Robert Levet[1]

Condemned to Hope's delusive mine,
    As on we toil from day to day,
By sudden blasts, or slow decline,
    Our social comforts drop away.

5   Well tried through many a varying year,
    See Levet to the grave descend;
Officious,° innocent, sincere,   *dutiful*
    Of every friendless name the friend.

Yet still he fills Affection's eye,
10   Obscurely wise, and coarsely kind;
Nor, lettered Arrogance, deny
    Thy praise to merit unrefined.

When fainting Nature called for aid,
    And hovering Death prepared the blow,
15   His vigorous remedy displayed
    The power of art without the show.

In Misery's darkest cavern known,
    His useful care was ever nigh,
Where hopeless Anguish poured his groan,
20   And lonely Want retired to die.

No summons mocked by chill delay,
    No petty gain disdained by pride,
The modest wants of every day
    The toil of every day supplied.

25   His virtues walked their narrow round,
    Nor made a pause, nor left a void;
And sure the Eternal Master found
    The single talent[2] well employed.

---

10. A pagan shrine; specifically the cart of Juggernaut (a form of the Hindu deity Vishnu), under the wheels of which devotees hurled themselves and were crushed.
1. An unlicensed physician practicing among the poor, who had long lived in Dr. Johnson's house. He was uncouth in appearance and stiff in manner.
2. An allusion to the portion of wealth given in trust in the parable of the talents, Matthew xxv.14–30.

The busy day, the peaceful night,
30   Unfelt, uncounted, glided by;
His frame was firm, his powers were bright,
    Though now his eightieth year was nigh.

Then with no throbbing fiery pain,
    No cold gradations of decay,
35 Death broke at once the vital chain,
    And freed his soul the nearest way.

1783

THOMAS GRAY
(1716–1771)

Ode

ON THE DEATH OF A FAVORITE CAT,
DROWNED IN A TUB OF GOLDFISHES

'Twas on a lofty vase's side,
Where China's gayest art had dyed
    The azure flowers that blow;°   *bloom*
Demurest of the tabby kind,
5   The pensive Selima, reclined,
    Gazed on the lake below.

Her conscious tail her joy declared;
The fair round face, the snowy beard,
    The velvet of her paws,
10 Her coat, that with the tortoise vies,
Her ears of jet, and emerald eyes,
    She saw; and purred applause.

Still had she gazed; but 'midst the tide
Two angel forms were seen to glide,
15   The genii° of the stream: *guardian spirits*
Their scaly armor's Tyrian hue
Through richest purple to the view
    Betrayed a golden gleam.[1]

The hapless nymph with wonder saw:
20 A whisker first and then a claw,
    With many an ardent wish,
She stretched in vain to reach the prize.
What female heart can gold despise?
    What cat's averse to fish?

25 Presumptuous maid! with looks intent
Again she stretched, again she bent,
    Nor knew the gulf between.
(Malignant Fate sat by and smiled)
The slippery verge her feet beguiled,
30   She tumbled headlong in.

---

1. "Tyrian" and (in classical reference) "purple" cover a considerable spectrum, including crimson. The fish are seen, through red highlights, as golden.

Eight times emerging from the flood
She mewed to every watery god,
   Some speedy aid to send.
No dolphin came, no Nereid stirred;[2]
35 Nor cruel Tom, nor Susan heard;
   A favorite has no friend!

From hence, ye beauties, undeceived,
Know, one false step is ne'er retrieved,
   And be with caution bold.
40 Not all that tempts your wandering eyes
And heedless hearts, is lawful prize;
   Nor all that glisters, gold.

1748

Elegy Written in a Country Churchyard

The curfew tolls the knell of parting day,
   The lowing herd wind slowly o'er the lea,
The plowman homeward plods his weary way,
   And leaves the world to darkness and to me.

5 Now fades the glimmering landscape on the sight,
   And all the air a solemn stillness holds,
Save where the beetle wheels his droning flight,
   And drowsy tinklings lull the distant folds;

Save that from yonder ivy-mantled tower
10   The moping owl does to the moon complain
Of such, as wandering near her secret bower,
   Molest her ancient solitary reign.

Beneath those rugged elms, that yew tree's shade,
   Where heaves the turf in many a moldering heap,
15 Each in his narrow cell forever laid,
   The rude° forefathers of the hamlet sleep.   *rustic*

The breezy call of incense-breathing morn,
   The swallow twittering from the straw-built shed,
The cock's shrill clarion, or the echoing horn,°   *hunting horn*
20   No more shall rouse them from their lowly bed.

For them no more the blazing hearth shall burn,
   Or busy housewife ply her evening care;
No children run to lisp their sire's return,
   Or climb his knees the envied kiss to share.

25 Oft did the harvest to their sickle yield,
   Their furrow oft the stubborn glebe° has broke;   *soil*
How jocund did they drive their team afield!
   How bowed the woods beneath their sturdy stroke!

Let not Ambition mock their useful toil,
30   Their homely joys, and destiny obscure;
Nor Grandeur hear with a disdainful smile
   The short and simple annals of the poor.

The boast of heraldry,[3] the pomp of power,
   And all that beauty, all that wealth e'er gave,
35 Awaits alike the inevitable hour.
   The paths of glory lead but to the grave.

2. A dolphin appeared to save the singer   3. I.e., noble family.
Arion when he was cast overboard. Nereids
are sea-nymphs.

Nor you, ye proud, impute to these the fault,
    If Memory o'er their tomb no trophies[4] raise,
Where through the long-drawn aisle and fretted° vault   *ornamented*
40   The pealing anthem swells the note of praise.

Can storied urn[5] or animated° bust   *lifelike*
    Back to its mansion call the fleeting breath?
Can Honor's voice provoke° the silent dust,   *call forth*
    Or Flattery soothe the dull cold ear of Death?

45 Perhaps in this neglected spot is laid
    Some heart once pregnant with celestial fire;
Hands that the rod of empire might have swayed,
    Or waked to ecstasy the living lyre.

But Knowledge to their eyes her ample page
50   Rich with the spoils of time did ne'er unroll;
Chill Penury repressed their noble rage,
    And froze the genial current of the soul.

Full many a gem of purest ray serene,
    The dark unfathomed caves of ocean bear:
55 Full many a flower is born to blush unseen,
    And waste its sweetness on the desert air.

Some village Hampden,[6] that with dauntless breast
    The little tyrant of his fields withstood;
Some mute inglorious Milton here may rest,
60   Some Cromwell guiltless of his country's blood.

The applause of listening senates to command,
    The threats of pain and ruin to despise,
To scatter plenty o'er a smiling land,
    And read their history in a nation's eyes,

65 Their lot forbade: nor circumscribed alone
    Their growing virtues, but their crimes confined;
Forbade to wade through slaughter to a throne,
    And shut the gates of mercy on mankind,

The struggling pangs of conscious truth to hide,
70   To quench the blushes of ingenuous shame,
Or heap the shrine of Luxury and Pride
    With incense kindled at the Muse's flame.

Far from the madding° crowd's ignoble strife,   *milling*
    Their sober wishes never learned to stray;
75 Along the cool sequestered vale of life
    They kept the noiseless tenor of their way.

Yet even these bones from insult to protect
    Some frail memorial still erected nigh,
With uncouth rhymes and shapeless sculpture decked,
80   Implores the passing tribute of a sigh.

Their name, their years, spelt by the unlettered Muse,
    The place of fame and elegy supply:
And many a holy text around she strews,
    That teach the rustic moralist to die.

---

4. Memorials to military heroes; typically, statuary representations of arms captured in battle.
5. Funeral urn with descriptive epitaph.
6. Leader of the opposition to Charles I in the controversy over ship money; killed in battle in the Civil Wars.

85 For who to dumb Forgetfulness a prey,
    This pleasing anxious being e'er resigned,
Left the warm precincts of the cheerful day,
    Nor cast one longing lingering look behind?

On some fond breast the parting soul relies,
90   Some pious drops the closing eye requires;
Even from the tomb the voice of Nature cries,
    Even in our ashes live their wonted fires.

For thee, who mindful of the unhonored dead
    Dost in these lines their artless tale relate;
95 If chance, by lonely contemplation led,
    Some kindred spirit shall inquire thy fate,

Haply some hoary-headed swain may say,
    "Oft have we seen him at the peep of dawn
Brushing with hasty steps the dews away
100   To meet the sun upon the upland lawn.

"There at the foot of yonder nodding beech
    That wreathes its old fantastic roots so high,
His listless length at noontide would he stretch,
    And pore upon the brook that babbles by.

105 "Hard by yon wood, now smiling as in scorn,
    Muttering his wayward fancies he would rove,
Now drooping, woeful wan, like one forlorn,
    Or crazed with care, or crossed in hopeless love.

"One morn I missed him on the customed hill,
110   Along the heath and near his favorite tree;
Another came; nor yet beside the rill,
    Nor up the lawn, nor at the wood was he;

"The next with dirges due in sad array
    Slow through the churchway path we saw him borne.
115 Approach and read (for thou canst read) the lay,
    Graved on the stone beneath yon aged thorn."

      The Epitaph

*Here rests his head upon the lap of Earth
    A youth to Fortune and to Fame unknown.
Fair Science° frowned not on his humble birth,*   Learning
120   *And Melancholy marked him for her own.*

*Large was his bounty, and his soul sincere,
    Heaven did a recompense as largely send:
He gave to Misery all he had, a tear,
    He gained from Heaven ('twas all he wished) a friend.*

125 *No farther seek his merits to disclose,
    Or draw his frailties from their dread abode
(There they alike in trembling hope repose),
    The bosom of his Father and his God.*

            ca. 1742–50   1751

Stanzas to Mr. Bentley[7]

In silent gaze the tuneful choir among,
  Half pleased, half blushing, let the Muse admire,
While Bentley leads her sister-art along,
  And bids the pencil° answer to the lyre.   *painter's brush*

5 See, in their course, each transitory thought
    Fixed by his touch a lasting essence take;
Each dream, in fancy's airy coloring wrought,
    To local symmetry and life awake!

The tardy rhymes that used to linger on,
10   To censure cold, and negligent of fame,
In swifter measures animated run,
    And catch a luster from his genuine flame.

Ah! could they catch his strength, his easy grace,
    His quick creation, his unerring line;
15 The energy of Pope they might efface,
    And Dryden's harmony submit to mine.

But not to one in this benighted age
    Is that diviner inspiration given,
That burns in Shakespeare's or in Milton's page,
20   The pomp and prodigality of Heaven.

As when, conspiring in the diamond's blaze,
    The meaner gems that singly charm the sight
Together dart their intermingled rays,
    And dazzle with a luxury of light.

25 Enough for me, if to some feeling breast,
    My lines a secret sympathy [impart;]
And as their pleasing influence [is confessed,]
    A sigh of soft reflection [stirs the heart.]

      ca. 1752   1775

The Fatal Sisters[8]

Now the storm begins to lower,
(Haste, the loom of Hell prepare!)
Iron-sleet of arrowy shower
Hurtles in the darkened air.

5 Glittering lances are the loom,
Where the dusky warp we strain,
Weaving many a soldier's doom,
Orkney's woe and Randver's bane.

7. Written while Richard Bentley was preparing the designs for *Six Poems by Mr. T. Gray.* The manuscript in which this poem was preserved was torn in its lower right-hand corner. The missing words are here conjecturally supplied in brackets.
8. These are the Valkyries, of whom five (Mista, Sangrida, Hilda, Gondula, and Geira) are named in the fifth and eighth stanzas. Gray's poem, based on a Latin translation of a Norse poem, treats of the Battle of Clontarf (A.D. 1014). According to Gray's headnote, Sigurd, Earl of the Orkney Islands, went to Ireland with a troop of soldiers to aid the young king Sictryg, who was warring against his father-in-law, King Brian. Sigurd and his men were cut to pieces, but Sictryg narrowly prevailed over Brian, who was killed in the action. On the day of the battle, a native of Caithness, the county of the Scottish mainland nearest the Orkneys, saw a troop on horseback ride up to a mountain and seemingly enter it. He followed them and observed, through a cleft in the rocks, twelve gigantic female figures employed about a loom. As they wove, they sang the song which follows. Upon finishing their work, they tore the web into twelve parts and galloped off, each one with a piece, six to the north and six to the south.

See the grisly texture grow,
10   ('Tis of human entrails made!)
And the weights that play below,
Each a gasping warrior's head.

Shafts for shuttles, dipped in gore,
Shoot° the trembling cords along.   *thrust*
15   Sword, that once a monarch bore,
Keep the tissue° close and strong.   *fabric*

Mista black, terrific° maid,   *fear-inspiring*
Sangrida, and Hilda, see,
Join the wayward° work to aid;   *self-determining*
20   'Tis the woof of victory.

Ere the ruddy sun be set,
Pikes must shiver, javelins sing,
Blade with clattering buckler° meet,   *shield*
Hauberk° crash, and helmet ring.   *coat of mail*

25   (Weave the crimson web of war!)
Let us go, and let us fly
Where our friends the conflict share,
Where they triumph, where they die.

As the paths of fate we tread,
30   Wading through the ensanguined field,
Gondula and Geira, spread
O'er the youthful king⁹ your shield.

We the reins to slaughter give;
Ours to kill, and ours to spare;
35   Spite of danger he shall live.
(Weave the crimson web of war!)

They whom once the desert beach
Pent within its bleak domain,
Soon their ample sway shall stretch
40   O'er the plenty of the plain.

Low the dauntless earl is laid,
Gored with many a gaping wound;
Fate demands a nobler head;
Soon a king¹ shall bite the ground.

45   Long his loss shall Eirin° weep,   *Ireland*
Ne'er again his likeness see;
Long her strains in sorrow steep,
Strains of immortality!

Horror covers all the heath;
50   Clouds of carnage blot the sun.
Sisters, weave the web of death;
Sisters, cease, the work is done.

Hail the task, and hail the hands!
Songs of joy and triumph sing!
55   Joy to the victorious bands,
Triumph to the younger king.

9. I.e., Sictryg.   1. I.e., Brian.

Mortal, thou that hear'st the tale,
Learn the tenor of our song.
Scotland, through each winding vale
60 Far and wide the notes prolong.

Sisters, hence with spurs of speed;
Each her thundering falchion° wield;   *sword*
Each bestride her sable steed.
Hurry, hurry to the field!

    1761   1768

WILLIAM COLLINS
(1721–1759)

Ode Written in the Beginning of the Year 1746[1]

How sleep the brave who sink to rest
By all their country's wishes blest!
When Spring, with dewy fingers cold,
Returns to deck their hallowed mold,
5 She there shall dress a sweeter sod
Than Fancy's feet have ever trod.

By fairy hands their knell is rung,
By forms unseen their dirge is sung;
There Honor comes, a pilgrim gray,
10 To bless the turf that wraps their clay,
And Freedom shall awhile repair,
To dwell a weeping hermit there!

    1746

Ode to Evening

If aught of oaten stop,[2] or pastoral song,
May hope, chaste Eve, to soothe thy modest ear,
   Like thy own solemn springs,
   Thy springs and dying gales,
5 O nymph reserved, while now the bright-haired sun
Sits in yon western tent, whose cloudy skirts,
   With brede° ethereal wove,   *braid*
   O'erhang his wavy bed:
Now air is hushed, save where the weak-eyed bat,
10 With short shrill shriek flits by on leathern wing,
   Or where the beetle winds
   His small but sullen horn,
As oft he rises 'midst the twilight path,
Against the pilgrim° borne in heedless hum: *wayfarer*
15   Now teach me, maid composed,
   To breathe some softened strain,
Whose numbers, stealing through thy darkening vale,
May not unseemly with its stillness suit,
   As, musing slow, I hail
20   Thy genial loved return!
For when thy folding-star[3] arising shows

1. The poem celebrates Englishmen who fell resisting the pretender to the throne ("Bonnie Prince Charlie," the grandson of James II) in the previous year.
2. "If any modulation of a (shepherd's) reed."
3. The evening star, which, when it becomes visible, tells the shepherd to drive his flock to the sheepfold.

His paly circlet, at his warning lamp
    The fragrant Hours, and elves
    Who slept in flowers the day,
25 And many a nymph who wreaths her brows with sedge,
And sheds the freshening dew, and, lovelier still,
    The pensive Pleasures sweet,
    Prepare thy shadowy car.
Then lead, calm votaress, where some sheety lake
30 Cheers the lone heath, or some time-hallowed pile
    Or upland fallows gray
    Reflect its last cool gleam.
But when chill blustering winds, or driving rain,
Forbid my willing feet, be mine the hut
35   That from the mountain's side
    Views wilds, and swelling floods,
And hamlets brown, and dim-discovered spires,
And hears their simple bell, and marks o'er all
    Thy dewy fingers draw
40   The gradual dusky veil.
While Spring shall pour his showers, as oft he wont,
And bathe thy breathing tresses, meekest Eve;
    While Summer loves to sport
    Beneath thy lingering light;
45 While sallow Autumn fills thy lap with leaves;
Or Winter, yelling through the troublous air,
    Affrights thy shrinking train,
    And rudely rends thy robes;
So long, sure-found beneath the sylvan shed,[4]
50 Shall Fancy, Friendship, Science, rose-lipped Health,
    Thy gentlest influence own,
    And hymn thy favorite name!

1746, 1748

CHRISTOPHER SMART
(1722–1771)

From Jubilate Agno[1]

For I will consider my Cat Jeoffry.
For he is the servant of the Living God, duly and daily serving him.
For at the first glance of the glory of God in the East he worships in his way.
700 For is this done by wreathing his body seven times round with elegant
    quickness.
For then he leaps up to catch the musk,[2] which is the blessing of God upon
    his prayer.
For he rolls upon prank to work it in.
For having done duty and received blessing he begins to consider himself.
For this he performs in ten degrees.
705 For first he looks upon his forepaws to see if they are clean.
For secondly he kicks up behind to clear away there.
For thirdly he works it upon stretch with the forepaws extended.
For fourthly he sharpens his paws by wood.
For fifthly he washes himself.
710 For sixthly he rolls upon wash.
For seventhly he fleas himself, that he may not be interrupted upon the beat.[3]

---

4. I.e., securely attained beneath the shelter of the forest.
1. "Rejoice in the Lamb"; i.e., in Jesus, the Lamb of God; written while Smart was confined for insanity.
2. Perhaps a scented plant, played with like catnip.
3. Upon his daily round, possibly of hunting.

For eighthly he rubs himself against a post.

For ninthly he looks up for his instructions.

For tenthly he goes in quest of food.

715 For having considered God and himself he will consider his neighbor.

For if he meets another cat he will kiss her in kindness.

For when he takes his prey he plays with it to give it a chance.

For one mouse in seven escapes by his dallying.

For when his day's work is done his business more properly begins.

720 For he keeps the Lord's watch in the night against the adversary.

For he counteracts the powers of darkness by his electrical skin and glaring
eyes.

For he counteracts the Devil, who is death, by brisking about the life.

For in his morning orisons he loves the sun and the sun loves him.

For he is of the tribe of Tiger.

725 For the Cherub Cat is a term of the Angel Tiger.[1]

For he has the subtlety and hissing of a serpent, which in goodness he
suppresses.

For he will not do destruction if he is well-fed, neither will he spit without
provocation.

For he purrs in thankfulness when God tells him he's a good Cat.

For he is an instrument for the children to learn benevolence upon.

730 For every house is incomplete without him, and a blessing is lacking in the
spirit.

For the Lord commanded Moses concerning the cats at the departure of the
Children of Israel from Egypt.

For every family had one cat at least in the bag.[5]

For the English Cats are the best in Europe.

For he is the cleanest in the use of his forepaws of any quadruped.

735 For the dexterity of his defense is an instance of the love of God to him
exceedingly.

For he is the quickest to his mark of any creature.

For he is tenacious of his point.

For he is a mixture of gravity and waggery.

For he knows that God is his Saviour.

740 For there is nothing sweeter than his peace when at rest.

For there is nothing brisker than his life when in motion.

For he is of the Lord's poor, and so indeed is he called by benevolence
perpetually—Poor Jeoffry! poor Jeoffry! the rat has bit thy throat.

For I bless the name of the Lord Jesus that Jeoffry is better.

For the divine spirit comes about his body to sustain it in complete cat.

745 For his tongue is exceeding pure so that it has in purity what it wants in
music.

For he is docile and can learn certain things.

For he can sit up with gravity, which is patience upon approbation.

For he can fetch and carry, which is patience in employment.

For he can jump over a stick, which is patience upon proof positive.

750 For he can spraggle upon waggle at the word of command.

For he can jump from an eminence into his master's bosom.

For he can catch the cork and toss it again.

For he is hated by the hypocrite and miser.

For the former is afraid of detection.

755 For the latter refuses the charge.

For he camels his back to bear the first notion of business.

For he is good to think on, if a man would express himself neatly.

For he made a great figure in Egypt for his signal services.

For he killed the Icneumon rat, very pernicious by land.[6]

---

4. Smart apparently thinks of Jeoffry as an immature or diminutive phase of a larger creature—cherubs being by artistic convention small and childlike.

5. The Israelites took with them silver and gold ornaments and raiment, as well as flocks and herds (Exodus xi.2 and xii.32,35). Smart adds the cats.

6. The rats encountered by Jeoffry may have impressed Smart as resembling mongooses (one sense of *ichneumon*); or there may be some reference to the ichneumon fly, a wasplike insect parasitic upon caterpillers.

760 For his ears are so acute that they sting again.
For from this proceeds the passing quickness of his attention.
For by stroking of him I have found out electricity.
For I perceived God's light about him both wax and fire.
For the electrical fire is the spiritual substance which God sends from heaven
    to sustain the bodies both of man and beast.
765 For God has blessed him in the variety of his movements.
For, though he cannot fly, he is an excellent clamberer.
For his motions upon the face of the earth are more than any other
    quadruped.
For he can tread to all the measures upon the music.
For he can swim for life.
780 For he can creep.

                          ca. 1760   1939

OLIVER GOLDSMITH
(1730–1774)

When Lovely Woman Stoops to Folly

When lovely woman stoops to folly,
    And finds too late that men betray,
What charm can soothe her melancholy,
    What art can wash her guilt away?

5 The only art her guilt to cover,
    To hide her shame from every eye,
To give repentance to her lover,
    And wring his bosom—is to die.

                                    1766

WILLIAM COWPER
(1731–1800)

From Olney Hymns

14. Jehovah-Shammah[1] (Ezekiel xlviii.35)

As birds their infant brood protect,[2]
And spread their wings to shelter them;
Thus saith the Lord to his elect,
"So will I guard Jerusalem."

5 And what then is Jerusalem,
This darling object of his care?
Where is its worth in God's esteem?
Who built it? who inhabits there?

Jehovah founded it in blood,
10 The blood of his incarnate Son;
There dwell the saints, once foes to God,
The sinners, whom he calls his own.

---

1. Translated (in Ezekiel xlviii.35 and in line 19 below), "The Lord is there."

2. Cowper notes that this simile is from Isaiah xxxi.5.

There, though besieged on every side,
Yet much beloved and guarded well;
15 From age to age they have defied
The utmost force of earth and hell.

Let earth repent, and hell despair,
This city has a sure defence;
Her name is called. The Lord is there,
20 And who has power to drive him thence?

                        ca. 1772   1779

67. I Will Praise the Lord at All Times

Winter has a joy for me,
While the Saviour's charms I read,
Lowly, meek, from blemish free,
In the snowdrop's pensive head.

5 Spring returns, and brings along
Life-invigorating suns:
Hark! the turtle's° plaintive song   *turtledove's*
Seems to speak his dying groans!

Summer has a thousand charms,
10 All expressive of his worth;
'Tis his sun that lights and warms,
His the air that cools the earth.

What! has autumn left to say
Nothing of a Saviour's grace?
15 Yes, the beams of milder day
Tell me of his smiling face.

Light appears with early dawn,
While the sun makes haste to rise,
See his bleeding beauties, drawn
20 On the blushes of the skies.

Evening, with a silent pace,
Slowly moving in the west,
Shows an emblem of his grace,
Points to an eternal rest.

                                   1779

Epitaph on a Hare

Here lies, whom hound did ne'er pursue,
    Nor swifter greyhound follow,
Whose foot ne'er tainted morning dew,
    Nor ear heard huntsman's hallo',

5 Old Tiney, surliest of his kind,
    Who, nursed with tender care,
And to domestic bounds confined,
    Was still a wild jack-hare.

Though duly from my hand he took
10   His pittance every night,
He did it with a jealous look,
    And, when he could, would bite.

His diet was of wheaten bread,
  And milk, and oats, and straw,
15 Thistles, or lettuces instead,
  With sand to scour his maw.

On twigs of hawthorn he regaled,°   *feasted*
  On pippins' russet peel;
And, when his juicy salads failed,
20   Sliced carrot pleased him well.

A Turkey carpet was his lawn,[3]
  Whereon he loved to bound,
To skip and gambol like a fawn,
  And swing his rump around.

25 His frisking was at evening hours,
  For then he lost his fear;
But most before approaching showers,
  Or when a storm drew near.

Eight years and five round-rolling moons
30   He thus saw steal away,
Dozing out all his idle noons,
  And every night at play.

I kept him for his humor's sake,
  For he would oft beguile
35 My heart of thoughts that made it ache,
  And force me to a smile.

But now, beneath this walnut-shade
  He finds his long, last home,
And waits in snug concealment laid,
40   Till gentler Puss shall come.

He,[4] still more agéd, feels the shocks
  From which no care can save,
And, partner once of Tiney's box,
  Must soon partake his grave.

                              1783   1784

From The Task[5]

From *Book I: The Sofa*

I sing the Sofa. I, who lately sang
Truth, Hope, and Charity,[6] and touched with awe
The solemn chords, and with a trembling hand,
Escaped with pain from that adventurous flight,
5 Now seek repose upon an humbler theme;
The theme though humble, yet august and proud
The occasion—for the fair commands the song.
   Time was, when clothing sumptuous or for use,
Save their own painted skins, our sires had none.
10 As yet black breeches were not; satin smooth,
Or velvet soft, or plush with shaggy pile:
The hardy chief upon the rugged rock

3. Cowper exercised his hares on his parlor carpet of Turkey red.
4. Puss, the longest-lived of Cowper's three hares.
5. So called because, when he complained of the want of a poetic topic, a friend, Lady Austen (the "fair" of line 7), set him the task of writing about the parlor sofa. The completed work, of which some one-quarter of the first book is here printed, ran to six books and ranged over a diversity of subjects.
6. Topics of poems in an earlier volume.

Washed by the sea, or on the gravelly bank
Thrown up by wintry torrents roaring loud,
15   Fearless of wrong, reposed his weary strength.
Those barbarous ages past, succeeded next
The birthday of invention; weak at first,
Dull in design, and clumsy to perform.
Joint-stools were then created; on three legs
20   Upborn they stood. Three legs upholding firm
A massy slab, in fashion square or round.
On such a stool immortal Alfred sat,[7]
And swayed the scepter of his infant realms:
And such in ancient halls and mansions drear
25   May still be seen; but perforated sore,
And drilled in holes, the solid oak is found,
By worms voracious eating through and through.
    At length a generation more refined
Improved the simple plan; made three legs four,
30   Gave them a twisted form vermicular,°   *worm-shaped*
And o'er the seat, with plenteous wadding stuffed,
Induced° a splendid cover, green and blue,   *drew*
Yellow and red, of tapestry richly wrought,
And woven close, or needle-work sublime.
35   There might ye see the peony spread wide,
The full-blown rose, the shepherd and his lass,
Lapdog and lambkin with black staring eyes,
And parrots with twin cherries in their beak.
    Now came the cane from India, smooth and bright
40   With Nature's varnish; severed into stripes
That interlaced each other, these supplied
Of texture firm a lattice-work, that braced
The new machine, and it became a chair.
But restless was the chair; the back erect
45   Distressed the weary loins, that felt no ease;
The slippery seat betrayed the sliding part
That pressed it, and the feet hung dangling down,
Anxious in vain to find the distant floor.
These for the rich: the rest, whom fate had placed
50   In modest mediocrity,[8] content
With base materials, sat on well-tanned hides,
Obdúrate and unyielding, glassy smooth,
With here and there a tuft of crimson yarn,
Or scarlet crewel,[9] in the cushion fixt;
55   If cushion might be called, what harder seemed
Than the firm oak of which the frame was formed.
No want of timber then was felt or feared
In Albion's happy isle. The lumber stood
Pond'rous and fixt by its own massy° weight.   *massive*
60   But elbows still were wanting; these, some say,
An alderman of Cripplegate contrived:
And some ascribe the invention to a priest
Burly and big, and studious of his ease.
But, rude at first, and not with easy slope
65   Receding wide, they pressed against the ribs,
And bruised the side; and, elevated high,
Taught the raised shoulders to invade the ears.
Long time elapsed or e'er our rugged sires
Complained, though incommodiously pent in,
7°   And ill at ease behind. The ladies first
'Gan murmur, as became the softer sex.

---

7. Alfred the Great (849–901) sat on such a   8. Middling income.
stool while hiding from the Danes in a peas-   9. Loosely wound worsted.
ant's cottage.

Ingenious fancy, never better pleased
Than when employed to accommodate the fair,
Heard the sweet moan with pity, and devised
75 The soft settee; one elbow at each end,
And in the midst an elbow it received,
United yet divided, twain at once.
So sit two kings of Brentford on one throne;[1]
And so two citizens who take the air,
80 Close packed, and smiling, in a chaise and one.[2]
But relaxation of the languid frame,
By soft recumbency of outstretched limbs,
Was bliss reserved for happier days. So slow
The growth of what is excellent; so hard
85 To attain perfection in this nether world.
Thus first necessity invented stools,
Convenience next suggested elbow-chairs,
And luxury the accomplished Sofa last.
        The nurse sleeps sweetly, hired to watch the sick,
90 Whom snoring she disturbs. As sweetly he
Who quits the coach-box at the midnight hour
To sleep within the carriage more secure,
His legs depending at the open door.
Sweet sleep enjoys the curate in his desk,
95 The tedious rector drawling o'er his head;
And sweet the clerk below.[3] But neither sleep
Of lazy nurse, who snores the sick man dead,
Nor his who quits the box at midnight hour
To slumber in the carriage more secure,
100 Nor sleep enjoyed by curate in his desk,
Nor yet the dozings of the clerk, are sweet,
Compared with the repose the Sofa yields.
        Oh may I live exempted (while I live
Guiltless of pampered appetite obscene)
105 From pangs arthritic, that infest the toe
Of libertine excess. The Sofa suits
The gouty limb, 'tis true; but gouty limb,
Though on a Sofa, may I never feel:
For I have loved the rural walk through lanes
110 Of grassy swarth,° close cropt by nibbling sheep,   *sward*
And skirted thick with intertexture firm
Of thorny boughs; have loved the rural walk
O'er hills, through valleys, and by rivers' brink,
E'er since a truant boy I passed my bounds
115 To enjoy a ramble on the banks of Thames;
And still remember, nor without regret
Of hours that sorrow since has much endeared,
How oft, my slice of pocket store consumed,
Still hungering, penniless and far from home,
120 I fed on scarlet hips and stony haws,
Or blushing crabs,[4] or berries, that emboss
The bramble, black as jet, or sloes austere.
Hard fare! but such as boyish appetite
Disdains not; nor the palate, undepraved
125 By culinary arts, unsavory deems.
No Sofa then awaited my return;
Nor Sofa then I needed. Youth repairs
His wasted spirits quickly, by long toil

---

1. In the Duke of Buckingham's burlesque play *The Rehearsal* (1672).
2. "Chaise and one": one-horse shay.
3. While the rector drones on, his clerical assistant (the curate) sleeps behind the lectern opposite the pulpit ("in his desk"), and the lay assistant (the clerk) sleeps in the front pew beneath. This verse paragraph is a parody of Eve's lyrical expression of joy in the creation and in Adam (*Paradise Lost* IV.641–56).
4. Hips are fruits of the rosebush, haw of the hawthorn, and crab of the crab-apple.

Incurring short fatigue; and, though our years
130 As life declines speed rapidly away,
And not a year but pilfers as he goes
Some youthful grace that age would gladly keep;
A tooth or auburn lock, and by degrees
Their length and color from the locks they spare;
135 The elastic spring of an unwearied foot
That mounts the stile with ease, or leaps the fence,
That play of lungs, inhaling and again
Respiring freely the fresh air, that makes
Swift pace or steep ascent no toil to me,
140 Mine have not pilfered yet; nor yet impaired
My relish of fair prospect; scenes that soothed
Or charmed me young, no longer young, I find
Still soothing and of power to charm me still.
And witness, dear companion of my walks,[5]
145 Whose arm this twentieth winter I perceive
Fast locked in mine, with pleasure such as love,
Confirmed by long experience of thy worth
And well-tried virtues, could alone inspire—
Witness a joy that thou hast doubled long.
150 Thou know'st my praise of nature most sincere,
And that my raptures are not conjured up
To serve occasions of poetic pomp,
But genuine, and art partner of them all.
How oft upon yon eminence our pace
155 Has slackened to a pause, and we have borne
The ruffling wind, scarce conscious that it blew,
While admiration, feeding at the eye,
And still unsated, dwelt upon the scene.
Thence with what pleasure have we just discerned
160 The distant plough slow moving, and beside
His laboring team, that swerved not from the track,
The sturdy swain diminished to a boy!
Here Ouse, slow winding through a level plain
Of spacious meads with cattle sprinkled o'er,
165 Conducts the eye along its sinuous course
Delighted. There, fast rooted in his bank,
Stand, never overlooked, our favorite elms,
That screen the herdsman's solitary hut;
While far beyond, and overthwart the stream
170 That, as with molten glass, inlays the vale,
The sloping land recedes into the clouds;
Displaying on its varied side the grace
Of hedgerow beauties numberless, square tower,
Tall spire, from which the sound of cheerful bells
175 Just undulates upon the listening ear,
Groves, heaths, and smoking villages, remote.
Scenes must be beautiful, which, daily viewed,
Please daily, and whose novelty survives
Long knowledge and the scrutiny of years.
180 Praise justly due to those that I describe.
    Nor rural sights alone, but rural sounds,
Exhilarate the spirit, and restore
The tone of languid Nature. Mighty winds,
That sweep the skirt of some far-spreading wood
185 Of ancient growth, make music not unlike
The dash of ocean on his winding shore,
And lull the spirit while they fill the mind;

5. Mary Unwin, a devoted friend of many years whom only his fits of insanity (it is thought) kept him from marrying. The scenes described below recall their walks between the localities of Weston and Olney.

Unnumbered branches waving in the blast,
And all their leaves fast fluttering, all at once.
190 Nor less composure waits upon the roar
Of distant floods, or on the softer voice
Of neighboring fountain, or of rills that slip
Through the cleft rock, and, chiming as they fall
Upon loose pebbles, lose themselves at length
195 In matted grass, that with a livelier green
Betrays the secret of their silent course.
Nature inanimate employs sweet sounds,
But animated nature sweeter still,
To soothe and satisfy the human ear.
200 Ten thousand warblers cheer the day, and one
The live-long night: nor these alone, whose notes
Nice-fingered art must emulate in vain,
But cawing rooks, and kites that swim sublime°   *aloft*
In still repeated circles, screaming loud,
205 The jay, the pie, and even the boding owl
That hails the rising moon, have charms for me.
Sounds inharmonious in themselves and harsh,
Yet heard in scenes where peace forever reigns,
And only there, please highly for their sake.

                                          1783   1785

The Castaway

Obscurest night involved the sky,
    The Atlantic billows roared,
When such a destined wretch as I,
    Washed headlong from on board,
5 Of friends, of hope, of all bereft,
His floating home forever left.

No braver chief could Albion boast
    Than he with whom he went,[6]
Nor ever ship left Albion's coast,
10   With warmer wishes sent.
He loved them both, but both in vain,
Nor him beheld, nor her again.

Not long beneath the whelming brine,
    Expert to swim, he lay;
15 Nor soon he felt his strength decline,
    Or courage die away;
But waged with death a lasting strife,
Supported by despair of life.

He shouted; nor his friends had failed
20   To check the vessel's course,
But so the furious blast prevailed,
    That, pitiless perforce,
They left their outcast mate behind,
And scudded still before the wind.

25 Some succor yet they could afford;
    And, such as storms allow,
The cask, the coop, the floated cord,
    Delayed not to bestow.
But he (they knew) nor ship, nor shore,
30 Whate'er they gave, should visit more.

---

6. Namely, George, Lord Anson, who told the castaway's story in his *Voyage Round the World* (1748).

Nor, cruel as it seemed, could he
　　Their haste himself condemn,
Aware that flight, in such a sea,
　　Alone could rescue them;
35　Yet bitter felt it still to die
Deserted, and his friends so nigh.

He long survives, who lives an hour
　　In ocean, self-upheld;
And so long he, with unspent power,
40　　His destiny repelled;
And ever, as the minutes flew,
Entreated help, or cried, "Adieu!"

At length, his transient respite past,
　　His comrades, who before
45　Had heard his voice in every blast,
　　Could catch the sound no more.
For then, by toil subdued, he drank
The stifling wave, and then he sank.

No poet wept him; but the page
50　　Of narrative sincere,
That tells his name, his worth, his age,
　　Is wet with Anson's tear.
And tears by bards or heroes shed
Alike immortalize the dead.

55　I therefore purpose not, or dream,
　　Descanting on his fate,
To give the melancholy theme
　　A more enduring date:
But misery still delights to trace
60　Its semblance in another's case.

No voice divine the storm allayed,
　　No light propitious shone,
When, snatched from all effectual aid,
　　We perished, each alone;
65　But I beneath a rougher sea,
And whelmed in deeper gulfs than he.

　　　　　　　　　　　　　　1799　　　　1803

WILLIAM BLAKE
(1757–1827)

From POETICAL SKETCHES

To the Muses[1]

Whether on Ida's[2] shady brow,
　　Or in the chambers of the East,
The chambers of the sun, that now
　　From antient melody have ceas'd;

---

1. Nine goddesses who, in Greek myth, preside over the arts and sciences, especially poetry.

2. Mountain in Asia Minor, distant from the mountains sacred to the Muses (Helicon and Parnassus) in Greece.

5   Whether in Heav'n ye wander fair,
         Or the green corners of the earth,
     Or the blue regions of the air,
         Where the melodious winds have birth;

     Whether on chrystal rocks ye rove,
10   Beneath the bosom of the sea
     Wand'ring in many a coral grove,
         Fair Nine, forsaking Poetry!

     How have you left the antient love
         That bards of old enjoy'd in you!
15   The languid strings do scarcely move!
         The sound is forc'd, the notes are few!

                                                            1783

Song

     How sweet I roam'd from field to field,
         And tasted all the summer's pride,
     'Till I the prince of love beheld,
         Who in the sunny beams did glide!

5   He shew'd me lilies for my hair,
         And blushing roses for my brow;
     He led me through his gardens fair,
         Where all his golden pleasures grow.

     With sweet May dews my wings were wet,
10   And Phoebus fir'd my vocal rage;[3]
     He caught me in his silken net,
         And shut me in his golden cage.

     He loves to sit and hear me sing,
         Then, laughing, sports and plays with me;
15   Then stretches out my golden wing,
         And mocks my loss of liberty.

                                                            1783

To the Evening Star

     Thou fair-hair'd angel of the evening,
     Now, while the sun rests on the mountains, light
     Thy bright torch of love; thy radiant crown
     Put on, and smile upon our evening bed!
5   Smile on our loves; and, while thou drawest the
     Blue curtains of the sky, scatter thy silver dew
     On every flower that shuts its sweet eyes
     In timely sleep. Let thy west wind sleep on
     The lake; speak silence with thy glimmering eyes,
10   And wash the dusk with silver. Soon, full soon,
     Dost thou withdraw; then the wolf rages wide,
     And the lion glares thro' the dun forest:
     The fleeces of our flocks are cover'd with
     Thy sacred dew: protect them with thin influence.[4]

                                                            1783

3. Impassioned song. Phoebus is Apollo, god of poetic inspiration.   4. In astrology, the effect that heavenly bodies exert on earthly things and creatures.

From SONGS OF INNOCENCE

The Lamb

Little Lamb, who made thee?
Dost thou know who made thee?
Gave thee life & bid thee feed,
By the stream & o'er the mead;
5   Gave thee clothing of delight,
Softest clothing wooly bright;
Gave thee such a tender voice,
Making all the vales rejoice!
   Little Lamb who made thee?
10 Dost thou know who made thee?

   Little Lamb I'll tell thee,
   Little Lamb I'll tell thee!
He° is calléd by thy name,   *Christ*
For he calls himself a Lamb:
15 He is meek & he is mild,
He became a little child:
I a child & thou a lamb,
We are calléd by his name.
   Little Lamb God bless thee.
20 Little Lamb God bless thee.

                         1789

Holy Thursday [I.]

'Twas on a Holy Thursday,[5] their innocent faces clean,
The children[6] walking two & two, in red & blue & green,
Grey headed beadles[7] walkd before with wands as white as snow,
Till into the high dome of Paul's they like Thames' waters flow.

5 O what a multitude they seemd, these flowers of London town!
Seated in companies they sit with radiance all their own
The hum of multitudes was there, but multitudes of lambs,
Thousands of little boys & girls raising their innocent hands.

Now like a mighty wind they raise to heaven the voice of song,
10 Or like harmonious thunderings the seats of heaven among.
Beneath them sit the aged men, wise guardians of the poor;
Then cherish pity, lest you drive an angel from your door.

                         1789

The Little Black Boy

My mother bore me in the southern wild,
And I am black, but O! my soul is white;
White as an angel is the English child:
But I am black as if bereav'd of light.

5 My mother taught me underneath a tree,
And sitting down before the heat of day,
She took me on her lap and kisséd me,
And pointing to the east, began to say:

5. Probably Ascension Day (40 days after Easter).
6. Here the children of charity schools are depicted in St. Paul's Cathedral, London.
7. Ushers charged with keeping order.

"Look on the rising sun: there God does live,
10 And gives his light, and gives his heat away;
And flowers and trees and beasts and men receive
Comfort in morning, joy in the noon day.

"And we are put on earth a little space,
That we may learn to bear the beams of love,
15 And these black bodies and this sun-burnt face
Is but a cloud, and like a shady grove.

"For when our souls have learn'd the heat to bear,
The cloud will vanish; we shall hear his voice,
Saying: 'Come out from the grove, my love & care,
20 And round my golden tent like lambs rejoice.' "

Thus did my mother say, and kisséd me;
And thus I say to little English boy:
When I from black and he from white cloud free,
And round the tent of God like lambs we joy,

25 I'll shade him from the heat till he can bear
To lean in joy upon our father's knee;
And then I'll stand and stroke his silver hair,
And be like him, and he will then love me.

1789

From Songs of Experience

Holy Thursday [II.]

Is this a holy thing to see,
In a rich and fruitful land,
Babes reducd to misery,
Fed with cold and usurous hand?

5 Is that trembling cry a song?
Can it be a song of joy?
And so many children poor?
It is a land of poverty!

And their sun does never shine,
10 And their fields and bleak & bare,
And their ways are fill'd with thorns;
It is eternal winter there.

For where-e'er the sun does shine,
And where-e'er rain does fall,
15 Babe can never hunger there,
Nor poverty the mind appall.

1794

The Sick Rose

O Rose, thou art sick.
The invisible worm
That flies in the night
In the howling storm

5   Has found out thy bed
Of crimson joy,
And his dark secret love
Does thy life destroy.

1794

A Poison Tree

I was angry with my friend:
I told my wrath, my wrath did end.
I was angry with my foe:
I told it not, my wrath did grow.

5   And I waterd it in fears,
Night & morning with my tears;
And I sunnéd it with smiles,
And with soft deceitful wiles.

And it grew both day and night,
10   Till it bore an apple bright.
And my foe beheld it shine,
And he knew that it was mine,

And into my garden stole,
When the night had veild the pole;
15   In the morning glad I see
My foe outstretchd beneath the tree.

1794

The Tyger

Tyger! Tyger! burning bright
In the forests of the night,
What immortal hand or eye
Could frame thy fearful symmetry?

5   In what distant deeps or skies
Burnt the fire of thine eyes?
On what wings dare he aspire?
What the hand, dare seize the fire?

10   And what shoulder, & what art,
Could twist the sinews of thy heart?
And when thy heart began to beat,
What dread hand? & what dread feet?

What the hammer? what the chain?
In what furnace was thy brain?
15   What the anvil? what dread grasp
Dare its deadly terrors clasp?

When the stars threw down their spears,
And water'd heaven with their tears,
Did he smile his work to see?
20   Did he who made the Lamb make thee?

Tyger! Tyger! burning bright
In the forests of the night,
What immortal hand or eye
Dare frame thy fearful symmetry?

1794

Ah Sun-flower

Ah Sun-flower! weary of time,
Who countest the steps of the Sun,
Seeking after that sweet golden clime
Where the traveller's journey is done;

5   Where the Youth pined away with desire,
And the pale Virgin shrouded in snow,
Arise from their graves and aspire,
Where my Sun-flower wishes to go.

1794

The Garden of Love

I went to the Garden of Love,
And saw what I never had seen:
A Chapel was built in the midst,
Where I used to play on the green.

5   And the gates of this Chapel were shut,
And "Thou shalt not" writ over the door;
So I turn'd to the Garden of Love,
That so many sweet flowers bore,

And I saw it was filled with graves,
10   And tomb-stones where flowers should be:
And Priests in black gowns were walking their rounds,
And binding with briars my joys & desires.

1794

London

I wander thro' each charter'd[8] street,
Near where the charter'd Thames does flow,
And mark in every face I meet
Marks of weakness, marks of woe.

5   In every cry of every man,
In every Infant's cry of fear,
In every voice, in every ban,[9]
The mind-forg'd manacles I hear.

How the Chimney-sweeper's cry
10   Every blackning Church appalls;
And the hapless Soldier's sigh
Runs in blood down Palace walls.

But most thro' midnight streets I hear
How the youthful Harlot's curse
15   Blasts the new-born Infant's tear,
And blights with plagues the Marriage hearse.

1794

8. Mapped out, legally defined, constricted.   9. A law or notice commanding or forbidding;
a published penalty.

From SONGS AND BALLADS

I Askéd a Thief

I askéd a thief to steal me a peach,
He turned up his eyes;
I ask'd a lithe lady to lie her down,
Holy & meek she cries.

5   As soon as I went
An angel came.
He wink'd at the thief
And smild at the dame—

And without one word said
10 Had a peach from the tree
And still as a maid
Enjoy'd the lady.

1796   1863

Mock on, Mock on, Voltaire, Rousseau

Mock on, Mock on, Voltaire, Rousseau;[1]
Mock on, Mock on, 'tis all in vain.
You throw the sand against the wind,
And the wind blows it back again.

5   And every sand becomes a Gem
Reflected in the beams divine;
Blown back, they blind the mocking Eye,
But still in Israel's paths they shine.

The Atoms of Democritus
10 And Newton's Particles of light[2]
Are sands upon the Red sea shore,[3]
Where Israel's tents do shine so bright.

1800–08   1863

From MILTON

And Did Those Feet

And did those feet in ancient time
Walk upon England's mountains green?
And was the holy Lamb of God
On England's pleasant pastures seen?

5   And did the Countenance Divine
Shine forth upon our clouded hills?
And was Jerusalem builded here,
Among these dark Satanic Mills?[4]

1. Leaders of the pre-Revolutionary French "Enlightenment"; critics of the established order, here representing thinkers who destroy without creating.
2. Democritus (Greek philosopher, fifth century B.C.) and Sir Isaac Newton (1642–1727), both represented as nonsensically reducing nature to inanimate matter.
3. Where God delivered the Israelites from the Egyptians (Exodus xiv).
4. The primary meaning is "millstone"—two heavy cylindrical stones that grind grain into meal between them; "factory" is an extended meaning.

Bring me my Bow of burning gold:
10 Bring me my Arrows of desire:
Bring me my Spear: O clouds unfold!
Bring me my Chariot of fire!

I will not cease from Mental Fight,
Nor shall my Sword sleep in my hand,
15 Till we have built Jerusalem
In England's green & pleasant Land.

1804–10

From JERUSALEM

England! Awake! Awake! Awake!

England! awake! awake! awake!
  Jerusalem thy Sister calls!
Why wilt thou sleep the sleep of death?
  And close her from thy ancient walls.

5   Thy hills & valleys felt her feet,
                        Gently upon their bosoms move:
                    Thy gates beheld sweet Zions ways;
                        Then was a time of joy and love.

And now the time returns again:
10   Our souls exult & Londons towers,
    Receive the Lamb of God to dwell
        In Englands green & pleasant bowers.

1804–09   1818

From FOR THE SEXES: *The Gates of Paradise*

To The Accuser who is
The God of This World[5]

Truly My Satan thou art but a Dunce,
And dost not know the Garment from the Man;
Every Harlot was a Virgin once,
Nor canst thou ever change Kate into Nan.

5   Tho thou are Worshipd by the Names Divine
Of Jesus & Jehovah: thou art still
The Son of Morn in weary Night's decline,
The lost Traveller's Dream under the Hill.

1793–1818

5. God conceived of as a harsh taskmaster and merciless judge; Blake rejected this concept as "Satanic."

ROBERT BURNS
(1759–1796)

To a Mouse

ON TURNING HER UP IN HER NEST WITH THE PLOUGH,
NOVEMBER, 1785

Wee, sleekit,° cow'rin, tim'rous beastie,   *sleek*
O, what a panic's in thy breastie!
Thou need na start awa sae hasty,
          Wi' bickering° brattle!°   *hurried / scamper*
5 I wad be laith to rin an' chase thee,
          Wi' murd'ring pattle!°   *plowstaff ("paddle")*

I'm truly sorry man's dominion
Has broken Nature's social union,
An' justifies that ill opinion
10   Which makes thee startle
At me, thy poor earth-born companion,
          An' fellow-mortal!

I doubt na, whiles,° but thou may thieve;   *sometimes*
What then? poor beastie, thou maun° live!   *must*
15 A daimen° icker° in a thrave°   *random / corn-ear / shock*
          'S a sma' request:
I'll get a blessin wi' the lave,°   *rest*
          And never miss't!

Thy wee bit housie, too, in ruin!
20 Its silly° wa's the win's are strewin!   *frail*
An' naething, now, to big° a new ane,   *build*
          O' foggage° green!   *mosses*
An' bleak December's winds ensuin,
          Baith snell° an' keen!   *bitter*

25 Thou saw the fields laid bare and waste,
An' weary winter comin fast,
An' cozie here, beneath the blast,
          Thou thought to dwell,
Till crash! the cruel coulter° past   *plowshare*
30   Out thro' thy cell.

That wee bit heap o' leaves an' stibble°   *stubble*
Has cost thee mony a weary nibble!
Now thou's turned out, for a' thy trouble,
          But° house or hald,°   *without / home ("hold")*
35 To thole° the winter's sleety dribble,   *endure*
          An' cranreuch° cauld!   *hoarfrost*

But, Mousie, thou art no thy lane,[1]
In proving foresight may be vain:
The best laid schemes o' mice an' men
40   Gang° aft a-gley.°   *go / astray*
An' lea'e us nought but grief an' pain
          For promised joy.

---

1. "No thy lane": not alone.

Still thou art blest, compared wi' me!
The present only toucheth thee:
45   But och! I backward cast my e'e
                On prospects drear!
An' forward, tho' I canna see,
                I guess an' fear!

1785, 1786

Holy Willie's² Prayer

O Thou, wha in the heavens dost dwell,
Wha, as it pleases best thysel',
Sends ane to heaven and ten to hell,
                A' for thy glory,
5   And no for ony guid or ill
                They've done afore thee!

I bless and praise thy matchless might,
Whan thousands thou hast left in night,
That I am here afore thy sight,
10   For gifts an' grace
A burnin' an' a shinin' light,
                To a' this place.

What was I, or my generation,
That I should get sic exaltation?
15   I, wha deserve most just damnation,
                For broken laws,
Sax thousand years 'fore my creation,
                Thro' Adam's cause.

When frae my mither's womb I fell,
20   Thou might hae plungéd me in hell,
To gnash my gums, to weep and wail,
                In burnin lakes,
Where damnéd devils roar and yell,
                Chained to their stakes;

25   Yet I am here a chosen sample,
To show thy grace is great and ample;
I'm here a pillar in thy temple,
                Strong as a rock,
A guide, a buckler, an example
30   To a' thy flock.

O Lord, thou kens what zeal I bear,
When drinkers drink, and swearers swear.
And singin' there and dancin' here,
                Wi' great an' sma':
35   For I am keepit by thy fear
                Free frae them a'.

But yet, O Lord! confess I must
At times I'm fashed° wi' fleshy lust;   *troubled*
An' sometimes too, wi' warldly trust,
40   Vile self gets in;
But thou remembers we are dust,
                Defiled in sin.

2. One William Fisher, an elder in the church at Mauchline, the seat of Burns's farm. He habitually censured other men's behavior and doctrine, but was himself rebuked for drunkenness and was suspected of stealing church funds.

O Lord! yestreen,° thou kens, wi' Meg—   *last night*
Thy pardon I sincerely beg;
45   O! may't ne'er be a livin' plague
                To my dishonour,
An' I'll ne'er lift a lawless leg
                Again upon her.

Besides I farther maun allow,
50   Wi' Lizzie's lass, three times I trow—
But, Lord, that Friday I was fou,°   *full (of liquor)*
                When I cam near her,
Or else thou kens thy servant true
                Wad never steer° her   *touch ("stir")*

55   May be thou lets this fleshly thorn
Beset thy servant e'en and morn
Lest he owre high and proud should turn,
                That he's sae gifted;
If sae, thy hand maun e'en be borne,
60   Until thou lift it.

Lord, bless thy chosen in this place,
For here thou hast a chosen race;
But God confound their stubborn face,
                And blast their name,
65   Wha bring thy elders to disgrace
                An' public shame.

Lord, mind Gawn Hamilton's³ deserts,
He drinks, an' swears, an' plays at cartes,
Yet has sae mony takin arts
70   Wi' great an' sma',
Frae God's ain priest the people's hearts
                He steals awa'.

An' when we chastened him therefor,
Thou kens how he bred sic a splorc°   *row*
75   As set the warld in a roar
                O' laughin' at us;
Curse thou his basket and his store,
                Kail° and potatoes.   *cabbage*

Lord, hear my earnest cry an' pray'r,
80   Against that presbytery o' Ayr;
Thy strong right hand, Lord, make it bare
                Upo' their heads;
Lord, weigh it down, and dinna spare,
                For their misdeeds.

85   O Lord my God, that glib-tongued Aiken,
My very heart and soul are quakin',
To think how we stood sweatin, shakin,
                An' pissed wi' dread,
While he, wi' hingin° lips and snakin,°   *hanging / sneering*
90   Held up his head.

---

3. Gavin Hamilton, a convivial lawyer friend
of Burns's. Accused of Sabbath-breaking and
other offenses by the elders of Mauchline
church, he was cleared by the Presbytery of
Ayr (line 80) with the help of his counsel
Robert Aiken (line 85).

Lord in the day of vengeance try him;
Lord, visit them wha did employ him,
And pass not in thy mercy by them,
    Nor hear their pray'r:
95 But, for thy people's sake, destroy them,
    And dinna spare.

But, Lord, remember me and mine
Wi' mercies temp'ral and divine,
That I for gear° and grace may shine   *wealth*
100   Excelled by nane,
And a' the glory shall be thine,
    Amen, Amen!

                  1785   1808

The Jolly Beggars[4]

A CANTATA RECITATIVO

When lyart° leaves bestrow the yird,°   *faded / earth*
Or, wavering like the bauckie-bird,°   *bat*
  Bedim cauld Boreas' blast;
When hailstanes drive wi' bitter skyte,°   *rush*
5 And infant frosts begin to bite,
    In hoary cranreuch° drest;   *frost*
Ae night at e'en a merry core°   *company*
  O' randie,° gangrel° bodies   *rough / vagabond*
In Poosie Nansie's held the splore,°   *spree*
10 To drink their orra duddies:[5]
    Wi' quaffing and laughing,
      They ranted and they sang,
    Wi' jumping and thumping
      The very girdle° rang.   *griddle*

15 First, niest the fire, in auld red rags
Ane sat, weel braced wi' mealy° bags   *meal*
  And knapsack a' in order;
His doxy° lay within his arm;   *girl*
Wi' usquebae° an blankets warm,   *whisky*
20 She blinket on her sodger;
An' aye he gies the tosy° drab   *tipsy*
  The tither° skelpin'° kiss,   *another / smacking*
While she held up her greedy gab,°   *mouth*
Just like an aumous dish:°   *alms-dish*
25   Ilk° smack still did crack still   *each*
      Just like a cadger's° whip;   *carrier's*
    Then staggering, and swaggering,
      He roared this ditty up:

      Air
      Tune: Soldier's Joy

I am a son of Mars, who have been in many wars,
30 And show my cuts and scars wherever I come:
This here was for a wench, and that other in a trench
  When welcoming the French at the sound of the drum.
              Lal de dauble . . .

---

4. The scene is "Poosie Nansie's," a brothel in Mauchline, Ayrshire, which served also as an inn and tavern for disreputable travelers.

5. I.e., to drink as long as they could offer spare clothing ("duds") in payment.

My 'prenticeship I passed, where my leader breathed his last,
   When the bloody die was cast on the heights of Abrám;[6]
35 And I servéd out my trade when the gallant game was played,
   And the Moro[7] low was laid at the sound of the drum.

I lastly was with Curtis, among the floating batt'ries,[8]
   And there I left for witness an arm and a limb;
40 Yet let my country need me, with Elliott[9] to head me
   I'd clatter on my stumps at the sound of a drum.

And now tho' I must beg with a wooden arm and leg
   And many a tattered rag hanging over my bum,
I'm as happy with my wallet, my bottle, and my callet°   *woman*
45 As when I used in scarlet to follow a drum.

What tho' with hoary locks I must stand the winter shocks,
   Beneath the woods and rocks oftentimes for a home?
When the t' other bag I sell, and the t' other bottle tell,°   *count*
   I could meet a troop of hell at the sound of the drum.

Recitativo

50 He ended; and the kebars° sheuk°	*rafters / shook*
Aboon the chorus roar;	
While frighted rattons° backward leuk,	*rats*
And seek the benmost° bore:°	*inmost / cranny*
A fairy° fiddler frae the neuk,	*"transported"*
55 He skirled° out *Encore!*	*shrilled*
But up arose the martial chuck,°	*lass ("chick")*
An laid the loud uproar:	

Air
Tune: Soldier Laddie

I once was a maid, tho' I cannot tell when,
And still my delight is in proper young men;
60 Some one of a troop of dragoons was my daddie,
No wonder I'm fond of a sodger laddie!
         Sing, Lal de dal . . .

The first of my loves was a swaggering blade,
To rattle the thundering drum was his trade;
65 His leg was so tight, and his cheek was so ruddy,
Transported I was with my sodger laddie.

But the godly old chaplain left him in the lurch,
The sword I forsook for the sake of the church;
He ventured the soul, and I riskéd the body,
70 'Twas then I proved false to my sodger laddie.

Full soon I grew sick of my sanctified sot,
The regiment at large for a husband I got;
From the gilded spontoon to the fife[1] I was ready.
I askéd no more but a sodger laddie.

75 But the peace it reduced me to beg in despair,
Till I met my old boy at a Cunningham fair;[2]
His rags regimental they fluttered so gaudy,
My heart it rejoiced at a sodger laddie.

6. Stormed when the British captured Quebec in 1759.
7. El Moro castle at Santiago de Cuba, captured in 1762.
8. Admiral Curtis destroyed the floating batteries of the French before Gibraltar in 1782.
9. Sir George Elliott, the heroic defender of Gibraltar from 1779 to 1783.
1. I.e., from officer to drum corpsman. The spontoon was an officer's short spear, a badge of rank.
2. A fair in the northern district of Ayrshire.

And now I have lived—I know not how long!
80 And still I can join in a cup or a song;
But whilst with both hands I can hold the glass steady,
Here's to thee, my hero, my sodger laddie!

Recitativo

Then niest° outspak a raucle° carlin,°   *next / coarse / old woman*
Wha kent° fu' weel to cleek° the sterling,[3]   *knew / snatch*
85 For mony a pursie she had hookéd,
And had in mony a well been doukéd.
Her love had been a Highland laddie,
But weary fa'° the waefu' woodie!°   *woe befall / gallows*
Wi' sighs and sobs, she thus began
90 To wail her braw° John Highlandman: *fine*

        Air
    Tune: O, An' Ye Were Dead, Guidman

A Highland lad my love was born,
The Lawlan' laws he held in scorn,
But he still was faithfu' to his clan,
My gallant, braw John Highlandman.

        chorus

95 Sing hey, my braw John Highlandman!
Sing ho, my braw John Highlandman!
There's no a lad in a' the lan'
Was match for my John Highlandman!

With his philibeg° an' tartan plaid,   *kilt*
100 And gude claymore° down by his side,   *sword*
The ladies' hearts he did trepan,°   *seduce*
My gallant, braw John Highlandman.

We rangéd a' from Tweed to Spey,[4]
And lived like lords and ladies gay,
105 For a Lawlan' face he feåréd none,
My gallant, braw John Highlandman.

They banished him beyond the sea,
But ere the bud was on the tree,
Adown my cheeks the pearls ran,
110 Embracing my John Highlandman.

But, Och! they catched him at the last,
And bound him in a dungeon fast.
My curse upon them every one—
They hanged my braw John Highlandman.

115 And now a widow, I must mourn
The pleasures that will ne'er return;
No comfort but a hearty can,
When I think on John Highlandman.

Recitativo

A pigmy scraper wi' his fiddle,
120 Wha used at trysts° and fairs to driddle,°   *markets / loiter*
Her strappin' limb and gawsie° middle   *buxom*
        (He reached nae higher)
Had holed his heartie like a riddle,°   *sieve*
        And blawn't on fire.

3. I.e., she picked pockets of silver coins.   4. From a southern river to a northern.

125 Wi' hand on hainch, and upward e'e,
    He crooned° his gamut, one, two, three,   *hummed*
    Then, in an arioso key,
            The wee Apollo
    Set aff, wi' allegretto glee,
130   His giga° solo.   *jigging*

                    Air
            Tune: Whistle Owre the Lave O't[5]

    Let me ryke° up to dight° that tear;   *reach / wipe*
    And go wi' me and be my dear,
    And then your every care and fear
        May whistle owre the lave o't.

                    chorus

135 I am a fiddler to my trade,
    And a' the tunes that e'er I played,
    The sweetest still to wife or maid
        Was *Whistle Owre the Lave O't.*

    At kirns° and weddings we'se be there,   *harvest-homes*
140 And O, sae nicely's we will fare!
    We'll bowse° about till Daddie Care   *booze*
        Sings *Whistle Owre the Lave O't.*

    Sae merrily's the banes we'll pyke,°   *pick*
    And sun oursels about the dyke;
145 And at our leisure, when ye like,
        We'll—whistle owre the lave o't!

    But bless me wi' your heav'n o' charms,
    And while I kittle° hair on thairms,°   *tickle / fiddle strings*
    Hunger, cauld, an a' sic harms,
150   May whistle owre the lave o't.

                    Recitativo

    Her charms had struck a sturdy caird,°   *tinker*
        As well as poor gut-scraper;
    He taks the fiddler by the beard,
        And draws a roosty rapier;
155 He swoor by a' was swearing worth
        To speet° him like a pliver,°   *spit / plover*
    Unless he would from that time forth
        Relinquish her for ever.

    Wi' ghastly ee, poor Tweedle-Dee
160   Upon his hunkers° bended,   *haunches*
    And prayed for grace wi' ruefu' face,
        And sae the quarrel ended.
    But tho' his little heart did grieve
        When round the tinkler prest her,
165 He feigned to snirtle° in his sleeve,   *snicker*
        When thus the caird addressed her:

                    Air
            Tune: Clout the Cauldron

    My bonie lass, I work in brass,
        A tinkler is my station;
    I've travelled round all Christian ground
170   In this my occupation;

5. "The Lave O't": the rest of it.

I've ta'en the gold[6] an' been enrolled
   In many a noble squadron;
But vain they searched, when off I marched
   To go and clout° the cauldron.   *patch*
175 Despise that shrimp, that withered imp,
   Wi' a' his noise and cap'rin,
And tak a share wi' those that bear
   The budget° and the apron!   *tool bag*
And by that stowp,° my faith and houpe!   *cup*
180   And by that dear Kilbaigie![7]
If e'er ye want, or meet wi' scant,
   May I ne'er weet my craigie!°   *throat*

     Recitativo

The caird prevailed: th' unblushing fair
   In his embraces sunk,
185 Partly wi' love o'ercome sae sair,°   *forcibly*
   An partly she was drunk.
Sir Violino, with an air
   That showed a man o' spunk,
Wished unison between the pair,
190   And made the bottle clunk
         To their health that night.

But hurchin° Cupid shot a shaft,   *urchin*
   That played a dame a shavie:°   *trick*
The fiddler raked her fore and aft,
195   Behint the chicken cavie.°   *coop*
Her lord, a wight of Homer's craft,
   Tho' limpin' wi' the spavie,°   *spavin*
He hirpled° up, and lap° like daft,° *limped / leaped / mad*
   And shored° them "Dainty Davie"[8]   *offered*
200   O' boot° that night.   *gratis*

He was a care-defying blade
   As ever Bacchus listed!°   *enlisted*
Tho' Fortune sair° upon him laid,   *sorely*
   His heart, she ever missed it.
205 He had nae wish but—to be glad,
   Nor want but—when he thirsted;
He hated nought but—to be sad,
   And thus the Muse suggested
         His sang that night.

     Air
     Tune: For A' That, An' A' That

210 I am a bard of no regard
   Wi' gentlefolks, and a' that,
But Homer-like, the glowrin° byke,° *staring / crowd*
   Frae town to town I draw that.

     chorus

For a' that, and a' that,
215   And twice as muckle's° a' that;   *much as*
I've lost but ane,[9] I've twa behin',
   I've wife eneugh for a' that.

---

6. The enlistment bonus.
7. A whisky.
8. "A bed together." The euphemism "Daintie Davie" recalls a 17th-century Scotsman, Mass

David Williamson, who escaped pursuing troopers by donning a feminine nightdress and sharing a woman's bed.
9. I.e., I've lost only one wife (to the fiddler).

I never drank the Muses' stank,°   pool
  Castalia's burn,° and a' that;   stream
220 But there it streams, and richly reams°—   foams
  My Helicon I ca' that.

Great love I bear to a' the fair,
  Their humble slave, and a' that;
But lordly will, I hold it still
225   A mortal sin to thraw° that.   thwart

In raptures sweet this hour we meet
  Wi' mutual love, and a' that;
But for how lang the flie may stang,
  Let inclination law° that.   determine

230 Their tricks and craft hae put me daft.
  They've ta'en me in, and a' that;
But clear your decks, an' here's the sex!
  I like the jads° for a' that.   jades

For a' that, and a' that,
235   And twice as muckle's a' that,
My dearest bluid, to do them guid,
  They're welcome till't,° for a' that!   to it

    Recitativo

So sung the bard, and Nansie's wa's
Shook with a thunder of applause,
240   Re-echoed from each mouth!
They toomed° their pocks,° an' pawned their duds,   emptied / pockets
They scarcely left to co'er their fuds,°   backsides
  To quench their lowin° drouth.   burning
Then owre° again the jovial thrang   over
245   The poet did request
To lowse° his pack, an' wale° a sang,   open / choose
  A ballad o' the best:
    He rising, rejoicing,
      Between his twa Deborahs,
250   Looks round him, an' found them
    Impatient for the chorus:

    Air
    Tune: Jolly Mortals, Fill Your Glasses

See the smoking bowl before us!
  Mark our jovial, ragged ring!
Round and round take up the chorus,
255   And in raptures let us sing:

    chorus

A fig for those by law protected!
  Liberty's a glorious feast,
Courts for cowards were erected,
  Churches built to please the priest!

260 What is title, what is treasure?
  What is reputation's care?
If we lead a life of pleasure,
  'Tis no matter how or where!

With the ready trick and fable
265   Round we wander all the day;
And at night, in barn or stable,
  Hug our doxies on the hay.

Does the train-attended carriage
    Thro' the country lighter rove?
270 Does the sober bed of marriage
    Witness brighter scenes of love?

Life is all a variorum,
    We regard not how it goes;
Let them cant about decorum
275   Who have characters to lose.

Here's to budgets,° bags, and wallets!	*satchels*
Here's to all the wandering train!	
Here's our ragged brats and callets!°	*women*
One and all, cry out, Amen!	

                              1785   1799

Of A' the Airts[1]

Of a' the airts° the wind can blaw,	*quarters*
I dearly like the west,	
For there the bonie lassie lives,	
The lassie I lo'e best:	
5 There's wild woods grow, and rivers row,°	*flow*
And mony a hill between;	
But day and night my fancy's flight	
Is ever wi' my Jean.	

I see her in the dewy flowers,	
10 I see her sweet and fair;	
I hear her in the tunefu' birds,	
I hear her charm the air:	
There's not a bonie flower that springs	
By fountain, shaw,° or green,	*wood*
15 There's not a bonie bird that sings,	
But minds me o' my Jean.	

                              1788   1790

Merry Hae I Been Teethin a Heckle

O merry hae I been teethin a heckle,°	*flax combs*
An' merry hae I been shapin a spoon:	
O merry hae I been cloutin° a kettle,	*patching*
An' kissin my Katie when a' was done.	
5 O, a' the lang day I ca,° at my hammer,	*knock*
An' a' the lang day I whistle and sing,	
O, a' the lang night I cuddle my kimmer,°	*lass*
An' a' the lang nights as happy's a king.	

Bitter in dool° I lickit my winnins[2]	*sorrow*
10 O' marrying Bess, to gie her a slave:	
Blest be the hour she cooled in her linnens,°	*shroud*
And blythe be the bird that sings on her grave!	

Come to my arms, my Katie, my Katie,	
An' come to my arms and kiss me again!	
15 Druken° or sober here's to thee, Katie!	*drunken*
And blest be the day I did it again.	

                                          1790

1. Written from Dumfriesshire to Burns's wife, Jean Armour, in Ayrshire, the county to the west.

2. "Licked my winnins": enjoyed what I had; made the best of bad luck.

Bonie Doon

Ye flowery banks o' bonie Doon,
  How can ye blume sae fair?
How can ye chant, ye little birds,
  And I sae fu' o' care?

5 Thou'll break my heart, thou bonie bird,
    That sings upon the bough;
  Thou minds me o' the happy days,
    When my fause° luve was true.   *false*

  Thou'll break my heart, thou bonie bird,
10   That sings beside thy mate;
  For sae I sat, and sae I sang,
    And wist° na o' my fate.   *knew*

  Aft hae I roved by bonie Doon
    To see the wood-bine twine,
15 And ilka° bird sang o' its luve,   *every*
    And sae did I o' mine.

  Wi' lightsome heart I pu'd a rose
    Frae aff its thorny tree;
  And my fause luver staw° my rose   *stole*
20   But left the thorn wi' me.

                                        1791   1792

WILLIAM WORDSWORTH
(1770–1850)

Lines

COMPOSED A FEW MILES ABOVE TINTERN ABBEY ON REVISITING THE
BANKS OF THE WYE DURING A TOUR. JULY 13, 1798[1]

Five years have passed; five summers, with the length
Of five long winters! and again I hear
These waters, rolling from their mountain-springs
With a soft inland murmur. Once again
5 Do I behold these steep and lofty cliffs,
That on a wild secluded scene impress
Thoughts of more deep seclusion; and connect
The landscape with the quiet of the sky.
The day is come when I again repose
10 Here, under this dark sycamore, and view
These plots of cottage ground, these orchard tufts,
Which at this season, with their unripe fruits,
Are clad in one green hue, and lose themselves
'Mid groves and copses. Once again I see
15 These hedgerows, hardly hedgerows, little lines
Of sportive wood run wild; these pastoral farms,
Green to the very door; and wreaths of smoke
Sent up, in silence, from among the trees!
With some uncertain notice, as might seem
20 Of vagrant dwellers in the houseless woods,
Or of some Hermit's cave, where by his fire
The Hermit sits alone.

---

1. Ruins of a medieval abbey situated in the valley of the river Wye, in Monmouthshire, noted
for its scenery.

These beauteous forms,

Through a long absence, have not been to me
As is a landscape to a blind man's eye;
25 But oft, in lonely rooms, and 'mid the din
Of towns and cities, I have owed to them,
In hours of weariness, sensations sweet,
Felt in the blood, and felt along the heart;
And passing even into my purer mind,
30 With tranquil restoration—feelings too
Of unremembered pleasure; such, perhaps,
As have no slight or trivial influence
On that best portion of a good man's life,
His little, nameless, unremembered, acts
35 Of kindness and of love. Nor less, I trust,
To them I may have owed another gift,
Of aspect more sublime; that blessed mood,
In which the burthen of the mystery,
In which the heavy and the weary weight
40 Of all this unintelligible world,
Is lightened—that serene and blessed mood,
In which the affections gently lead us on—
Until, the breath of this corporeal frame
And even the motion of our human blood
45 Almost suspended, we are laid asleep
In body, and become a living soul;
While with an eye made quiet by the power
Of harmony, and the deep power of joy,
We see into the life of things.

If this

50 Be but a vain belief, yet, oh! how oft—
In darkness and amid the many shapes
Of joyless daylight; when the fretful stir
Unprofitable, and the fever of the world,
Have hung upon the beatings of my heart—
55 How oft, in spirit, have I turned to thee,
O sylvan Wye! thou wanderer through the woods,
How often has my spirit turned to thee!

    And now, with gleams of half-extinguished thought,
With many recognitions dim and faint,
60 And somewhat of a sad perplexity,
The picture of the mind revives again;
While here I stand, not only with the sense
Of present pleasure, but with pleasing thoughts
That in this moment there is life and food
65 For future years. And so I dare to hope,
Though changed, no doubt, from what I was when first
I came among these hills; when like a roe
I bounded o'er the mountains, by the sides
Of the deep rivers, and the lonely streams,
70 Wherever nature led—more like a man
Flying from something that he dreads than one
Who sought the thing he loved. For nature then
(The coarser[2] pleasures of my boyish days,
And their glad animal movements all gone by)
75 To me was all in all.—I cannot paint
What then I was. The sounding cataract
Haunted me like a passion; the tall rock,
The mountain, and the deep and gloomy wood,
Their colors and their forms, were then to me

2. I.e., primarily physical.

80 An appetite; a feeling and a love,
 That had no need of a remoter charm,
 By thought supplied, nor any interest
 Unborrowed from the eye.—That time is past,
 And all its aching joys are now no more,
85 And all its dizzy raptures. Not for this
 Faint° I, nor mourn nor murmur; other gifts   *become discouraged*
 Have followed; for such loss, I would believe,
 Abundant recompense. For I have learned
 To look on nature, not as in the hour
90 Of thoughtless youth; but hearing oftentimes
 The still, sad music of humanity,
 Nor harsh nor grating, though of ample power
 To chasten and subdue. And I have felt
 A presence that disturbs me with the joy
95 Of elevated thoughts; a sense sublime
 Of something far more deeply interfused,
 Whose dwelling is the light of setting suns,
 And the round ocean and the living air,
 And the blue sky, and in the mind of man:
100 A motion and a spirit, that impels
 All thinking things, all objects of all thought,
 And rolls through all things. Therefore am I still
 A lover of the meadows and the woods,
 And mountains; and of all that we behold
105 From this green earth; of all the mighty world
 Of eye, and ear—both what they half create,
 And what perceive; well pleased to recognize
 In nature and the language of the sense
 The anchor of my purest thoughts, the nurse,
110 The guide, the guardian of my heart, and soul
 Of all my moral being.

       Nor perchance,
 If I were not thus taught, should I the more
 Suffer my genial spirits° to decay: *vital energies*
 For thou art with me here upon the banks
115 Of this fair river; thou my dearest Friend,[3]
 My dear, dear Friend; and in thy voice I catch
 The language of my former heart, and read
 My former pleasures in the shooting lights
 Of thy wild eyes. Oh! yet a little while
120 May I behold in thee what I was once,
 My dear, dear Sister! and this prayer I make,
 Knowing that Nature never did betray
 The heart that loved her; 'tis her privilege,
 Through all the years of this our life, to lead
125 From joy to joy: for she can so inform
 The mind that is within us, so impress
 With quietness and beauty, and so feed
 With lofty thoughts, that neither evil tongues,
 Rash judgments, nor the sneers of selfish men,
130 Nor greetings where no kindness is, nor all
 The dreary intercourse of daily life,
 Shall e'er prevail against us, or disturb
 Our cheerful faith, that all which we behold
 Is full of blessings. Therefore let the moon
135 Shine on thee in thy solitary walk;
 And let the misty mountain winds be free
 To blow against thee: and, in after years,
 When these wild ecstasies shall be matured

---

3. Wordsworth's sister Dorothy, who accompanied him on the walking trip here commemorated.

Into a sober pleasure; when thy mind
140 Shall be a mansion for all lovely forms,
Thy memory be as a dwelling place
For all sweet sounds and harmonies; oh! then,
If solitude, or fear, or pain, or grief
Should be thy portion, with what healing thoughts
145 Of tender joy wilt thou remember me,
And these my exhortations! Nor, perchance—
If I should be where I no more can hear
Thy voice, nor catch from thy wild eyes these gleams
Of past existence—wilt thou then forget
150 That on the banks of this delightful stream
We stood together; and that I, so long
A worshiper of Nature, hither came
Unwearied in that service; rather say
With warmer love—oh! with far deeper zeal
155 Of holier love. Nor wilt thou then forget,
That after many wanderings, many years
Of absence, these steep woods and lofty cliffs,
And this green pastoral landscape, were to me
More dear, both for themselves and for thy sake!

1798

From The Prelude

From *Book I*

Fair seedtime had my soul, and I grew up
Fostered alike by beauty and by fear:
Much favored in my birthplace,[4] and no less
In that belovéd Vale[5] to which erelong
305 We were transplanted—there were we let loose
For sports of wider range. Ere I had told
Ten birthdays, when among the mountain slopes
Frost, and the breath of frosty wind, had snapped
The last autumnal crocus, 'twas my joy
310 With store of springes° o'er my shoulder hung   *snares*
To range the open heights where woodcocks run
Along the smooth green turf. Through half the night,
Scudding away from snare to snare, I plied
That anxious visitation—moon and stars
315 Were shining o'er my head. I was alone,
And seemed to be a trouble to the peace
That dwelt among them. Sometimes it befell
In these night wanderings, that a strong desire
O'erpowered my better reason, and the bird
320 Which was the captive of another's toil
Became my prey; and when the deed was done
I heard among the solitary hills
Low breathings coming after me, and sounds
Of undistinguishable motion, steps
325 Almost as silent as the turf they trod.

Nor less, when spring had warmed the cultured° Vale,   *cultivated*
Moved we as plunderers where the mother bird
Had in high places built her lodge; though mean
Our object and inglorious, yet the end
330 Was not ignoble. Oh! when I have hung
Above the raven's nest, by knots of grass

---

4. Cockermouth, in the northern part of the   5. Esthwaite, also in the Lakes.
English Lake District.

And half-inch fissures in the slippery rock
But ill sustained, and almost (so it seemed)
Suspended by the blast that blew amain,
335 Shouldering the naked crag, oh, at that time
While on the perilous ridge I hung alone,
With what strange utterance did the loud dry wind
Blow through my ear! the sky seemed not a sky
Of earth—and with what motion moved the clouds!

340   Dust as we are, the immortal spirit grows
Like harmony in music; there is a dark
Inscrutable workmanship that reconciles
Discordant elements, makes them cling together
In one society. How strange that all
345 The terrors, pains, and early miseries,
Regrets, vexations, lassitudes interfused
Within my mind, should e'er have borne a part,
And that a needful part, in making up
The calm existence that is mine when I
350 Am worthy of myself! Praise to the end!
Thanks to the means which Nature deigned to employ;
Whether her fearless visitings, or those
That came with soft alarm, like hurtless light
Opening the peaceful clouds; or she may use
355 Severer interventions, ministry
More palpable, as best might suit her aim.

        One summer evening (led by her) I found
A little boat tied to a willow tree
Within a rocky cave, its usual home.
360 Straight I unloosed her chain, and stepping in
Pushed from the shore. It was an act of stealth
And troubled pleasure, nor without the voice
Of mountain echoes did my boat move on;
Leaving behind her still, on either side,
365 Small circles glittering idly in the moon,
Until they melted all into one track
Of sparkling light. But now, like one who rows,
Proud of his skill, to reach a chosen point
With an unswerving line, I fixed my view
370 Upon the summit of a craggy ridge,
The horizon's utmost boundary; for above
Was nothing but the stars and the gray sky.
She was an elfin pinnace; lustily
I dipped my oars into the silent lake,
375 And, as I rose upon the stroke, my boat
Went heaving through the water like a swan;
When, from behind that craggy steep till then
The horizon's bound, a huge peak, black and huge,
As if with voluntary power instinct,
380 Upreared its head. I struck and struck again,
And growing still in stature the grim shape
Towered up between me and the stars, and still,
For so it seemed, with purpose of its own
And measured motion like a living thing,
385 Strode after me. With trembling oars I turned,
And through the silent water stole my way
Back to the covert of the willow tree;
There in her mooring place I left my bark,
And through the meadows homeward went, in grave
390 And serious mood; but after I had seen
That spectacle, for many days, my brain

Worked with a dim and undetermined sense
Of unknown modes of being; o'er my thoughts
There hung a darkness, call it solitude
395 Or blank desertion. No familiar shapes
Remained, no pleasant images of trees,
Of sea or sky, no colors of green fields;
But huge and mighty forms, that do not live
Like living men, moved slowly through the mind
400 By day, and were a trouble to my dreams.

    Wisdom and Spirit of the universe!
Thou Soul that art the eternity of thought,
That givest to forms and images a breath
And everlasting motion, not in vain
405 By day or starlight thus from my first dawn
Of childhood didst thou intertwine for me
The passions that build up our human soul;
Not with the mean and vulgar works of man,
But with high objects, with enduring things—
410 With life and nature—purifying thus
The elements of feeling and of thought,
And sanctifying, by such discipline,
Both pain and fear, until we recognize
A grandeur in the beating of the heart.
415 Nor was this fellowship vouchsafed to me
With stinted kindness. In November days,
When vapors rolling down the valley made
A lonely scene more lonesome, among woods,
At noon and 'mid the calm of summer nights,
420 When, by the margin of the trembling lake,
Beneath the gloomy hills homeward I went
In solitude, such intercourse was mine;
Mine was it in the fields both day and night,
And by the waters, all the summer long.

425   And in the frosty season, when the sun
Was set, and visible for many a mile
The cottage windows blazed through twilight gloom,
I heeded not their summons: happy time
It was indeed for all of us—for me
430 It was a time of rapture! Clear and loud
The village clock tolled six—I wheeled about,
Proud and exulting like an untired horse
That cares not for his home. All shod with steel,
We hissed along the polished ice in games
435 Confederate, imitative of the chase
And woodland pleasures—the resounding horn,
The pack loud chiming, and the hunted hare.
So through the darkness and the cold we flew,
And not a voice was idle; with the din
440 Smitten, the precipices rang aloud;
The leafless trees and every icy crag
Tinkled like iron; while far distant hills
Into the tumult sent an alien sound
Of melancholy not unnoticed, while the stars
445 Eastward were sparkling clear, and in the west
The orange sky of evening died away.
Not seldom from the uproar I retired
Into a silent bay, or sportively
Glanced sideway, leaving the tumultuous throng,
450 To cut across the reflex° of a star   *reflection*
That fled, and, flying still before me, gleamed

Upon the glassy plain; and oftentimes,
When we had given our bodies to the wind,
And all the shadowy banks on either side
455 Came sweeping through the darkness, spinning still
The rapid line of motion, then at once
Have I, reclining back upon my heels,
Stopped short; yet still the solitary cliffs
Wheeled by me—even as if the earth had rolled
460 With visible motion her diurnal round!
Behind me did they stretch in solemn train,
Feebler and feebler, and I stood and watched
Till all was tranquil as a dreamless sleep.

    Ye Presences of Nature in the sky
465 And on the earth! Ye Visions of the hills!
And Souls of lonely places! can I think
A vulgar° hope was yours when ye employed   *lowly*
Such ministry, when ye, through many a year
Haunting me thus among my boyish sports,
470 On caves and trees, upon the woods and hills,
Impressed upon all forms the characters
Of danger or desire; and thus did make
The surface of the universal earth
With triumph and delight, with hope and fear,
Work like a sea?

                           1798–1800   1850

She Dwelt Among the Untrodden Ways

She dwelt among the untrodden ways
    Beside the springs of Dove.[6]
A Maid whom there were none to praise
    And very few to love;

5 A violet by a mossy stone
    Half hidden from the eye!
—Fair as a star, when only one
    Is shining in the sky.

She lived unknown, and few could know
10   When Lucy ceased to be;
But she is in her grave, and, oh,
    The difference to me!

                                     1800

Three Years She Grew

Three years she grew in sun and shower,
Then Nature said, "A lovelier flower
On earth was never sown;
This Child I to myself will take;
5 She shall be mine, and I will make
A Lady of my own.

"Myself will to my darling be
Both law and impulse: and with me
The Girl, in rock and plain,
10 In earth and heaven, in glade and bower,
Shall feel an overseeing power
To kindle or restrain.

---

6. Several rivers in England are named Dove.

"She shall be sportive as the fawn
That wild with glee across the lawn
15   Or up the mountain springs;
And hers shall be the breathing balm,
And hers the silence and the calm
Of mute insensate things.

"The floating clouds their state shall lend
20   To her; for her the willow bend;
Nor shall she fail to see
Even in the motions of the Storm
Grace that shall mold the Maiden's form
By silent sympathy.

25   "The stars of midnight shall be dear
To her; and she shall lean her ear
In many a secret place
Where rivulets dance their wayward round,
And beauty born of murmuring sound
30   Shall pass into her face.

"And vital feelings of delight
Shall rear her form to stately height,
Her virgin bosom swell;
Such thoughts to Lucy I will give
35   While she and I together live
Here in this happy dell."

Thus Nature spake—the work was done—
How soon my Lucy's race was run!
She died, and left to me
40   This health, this calm, and quiet scene;
The memory of what has been,
And never more will be.

                                                    1800

A Slumber Did My Spirit Seal

A slumber did my spirit seal;
   I had no human fears:
She seemed a thing that could not feel
   The touch of earthly years.

5   No motion has she now, no force;
   She neither hears nor sees;
Rolled round in earth's diurnal course,
   With rocks, and stones, and trees.

                                                    1800

It Is a Beauteous Evening

It is a beauteous evening, calm and free,
The holy time is quiet as a Nun
Breathless with adoration; the broad sun
Is sinking down in its tranquility;
5   The gentleness of heaven broods o'er the Sea:
Listen! the mighty Being is awake,
And doth with his eternal motion make
A sound like thunder—everlastingly.
Dear Child! dear Girl! that walkest with me here,
10   If thou appear untouched by solemn thought,

Thy nature is not therefore less divine:
Thou liest in Abraham's bosom[7] all the year,
And worship'st at the Temple's inner shrine,[8]
God being with thee when we know it not.

1807

London, 1802

Milton! thou shouldst be living at this hour:
England hath need of thee: she is a fen
Of stagnant waters: altar, sword, and pen,
Fireside, the heroic wealth of hall and bower,
5   Have forfeited their ancient English dower
Of inward happiness. We are selfish men;
Oh! raise us up, return to us again;
And give us manners, virtue, freedom, power.
Thy soul was like a Star, and dwelt apart;
10   Thou hadst a voice whose sound was like the sea:
Pure as the naked heavens, majestic, free,
So didst thou travel on life's common way,
In cheerful godliness; and yet thy heart
The lowliest duties on herself did lay.

1807

Composed upon Westminster Bridge, September 3, 1802

Earth has not anything to show more fair:
Dull would he be of soul who could pass by
A sight so touching in its majesty;
This City now doth, like a garment, wear
5   The beauty of the morning; silent, bare,
Ships, towers, domes, theaters, and temples lie
Open unto the fields, and to the sky;
All bright and glittering in the smokeless air.
Never did sun more beautifully steep
10   In his first splendor, valley, rock, or hill;
Ne'er saw I, never felt, a calm so deep!
The river glideth at his own sweet will:
Dear God! the very houses seem asleep;
And all that mighty heart is lying still!

1807

Nuns Fret Not at Their Convent's Narrow Room

Nuns fret not at their convent's narrow room;
And hermits are contented with their cells;
And students with their pensive citadels;
Maids at the wheel, the weaver at his loom,
5   Sit blithe and happy; bees that soar for bloom,
High as the highest Peak of Furness-fells,[9]
Will murmur by the hour in foxglove bells:
In truth the prison, into which we doom
Ourselves, no prison is: and hence for me,
10   In sundry moods, 'twas pastime to be bound
Within the Sonnet's scanty plot of ground;
Pleased if some Souls (for such there needs must be)
Who have felt the weight of too much liberty,
Should find brief solace there, as I have found.

1807

---

7. Where souls in heaven rest (as in Luke, xvi.22).
8. The holy of holies (as in the ancient temple in Jerusalem); where God is present.
9. Mountains in the English Lake District.

My Heart Leaps Up

My heart leaps up when I behold
  A rainbow in the sky:
So was it when my life began;
So is it now I am a man;
5 So be it when I shall grow old,
    Or let me die!
The Child is father of the Man;
And I could wish my days to be
Bound each to each by natural piety.

1807

Ode

INTIMATIONS OF IMMORTALITY FROM
RECOLLECTIONS OF EARLY CHILDHOOD

The Child is father of the Man;
And I could wish my days to be
Bound each to each by natural piety.[1]

1

There was a time when meadow, grove, and stream,
The earth, and every common sight,
    To me did seem
    Appareled in celestial light,
5 The glory and the freshness of a dream.
It is not now as it hath been of yore—
    Turn whereso'er I may,
    By night or day,
The things which I have seen I now can see no more.

2

10   The Rainbow comes and goes,
    And lovely is the Rose,
    The Moon doth with delight
Look round her when the heavens are bare,
    Waters on a starry night
15   Are beautiful and fair;
  The sunshine is a glorious birth;
  But yet I know, where'er I go,
That there hath passed away a glory from the earth.

3

Now, while the birds thus sing a joyous song,
20 And while the young lambs bound
    As to the tabor's sound,[2]
To me alone there came a thought of grief:
A timely utterance gave that thought relief,
    And I again am strong:
25 The cataracts blow their trumpets from the steep;
No more shall grief of mine the season wrong;
I hear the Echoes through the mountains throng,
The Winds come to me from the fields of sleep,
    And all the earth is gay;
30   Land and sea
    Give themselves up to jollity,
    And with the heart of May
    Doth every Beast keep holiday—
    Thou Child of Joy,
35 Shout round me, let me hear thy shouts, thou happy Shepherd-boy!

1. Final lines of Wordsworth's *My Heart Leaps Up*. 2. "Tabor": a small drum.

4
Ye blesséd Creatures, I have heard the call
  Ye to each other make; I see
The heavens laugh with you in your jubilee;
40   My heart is at your festival,
      My head hath its coronal,
The fullness of your bliss, I feel—I feel it all.
      Oh, evil day! if I were sullen
      While Earth herself is adorning,
45   This sweet May morning,
      And the Children are culling
        On every side,
      In a thousand valleys far and wide,
      Fresh flowers; while the sun shines warm,
50 And the Babe leaps up on his Mother's arm—
      I hear, I hear, with joy I hear!
     —But there's a Tree, of many, one,
A single Field which I have looked upon,
Both of them speak of something that is gone:
55   The Pansy at my feet
       Doth the same tale repeat:
Whither is fled the visionary gleam?
Where is it now, the glory and the dream?

5
Our birth is but a sleep and a forgetting:
60 The Soul that rises with us, our life's Star,
      Hath had elsewhere its setting,
       And cometh from afar:
      Not in entire forgetfulness,
      And not in utter nakedness,
65 But trailing clouds of glory do we come
      From God, who is our home:
Heaven lies about us in our infancy!
Shades of the prison-house begin to close
      Upon the growing Boy
70   But he
Beholds the light, and whence it flows,
      He sees it in his joy;
The Youth, who daily farther from the east
      Must travel, still is Nature's Priest,
75   And by the vision splendid
      Is on his way attended;
At length the Man perceives it die away,
And fade into the light of common day.

6
Earth fills her lap with pleasures of her own;
80 Yearnings she hath in her own natural kind,
And, even with something of a Mother's mind,
      And no unworthy aim,
      The homely° Nurse doth all she can   *simple, kindly*
To make her foster child, her Inmate Man,
85   Forget the glories he hath known,
And that imperial palace whence he came.

7
Behold the Child among his newborn blisses,
A six-years' Darling of a pygmy size!
See, where 'mid work of his own hand he lies,
90 Fretted° by sallies of his mother's kisses,   *vexed*
With light upon him from his father's eyes!
See, at his feet, some little plan or chart,
Some fragment from his dream of human life,
Shaped by himself with newly-learnéd art;

95   A wedding or a festival,
        A mourning or a funeral;
            And this hath now his heart,
            And unto this he frames his song;
            Then will he fit his tongue
100 To dialogues of business, love, or strife;
            But it will not be long
            Ere this be thrown aside,
            And with new joy and pride
    The little Actor cons another part;
105 Filling from time to time his "humorous stage"[3]
    With all the Persons, down to palsied Age,
    That Life brings with her in her equipage;
            As if his whole vocation
            Were endless imitation.
                8
110 Thou, whose exterior semblance doth belie
            Thy Soul's immensity;
    Thou best Philosopher, who yet dost keep
    Thy heritage, thou Eye among the blind,
    That, deaf and silent, read'st the eternal deep,
115 Haunted forever by the eternal mind—
            Mighty Prophet! Seer blest!
            On whom those truths do rest,
    Which we are toiling all our lives to find,
    In darkness lost, the darkness of the grave;
120 Thou, over whom thy Immortality
    Broods like the Day, a Master o'er a Slave,
    A Presence which is not to be put by;
    Thou little Child, yet glorious in the might
    Of heaven-born freedom on thy being's height,
125 Why with such earnest pains dost thou provoke
    The years to bring the inevitable yoke,
    Thus blindly with thy blessedness at strife?
    Full soon thy Soul shall have her earthly freight,
    And custom lie upon thee with a weight,
130 Heavy as frost, and deep almost as life!
                9
            O joy! that in our embers
            Is something that doth live,
            That nature yet remembers
            What was so fugitive!
135 The thought of our past years in me doth breed
    Perpetual benediction: not indeed
    For that which is most worthy to be blest;
    Delight and liberty, the simple creed
    Of Childhood, whether busy or at rest,
140 With new-fledged hope still fluttering in his breast—
            Not for these I raise
            The song of thanks and praise;
            But for those obstinate questionings
            Of sense and outward things,
145   Fallings from us, vanishings;
            Blank misgivings of a Creature
    Moving about in worlds not realized,
    High instincts before which our mortal Nature
    Did tremble like a guilty Thing surprised;
150   But for those first affections,
            Those shadowy recollections,
            Which, be they what they may,

3. I.e., playing the parts of characters with various temperaments, called "humors" by Elizabethan poets and playwrights.

Are yet the fountain light of all our day,
Are yet a master light of all our seeing;
155   Uphold us, cherish, and have power to make
Our noisy years seem moments in the being
Of the eternal Silence: truths that wake,
       To perish never;
Which neither listlessness, nor mad endeavor,
160   Nor Man nor Boy,
Nor all that is at enmity with joy,
Can utterly abolish or destroy!
       Hence in a season of calm weather
       Though inland far we be,
165 Our Souls have sight of that immortal sea
       Which brought us hither,
       Can in a moment travel thither,
And see the Children sport upon the shore,
And hear the mighty waters rolling evermore.

10

170 Then sing, ye Birds, sing, sing a joyous song!
       And let the young Lambs bound
       As to the tabor's sound!
We in thought will join your throng,
       Ye that pipe and ye that play,
175   Ye that through your hearts today
       Feel the gladness of the May!
What though the radiance which was once so bright
Be now forever taken from my sight,
       Though nothing can bring back the hour
180 Of splendor in the grass, of glory in the flower;
       We will grieve not, rather find
       Strength in what remains behind;
       In the primal sympathy
       Which having been must ever be;
185   In the soothing thoughts that spring
       Out of human suffering;
       In the faith that looks through death,
In years that bring the philosophic mind.

11

And O, ye Fountains, Meadows, Hills, and Groves,
190 Forebode not any severing of our loves!
Yet in my heart of hearts I feel your might;
I only have relinquished one delight
To live beneath your more habitual sway.
I love the Brooks which down their channels fret,
195 Even more than when I tripped lightly as they;
The innocent brightness of a newborn Day
       Is lovely yet;
The clouds that gather round the setting sun
Do take a sober coloring from an eye
200 That hath kept watch o'er man's mortality;
Another race hath been, and other palms° are won.   *symbols of victory*
Thanks to the human heart by which we live,
Thanks to its tenderness, its joys, and fears,
To me the meanest° flower that blows° can give   *most ordinary / blooms*
205 Thoughts that do often lie too deep for tears.

1802–4   1807

Ode to Duty

Jam non consilio bonus, sed more eo perductus, ut non tantum recte facere possim, sed nisi recte facere non possim.

—SENECA[4]

Stern Daughter of the Voice of God!
O Duty! if that name thou love
Who are a light to guide, a rod
To check the erring, and reprove;
5   Thou, who art victory and law
When empty terrors overawe;
From vain temptations dost set free;
And calm'st the weary strife of frail humanity!

There are who ask not if thine eye
10   Be on them; who, in love and truth,
Where no misgiving is, rely
Upon the genial sense[5] of youth:
Glad Hearts! without reproach or blot;
Who do thy work, and know it not:
15   Oh! if through confidence misplaced
They fail, thy saving arms, dread Power! around them cast.

Serene will be our days and bright,
And happy will our nature be,
When love is an unerring light,
20   And joy its own security.
And they a blissful course may hold
Even now, who, not unwisely bold,
Live in the spirit of this creed;
Yet seek thy firm support, according to their need.

25   I, loving freedom, and untried,
No sport of every random gust,
Yet being to myself a guide,
Too blindly have reposed my trust;
And oft, when in my heart was heard
30   Thy timely mandate, I deferred
The task, in smoother walks to stray;
But thee I now would serve more strictly, if I may.

Through no disturbance of my soul,
Or strong compunction° in me wrought,   *remorse*
35   I supplicate for thy control;
But in the quietness of thought:
Me this unchartered freedom tires;
I feel the weight of chance desires:
My hopes no more must change their name,
40   I long for a repose that ever is the same.

Stern Lawgiver! yet thou dost wear
The Godhead's most benignant grace;
Nor know we anything so fair
As is the smile upon thy face:
45   Flowers laugh before thee on their beds
And fragrance in thy footing treads;
Thou dost preserve the stars from wrong
And the most ancient heavens, through thee, are fresh and strong.

---

4. From the Roman philosopher and dramatist's *Moral Epistles* (CXX.10): "Now am I good not by taking thought but urged on by habit, to this effect: not so much can I act rightly as other than rightly I cannot act."
5. Generous impulse; innate good nature.

To humbler functions, awful Power!
50 I call thee: I myself commend
Unto thy guidance from this hour;
Oh, let my weakness have an end!
Give unto me, made lowly wise,
The spirit of self-sacrifice;
55 The confidence of reason give;
And in the light of truth thy Bondman let me live!

1807

I Wandered Lonely As a Cloud

I wandered lonely as a cloud
That floats on high o'er vales and hills,
When all at once I saw a crowd,
A host, of golden daffodils;
5 Beside the lake, beneath the trees,
Fluttering and dancing in the breeze.

Continuous as the stars that shine
And twinkle on the milky way,
They stretched in never-ending line
10 Along the margin of a bay:
Ten thousand saw I at a glance,
Tossing their heads in sprightly dance.

The waves beside them danced; but they
Outdid the sparkling waves in glee;
15 A poet could not but be gay,
In such a jocund° company;   *cheerful*
I gazed—and gazed—but little thought
What wealth the show to me had brought:

For oft, when on my couch I lie
20 In vacant or in pensive mood,
They flash upon that inward eye
Which is the bliss of solitude;
And then my heart with pleasure fills,
And dances with the daffodils.

1807

Elegiac Stanzas[6]

SUGGESTED BY A PICTURE OF PEELE CASTLE, IN A STORM, PAINTED BY
SIR GEORGE BEAUMONT

I was thy neighbor once, thou rugged Pile!
Four summer weeks I dwelt in sight of thee:
I saw thee every day; and all the while
Thy Form was sleeping on a glassy sea.

5 So pure the sky, so quiet was the air!
So like, so very like, was day to day!
Whene'er I looked, thy Image still was there;
It trembled, but it never passed away.

How perfect was the calm! it seemed no sleep;
10 No mood, which season takes away, or brings:
I could have fancied that the mighty Deep
Was even the gentlest of all gentle Things.

6. In memory of the poet's brother, John, who had recently died in a shipwreck (see lines 36–39).

Ah! THEN, if mine had been the Painter's hand,
To express what then I saw; and add the gleam,
The light that never was, on sea or land,
The consecration, and the Poet's dream;

15

I would have planted thee, thou hoary Pile
Amid a world how different from this!
Beside a sea that could not cease to smile;
On tranquil land, beneath a sky of bliss.

20

Thou shouldst have seemed a treasure house divine
O peaceful years; a chronicle of heaven—
Of all the sunbeams that did ever shine
The very sweetest had to thee been given.

A Picture had it been of lasting ease,
Elysian⁷ quiet, without toil or strife;
No motion but the moving tide, a breeze,
Or merely silent Nature's breathing life.

Such, in the fond illusion of my heart,
Such Picture would I at that time have made,
And seen the soul of truth in every part,
A steadfast peace that might not be betrayed.

So once it would have been—'tis so no more;
I have submitted to a new control:
A power is gone, which nothing can restore;
A deep distress hath humanized my Soul.

Not for a moment could I now behold
A smiling sea, and be what I have been:
The feeling of my loss will ne'er be old;
This, which I know, I speak with mind serene.

Then, Beaumont, Friend! who would have been the Friend,
If he had lived, of him whom I deplore,°   lament
This work of thine I blame not, but commend;
This sea in anger, and that dismal shore.

O 'tis a passionate Work!—yet wise and well,
Well chosen is the spirit that is here;
That Hulk which labors in the deadly swell,
This rueful sky, this pageantry of fear!

And this huge Castle, standing here sublime,
I love to see the look with which it braves,
Cased in the unfeeling armor of old time,
The lightning, the fierce wind, and trampling waves.

Farewell, farewell the heart that lives alone,
Housed in a dream, at distance from the Kind!°   mankind
Such happiness, wherever it be known,
Is to be pitied; for 'tis surely blind.

But welcome fortitude, and patient cheer,
And frequent sights of what is to be borne!
Such sights, or worse, as are before me here.
Not without hope we suffer and we mourn.

1807

---

7. In Greek myth the souls of the blest dwelt in the Elysian Fields.

The World Is Too Much with Us

The world is too much with us; late and soon,
Getting and spending, we lay waste our powers;
Little we see in Nature that is ours;
We have given our hearts away, a sordid boon!°   *gift*
5 This Sea that bares her bosom to the moon,
The winds that will be howling at all hours,
And are up-gathered now like sleeping flowers,
For this, for everything, we are out of tune;
It moves us not.—Great God! I'd rather be
10 A Pagan suckled in a creed outworn;
So might I, standing on this pleasant lea,
Have glimpses that would make me less forlorn;
Have sight of Proteus rising from the sea;
Or hear old Triton blow his wreathéd horn.[8]

1807

The Solitary Reaper

Behold her, single in the field,
Yon solitary Highland Lass!
Reaping and singing by herself;
Stop here, or gently pass!
5 Alone she cuts and binds the grain,
And sings a melancholy strain;
O listen! for the Vale profound
Is overflowing with the sound.

No Nightingale did ever chaunt
10 More welcome notes to weary bands
Of travelers in some shady haunt,
Among Arabian sands;
A voice so thrilling ne'er was heard
In springtime from the Cuckoo bird,
15 Breaking the silence of the seas
Among the farthest Hebrides.

Will no one tell me what she sings?—
Perhaps the plaintive numbers flow
For old, unhappy, far-off things,
20 And battles long ago;
Or is it some more humble lay,
Familiar matter of today?
Some natural sorrow, loss, or pain,
That has been, and may be again?

25 Whate'er the theme, the Maiden sang
As if her song could have no ending;
I saw her singing at her work,
And o'er the sickle bending—
I listened, motionless and still;
30 And, as I mounted up the hill,
The music in my heart I bore,
Long after it was heard no more.

1807

8. In Greek myth Proteus, the "Old Man of the Sea," rises from the sea at midday and can be forced to read the future by anyone who holds him while he takes many frightening shapes. Triton is the son of the sea-god Neptune; the sound of his conch-shell horn calms the waves.

Surprised by Joy

Surprised by joy—impatient as the Wind
I turned to share the transport—Oh! with whom
But thee,[9] deep buried in the silent tomb,
That spot which no vicissitude can find?
5   Love, faithful love, recalled thee to my mind—
But how could I forget thee? Through what power,
Even for the least division of an hour,
Have I been so beguiled as to be blind
To my most grievous loss!—That thought's return
10   Was the worst pang that sorrow ever bore,
Save one, one only, when I stood forlorn,
Knowing my heart's best treasure was no more;
That neither present time, nor years unborn
Could to my sight that heavenly face restore.

                                                    1815

Mutability

From low to high doth dissolution climb,
And sink from high to low, along a scale
Of awful notes, whose concord shall not fail;
A musical but melancholy chime,
5   Which they can hear who meddle not with crime,
Nor avarice, nor over-anxious care.
Truth fails not; but her outward forms that bear
The longest date do melt like frosty rime,°   *thin coating*
That in the morning whitened hill and plain
10   And is no more; drop like the tower sublime
Of yesterday, which royally did wear
His crown of weeds, but could not even sustain
Some casual shout that broke the silent air,
Or the unimaginable touch of Time.

                                                    1822

Extempore Effusion upon the Death of James Hogg[1]

When first, descending from the moorlands,
I saw the Stream of Yarrow glide
Along a bare and open valley,
The Ettrick Shepherd was my guide.

5   When last along its banks I wandered,
Through groves that had begun to shed
Their golden leaves upon the pathways,
My steps the Border-minstrel[2] led.

The mighty Minstrel breathes no longer,
10   'Mid moldering ruins low he lies;
And death upon the braes° of Yarrow,   *banks*
Has closed the Shepherd-poet's eyes:

Nor has the rolling year twice measured,
From sign to sign, its steadfast course,
15   Since every mortal power of Coleridge[3]
Was frozen at its marvelous source;

9. The poet's daughter Catharine, who died
at the age of four, in 1812.
1. Scottish poet (1770–1835) born in Ettrick;
for a time he was a shepherd. An *extempore
effusion* is a poem composed rapidly, without
premeditation.

2. Sir Walter Scott, famous Scottish poet and
novelist (1771–1832).
3. Wordsworth's friend and collaborator, who
died in 1834.

The rapt One,[4] of the godlike forehead,
The heaven-eyed creature sleeps in earth:
And Lamb,[5] the frolic and the gentle,
20   Has vanished from his lonely hearth.

Like clouds that rake the mountain summits,
Or waves that own no curbing hand,
How fast has brother followed brother,
From sunshine to the sunless land!

25   Yet I, whose lids from infant slumber
Were earlier raised, remain to hear
A timid voice, that asks in whispers,
"Who next will drop and disappear?"

Our haughty life is crowned with darkness,
30   Like London with its own black wreath,
On which with thee, O Crabbe![6] forth-looking,
I gazed from Hampstead's breezy heath.

As if but yesterday departed,
Thou too art gone before; but why,
35   O'er ripe fruit, seasonably gathered,
Should frail survivors heave a sigh?

Mourn rather for that holy Spirit,
Sweet as the spring, as ocean deep;
For her[7] who, ere her summer faded,
40   Has sunk into a breathless sleep.

No more of old romantic sorrows,
For slaughtered Youth or lovelorn Maid!
With sharper grief is Yarrow smitten,
And Ettrick mourns with her their Poet dead.

                                                        1835

So Fair, So Sweet, Withal So Sensitive

So fair, so sweet, withal so sensitive,
Would that the little Flowers were born to live,
Conscious of half the pleasure which they give;

That to this mountain-daisy's self were known
5   The beauty of its star-shaped shadow, thrown
On the smooth surface of this naked stone!

And what if hence a bold desire should mount
High as the Sun, that he could take account
Of all that issues from his glorious fount!

10   So might he ken how by his sovereign aid
These delicate companionships are made;
And how he rules the pomp of light and shade;

And were the Sister-power that shines by night
So privileged, what a countenance of delight
15   Would through the clouds break forth on human sight!

Fond fancies! wheresoe'er shall turn thine eye
On earth, air, ocean, or the starry sky,
Converse with Nature in pure sympathy;

---

4. Coleridge (alluding to his "mystical" philosophy).
5. Charles Lamb (1775–1834), essayist and critic, friend of Wordsworth and Coleridge.
6. George Crabbe (1754–1832), poet, acquaintance of Wordsworth.
7. Felicia Hemans (1793–1835), popular poetess, noted for her beauty and conversation.

20 All vain desires, all lawless wishes quelled,
Be Thou to love and praise alike impelled,
Whatever boon° is granted or withheld.

gift
1845

SAMUEL TAYLOR COLERIDGE
(1772–1834)

Kubla Khan[1]

OR A VISION IN A DREAM. A FRAGMENT

In Xanadu did Kubla Khan
A stately pleasure dome decree:
Where Alph, the sacred river, ran
Through caverns measureless to man
5   Down to a sunless sea.
So twice five miles of fertile ground
With walls and towers were girdled round:
And there were gardens bright with sinuous rills,
Where blossomed many an incense-bearing tree;
10 And here were forests ancient as the hills,
Enfolding sunny spots of greenery.

But oh! that deep romantic chasm which slanted
Down the green hill athwart a cedarn cover!
A savage place! as holy and enchanted
15 As e'er beneath a waning moon was haunted
By woman wailing for her demon lover!
And from this chasm, with ceaseless turmoil seething,
As if this earth in fast thick pants were breathing,
A mighty fountain momently was forced:
20 Amid whose swift half-intermitted burst
Huge fragments vaulted like rebounding hail,
Or chaffy grain beneath the thresher's flail:
And 'mid these dancing rocks at once and ever
It flung up momently the sacred river.
25 Five miles meandering with a mazy motion
Through wood and dale the sacred river ran,
Then reached the caverns measureless to man,
And sank in tumult to a lifeless ocean:
And 'mid this tumult Kubla heard from far
30 Ancestral voices prophesying war!

The shadow of the dome of pleasure
Floated midway on the waves;
Where was heard the mingled measure
From the fountain and the caves.
35 It was a miracle of rare device,
A sunny pleasure dome with caves of ice!

1. The first *khan,* or ruler, of the Mongol dynasty in 13th-century China. The topography and place-names are fictitious. In a prefatory note to the poem, Coleridge gave the following background: "In the summer of the year 1797, the author, then in ill health, had retired to a lonely farmhouse between Porlock and Linton, on the Exmoor confines of Somerset and Devonshire. In consequence of a slight indisposition, an anodyne had been prescribed, from the effects of which he fell asleep in his chair at the moment that he was reading the following sentence, or words of the same substance, in *Purchas's Pilgrimage:* "Here the Khan Kubla commanded a palace to be built, and a·stately garden thereunto. And thus ten miles of fertile ground were inclosed with a wall." The author continued for about three hours in a profound sleep, at least of the external sense, during which time he has the most vivid confidence that he could not have composed less than from two to three hundred lines; if that indeed can be called composition in which all the images rose up before him as *things,* with a parallel production of the correspondent expressions, without any sensation or consciousness of effort. On awaking he appeared to himself to have a distinct recollection of the whole, and taking his pen, ink, and paper, instantly and eagerly wrote down the lines that are here preserved. At this moment he was unfortunately called out by a person on business from Porlock, and detained by him above an hour, and on his return to his room, found, to his no small surprise and mortification, that though he still retained some vague and dim recollection of the general purport of the vision, yet, with the exception of some eight or ten scattered lines and images, all the rest had passed away like the images on the surface of a stream into which a stone has been cast, but, alas! without the after restoration of the latter!"

A damsel with a dulcimer[2]
In a vision once I saw:
It was an Abyssinian maid,
40 And on her dulcimer she played,
Singing of Mount Abora.
Could I revive within me
Her symphony and song,
To such a deep delight 'twould win me,
45 That with music loud and long,
I would build that dome in air,
That sunny dome! those caves of ice!
And all who heard should see them there,
And all should cry, Beware! Beware!
50 His flashing eyes, his floating hair!
Weave a circle round him thrice,
And close your eyes with holy dread,
For he on honey-dew hath fed,
And drunk the milk of Paradise.

1797–98   1816

Frost at Midnight

The Frost performs its secret ministry,
Unhelped by any wind. The owlet's cry
Came loud—and hark, again! loud as before.
The inmates of my cottage, all at rest,
5 Have left me to that solitude, which suits
Abstruser musings: save that at my side
My cradled infant[3] slumbers peacefully.
'Tis calm indeed! so calm, that it disturbs
And vexes meditation with its strange
10 And extreme silentness. Sea, hill, and wood,
This populous village! Sea, and hill, and wood,
With all the numberless goings-on of life,
Inaudible as dreams! the thin blue flame
Lies on my low-burnt fire, and quivers not;
15 Only that film,[4] which fluttered on the grate,
Still flutters there, the sole unquiet thing.
Methinks its motion in this hush of nature
Gives it dim sympathies with me who live,
Making it a companionable form,
20 Whose puny flaps and freaks the idling Spirit
By its own moods interprets, everywhere
Echo or mirror seeking of itself,
And makes a toy of Thought.

But O! how oft,
How oft, at school, with most believing mind,
25 Presageful,° have I gazed upon the bars,   *foretelling*
To watch that fluttering *stranger!* and as oft
With unclosed lids, already had I dreamt
Of my sweet birthplace, and the old church tower,
Whose bells, the poor man's only music, rang
30 From morn to evening, all the hot Fair-day,[5]
So sweetly, that they stirred and haunted me
With a wild pleasure, falling on mine ear
Most like articulate sounds of things to come!
So gazed I, till the soothing things, I dreamt,
35 Lulled me to sleep, and sleep prolonged my dreams!
And so I brooded all the following morn,
Awed by the stern preceptor's° face, mine eye   *schoolmaster's*

2. A harp-like instrument.
3. Coleridge's son Hartley.
4. Embers flickering in the grate of a fire-place; in folklore said to forecast the arrival of an unexpected guest; hence called *strangers* (lines 26, 41).
5. Market-day, often a time of festivities.

Fixed with mock study on my swimming book:[6]
Save if the door half opened, and I snatched
40 A hasty glance, and still my heart leaped up,
For still I hoped to see the *stranger's* face,
Townsman, or aunt, or sister more beloved,
My playmate when we both were clothed alike![7]

Dear Babe, that sleepest cradled by my side,
45 Whose gentle breathings, heard in this deep calm,
Fill up the interspersèd vacancies
And momentary pauses of the thought!
My babe so beautiful! it thrills my heart
With tender gladness, thus to look at thee,
50 And think that thou shalt learn far other lore,
And in far other scenes! For I was reared
In the great city, pent 'mid cloisters dim,
And saw nought lovely but the sky and stars.
But *thou*, my babe! shalt wander like a breeze
55 By lakes and sandy shores, beneath the crags
Of ancient mountain, and beneath the clouds,
Which image in their bulk both lakes and shores
And mountain crags: so shalt thou see and hear
The lovely shapes and sounds intelligible
60 Of that eternal language, which thy God
Utters, who from eternity doth teach
Himself in all, and all things in himself.
Great universal Teacher! he shall mold
Thy spirit, and by giving make it ask.

65 Therefore all seasons shall be sweet to thee,
Whether the summer clothe the general° earth   *generative, vernal*
With greenness, or the redbreast sit and sing
Betwixt the tufts of snow on the bare branch
Of mossy apple tree, while the nigh thatch
70 Smokes in the sun-thaw; whether the eave-drops fall
Heard only in the trances of the blast,
Or if the secret ministry of frost
Shall hang them up in silent icicles,
Quietly shining to the quiet Moon.

1798

The Rime of the Ancient Mariner

IN SEVEN PARTS

Facile credo, plures esse Naturas invisibiles quam visibiles in rerum universitate. Sed horum [sic]
omnium familiam quis nobis enarrabit? et gradus et cognationes et discrimina et singulorum
munera? Quid agunt? quae loca habitant? Harum rerum notitiam semper ambivit ingenium
humanum, nunquam attigit. Juvat, interea, non diffiteor, quandoque in animo, in tabulâ, majoris
et melioris mundi imaginem contemplari: ne mens assuefacta hodiernae vitae minutiis se
contrahat nimis, et tota subsidat in pusillas cogitationes. Sed veritati interea invigilandum est,
modusque servandus, ut certa ab incertis, diem a nocte, distinguamus.

—T. BURNET[8]

Part I

An ancient Mar-   It is an ancient Mariner
iner meeteth   And he stoppeth one of three.
three Gallants
bidden to a wed-   —"By thy long gray beard and glittering eye,
ding feast, and   Now wherefore stopp'st thou me?
detaineth one.

6. I.e., seen unclearly because of emotion.
7. In early childhood, when boys and girls wore the same kind of infants' clothing.
8. From *Archaeologiae Philosophiae*, p. 68. "I can easily believe that there are more invisible than visible beings in the universe. But of their families, degrees, connections, distinctions, and functions, who shall tell us? How do they act? Where are they found? About such matters the human mind has always circled without attaining knowledge. Yet I do not doubt that sometimes it is well for the soul to contemplate as in a picture the image of a larger and better world, lest the mind, habituated to the small concerns of daily life, limit itself too much and sink entirely into trivial thinking. But meanwhile we must be on watch for the truth, avoiding extremes, so that we may distinguish certain from uncertain, day from night." Burnet was a 17th-century English theologian.

The Bridegroom's doors are opened wide,   5
And I am next of kin;
The guests are met, the feast is set:
May'st hear the merry din."

He holds him with his skinny hand,
"There was a ship," quoth he.   10
"Hold off! unhand me, graybeard loon!"
Eftsoons° his hand dropped he.   *straightway*

*The Wedding
Guest is spell-
bound by the eye
of the old seafar-
ing man, and
constrained to
hear his tale.*
He holds him with his glittering eye—
The Wedding Guest stood still,
And listens like a three years' child: 15
The Mariner hath his will.

The Wedding Guest sat on a stone:
He cannot choose but hear;
And thus spake on that ancient man,
The bright-eyed Mariner.   20

"The ship was cheered, the harbor cleared,
Merrily did we drop
Below the kirk,° below the hill,   *church*
*The Mariner
tells how the
ship sailed south-
ward with a good
wind and fair
weather, till it
reached the line.*
Below the lighthouse top.

The Sun came up upon the left,   25
Out of the sea came he!
And he shone bright, and on the right
Went down into the sea.

Higher and higher every day,
Till over the mast at noon—"   30
The Wedding Guest here beat his breast,
For he heard the loud bassoon.

*The Wedding
Guest heareth
the bridal music;
but the Mariner
continueth his
tale.*
The bride hath paced into the hall,
Red as a rose is she;
Nodding their heads before her goes   35
The merry minstrelsy.

The Wedding Guest he beat his breast,
Yet he cannot choose but hear;
And thus spake on that ancient man,
The bright-eyed Mariner.   40

*The ship driven
by a storm to-
ward the South
Pole.*
"And now the STORM-BLAST came, and he
Was tyrannous and strong;
He struck with his o'ertaking wings,
And chased us south along.

With sloping masts and dipping prow,   45
As who pursued with yell and blow
Still treads the shadow of his foe,
And forward bends his head,
The ship drove fast, loud roared the blast,
And southward aye we fled.   50

And now there came both mist and snow,
And it grew wondrous cold:
And ice, mast-high, came floating by,
As green as emerald.

The land of ice,
and of fearful
sounds where no
living thing was
to be seen.

And through the drifts the snowy clifts°   cliffs   55
Did send a dismal sheen:
Nor shapes of men nor beasts we ken—
The ice was all between.

The ice was here, the ice was there,
The ice was all around: 60
It cracked and growled, and roared and howled,
Like noises in a swound!°   *swoon*

Till a great sea
bird, called the
Albatross, came
through the
snow-fog, and
was received
with great joy
and hospitality.

At length did cross an Albatross,
Thorough the fog it came;
As if it had been a Christian soul,   65
We hailed it in God's name.

It ate the food it ne'er had eat,
And round and round it flew.
The ice did split with a thunder-fit;
The helmsman steered us through!   70

And lo! the Al-
batross proveth
a bird of good
omen, and fol-
loweth the ship
as it returned
northward
through fog and
floating ice.

And a good south wind sprung up behind;
The Albatross did follow,
And every day, for food or play,
Came to the mariners' hollo!

In mist or cloud, on mast or shroud,   75
It perched for vespers nine;
Whiles all the night, through fog-smoke white,
Glimmered the white Moon-shine."

The ancient
Mariner inhospi-
tably killeth the
pious bird of
good omen.

"God save thee, ancient Mariner!
From the fiends, that plague thee thus!—   80
Why look'st thou so?"—With my crossbow
I shot the ALBATROSS.

Part II

The Sun now rose upon the right:
Out of the sea came he,
Still hid in mist, and on the left   85
Went down into the sea.

And the good south wind still blew behind,
But no sweet bird did follow,
Nor any day for food or play
Came to the mariners' hollo!   90

His shipmates
cry out against
the ancient Mar-
iner, for killing
the bird of good
luck.

And I had done a hellish thing,
And it would work 'em woe:
For all averred, I had killed the bird
That made the breeze to blow.
Ah wretch! said they, the bird to slay,   95
That made the breeze to blow!

But when the
fog cleared off,
they justify the
same, and thus
make themselves
accomplices in
the crime.

Nor dim nor red, like God's own head,
The glorious Sun uprist:°   *arose*
Then all averred, I had killed the bird
That brought the fog and mist.   100
'Twas right, said they, such birds to slay,
That bring the fog and mist.

The fair breeze blew, the white foam flew,
The furrow followed free;
We were the first that ever burst   105
Into that silent sea.

Down dropped the breeze, the sails dropped down,
'Twas sad as sad could be;
And we did speak only to break
The silence of the sea!   110

All in a hot and copper sky,
The bloody Sun, at noon,
Right up above the mast did stand,
No bigger than the Moon.

Day after day, day after day,   115
We stuck, nor breath nor motion;
As idle as a painted ship
Upon a painted ocean.

Water, water, everywhere,
And all the boards did shrink;   120
Water, water, everywhere,
Nor any drop to drink.

The very deep did rot: O Christ!
That ever this should be!
Yea, slimy things did crawl with legs   125
Upon the slimy sea.

About, about, in reel and rout
The death-fires danced at night;
The water, like a witch's oils,
Burnt green, and blue and white.   130

And some in dreams assuréd were
Of the Spirit that plagued us so;
Nine fathom deep he had followed us
From the land of mist and snow.

And every tongue, through utter drought,   135
Was withered at the root;
We could not speak, no more than if
We had been choked with soot.

Ah! well-a-day! what evil looks
Had I from old and young!   140
Instead of the cross, the Albatross
About my neck was hung.

Part III

There passed a weary time. Each throat
Was parched, and glazed each eye.
A weary time! a weary time!   145
How glazed each weary eye,
When looking westward, I beheld
A something in the sky.

At first it seemed a little speck,
And then it seemed a mist;   150
It moved and moved, and took at last
A certain shape, I wist.°   *knew*

A speck, a mist, a shape, I wist!
And still it neared and neared:
As if it dodged a water sprite,   155
It plunged and tacked and veered.

At its nearer ap- With throats unslaked, with black lips baked,
proach, it seem- We could nor laugh nor wail;
eth him to be a Through utter drought all dumb we stood!
ship; and at a I bit my arm, I sucked the blood,   160
dear ransom he And cried, A sail! a sail!
freeth his speech
from the bonds
of thirst.

With throats unslaked, with black lips baked,
Agape they heard me call:
A flash of joy; Gramercy!° they for joy did grin,   *thank heavens!*
And all at once their breath drew in,   165
As they were drinking all.

And horror fol- See! see! (I cried) she tacks no more!
lows. For can it Hither to work us weal;°   *benefit*
be a ship that Without a breeze, without a tide,
comes onward She steadies with upright keel!   170
without wind or
tide?

The western wave was all aflame.
The day was well nigh done!
Almost upon the western wave
Rested the broad bright Sun;
When that strange shape drove suddenly   175
Betwixt us and the Sun.

It seemeth him And straight the Sun was flecked with bars,
but the skeleton (Heaven's Mother send us grace!)
of a ship. As if through a dungeon grate he peered
With broad and burning face.   180

Alas! (thought I, and my heart beat loud)
And its ribs are How fast she nears and nears!
seen as bars on Are those *her* sails that glance in the Sun,
the face of the Like restless gossameres?
setting Sun.

The Specter- Are those *her* ribs through which the Sun   185
Woman and her Did peer, as through a grate?
Deathmate, and And is that Woman all her crew?
no other on Is that a DEATH? and are there two?
board the skele- Is DEATH that woman's mate?
ton ship.

Like vessel, like *Her* lips were red, *her* looks were free, 190
crew! Her locks were yellow as gold:
Her skin was as white as leprosy,
The Nightmare LIFE-IN-DEATH was she,
Who thicks man's blood with cold.

Death and Life- The naked hulk alongside came,   195
in-Death have And the twain were casting dice;
diced for the "The game is done! I've won! I've won!"
ship's crew, and Quoth she, and whistles thrice.
she (the latter)
winneth the an-
cient Mariner.

<table>
<tr><td>*No twilight within the courts of the Sun.*</td><td>The Sun's rim dips; the stars rush out:
At one stride comes the dark;
With far-heard whisper, o'er the sea,
Off shot the specter-bark.</td><td>200</td></tr>
</table>

At the rising of the Moon,

We listened and looked sideways up!
Fear at my heart, as at a cup,
My lifeblood seems to sip!　　　　　　　　　205
The stars were dim, and thick the night,
The steersman's face by his lamp gleamed white;
From the sails the dew did drip—
Till clomb above the eastern bar
The hornéd Moon, with one bright star　　210
Within the nether tip.

*One after an-
other,*

One after one, by the star-dogged Moon,
Too quick for groan or sigh,
Each turned his face with ghastly pang,
And cursed me with his eye.　　　　　　215

*His shipmates
drop down dead.*

Four times fifty living men,
(And I heard nor sigh nor groan)
With heavy thump, a lifeless lump,
They dropped down one by one.

*But Life-in-
Death begins her
work on the an-
cient Mariner.*

The souls did from their bodies fly—　　220
They fled to bliss or woe!
And every soul, it passed me by,
Like the whizz of my cross-bow!

Part IV

*The Wedding
Guest feareth
that a Spirit is
talking to him;*

"I fear thee, ancient Mariner!
I fear thy skinny hand!　　　　　　　　225
And thou art long, and lank, and brown,
As is the ribbed sea-sand.

*But the ancient
Mariner assureth
him of his bodily
life, and pro-
ceedeth to relate
his horrible pen-
ance.*

I fear thee and thy glittering eye,
And thy skinny hand, so brown."—
Fear not, fear not, thou Wedding Guest!　230
This body dropped not down.

Alone, alone, all, all alone,
Alone on a wide wide sea!
And never a saint took pity on
My soul in agony.　　　　　　　　　　235

*He despiseth the
creatures of the
calm,*

The many men, so beautiful!
And they all dead did lie:
And a thousand thousand slimy things
Lived on; and so did I.

*And envieth that
they should live,
and so many lie
dead.*

I looked upon the rotting sea,　　　　　240
And drew my eyes away;
I looked upon the rotting deck,
And there the dead men lay.

I looked to heaven, and tried to pray;
But or ever a prayer had gushed,　　　245
A wicked whisper came, and made
My heart as dry as dust.

I closed my lids, and kept them close,
And the balls like pulses beat,
For the sky and the sea, and the sea and the sky   250
Lay like a load on my weary eye,
And the dead were at my feet.

But the curse liveth for him in the eye of the dead men.

The cold sweat melted from their limbs,
Nor rot nor reek did they:
The look with which they looked on me   255
Had never passed away.

An orphan's curse would drag to hell
A spirit from on high;
But oh! more horrible than that
Is the curse in a dead man's eye!   260
Seven days, seven nights, I saw that curse,
And yet I could not die.

The moving Moon went up the sky,
And nowhere did abide:

In his loneliness and fixedness he yearneth towards the journeying Moon, and the stars that still sojourn, yet still move onward; and everywhere the blue sky belongs to them, and is their appointed rest, and their native country and their own natural homes, which they enter unannounced, as lords that are certainly expected and yet there is a silent joy at their arrival.

Softly she was going up,   265
And a star or two beside—

Her beams bemocked the sultry main,
Like April hoar-frost spread;
But where the ship's huge shadow lay,
The charmèd water burnt alway   270
A still and awful red.

By the light of the Moon he beholdeth God's creatures of the great calm.

Beyond the shadow of the ship,
I watched the water snakes:
They moved in tracks of shining white,
And when they reared, the elfish light   275
Fell off in hoary° flakes.   gray or white

Within the shadow of the ship
I watched their rich attire:
Blue, glossy green, and velvet black,
They coiled and swam; and every track   280
Was a flash of golden fire.

Their beauty and their happiness.

O happy living things! no tongue
Their beauty might declare:
A spring of love gushed from my heart,

He blesseth them in his heart.

And I blessed them unaware: 285
Sure my kind saint took pity on me,
And I blessed them unaware.

The spell begins to break.

The self-same moment I could pray;
And from my neck so free
The Albatross fell off, and sank   290
Like lead into the sea.

Part V

Oh sleep! it is a gentle thing,
Beloved from pole to pole!
To Mary Queen the praise be given!
She sent the gentle sleep from Heaven,   295
That slid into my soul.

By grace of the
holy Mother, the
ancient Mariner
is refreshed with
rain.

The silly° buckets on the deck,   *lowly, harmless*
That had so long remained,
I dreamt that they were filled with dew;
And when I awoke, it rained.   300

My lips were wet, my throat was cold,
My garments all were dank;
Sure I had drunken in my dreams,
And still my body drank.

I moved, and could not feel my limbs: 305
I was so light—almost
I thought that I had died in sleep,
And was a blessèd ghost.

He heareth
sounds and seeth
strange sights
and commotions
in the sky and
the element.

And soon I heard a roaring wind:
It did not come anear;   310
But with its sound it shook the sails,
That were so thin and sere.

The upper air burst into life!
And a hundred fire-flags sheen,°   *shone*
To and fro they were hurried about!   315
And to and fro, and in and out,
The wan stars danced between.

And the coming wind did roar more loud,
And the sails did sigh like sedge;[9]
And the rain poured down from one black cloud;   320
The Moon was at its edge.

The thick black cloud was cleft, and still
The Moon was at its side:
Like waters shot from some high crag,
The lightning fell with never a jag,   325
A river steep and wide.

The bodies of
the ship's crew
are inspirited,
and the ship
moves on;

The loud wind never reached the ship,
Yet now the ship moved on!
Beneath the lightning and the Moon
The dead men gave a groan.   330

They groaned, they stirred, they all uprose,
Nor spake, nor moved their eyes;
It had been strange, even in a dream,
To have seen those dead men rise.

The helmsman steered, the ship moved on;   335
Yet never a breeze up-blew;
The mariners all 'gan work the ropes,
Where they were wont to do;
They raised their limbs like lifeless tools—
We were a ghastly crew.   340

The body of my brother's son
Stood by me, knee to knee:
The body and I pulled at one rope,
But he said nought to me.

9. Rushlike plants bordering streams and lakes.

"I fear thee, ancient Mariner!"   345

*But not by the
souls of the men,
nor by demons
of earth or mid-
dle air, but by a
blesséd troop of
angelic spirits,
sent down by
the invocation of
the guardian
saint.*

Be calm, thou Wedding Guest!
'Twas not those souls that fled in pain,
Which to their corses° came again,   *corpses*
But a troop of spirits blest:

For when it dawned—they dropped their arms,   350
And clustered round the mast;
Sweet sounds rose slowly through their mouths,
And from their bodies passed.

Around, around, flew each sweet sound,
Then darted to the Sun;   355
Slowly the sounds came back again,
Now mixed, now one by one.

Sometimes a-dropping from the sky
I heard the sky-lark sing;
Sometimes all little birds that are,   360
How they seemed to fill the sea and air
With their sweet jargoning!°   *warbling*

And now 'twas like all instruments,
Now like a lonely flute;
And now it is an angel's song,   365
That makes the heavens be mute.

It ceased; yet still the sails made on
A pleasant noise till noon,
A noise like of a hidden brook
In the leafy month of June,   370
That to the sleeping woods all night
Singeth a quiet tune.

Till noon we quietly sailed on,
Yet never a breeze did breathe:
Slowly and smoothly went the ship,   375
Moved onward from beneath.

*The lonesome
Spirit from the
South Pole car-
ries on the ship
as far as the
Line, in obedi-
ence to the an-
gelic troop, but
still requireth
vengeance.*

Under the keel nine fathom deep,
From the land of mist and snow,
The spirit slid: and it was he
That made the ship to go.   380
The sails at noon left off their tune,
And the ship stood still also.

The Sun, right up above the mast,
Had fixed her to the ocean:
But in a minute she 'gan stir,   385
With a short uneasy motion—
Backwards and forwards half her length
With a short uneasy motion.

Then like a pawing horse let go,
She made a sudden bound: 390
It flung the blood into my head,
And I fell down in a swound.

The Polar Spirit's fellow demons, the invisible inhabitants of the element, take part in his wrong; and two of them relate, one to the other, that penance long and heavy for the ancient Mariner hath been accorded to the Polar Spirit, who returneth southward.

How long in that same fit I lay,
I have not° to declare;   *cannot*
But ere my living life returned,   395
I heard and in my soul discerned
Two voices in the air.

"Is it he?" quoth one, "Is this the man?
By him who died on cross,
With his cruel bow he laid full low   400
The harmless Albatross.

The spirit who bideth by himself
In the land of mist and snow,
He loved the bird that loved the man
Who shot him with his bow."   405

The other was a softer voice,
As soft as honey-dew:
Quoth he, "The man hath penance done,
And penance more will do."

Part VI

FIRST VOICE
"But tell me, tell me! speak again,   410
Thy soft response renewing—
What makes that ship drive on so fast?
What is the ocean doing?"

SECOND VOICE
"Still as a slave before his lord,
The ocean hath no blast;   415
His great bright eye most silently
Up to the Moon is cast—

If he may know which way to go;
For she guides him smooth or grim.
See, brother, see! how graciously   420
She looketh down on him."

FIRST VOICE
The Mariner hath been cast into a trance; for the angelic power causeth the vessel to drive northward faster than human life could endure.
"But why drives on that ship so fast,
Without or wave or wind?"

SECOND VOICE
"The air is cut away before,
And closes from behind.   425

Fly, brother, fly! more high, more high!
Or we shall be belated:
For slow and slow that ship will go,
When the Mariner's trance is abated."

The supernatural motion is retarded; the Mariner awakes, and his penance begins anew.
I woke, and we were sailing on   430
As in a gentle weather:
'Twas night, calm night, the moon was high;
The dead men stood together.

All stood together on the deck,
For a charnel-dungeon fitter: 435
All fixed on me their stony eyes,
That in the Moon did glitter.

The pang, the curse, with which they died,
Had never passed away:
I could not draw my eyes from theirs,   440
Nor turn them up to pray.

The curse is And now this spell was snapped: once more
finally expiated. I viewed the ocean green,
And looked far forth, yet little saw
Of what had else been seen—   445

Like one, that on a lonesome road
Doth walk in fear and dread,
And having once turned round walks on,
And turns no more his head;
Because he knows, a frightful fiend   450
Doth close behind him tread.

But soon there breathed a wind on me,
Nor sound nor motion made:
Its path was not upon the sea,
In ripple or in shade.   455

It raised my hair, it fanned my cheek
Like a meadow-gale of spring—
It mingled strangely with my fears,
Yet it felt like a welcoming.

Swiftly, swiftly flew the ship,   460
Yet she sailed softly too:
Sweetly, sweetly blew the breeze—
On me alone it blew.

And the ancient Oh! dream of joy! is this indeed
Mariner behold- The lighthouse top I see?   465
eth his native Is this the hill? is this the kirk?
country. Is this mine own countree?

We drifted o'er the harbor-bar,
And I with sobs did pray—
O let me be awake, my God!   470
Or let me sleep alway.

The harbor-bay was clear as glass,
So smoothly it was strewn!
And on the bay the moonlight lay,
And the shadow of the Moon.   475

The rock shone bright, the kirk no less,
That stands above the rock:
The moonlight steeped in silentness
The steady weathercock.

And the bay was white with silent light,   480
Till rising from the same,
The angelic Full many shapes, that shadows were,
spirits leave the In crimson colors came.
dead bodies,

A little distance from the prow
Those crimson shadows were: 485
And appear in I turned my eyes upon the deck—
their own forms Oh, Christ! what saw I there!
of light.

Each corse lay flat, lifeless and flat,
And, by the holy rood!°   *cross of Christ*
A man all light, a seraph°-man,   *angel-like*   490
On every corse there stood.

This seraph-band, each waved his hand:
It was a heavenly sight!
They stood as signals to the land,
Each one a lovely light;   495

This seraph-band, each waved his hand,
No voice did they impart—
No voice; but oh! the silence sank
Like music on my heart.

But soon I heard the dash of oars,   500
I heard the Pilot's cheer;
My head was turned perforce away
And I saw a boat appear.

The Pilot and the Pilot's boy,
I heard them coming fast: 505
Dear Lord in Heaven! it was a joy
The dead men could not blast.

I saw a third—I heard his voice:
It is the Hermit good!
He singeth loud his godly hymns   510
That he makes in the wood.
He'll shrieve[1] my soul, he'll wash away
The Albatross's blood.

Part VII

The Hermit of the Wood

This Hermit good lives in that wood
Which slopes down to the sea.   515
How loudly his sweet voice he rears!
He loves to talk with marineres
That come from a far countree.

He kneels at morn, and noon, and eve—
He hath a cushion plump: 520
It is the moss that wholly hides
The rotted old oak stump.

The skiff-boat neared: I heard them talk,
"Why, this is strange, I trow!
Where are those lights so many and fair,   525
That signal made but now?"

Approacheth the ship with wonder.

"Strange, by my faith!" the Hermit said—
"And they answered not our cheer!
The planks looked warped! and see those sails,
How thin they are and sere!   530
I never saw aught like to them,
Unless perchance it were

Brown skeletons of leaves that lag
My forest-brook along;
When the ivy tod° is heavy with snow,   *bushy clump*   535
And the owlet whoops to the wolf below,
That eats the she-wolf's young."

---

1. Set free from sin.

"Dear Lord! it hath a fiendish look,"
The Pilot made reply,
"I am a-feared"—"Push on, push on!"   540
Said the Hermit cheerily.

The boat came closer to the ship,
But I nor spake nor stirred;
The boat came close beneath the ship,
And straight a sound was heard.   545

The ship sud-
denly sinketh.
Under the water it rumbled on,
Still louder and more dread:
It reached the ship, it split the bay;
The ship went down like lead.

The ancient
Mariner is saved
in the Pilot's
boat.
Stunned by that loud and dreadful sound,   550
Which sky and ocean smote,
Like one that hath been seven days drowned
My body lay afloat;
But swift as dreams, myself I found
Within the Pilot's boat.   555

Upon the whirl, where sank the ship,
The boat spun round and round;
And all was still, save that the hill
Was telling of the sound.

I moved my lips—the Pilot shrieked   560
And fell down in a fit;
The holy Hermit raised his eyes,
And prayed where he did sit.

I took the oars: the Pilot's boy,
Who now doth crazy go,   565
Laughed loud and long, and all the while
His eyes went to and fro.
"Ha! ha!" quoth he, "full plain I see,
The Devil knows how to row."

And now, all in my own countree,   570
I stood on the firm land!
The Hermit stepped forth from the boat,
And scarcely he could stand.

The ancient
Mariner ear-
nestly entreateth
the Hermit to
shrieve him; and
the penance of
life falls on him.
"O shrieve me, shrieve me, holy man!"
The Hermit crossed[2] his brow.   575
"Say quick," quoth he, "I bid thee say—
What manner of man art thou?"

Forthwith this frame of mine was wrenched
With a woeful agony,
Which forced me to begin my tale;   580
And then it left me free.

And ever and
anon throughout
his future life
an agony con-
straineth him to
travel from
land to land;
Since then, at an uncertain hour,
That agony returns:
And till my ghastly tale is told,
This heart within me burns.   585

I pass, like night, from land to land;
I have strange power of speech;

2. Made the sign of the cross upon.

That moment that his face I see,
I know the man that must hear me:
To him my tale I teach.   590

What loud uproar bursts from that door!
The wedding guests are there:
But in the garden-bower the bride
And bridemaids singing are:
And hark the little vesper bell,   595
Which biddeth me to prayer!

O Wedding Guest! this soul hath been
Alone on a wide wide sea:
So lonely 'twas, that God himself
Scarce seeméd there to be.   600

O sweeter than the marriage feast,
'Tis sweeter far to me,
To walk together to the kirk
With a goodly company!

To walk together to the kirk,   605
And all together pray,
While each to his great Father bends,
Old men, and babes, and loving friends
And youths and maidens gay!

And to teach, by Farewell, farewell! but this I tell   610
his own exam-   To thee, thou Wedding Guest!
ple, love and   He prayeth well, who loveth well
reverence to all Both man and bird and beast.
things that God
made and loveth.

He prayeth best, who loveth best
All things both great and small;   615
For the dear God who loveth us,
He made and loveth all.

The Mariner, whose eye is bright,
Whose beard with age is hoar,
Is gone: and now the Wedding Guest   620
Turned from the bridegroom's door.

He went like one that hath been stunned,
And is of sense forlorn:°   *deprived*
A sadder and a wiser man,
He rose the morrow morn.

                                        1798   1817

Dejection: An Ode

Late, late yestreen I saw the new Moon,
With the old Moon in her arms;
And I fear, I fear, my master dear!
We shall have a deadly storm.
          Ballad of Sir Patrick Spence

                    1

Well! If the bard was weather-wise, who made
   The grand old ballad of Sir Patrick Spence,
   This night, so tranquil now, will not go hence
Unroused by winds, that ply a busier trade
5   Than those which mold yon cloud in lazy flakes,
   Or the dull sobbing draft, that moans and rakes

Upon the strings of this Aeolian lute,[3]
     Which better far were mute.
     For lo! the New-moon winter-bright!
10   And overspread with phantom light,
       (With swimming phantom light o'erspread
       But rimmed and circled by a silver thread)
     I see the old Moon in her lap, foretelling
       The coming-on of rain and squally blast.
15   And oh! that even now the gust were swelling,
       And the slant night shower driving loud and fast!
     Those sounds which oft have raised me, whilst they awed,
       And sent my soul abroad,
     Might now perhaps their wonted° impulse give,   *usual*
20   Might startle this dull pain, and make it move and live!

                          2
     A grief without a pang, void, dark, and drear,
       A stifled, drowsy, unimpassioned grief,
       Which finds no natural outlet, no relief,
         In word, or sigh, or tear—
25   O Lady! in this wan and heartless mood,
     To other thoughts by yonder throstle wooed,
       All this long eve, so balmy and serene,
     Have I been gazing on the western sky,
       And its peculiar tint of yellow green:
30   And still I gaze—and with how blank an eye!
     And those thin clouds above, in flakes and bars,
     That give away their motion to the stars;
     Those stars, that glide behind them or between,
     Now sparkling, now bedimmed, but always seen:
35   Yon crescent Moon, as fixed as if it grew
     In its own cloudless, starless lake of blue;
     I see them all so excellently fair,
     I see, not feel, how beautiful they are!

                          3
         My genial spirits° fail;   *vital energies*
40   And what can these avail
     To lift the smothering weight from off my breast?
         It were a vain endeavor,
           Though I should gaze forever
     On that green light that lingers in the west:
45   I may not hope from outward forms to win
     The passion and the life, whose fountains are within.

                          4
     O Lady! we receive but what we give,
     And in our life alone does Nature live:
     Ours is her wedding garment, ours her shroud!
50   And would we aught behold, of higher worth,
     Than that inanimate cold world allowed
     To the poor loveless ever-anxious crowd,
       Ah! from the soul itself must issue forth
     A light, a glory, a fair luminous cloud
55   Enveloping the Earth—
     And from the soul itself must there be sent
       A sweet and potent voice, of its own birth,
     Of all sweet sounds the life and element!

                          5
     O pure of heart! thou need'st not ask of me
60   What this strong music in the soul may be!
     What, and wherein it doth exist,
     This light, this glory, this fair luminous mist,

---

3. The wind-harp (named after Aeolus, classi-   equipped with a set of strings that vibrate in
cal god of winds) has a sounding board   response to air currents.

This beautiful and beauty-making power.
Joy, virtuous Lady! Joy that ne'er was given,
65 Save to the pure, and in their purest hour,
Life, and Life's effluence, cloud at once and shower,
Joy, Lady! is the spirit and the power,
Which wedding Nature to us gives in dower
    A new Earth and new Heaven,
70 Undreamt of by the sensual and the proud—
Joy is the sweet voice, Joy the luminous cloud—
    We in ourselves rejoice!
And thence flows all that charms or ear or sight,
    All melodies the echoes of that voice,
75 All colors a suffusion from that light.
                6
There was a time when, though my path was rough,
    This joy within me dallied with distress,
And all misfortunes were but as the stuff
    Whence Fancy made me dreams of happiness:
80 For hope grew round me, like the twining vine,
And fruits, and foliage, not my own, seemed mine.
But now afflictions bow me down to earth:
Nor care I that they rob me of my mirth;
    But oh! each visitation
85 Suspends what nature gave me at my birth,
    My shaping spirit of Imagination.

For not to think of what I needs must feel,
    But to be still and patient, all I can;
And happily by abstruse research to steal
90   From my own nature all the natural man—
This was my sole resource, my only plan:
Till that which suits a part infects the whole,
And now is almost grown the habit of my soul.
                7
Hence, viper thoughts, that coil around my mind,
95   Reality's dark dream!
I turn from you, and listen to the wind,
    Which long has raved unnoticed. What a scream
Of agony by torture lengthened out
That lute sent forth! Thou Wind, that rav'st without,
100   Bare crag, or mountain tairn,° or blasted tree,   *pool*
Or pine grove whither woodman never clomb,
Or lonely house, long held—the witches' home,
    Methinks were fitter instruments for thee,
Mad lutanist! who in this month of showers,
105 Of dark-brown gardens, and of peeping flowers,
Mak'st devils' yule,[4] with worse than wintry song,
The blossoms, buds, and timorous leaves among.
    Thou actor, perfect in all tragic sounds!
Thou mighty poet, e'en to frenzy bold!
110   What tell'st thou now about?
    'Tis of the rushing of an host in rout,
With groans, of trampled men, with smarting wounds—
At once they groan with pain, and shudder with the cold!
But hush! there is a pause of deepest silence!
115   And all that noise, as of a rushing crowd,
With groans, and tremulous shudderings—all is over—
    It tells another tale, with sounds less deep and loud!
        A tale of less affright,
        And tempered with delight,

4. A winter storm in spring; hence, an unnatural or "devils' " Christmas.

120 As Otway's[5] self had framed the tender lay—
       'Tis of a little child
       Upon a lonesome wild,
   Not far from home, but she hath lost her way:
   And now moans low in bitter grief and fear,
125 And now screams loud, and hopes to make her mother hear.
               8
   'Tis midnight, but small thoughts have I of sleep:
   Full seldom may my friend such vigils keep!
   Visit her, gentle Sleep! with wings of healing,
       And may this storm be but a mountain birth,
130 May all the stars hang bright above her dwelling,
       Silent as though they watched the sleeping Earth!
           With light heart may she rise,
           Gay fancy, cheerful eyes,
       Joy lift her spirit, joy attune her voice;
135 To her may all things live, from pole to pole,
   Their life the eddying of her living soul!
       O simple spirit, guided from above,
   Dear Lady! friend devoutest of my choice,
   Thus mayest thou ever, evermore rejoice.

                                    1802   1817

WALTER SAVAGE LANDOR
(1775–1864)

Rose Aylmer[1]

Ah what avails the sceptered race,
    Ah what the form divine!
What every virtue, every grace!
    Rose Aylmer, all were thine.
5 Rose Aylmer, whom these wakeful eyes
    May weep, but never see,
A night of memories and of sighs
    I consecrate to thee.

                                  1806, 1831, 1846

Mild Is the Parting Year, and Sweet

Mild is the parting year, and sweet
    The odor of the falling spray;
Life passes on more rudely fleet,
    And balmless is its closing day.

5 I wait its close, I court its gloom,
    But mourn that never must there fall
Or on my breast or on my tomb
    The tear that would have soothed it all.

                                    1831, 1846

5. A 17th-century English dramatist, noted for his power to evoke pathos.
1. The Honorable Rose Whitworth Aylmer (1779–1800), whom Landor had known in Wales, died suddenly in Calcutta on March 2, 1800.

Past Ruined Ilion Helen[2] Lives

Past ruined Ilion Helen lives,
   Alcestis[3] rises from the shades;
Verse calls them forth; 'tis verse that gives
   Immortal youth to mortal maids.

5 Soon shall Oblivion's deepening veil
   Hide all the peopled hills you see,
The gay, the proud, while lovers hail
   In distant ages you and me.

10 The tear for fading beauty check,
   For passing glory cease to sigh;
One form shall rise above the wreck,
   One name, Ianthe, shall not die.

1831

Dirce

Stand close around, ye Stygian set,[4]
   With Dirce in one boat conveyed!
Or Charon, seeing may forget
   That he is old and she a shade.

1831, 1846

To My Child Carlino[5]

> They are verses written by a gentleman who resided long in this country.
> and who much regretted the necessity of leaving it.
> —BOCCACCIO

Carlino! what art thou about, my boy?
Often I ask that question, though in vain;
For we are far apart: ah! therefore 'tis
I often ask it; not in such a tone
5 As wiser fathers do, who know too well.
Were we not children, you and I together?
Stole we not glances from each other's eyes?
Swore we not secrecy in such misdeeds?
Well could we trust each other. Tell me, then,
10 What thou art doing. Carving out thy name,
Or haply mine, upon my favorite seat,
With the new knife I sent thee oversea?
Or hast thou broken it, and hid the hilt
Among the myrtles, starred with flowers, behind?
15 Or under that high throne whence fifty lilies
(With sworded tuberoses dense around)
Lift up their heads at once . . . not without fear
That they were looking at thee all the while?
   Does Cincirillo follow thee about?
20 Inverting one swart foot suspensively,
And wagging his dread jaw, at every chirp
Of bird above him on the olive-branch?
Frighten him then away! 'twas he who slew
Our pigeons, our white pigeons, peacock-tailed,
25 That feared not you and me . . . alas, nor him!

2. Helen of Troy ("Ilion").
3. Alcestis sacrificed her life for her husband,
who was stricken with a mortal illness. She
acted in accordance with Apollo's promise that
he might thus be saved; she was then brought
back from the underworld by Hercules.

4. The shades of the dead who were ferried by
Charon over the river Styx to Hades.
5. The poem is addressed to Charles Savage
Landor (1825–1917), youngest of Landor's
three sons, at a time when Landor was in
England and the three boys were in Italy.

I flattened his striped sides along my knee,
And reasoned with him on his bloody mind,
Till he looked blandly, and half-closed his eyes
To ponder on my lecture in the shade.
30 I doubt his memory much, his heart a little,
And in some minor matters (may I say it?)
Could wish him rather sager. But from thee
God hold back wisdom yet for many years!
Whether in early season or in late
35 It always comes high priced. For thy pure breast
I have no lesson; it for me has many.
Come, throw it open then! What sports, what cares
(Since there are none too young for these) engage
Thy busy thoughts? Are you again at work,
40 Walter[6] and you, with those sly laborers,
Geppo, Giovanni, Cecco, and Poeta,
To build more solidly your broken dam
Among the poplars, whence the nightingale
Inquisitively watched you all day long?
45 I was not of your council in the scheme,
Or might have saved you silver without end,
And sighs too without number. Art thou gone
Below the mulberry, where that cold pool
Urged to devise a warmer, and more fit
50 For mighty swimmers, swimming three abreast?
Or art thou panting in this summer noon
Upon the lowest step before the hall,
Drawing a slice of watermelon, long
As Cupid's bow, athwart thy wetted lips
(Like one who plays Pan's pipe) and letting drop
The sable seeds from all their separate cells,
And leaving bays profound and rocks abrupt,
Redder than coral round Calypso's[7] cave?

1837   1846

Dying Speech of an Old Philosopher

I strove with none, for none was worth my strife:
  Nature I loved, and, next to Nature, Art:
I warmed both hands before the fire of Life;
  It sinks; and I am ready to depart.

1849

GEORGE GORDON, LORD BYRON
(1788–1824)

Written After Swimming from Sestos to Abydos[1]

1
If, in the month of dark December,
  Leander, who was nightly wont
(What maid will not the tale remember?)
  To cross thy stream, broad Hellespont!

6. Walter Savage Landor (1822–99), the poet's second son.
7. The nymph or goddess who welcomed Odysseus in her island, Ogygia, after the wreck of his ship, and held him there for seven years.

1. The Hellespont, or Dardanelles, is the strait separating Europe from Asia Minor, between Abydos on the Greek shore and Sestos on the Asian. In Greek legend, Leander used to swim from Abydos to visit his sweetheart Hero at Sestos.

2

5 If, when the wintry tempest roared,
 He sped to Hero, nothing loath,
And thus of old thy current poured,
 Fair Venus! how I pity both!

3

For *me*, degenerate modern wretch,
10 Though in the genial month of May,
My dripping limbs I faintly stretch,
 And think I've done a feat today.

4

But since he crossed the rapid tide,
 According to the doubtful story,
15 To woo—and—Lord knows what beside,
 And swam for Love, as I for Glory;

5

'Twere hard to say who fared the best:
 Sad mortals! thus the gods still plague you!
He lost his labor, I my jest;
 For he was drowned, and I've the ague.°   *chills and fever*
                          1812

The Destruction of Sennacherib[2]

1

The Assyrian came down like the wolf on the fold,
And his cohorts were gleaming in purple and gold;
And the sheen of their spears was like stars on the sea,
When the blue wave rolls nightly on deep Galilee.

2

5 Like the leaves of the forest when summer is green,
That host with their banners at sunset were seen:
Like the leaves of the forest when autumn hath blown,
That host on the morrow lay withered and strown.

3

10 For the Angel of Death spread his wings on the blast,
And breathed in the face of the foe as he passed;
And the eyes of the sleepers waxed deadly and chill,
And their hearts but once heaved, and forever grew still!

4

And there lay the steed with his nostril all wide,
But through it there rolled not the breath of his pride;
15 And the foam of his gasping lay white on the turf,
And cold as the spray of the rock-beating surf.

5

And there lay the rider distorted and pale,
With the dew on his brow, and the rust on his mail:
And the tents wer all silent, the banners alone,
20 The lances unlifted, the trumpet unblown.

6

And the widows of Ashur[3] are loud in their wail,
And the idols are broke in the temple of Baal;[4]
And the might of the Gentile,[5] unsmote by the sword,
Hath melted like snow in the glance of the Lord!

                           1815

---

2. Assyrian king, whose armies, while besieging Jerusalem (701 B.C.), were attacked by a violent plague (II Kings xix.35).

3. Assyria.
4. Deity of the Assyrians.
5. Here, Sennacherib; anyone not a Hebrew.

She Walks in Beauty

1

She walks in beauty, like the night
  Of cloudless climes and starry skies;
And all that's best of dark and bright
  Meet in her aspect and her eyes:
5 Thus mellowed to that tender light
  Which heaven to gaudy day denies.

2

One shade the more, one ray the less,
  Had half impaired the nameless grace
Which waves in every raven tress,
10   Or softly lightens o'er her face;
Where thoughts serenely sweet express
  How pure, how dear their dwelling place.

3

And on that cheek, and o'er that brow,
  So soft, so calm, yet eloquent,
15 The smiles that win, the tints that glow,
  But tell of days in goodness spent,
A mind at peace with all below,
  A heart whose love is innocent!

1815

So We'll Go No More A-Roving

1

So we'll go no more a-roving
  So late into the night,
Though the heart be still as loving,
  And the moon be still as bright.

2

5 For the sword outwears its sheath,
  And the soul wears out the breast,
And the heart must pause to breathe,
  And Love itself have rest.

3

Though the night was made for loving,
10   And the day returns too soon,
Yet we'll go no more a-roving
  By the light of the moon.

1817   1836

Stanzas

COULD LOVE FOR EVER

Could Love for ever
  Run like a river,
  And Time's endeavor
    Be tried in vain—
5 No other pleasure
  With this could measure;
  And like a treasure
    We'd hug the chain.
But since our sighing
10   Ends not in dying,
  And, formed for flying,
    Love plumes his wing;

Then for this reason
Let's love a season;
15 But let that season be only Spring.

When lovers parted
Feel broken-hearted,
And, all hopes thwarted,
   Expect to die;
20 A few years older,
Ah! how much colder
They might behold her
   For whom they sigh!
When linked together,
25 In every weather,
They pluck Love's feather
   From out his wing—
He'll stay for ever,
But sadly shiver
30 Without his plumage, when past the Spring.

Like chiefs of Faction,[6]
His life is action—
A formal paction°   *settlement, contract*
   That curbs his reign,
36 Obscures his glory,
Despot no more, he
Such territory
   Quits with disdain.
Still, still advancing,
40 With banners glancing,
His power enhancing,
   He must move on—
Repose but cloys him,
Retreat destroys him,
45 Love brooks not a degraded throne.

Wait not, fond lover!
Till years are over,
And then recover
   As from a dream.
50 While each bewailing
The other's failing,
With wrath and railing,
   All hideous seem—
While first decreasing,
55 Yet not quite ceasing,
Wait not till teasing
   All passion blight:
If once diminished,
Love's reign is finished—
60 Then part in friendship—and bid good night.

So shall Affection
To recollection
The dear connection
   Bring back with joy:
65 You had not waited
Till, tired or hated,
Your passions sated
   Began to cloy.

6. Militant party or clique.

Your last embraces
70 Leave no cold traces—
The same fond faces
        As through the past:
And eyes, the mirrors
Of your sweet errors,
75 Reflect but rapture—not least though last.

True, separations
Ask more than patience;
What desperations
        From such have risen!
80 But yet remaining,
What is't but chaining
Hearts which, once waning,
        Beat 'gainst their prison?
Time can but cloy love
85 And use destroy love:
The wingéd boy, Love,
        Is but for boys—
You'll find it torture,
Though sharper, shorter,
90 To wean, and not wear out your joys.

                                        1819

Stanzas

WHEN A MAN HATH NO FREEDOM TO FIGHT FOR AT HOME

When a man hath no freedom to fight for at home,
    Let him combat for that of his neighbors;
Let him think of the glories of Greece and of Rome,
    And get knocked on his head for his labors.

5   To do good to mankind is the chivalrous plan,
    And is always as nobly requited;
Then battle for freedom wherever you can,
    And, if not shot or hanged, you'll get knighted.

                                        1824

On This Day I Complete My Thirty-sixth Year

Missolonghi,[7] January 22, 1824

'Tis time this heart should be unmoved,
    Since others it hath ceased to move:
Yet, though I cannot be beloved,
        Still let me love!

5   My days are in the yellow leaf;
    The flowers and fruits of love are gone;
The worm, the canker,° and the grief   *deep infection*
        Are mine alone!

The fire that on my bosom preys
10 Is lone as some volcanic isle;
No torch is kindled at its blaze—
        A funeral pile.

7. In Greece, where Byron had gone to support the Greek war for independence from Turkey, and where he died, April 19, 1824.

The hope, the fear, the jealous care,
  The exalted portion of the pain
15 And power of love, I cannot share,
      But wear the chain.

But 'tis not *thus*—and 'tis not *here*—
  Such thoughts should shake my soul, nor *now*,
Where glory decks the hero's bier,
20   Or binds his brow.

The sword, the banner, and the field,
  Glory and Greece, around me see!
The Spartan, borne upon his shield,
      Was not more free.

25 Awake! (not Greece—she *is* awake!)
  Awake, my spirit! Think through *whom*
Thy life-blood tracks its parent lake,
      And then strike home!

Tread those reviving passions down,
30 Unworthy manhood!—unto thee
Indifferent should the smile or frown
      Of beauty be.

If thou regrett'st thy youth, *why live?*
  The land of honorable death
35 Is here:—up to the field, and give
      Away thy breath!

Seek out—less often sought than found—
  A soldier's grave, for thee the best;
Then look around, and choose thy ground,
40   And take thy rest.

1824

PERCY BYSSHE SHELLEY
(1792–1822)

Hymn to Intellectual Beauty[1]

1
The awful shadow of some unseen Power
  Floats though unseen among us—visiting
  This various world with as inconstant wing
As summer winds that creep from flower to flower—
5 Like moonbeams that behind some piny mountain shower,
      It visits with inconstant glance
      Each human heart and countenance;
Like hues and harmonies of evening—
      Like clouds in starlight widely spread—
10   Like memory of music fled—
      Like aught that for its grace may be
Dear, and yet dearer for its mystery.

---

1. Beauty perceived not by the senses but by spiritual illumination.

2

Spirit of BEAUTY, that dost consecrate
   With thine own hues all thou dost shine upon
15   Of human thought or form—where art thou gone?
Why dost thou pass away and leave our state,
This dim vast vale of tears, vacant and desolate?
      Ask why the sunlight not forever
      Weaves rainbows o'er yon mountain river,
20 Why aught should fail and fade that once is shown,
      Why fear and dream and death and birth
      Cast on the daylight of this earth
      Such gloom—why man has such a scope
For love and hate, despondency and hope?

3

25 No voice from some sublimer world hath ever
     To sage or poet these responses given—
     Therefore the names of Daemon, Ghost, and Heaven,
Remain the records of their vain endeavor,
Frail spells—whose uttered charm might not avail to sever,
30   From all we hear and all we see,
      Doubt, chance, and mutability.
Thy light alone—like mist o'er mountains driven,
      Or music by the night wind sent
      Through strings of some still instrument,
35   Or moonlight on a midnight stream,
Gives grace and truth to life's unquiet dream.

4

Love, Hope, and Self-esteem, like clouds depart
   And come, for some uncertain moments lent.
   Man were immortal, and omnipotent,
40 Didst thou, unknown and awful as thou art,
Keep with thy glorious train° firm state within his heart.   *company*
      Thou messenger of sympathies,
      That wax and wane in lovers' eyes—
Thou—that to human thought art nourishment,
45   Like darkness to a dying flame!
      Depart not as thy shadow came,
      Depart not—lest the grave should be,
Like life and fear, a dark reality.

5

While yet a boy I sought for ghosts, and sped
50   Through many a listening chamber, cave and ruin,
     And starlight wood, with fearful steps pursuing
Hopes of high talk with the departed dead.
I called on poisonous names[2] with which our youth is fed;
      I was not heard—I saw them not—
55   When musing deeply on the lot
Of life, at that sweet time when winds are wooing
      All vital things that wake to bring
      News of birds and blossoming—
      Sudden, thy shadow fell on me;
60 I shrieked, and clasped my hands in ecstasy!

6

I vowed that I would dedicate my powers
   To thee and thine—have I not kept the vow?
   With beating heart and streaming eyes, even now
I call the phantoms of a thousand hours
65 Each from his voiceless grave: they have in visioned bowers
     Of studious zeal or love's delight
     Outwatched with me the envious night—

---

2. Possibly alluding to attempts to summon spirits of the dead by means of magic rites.

They know that never joy illumed my brow
    Unlinked with hope that thou wouldst free
70   This world from its dark slavery,
    That thou—O awful LOVELINESS,
Wouldst give whate'er these words cannot express.

7

The day becomes more solemn and serene
    When noon is past—there is a harmony
75   In autumn, and a luster in its sky,
Which through the summer is not heard or seen,
As if it could not be, as if it had not been!
    Thus let thy power, which like the truth
    Of nature on my passive youth
80 Descended, to my onward life supply
    Its calm—to one who worships thee,
    And every form containing thee,
    Whom, SPIRIT fair, thy spells did bind
To fear himself, and love all human kind.

1817

Ozymandias[3]

I met a traveler from an antique land
Who said: Two vast and trunkless legs of stone
Stand in the desert . . . Near them, on the sand,
Half sunk, a shattered visage lies, whose frown,
5 And wrinkled lip, and sneer of cold command,
Tell that its sculptor well those passions read
Which yet survive, stamped on these lifeless things,
The hand that mocked them, and the heart that fed:
And on the pedestal these words appear:
10 "My name is Ozymandias, king of kings:
Look on my works, ye Mighty, and despair!"
Nothing beside remains. Round the decay
Of that colossal wreck, boundless and bare
The lone and level sands stretch far away.

1818

Stanzas Written in Dejection, Near Naples

1

The sun is warm, the sky is clear,
    The waves are dancing fast and bright,
Blue isles and snowy mountains wear
    The purple noon's transparent might,
5   The breath of the moist earth is light,
Around its unexpanded buds;
    Like many a voice of one delight,
The winds, the birds, the ocean floods,
The City's voice itself is soft like Solitude's.

2

10 I see the Deep's untrampled floor
    With green and purple seaweeds strown;
I see the waves upon the shore,
    Like light dissolved in star-showers, thrown:
    I sit upon the sands alone—
15 The lightning of the noontide ocean
    Is flashing round me, and a tone
    Arises from its measured motion;
How sweet! did any heart now share in my emotion.

3. Greek name for the Egyptian monarch Ramses II (13th century B.C.), who is said to have erected a huge statue of himself.

3

20   Alas! I have nor hope nor health,
        Nor peace within nor calm around,
    Nor that content surpassing wealth
        The sage in meditation found,
        And walked with inward glory crowned—
    Nor fame, nor power, nor love, nor leisure.
25   Others I see whom these surround—
    Smiling they live, and call life pleasure;
    To me that cup has been dealt in another measure.

4

    Yet now despair itself is mild,
        Even as the winds and waters are;
30   I could lie down like a tired child,
        And weep away the life of care
        Which I have borne and yet must bear,
    Till death like sleep might steal on me,
        And I might feel in the warm air
35   My cheek grow cold, and hear the sea
    Breathe o'er my dying brain its last monotony.

5

    Some might lament that I were cold,
        As I, when this sweet day is gone,
    Which my lost heart, too soon grown old,
40   Insults with this untimely moan;
        They might lament—for I am one
    Whom men love not—and yet regret,
        Unlike this day, which, when the sun
    Shall on its stainless glory set,
    Will linger, though enjoyed, like joy in memory yet.

                                    1818   1824

Ode to the West Wind

1

O wild West Wind, thou breath of Autumn's being,
Thou, from whose unseen presence the leaves dead
Are driven, like ghosts from an enchanter fleeing,

Yellow, and black, and pale, and hectic red,
5   Pestilence-stricken multitudes: O thou,
Who chariotest to their dark wintry bed

The wingéd seeds, where they lie cold and low,
Each like a corpse within its grave, until
Thine azure sister of the Spring shall blow

10   Her clarion[4] o'er the dreaming earth, and fill
(Driving sweet buds like flocks to feed in air)
With living hues and odors plain and hill:

Wild Spirit, which art moving everywhere;
Destroyer and preserver; hear, oh, hear!

2

15   Thou on whose stream, mid the steep sky's commotion,
Loose clouds like earth's decaying leaves are shed,
Shook from the tangled boughs of Heaven and Ocean,

---

4. Melodious trumpet-call.

Angels[5] of rain and lightning: there are spread
On the blue surface of thine aëry surge,
20 Like the bright hair uplifted from the head

Of some fierce Maenad,[6] even from the dim verge
Of the horizon to the zenith's height,
The locks of the approaching storm. Thou dirge

Of the dying year, to which this closing night
25 Will be the dome of a vast sepulcher,
Vaulted with all thy congregated might

Of vapors, from whose solid atmosphere
Black rain, and fire, and hail will burst: oh, hear!

3

Thou who didst waken from his summer dreams
30 The blue Mediterranean, where he lay,
Lulled by the coil of his crystálline streams,

Beside a pumice isle in Baiae's bay,[7]
And saw in sleep old palaces and towers
Quivering within the wave's intenser day,

35 All overgrown with azure moss and flowers
So sweet, the sense faints picturing them! Thou
For whose path the Atlantic's level powers

Cleave themselves into chasms, while far below
The sea-blooms and the oozy woods which wear
40 The sapless foliage of the ocean, know

Thy voice, and suddenly grow gray with fear,
And tremble and despoil themselves: oh, hear!

4

If I were a dead leaf thou mightest bear;
If I were a swift cloud to fly with thee;
45 A wave to pant beneath thy power, and share

The impulse of thy strength, only less free
Than thou, O uncontrollable! If even
I were as in my boyhood, and could be

The comrade of thy wanderings over Heaven,
50 As then, when to outstrip thy skyey speed
Scarce seem a vision; I would ne'er have striven

As thus with thee in prayer in my sore need.
Oh, lift me as a wave, a leaf, a cloud!
I fall upon the thorns of life! I bleed!

55 A heavy weight of hours has chained and bowed
One too like thee: tameless, and swift, and proud.

5

Make me thy lyre,[8] even as the forest is:
What if my leaves are falling like its own!
The tumult of thy mighty harmonies

5. In Greek derivation, messengers or divine
messengers.
6. Frenzied dancer, worshipper of Dionysus,
a god of wine and fertility.

7. Near Naples, Italy.
8. Small harp traditionally used to accompany
songs and recited poems.

60 Will take from both a deep, autumnal tone,
   Sweet though in sadness. Be thou, Spirit fierce,
   My spirit! Be thou me, impetuous one!

   Drive my dead thoughts over the universe
   Like withered leaves to quicken a new birth!
65 And, by the incantation of this verse,

   Scatter, as from an unextinguished hearth
   Ashes and sparks, my words among mankind!
   Be through my lips to unawakened earth

   The trumpet of a prophecy! O Wind,
70 If Winter comes, can Spring be far behind?

                                            1820

The Cloud

   I bring fresh showers for the thirsting flowers,
       From the seas and the streams;
   I bear light shade for the leaves when laid
       In their noonday dreams.
5 From my wings are shaken the dews that waken
       The sweet buds every one,
   When rocked to rest on their mother's breast,
       As she dances about the sun.
   I wield the flail of the lashing hail,
10   And whiten the green plains under,
   And then again I dissolve it in rain,
       And laugh as I pass in thunder.

   I sift the snow on the mountains below,
       And their great pines groan aghast;
15 And all the night 'tis my pillow white,
       While I sleep in the arms of the blast.
   Sublime on the towers of my skyey bowers,
       Lightning my pilot[9] sits;
   In a cavern under is fettered the thunder,
20   It struggles and howls at fits;°   *intermittently*
   Over earth and ocean, with gentle motion,
       This pilot is guiding me,
   Lured by the love of the genii that move
       In the depths of the purple sea;
25 Over the rills, and the crags, and the hills,
       Over the lakes and the plains,
   Wherever he dream, under mountain or stream,
       The Spirit he loves remains;
   And I all the while bask in Heaven's blue smile,
30   Whilst he is dissolving in rains.

   The sanguine Sunrise, with his meteor eyes,
       And his burning plumes outspread,
   Leaps on the back of my sailing rack,[1]
       When the morning star shines dead;
35 As on the jag of a mountain crag,
       Which an earthquake rocks and swings,
   An eagle alit one moment may sit
       In the light of its golden wings.

---

9. Electrical energy, here represented as direct-
ing the cloud in response to the attraction of
opposite charges ("genii," line 23) under the
sea.
1. Wind-driven clouds.

And when Sunset may breathe, from the lit sea beneath,
40   Its ardors of rest and of love,
And the crimson pall of eve may fall
     From the depth of Heaven above,
With wings folded I rest, on mine aëry nest,
     As still as a brooding dove.

45   That orbéd maiden with white fire laden,
     Whom mortals call the Moon,
Glides glimmering o'er my fleecelike floor,
     By the midnight breezes strewn;
And wherever the beat of her unseen feet,
50   Which only the angels hear,
May have broken the woof° of my tent's thin roof,   *fabric*
     The stars peep behind her and peer;
And I laugh to see them whirl and flee,
     Like a swarm of golden bees,
55   When I widen the rent in my wind-built tent,
     Till the calm rivers, lakes, and seas,
Like strips of the sky fallen through me on high,
     Are each paved with the moon and these.

60   I bind the Sun's throne with a burning zone,°   *belt*
     And the Moon's with a girdle of pearl;
The volcanoes are dim, and the stars reel and swim,
     When the whirlwinds my banner unfurl.
From cape to cape, with a bridgelike shape,
     Over a torrent sea,
65   Sunbeam-proof, I hang like a roof—
     The mountains its columns be.
The triumphal arch through which I march
     With hurricane, fire, and snow,
When the Powers of the air are chained to my chair,
70   Is the million-colored bow;
The sphere-fire above its soft colors wove,
     While the moist Earth was laughing below.

I am the daughter of Earth and Water,
     And the nursling of the Sky;
75   I pass through the pores of the ocean and shores;
     I change, but I cannot die.
For after the rain when with never a stain
     The pavilion of Heaven is bare,
And the winds and sunbeams with their convex° gleams   *upward-arching*
80   Build up the blue dome of air,
I silently laugh at my own cenotaph,[2]
     And out of the caverns of rain,
Like a child from the womb, like a ghost from the tomb,
     I arise and unbuild it again.

                                        1820

---

2. Monument honoring a person who is buried elsewhere.

Adonais[3]

AN ELEGY ON THE DEATH OF JOHN KEATS,
AUTHOR OF ENDYMION, HYPERION, ETC.

'Αστὴρ πρὶν μὲν ἔλαμπες ἐνὶ ζωοῖσιν 'Εῷος·
νῦν δὲ θανὼν λάμπεις "Εσπερος ἐν φθιμένοις.[4]
—PLATO

1

I weep for Adonais—he is dead!
Oh, weep for Adonais! though our tears
Thaw not the frost which binds so dear a head!
And thou, sad Hour, selected from all years
To mourn our loss, rouse thy obscure compeers,
And teach them thine own sorrow, say: with me
Died Adonais; till the Future dares
Forget the Past, his fate and fame shall be
An echo and a light unto eternity!

2

Where wert thou mighty Mother,[5] when he lay,
When thy Son lay, pierced by the shaft which flies
In darkness? where was lorn Urania
When Adonais died? With veiléd eyes,
'Mid listening Echoes, in her Paradise
She sate, while one, with soft enamored breath,
Rekindled all the fading melodies,
With which, like flowers that mock the corse° beneath,   *corpse*
He had adorned and hid the coming bulk of death.

3

Oh, weep for Adonais—he is dead!
Wake, melancholy Mother, wake and weep!
Yet wherefore? Quench within their burning bed
Thy fiery tears, and let thy loud heart keep
Like his, a mute and uncomplaining sleep;
For he is gone, where all things wise and fair
Descend:—oh, dream not that the amorous Deep
Will yet restore him to the vital air;
Death feeds on his mute voice, and laughs at our despair.

4

Most musical of mourners, weep again!
Lament anew, Urania!—He[6] died,
Who was the Sire of an immortal strain,
Blind, old, and lonely, when his country's pride,
The priest, the slave, and the liberticide,
Trampled and mocked with many a loathéd rite
Of lust and blood; he went, unterrified,
Into the gulf of death; but his clear Sprite°   *spirit*
Yet reigns o'er earth; the third among the sons of light.[7]

5

Most musical of mourners, weep anew!
Not all to that bright station dared to climb;
And happier they their happiness who knew,
Whose tapers yet burn through that night of time
In which suns perished; others more sublime,

---

3. A name derived from *Adonis,* in Greek legend a young hunter beloved of Aphrodite (Venus) and killed by a wild boar. The root meaning of his name, *Adon,* is "the lord," and in the form *Adonai* appears in Hebrew scriptures as a synonym for *God.*
4. "Thou wert the morning star among the living,/Ere thy fair light had fled—/Now, having died, thou art as Hesperus, giving/New splendor to the dead" [Shelley's translation];

Venus is both Hesperus, the evening star, and also the morning star.
5. Urania, "heavenly one," Venus invoked as the Muse of noble poetry. Adonais is represented as her son.
6. Milton, who also invoked the aid of Urania (see *Paradise Lost,* I.6–16).
7. Rivaled as a poet by only two predecessors, Homer and Dante.

Struck by the envious wrath of man or God,
Have sunk, extinct in their refulgent prime;
And some yet live, treading the thorny road,
45　　Which leads, through toil and hate, to Fame's serene abode.

6

But now, thy youngest, dearest one, has perished,
The nursling of thy widowhood, who grew,
Like a pale flower by some sad maiden cherished,
And fed with true-love tears, instead of dew;
50　　Most musical of mourners, weep anew!
Thy extreme° hope, the loveliest and the last,　　　　　　　*highest, latest*
The bloom, whose petals nipped before they blew
Died on the promise of the fruit, is waste;
The broken lily lies—the storm is overpast.

7

55　　To that high Capital,[8] where kingly Death
Keeps his pale court in beauty and decay,
He came; and bought, with price of purest breath,
A grave among the eternal.—Come away!
Haste, while the vault of blue Italian day
60　　Is yet his fitting charnel-roof! while still
He lies, as if in dewy sleep he lay;
Awake him not! surely he takes his fill
Of deep and liquid rest, forgetful of all ill.

8

He will awake no more, oh, never more!—
65　　Within the twilight chamber spreads apace
The shadow of white Death, and at the door
Invisible Corruption waits to trace
His extreme way to her dim dwelling-place;
The eternal Hunger sits, but pity and awe
70　　Soothe her pale rage, nor dares she to deface
So fair a prey, till darkness and the law
Of change, shall o'er his sleep the mortal curtain draw.

9

Oh, weep for Adonais!—The quick Dreams,
The passion-wingéd Ministers of thought,
75　　Who were his flocks, whom near the living streams
Of his young spirit he fed, and whom he taught
The love which was its music, wander not—
Wander no more, from kindling brain to brain,
But droop there, whence they sprung; and mourn their lot
80　　Round the cold heart, where, after their sweet pain,
They ne'er will gather strength, or find a home again.

10

And one with trembling hand clasps his cold head,
And fans him with her moonlight wings, and cries,
"Our love, our hope, our sorrow, is not dead;
85　　See, on the silken fringe of his faint eyes,
Like dew upon a sleeping flower, there lies
A tear some Dream has loosened from his brain."
Lost Angel of a ruined Paradise!
She knew not 'twas her own; as with no stain
90　　She faded, like a cloud which had outwept its rain.

11

One from a lucid urn of starry dew
Washed his light limbs as if embalming them;
Another clipped her profuse locks, and threw
The wreath upon him, like an anadem,°　　　　　　　　*garland*
95　　Which frozen tears instead of pearls begem;

8. Rome, where Keats died.

Another in her willful grief would break
Her bow and wingéd reeds, as if to stem
A greater loss with one which was more weak;
And dull the barbéd fire against his frozen cheek.

12

100 Another Splendor on his mouth alit,
That mouth, whence it was wont to draw the breath
Which gave it strength to pierce the guarded wit,[9]
And pass into the panting heart beneath
With lightning and with music: the damp death
105 Quenched its caress upon its icy lips;
And, as a dying meteor stains a wreath
Of moonlight vapor, which the cold night clips,°   *envelops*
It flushed through his pale limbs, and passed to its eclipse.

13

And others came . . . Desires and Adorations,
110 Wingéd Persuasions and veiled Destinies,
Splendors, and Glooms, and glimmering Incarnations
Of hopes and fears, and twilight Phantasies;
And Sorrow, with her family of Sighs,
And Pleasure, blind with tears, led by the gleam
115 Of her own dying smile instead of eyes,
Came in slow pomp;—the moving pomp might seem
Like pageantry of mist on an autumnal stream.

14

All he had loved, and molded into thought
From shape, and hue, and odor, and sweet sound,
120 Lamented Adonais. Morning sought
Her eastern watch-tower, and her hair unbound,
Wet with the tears which should adorn the ground,
Dimmed the aërial eyes that kindle day;
Afar the melancholy thunder moaned,
125 Pale Ocean in unquiet slumber lay,
And the wild Winds flew round, sobbing in their dismay.

15

Lost Echo[1] sits amid the voiceless mountains,
And feeds her grief with his remembered lay,
And will no more reply to winds or fountains,
130 Or amorous birds perched on the young green spray,
Or herdsman's horn, or bell at closing day;
Since she can mimic not his lips, more dear
Than those for whose disdain she pined away
Into a shadow of all sounds:—a drear
135 Murmur, between their songs, is all the woodmen hear.

16

Grief made the young Spring wild, and she threw down
Her kindling buds, as if she Autumn were,
Or they dead leaves; since her delight is flown
For whom should she have waked the sullen year?
140 To Phoebus was not Hyacinth[2] so dear,
Nor to himself Narcissus, as to both
Thou, Adonais; wan they stand and sere
Amid the faint companions of their youth,
With dew all turned to tears; odor, to sighing ruth.°   *pity*

17

145 Thy spirit's sister, the lorn nightingale,
Mourns not her mate with such melodious pain;
Not so the eagle, who like thee could scale
Heaven, and could nourish in the sun's domain

---

9. The defensive analytical mind.
1. A nymph who loved Narcissus and who pined away into a mere voice when that youth fell in love with his own reflection in a pool.
2. Youth loved by Apollo ("Phoebus"), who killed him by accident.

Her mighty youth,[3] with morning, doth complain,
150 Soaring and screaming round her empty nest,
As Albion° wails for thee: the curse of Cain[4]   *England*
Light on his head who[5] pierced thy innocent breast,
And scared the angel soul that was its earthly guest!

18

Ah, woe is me! Winter is come and gone,
155 But grief returns with the revolving year;
The airs and streams renew their joyous tone;
The ants, the bees, the swallows reappear;
Fresh leaves and flowers deck the dead Seasons' bier;
The amorous birds now pair in every brake,°   *thicket*
160 And build their mossy homes in field and brere;°   *briar*
And the green lizard, and the golden snake,
Like unimprisoned flames, out of their trance awake.

19

Through wood and stream and field and hill and Ocean,
A quickening life from the Earth's heart has burst
165 As it has ever done, with change and motion,
From the great morning of the world when first
God dawned on Chaos; in its stream immersed
The lamps of Heaven flash with a softer light;
All baser things pant with life's sacred thirst;
170 Diffuse themselves; and spend in love's delight,
The beauty and the joy of their renewéd might.

20

The leprous corpse touched by this spirit tender
Exhales itself in flowers of gentle breath;
Like incarnations of the stars, when splendor
175 Is changed to fragrance, they illumine death
And mock the merry worm that wakes beneath;
Nought we know, dies. Shall that alone which knows
Be as a sword consumed before the sheath
By sightless[6] lightning?—the intense atom[7] glows
180 A moment, then is quenched in a most cold repose.

21

Alas! that all we loved of him should be,
But for our grief, as if it had not been,
And grief itself be mortal! Woe is me!
Whence are we, and why are we? of what scene
185 The actors or spectators? Great and mean
Meet massed in death, who lends what life must borrow.
As long as skies are blue, and fields are green,
Evening must usher night, night urge the morrow,
Month follow month with woe, and year wake year to sorrow.

22

190 *He* will awake no more, oh, never more!
"Wake thou," cried Misery, "childless Mother, rise
Out of thy sleep, and slake, in thy heart's core,
A wound more fierce than his with tears and sighs."
And all the Dreams that watched Urania's eyes,
195 And all the Echoes whom their sister's song
Had held in holy silence, cried, "Arise!"
Swift as a Thought by the snake Memory stung,
From her ambrosial rest the fading Splendor sprung.

3. In folklore an eagle could recapture its youth by soaring close to the sun.
4. God's curse upon Cain for having slain his brother Abel was that nothing should grow for him and that he should be homeless (Genesis iii.11–12).
5. The anonymous critic whose venomous review of Keats's *Endymion* had hastened, Shelley believed, Keats's death.
6. Unseeing and unseen.
7. Indivisible and indestructible unit of anything that exists.

23

She rose like an autumnal Night, that springs
Out of the East, and follows wild and drear
The golden Day, which, on eternal wings,
Even as a ghost abandoning a bier,
Has left the Earth a corpse. Sorrow and fear
So struck, so roused, so rapt Urania;
So saddened round her like an atmosphere
Of stormy mist; so swept her on her way
Even to the mournful place where Adonais lay.

24

Out of her secret Paradise she sped,
Through camps and cities rough with stone, and steel,
And human hearts, which to her aery tread
Yielding not, wounded the invisible
Palms of her tender feet where'er they fell:
And barbéd tongues, and thoughts more sharp than they,
Rent the soft Form they never could repel,
Whose sacred blood, like the young tears of May,
Paved with eternal flowers that undeserving way.

25

In the death-chamber for a moment Death,
Shamed by the presence of that living Might,
Blushed to annihilation, and the breath
Revisited those lips, and life's pale light
Flashed through those limbs, so late her dear delight.
"Leave me not wild and drear and comfortless,
As silent lightning leaves the starless night!
Leave me not!" cried Urania: her distress
Roused Death: Death rose and smiled, and met her vain caress.

26

"Stay yet awhile! speak to me once again;
Kiss me, so long but as a kiss may live;
And in my heartless breast and burning brain
That word, that kiss, shall all thoughts else survive,
With food of saddest memory kept alive,
Now thou art dead, as if it were a part
Of thee, my Adonais! I would give
All that I am to be as thou now art,
But I am chained to Time, and cannot thence depart!

27

"O gentle child, beautiful as thou wert,
Why didst thou leave the trodden paths of men
Too soon, and with weak hands though mighty heart
Dare the unpastured dragon in his den?
Defenseless as thou wert, oh! where was then
Wisdom the mirrored shield, or scorn the spear?[8]
Or hadst thou waited the full cycle, when
Thy spirit should have filled its crescent sphere,
The monsters of life's waste had fled from thee like deer.

28

"The herded wolves, bold only to pursue;
The obscene ravens, clamorous o'er the dead;
The vultures, to the conqueror's banner true,
Who feed where Desolation first has fed,
And whose wings rain contagion;—how they[9] fled,
When like Apollo, from his golden bow,

---

8. An allusion to Perseus, who killed the monster Medusa, evading her gaze, which could turn him into stone, by using his shield as a mirror.

9. Critics, here characterized as beasts and birds of prey.

250   The Pythian of the age[1] one arrow sped
        And smiled!—The spoilers tempt no second blow,
    They fawn on the proud feet that spurn them lying low.

                    29
        "The sun comes forth, and many reptiles spawn;
        He sets, and each ephemeral insect then
255   Is gathered into death without a dawn,
        And the immortal stars awake again;
        So is it in the world of living men:
        A godlike mind soars forth, in its delight
        Making earth bare and veiling heaven, and when
260   It sinks, the swarms that dimmed or shared its light
    Leave to its kindred lamps the spirit's awful night."

                    30
        Thus ceased she: and the mountain shepherds came
        Their garlands sere, their magic mantles rent;
        The Pilgrim of Eternity,[2] whose fame
265   Over his living head like Heaven is bent,
        An early but enduring monument,
        Came, veiling all the lightnings of his song
        In sorrow; from her wilds Ierne° sent   *Ireland*
        The sweetest lyrist of her saddest wrong,[3]
270 And love taught grief to fall like music from his tongue.

                    31
        Midst others of less note, came one frail Form,[4]
        A phantom among men; companionless
        As the last cloud of an expiring storm,
        Whose thunder is its knell; he, as I guess,
275   Had gazed on Nature's naked loveliness,
        Actaeon-like,[5] and now he fled astray
        With feeble steps o'er the world's wilderness,
        And his own thoughts, along that rugged way,
    Pursued, like raging hounds, their father and their prey.

                    32
280   A pardlike[6] Spirit beautiful and swift—
        A Love in desolation masked;—a Power
        Girt round with weakness;—it can scarce uplift
        The weight of the superincumbent hour;
        It is a dying lamp, a falling shower,
285   A breaking billow;—even whilst we speak
        Is it not broken? On the withering flower
        The killing sun smiles brightly: on a cheek
    The life can burn in blood, even while the heart may break.

                    33
        His head was bound with pansies overblown,
290   And faded violets, white, and pied,° and blue;   *multicolored*
        And a light spear topped with a cypress cone,
        Round whose rude shaft dark ivy-tresses grew
        Yet dripping with the forest's noonday dew,
        Vibrated, as the ever-beating heart
295   Shook the weak hand that grasped it; of that crew
        He came the last, neglected and apart;
    A herd-abandoned deer, struck by the hunter's dart.

---

1. Byron, Shelley's friend, who attacked the critics in *English Bards and Scotch Reviewers;* here compared to Apollo the Pythian, who slew the monster Python near Delphi.
2. Byron, as author of *Childe Harold's Pilgrimage.*
3. Thomas Moore (1779–1852), poet, author of *Irish Melodies.*
4. Shelley, as poet-mourner, here wearing emblems of the god Dionysus.
5. Actaeon, a young hunter, offended the goddess Diana by discovering her while she was bathing. She transformed him into a stag, and he was torn to pieces by his hounds.
6. Leopard-like; the leopard was sacred to Dionysus.

34

All stood aloof, and at his partial moan[7]
Smiled through their tears; well knew that gentle band
300   Who in another's fate now wept his own;
As in the accents of an unknown land,
He sung new sorrow; sad Urania scanned
The Stranger's mien, and murmured: "Who art thou?"
He answered not, but with a sudden hand
305   Made bare his branded and ensanguined brow,
Which was like Cain's or Christ's—oh! that it should be so!

35

What softer voice is hushed over the dead?
Athwart what brow is that dark mantle thrown?
What form leans sadly o'er the white death-bed,
310   In mockery° of monumental stone,   *imitation*
The heavy heart heaving without a moan?
If it be He,[8] who, gentlest of the wise,
Taught, soothed, loved, honored the departed one;
Let me not vex, with inharmonious sighs,
315   The silence of that heart's accepted sacrifice.

36

Our Adonais has drunk poison—oh!
What deaf and viperous murderer could crown
Life's early cup with such a draught of woe?
The nameless worm[9] would now itself disown:
320   It felt, yet could escape the magic tone
Whose prelude held° all envy, hate and wrong,   *held off*
But what was howling in one breast alone,
Silent with expectation of the song,
Whose master's hand is cold, whose silver lyre unstrung.

37

325   Live thou, whose infamy is not thy fame!
Live! fear no heavier chastisement from me,
Thou noteless blot on a remembered name!
But be thyself, and know thyself to be!
And ever at thy season be thou free
330   To spill the venom when thy fangs o'erflow:
Remorse and Self-contempt shall cling to thee;
Hot Shame shall burn upon thy secret brow,
And like a beaten hound tremble thou shalt—as now.

38

Nor let us weep that our delight is fled
335   Far from these carrion kites° that scream below;   *scavenger hawks*
He wakes or sleeps with the enduring dead;
Thou canst not soar where he is sitting now.
Dust to the dust! but the pure spirit shall flow
Back to the burning fountain whence it came,
340   A portion of the Eternal, which must glow
Through time and change, unquenchably the same,
Whilst thy[1] cold embers choke the sordid hearth of shame.

39

Peace, peace! he is not dead, he doth not sleep—
He hath awakened from the dream of life—
345   'Tis we, who lost in stormy visions, keep
With phantoms an unprofitable strife,
And in mad trance strike with our spirit's knife
Invulnerable nothings.—*We* decay

---

7. Expressing a bond of sympathy (partiality) toward Adonais.
8. Leigh Hunt (1784–1859), poet and critic, friend of Keats and Shelley.

9. Serpent; the anonymous reviewer (see line 152).
1. The reviewer's.

Like corpses in a charnel; fear and grief
350   Convulse us and consume us day by day,
And cold hopes swarm like worms within our living clay.

       40

He has outsoared the shadow of our night;
Envy and calumny and hate and pain,
And that unrest which men miscall delight,
355   Can touch him not and torture not again;
From the contagion of the world's slow stain
He is secure, and now can never mourn
A heart grown cold, a head grown gray in vain;
Nor, when the spirit's self has ceased to burn,
360 With sparkless ashes load an unlamented urn.

       41

He lives, he wakes—'tis Death is dead, not he;
Mourn not for Adonais.—Thou young Dawn,
Turn all thy dew to splendor, for from thee
The spirit thou lamentest is not gone;
365   Ye caverns and ye forests, cease to moan!
Cease ye faint flowers and fountains, and thou Air,
Which like a morning veil thy scarf hadst thrown
O'er the abandoned Earth, now leave it bare
Even to the joyous stars which smile on its despair!

       42

370 He is made one with Nature: there is heard
His voice in all her music, from the moan
Of thunder, to the song of night's sweet bird;
He is a presence to be felt and known
In darkness and in light, from herb and stone,
375   Spreading itself where'er that Power may move
Which has withdrawn his being to its own;
Which wields the world with never wearied love,
Sustains it from beneath, and kindles it above.

       43

He is a portion of the loveliness
380 Which once he made more lovely: he doth bear
His part, while the one Spirit's plastic° stress   *formative*
Sweeps through the dull dense world, compelling there
All new successions to the forms they wear;
Torturing the unwilling dross° that checks its flight   *coarse matter*
385   To its own likeness, as each mass may bear;
And bursting in its beauty and its might
From trees and beasts and men into the Heaven's light.

       44

The splendors of the firmament of time
May be eclipsed, but are extinguished not;
390 Like stars to their appointed height they climb,
And death is a low mist which cannot blot
The brightness it may veil. When lofty thought
Lifts a young heart above its mortal lair,
And love and life contend in it, for what
395   Shall be its earthly doom, the dead live there
And move like winds of light on dark and stormy air.

       45

The inheritors of unfulfilled renown
Rose from their thrones, built beyond mortal thought,
Far in the Unapparent. Chatterton[2]
400 Rose pale, his solemn agony had not
Yet faded from him; Sidney,[3] as he fought

---

2. Thomas Chatterton (1752–70), a gifted young poet who committed suicide.

3. Sir Philip Sidney (1554–1586), a poet, critic, courtier, and soldier, fatally wounded in battle.

And as he fell and as he lived and loved
Sublimely mild, a Spirit without spot,
Arose; and Lucan,[4] by his death approved:°   *vindicated*
405   Oblivion as they rose shrank like a thing reproved.

46

And many more, whose names on Earth are dark
But whose transmitted effluence cannot die
So long as fire outlives the parent spark,
Rose, robed in dazzling immortality.
410   "Thou art become as one of us," they cry,
"It was for thee yon kingless sphere has long
Swung blind in unascended majesty,
Silent alone amid an Heaven of Song.
Assume thy wingéd throne, thou Vesper of our throng!"

47

415   Who mourns for Adonais? Oh, come forth,
Fond wretch! and know thyself and him aright.
Clasp with thy panting soul the pendulous[5] Earth;
As from a center, dart thy spirit's light
Beyond all worlds, until its spacious might
420   Satiate the void circumference: then shrink
Even to a point within our day and night;
And keep thy heart light lest it make thee sink
When hope has kindled hope, and lured thee to the brink.

48

Or go to Rome, which is the sepulcher,
425   Oh, not of him, but of our joy: 'tis nought
That ages, empires, and religions there
Lie buried in the ravage they have wrought;
For such as he can lend—they borrow not
Glory from those who made the world their prey;
430   And he is gathered to the kings of thought
Who waged contention with their time's decay,
And of the past are all that cannot pass away.

49

Go thou to Rome,—at once the Paradise,
The grave, the city, and the wilderness;
435   And where its wrecks like shattered mountains rise,
And flowering weeds, and fragrant copses dress
The bones of Desolation's nakedness
Pass, till the Spirit of the spot shall lead
Thy footsteps to a slope of green access
440   Where, like an infant's smile, over the dead
A light of laughing flowers along the grass is spread,

50

And gray walls moulder round, on which dull Time
Feeds, like slow fire upon a hoary brand;
And one keen pyramid[6] with wedge sublime,
445   Pavilioning the dust of him who planned
This refuge for his memory, doth stand
Like flame transformed to marble; and beneath,
A field is spread, on which a newer band
Have pitched in Heaven's smile their camp of death,
450   Welcoming him we lose with scarce extinguished breath.

51

Here pause: these graves are all too young as yet
To have outgrown the sorrow which consigned
Its charge to each; and if the seal is set,

4. Lucan, a young Roman poet, took his own life rather than die under sentence of the notorious emperor Nero, against whom he had conspired.
5. Floating poised in space.
6. Tomb of Gaius Cestius, an officer of ancient Rome, beside the Protestant cemetery where Keats and Shelley are buried.

Here, on one fountain of a mourning mind,
455　Break it not thou! too surely shalt thou find
Thine own well full, if thou returnest home,
Of tears and gall. From the world's bitter wind
Seek shelter in the shadow of the tomb.
What Adonais is, why fear we to become?

52
460　The One remains, the many change and pass;
Heaven's light forever shines, Earth's shadows fly;
Life, like a dome of many-colored glass,
Stains the white radiance of Eternity,
Until Death tramples it to fragments.—Die,
465　If thou wouldst be with that which thou dost seek!
Follow where all is fled!—Rome's azure sky,
Flowers, ruins, statues, music, words, are weak
The glory they transfuse with fitting truth to speak.

53
Why linger, why turn back, why shrink, my Heart?
470　Thy hopes are gone before: from all things here
They have departed; thou shouldst now depart!
A light is past from the revolving year,
And man, and woman; and what still is dear
Attracts to crush, repels to make thee wither.
475　The soft sky smiles,—the low wind whispers near:
'Tis Adonais calls! oh, hasten thither,
No more let life divide what Death can join together.

54
That Light whose smile kindles the Universe,
That Beauty in which all things work and move,
480　That Benediction which the eclipsing Curse
Of birth can quench not, that sustaining Love
Which through the web of being blindly wove
By man and beast and earth and air and sea,
Burns bright or dim, as each are mirrors of
485　The fire for which all thirst; now beams on me,
Consuming the last clouds of cold mortality.

55
The breath whose might I have invoked in song
Descends on me; my spirit's bark is driven,
Far from the shore, far from the trembling throng
490　Whose sails were never to the tempest given;
The massy earth and spheréd skies are riven!
I am borne darkly, fearfully, afar;
Whilst burning through the inmost veil of Heaven,
The soul of Adonais, like a star,
495　Beacons from the abode where the Eternal are.

1821

To Jane:[7] The Keen Stars Were Twinkling

1
The keen stars were twinkling,
And the fair moon was rising among them,
　　Dear Jane!
The guitar was tinkling,
5　But the notes were not sweet till you sung them
　　Again.

---

7. Jane Williams and her husband Edward were intimate friends of Shelley's.

2

As the moon's soft splendor
O'er the faint cold starlight of Heaven
    Is thrown,
10 So your voice most tender
To the strings without soul had then given
    Its own.

3

The stars will awaken,
Though the moon sleep a full hour later,
15   Tonight;
No leaf will be shaken
Whilst the dews of your melody scatter
    Delight.

4

Though the sound overpowers,
20 Sing again, with your dear voice revealing
    A tone
Of some world far from ours,
Where music and moonlight and feeling
    Are one.

                                    1822   1832

From Hellas:[8] *Two Choruses*

Worlds on Worlds

Worlds on worlds are rolling ever
    From creation to decay,
Like the bubbles on a river
    Sparkling, bursting, borne away.
5   But they[9] are still immortal
    Who, through birth's orient portal
And death's dark chasm hurrying to and fro,
    Clothe their unceasing flight
    In the brief dust and light
10 Gathered around their chariots as they go;
    New shapes they still may weave,
    New gods, new laws receive,
Bright or dim are they as the robes they last
    On Death's bare ribs had cast.

15   A power from the unknown God,[1]
    A Promethean conqueror,[2] came;
Like a triumphal path he trod
    The thorns of death and shame.
    A mortal shape to him
    Was like the vapor dim
20 Which the orient planet animates with light;
    Hell, Sin, and Slavery came,
    Like bloodhounds mild and tame,
Nor preyed, until their Lord had taken flight;
25   The moon of Mahomet[3]
    Arose, and it shall set:
While blazoned as on Heaven's immortal noon
    The cross leads generations on.

8. *Hellas,* an ancient name for Greece, is the title of a drama in which Shelley celebrates the contemporary Greek struggle for independence, which he saw as heralding the return of the legendary "Age of Saturn" or "Age of Gold," the first, best period of human history.
9. "The first stanza contrasts the immortality of the living and thinking beings which inhabit the planets, and to use a common and inadequate phrase, *clothe themselves in matter,* with the transience of the noblest manifestations of the external world" [Shelley's note].
1. At Athens St. Paul proclaimed the "unknown god," i.e., the One God of the Hebraic and Christian faiths (Acts xvii.22–28).
2. Christ; likened to the Greek Titan Prometheus, who befriended and suffered for mankind.
3. Crescent moon, symbol of Mohammedanism.

Swift as the radiant shapes of sleep
30   From one whose dreams are Paradise
Fly, when the fond wretch wakes to weep,
   And Day peers forth with her blank eyes;
   So fleet, so fain, so fair,
   The Powers of earth and air
35 Fled from the folding-star[4] of Bethlehem:
   Apollo, Pan, and Love,
   And even Olympian Jove[5]
Grew weak, for killing Truth had glared on them;
40   Our hills and seas and streams,
      Dispeopled of their dreams,
Their waters turned to blood, their dew to tears,
   Wailed for the golden years.

                                        1822

The World's Great Age

The world's great age begins anew,
   The golden years return,
The earth doth like a snake[6] renew
   Her winter weeds[7] outworn:
5 Heaven smiles, and faiths and empires gleam,
Like wrecks of a dissolving dream.

A brighter Hellas rears its mountains
   From waves serener far;
A new Peneus[8] rolls his fountains
10   Against the morning star.
Where fairer Tempes[9] bloom, there sleep
Young Cyclads[1] on a sunnier deep.

A loftier Argo[2] cleaves the main,
   Fraught with a later prize;
15 Another Orpheus[3] sings again,
   And loves, and weeps, and dies.
A new Ulysses leaves once more
Calypso[4] for his native shore.

Oh, write no more the tale of Troy,
20   If earth Death's scroll must be!
Nor mix with Laian rage[5] the joy
   Which dawns upon the free:
Although a subtler Sphinx renew
Riddles of death Thebes never knew.

25 Another Athens shall arise,
   And to remoter time
Bequeath, like sunset to the skies,
   The splendor of its prime;
And leave, if nought so bright may live,
30 All earth can take or Heaven can give.

4. Star that rises at the hour when sheep are brought to the fold at evening.
5. Gods worshipped in Greece until Christianity displaced them.
6. Shedding its skin after hibernation, a symbol of regeneration.
7. Clothes, especially mourning garments.
8. Greek river of legendary beauty.
9. Valley of the Peneus.
1. Or Cyclades, islands in the Aegean Sea.
2. In Greek legend, the first of seagoing vessels, on which Jason sailed to gain the "prize" (line 14) of the Golden Fleece.
3. Legendary Greek poet and musician of magical genius whose playing on the lyre caused his wife, Eurydice, to be released from the realm of the dead on condition that he would not look at her until they had reached the upper world. Breaking his pledge at the last moment, he lost her forever.
4. Island-nymph with whom Ulysses (Odysseus) lived for seven years during his return to Ithaca from the Trojan War.
5. Ignorant of his own identity, Oedipus in a rage killed King Laius of Thebes (in fact his father). Oedipus then delivered Thebes from the power of a sphinx by answering her riddles and won Jocasta (in fact his mother) as his wife and queen.

Saturn and Love their long repose
   Shall burst, more bright and good
Than all who fell, than One who rose,
   Than many unsubdued:[6]
35 Not gold, not blood, their altar dowers,
But votive tears and symbol flowers.

Oh, cease! must hate and death return?
   Cease! must men kill and die?
Cease! drain not to its dregs the urn
40   Of bitter prophecy.
The world is weary of the past,
Oh, might it die or rest at last!

                                 1822

JOHN CLARE
(1793–1864)

Badger

When midnight comes a host of dogs and men
Go out and track the badger to his den,
And put a sack within the hole, and lie
Till the old grunting badger passes by.
5 He comes and hears—they let the strongest loose.
The old fox hears the noise and drops the goose.
The poacher shoots and hurries from the cry,
And the old hare half wounded buzzes by.
They get a forkéd stick to bear him down
10 And clap the dogs and take him to the town,
And bait him all the day with many dogs,
And laugh and shout and fright the scampering hogs.
He runs along and bites at all he meets:
They shout and hollo down the noisy streets.

15 He turns about to face the loud uproar
And drives the rebels to their very door.
The frequent stone is hurled where'er they go;
When badgers fight, then everyone's a foe.
The dogs are clapped and urged to join the fray;
20 The badger turns and drives them all away.
Though scarcely half as big, demure and small,
He fights with dogs for hours and beats them all.
The heavy mastiff, savage in the fray,
Lies down and licks his feet and turns away.
25 The bulldog knows his match and waxes cold,
The badger grins and never leaves his hold.
He drives the crowd and follows at their heels
And bites them through—the drunkard swears and reels.

The frighted women take the boys away,
30 The blackguard laughs and hurries on the fray.
He tries to reach the woods, an awkward race,
But sticks and cudgels quickly stop the chase.
He turns again and drives the noisy crowd
And beats the many dogs in noises loud.
35 He drives away and beats them every one,

6. Saturn and Love are the restored deities of the "world's great age"; "all who fell" are the deities who "fell" when Christ arose from the dead; the "many unsubdued" are idols still worshipped throughout the world.

And then they loose them all and set them on.
He falls as dead and kicked by boys and men,
Then starts and grins and drives the crowd again;
Till kicked and torn and beaten out he lies
40 And leaves his hold and crackles, groans, and dies.

                    1835–37   1920

Gypsies

The snow falls deep; the forest lies alone;
The boy goes hasty for his load of brakes,°   brushwood
Then thinks upon the fire and hurries back;
The gypsy knocks his hands and tucks them up,
5 And seeks his squalid camp, half hid in snow,
Beneath the oak which breaks away the wind,
And bushes close in snow like hovel warm;
There tainted mutton wastes upon the coals,
And the half-wasted dog squats close and rubs,
10 Then feels the heat too strong, and goes aloof;
He watches well, but none a bit can spare,
And vainly waits the morsel thrown away.
'Tis thus they live—a picture to the place,
A quiet, pilfering, unprotected race.

                    1837–41   1920

Song: Love Lives Beyond the Tomb

            Love lives beyond
The tomb, the earth, which fades like dew—
            I love the fond,
The faithful, and the true.

5   Love lives in sleep,
'Tis happiness of healthy dreams,
            Eve's dews may weep,
But love delightful seems.

            'Tis seen in flowers,
10 And in the even's pearly dew
            On earth's green hours,
And in the heaven's eternal blue.

            'Tis heard in spring
When light and sunbeams, warm and kind,
15   On angel's wing
Brings love and music to the wind.

            And where's the voice
So young, so beautiful, and sweet
            As nature's choice,
20 Where spring and lovers meet?

            Love lives beyond
The tomb, the earth, the flowers, and dew.
            I love the fond,
The faithful, young, and true.

                    1842–64   1873

First Love

I ne'er was struck before that hour
   With love so sudden and so sweet,
Her face it bloomed like a sweet flower
   And stole my heart away complete.
5 My face turned pale as deadly pale.
   My legs refused to walk away,
And when she looked, what could I ail?
   My life and all seemed turned to clay.

And then my blood rushed to my face
10   And took my eyesight quite away,
The trees and bushes round the place
   Seemed midnight at noonday.
I could not see a single thing,
   Words from my eyes did start—
15 They spoke as chords do from the string,
   And blood burnt round my heart.

Are flowers the winter's choice?
   Is love's bed always snow?
She seemed to hear my silent voice,
20   Not love's appeals to know.
I never saw so sweet a face
   As that I stood before.
My heart has left its dwelling-place
   And can return no more.

               1842–64   1920

Farewell

Farewell to the bushy clump close to the river
And the flags where the butter-bump° hides in forever;   *bittern*
Farewell to the weedy nook, hemmed in by waters;
Farewell to the miller's brook and his three bonny daughters;
5 Farewell to them all while in prison I lie—
In the prison a thrall sees naught but the sky.

Shut out are the green fields and birds in the bushes;
In the prison yard nothing builds, blackbirds or thrushes.
Farewell to the old mill and dash of the waters,
10 To the miller and, dearer still, to his three bonny daughters.

In the nook, the larger burdock grows near the green willow;
In the flood, round the moor-cock dashes under the billow;
To the old mill farewell, to the lock, pens, and waters,
To the miller himsel', and his three bonny daughters.

               1842–64   1920

I Am

I am: yet what I am none cares or knows
   My friends forsake me like a memory lost,
I am the self-consumer of my woes—
   They rise and vanish in oblivious host,
5 Like shadows in love's frenzied, stifled throes—
And yet I am, and live—like vapors tossed

Into the nothingness of scorn and noise,
　　Into the living sea of waking dreams,
Where there is neither sense of life or joys,
10　　But the vast shipwreck of my life's esteems;
Even the dearest, that I love the best,
Are strange—nay, rather stranger than the rest.

I long for scenes, where man hath never trod,
　　A place where woman never smiled or wept—
15 There to abide with my Creator, God,
　　And sleep as I in childhood sweetly slept,
Untroubling, and untroubled where I lie,
The grass below— above the vaulted sky.

　　　　　　　　　　　　　　1842–64　　　　　1865

JOHN KEATS
(1795–1821)

On First Looking into Chapman's Homer[1]

Much have I traveled in the realms of gold,
　　And many goodly states and kingdoms seen;
　　Round many western islands have I been
Which bards in fealty° to Apollo[2] hold.　　　　　　　*allegiance*
5 Oft of one wide expanse had I been told
　　That deep browed Homer ruled as his demesne;°　　*domain*
　　Yet did I never breathe its pure serene°　　　　　*atmosphere*
Till I heard Chapman speak out loud and bold:
Then felt I like some watcher of the skies
10　　When a new planet swims into his ken;
Or like stout Cortez[3] when with eagle eyes
　　He stared at the Pacific—and all his men
Looked at each other with a wild surmise—
　　Silent, upon a peak in Darien.

　　　　　　　　　　　　　　　　　　　　　1816

On the Sea

It keeps eternal whisperings around
　　Desolate shores, and with its mighty swell
　　Gluts twice ten thousand Caverns, till the spell
Of Hecate[4] leaves them their old shadowy sound.
5 Often 'tis in such gentle temper found,
　　That scarcely will the very smallest shell
　　Be moved for days from where it sometime fell,
When last the winds of Heaven were unbound.
Oh ye! who have your eyeballs vexed and tired,
10　　Feast them upon the wideness of the Sea;
　　　　Oh ye! whose ears are dinned with uproar rude,
　　Or fed too much with cloying melody—
　　　　Sit ye near some old Cavern's Mouth and brood,
Until ye start, as if the sea nymphs quired!°　　　*choired*
　　　　　　　　　　　　　　　　　　　　　1817

---

1. Translation of Homer's *Iliad* by George Chapman, a contemporary of Shakespeare's.
2. God of poetic inspiration.
3. Spanish conqueror of Mexico; in fact, Balboa, not Cortez, was the first European to see the Pacific, from Darien, in Panama.
4. Greek goddess associated with witchcraft and the underworld.

On Sitting Down to Read *King Lear* Once Again

O golden-tongued Romance with serene lute!
  Fair pluméd Siren!° Queen of far away!   *enchantress*
  Leave melodizing on this wintry day,
Shut up thine olden pages, and be mute:
5 Adieu! for once again the fierce dispute
  Betwixt damnation and impassioned clay
  Must I burn through; once more humbly assay
The bitter-sweet of this Shakespearean fruit.
Chief Poet! and ye clouds of Albion,[5]
10 Begetters of our deep eternal theme,
When through the old oak forest I am gone,
  Let me not wander in a barren dream,
But when I am consuméd in the fire,
Give me new Phoenix[6] wings to fly at my desire.

                                    1818   1838

When I Have Fears

When I have fears that I may cease to be
  Before my pen has gleaned my teeming brain,
Before high-piléd books, in charact'ry,°   *written symbols*
  Hold like rich garners the full-ripened grain;
5 When I behold, upon the night's starred face,
  Huge cloudy symbols of a high romance,
And think that I may never live to trace
  Their shadows, with the magic hand of chance;
And when I feel, fair creature of an hour,
10 That I shall never look upon thee more,
Never have relish in the faery° power   *magical*
  Of unreflecting love!—then on the shore
Of the wide world I stand alone, and think
Till Love and Fame to nothingness do sink.

                                    1818   1848

To Homer

Standing aloof in giant ignorance,
  Of thee I hear and of the Cyclades,[7]
As one who sits ashore and longs perchance
  To visit dolphin-coral in deep seas.
5 So thou wast blind! but then the veil was rent,
  For Jove[8] uncurtained Heaven to let thee live,
And Neptune[9] made for thee a spumy tent,
  And Pan[1] made sing for thee his forest-hive;
Aye, on the shores of darkness there is light,
10 And precipices show untrodden green;
There is a budding morrow in midnight,
  There is a triple sight in blindness keen;
Such seeing hadst thou, as it once befell
To Dian, Queen of Earth, and Heaven, and Hell.[2]

                                    1818   1848

5. Ancient name for England, especially referring to pre-Roman Britain, the era of King Lear.
6. Fabled Arabian bird that, after living for centuries, consumes itself in fire and is reborn.
7. Islands in the Aegean, famed for their beauty.
8. Monarch of all the Greek gods; ruler of the sky and the dwellings of the immortals.

9. God of oceans.
1. God of streams and woodlands and their visible and invisible inhabitants.
2. Diana came to be regarded as having three forms and realms: goddess of the earth and fertility, of the moon, and of the underworld ("Hell").

The Eve of St. Agnes[3]

1

St. Agnes' Eve—Ah, bitter chill it was!
The owl, for all his feathers, was a-cold;
The hare limped trembling through the frozen grass,
And silent was the flock in woolly fold:
Numb were the Beadsman's[4] fingers, while he told
His rosary, and while his frosted breath,
Like pious incense from a censer old,
Seemed taking flight for heaven, without a death,
Past the sweet Virgin's picture, while his prayer he saith.

2

His prayer he saith, this patient, holy man;
Then takes his lamp, and riseth from his knees,
And back returneth, meager, barefoot, wan,
Along the chapel aisle by slow degrees:
The sculptured dead, on each side, seem to freeze,
Imprisoned in black, purgatorial rails:
Knights, ladies, praying in dumb orat'ries,[5]
He passeth by; and his weak spirit fails
To think how they may ache in icy hoods and mails.

3

Northward he turneth through a little door,
And scarce three steps, ere Music's golden tongue
Flattered to tears this aged man and poor;
But no—already had his deathbell rung:
The joys of all his life were said and sung:
His was harsh penance on St. Agnes' Eve:
Another way he went, and soon among
Rough ashes sat he for his soul's reprieve,
And all night kept awake, for sinner's sake to grieve.

4

That ancient Beadsman heard the prelude soft;
And so it chanced, for many a door was wide,
From hurry to and fro. Soon, up aloft,
The silver, snarling trumpets 'gan to chide:
The level chambers, ready with their pride,
Were glowing to receive a thousand guests:
The carvéd angels, ever eager-eyed,
Stared, where upon their heads the cornice rests,
With hair blown back, and wings put crosswise on their breasts.

5

At length burst in the argent revelry,[6]
With plume, tiara, and all rich array,
Numerous as shadows haunting faerily
The brain, new stuffed, in youth, with triumphs gay
Of old romance. These let us wish away,
And turn, sole-thoughted, to one Lady there,
Whose heart had brooded, all that wintry day,
On love, and winged St. Agnes' saintly care,
As she had heard old dames full many times declare.

6

They told her how, upon St. Agnes' Eve,
Young virgins might have visions of delight,
And soft adorings from their loves receive

3. January 20, proverbially the coldest winter night. St. Agnes, martyred in the 4th century A.D., is patroness of virgins. Traditionally, a maiden who observes the ritual of St. Agnes' Eve will see a vision of her husband-to-be.
4. From Middle English *bede,* meaning *prayer.*
A needy dependent, paid a small stipend to pray regularly for his benefactor. "Rosary" (line 6): a string of beads on which a series of short prayers are counted ("told," line 5).
5. Small chapels in a larger one.
6. Brightly-dressed revelers.

Upon the honeyed middle of the night,
50   If ceremonies due they did aright;
As, supperless to bed they must retire,
And couch supine their beauties, lily white;
Nor look behind, nor sideways, but require
Of Heaven with upward eyes for all that they desire.

7

55   Full of this whim was thoughtful Madeline:
The music, yearning like a God in pain,
She scarcely heard: her maiden eyes divine,
Fixed on the floor, saw many a sweeping train
Pass by—she heeded not at all: in vain
60   Came many a tiptoe, amorous cavalier,
And back retired; not cooled by high disdain;
But she saw not: her heart was otherwhere:
She sighed for Agnes' dreams, the sweetest of the year.

8

She danced along with vague, regardless eyes,
65   Anxious her lips, her breathing quick and short:
The hallowed hour was near at hand: she sighs
Amid the timbrels,° and the thronged resort   *hand drums*
Of whisperers in anger, or in sport;
'Mid looks of love, defiance, hate, and scorn,
70   Hoodwinked with faery fancy; all amort,[7]
Save to St. Agnes and her lambs unshorn,[8]
And all the bliss to be before tomorrow morn.

9

So, purposing each moment to retire,
She lingered still. Meantime, across the moors,
75   Had come young Porphyro, with heart on fire
For Madeline. Beside the portal doors,
Buttressed from moonlight,[9] stands he, and implores
All saints to give him sight of Madeline,
But for one moment in the tedious hours,
80   That he might gaze and worship all unseen;
Perchance speak, kneel, touch, kiss—in sooth such things have been.

10

He ventures in: let no buzzed whisper tell:
All eyes be muffled, or a hundred swords
Will storm his heart, Love's fev'rous citadel:
85   For him, those chambers held barbarian hordes,
Hyena foemen, and hot-blooded lords,
Whose very dogs would execrations howl
Against his lineage: not one breast affords
Him any mercy, in that mansion foul,
90   Save one old beldame,° weak in body and in soul.   *old woman*

11

Ah, happy chance! the aged creature came,
Shuffling along with ivory-headed wand,
To where he stood, hid from the torch's flame,
Behind a broad hall-pillar, far beyond
95   The sound of merriment and chorus bland:°   *harmonizing*
He startled her; but soon she knew his face,
And grasped his fingers in her palsied hand,
Saying, "Mercy, Porphyro! hie thee from this place;
They are all here tonight, the whole bloodthirsty race!

12

100   "Get hence! get hence! there's dwarfish Hildebrand;
He had a fever late, and in the fit

---

7. Dead; i.e., oblivious.
8. Symbolically associated with St. Agnes; new wool offered at the Mass commemorating the saint was later spun and woven by the nuns (lines 115–117).
9. I.e., concealed in dark shadows.

He curséd thee and thine, both house and land:
Then there's that old Lord Maurice, not a whit
More tame for his gray hairs—Alas me! flit!
105   Flit like a ghost away."—"Ah, Gossip[1] dear,
We're safe enough; here in this armchair sit,
And tell me how"—"Good Saints! not here, not here;
Follow me, child, or else these stones will be thy bier."

          13

He followed through a lowly archéd way,
110   Brushing the cobwebs with his lofty plume,
And as she muttered "Well-a—well-a-day!"
He found him in a little moonlight room,
Pale, latticed, chill, and silent as a tomb.
"Now tell me where is Madeline," said he,
115   "O tell me, Angela, by the holy loom
Which none but secret sisterhood may see,
When they St. Agnes' wool are weaving piously."

          14

"St Agnes! Ah! it is St. Agnes' Eve—
Yet men will murder upon holy days:
120   Thou must hold water in a witch's sieve,
And be liege lord of all the Elves and Fays,[2]
To venture so: it fills me with amaze
To see thee, Porphyro!—St. Agnes' Eve!
God's help! my lady fair the conjuror plays[3]
125   This very night: good angels her deceive!
But let me laugh awhile, I've mickle° time to grieve."   *much*

          15

Feebly she laugheth in the languid moon,
While Porphyro upon her face doth look,
Like puzzled urchin on an aged crone
130   Who keepeth closed a wondrous riddle-book,
As spectacled she sits in chimney nook.
But soon his eyes grew brilliant, when she told
His lady's purpose; and he scarce could brook°   *check*
Tears, at the thought of those enchantments cold,
135 And Madeline asleep in lap of legends old.

          16

Sudden a thought came like a full-blown rose,
Flushing his brow, and in his painéd heart
Made purple riot: then doth he propose
A stratagem, that makes the beldame start:
140   "A cruel man and impious thou art:
Sweet lady, let her pray, and sleep, and dream
Alone with her good angels, far apart
From wicked men like thee. Go, go!—I deem
Thou canst not surely be the same that thou didst seem."

          17

145   "I will not harm her, by all saints I swear,"
Quoth Porphyro: "O may I ne'er find grace
When my weak voice shall whisper its last prayer,
If one of her soft ringlets I displace,
Or look with ruffian passion in her face:
150   Good Angela, believe me by these tears;
Or I will, even in a moment's space,
Awake, with horrid shout, my foemen's ears,
And beard them, though they be more fanged than wolves and bears."

---

1. Old kinswoman or household retainer.
2. I.e., to hold water in a sieve and to com-
mand elves and fairies ("Fays"), Porphyro
would have to be a magician.
3. I.e., is trying magic spells.

18

"Ah! why wilt thou affright a feeble soul?
155   A poor, weak, palsy-stricken, churchyard thing,[4]
Whose passing bell[5] may ere the midnight toll;
Whose prayers for thee, each morn and evening,
Were never missed."—Thus plaining,° doth she bring   *complaining*
A gentler speech from burning Porphyro;
160   So woeful and of such deep sorrowing,
That Angela gives promise she will do
Whatever he shall wish, betide her weal or woe.

19

Which was, to lead him, in close secrecy,
Even to Madeline's chamber, and there hide
165   Him in a closet, of such privacy
That he might see her beauty unespied,
And win perhaps that night a peerless bride,
While legioned faeries paced the coverlet,
And pale enchantment held her sleepy-eyed.
170   Never on such a night have lovers met,
Since Merlin paid his Demon all the monstrous debt.[6]

20

"It shall be as thou wishest," said the Dame:
"All cates° and dainties shall be storéd there   *delicacies*
Quickly on this feast[7] night: by the tambour frame[8]
175   Her own lute thou wilt see: no time to spare,
For I am slow and feeble, and scarce dare
On such a catering trust my dizzy head.
Wait here, my child, with patience; kneel in prayer
The while: Ah! thou must needs the lady wed,
180   Or may I never leave my grave among the dead."

21

So saying, she hobbled off with busy fear.
The lover's endless minutes slowly passed:
The dame returned, and whispered in his ear
To follow her; with aged eyes aghast
185   From fright of dim espial. Safe at last,
Through many a dusky gallery, they gain
The maiden's chamber, silken, hushed, and chaste;
Where Porphyro took covert, pleased amain.°   *greatly*
His poor guide hurried back with agues in her brain.

22

190   Her falt'ring hand upon the balustrade,
Old Angela was feeling for the stair,
When Madeline, St. Agnes' charméd maid,
Rose, like a missioned spirit, unaware:
With silver taper's light, and pious care,
195   She turned, and down the aged gossip led
To a safe level matting. Now prepare,
Young Porphyro, for gazing on that bed;
She comes, she comes again, like ringdove frayed° and fled.   *affrighted*

23

Out went the taper as she hurried in;
200   Its little smoke, in pallid moonshine, died:
She closed the door, she panted, all akin
To spirits of the air, and visions wide:
No uttered syllable, or, woe betide!

4. I.e., soon to die.
5. Tolled when a person died ("passed away").
6. Possibly alluding to the tale that Merlin, in Arthurian legend a great wizard, lies bound for ages by a spell that he gave to an evil woman to buy her love.
7. The festival, or Mass, honoring St. Agnes.
8. A circular embroidery frame.

But to her heart, her heart was voluble,
205   Paining with eloquence her balmy side;
    As though a tongueless nightingale should swell
Her throat in vain, and die, heart-stifled, in her dell.

24

    A casement high and triple-arched there was,
    All garlanded with carven imag'ries
210   Of fruits, and flowers, and bunches of knot-grass,
    And diamonded with panes of quaint device,
    Innumerable of stains and splendid dyes,
    As are the tiger-moth's deep-damasked wings;
    And in the midst, 'mong thousand heraldries,
215   And twilight saints, and dim emblazonings,
A shielded scutcheon blushed with blood of queens and kings.[9]

25

    Full on this casement shone the wintry moon,
    And threw warm gules[1] on Madeline's fair breast,
    As down she knelt for heaven's grace and boon;°   *gift*
220   Rose-bloom fell on her hands, together pressed,
    And on her silver cross soft amethyst,
    And on her hair a glory, like a saint:
    She seemed a splendid angel, newly dressed,
    Save wings, for heaven—Porphyro grew faint:
225 She knelt, so pure a thing, so free from mortal taint.

26

    Anon his heart revives: her vespers done,
    Of all its wreathéd pearls her hair she frees;
    Unclasps her warméd jewels one by one;
    Loosens her fragrant bodice; by degrees
230   Her rich attire creeps rustling to her knees:
    Half-hidden, like a mermaid in sea-weed,
    Pensive awhile she dreams awake, and sees,
    In fancy, fair St. Agnes in her bed,
But dares not look behind, or all the charm is fled.

27

235   Soon, trembling in her soft and chilly nest,
    In sort of wakeful swoon, perplexed she lay,
    Until the poppied warmth of sleep oppressed
    Her soothéd limbs, and soul fatigued away;
    Flown, like a thought, until the morrow-day;
240   Blissfully havened both from joy and pain;
    Clasped like a missal where swart Paynims[2] pray;
    Blinded alike from sunshine and from rain,
As though a rose should shut, and be a bud again.

28

    Stol'n to this paradise, and so entranced,
245   Porphyro gazed upon her empty dress,
    And listened to her breathing, if it chanced
    To wake into a slumberous tenderness;
    Which when he heard, that minute did he bless,
    And breathed himself: then from the closet crept,
250   Noiseless as fear in a wide wilderness,
    And over the hushed carpet, silent, stepped,
And 'tween the curtains peeped, where, lo!—how fast she slept.

29

    Then by the bedside, where the faded moon
    Made a dim, silver twilight, soft he set
255   A table, and, half anguished, threw thereon
    A cloth of woven crimson, gold, and jet—

---

9. A shield representing a coat of arms ("scutcheon") showed the red pigments ("blushed") indicating royal ancestry.

1. Heraldic red; here, in stained glass.
2. Dark pagans.

O for some drowsy Morphean amulet![3]
The boisterous, midnight, festive clarion,
The kettledrum, and far-heard clarinet,
260   Affray his ears, though but in dying tone—
The hall door shuts again, and all the noise is gone.

30
And still she slept an azure-lidded sleep,
In blanchéd linen, smooth, and lavendered,
While he from forth the closet brought a heap
265   Of candied apple, quince, and plum, and gourd;
With jellies soother than the creamy curd,
And lucent syrups, tinct° with cinnamon;   *tinctured*
Manna and dates, in argosy transferred
From Fez;[4] and spicéd dainties, every one,
270 From silken Samarcand to cedared Lebanon.[5]

31
These delicates he heaped with glowing hand
On golden dishes and in baskets bright
Of wreathéd silver: sumptuous they stand
In the retiréd quiet of the night,
275   Filling the chilly room with perfume light.—
"And now, my love, my seraph° fair, awake!   *angel*
Thou art my heaven, and I thine eremite:[6]
Open thine eyes, for meek St. Agnes' sake,
Or I shall drowse beside thee, so my soul doth ache."

32
280   Thus whispering, his warm, unnervéd arm
Sank in her pillow. Shaded was her dream
By the dusk curtains: 'twas a midnight charm
Impossible to melt as icéd stream:
The lustrous salvers° in the moonlight gleam;   *serving dishes*
285   Broad golden fringe upon the carpet lies:
It seemed he never, never could redeem
From such a steadfast spell his lady's eyes;
So mused awhile, entoiled in wooféd° fantasies.   *enwoven*

33
Awakening up, he took her hollow lute—
290   Tumultuous—and, in chords that tenderest be,
He played an ancient ditty, long since mute,
In Provence called "*La belle dame sans merci*"[7]
Close to her ear touching the melody;
Wherewith disturbed, she uttered a soft moan:
295   He ceased—she panted quick—and suddenly
Her blue affrayéd eyes wide open shone:
Upon his knees he sank, pale as smooth-sculptured stone.

34
Her eyes were open, but she still beheld,
Now wide awake, the vision of her sleep:
300   There was a painful change, that nigh expelled
The blisses of her dream so pure and deep,
At which fair Madeline began to weep,
And moan forth witless words with many a sigh;
While still her gaze on Porphyro would keep,
305   Who knelt, with joinéd hands and piteous eye,
Fearing to move or speak, she looked so dreamingly.

35
"Ah, Porphyro!" said she, "but even now ·
Thy voice was at sweet tremble in mine ear,
Made tunable with every sweetest vow;

3. An object, such as an engraved stone, ex-   5. Places associated with ancient luxury and
erting the power of Morpheus, god of sleep.   wealth.
4. Morocco.   6. Hermit, religious devotee.
                                                   7. The lady beautiful but without mercy.

310   And those sad eyes were spiritual and clear:
       How changed thou art! how pallid, chill, and drear!
       Give me that voice again, my Porphyro,
       Those looks immortal, those complainings dear!
       Oh leave me not in this eternal woe,
315 For if thou diest, my Love, I know not where to go."
              36
       Beyond a mortal man impassioned far
       At these voluptuous accents, he arose,
       Ethereal, flushed, and like a throbbing star
       Seen mid the sapphire heaven's deep repose;
320   Into her dream he melted, as the rose
       Blendeth its odor with the violet—
       Solution sweet: meantime the frost-wind blows
       Like Love's alarum° pattering the sharp sleet   *signal, call to arms*
Against the windowpanes; St. Agnes' moon hath set.
              37
325 'Tis dark: quick pattereth the flaw-blown° sleet: *gust-blown*
       "This is no dream, my bride, my Madeline!"
       'Tis dark: the icéd gusts still rave and beat:
       "No dream, alas! alas! and woe is mine!
       Porphyro will leave me here to fade and pine.—
330   Cruel! what traitor could thee hither bring?
       I curse not, for my heart is lost in thine,
       Though thou forsakest a deceivéd thing—
A dove forlorn and lost with sick unprunéd[8] wing."
              38
       "My Madeline! sweet dreamer! lovely bride!
335 Say, may I be for aye thy vassal blest?
       Thy beauty's shield, heart-shaped and vermeil° dyed?   *vermilion*
       Ah, silver shrine, here will I take my rest
       After so many hours of toil and quest,
       A famished pilgrim—saved by miracle.
340   Though I have found, I will not rob thy nest
       Saving of thy sweet self; if thou think'st well
To trust, fair Madeline, to no rude infidel.
              39
       "Hark! 'tis an elfin-storm from faery land,
       Of haggard° seeming, but a boon indeed: *wild, ugly*
345 Arise—arise! the morning is at hand—
       The bloated wassaillers° will never heed—   *drunken revelers*
       Let us away, my love, with happy speed;
       There are no ears to hear, or eyes to see—
       Drowned all in Rhenish and the sleepy mead:[9]
350   Awake! arise! my love, and fearless be,
For o'er the southern moors I have a home for thee."
              40
       She hurried at his words, beset with fears,
       For there were sleeping dragons all around,
       At glaring watch, perhaps, with ready spears—
355 Down the wide stairs a darkling way they found.—
       In all the house was heard no human sound.
       A chain-dropped lamp was flickering by each door;
       The arras, rich with horseman, hawk, and hound,
       Fluttered in the besieging wind's uproar;
360 And the long carpets rose along the gusty floor.
              41
       They glide, like phantoms, into the wide hall;
       Like phantoms, to the iron porch, they glide;
       Where lay the Porter, in uneasy sprawl,

8. Unpreened; i.e., disarranged, rumpled.   9. Rhine wine, and fermented honey and
                                                    water.

With a huge empty flagon by his side:
365   The wakeful bloodhound rose, and shook his hide,
But his sagacious eye an inmate owns:°   *recognizes*
By one, and one, the bolts full easy slide:
The chains lie silent on the footworn stones;
The key turns, and the door upon its hinges groans.

                        42
370   And they are gone: aye, ages long ago
These lovers fled away into the storm.
That night the Baron dreamt of many a woe,
And all his warrior-guests, with shade and form
Of witch, and demon, and large coffin-worm,
375   Were long be-nightmared. Angela the old
Died palsy-twitched, with meager face deform;
The Beadsman, after thousand aves¹ told,
For aye unsought for slept among his ashes cold.

                                          1819   1820

La Belle Dame sans Merci²

O what can ail thee, Knight at arms,
   Alone and palely loitering?
The sedge has withered from the Lake
   And no birds sing!

5   O what can ail thee, Knight at arms,
   So haggard, and so woebegone?
The squirrel's granary is full
   And the harvest's done.

I see a lily on thy brow
10   With anguish moist and fever dew,
And on thy cheeks a fading rose
   Fast withereth too.

"I met a Lady in the Meads,°   *meadows*
   Full beautiful, a faery's child,
15   Her hair was long, her foot was light
   And her eyes were wild.

"I made a Garland for her head,
   And bracelets too, and fragrant Zone;°   *girdle*
She looked at me as she did love
20   And made sweet moan.

"I set her on my pacing steed
   And nothing else saw all day long,
For sidelong would she bend and sing
   A faery's song.

25   "She found me roots of relish sweet,
   And honey wild, and manna dew,
And sure in language strange she said
   'I love thee true.'

"She took me to her elfin grot
30   And there she wept and sighed full sore,
And there I shut her wild wild eyes
   With kisses four.

1. As in *Ave Maria* (Hail Mary), a saluta-   This is an earlier (and widely preferred) ver-
tion to the Virgin.   sion of a poem first published in 1820.
2. The lady beautiful but without mercy.

"And there she lulléd me asleep,
　　And there I dreamed, Ah Woe betide!
35　The latest° dream I ever dreamt　　　　　　　　　　　　　　*last*
　　　　On the cold hill side.

"I saw pale Kings, and Princes too,
　　Pale warriors, death-pale were they all;
They cried, 'La belle dame sans merci
40　　　Thee hath in thrall!'

"I saw their starved lips in the gloam
　　With horrid warning gapéd wide,
And I awoke, and found me here
　　　On the cold hill's side.

45　"And this is why I sojourn here,
　　Alone and palely loitering;
Though the sedge is withered from the Lake
　　　And no birds sing."

　　　　　　　　　　　　　　　　　April 1819　　　　1888

Ode to a Nightingale

1

My heart aches, and a drowsy numbness pains
　　My sense, as though of hemlock[3] I had drunk,
Or emptied some dull opiate to the drains
　　One minute past, and Lethe-wards[4] had sunk:
5　'Tis not through envy of thy happy lot,
　　But being too happy in thine happiness—
　　　　That thou, light-wingéd Dryad of the trees,
　　　　　In some melodious plot
　　Of beechen green, and shadows numberless,
10　　　Singest of summer in full-throated ease.

2

O, for a draught of vintage! that hath been
　　Cooled a long age in the deep-delvéd earth,
Tasting of Flora[5] and the country green,
　　Dance, and Provençal song,[6] and sunburnt mirth!
15　O for a beaker full of the warm South,
　　Full of the true, the blushful Hippocrene,[7]
　　　　With beaded bubbles winking at the brim,
　　　　　And purple-stainéd mouth;
　　That I might drink, and leave the world unseen,
20　　　And with thee fade away into the forest dim:

3

Fade far away, dissolve, and quite forget
　　What thou among the leaves hast never known,
The weariness, the fever, and the fret
　　Here, where men sit and hear each other groan;
25　Where palsy shakes a few, sad, last gray hairs,
　　Where youth grows pale, and specter-thin, and dies,
　　　　Where but to think is to be full of sorrow
　　　　　And leaden-eyed despairs,
　　Where Beauty cannot keep her lustrous eyes,
30　　　Or new Love pine at them beyond tomorrow.

3. Opiate made from a poisonous herb.
4. Towards the river Lethe, whose waters in Hades bring the dead forgetfulness.
5. Roman goddess of springtime and flowers.
6. Of the late-medieval troubadours of Provence, in southern France.
7. The fountain of the Muses (goddesses of poetry and the arts) on Mt. Helicon in Greece; its waters induce poetic inspiration.

4

Away! away! for I will fly to thee,
  Not charioted by Bacchus and his pards,[8]
But on the viewless° wings of Poesy,   *invisible*
  Though the dull brain perplexes and retards:
35 Already with thee! tender is the night,
  And haply the Queen-Moon is on her throne,
    Clustered around by all her starry Fays;°   *fairies*
      But here there is no light,
  Save what from heaven is with the breezes blown
40   Through verdurous glooms and winding mossy ways.

5

I cannot see what flowers are at my feet,
  Nor what soft incense hangs upon the boughs,
But, in embalméd° darkness, guess each sweet   *perfumed*
  Wherewith the seasonable month endows
45 The grass, the thicket, and the fruit tree wild;
  White hawthorn, and the pastoral eglantine;[9]
    Fast fading violets covered up in leaves;
      And mid-May's eldest child,
  The coming musk-rose, full of dewy wine,
50   The murmurous haunt of flies on summer eves.

6

Darkling° I listen; and for many a time   *in darkness*
  I have been half in love with easeful Death,
Called him soft names in many a muséd rhyme,
  To take into the air my quiet breath;
55 Now more than ever seems it rich to die,
  To cease upon the midnight with no pain,
    While thou art pouring forth thy soul abroad
      In such an ecstasy!
  Still wouldst thou sing, and I have ears in vain—
60   To thy high requiem become a sod.

7

Thou wast not born for death, immortal Bird!
  No hungry generations tread thee down;
The voice I hear this passing night was heard
  In ancient days by emperor and clown:
65 Perhaps the selfsame song that found a path
  Through the sad heart of Ruth,[1] when, sick for home,
    She stood in tears amid the alien corn;
      The same that ofttimes hath
  Charmed magic casements, opening on the foam
70   Of perilous seas, in faery lands forlorn.

8

Forlorn! the very word is like a bell
  To toll me back from thee to my sole self!
Adieu! the fancy cannot cheat so well
  As she is famed to do, deceiving elf.
75 Adieu! adieu! thy plaintive anthem fades
  Past the near meadows, over the still stream,
    Up the hill side; and now 'tis buried deep
      In the next valley-glades:
  Was it a vision, or a waking dream?
80   Fled is that music:—Do I wake or sleep?

                                    May 1819   1820

8. "Bacchus": god of wine, often depicted in a chariot drawn by leopards ("pards").
9. Sweetbriar; wood roses.
1. In the Old Testament, a woman of great loyalty and modesty who, as a stranger in Judah, won a husband while gleaning in the barley-fields ("the alien corn," line 67).

Ode on Melancholy

1

No, no, go not to Lethe,[2] neither twist
    Wolfsbane, tight-rooted, for its poisonous wine;
Nor suffer thy pale forehead to be kissed
    By nightshade,[3] ruby grape of Proserpine;[4]
Make not your rosary of yew-berries,[5]
    Nor let the beetle, nor the death-moth be
        Your mournful Psyche, nor the downy owl[6]
A partner in your sorrow's mysteries;
    For shade to shade will come too drowsily,
        And drown the wakeful anguish of the soul.

2

But when the melancholy fit shall fall
    Sudden from heaven like a weeping cloud,
That fosters the droop-headed flowers all,
    And hides the green hill in an April shroud;
Then glut thy sorrow on a morning rose,
    Or on the rainbow of the salt sand-wave,
    Or on the wealth of globéd peonies;
Or if thy mistress some rich anger shows,
    Imprison her soft hand, and let her rave,
        And feed deep, deep upon her peerless eyes.

3

She[7] dwells with Beauty—Beauty that must die;
    And Joy, whose hand is ever at his lips
Bidding adieu; and aching Pleasure nigh,
    Turning to Poison while the bee-mouth sips:
Aye, in the very temple of Delight
    Veiled Melancholy has her sov'reign shrine,
        Though seen of none save him whose strenuous tongue
Can burst Joy's grape against his palate fine;[8]
His soul shall taste the sadness of her might,
        And be among her cloudy trophies[9] hung.

                May 1819   1820

Ode on a Grecian Urn

1

Thou still unravished bride of quietness,
    Thou foster child of silence and slow time,
Sylvan historian, who canst thus express
    A flowery tale more sweetly than our rhyme:
What leaf-fringed legend haunts about thy shape
    Of deities or mortals, or of both,
        In Tempe or the dales of Arcady?[1]
What men or gods are these? What maidens loath?
What mad pursuit? What struggle to escape?
        What pipes and timbrels? What wild ecstasy?

2

Heard melodies are sweet, but those unheard
    Are sweeter; therefore, ye soft pipes, play on;

2. River whose waters in Hades bring forgetfulness to the dead.
3. "Nightshade" and "wolfsbane" are poisonous herbs from which sedatives and opiates were extracted.
4. Queen of Hades.
5. Symbols of mourning; often growing in cemeteries.
6. Beetles, moths, and owls have been traditionally associated with darkness, death and burial; "Psyche" means *Soul*, sometimes symbolized by a moth that escapes the mouth in sleep or at death.
7. The goddess Melancholy.
8. Keen, subtle.
9. Symbols of victory, such as banners, hung in religious shrines.
1. Tempe and Arcady (or Arcadia), in Greece, are traditional symbols of perfect pastoral landscapes.

Not to the sensual ear, but, more endeared,
    Pipe to the spirit ditties of no tone:
15 Fair youth, beneath the trees, thou canst not leave
    Thy song, nor ever can those trees be bare;
        Bold Lover, never, never canst thou kiss,
Though winning near the goal—yet, do not grieve;
        She cannot fade, though thou hast not thy bliss,
20   Forever wilt thou love, and she be fair!

        3
Ah, happy, happy boughs! that cannot shed
    Your leaves, nor ever bid the Spring adieu;
And, happy melodist, unweariéd,
    Forever piping songs forever new;
25 More happy love! more happy, happy love!
    Forever warm and still to be enjoyed,
        Forever panting, and forever young;
All breathing human passion far above,
    That leaves a heart high-sorrowful and cloyed,
30   A burning forehead, and a parching tongue.

        4
Who are these coming to the sacrifice?
    To what green altar, O mysterious priest,
Lead'st thou that heifer lowing at the skies,
    And all her silken flanks with garlands dressed?
35 What little town by river or sea shore,
    Or mountain-built with peaceful citadel,
        Is emptied of this folk, this pious morn?
And, little town, thy streets forevermore
    Will silent be; and not a soul to tell
40   Why thou art desolate, can e'er return.

        5
O Attic² shape! Fair attitude! with brede°   *woven pattern*
    Of marble men and maidens overwrought,
With forest branches and the trodden weed;
    Thou, silent form, dost tease us out of thought
45 As doth eternity: Cold Pastoral!
    When old age shall this generation waste,
        Thou shalt remain, in midst of other woe
Than ours, a friend to man, to whom thou say'st,
    "Beauty is truth, truth beauty,"³—that is all
50   Ye know on earth, and all ye need to know.
                  May 1819   1820

To Autumn

        1
Season of mists and mellow fruitfulness,
    Close bosom-friend of the maturing sun;
Conspiring with him how to load and bless
    With fruit the vines that round the thatch-eaves run;
5 To bend with apples the mossed cottage-trees,
    And fill all fruit with ripeness to the core;
        To swell the gourd, and plump the hazel shells
    With a sweet kernel; to set budding more,
And still more, later flowers for the bees,
10   Until they think warm days will never cease,
        For Summer has o'er-brimmed their clammy cells.

---

2. Greek, especially Athenian.
3. The quotation marks around this phrase are absent from some other versions also having good authority. This discrepancy has led some readers to ascribe only this phrase to the voice of the Urn; others ascribe to the Urn the whole of the two concluding lines.

2
Who hath not seen thee oft amid thy store?
    Sometimes whoever seeks abroad may find
Thee sitting careless on a granary floor,
15   Thy hair soft-lifted by the winnowing wind;[4]
Or on a half-reaped furrow sound asleep,
    Drowsed with the fume of poppies, while thy hook[5]
        Spares the next swath and all its twinéd flowers:
And sometimes like a gleaner thou dost keep
20   Steady thy laden head across a brook;
    Or by a cider-press, with patient look,
        Thou watchest the last oozings hours by hours.

3
Where are the songs of Spring? Aye, where are they?
    Think not of them, thou hast thy music too—
25 While barréd clouds bloom the soft-dying day,
    And touch the stubble-plains with rosy hue;
Then in a wailful choir the small gnats mourn
    Among the river sallows,° borne aloft   *low-growing willows*
        Or sinking as the light wind lives or dies;
30 And full-grown lambs loud bleat from hilly bourn;°   *field*
    Hedge crickets sing; and now with treble soft
    The redbreast whistles from a garden-croft;[6]
        And gathering swallows twitter in the skies.

                                September 19, 1819   1820

Bright Star

Bright star, would I were steadfast as thou art—
    Not in lone splendor hung aloft the night
And watching, with eternal lids apart,
    Like nature's patient, sleepless Eremite,°   *hermit, devotee*
5 The moving waters at their priestlike task
    Of pure ablution round earth's human shores,
Or gazing on the new soft fallen mask
    Of snow upon the mountains and the moors—
No—yet still steadfast, still unchangeable,
10   Pillowed upon my fair love's ripening breast,
    To feel forever its soft fall and swell,
        Awake forever in a sweet unrest,
Still, still to hear her tender-taken breath,
And so live ever—or else swoon to death.

                                1819   1838

This Living Hand[7]

This living hand, now warm and capable
Of earnest grasping, would, if it were cold
And in the icy silence of the tomb,
So haunt thy days and chill thy dreaming nights
5 That thou wouldst wish thine own heart dry of blood
So in my veins red life might stream again,
And thou be conscience-calmed—see here it is—
I hold it towards you.

                                1819?   1898

4. "Winnowing": blowing the grain clear of the lighter chaff.
5. Small curved blade for cutting grain; sickle.
6. Small field, as for a vegetable garden, near a house.
7. Written on a manuscript page of Keats's unfinished poem, *The Cap and Bells*.

RALPH WALDO EMERSON
(1803–1882)

Concord Hymn

SUNG AT THE COMPLETION OF THE BATTLE MONUMENT,[1] JULY 4, 1837

By the rude bridge that arched the flood,
  Their flag to April's breeze unfurled,
Here once the embattled farmers stood
  And fired the shot heard round the world.

5 The foe long since in silence slept;
  Alike the conqueror silent sleeps;
And Time the ruined bridge has swept
  Down the dark stream which seaward creeps.

On this green bank, by this soft stream,
10   We set to-day a votive stone;
That memory may their deed redeem,
  When, like our sires, our sons are gone.

Spirit, that made those heroes dare
  To die, and leave their children free,
15 Bid Time and Nature gently spare
  The shaft we raise to them and thee.

                                        1837, 1876

The Rhodora

ON BEING ASKED, WHENCE IS THE FLOWER?

In May, when sea-winds pierced our solitudes,
I found the fresh Rhodora in the woods,
Spreading its leafless blooms in a damp nook,
To please the desert and the sluggish brook.
5 The purple petals, fallen in the pool,
Made the black water with their beauty gay;
Here might the red-bird come his plumes to cool,
And court the flower that cheapens his array.
Rhodora! if the sages ask thee why
10 This charm is wasted on the earth and sky,
Tell them, dear, that if eyes were made for seeing,
Then Beauty is its own excuse for being:
Why thou wert there, O rival of the rose!
I never thought to ask, I never knew;
15 But, in my simple ignorance, suppose
The self-same Power that brought me there brought you.
              1834   1839, 1847

Hamatreya[2]

Bulkeley, Hunt, Willard, Hosmer, Meriam, Flint,[3]
Possessed the land which rendered to their toil
Hay, corn, roots, hemp, flax, apples, wool and wood.
Each of these landlords walked amidst his farm,

1. Commemorating the battles of Lexington and Concord, April 19, 1775.   2. A variant of the Hindu name *Maitreya*.
3. First settlers of Concord, Massachusetts.

5   Saying, ' 'T is mine, my children's and my name's.
How sweet the west wind sounds in my own trees!
How graceful climb those shadows on my hill!
I fancy these pure waters and the flags°   *plants, grass*
Know me, as does my dog: we sympathize;
10   And, I affirm, my actions smack of the soil.'

Where are these men? Asleep beneath their grounds:
And strangers, fond as they, their furrows plough.
Earth laughs in flowers, to see her boastful boys
Earth proud, proud of the earth which is not theirs;
15   Who steer the plough, but cannot steer their feet
Clear of the grave.
They added ridge to valley, brook to pond,
And sighed for all that bounded their domain;
'This suits me for a pasture, that's my park;
20   We must have clay, lime, gravel, granite-ledge,
And misty lowland, where to go for peat.
The land is well—lies fairly to the south.
'T is good, when you have crossed the sea and back,
To find the sitfast acres where you left them.'
25   Ah! the hot owner sees not Death, who adds
Him to his land, a lump of mould the more.
Hear what the Earth says:

     Earth-song

     Mine and yours;
     Mine, not yours.
30   Earth endures;
     Stars abide—
     Shine down in the old sea;
     Old are the shores;
     But where are old men?
35   I who have seen much,
     Such have I never seen.

     The lawyer's deed
     Ran sure,
     In tail,[4]
40   To them, and to their heirs
     Who shall succeed,
     Without fail,
     Forevermore.

     Here is the land,
45   Shaggy with wood,
     With its old valley,
     Mound and flood.
     But the heritors?
     Fled like the flood's foam.
50   The lawyer, and the laws,
     And the kingdom,
     Clean swept herefrom.

     They called me theirs.
     Who so controlled me;
55   Yet every one
     Wished to stay, and is gone,
     How am I theirs,
     If they cannot hold me,
     But I hold them?

4. I.e., entailed; to *entail* is to limit by legal means (usually a will) the inheritance of an estate to a specified line of heirs.

60 When I heard the Earth-song,
    I was no longer brave;
    My avarice cooled
    Like lust in the chill of the grave.

                                                    1847

Ode

INSCRIBED TO W. H. CHANNING[5]

    Though loath to grieve
    The evil time's sole patriot,
    I cannot leave
    My honied thought
5   For the priest's cant,
    Or statesman's rant.

    If I refuse
    My study for their politique,
10 Which at the best is trick,
    The angry Muse
    Puts confusion in my brain.

    But who is he that prates
    Of the culture of mankind,
    Of better arts and life?
15 Go, blindworm, go,
    Behold the famous States
    Harrying Mexico
    With rifle and with knife![6]

    Or who, with accent bolder,
20 Dare praise the freedom-loving mountaineer?
    I found by thee, O rushing Contoocook![7]
    And in thy valleys, Agiochook![8]
    The jackals of the Negro-holder.

    The God who made New Hampshire
25 Taunted the lofty land
    With little men;
    Small bat and wren
    House in the oak:
    If earth-fire cleave

30 The upheaved land, and bury the folk,
    The southern crocodile would grieve.
    Virtue palters;° Right is hence;   *hesitates, equivocates*
    Freedom praised, but hid;
    Funeral eloquence
35 Rattles the coffin-lid.

    What boots thy zeal,
    O glowing friend,
    That would indignant rend
    The northland from the south?
40 Wherefore? to what good end?

---

5. Unitarian clergyman, transcendentalist, and activist in social causes, particularly the anti-slavery movement.
6. A reference to the war between the United States and Mexico (1846–48) chiefly over the question of the boundaries of Texas. To some Americans, the United States' position was immoral.
7. Part of the Merrimack River in New Hampshire.
8. The White Mountains of New Hampshire.

Boston Bay and Bunker Hill
Would serve things still;
Things are of the snake.

The horseman serves the horse,
45 The neatherd serves the neat,[9]
The merchant serves the purse,
The eater serves his meat;
'T is the day of the chattel,
Web to weave, and corn to grind;
50 Things are in the saddle,
And ride mankind.

There are two laws discrete,
Not reconciled,
Law for man, and law for things;
55 The last builds town and fleet,
But it runs wild,
And doth the man unking.

'T is fit the forest fall,
The steep be graded,
60 The mountain tunnelled,
The sand shaded,
The orchard planted,
The glebe tilled,
The prairie granted,
65 The steamer built.

Let man serve law for man;
Live for friendship, live for love,
For truth's and harmony's behoof;°   *benefit*
The state may follow how it can,
70 As Olympus follows Jove.

   Yet do not I implore
The wrinkled shopman to my surrounding woods,
Nor bid the unwilling senator
Ask votes of thrushes in the solitudes.
75 Every one to his chosen work;
Foolish hands may mix and mar;
Wise and sure the issues are.
Round they roll till dark is light,
Sex to sex, and even to odd;
80 The over-god
Who marries Right to Might,
Who peoples, unpeoples,
He who exterminates
Races by stronger races,
85 Black by white faces,
Knows to bring honey
Out of the lion;[1]
Grafts gentlest scion
On pirate and Turk.

90 The Cossack eats Poland,[2]
Like stolen fruit;
Her last noble is ruined,
Her last poet mute:

9. Archaic terms for *cowherd* and *cow*.
1. The allusion in lines 83–87 is to Samson, who killed a lion and returned later to find the carcass filled with honey (Judges xiv.5–10).
2. Russian military despotism, established in Poland after the popular insurrections of 1830–31, was challenged by a new Polish uprising (lines 94–96) in 1846.

Straight, into double band
95   The victors divide;
Half for freedom strike and stand;—
The astonished Muse finds thousands at her side.

                                                                1847

Brahma[3]

If the red slayer think he slays,
    Or if the slain think he is slain,
They know not well the subtle ways
    I keep, and pass, and turn again.

5   Far or forgot to me is near;
    Shadow and sunlight are the same;
The vanished gods to me appear;
    And one to me are shame and fame.

They reckon ill who leave me out;
10   When me they fly, I am the wings;
I am the doubter and the doubt,
    And I the hymn the Brahmin sings.

The strong gods pine for my abode,
    And pine in vain the sacred Seven,[4]
15 But thou, meek lover of the good!
    Find me, and turn thy back on heaven.

                        1856   1857, 1867

Days

Daughters of Time, the hypocritic Days,
Muffled and dumb like barefoot dervishes,
And marching single in an endless file,
Bring diadems and fagots in their hands.
5   To each they offer gifts after his will,
Bread, kingdom, stars, and sky that holds them all.

I, in my pleached garden,[5] watched the pomp,
Forgot my morning wishes, hastily
Took a few herbs and apples, and the Day
10 Turned and departed silent. I, too late,
Under her solemn fillet° saw the scorn.

                                              hair band
                                              1857, 1867

3. The supreme God of Hindu mythology and, in later theological developments, the divine reality itself, once thought to comprehend the entire universe which is the manifestation of that reality.
4. Perhaps the seven saints high in the Brahman hierarchy, but lesser than Brahma.
5. To pleach is to entwine, plait, or arrange foliage artificially.

HENRY WADSWORTH LONGFELLOW
(1807–1882)

Mezzo Cammin[1]

WRITTEN AT BOPPARD ON THE RHINE AUGUST 25, 1842, JUST BEFORE
LEAVING FOR HOME

Half of my life is gone, and I have let
　　The years slip from me and have not fulfilled
　　The aspiration of my youth, to build
　　Some tower of song with lofty parapet.
5　Not indolence, nor pleasure, nor the fret
　　Of restless passions that would not be stilled,
　　But sorrow, and care that almost killed,[2]
　　Kept me from what I may accomplish yet;
Though, halfway up the hill, I see the Past
10　Lying beneath me with its sounds and sights,
　　A city in the twilight dim and vast,
With smoking roofs, soft bells, and gleaming lights,
　　And hear above me on the autumnal blast
The cataract of Death far thundering from the heights.

　　　　　　　　　　　　　　　　1842　　　　1846

Divina Commedia[3]

1

Oft have I seen at some cathedral door
　　A laborer, pausing in the dust and heat,
　　Lay down his burden, and with reverent feet
　　Enter, and cross himself, and on the floor
5　Kneel to repeat his paternoster[4] o'er;
　　Far off the noises of the world retreat;
　　The loud vociferations of the street
　　Become an undistinguishable roar.
So, as I enter here from day to day,
10　And leave my burden at this minster gate,
　　Kneeling in prayer, and not ashamed to pray,
The tumult of the time disconsolate
　　To inarticulate murmurs dies away,
　　While the eternal ages watch and wait.

2

How strange the sculptures that adorn these towers!
　　This crowd of statues, in whose folded sleeves
　　Birds build their nests; while canopied with leaves
　　Parvis[5] and portal bloom like trellised bowers,
5　And the vast minster seems a cross of flowers!
　　But fiends and dragons on the gargoyled eaves
　　Watch the dead Christ between the living thieves,
　　And, underneath, the traitor Judas lowers!
Ah! from what agonies of heart and brain,
10　What exultations trampling on despair,
　　What tenderness, what tears, what hate of wrong,

---

1. A phrase from the first line of Dante's
*Divina Commedia: "Nel mezzo del cammin di
nostra vita"* (midway upon the journey of our
life).
2. Probably an allusion to the death of Long-
fellow's wife in 1835.

3. Divine Comedy.
4. Literally, the Latin "our father," the first
words of the Lord's Prayer.
5. The court or portico in front of a church
or cathedral.

What passionate outcry of a soul in pain,
 Uprose this poem of the earth and air,
 This mediaeval miracle of song!

3

I enter, and I see thee in the gloom
 Of the long aisles, O poet saturnine![6]
 And strive to make my steps keep pace with thine.
 The air is filled with some unknown perfume;
The congregation of the dead make room
 For thee to pass; the votive tapers shine;
 Like rooks that haunt Ravenna's[7] groves of pine
 The hovering echoes fly from tomb to tomb.
From the confessionals I hear arise
 Rehearsals of forgotten tragedies,
 And lamentations from the crypts below;
And then a voice celestial that begins
 With the pathetic words, "Although your sins
 As scarlet be," and ends with "as the snow."[8]

4

With snow-white veil and garments as of flame,
 She stands before thee, who so long ago
 Filled thy young heart with passion and the woe
 From which thy song and all its splendors came;[9]
And while with stern rebuke she speaks thy name,
 The ice about thy heart melts as the snow
 On mountain heights, and in swift overflow
 Comes gushing from thy lips in sobs of shame.
Thou makest full confession; and a gleam,
 As of the dawn on some dark forest cast,
 Seems on thy lifted forehead to increase;
Lethe and Eunoë[1]—the remembered dream
 And the forgotten sorrow—bring at last
 That perfect pardon which is perfect peace.

5

I lift mine eyes, and all the windows blaze
 With forms of saints and holy men who died,
 Here martyred and hereafter glorified;
 And the great Rose[2] upon its leaves displays
Christ's Triumph, and the angelic roundelays,
 With splendor upon splendor multiplied;
 And Beatrice again at Dante's side
 No more rebukes, but smiles her words of praise.
And then the organ sounds, and unseen choirs
 Sing the old Latin hymns of peace and love
 And benedictions of the Holy Ghost;
And the melodious bells among the spires
 O'er all the housetops and through heaven above
 Proclaim the elevation of the Host![3]

6

O star of morning and of liberty![4]
 O bringer of the light, whose splendor shines
 Above the darkness of the Apennines,
 Forerunner of the day that is to be!

---

6. A reference to Dante himself.
7. A city in northeastern Italy, much admired by Dante and in which he died after having fled Florence in 1301.
8. "Come now, and let us reason together, saith the Lord: though your sins be as scarlet, they shall be as white as snow" (Isaiah i.18).
9. A reference to Beatrice, who, whether as a real person in his youth or as a vision, was Dante's inspiration in *Vita Nuova* and *Divina Commedia*.

1. In classical myth and literature, Lethe is the river of forgetfulness; Eunoë, of good memories.
2. A many-petaled rose is, in the *Paradiso* section of *Divina Commedia*, Dante's vision of Christ triumphant, with the Virgin and the saints.
3. The consecrated bread in the Eucharist, or communion sacrament.
4. A direct address to Dante as symbol of the rising spirit of freedom in the Renaissance.

5 The voices of the city and the sea,
The voices of the mountains and the pines,
Repeat thy song, till the familiar lines
Are footpaths for the thought of Italy!
Thy flame is blown abroad from all the heights,
10 Through all the nations, and a sound is heard,
As of a mighty wind, and men devout,
Strangers of Rome, and the new proselytes,
In their own language hear thy wondrous word,
And many are amazed and many doubt.

1864–67   1865–67

EDWARD FITZGERALD
(1809–1883)

The Rubáiyát of Omar Khayyám of Naishápúr[1]

1

Wake! For the Sun, who scattered into flight
The Stars before him from the Field of Night,
    Drives Night along with them from Heav'n, and strikes
The Sultán's Turret with a Shaft of Light.

2

5 Before the phantom of False morning died,
Methought a Voice within the Tavern cried,
    "When all the Temple is prepared within,
"Why nods the drowsy Worshipper outside?"

3

And, as the Cock crew, those who stood before
10 The Tavern shouted—"Open then the Door!
    "You know how little while we have to stay,
"And, once departed, may return no more."

4

Now the New Year[2] reviving old Desires,
The thoughtful Soul to Solitude retires,
15   Where the WHITE HAND OF MOSES on the Bough
Puts out, and Jesus from the Ground suspires.[3]

5

Irám[4] indeed is gone with all his Rose,
And Jamshýd's Sev'n-ringed Cup[5] where no one knows;
    But still a Ruby kindles in the Vine,
20 And many a Garden by the Water blows.

6

And David's lips are lockt; but in divine
High-piping Pehleví,[6] with "Wine! Wine! Wine!
    "Red Wine!"—the Nightingale cries to the Rose
That sallow cheek of hers to incarnadine.

1. Omar Khayyám, Persian poet, mathematician, and astronomer (ca. 1050–1132?), lived at Nishapur, in the province of Khurasan. FitzGerald translated his epigrammatic quatrains (*Rubáiyát*, plural of *ruba'i,* quatrain) which he first published in 1859; in three subsequent editions (the fourth edition is printed here) FitzGerald made many alterations of detail, arrangement, and number of stanzas.
2. "Beginning with the Vernal Equinox, it must be remembered" [FitzGerald's note].
3. The blossoming of trees is compared to the whiteness of Moses' hand as it is described in Exodus iv.6, and the sweetness of flowers to the sweetness of the breath of Jesus.
4. "A royal Garden now sunk somewhere in the Sands of Arabia" [FitzGerald's note].
5. In Persian mythology, Jamshýd was a king of the peris (celestial beings), who, because he had boasted of his immortality, was compelled to live on earth in human form for 700 years, becoming one of the kings of Persia. His cup, the invention of Kai-Kosru (line 38), another Persian king, great-grandson of Kai-Kobad (line 36), was decorated with signs enabling its possessor to foretell the future.
6. The ancient literary language of Persia.

7

25 Come, fill the Cup, and in the fire of Spring
     Your Winter-garment of Repentance fling:
         The Bird of Time has but a little way
     To flutter—and the Bird is on the Wing.

8

     Whether at Naishápúr or Babylon,
30 Whether the Cup with sweet or bitter run,
         The Wine of Life keeps oozing drop by drop,
     The Leaves of Life keep falling one by one.

9

     Each Morn a thousand Roses brings, you say;
     Yes, but where leaves the Rose of Yesterday?
35   And this first Summer month that brings the Rose
     Shall take Jamshýd and Kaikobád away.

10

     Well, let it take them! What have we to do
     With Kaikobád the Great, or Kaikhosrú?
         Let Zál and Rustum[7] bluster as they will,
40 Or Hátim[8] call to Supper—heed not you.

11

     With me along the strip of Herbage strown
     That just divides the desert from the sown,
         Where name of Slave and Sultán is forgot—
     And Peace to Mahmúd[9] on his golden Throne!

12

45 A Book of Verses underneath the Bough,
     A Jug of Wine, a Loaf of Bread—and Thou
         Beside me singing in the Wilderness—
     Oh, Wilderness were Paradise enow!

13

     Some for the Glories of This World; and some
50 Sigh for the Prophet's[1] Paradise to come;
         Ah, take the Cash, and let the Credit go,
     Nor heed the rumble of a distant Drum!

14

     Look to the blowing Rose about us—"Lo,
     "Laughing," she says, "into the world I blow,
55   "At once the silken tassel of my Purse
     "Tear, and its Treasure on the Garden throw."

15

     And those who husbanded the Golden grain,
     And those who flung it to the winds like Rain,
         Alike to no such aureate Earth are turned
60 As, buried once, Men want dug up again.

16

     The Worldly Hope men set their Hearts upon
     Turns Ashes—or it prospers; and anon,
         Like Snow upon the Desert's dusty Face,
     Lighting a little hour or two—is gone.

17

65 Think, in this battered Caravanserai°   *inn*
     Whose Portals are alternate Night and Day,
         How Sultán after Sultán with his Pomp
     Abode his destined Hour, and went his way.

---

7. "The 'Hercules' of Persia, and Zál his   9. Sultan Máhmúd of Ghazni, in Afghan-
Father" [FitzGerald's note].   istan (971–1031), renowned both as ruler and
8. Hátim Tai: a Persian chieftain, an arche- as the conqueror of India.
type of oriental hospitality.   1. I.e., Mohammed's.

18

They say the Lion and the Lizard keep
70 The Courts where Jamshýd gloried and drank deep:
    And Bahrám,[2] that great Hunter—the Wild Ass
Stamps o'er his Head, but cannot break his Sleep.

19

I sometimes think that never blows so red
The Rose as where some buried Caesar bled;
75   That every Hyacinth the Garden wears
Dropt in her Lap from some once lovely Head.

20

And this reviving Herb whose tender Green
Fledges the river-lip on which we lean—
    Ah, lean upon it lightly! for who knows
80 From what once lovely Lip it springs unseen!

21

Ah, my Belovéd, fill the Cup that clears
TODAY of past Regrets and future Fears:
    Tomorrow!—Why, Tomorrow I may be
Myself with Yesterday's Sev'n thousand Years.

22

85 For some we loved, the loveliest and the best
That from his Vintage rolling Time hath prest,
    Have drunk their Cup a Round or two before,
And one by one crept silently to rest.

23

And we, that make merry in the Room
90 They left, and Summer dresses in new bloom,
    Ourselves must we beneath the Couch of Earth
Descend—ourselves to make a Couch—for whom?

24

Ah, make the most of what we yet may spend,
Before we too into the Dust descend;
95   Dust into Dust, and under Dust to lie,
Sans Wine, sans Song, sans Singer, and sans End!

25

Alike for those who for TODAY prepare,
And those that after some TOMORROW stare,
    A Muezzín[3] from the Tower of Darkness cries,
100 "Fools! your Reward is neither Here nor There."

26

Why, all the Saints and Sages who discussed
Of the Two Worlds so wisely—they are thrust
    Like foolish Prophets forth; their Words to Scorn
Are scattered, and their Mouths are stopt with Dust.

27

105 Myself when young did eagerly frequent
Doctor and Saint, and heard great argument
    About it and about: but evermore
Came out by the same door where in I went.

28

With them the seed of Wisdom did I sow,
110 And with mine own hand wrought to make it grow;
    And this was all the Harvest that I reaped—
"I came like Water, and like Wind I go."

29

Into this Universe, and *Why* not knowing
Nor *Whence*, like Water willy-nilly flowing;
115   And out of it, as Wind along the Waste,
I know not *Whither*, willy-nilly blowing.

---

2. A Sassanian king who, according to legend, met his death while hunting the wild ass.

3. The crier who calls the hours of prayer from tower or minaret.

30

What, without asking, hither hurried *Whence?*
And, without asking, *Whither* hurried hence!
   Oh, many a Cup of this forbidden Wine[4]
120 Must drown the memory of that insolence!

31

Up from Earth's Center through the Seventh Gate
I rose, and on the Throne of Saturn[5] sate,
   And many a Knot unraveled by the Road;
But not the Master-knot of Human Fate.

32

125 There was the Door to which I found no Key;
There was the Veil through which I might not see:
   Some little talk awhile of ME and THEE
There was—and then no more of THEE and ME.

33

Earth could not answer; nor the Seas that mourn
130 In flowing Purple, of their Lord forlorn;
   Nor rolling Heaven, with all his Signs revealed
And hidden by the sleeve of Night and Morn.

34

Then of the THEE IN ME who works behind
The Veil, I lifted up my hands to find
135   A lamp amid the Darkness; and I heard,
As from Without—"THE ME WITHIN THEE BLIND!"

35

Then to the Lip of this poor earthen Urn
I leaned, the Secret of my Life to learn:
   And Lip to Lip it murmured—"While you live,
140 "Drink! for, once dead, you never shall return."

36

I think the Vessel, that with fugitive
Articulation answered, once did live,
   And drink; and Ah! the passive Lip I kissed,
How many Kisses might it take—and give!

37

145 For I remember stopping by the way
To watch a Potter thumping his wet Clay:
   And with its all-obliterated Tongue
It murmured—"Gently, Brother, gently, pray!"

38

And has not such a Story from of Old
150 Down Man's successive generations rolled
   Of such a clod of saturated Earth
Cast by the Maker into Human mold?

39

And not a drop that from our Cups we throw
For Earth to drink of, but may steal below
155   To quench the fire of Anguish in some Eye
There hidden—far beneath, and long ago.

40

As then the Tulip for her morning sup
Of Heav'nly Vintage from the soil looks up,
   Do you devoutly do the like, till Heav'n
160 To Earth invert you—like an empty Cup.

---

4. Alcohol is forbidden to Mohammedans.
5. "Lord of the Seventh Heaven" [FitzGerald's note]. In ancient astronomy, Saturn was the most remote of the seven known planets; hence, Omar had reached the bounds of astronomical knowledge.

41

Perplext no more with Human or Divine,
Tomorrow's tangle to the winds resign,
  And lose your fingers in the tresses of
The Cypress-slender Minister of Wine.[6]

42

165 And if the Wine you drink, the Lip you press,
End in what All begins and ends in—Yes;
  Think then you are TODAY what YESTERDAY
You were—TOMORROW you shall not be less.

43

So when that Angel of the darker Drink
170 At last shall find you by the river-brink,
  And, offering his Cup, invite your Soul
Forth to your Lips to quaff—you shall not shrink.

44

Why, if the Soul can fling the Dust aside,
And naked on the Air of Heaven ride,
175   Were't not a Shame—were't not a Shame for him
In this clay carcase crippled to abide?

45

'Tis but a Tent where takes his one day's rest
A Sultán to the realm of Death addrest;
  The Sultán rises, and the dark Ferrásh[7]
180 Strikes, and prepares it for another Guest.

46

And fear not lest Existence closing your
Account, and mine, should know the like no more;
  The Eternal Sáki° from that Bowl has poured   cup-bearer
Millions of Bubbles like us, and will pour.

47

185 When You and I behind the Veil are past,
Oh, but the long, long while the World shall last,
  Which of our Coming and Departure heeds
As the Sea's self should heed a pebble-cast.

48

190 A Moment's Halt—a momentary taste
Of BEING from the Well amid the Waste—
  And Lo!—the phantom Caravan has reached
The NOTHING it set out from—Oh, make haste!

49

Would you that spangle of Existence spend
About THE SECRET—quick about it, Friend!
195   A Hair perhaps divides the False and True—
And upon what, prithee, may life depend?

50

A Hair perhaps divides the False and True;
Yes; and a single Alif[8] were the clue—
  Could you but find it—to the Treasure-house,
200 And peradventure to THE MASTER too;

51

Whose secret Presence, through Creation's veins
Running Quicksilver-like eludes your pains;
  Taking all shapes from Máh to Máhi;[9] and
They change and perish all—but He remains;

---

6. The maidservant who pours the wine.
7. The servant charged with setting up and striking the tent.

8. First letter of Arabic alphabet, consisting of a single vertical stroke.
9. From lowest to highest.

52

²⁰⁵ A moment guessed—then back behind the Fold
Immerst of Darkness round the Drama rolled
　　Which, for the Pastime of Eternity,
He doth Himself contrive, enact, behold.

53

But if in vain, down on the stubborn floor
²¹⁰ Of Earth, and up to Heav'n's unopening Door,
　　You gaze TODAY, while You are You—how then
TOMORROW, You when shall be You no more?

54

Waste not your Hour, nor in the vain pursuit
Of This and That endeavor and dispute;
²¹⁵ 　　Better be jocund with the fruitful Grape
Than sadden after none, or bitter, Fruit.

55

You know, my Friends, with what a brave Carouse
I made a Second Marriage in my house;
　　Divorced old barren Reason from my Bed,
²²⁰ And took the Daughter of the Vine to Spouse.

56

For "Is" and "Is-NOT" though with Rule and Line
And "UP-AND-DOWN" by Logic I define,
　　Of all that one should care to fathom, I
Was never deep in anything but—Wine.

57

²²⁵ Ah, but my Computations, People say,
Reduced the Year to better reckoning?¹—Nay,
　　'Twas only striking from the Calendar
Unborn Tomorrow, and dead Yesterday.

58

And lately, by the Tavern Door agape,
²³⁰ Came shining through the Dusk an Angel Shape
　　Bearing a Vessel on his Shoulder; and
He bid me taste of it; and 'twas—the Grape!

59

The Grape that can with Logic absolute
The Two-and-Seventy jarring Sects² confute:
²³⁵ 　　The sovereign Alchemist that in a trice
Life's leaden metal into Gold transmute:

60

The mighty Mahmúd, Allah-breathing Lord,³
That all the misbelieving and black Horde
　　Of Fears and Sorrows that infest the Soul
²⁴⁰ Scatters before him with his whirlwind Sword.

61

Why, be this Juice the growth of God, who dare
Blaspheme the twisted tendril as a Snare?
　　A Blessing, we should use it, should we not?
And if a Curse—why, then, Who set it there?

62

²⁴⁵ I must abjure the Balm of Life, I must,
Scared by some After-reckoning ta'en on trust,
　　Or lured with Hope of some Diviner Drink,
To fill the Cup—when crumbled into Dust!

---

1. Omar was one of the learned men who had been charged with reforming the calendar.
2. "The 72 sects into which Islamism so soon split" [FitzGerald's note].
3. "This alludes to Máhmúd's Conquest of India and its swarthy Idolators" [FitzGerald's note].

63

Oh threats of Hell and Hopes of Paradise!
250   One thing at least is certain—*This* Life flies;
        One thing is certain and the rest is Lies;
The Flower that once has blown for ever dies.

64

Strange, is it not? that of the myriads who
Before us passed the door of Darkness through,
255   Not one returns to tell us of the Road,
Which to discover we must travel too.

65

The Revelations of Devout and Learned
Who rose before us, and as Prophets burned,
        Are all but Stories, which, awoke from Sleep
260   They told their comrades, and to Sleep returned.

66

I sent my Soul through the Invisible,
Some letter of that Afterlife to spell:
        And by and by my Soul returned to me,
And answered "I Myself am Heav'n and Hell:"

67

265   Heav'n but the Vision of fulfilled Desire,
And Hell the Shadow from a Soul on fire,
        Cast on the Darkness into which Ourselves,
So late emerged from, shall so soon expire.

68

We are no other than a moving row
270   Of Magic Shadow-shapes that come and go
        Round with the Sun-illumined Lantern held
In Midnight by the Master of the Show;

69

But helpless Pieces of the Game He plays
Upon his Checkerboard of Nights and Days;
275   Hither and thither moves, and checks, and slays,
And one by one back in the Closet lays.

70

The Ball no question makes of Ayes and Noes,
But Here or There as strikes the Player goes;
        And He that tossed you down into the Field,
280   *He* knows about it all—HE knows—HE knows!

71

The Moving Finger writes; and, having writ,
Moves on: nor all your Piety nor Wit
        Shall lure it back to cancel half a Line,
Nor all your Tears wash out a Word of it.

72

285   And that inverted Bowl they call the Sky,
Whereunder crawling cooped we live and die,
        Lift not your hands to *It* for help—for It
As impotently moves as you or I.

73

With Earth's first Clay They did the Last Man knead,
290   And there of the Last Harvest sowed the Seed:
        And the first Morning of Creation wrote
What the Last Dawn of Reckoning shall read.

74

YESTERDAY *This* Day's Madness did prepare;
TOMORROW's Silence, Triumph, or Despair:
295   Drink! for you know not whence you came, nor why:
Drink! for you know not why you go, nor where.

75

I tell you this—When, started from the Goal,
Over the flaming shoulders of the Foal[4]
   Of Heav'n, Parwín and Mushtarí[5] they flung,
In my predestined Plot of Dust and Soul.

76

The Vine had struck a fiber: which about
If clings my Being—let the Dervish[6] flout;
   Of my Base metal may be filed a Key,
That shall unlock the Door he howls without.

77

And this I know: whether the one True Light
Kindle to Love, or Wrath consume me quite,
   One Flash of It within the Tavern caught
Better than in the Temple lost outright.

78

What! out of senseless Nothing to provoke
A conscious Something to resent the yoke
   Of unpermitted Pleasure, under pain
Of Everlasting Penalties, if broke!

79

What! from his helpless Creature be repaid
Pure Gold for what he lent him dross-allayed—
   Sue for a Debt he never did contract,
And cannot answer—Oh the sorry trade!

80

Oh Thou, who didst with pitfall and with gin°   *trap*
Beset the Road I was to wander in,
   Thou wilt not with Predestined Evil round
Enmesh, and then impute my Fall to Sin!

81

Oh Thou, who Man of baser Earth didst make,
And ev'n with Paradise devise the Snake:
   For all the Sin wherewith the Face of Man
Is blackened—Man's forgiveness give—and take!

82

As under cover of departing Day
Slunk hunger-stricken Ramazán[7] away,
   Once more within the Potter's house alone
I stood, surrounded by the Shapes of Clay.

83

Shapes of all Sorts and Sizes, great and small,
That stood along the floor and by the wall;
   And some loquacious Vessels were; and some
Listened perhaps, but never talked at all.

84

Said one among them—"Surely not in vain
"My substance of the common Earth was ta'en
   "And to this Figure molded, to be broke,
"Or trampled back to shapeless Earth again."

85

Then said a Second—"Ne'er a peevish Boy
"Would break the Bowl from which he drank in joy;
   "And He that with his hand the Vessel made
"Will surely not in after Wrath destroy."

4. The constellation known as the Colt (*Equuleus*) or Foal.
5. "The Pleiads and Jupiter" [FitzGerald's note]; Omar ascribes his fate to the position of the stars and planets at the time of his birth.
6. Member of any of several Muslim orders taking vows of austerity and poverty.
7. The Mohammedans' annual thirty-day fast, during which no food may be taken from dawn to sunset.

86

After a momentary silence spake
Some Vessel of a more ungainly Make;
   "They sneer at me for leaning all awry:
"What! did the Hand then of the Potter shake?"

87

345 Whereat some one of the loquacious Lot—
I think a Súfi° pipkin—waxing hot—   *mystic*
   "All this of Pot and Potter—Tell me then,
"Who is the Potter, pray, and who the Pot?"

88

"Why," said another, "Some there are who tell
350 "Of one who threatens he will toss to Hell
   "The luckless Pots he marred in making—Pish!
"He's a Good Fellow, and 'twill all be well."

89

"Well," murmured one, "Let whoso make or buy,
"My Clay with long Oblivion is gone dry:
355   "But fill me with the old familiar Juice,
"Methinks I might recover by and by."

90

So while the Vessels one by one were speaking,
The little Moon[8] looked in that all were seeking:
   And then they jogged each other, "Brother! Brother!
360 "Now for the Porter's shoulder-knot[9] a-creaking!"

91

Ah, with the Grape my fading Life provide,
And wash the Body whence the Life has died,
   And lay men shrouded in the living Leaf,
By some not unfrequented Garden-side.

92

365 That ev'n my buried Ashes such a snare
Of Vintage shall fling up into the Air
   As not a True-believer passing by
But shall be overtaken unaware.

93

Indeed the Idols I have loved so long
370 Have done my credit in this World much wrong:
   Have drowned my Glory in a shallow Cup,
And sold my Reputation for a Song.

94

Indeed, indeed, Repentance oft before
I swore—but was I sober when I swore?
375   And then and then came Spring, and Rose-in-hand
My threadbare Penitence apieces tore.

95

And much as Wine has played the Infidel,
And robbed me of my Robe of Honor—Well,
   I wonder often what the Vintners buy
380 One half so precious as the stuff they sell.

96

Yet Ah, that Spring should vanish with the Rose!
That Youth's sweet-scented manuscript should close!
   The Nightingale that in the branches sang,
Ah whence, and whither flown again, who knows!

8. The new moon, which signaled the end of
Ramazán.

9. The knot on the porter's shoulder-strap
from which the wine-jars were hung.

97

385 Would but the Desert of the Fountain yield
One glimpse—if dimly, yet indeed, revealed,
   To which the fainting Traveler might spring,
As springs the trampled herbage of the field!

98

Would but some wingéd Angel ere too late
390 Arrest the yet unfolded Roll of Fate,
   And make the stern Recorder otherwise
Enregister, or quite obliterate!

99

Ah Love! could you and I with Him conspire
To grasp this sorry Scheme of Things entire,
395   Would not we shatter it to bits—and then
Remold it nearer to the Heart's Desire!

100

Yon rising Moon that looks for us again—
How oft hereafter will she wax and wane;
   How oft hereafter rising look for us
400 Through this same Garden—and for *one* in vain!

101

And when like her, oh Sákí, you shall pass
Among the Guests Star-scattered on the Grass,
   And in your joyous errand reach the spot
Where I made One—turn down an empty Glass!

TAMÁM[10]

1859, 1879

EDGAR ALLAN POE
(1809–1849)

Sonnet—To Science

Science! true daughter of Old Time thou art!
   Who alterest all things with thy peering eyes.
Why preyest thou thus upon the poet's heart,
   Vulture, whose wings are dull realities?
5 How should he love thee? or how deem thee wise?
   Who wouldst not leave him in his wandering
To seek for treasure in the jeweled skies,
   Albeit he soared with an undaunted wing?
Hast thou not dragged Diana[1] from her car?
10   And driven the Hamadryad[2] from the wood
To seek a shelter in some happier star?
   Hast thou not torn the Naiad° from her flood,   *river nymph*
The Elfin from the green grass, and from me
The summer dream beneath the tamarind tree?[3]

1829   1829, 1845

---

10. It is ended.
1. To the Romans, the virgin goddess of the hunt, revered for her chastity and protectiveness. Her "car" is the moon.

2. Wood nymph said to live and die with the tree she inhabits.
3. An oriental tree the fruit of which is used medicinally and for food.

To Helen

Helen, thy beauty is to me
　　Like those Nicean barks of yore,
That gently, o'er a perfumed sea,
　　The weary, way-worn wanderer bore
5　　To his own native shore.

On desperate seas long wont to roam,
　　Thy hyacinth hair,[4] thy classic face,
Thy Naiad airs have brought me home
　　To the glory that was Greece
10　And the grandeur that was Rome.

Lo! in yon brilliant window-niche
　　How statue-like I see thee stand!
　　The agate lamp within thy hand,
Ah! Psyche,[5] from the regions which
15　Are Holy Land!

　　　　　　　　　　　1823　　　　　1831, 1845

ALFRED, LORD TENNYSON
(1809–1892)

Song

1

A spirit haunts the year's last hours
Dwelling amid these yellowing bowers.
　　　To himself he talks;
For at eventide, listening earnestly,
5　At his work you may hear him sob and sigh
　　　In the walks;
　　Earthward he boweth the heavy stalks
Of the moldering flowers.
　　　Heavily hangs the broad sunflower
10　　　Over its grave i' the earth so chilly;
　　Heavily hangs the hollyhock,
　　　Heavily hangs the tiger-lily.

2

The air is damp, and hushed, and close,
As a sick man's room when he taketh repose
15　　　An hour before death;
My very heart faints and my whole soul grieves
At the moist rich smell of the rotting leaves,
　　　And the breath
　　Of the fading edges of box[1] beneath,
20　And the year's last rose.
　　　Heavily hangs the broad sunflower
　　　Over its grave i' the earth so chilly;
　　Heavily hangs the hollyhock,
　　　Heavily hangs the tiger-lily.

　　　　　　　　　　　　　　　　　1830

---

4. Presumably, hair like that of the slain youth Hyacinthus, beloved of Apollo.
5. Having lost her lover Cupid because she insisted on seeing him when he preferred to come to her unseen at night (she dropped oil accidentally from her lamp while he was sleep-ing), Psyche appealed for help in finding Cupid to Venus, who required, among other things, that Psyche bring back unopened a box from the underworld.
1. Evergreen shrub used in formal gardening.

The Lotos-Eaters[2]

"Courage!" he[3] said, and pointed toward the land,
"This mounting wave will roll us shoreward soon."
In the afternoon they came unto a land
In which it seeméd always afternoon.
5   All round the coast the languid air did swoon,
Breathing like one that hath a weary dream.
Full-faced above the valley stood the moon;
And, like a downward smoke, the slender stream
Along the cliff to fall and pause and fall did seem.

10 A land of streams! some, like a downward smoke,
Slow-dropping veils of thinnest lawn,[4] did go;
And some through wavering lights and shadows broke,
Rolling a slumbrous sheet of foam below.
They saw the gleaming river seaward flow
15 From the inner land; far off, three mountain-tops,
Three silent pinnacles of agéd snow,
Stood sunset-flushed; and, dewed with showery drops,
Up-clomb the shadowy pine above the woven copse.

The charméd sunset lingered low adown
20 In the red West; through mountain clefts the dale
Was seen far inland, and the yellow down
Bordered with palm, and many a winding vale
And meadow, set with slender galingale;[5]
A land where all things always seemed the same!
25 And round about the keel with faces pale,
Dark faces pale against that rosy flame,
The mild-eyed melancholy Lotos-eaters came.

Branches they bore of that enchanted stem,
Laden with flower and fruit, whereof they gave
30 To each, but whoso did receive of them
And taste, to him the gushing of the wave
Far far away did seem to mourn and rave
On alien shores; and if his fellow spake,
His voice was thin, as voices from the grave;
35 And deep-asleep he seemed, yet all awake,
And music in his ears his beating heart did make.

They sat them down upon the yellow sand,
Between the sun and moon upon the shore;
And sweet it was to dream of fatherland,
40 Of child, and wife, and slave; but evermore
Most weary seemed the sea, weary the oar,
Weary the wandering fields of barren foam.
Then someone said, "We will return no more;"
And all at once they sang, "Our island home
45 Is far beyond the wave; we will no longer roam."

Choric Song

1

There is sweet music here that softer falls
Than petals from blown roses on the grass,
Or night-dews on still waters between walls
Of shadowy granite, in a gleaming pass;

---

2. In Greek legend, a people who ate the fruit of the lotos, the effect of which was to induce drowsy languor and forgetfulness. The visit of Odysseus and his men to their island is described in the *Odyssey*, IX.82–97.

3. I.e., Odysseus.
4. Sheer cotton fabric.
5. A reed-like plant, a species of sedge.

50 Music that gentlier on the spirit lies,
Than tired eyelids upon tired eyes;
Music that brings sweet sleep down from the blissful skies.
Here are cool mosses deep,
And through the moss the ivies creep,
55 And in the stream the long-leaved flowers weep,
And from the craggy ledge the poppy hangs in sleep.

2

Why are we weighed upon with heaviness,
And utterly consumed with sharp distress,
While all things else have rest from weariness?
60 All things have rest: why should we toil alone,
We only toil, who are the first of things,
And make perpetual moan,
Still from one sorrow to another thrown;
Nor ever fold our wings,
65 And cease from wanderings,
Nor steep our brows in slumber's holy balm;
Nor harken what the inner spirit sings,
"There is no joy but calm!"—
Why should we only toil, the roof and crown of things?

3

70 Lo! in the middle of the wood,
The folded leaf is wooed from out the bud
With winds upon the branch, and there
Grows green and broad, and takes no care,
Sun-steeped at noon, and in the moon
75 Nightly dew-fed; and turning yellow
Falls, and floats adown the air.
Lo! sweetened with the summer light,
The full-juiced apple, waxing over-mellow,
80 Drops in a silent autumn night.
All its allotted length of days
The flower ripens in its place,
Ripens and fades, and falls, and hath no toil,
Fast-rooted in the fruitful soil.

4

Hateful is the dark-blue sky,
85 Vaulted o'er the dark-blue sea.
Death is the end of life; ah, why
Should life all labor be?
Let us alone. Time driveth onward fast
And in a little while our lips are dumb.
90 Let us alone. What is it that will last?
All things are taken from us, and become
Portions and parcels of the dreadful past.
Let us alone. What pleasure can we have
To war with evil? Is there any peace
95 In ever climbing up the climbing wave?
All things have rest, and ripen toward the grave
In silence—ripen, fall, and cease:
Give us long rest or death, dark death, or dreamful ease.

5

How sweet it were, hearing the downward stream,
100 With half-shut eyes ever to seem
Falling asleep in a half-dream!
To dream and dream, like yonder amber light,
Which will not leave the myrrh-bush on the height;
To hear each other's whispered speech;
105 Eating the Lotos day by day,
To watch the crisping ripples on the beach,
And tender curving lines of creamy spray;

To lend our hearts and spirits wholly
To the influence of mild-minded melancholy;
110 To muse and brood and live again in memory,
With those old faces of our infancy
Heaped over with a mound of grass,
Two handfuls of white dust, shut in an urn of brass!

6

Dear is the memory of our wedded lives,
115 And dear the last embraces of our wives
And their warm tears; but all hath suffered change;
For surely now our household hearths are cold,
Our sons inherit us, our looks are strange,
And we should come like ghosts to trouble joy.
120 Or else the island princes[6] over-bold
Have eat our substance, and the minstrel sings
Before them of the ten years' war in Troy,
And our great deeds, as half-forgotten things.
Is there confusion in the little isle?[7]
125 Let what is broken so remain.
The Gods are hard to reconcile;
'Tis hard to settle order once again.
There *is* confusion worse than death,
Trouble on trouble, pain on pain,
130 Long labor unto aged breath,
Sore tasks to hearts worn out by many wars
And eyes grown dim with gazing on the pilot-stars.

7

But, propt on beds of amaranth[8] and moly,
How sweet—while warm airs lull us, blowing lowly—
135 With half-dropt eyelid still,
Beneath a heaven dark and holy,
To watch the long bright river drawing slowly
His waters from the purple hill—
To hear the dewy echoes calling
140 From cave to cave through the thick-twined vine—
To watch the emerald-colored water falling
Through many a woven acanthus-wreath divine!
Only to hear and see the far-off sparkling brine,
Only to hear were sweet, stretched out beneath the pine.

8

145 The Lotos blooms below the barren peak,
The Lotos blows by every winding creek;
All day the wind breathes low with mellower tone;
Through every hollow cave and alley lone
Round and round the spicy downs the yellow Lotos-dust is blown.
150 We have had enough of action, and of motion we,
Rolled to starboard, rolled to larboard, when the surge was seething free,
Where the wallowing monster spouted his foam-fountains in the sea.
Let us swear an oath, and keep it with an equal mind,
In the hollow Lotos-land to live and lie reclined
155 On the hills like Gods together, careless of mankind.
For they lie beside their nectar, and the bolts are hurled
Far below them in the valleys, and the clouds are lightly curled
Round their golden houses, girdled with the gleaming world;
Where they smile in secret, looking over wasted lands,
160 Blight and famine, plague and earthquake, roaring deeps and fiery sands,
Clanging fights, and flaming towns, and sinking ships, and praying hands.
But they smile, they find a music centered in a doleful song
Steaming up, a lamentation and an ancient tale of wrong,

6. The princes who had remained behind in Ithaca while Odysseus was at Troy.
7. I.e., Ithaca.

8. A legendary flower, reputed not to fade; moly, an herb of magical properties.

Like a tale of little meaning though the words are strong;
165 Chanted from an ill-used race of men that cleave the soil,
Sow the seed, and reap the harvest with enduring toil,
Storing yearly little dues of wheat, and wine and oil;
Till they perish and they suffer—some, 'tis whispered—down in hell
Suffer endless anguish, others in Elysian valleys dwell,
170 Resting weary limbs at last on beds of asphodel.[9]
Surely, surely, slumber is more sweet than toil, the shore
Than labor in the deep mid-ocean, wind and wave and oar;
O, rest ye, brother mariners, we will not wander more.

1832, 1842

Break, Break, Break

Break, break, break,
    On thy cold gray stones, O Sea!
And I would that my tongue could utter
    The thoughts that arise in me.

5 O, well for the fisherman's boy,
    That he shouts with his sister at play!
O, well for the sailor lad,
    That he sings in his boat on the bay!

And the stately ships go on
10   To their haven under the hill;
But O for the touch of a vanished hand,
    And the sound of a voice that is still!

Break, break, break,
    At the foot of thy crags, O Sea!
15 But the tender grace of a day that is dead
    Will never come back to me.

1834   1842

Songs from The Princess

Tears, Idle Tears

Tears, idle tears, I know not what they mean,
Tears from the depth of some divine despair
Rise in the heart, and gather to the eyes,
In looking on the happy autumn-fields,
5 And thinking of the days that are no more.

Fresh as the first beam glittering on a sail,
That brings our friends up from the underworld,
Sad as the last which reddens over one
That sinks with all we love below the verge;
10 So sad, so fresh, the days that are no more.

Ah, sad and strange as in dark summer dawns
The earliest pipe of half-awakened birds
To dying ears, when unto dying eyes
The casement slowly grows a glimmering square;
15 So sad, so strange, the days that are no more.

Dear as remembered kisses after death,
And sweet as those by hopeless fancy feigned
On lips that are for others; deep as love,
Deep as first love, and wild with all regret;
20 O Death in Life, the days that are no more!

1847

9. Any one of a number of plants of the lily family.

Now Sleeps the Crimson Petal

Now sleeps the crimson petal, now the white;
Nor waves the cypress in the palace walk;
Nor winks the gold fin in the porphyry font.
The firefly wakens; waken thou with me.

5   Now droops the milk-white peacock like a ghost,
And like a ghost she glimmers on to me.

Now lies the Earth all Danaë[1] to the stars,
And all thy heart lies open unto me.

Now slides the silent meteor on, and leaves
10 A shining furrow, as thy thoughts in me.

Now folds the lily all her sweetness up,
And slips into the bosom of the lake.
So fold thyself, my dearest, thou, and slip
Into my bosom and be lost in me.

                                    1847

From In Memoriam A. H. H.[2]

OBIIT. MDCCCXXXIII

1

I held it truth, with him who sings
    To one clear harp in divers tones,[3]
    That men may rise on stepping-stones
Of their dead selves to higher things.

5 But who shall so forecast the years
    And find in loss a gain to match?
    Or reach a hand through time to catch
The far-off interest of tears?

Let Love clasp Grief lest both be drowned,
10   Let darkness keep her raven gloss.
    Ah, sweeter to be drunk with loss,
To dance with Death, to beat the ground,

Than that the victor Hours should scorn
    The long result of love, and boast,
15   "Behold the man that loved and lost,
But all he was is overworn."

2

Old yew, which graspest at the stones
    That name the underlying dead,
    Thy fibers net the dreamless head,
Thy roots are wrapt about the bones.

5 The seasons bring the flowers again,
    And bring the firstling to the flock;
    And in the dusk of thee the clock
Beats out the little lives of men.

1. Daughter of a king of Argos in ancient Greece who, warned by an oracle that she would bear a son who would kill him, shut her up in a bronze chamber, where she was visited by Zeus in a shower of gold.
2. Arthur Henry Hallam (1811–33) had been Tennyson's close friend at Cambridge; they had traveled together in France and Germany; and Hallam had been engaged to the poet's sister. To his associates at Cambridge, Hallam had seemed to give the most brilliant promise of future greatness. In the summer of 1833 Hallam had been traveling on the Continent with his father, when he died of stroke at Vienna.
3. I.e., Goethe.

O, not for thee the glow, the bloom,
10 Who changest not in any gale,
Nor branding summer suns avail
To touch thy thousand years of gloom;

And gazing on thee, sullen tree,
Sick for thy stubborn hardihood,
15 I seem to fail from out my blood
And grow incorporate into thee.

7

Dark house, by which once more I stand
Here in the long unlovely street,[4]
Doors, where my heart was used to beat
So quickly, waiting for a hand,

5 A hand that can be clasped no more—
Behold me, for I cannot sleep,
And like a guilty thing I creep
At earliest morning to the door.

He is not here; but far away
10 The noise of life begins again,
And ghastly through the drizzling rain
On the bald street breaks the blank day.

10

I hear the noise about thy keel;[5]
I hear the bell struck in the night;
I see the cabin-window bright;
I see the sailor at the wheel.

5 Thou bring'st the sailor to his wife,
And traveled men from foreign lands;
And letters unto trembling hands;
And, thy dark freight, a vanished life.

So bring him; we have idle dreams;
10 This look of quiet flatters thus
Our home-bred fancies. Oh, to us,
The fools of habit, sweeter seems

To rest beneath the clover sod,
That takes the sunshine and the rains,
15 Or where the kneeling hamlet drains
The chalice of the grapes of God;[6]

Than if with thee the roaring wells
Should gulf him fathom-deep in brine,
And hands so often clasped in mine,
20 Should toss with tangle and with shells.

11

Calm is the morn without a sound,
Calm as to suit a calmer grief,
And only through the faded leaf
The chestnut pattering to the ground;

5 Calm and deep peace on this high wold,°   *upland plain*
And on these dews that drench the furze,
And all the silvery gossamers
That twinkle into green and gold;

---

4. I.e., Wimpole St., where Hallam had been living after he left Cambridge.
5. Hallam's body had been brought back to England by ship from Trieste.

6. I.e., near the church where the villagers receive the wine of communion.

Calm and still light on yon great plain
10   That sweeps with all its autumn bowers,
        And crowded farms and lessening towers,
To mingle with the bounding main;

Calm and deep peace in this wide air,
        These leaves that redden to the fall,
15   And in my heart, if calm at all,
If any calm, a calm despair;

Calm on the seas, and silver sleep,
        And waves that sway themselves in rest,
        And dead calm in the noble breast
20   Which heaves but with the heaving deep.

19

The Danube to the Severn gave
        The darkened heart that beat no more;[7]
        They laid him by the pleasant shore,
And in the hearing of the wave.

5   There twice a day the Severn fills;
        The salt sea-water passes by,
        And hushes half the babbling Wye,[8]
And makes a silence in the hills.

The Wye is hushed nor moved along,
10   And hushed my deepest grief of all,
        When filled with tears that cannot fall,
I brim with sorrow drowning song.

The tide flows down, the wave again
        Is vocal in its wooded walls;
15   My deeper anguish also falls,
And I can speak a little then.

27

I envy not in any moods
        The captive void of noble rage,
        The linnet born within the cage,
That never knew the summer woods;

5   I envy not the beast that takes
        His license in the field of time,
        Unfettered by the sense of crime,
To whom a conscience never wakes;

Nor, what may count itself as blest,
10   The heart that never plighted troth
        But stagnates in the weeds of sloth;
Nor any want-begotten rest.[9]

I hold it true, whate'er befall;
        I feel it, when I sorrow most;
15   'Tis better to have loved and lost
Than never to have loved at all.

50

Be near me when my light is low,
        When the blood creeps, and the nerves prick
        And tingle; and the heart is sick,
And all the wheels of being slow.

7. Vienna, where Hallam died, is on the Danube; the Severn empties into the Bristol Channel near Clevedon, Somersetshire, Hallam's burial place.
8. The Wye, a tributary of the Severn, also runs into the Bristol Channel; the incoming tide deepens the river and makes it quiet, but as the tide ebbs the Wye once more becomes voluble.
9. I.e., rest that comes merely from ignorance or from deprivation of experience.

5   Be near me when the sensuous frame
     Is racked with pangs that conquer trust;
     And Time, a maniac scattering dust,
  And Life, a Fury slinging flame.

Be near me when my faith is dry,
10   And men the flies of latter spring,
     That lay their eggs, and sting and sing
  And weave their petty cells and die.

Be near me when I fade away,
    To point the term of human strife,
15   And on the low dark verge of life
  The twilight of eternal day.

67

When on my bed the moonlight falls,
    I know that in thy place of rest
    By that broad water of the west
  There comes a glory on the walls:[1]

5   Thy marble bright in dark appears,
    As slowly steals a silver flame
    Along the letters of thy name,
  And o'er the number of thy years.

The mystic glory swims away,
10   From off my bed the moonlight dies;
    And closing eaves of wearied eyes
  I sleep till dusk is dipped in gray;

And then I know the mist is drawn
    A lucid veil from coast to coast,
15   And in the dark church like a ghost
  Thy tablet glimmers to the dawn.

88

Wild bird, whose warble, liquid sweet,
    Rings Eden through the budded quicks,[2]
    O, tell me where the senses mix,
  O, tell me where the passions meet,

5   Whence radiate: fierce extremes employ
    Thy spirits in the darkening leaf,
    And in the midmost heart of grief
  Thy passion clasps a secret joy;

And I—my harp would prelude woe—
10   I cannot all command the strings;
    The glory of the sum of things
  Will flash along the chords and go.

95

By night we lingered on the lawn,
    For underfoot the herb was dry;
    And genial warmth; and o'er the sky
  The silvery haze of summer drawn;

5   And calm that let the tapers burn
    Unwavering: not a cricket chirred;
    The brook alone far-off was heard,
  And on the board the fluttering urn.[3]

1. Hallam's tomb was inside Clevedon Church, just south of Clevedon, Somersetshire, on a hill overlooking the Bristol Channel.
2. Hawthorn hedge-row.
3. I.e., on the table a tea- or coffee-urn heated by a fluttering flame beneath.

And bats went round in fragrant skies,
10   And wheeled or lit the filmy shapes
    That haunt the dusk, with ermine capes
And woolly breasts and beaded eyes;

While now we sang old songs that pealed
    From knoll to knoll, where, couched at ease,
15   The white kine glimmered, and the trees
Laid their dark arms about the field.

But when those others, one by one,
    Withdrew themselves from me and night,
    And in the house light after light
20 Went out, and I was all alone,

A hunger seized my heart; I read
    Of that glad year which once had been,
    In those fallen leaves which kept their green,
The noble letters of the dead.

25 And strangely on the silence broke
    The silent-speaking words, and strange
    Was love's dumb cry defying change
To test his worth; and strangely spoke

The faith, the vigor, bold to dwell
30   On doubts that drive the coward back,
    And keen through wordy snares to track
Suggestion to her inmost cell.

So word by word, and line by line,
    The dead man touched me from the past,
35   And all at once it seemed at last
The living soul was flashed on mine,

And mine in this was wound, and whirled
    About empyreal heights of thought,
    And came on that which is, and caught
40 The deep pulsations of the world,

Eonian music[4] measuring out
    The steps of Time—the shocks of Chance—
    The blows of Death. At length my trance
Was canceled, stricken through with doubt.

45 Vague words! but ah, how hard to frame
    In matter-molded forms of speech,
    Or even for intellect to reach
Through memory that which I became;

Till now the doubtful dusk revealed
50   The knolls once more where, couched at ease,
    The white kine glimmered, and the trees
Lain their dark arms about the field;

And sucked from out the distant gloom
    A breeze began to tremble o'er
55   The large leaves of the sycamore,
And fluctuate all the still perfume,

4. I.e., the rhythm of the universe which has persisted for eons.

And gathering freshlier overhead
　　Rocked the full-foliaged elms, and swung
　　The heavy-folded rose, and flung
60　The lilies to and fro, and said,

"The dawn, the dawn," and died away;
　　And East and West, without a breath,
　　Mixt their dim lights, like life and death,
To broaden into boundless day.
　　　　　105
Tonight ungathered let us leave
　　This laurel, let this holly stand:
　　We live within the stranger's land,
And strangely falls our Christmas-eve.[5]

5　Our father's dust is left alone
　　And silent under other snows:
　　There in due time the woodbine blows,
The violet comes, but we are gone.

No more shall wayward grief abuse
10　The genial hour with mask and mime;
　　For change of place, like growth of time,
Has broke the bond of dying use.

Let cares that petty shadows cast,
　　By which our lives are chiefly proved,
15　A little spare the night I loved,
And hold it solemn to the past.

But let no footstep beat the floor,
　　Nor bowl of wassail mantle warm;
　　For who would keep an ancient form
20　Through which the spirit breathes no more?

Be neither song, nor game, nor feast;
　　Nor harp be touched, nor flute be blown;
　　No dance, no motion, save alone
What lightens in the lucid East

25　Of rising worlds[6] by yonder wood.
　　Long sleeps the summer in the seed;
　　Rut out your measured arcs,[7] and lead
The closing cycle rich in good.
　　　　　119
Doors, where my heart was used to beat
　　So quickly, not as one that weeps
　　I come once more; the city sleeps;
I smell the meadow in the street;

5　I hear a chirp of birds; I see
　　Betwixt the black fronts long-withdrawn
　　A light-blue lane of early dawn,
And think of early days and thee,

And bless thee, for thy lips are bland,
10　And bright the friendship of thine eyes;
　　And in my thoughts with scarce a sigh
I take the pressure of thine hand.

5. The third Christmas since Hallam's death found the Tennysons living no longer at Somersby, Lincolnshire, associated with his visits, but in a new home in Epping Forest.

6. I.e., stars.
7. The measured courses of the stars, which will eventually usher in the final period of perfect good.

121

Sad Hesper o'er the buried sun
   And ready, thou, to die with him,
   Thou watchest all things ever dim
And dimmer, and a glory done.

5 The team is loosened from the wain,°   *wagon*
   The boat is drawn upon the shore;
   Thou listenest to the closing door,
And life is darkened in the brain.

Bright Phosphor, fresher for the night,
10   By thee the world's great work is heard
   Beginning, and the wakeful bird;
Behind thee comes the greater light.

The market boat is on the stream,
   And voices hail it from the brink;
15   Thou hear'st the village hammer clink,
And see'st the moving of the team.

Sweet Hesper-Phosphor, double name[8]
   For what is one, the first, the last,
   Thou, like my present and my past,
20 Thy place is changed; thou art the same.

130

Thy voice is on the rolling air;
   I hear thee where the waters run;
   Thou standest in the rising sun,
And in the setting thou art fair.

5 What are thou then? I cannot guess;
   But though I seem in star and flower
   To feel thee some diffusive power,
I do not therefore love thee less.

My love involves the love before;
10   My love is vaster passion now;
   Though mixed with God and Nature thou,
I seem to love thee more and more.

Far off thou art, but ever nigh;
   I have thee still, and I rejoice;
15   I prosper, circled with thy voice;
I shall not lose theee though I die.

                       1833–50   1850

The Eagle

FRAGMENT

He clasps the crag with crooked hands;
Close to the sun in lonely lands,
Ringed with the azure world, he stands.

The wrinkled sea beneath him crawls;
5 He watches from his mountain walls,
And like a thunderbolt he falls.

                                   1851

---

8. Hesper, the evening star, and Phosphor, the morning star, are both the planet Venus.

Tithonus[9]

The woods decay, the woods decay and fall,
The vapors weep their burthen to the ground,
Man comes and tills the field and lies beneath,
And after many a summer dies the swan.
5   Me only cruel immortality
Consumes; I wither slowly in thine arms,
Here at the quiet limit of the world,
A white-haired shadow roaming like a dream
The ever-silent spaces of the East,
10   Far-folded mists, and gleaming halls of morn.
     Alas! for this gray shadow, once a man—
So glorious in his beauty and thy choice,
Who madest him thy chosen, that he seemed
To his great heart none other than a God!
15   I asked thee, "Give me immortality."
Then didst thou grant mine asking with a smile,
Like wealthy men who care not how they give.
But thy strong Hours indignant worked their wills,
And beat me down and marred and wasted me,
20   And though they could not end me, left me maimed
To dwell in presence of immortal youth.
Immortal age beside immortal youth,
And all I was in ashes. Can thy love,
Thy beauty, make amends, though even now,
25   Close over us, the silver star[1] thy guide,
Shines in those tremulous eyes that fill with tears
To hear me? Let me go; take back thy gift.
Why should a man desire in any way
To vary from the kindly race of men,
30   Or pass beyond the goal of ordinance
Where all should pause, as is most meet for all?
     A soft air fans the cloud apart; there comes
A glimpse of that dark world where I was born.
Once more the old mysterious glimmer steals
35   From thy pure brows, and from thy shoulders pure,
And bosom beating with a heart renewed.
Thy cheek begins to redden through the gloom,
Thy sweet eyes brighten slowly close to mine,
Ere yet they blind the stars, and the wild team
40   Which love thee, yearning for thy yoke, arise,
And shake the darkness from their loosened manes,
And beat the twilight into flakes of fire.
     Lo! ever thus thou growest beautiful
In silence, then before thine answer given
45   Departest, and thy tears are on my cheek.
     Why wilt thou ever scare me with thy tears,
And make me tremble lest a saying learnt,
In days far-off, on that dark earth, be true?
"The Gods themselves cannot recall their gifts."
50   Ay me! ay me! with what another heart
In days far-off, and with what other eyes
I used to watch—if I be he that watched—
The lucid outline forming round thee; saw
The dim curls kindle into sunny rings;
55   Changed with thy mystic change, and felt my blood

---

9. A Trojan prince beloved by Aurora (Greek
Eos), goddess of the dawn, who took him as
her spouse. She begged Zeus to grant him
eternal life, but forgot to ask also for the gift
of eternal youth.
1. I.e., the morning star.

Glow with the glow that slowly crimsoned all
Thy presence and thy portals, while I lay,
Mouth, forehead, eyelids, growing dewy-warm
With kisses balmier than half-opening buds
60   Of April, and could hear the lips that kissed
Whispering I knew not what of wild and sweet,
Like that strange song I heard Apollo sing,
While Ilion like a mist rose into towers.[2]
        Yet hold me not for ever in thine East;
65   How can my nature longer mix with thine?
Coldly thy rosy shadows bathe me, cold
Are all thy lights, and cold my wrinkled feet
Upon thy glimmering thresholds, when the steam
Floats up from those dim fields about the homes
70   Of happy men that have the power to die,
And grassy barrows of the happier dead.
Release me, and restore me to the ground.
Thou seest all things, thou wilt see my grave;
Thou wilt renew thy beauty morn by morn,
75   I earth in earth forget these empty courts,
And thee returning on thy silver wheels.

1833, 1859   1860

Milton

ALCAICS[3]

O mighty-mouthed inventor of harmonies,
O skilled to sing of Time or Eternity,
    God-gifted organ-voice of England,
        Milton, a name to resound for ages;
5   Whose Titan[4] angels, Gabriel, Abdiel,[5]
Starred from Jehovah's gorgeous armories,
    Tower, as the deep-domed empyrëan
        Rings to the roar of an angel onset—
Me rather all that bowery loneliness,
10   The brooks of Eden mazily murmuring,
    And bloom profuse and cedar arches
        Charm, as a wanderer out in ocean,
Where some refulgent sunset of India
Streams o'er a rich ambrosial ocean isle,
15   And crimson-hued the stately palm-woods
            Whisper in odorous heights of even.

1863

---

2. According to legend, the walls and towers
of Ilion (Troy) were raised by the sound
of Apollo's song, as related by Ovid, *He-
roides*, XVI.179.
3. The Alcaic ode, named after the Greek
lyric poet Alcaeus, ca. 600 B.C. See Glossary,
entry on **Alcaic strophe**, at the end of this
anthology.

4. Gigantic in size and power.
5. "Gabriel": one of the seven archangels; in
Paradise Lost, one of the four angels who
guard Paradise and who oppose Satan's at-
tacks on it. "Abdiel": in *Paradise Lost*, one of
the faithful angels who resisted Satan's revolt,
striking the first sword-blow against him.

To Virgil

WRITTEN AT THE REQUEST OF THE MANTUANS FOR THE NINETEENTH
CENTENARY OF VIRGIL'S DEATH[6]

1
Roman Virgil, thou that singest[7]
    Ilion's lofty temples robed in fire,
Ilion falling, Rome arising,
    wars, and filial faith, and Dido's pyre;[8]

2
5 Landscape-lover, lord of language
    more than he that sang the Works and Days,[9]
All the chosen coin of fancy
    flashing out from many a golden phrase;

3
Thou that singest wheat and woodland,
10   tilth and vineyard, hive and horse and herd;
All the charm of all the Muses
    often flowering in a lonely word;

4
Poet of the happy Tityrus
    piping underneath his beechen bowers;[1]
15 Poet of the poet-satyr[2]
    whom the laughing shepherd bound with flowers;

5
Chanter of the Pollio,[3] glorying
    in the blissful years again to be,
Summers of the snakeless meadow,
20   unlaborious earth and oarless sea;

6
Thou that seest Universal
    Nature moved by Universal Mind;
Thou majestic in thy sadness
    at the doubtful doom of human kind;

7
25 Light among the vanished ages;
    star that gildest yet this phantom shore;
Golden branch[4] amid the shadows,
    kings and realms that pass to rise no more;

8
Now thy Forum roars no longer,
30   fallen every purple Caesar's dome—
Though thine ocean-roll of rhythm
    sound forever of Imperial Rome—

9
Now the Rome of slaves hath perished,
    and the Rome of freemen holds her place,[5]
35 I, from out the North Island
    sundered once from all the human race,

6. The Roman poet Virgil was born near Mantua, in northern Italy, on October 19, 70 B.C., and died at Brundisium (modern Brindisi), on September 20, 19 B.C.
7. In the *Aeneid,* Virgil's last and greatest work: Aeneas, who fought against the Greeks in the Trojan War and who escaped after the fall of Troy (Ilion) with his father Anchises, was destined after his wanderings to be the founder of Rome.
8. Dido, Queen of Carthage, loved by Aeneas and deserted by him when he was ordered by Mercury to continue on his way and to fulfill his imperial mission: she immolates herself.
9. The Greek poet Hesiod, whose didactic poem of occupations is here compared with Virgil's *Georgics,* descriptive of country life and farm pursuits.
1. In Virgil's *Eclogues* or Pastorals, especially the opening of *Eclogue* I.
2. Silenus, in *Eclogue* VI.
3. Gaius Asinus Pollio, Roman consul and man of letters, to whom Virgil dedicated the fourth Eclogue, in which he identifies the return of the world's golden age with the time of Pollio's consulate.
4. In the *Aeneid* VI.136 ff. Aeneas, prior to his journey to the underworld, is warned by the Sibyl that his safety depends on his finding and breaking off the golden bough which must be presented to Proserpine, goddess of the underworld.
5. Italy had finally achieved its freedom and unification in 1870.

10

I salute thee, Mantovano,°   *Mantuan*
    I that loved thee since my day began,
Wielder of the stateliest measure
40   ever molded by the lips of man.

                  1880   1883

Frater Ave Atque Vale[6]

Row us out from Desenzano, to your Sirmione row!
So they rowed, and there we landed—"O venusta Sirmio!"[7]
There to me through all the groves of olive in the summer glow,
There beneath the Roman ruin where the purple flowers grow,
5 Came that "Ave atque Vale" of the poet's hopeless woe,
Tenderest of Roman poets nineteen-hundred years ago,
"Frater Ave atque Vale"—as we wandered to and fro
Gazing at the Lydian laughter of the Garda Lake below[8]
Sweet Catullus's all-but-island, olive-silvery Sirmio!

                  1880   1885

Crossing the Bar

Sunset and evening star,
    And one clear call for me!
And may there be no moaning of the bar,
    When I put out to sea,

5 But such a tide as moving seems asleep,
    Too full for sound and foam,
When that which drew from out the boundless deep
    Turns again home.

Twilight and evening bell,
10   And after that the dark!
And may there be no sadness of farewell,
    When I embark;

For though from out our bourne of Time and Place
    The flood may bear me far,
15 I hope to see my Pilot face to face
    When I have crossed the bar.

                              1889

6. The title (Brother, hail and farewell) repeats the concluding phrase of poem number CI, in which Catullus records the journey to visit his brother's tomb in Asia Minor. Tennyson's poem, written on a visit to the little peninsula of Sirmio, on Lake Garda in Northern Italy, shortly after his own brother had died, echoes phrases from another poem (XXXI) in which Catullus describes his pleasure in returning to Sirmio after a long absence.
7. O lovely Sirmio.
8. Catullus's line, "And rejoice, O Lydian waves of the lake" (XXXI: 13) alludes to the old belief that the Estruscans of the Garda region had originated in Lydia, in Asia Minor.

ROBERT BROWNING
1812–1889

My Last Duchess[1]

FERRARA

That's my last duchess painted on the wall,
Looking as if she were alive. I call
That piece a wonder, now: Frà Pandolf's hands
Worked busily a day, and there she stands.
5   Will't please you sit and look at her? I said
"Frà Pandolf" by design, for never read
Strangers like you that pictured countenance,
The depth and passion of its earnest glance,
But to myself they turned (since none puts by
10   The curtain I have drawn for you, but I)
And seemed as they would ask me, if they durst,
How such a glance came there; so, not the first
Are you to turn and ask thus. Sir, 'twas not
Her husband's presence only, called that spot
15   Of joy into the Duchess' cheek: perhaps
Frà Pandolf chanced to say "Her mantle laps
"Over my lady's wrist too much," or "Paint
"Must never hope to reproduce the faint
"Half-flush that dies along her throat": such stuff
20   Was courtesy, she thought, and cause enough
For calling up that spot of joy. She had
A heart—how shall I say?—too soon made glad,
Too easily impressed; she like whate'er
She looked on, and her looks went everywhere.
25   Sir, 'twas all one! My favor at her breast,
The dropping of the daylight in the West,
The bough of cherries some officious fool
Broke in the orchard for her, the white mule
She rode with round the terrace—all and each
30   Would draw from her alike the approving speech,
Or blush, at least. She thanked men—good! but thanked
Somehow—I know not how—as if she ranked
My gift of a nine-hundred-years-old name
With anybody's gift. Who'd stoop to blame
35   This sort of trifling? Even had you skill
In speech—which I have not—to make your will
Quite clear to such an one, and say, "Just this
"Or that in you disgusts me; here you miss,
"Or there exceed the mark"—and if she let
40   Herself be lessoned so, nor plainly set
Her wits to yours, forsooth, and made excuse,
—E'en then would be some stooping; and I choose
Never to stoop. Oh sir, she smiled, no doubt,
Whene'er I passed her; but who passed without
45   Much the same smile? This grew; I gave commands;
Then all smiles stopped together. There she stands

1. The events of Browning's poem parallel historical events, but its emphasis is rather on truth to Renaissance attitudes than on historic specificity. Alfonso II d'Este, Duke of Ferrara (born 1533), in Northern Italy, had married his first wife, daughter of Cosimo I de'Medici, Duke of Florence, in 1558, when she was fourteen; she died on April 21, 1561, under suspicious circumstances, and soon afterwards he opened negotiations for the hand of the niece of the Count of Tyrol, the seat of whose court was at Innsbruck, in Austria. "Fra Pandolf" and "Claus of Innsbruck" are types rather than specific artists.

As if alive. Will 't please you rise? We'll meet
The company below, then. I repeat,
The Count your master's known munificence
50 Is ample warrant that no just pretense
Of mine for dowry will be disallowed;
Though his fair daughter's self, as I avowed
At starting, is my object. Nay, we'll go
Together down, sir. Notice Neptune, though,
55 Taming a sea-horse, thought a rarity,
Which Claus of Innsbruck cast in bronze for me!

1842

Home-Thoughts, From Abroad

1

Oh, to be in England
Now that April's there,
And whoever wakes in England
Sees, some morning, unaware,
5 That the lowest boughs and the brushwood sheaf
Round the elm-tree bole are in tiny leaf,
While the chaffinch sings on the orchard bough
In England—now!

2

And after April, when May follows,
10 And the whitethroat builds, and all the swallows!
Hark, where my blossomed pear-tree in the hedge
Leans to the field and scatters on the clover
Blossoms and dewdrops—at the bent spray's edge—
That's the wise thrush; he sings each song twice over,
15 Lest you should think he never could recapture
The first fine careless rapture!
And though the fields look rough with hoary dew
All will be gay when noontide wakes anew
The buttercups, the little children's dower
—Far brighter than this gaudy melon-flower!

1845

The Bishop Orders His Tomb at Saint Praxed's Church[2]

ROME, 15—

Vanity, saith the preacher, vanity![3]
Draw round my bed: is Anselm keeping back?
Nephews—sons mine . . . ah God, I know not! Well—
She, men would have to be your mother once,
5 Old Gandolf envied me, so fair she was!
What's done is done, and she is dead beside,
Dead long ago, and I am Bishop since,
And as she died so must we die ourselves,
And thence ye may perceive the world's a dream.
10 Life, how and what is it? As here I lie
In this state-chamber, dying by degrees,
Hours and long hours in the dead night, I ask
"Do I live, am I dead?" Peace, peace seems all.
Saint Praxed's ever was the church for peace;
15 And so, about this tomb of mine. I fought
With tooth and nail to save my niche, ye know:

2. The church of Santa Prassede, in Rome, dedicated to a Roman virgin, dates from the fifth century but was rebuilt early in the ninth and restored at later times. The 16th-century Bishop who speaks here is a fictional figure, as is his predecessor, Gandolf.

3. An echo of Ecclesiastes i.2: "Vanity of vanities, saith the Preacher, vanity of vanities; all is vanity."

—Old Gandolf cozened° me, despite my care;   *cheated*
Shrewd was that snatch from out the corner south
He graced his carrion with, God curse the same!
20 Yet still my niche is not so cramped but thence
One sees the pulpit o' the epistle-side,[4]
And somewhat of the choir, those silent seats,
And up into the aery dome where live
The angels, and a sunbeam's sure to lurk:
25 And I shall fill my slab of basalt there,
And 'neath my tabernacle[5] take my rest,
With those nine columns round me, two and two,
The odd one at my feet where Anselm stands:
Peach-blossom marble all, the rare, the ripe
30 As fresh-poured red wine of a mighty pulse.
—Old Gandolf with his paltry onion-stone,
Put me where I may look at him! True peach,
Rosy and flawless: how I earned the prize!
Draw close: that conflagration of my church
35 —What then? So much was saved if aught were missed!
My sons, ye would not be my death? Go dig
The white-grape vineyard where the oil-press stood,
Drop water gently till the surface sink,
And if ye find . . . Ah God, I know not, I! . . .
40 Bedded in store of rotten fig-leaves soft,
And corded up in a tight olive-frail,°   *olive basket*
Some lump, ah God, of *lapis lazuli*,[6]
Big as a Jew's head cut off at the nape,
Blue as a vein o'er the Madonna's breast . . .
45 Sons, all have I bequeathed you, villas, all,
That brave Frascati[7] villa with its bath,
So, let the blue lump poise between my knees,
Like God the Father's globe on both his hands
Ye worship in the Jesu Church[8] so gay,
50 For Gandolf shall not choose but see and burst!
Swift as a weaver's shuttle fleet our years:[9]
Man goeth to the grave, and where is he?
Did I say basalt for my slab, sons? Black—
'Twas ever antique-black I meant! How else
55 Shall ye contrast my frieze to come beneath?
The bas-relief in bronze ye promised me,
Those Pans and Nymphs ye wot of, and perchance
Some tripod, thyrsus,[1] with a vase or so,
The Saviour at his sermon on the mount,
60 Saint Praxed in a glory,[2] and one Pan
Ready to twitch the Nymph's last garment off,
And Moses with the tables . . . but I know
Ye mark me not! What do they whisper thee,
Child of my bowels, Anselm? Ah, ye hope
65 To revel down my villas while I gasp
Bricked o'er with beggar's moldy travertine[3]
Which Gandolf from his tomb-top chuckles at!
Nay, boys, ye love me—all of jasper, then!
'T is jasper ye stand pledged to, lest I grieve
70 My bath must needs be left behind, alas!
One block, pure green as a pistachio-nut,

---

4. The right-hand side as one faces the altar, the side from which the Epistles of the New Testament were read.
5. Canopy over his tomb.
6. A vivid blue stone, one of the so-called hard stones, used for ornament.
7. A resort town in the mountains.
8. The splendid baroque church, Il Gesù. The sculptured group of the Trinity includes a terrestrial globe carved from the largest known block of lapis lazuli.

9. See Job vii.6 ("My days are swifter than a weaver's shuttle, and are spent without hope").
1. A staff ornamented with ivy or vine-leaves, carried by followers of Bacchus, the Roman god of wine and revelry.
2. Rays of gold, signifying sanctity, around the head or body of the saint portrayed.
3. Ordinary limestone used in building.

There's plenty jasper somewhere in the world—
And have I not Saint Praxed's ear to pray
Horses for ye, and brown Greek manuscripts,
75   And mistresses with great smooth marbly limbs?
—That's if ye carve my epitaph aright,
Choice Latin, picked phrase, Tully's[4] every word,
No gaudy ware like Gandolf's second line—
Tully, my masters? Ulpian[5] serves his need!
80   And then how I shall lie through centuries,
And hear the blessed mutter of the mass,
And see God made and eaten all day long,[6]
And feel the steady candle-flame, and taste
Good strong thick stupefying incense-smoke!
85   For as I lie here, hours of the dead night,
Dying in state and by such slow degrees,
I fold my arms as if they clasped a crook,[7]
And stretch my feet forth straight as stone can point,
And let the bedclothes, for a mortcloth,[8] drop
90   Into great laps and folds of sculptor's-work:
And as yon tapers dwindle, and strange thoughts
Grow, with a certain humming in my ears,
About the life before I lived this life,
And this life too, popes, cardinals and priests,
95   Saint Praxed at his sermon on the mount,[9]
Your tall pale mother with her talking eyes,
And new-found agate urns as fresh as day,
And marble's language, Latin pure, discreet,
—Aha, ELUCESCEBAT[1] quoth our friend?
100   No Tully, said I, Ulpian at the best!
Evil and brief hath been my pilgrimage.
All *lapis*, all, son! Else I give the Pope
My villas! Will ye ever eat my heart?
Ever your eyes were as a lizard's quick,
105   They glitter like your mother's for my soul,
Or ye would heighten my impoverished frieze,
Piece out its starved design, and fill my vase
With grapes, and add a vizor and a Term,[2]
And to the tripod ye would tie a lynx
110   That in his struggle throws the thyrsus down,
To comfort me on my entablature
Whereon I am to lie till I must ask
"Do I live, am I dead?" There, leave me, there!
For ye have stabbed me with ingratitude
115   To death—ye wish it—God, ye wish it! Stone—
Gritstone, a-crumble! Clammy squares which sweat
As if the corpse they keep were oozing through—
And no more *lapis* to delight the world!
Well, go! I bless ye. Fewer tapers there,
120   But in a row: and, going, turn your backs
—Ay, like departing altar-ministrants,
And leave me in my church, the church for peace,
That I may watch at leisure if he leers—
Old Gandolf, at me, from his onion-stone,
125   As still he envied me, so fair she was!

1845, 1849

4. Familiar name for Cicero (Marcus Tullius Cicero).
5. His Latin would be stylistically inferior to that of Cicero.
6. Refers to the doctrine of transubstantiation.
7. I.e., the Bishop's crozier, with its emblematic resemblance to a shepherd's crook.
8. The pall with which the coffin is draped.
9. As the Bishop's mind wanders, he attributes Christ's Sermon on the Mount to Santa Prassede.
1. A word from Gandolf's epitaph (a form of the Latin verb meaning "to shine forth"); the Bishop claims that this form is inferior to *elucebat*, which Cicero would have used.
2. "Vizor": a mask; "Term": a pillar adorned with a bust. Both are motifs of classical sculpture imitated by the Renaissance.

Fra Lippo Lippi[3]

I am poor brother Lippo, by your leave!
You need not clap your torches to my face.
Zooks, what's to blame? you think you see a monk!
What, 'tis past midnight, and you go the rounds,
5 And here you catch me at an alley's end
Where sportive ladies leave their doors ajar?
The Carmine's my cloister:[4] hunt it up,
Do—harry out, if you must show your zeal,
Whatever rat, there, haps on his wrong hole,
10 And nip each softling of a wee white mouse,
Weke, weke, that's crept to keep him company!
Aha, you know your betters! Then, you'll take
Your hand away that's fiddling on my throat,
And please to know me likewise. Who am I?
15 Why, one, sir, who is lodging with a friend
Three streets off—he's a certain . . . how d'ye call?
Master—a . . . Cosimo of the Medici,[5]
I' the house that caps the corner. Boh! you were best!
Remember and tell me, the day you're hanged,
20 How you affected such a gullet's-gripe![6]
But you, sir, it concerns you that your knaves
Pick up a manner nor discredit you:
Zooks, are we pilchards,° that they sweep the streets   fish
And count fair prize what comes into their net?
25 He's Judas to a tittle, that man is![7]
Just such a face! Why, sir, you make amends.
Lord, I'm not angry! Bid your hangdogs go
Drink out this quarter-florin to the health
Of the munificent House that harbors me
30 (And many more beside, lads! more beside!)
And all's come square again. I'd like his face—
His, elbowing on his comrade in the door
With the pike and lantern—for the slave that holds
John Baptist's head a-dangle by the hair
35 With one hand ("Look you, now," as who should say)
And his weapon in the other, yet unwiped!
It's not your chance to have a bit of chalk,
A wood-coal or the like? or you should see!
Yes, I'm the painter, since you style me so.
40 What, brother Lippo's doings, up and down,
You know them and they take you? like enough!
I saw the proper twinkle in your eye—
'Tell you, I liked your looks at very first.
Let's sit and set things straight now, hip to haunch.
45 Here's spring come, and the nights one makes up bands
To roam the town and sing out carnival,
And I've been three weeks shut within my mew,[8]
A-painting for the great man, saints and saints
And saints again. I could not paint all night—
50 Ouf! I leaned out of window for fresh air.

3. Florentine painter (ca. 1406–69), whose life Browning knew from Vasari's *Lives of the Most Eminent Painters, Sculptors, and Architects,* and from other sources, and whose paintings he had learned to know at first hand during his years in Florence.
4. Fra Lippo had entered the Carmelite cloister while still a boy. He gave up monastic vows on June 6, 1421, but was clothed by the monastery until 1431 and was called "Fra Filippo" in documents until his death.
5. Cosimo de'Medici (1389–1464), Fra Lippo's wealthy patron and an important political power in Florence.
6. I.e., grip on my throat.
7. Of one of the watchmen who have arrested him, he says he looks exactly like Judas.
8. I.e., within the confines of my quarters (in the Medici palace).

There came a hurry of feet and little feet,
A sweep of lute-strings, laughs, and whiffs of song—
Flower o' the broom,
Take away love, and our earth is a tomb!
55 *Flower o' the quince,*
I let Lisa go, and what good in life since?
Flower o' the thyme—and so on. Round they went.
Scarce had they turned the corner when a titter
Like the skipping of rabbits by moonlight—
        three slim shapes,
60 And a face that looked up . . . zooks, sir, flesh and blood,
That's all I'm made of! Into shreds it went,
Curtain and counterpane and coverlet,
All the bed-furniture—a dozen knots,
There was a ladder! Down I let myself,
65 Hands and feet, scrambling somehow, and so dropped,
And after them. I came up with the fun
Hard by Saint Laurence,[9] hail fellow, well met—
Flower o' the rose,
If I've been merry, what matter who knows?
70 And so as I was stealing back again
To get to bed and have a bit of sleep
Ere I rise up to-morrow and go work
On Jerome knocking at his poor old breast[1]
With his great round stone to subdue the flesh,
75 You snap me of the sudden. Ah, I see!
Though your eye twinkles still, you shake your head—
Mine's shaved—a monk, you say—the sting's in that!
If Master Cosimo announced himself,
Mum's the word naturally; but a monk!
80 Come, what am I a beast for? tell us, now!
I was a baby when my mother died
And father died and left me in the street.
I starved there, God knows how, a year or two
On fig-skins, melon-parings, rinds and shucks,
85 Refuse and rubbish. One fine frosty day,
My stomach being empty as your hat,
The wind doubled me up and down I went.
Old Aunt Lapaccia trussed me with one hand,
(Its fellow was a stinger as I knew)
90 And so along the wall, over the bridge,
By the straight cut to the convent. Six words there,
While I stood munching my first bread that month:
"So, boy, you're minded," quoth the good fat father
Wiping his own mouth, 't was refection-time—
95 "To quit this very miserable world?
"Will you renounce" . . . "the mouthful of bread?" thought I;
By no means! Brief, they made a monk of me;
I did renounce the world, its pride and greed,
Palace, farm, villa, shop and banking-house,
100 Trash, such as these poor devils of Medici
Have given their hearts to—all at eight years old.
Well, sir, I found in time, you may be sure,
'T was not for nothing—the good bellyful,
The warm serge and the rope that goes all round,
105 And day-long blessed idleness beside!
"Let's see what the urchin's fit for"—that came next.
Not overmuch their way, I must confess.
Such a to-do! They tried me with their books:

9. The church of San Lorenzo, not far from the Medici palace.

1. I.e., on a painting of St. Jerome in the Desert.

Lord, they'd have taught me Latin in pure waste!
110 *Flower o' the clove,*
All the Latin I construe is, "amo" I love!
But, mind you, when a boy starves in the streets
Eight years together, as my fortune was,
Watching folk's faces to know who will fling
115 The bit of half-stripped grape-bunch he desires,
And who will curse or kick him for his pains—
Which gentleman processional and fine,
Holding a candle to the Sacrament,
Will wink and let him lift a plate and catch
125 The droppings of the wax to sell again,
Or holla for the Eight[2] and have him whipped—
How say I? nay, which dog bites, which lets drop
His bone from the heap of offal in the street—
Why, soul and sense of him grow sharp alike,
125 He learns the look of things, and none the less
For admonition from the hunger-pinch.
I had a store of such remarks, be sure,
Which, after I found leisure, turned to use.
I drew men's faces on my copy-books,
130 Scrawled them within the antiphonary's[3] marge,
Joined legs and arms to the long music-notes,
Found eyes and nose and chin for A's and B's,
And made a string of pictures of the world
Betwixt the ins and outs of verb and noun,
135 On the wall, the bench, the door. The monks looked black.
"Nay," quoth the Prior, "turn him out, d'ye say?
"In no wise. Lose a crow and catch a lark.
"What if at last we get our man of parts,
"We Carmelites, like those Camaldolese[4]
140 "And Preaching Friars,[5] to do our church up fine
"And put the front on it that ought to be!"
And hereupon he bade me daub away.
Thank you! my head being crammed, the walls a blank,
Never was such prompt disemburdening.
145 First, every sort of monk, the black and white,
I drew them, fat and lean: then, folk at church,
From good old gossips waiting to confess
Their cribs of barrel-droppings, candle-ends—
To the breathless fellow at the altar-foot,
150 Fresh from his murder, safe and sitting there
With the little children round him in a row
Of admiration, half for his beard and half
For that white anger of his victim's son
Shaking a fist at him with one fierce arm,
155 Signing[6] himself with the other because of Christ
(Whose sad face on the cross sees only this
After the passion of a thousand years)
Till some poor girl, her apron o'er her head,
(Which the intense eyes looked through) came at eve
160 On tiptoe, said a word, dropped in a loaf,
Her pair of earrings and a bunch of flowers
(The brute took growling), prayed, and so was gone.
I painted all, then cried " 'Tis ask and have;
"Choose, for more's ready!"—laid the ladder flat,
165 And showed my covered bit of cloister-wall.

---

2. The Florentine magistrates.
3. The book containing the antiphons, or responses chanted in the liturgy.
4. Members of a religious order at Camaldoli, in the Apennines.

5. I.e., Dominicans.
6. Making the sign of the cross with one hand, because of the image of Christ on the altar.

The monks closed in a circle and praised loud
Till checked, taught what to see and not to see,
Being simple bodies—"That's the very man!
"Look at the boy who stoops to pat the dog!
170 "That woman's like the Prior's niece who comes
"To care about his asthma: it's the life!"
But there my triumph's straw-fire flared and funked;
Their betters took their turn to see and say:
The Prior and the learned pulled a face
175 And stopped all that in no time. "How? what's here?
"Quite from the mark of painting, bless us all!
"Faces, arms, legs and bodies like the true
"As much as pea and pea! it's devil's-game!
"Your business is not to catch men with show,
180 "With homage to the perishable clay,
"But lift them over it, ignore it all,
"Make them forget there's such a thing as flesh.
"Your business is to paint the souls of men—
"Man's soul, and it's a fire, smoke . . . no, it's not . . .
185 "It's vapor done up like a new-born babe—
"(In that shape when you die it leaves your mouth)
"It's . . . well, what matters talking, it's the soul!
"Give us no more of body than shows soul!
"Here's Giotto,[7] with his Saint a-praising God,
190 "That sets us praising—why not stop with him?
"Why put all thoughts of praise out of our head
"With wonder at lines, colors, and what not?
"Paint the soul, never mind the legs and arms!
"Rub all out, try at it a second time.
195 "Oh, that white smallish female with the breasts,
"She's just my niece . . . Herodias,[8] I would say—
"Who went and danced and got men's heads cut off!
"Have it all out!" Now, is this sense, I ask?
A fine way to paint soul, by painting body
200 So ill, the eye can't stop there, must go further
And can't fare worse! Thus, yellow does for white
When what you put for yellow's simply black,
And any sort of meaning looks intense
When all beside itself means and looks nought.
205 Why can't a painter lift each foot in turn,
Left foot and right foot, go a double step,
Make his flesh liker and his soul more like,
Both in their order? Take the prettiest face,
The Prior's niece . . . patron-saint—is it so pretty
210 You can't discover if it means hope, fear,
Sorrow or joy? won't beauty go with these?
Suppose I've made her eyes all right and blue,
Can't I take breath and try to add life's flash,
And then add soul and heighten them threefold?
215 Or say there's beauty with no soul at all—
(I never saw it—put the case the same—)
If you get simple beauty and nought else,
You get about the best thing God invents:
That's somewhat: and you'll find the soul you have missed,
220 Within yourself, when you return him thanks.
"Rub all out!" Well, well, there's my life, in short,
And so the thing has gone on ever since.
I'm grown a man no doubt, I've broken bounds:

7. The great Florentine painter (1267–1337).
8. Sister-in-law of the tetrarch Herod. She had demanded that John the Baptist be imprisoned: when her daughter Salome so pleased the king with her dancing that he promised her anythink she asked, Herodias instructed her to ask for the head of a Baptist on a platter (Matthew xiv.1–12).

You should not take a fellow eight years old
225 And make him swear to never kiss the girls.
I'm my own master, paint now as I please—
Having a friend, you see, in the Corner-house![9]
Lord, it's fast holding by the rings in front—
Those great rings serve more purposes than just
230 To plant a flag in, or tie up a horse!
And yet the old schooling sticks, the old grave eyes
Are peeping o'er my shoulder as I work,
The heads shake still—"It's art's decline, my son!
"You're not of the true painters, great and old;
235 "Brother Angelico's the man, you'll find;
"Brother Lorenzo[1] stands his single peer:
"Fag on at flesh, you'll never make the third!"
Flower o' the pine,
You keep your mistr . . . manners, and I'll stick to mine!
240 I'm not the third, then: bless us, they must know!
Don't you think they're the likeliest to know,
They with their Latin? So, I swallow my rage,
Clench my teeth, suck my lips in tight, and paint
To please them—sometimes do and sometimes don't;
245 For, doing most, there's pretty sure to come
A turn, some warm eve finds me at my saints—
A laugh, a cry, the business of the world—
(*Flower o' the peach,*
Death for us all, and his own life for each!)
250 And my whole soul revolves, the cup runs over,
The world and life's too big to pass for a dream,
And I do these wild things in sheer despite,
And play the fooleries you catch me at,
In pure rage! The old mill-horse, out at grass
255 After hard years, throws up his stiff heels so,
Although the miller does not preach to him
The only good of grass is to make chaff.
What would men have? Do they like grass or no—
May they or mayn't they? all I want's the thing
260 Settled for ever one way. As it is,
You tell too many lies and hurt yourself:
You don't like what you only like too much,
You do like what, if given you at your word,
You find abundantly detestable.
265 For me, I think I speak as I was taught;
I always see the garden and God there
A-making man's wife: and, my lesson learned,
The value and significance of flesh,
I can't unlearn ten minutes afterwards.

270   You understand me: I'm a beast, I know.
But see, now—why, I see as certainly
As that the morning-star's about to shine,
What will hap some day. We've a youngster here
Comes to our convent, studies what I do,
275 Slouches and stares and lets no atom drop:
His name is Guidi—he'll not mind the monks—
They call him Hulking Tom,[2] he lets them talk—
He picks my practice up—he'll paint apace,

9. I.e., the Medici palace.
1. Fra   Angelico   (1387–1455),   and   Fra
Lorenzo Monaco (1370–1425).
2. The painter Tommaso Guidi (1401–28),
known as Masaccio (from *Tomasaccio,* mean-
ing "Big Tom" or "Hulking Tom"). The series
of frescoes which he painted in Santa Maria
del Carmine, of key importance in the history
of Florentine painting, was completed by Fra
Lippo's son, Filippino Lippi, and it is in fact
more likely that Fra Lippo learned from
Masaccio than that he saw him as a promising
newcomer.

I hope so—though I never live so long,
280 I know what's sure to follow. You be judge!
You speak no Latin more than I, belike;
However, you're my man, you've seen the world
—The beauty and the wonder and the power,
The shapes of things, their colors, lights and shades,
285 Changes, surprises—and God made it all!
—For what? Do you feel thankful, ay or no,
For this fair town's face, yonder river's line,
The mountain round it and the sky above,
Much more the figures of man, woman, child,
290 These are the frame to? What's it all about?
To be passed over, despised? or dwelt upon,
Wondered at? oh, this last of course!—you say.
But why not do as well as say, paint these
Just as they are, careless what comes of it?
295 God's works—paint anyone, and count it crime
To let a truth slip. Don't object, "His works
"Are here already; nature is complete:
"Suppose you reproduce her (which you can't)
"There's no advantage! you must beat her, then."
300 For, don't you mark? we're made so that we love
First when we see them painted, things we have passed
Perhaps a hundred times nor cared to see;
And so they are better, painted—better to us,
Which is the same thing. Art was given for that;
305 God uses us to help each other so,
Lending our minds out. Have you noticed, now,
Your cullion's hanging face? A bit of chalk,
And trust me but you should, though! How much more,
If I drew higher things with the same truth!
310 That were to take the Prior's pulpit-place,
Interpret God to all of you! Oh, oh,
It makes me mad to see what men shall do
And we in our graves! This world's no blot for us,
Nor blank; it means intensely, and means good:
315 To find its meaning is my meat and drink.
"Ay, but you don't so instigate to prayer!"
Strikes in the Prior: "when your meaning's plain
"It does not say to folk—remember matins,
"Or, mind you fast next Friday!" Why, for this
320 What need of art at all? A skull and bones,
Two bits of stick nailed crosswise, or, what's best,
A bell to chime the hour with, does as well.
I painted a Saint Laurence six months since
At Prato,[3] splashed the fresco in fine style:
325 "How looks my painting, now the scaffold's down?"
I ask a brother: "Hugely," he returns—
"Already not one phiz of your three slaves
"Who turn the Deacon off his toasted side,[4]
"But's scratched and prodded to our heart's content,
330 "The pious people have so eased their own
"With coming to say prayers there in a rage:
"We get on fast to see the bricks beneath.
"Expect another job this time next year,
"For pity and religion grow i' the crowd—
355 "Your painting serves its purpose!" Hang the fools!

3. Smaller town near Florence, where Fra Lippo painted some of his most important pictures.
4. Saint Lawrence was martyred by being roasted on a gridiron; according to legend, he urged his executioners to turn him over, saying that he was done on one side.

—That is—you'll not mistake an idle word
Spoke in a huff by a poor monk, God wot,
Tasting the air this spicy night which turns
The unaccustomed head like Chianti wine!
340 Oh, the church knows! don't misreport me, now!
It's natural a poor monk out of bounds
Should have his apt word to excuse himself:
And hearken how I plot to make amends.
I have bethought me: I shall paint a piece
345 . . . There's for you! Give me six months, then go, see
Something in Sant' Ambrogio's![5] Bless the nuns!
They want a cast o' my office. I shall paint
God in the midst, Madonna and her babe,
Ringed by a bowery flowery angel-brood,
350 Lilies and vestments and white faces, sweet
As puff on puff of grated orris-root
When ladies crowd to Church at midsummer.
And then i' the front, of course a saint or two—
Saint John, because he saves the Florentines,[6]
355 Saint Ambrose, who puts down in black and white
The convent's friends and gives them a long day,
And Job, I must have him there past mistake,
The man of Uz (and Us without the z,
Painters who need his patience). Well, all these
360 Secured at their devotion, up shall come
Out of a corner when you least expect,
As one by a dark stair into a great light,
Music and talking, who but Lippo! I!
Mazed, motionless and moonstruck—I'm the man!
365 Back I shrink—what is this I see and hear?
I, caught up with my monk's-things by mistake,
My old serge gown and rope that goes all round,
I, in this presence, this pure company!
Where's a hole, where's a corner for escape?
370 Then steps a sweet angelic slip of a thing
Forward, puts out a soft palm—"Not so fast!"
—Addresses the celestial presence, "nay—
"He made you and devised you, after all,
"Though he's none of you! Could Saint John there draw—
375 "His camel-hair[7] make up a painting-brush?
"We come to brother Lippo for all that,
"*Iste perfecit opus!*"[8] So, all smile—
I shuffle sideways with my blushing face
Under the cover of a hundred wings
380 Thrown like a spread of kirtles[9] when you're gay
And play hot cockles,[1] all the doors being shut,
Till, wholly unexpected, in there pops
The hothead husband! Thus I scuttle off
To some safe bench behind, not letting go
285 The palm of her, the little lily thing
That spoke the good word for me in the nick,
Like the Prior's niece . . . Saint Lucy, I would say.
And so all's saved for me, and for the church

5. Fra Lippo painted the *Coronation of the Virgin*, here described, for the high altar of Sant' Ambrogio in 1447.
6. San Giovanni is the patron saint of Florence.
7. John the Baptist is often portrayed wearing a rough robe of camel's hair, in accord with Mark i.6.
8. It is more likely that the figure which Browning took to be that of the painter is that of the patron, the Very Reverend Francesco Marenghi, who ordered the painting in 1441, and that the words on the scroll before him ("*Is [te] perfecit opus*," This man accomplished the work) refer to the commissioning of the project.
9. Women's gowns or skirts.
1. A game in which a blindfolded player must guess who has struck him.

A pretty picture gained. Go, six months hence!
390   Your hand, sir, and good-bye: no lights, no lights!
The street's hushed, and I know my own way back,
Don't fear me! there's the gray beginning. Zooks!

1855

A Toccata of Galuppi's[2]

1
Oh Galuppi, Baldassare, this is very sad to find!
I can hardly misconceive you; it would prove me deaf and blind;
But although I take your meaning, 'tis with such a heavy mind!

2
Here you come with your old music, and here's all the good it brings.
5   What, they lived once thus at Venice where the merchants were the kings,
Where Saint Mark's is, where the Doges used to wed the sea with rings?[3]

3
Ay, because the sea's the street there; and 'tis arched by . . . what you
call
. . . Shylock's bridge[4] with houses on it, where they kept the carnival:
I was never out of England—it's as if I saw it all.

4
10   Did young people take their pleasure when the sea was warm in May?
Balls and masks begun at midnight, burning ever to mid-day,
When they made up fresh adventures for the morrow, do you say?

5
Was a lady such a lady, cheeks so round and lips so red—
On her neck the small face bouyant, like a bellflower on its bed,
15   O'er the breast's superb abundance where a man might base his head?

6
Well, and it was graceful of them—they'd break talk off and afford
—She, to bite her mask's black velvet—he, to finger on his sword,
While you sat and played Toccatas, stately at the clavichord?[5]

7
What? Those lesser thirds so plaintive, sixths diminished, sigh on sigh,
20   Told them something? Those suspensions, those solutions—"Must we die?"
Those commiserating sevenths—"Life might last! we can but try!"

8
"Were you happy?" "Yes." "And are you still as happy?" "Yes. And you?"
"Then, more kisses!" "Did *I* stop them, when a million seemed so few?"
Hark, the dominant's persistence till it must be answered to!

9
25   So, an octave struck the answer. Oh, they praised you, I dare say!
"Brave Galuppi! that was music! good alike at grave and gay!
"I can always leave off talking when I hear a master play!"

10
Then they left you for their pleasure: till in due time, one by one,
Some with lives that came to nothing, some with deeds as well undone,
30   Death stepped tacitly and took them where they never see the sun.

11
But when I sit down to reason, think to take my stand nor swerve,
While I triumph o'er a secret wrung from nature's close reserve,
In you come with your cold music[6] till I creep through every nerve.

2. The poem presents the reflections of a 19th-century Englishman, as he plays a toccata by the 18th-century Venetian composer Baldassare Galuppi. (A toccata is a "touch-piece," the word derived from the Italian verb *toccare*, to touch: "a composition intended to exhibit the touch and exhibition of the performer," and hence often having the character of "showy improvisation" [*Grove's Dictionary of Music and Musicians*]. In stanzas 7–9, the quoted words represent the thoughts, feelings, or casual remarks of the earlier Venetian audience, now dispersed by death.

3. Each year the Doge, chief magistrate of the Venetian republic, threw a ring into the sea with the ceremonial words, "We wed thee, O sea, in sign of true and everlasting dominion."
4. The Rialto Bridge over the Grand Canal.
5. "A keyboard instrument, precursor of the piano" [Webster].
6. In stanzas 12–15, the quoted words are the words he imagines the composer as speaking to him.

12

Yes, you, like a ghostly cricket, creaking where a house was burned:
35   "Dust and ashes, dead and done with, Venice spent what Venice earned.
"The soul, doubtless, is immortal—where a soul can be discerned.

13

"Yours for instance: you know physics, something of geology,
"Mathematics are your pastime; souls shall rise in their degree;
"Butterflies may dread extinction—you'll not die, it cannot be!

14

40   "As for Venice and her people, merely born to bloom and drop,
"Here on earth they bore their fruitage, mirth and folly were the crop:
"What of soul was left, I wonder, when the kissing had to stop?

15

"Dust and ashes!" So you creak it, and I want the heart to scold.
Dear dead women, with such hair, too—what's become of all the gold
45   Used to hang and brush their bosoms? I feel chilly and grown old.

                                        ca. 1847   1855

Memorabilia

1

Ah, did you once see Shelley plain,
    And did he stop and speak to you
And did you speak to him again?
    How strange it seems and new!

2

5   But you were living before that,
    And also you are living after;
And the memory I started at—
    My starting moves your laughter.

3

I crossed a moor, with a name of its own
10   And a certain use in the world no doubt,
Yet a hand's-breadth of it shines alone
    'Mid the blank miles round about:

4

For there I picked up on the heather
    And there I put inside my breast
15   A moulted feather, an eagle-feather!
    Well, I forget the rest.

                                                    1855

Two in the Campagna[7]

1

I wonder do you feel today
    As I have felt since, hand in hand,
We sat down on the grass, to stray
    In spirit better through the land,
5   This morn of Rome and May?

2

For me, I touched a thought, I know,
    Has tantalized me many times,
(Like turns of thread the spiders throw
    Mocking across our path) for rhymes
10   To catch at and let go.

---

7. The grassy, rolling countryside around Rome; it was malarial, and hence semi-deserted, until Mussolini reclaimed the Pontine marshes.

3

Help me to hold it! First it left
    The yellowing fennel,[8] run to seed
There, branching from the brickwork's cleft,
    Some old tomb's ruin: yonder weed
15 Took up the floating weft,°   *spider-web*

4

Where one small orange cup amassed
    Five beetles—blind and green they grope
Among the honey-meal: and last,
    Everywhere on the grassy slope
20 I traced it. Hold it fast!

5

The champaign[9] with its endless fleece
    Of feathery grasses everywhere!
Silence and passion, joy and peace,
    An everlasting wash of air—
25 Rome's ghost since her decease.

6

Such life here, through such lengths of hours,
    Such miracles performed in play,
Such primal naked forms of flowers,
    Such letting nature have her way
30 While heaven looks from its towers!

7

How say you? Let us, O my dove,
    Let us be unashamed of soul,
As earth lies bare to heaven above!
    How is it under our control
35 To love or not to love?

8

I would that you were all to me,
    You that are just so much, no more.
Nor yours nor mine, nor slave nor free!
    Where does the fault lie? What the core
40 O' the wound, since wound must be?

9

I would I could adopt your will,
    See with your eyes, and set my heart
Beating by yours, and drink my fill
    At your soul's springs—your part my part
45 In life, for good and ill.

10

No. I yearn upward, touch you close,
    Then stand away. I kiss your cheek,
Catch your soul's warmth—I pluck the rose
    And love it more than tongue can speak—
50 Then the good minute goes.

11

Already how am I so far
    Out of that minute? Must I go
Still like the thistle-ball, no bar,
    Onward, whenever light winds blow,
55 Fixed by no friendly star?

12

Just when I seemed about to learn!
    Where is the thread now? Off again!
The old trick! Only I discern—
    Infinite passion, and the pain
60 Of finite hearts that yearn.

1855

---

8. A yellow-flowered plant, whose aromatic   9. I.e., grassland—here, the Campagna itself.
seeds are used as a condiment.

Abt Vogler[1]

AFTER HE HAS BEEN EXTEMPORIZING UPON THE MUSICAL INSTRUMENT
OF HIS INVENTION

1

Would that the structure brave, the manifold music I build,
    Bidding my organ obey, calling its keys to their work,
Claiming each slave of the sound, at a touch, as when Solomon willed
    Armies of angels that soar, legions of demons that lurk,
5 Man, brute, reptile, fly—alien of end and of aim,
    Adverse, each from the other heaven-high, hell-deep removed—
Should rush into sight at once as he named the ineffable Name,[2]
    And pile him a palace straight, to pleasure the princess he loved![3]

2

Would it might tarry like his, the beautiful building of mine,
10   This which my keys in a crowd pressed and importuned to raise!
Ah, one and all, how they helped, would dispart now and now combine,
    Zealous to hasten the work, heighten their master his praise!
And one would bury his brow with a blind plunge down to hell,
    Burrow awhile and build, broad on the roots of things,
15 Then up again swim into sight, having based me my palace well,
    Founded it, fearless of flame, flat on the nether springs.

3

And another would mount and march, like the excellent minion he was,
    Ay, another and yet another, one crowd but with many a crest,
Raising my rampired[4] walls of gold as transparent as glass,
20   Eager to do and die, yield each his place to the rest:
For higher still and higher (as a runer tips with fire,
    When a great illumination surprises a festal night—
Outlining round anad round Rome's dome from space to spire)[5]
    Up, the pinnacled glory reached, and the pride of my soul was in sight.

4

25 In sight? Not half! for it seemed, it was certain, to match man's birth,
    Nature in turn conceived, obeying an impulse as I;
And the emulous heaven yearned down, made effort to reach the earth,
    As the earth had done her best, in my passion, to scale the sky:
Novel splendors burst forth, grew familiar and dwelt with mine,
30   Not a point nor peak but found and fixed its wandering star;
Meteor-moons, balls of blaze: and they did not pale nor pine,
    For earth had attained to heaven, there was no more near nor far.

5

Nay more; for there wanted not who walked in the glare and glow,
    Presences plain in the place; or, fresh from the Protoplast[6]
35 Furnished for ages to come, when a kindlier wind should blow,
    Lured now to begin and live, in a house to their liking at last;
Or else the wonderful Dead who have passed through the body and gone,
    But were back once more to breathe in an old world worth their new:
What never had been, was now; what was, as it shall be anon;
40   And what is—shall I say, matched both? for I was made perfect too.

1. Georg Joseph Vogler (1749–1814), German composer, organist, music theorist, and teacher of composition, had been ordained in Rome in 1773 and bore the honorary title of *Abbé* [Abt] throughout his life. A widely traveled performer, he was most famous as an extemporizer. He was the inventor of a portable organ called the Orchestrion.
2. Solomon, son of David and Bathsheba, and David's successor as king of Israel, was reputed to possess a seal bearing "the ineffable Name"—the unspeakable name of God—which gave him great wisdom and power not only over men but also over good and evil spirits and the forces of nature.
3. Besides building the Temple and his own houses, Solomon "made also a house for Pharaoh's daughter, whom he had taken to wife * * *" (I Kings vii.).
4. Strengthened as with ramparts.
5. The dome of St. Peter's, outlined in lights on a festival night.
6. I.e., That which was first formed, the original archetypal being.

6

All through my keys that gave their sounds to a wish of my soul,
    All through my soul that praised as its wish flowed visibly forth,
All through music and me! For think, had I painted the whole,
    Why, there it had stood, to see, nor the process so wonder-worth:
45 .Had I written the same, made verse—still,° effect proceeds from cause,   *ever*
    Ye know why the forms are fair, ye hear how the tale is told;
It is all triumphant art, but art in obedience to laws,
    Painter and poet are proud in the artist-list enrolled:

7

But here is the finger of God, a flash of the will that can,
50   Existent behind all laws, that made them and, lo, they are!
And I know not if, save in this, such gift be allowed to man,
    That out of three sounds he frame, not a fourth sound, but a star.
Consider it well: each tone of our scale in itself is nought;
    It is everywhere in the world—loud, soft, and all is said:
55 Give it to me to use! I mix it with two in my thought:
    And, there! Ye have heard and seen: consider and bow the head!

8

Well, it is gone at last, the palace of music I reared;
    Gone! and the good tears start, the praises that come too slow;
For one is assured at first, one scarce can say that he feared,
60   That he even gave it a thought, the gone thing was to go.
Never to be again! But many more of the kind
    As good, nay, better perchance: is this your comfort to me?
To me, who must be saved because I cling with my mind
    To the same, same self, same love, same God: ay, what was, shall be.

9

65 Therefore to whom turn I but to thee, the ineffable Name?
    Builder and maker, thou, of houses not made with hands![7]
What, have fear of change from thee who art ever the same?
    Doubt that thy power can fill the heart that thy power expands?
There shall never be one lost good! What was, shall live as before;
70   The evil is null, is nought, is silence implying sound;
What was good shall be good, with, for evil, so much good more;
    On the earth the broken arcs; in the heaven, a perfect round.

10

All we have willed or hoped or dreamed of good shall exist;
    Not its semblance, but itself; no beauty, nor good, nor power
75 Whose voice has gone forth, but each survives for the melodist
    When eternity affirms the conception of an hour.
The high that proved too high, the heroic for earth too hard,
    The passion that left the ground to lose itself in the sky,
Are music sent up to God by the lover and the bard;
80   Enough that he heard it once: we shall hear it by-and-by.

11

And what is our failure here but a triumph's evidence
    For the fullness of the days? Have we withered or agonized?
Why else was the pause prolonged but that singing might issue thence?
    Why rushed the discords in but that harmony should be prized?
85 Sorrow is hard to bear, and doubt is slow to clear,
    Each sufferer says his say, his scheme of the weal and woe:
But God has a few of us whom he whispers in the ear;
    The rest may reason and welcome: 'tis we musicians know.

12

Well, it is earth with me; silence resumes her reign:
90   I will be patient and proud, and soberly acquiesce.
Give me the keys. I feel for the common chord again,
    Sliding by semitones, till I sink to the minor—yes,

---

7. See I Corinthians v.1 ("For we know that if our earthly house of this tabernacle were dissolved, we have a building of God, a house not made with hands, eternal in the heavens").

And I blunt it into a ninth, and I stand on alien ground,
   Surveying awhile the heights rolled from into the deep;
95 Which, hark, I have dared and done, for my resting-place is found,
   The C Major of this life:[8] so, now I will try to sleep.

1864

HENRY DAVID THOREAU
(1817–1862)

I Am a Parcel of Vain Strivings Tied

I am a parcel of vain strivings tied
   By a chance bond together,
   Dangling this way and that, their links
     Were made so loose and wide,
5   Methinks,
     For milder weather.

A bunch of violets without their roots,
   And sorrel intermixed,
   Encircled by a wisp of straw
10   Once coiled about their shoots,
     The law
    By which I'm fixed.

A nosegay which Time clutched from out
   Those fair Elysian fields,[1]
15 With weeds and broken stems, in haste,
   Doth make the rabble rout
     That waste
    The day he yields.

And here I bloom for a short hour unseen,
20   Drinking my juices up,
   With no root in the land
    To keep my branches green,
     But stand
    In a bare cup.

1841

The Inward Morning

Packed in my mind lie all the clothes
   Which outward nature wears,
And in its fashion's hourly change
   It all things else repairs.

5 In vain I look for change abroad,
   And can no difference find,
Till some new ray of peace uncalled
   Illumes my inmost mind.

---

8. Vogler moves from the common or "perfect" chord ("the combination of any note with its third [major or minor], perfect fifth, and octave," O.E.D.); through the minor chord, which would shadow the full harmony of the common chord; altering the minor chord to a ninth ("the interval of an octave and a second") with its suggestion of standing momentarily detached "on alien ground" (line 93), until he concludes by returning to C Major—"the key-note of the 'natural' major scale."
1. In Greek mythology, the home of the blessed in the afterlife.

What is it gilds the trees and clouds,
10   And paints the heavens so gay,
But yonder fast-abiding light
    With its unchanging ray?

Lo, when the sun streams through the wood,
    Upon a winter's morn,
15 Where'er his silent beams intrude
    The murky night is gone.

How could the patient pine have known
    The morning breeze would come,
Or humble flowers anticipate
20   The insect's noonday hum,

Till the new light with morning cheer
    From far streamed through the aisles,
And nimbly told the forest trees
    For many stretching miles?

25 I've heard within my inmost soul
    Such cheerful morning news,
In the horizon of my mind
    Have seen such orient hues,

As in the twilight of the dawn,
30   When the first birds awake,
Are heard within some silent wood,
    Where they the small twigs break,

Or in the eastern skies are seen,
    Before the sun appears,
35 The harbingers of summer heats
    Which from afar he bears.

                                        1842,   1849

Haze

Woof of the sun, ethereal gauze,
Woven of Nature's richest stuffs,
Visible heat, air-water and dry sea,
Last conquest of the eye;
5 Toil of the day displayed, sun-dust,
Aerial surf upon the shores of earth,
Ethereal estuary, frith[2] of light,
Breakers of air, billows of heat,
Fine summer spray on inland seas;
10 Bird of the sun, transparent-winged
Owlet of noon, soft-pinioned,
From heath or stubble rising without song,
Establish thy serenity o'er the fields.

                                        1843,   1849

Love Equals Swift and Slow

Love equals swift and slow,
    And high and low,
Racer and lame,
    The hunter and his game.

                                        1849

_____
2. In this context of sea-land imagery, a narrow channel.

HERMAN MELVILLE
(1819–1891)

The March into Virginia

ENDING IN THE FIRST MANASSAS[1] (JULY 1861)

Did all the lets and bars appear
  To every just or larger end,
Whence should come the trust and cheer?
Youth must its ignorant impulse lend—
5 Age finds place in the rear.
  All wars are boyish, and are fought by boys,
The champions and enthusiasts of the state:
  Turbid ardours and vain joys
    Not barrenly abate—
10 Stimulants to the power mature,
    Preparatives of fate.

Who here forecasteth the event?
What heart but spurns at precedent
And warnings of the wise,
15 Contemned foreclosures of surprise?
The banners play, the bugles call,
The air is blue and prodigal.
  No berrying party, pleasure-wooed,
No picnic party in the May,
20 Ever went less loth than they
    Into that leafy neighbourhood.
In Bacchic glee they file toward Fate,
Moloch's[2] uninitiate;
Expectancy, and glad surmise
25 Of battle's unknown mysteries.

All they feel is this: 'tis glory,
A rapture sharp, though transitory,
Yet lasting in belaureled story.
So they gaily go to fight,
30 Chatting left and laughing right.

But some who this blithe mood present,
  As on in lightsome files they fare,
Shall die experienced ere three days are spent—
  Perish, enlightened by the volleyed glare;
35 Or shame survive, and, like to adamant,[3]
  The throe of Second Manassas[4] share.

              1861   1866

1. The battle on July 21, 1861, at Bull Run, where the Union forces were routed.
2. Idol to whom children were sacrificed in Old Testament days.
3. Hard, unbreakable substance.
4. The second defeat of the Union forces at Manassas was on August 30, 1862.

Shiloh[5]

A REQUIEM (APRIL 1862)

Skimming lightly, wheeling still,
   The swallows fly low
Over the field in clouded days,
   The forest-field of Shiloh—
5 Over the field where April rain
Solaced the parched one stretched in pain
Through the pause of night
That followed the Sunday fight
   Around the church of Shiloh—
10 The church so lone, the log-built one,
That echoed to many a parting groan
     And natural prayer
   Of dying foemen mingled there—
Foemen at morn, but friends at eve—
15   Fame or country least their care:
(What like a bullet can undeceive!)
   But now they lie low,
While over them the swallows skim,
   And all is hushed at Shiloh.

                             1866

The Maldive Shark

About the Shark, phlegmatical one,
Pale sot of the Maldive sea,
The sleek little pilot-fish, azure and slim,
How alert in attendance be.
5 From his saw-pit of mouth, from his charnel of maw,
They have nothing of harm to dread,
But liquidly glide on his ghastly flank
Or before his Gorgonian[6] head;
Or lurk in the port of serrated teeth
10 In white triple tiers of glittering gates,
And there find a haven when peril's abroad,
An asylum in jaws of the Fates!
They are friends; and friendly they guide him to prey,
Yet never partake of the treat—
15 Eyes and brains to the dotard lethargic and dull,
Pale ravener of horrible meat.

                             1888

5. The battle at Shiloh church in Tennessee on April 6 and 7, 1862, was one of the bloodiest of the Civil War.
6. In classical mythology, Gorgon was one of three sisters (Medusa was another) whose face and snake-entwined hair could turn the viewer to stone; hence, a thing so frightening as to freeze its beholder.

WALT WHITMAN
(1819–1892)

Vigil Strange I Kept on the Field One Night

Vigil strange I kept on the field one night;
When you my son and my comrade dropt at my side that day,
One look I but gave which your dear eyes return'd with a look I shall never
    forget,
One touch of your hand to mine O boy, reach'd up as you lay on the ground,
5 Then onward I sped in the battle, the even-contested battle,
Till late in the night reliev'd to the place at last again I made my way,
Found you in death so cold dear comrade, found your body son of respond-
    ing kisses, (never again on earth responding,)
Bared your face in the starlight, curious the scene, cool blew the moderate
    night-wind,
Long there and then in vigil I stood, dimly around me the battle-field
    spreading,
10 Vigil wondrous and vigil sweet there in the fragrant silent night,
But not a tear fell, not even a long-drawn sigh, long I gazed,
Then on the earth partially reclining sat by your side leaning my chin in my
    hands,
Passing sweet hours, immortal and mystic hours with you dearest comrade –
    not a tear, not a word,
Vigil of silence, love and death, vigil for you my son and my soldier,
15 As onward silently stars aloft, eastward new ones upward stole,
Vigil finally for you brave boy, (I could not save you, swift was your death,
I faithfully loved you and cared for you living, I think we shall surely meet
    again,)
Till at latest lingering of the night, indeed just as the dawn appear'd,
My comrade I wrapt in his blanket, envelop'd well his form,
20 Folded the blanket well, tucking it carefully over head and carefully under
    feet,
And there and then and bathed by the rising sun, my son in his grave, in his
    rude-dug grave I deposited,
Ending my vigil strange with that, vigil of night and battle-field dim,
Vigil for boy of responding kisses, (never again on earth responding,)
Vigil for comrade swiftly slain, vigil I never forget, how as day brighten'd,
25 I rose from the chill ground and folded my soldier well in his blanket,
And buried him where he fell.

                              1865   1867

Beat! Beat! Drums!

Beat! beat! drums! blow! bugles! blow!
Through the windows—through doors—burst like a ruthless force,
Into the solemn church, and scatter the congregation,
Into the school where the scholar is studying;
5 Leave not the bridegroom quiet—no happiness must he have now with his
    bride,
Nor the peaceful farmer any peace, ploughing his field or gathering his grain,
So fierce you whirr and pound you drums—so shrill you bugles blow.

Beat! beat! drums!—blow! bugles! blow!
Over the traffic of cities—over the rumble of wheels in the streets;
10 Are beds prepared for sleepers at night in the houses? no sleepers must sleep
    in those beds,

No bargainers' bargains by day—no brokers or speculators—would they
    continue?
Would the talkers be talking? would the singer attempt to sing?
Would the lawyer rise in the court to state his case before the judge?
Then rattle quicker, heavier drums—you bugles wilder blow.
15 Beat! beat! drums!—blow! bugles! blow!
Make no parley—stop for no expostulation,
Mind not the timid—mind not the weeper or prayer,
Mind not the old man beseeching the young man,
Let not the child's voice be heard, nor the mother's entreaties,
20 Make even the trestles to shake the dead where they lie awaiting the hearses,
So strong you thump O terrible drums—so loud you bugles blow.

                                       1861   1867

Out of the Cradle Endlessly Rocking

Out of the cradle endlessly rocking,
Out of the mocking-bird's throat, the musical shuttle,
Out of the Ninth-month[1] midnight,
Over the sterile sands and the fields beyond, where the child leaving his bed
    wander'd alone, bareheaded, barefoot,
5 Down from the shower'd halo,
Up from the mystic play of shadows twining and twisting as if they were
    alive,
Out from the patches of briers and blackberries,
From the memories of the bird that chanted to me,
From your memories sad brother, from the fitful risings and fallings I heard,
10 From under that yellow half-moon late-risen and swollen as if with tears,
From those beginning notes of yearning and love there in the mist,
From the thousand responses of my heart never to cease,
From the myriad thence-arous'd words,
From the word stronger and more delicious than any,
15 From such as now they start the scene revisiting,
As a flock, twittering, rising, or overhead passing,
Borne hither, ere all eludes me, hurriedly,
A man, yet by these tears a little boy again,
Throwing myself on the sand, confronting the waves,
20 I, chanter of pains and joys, uniter of here and hereafter,
Taking all hints to use them, but swiftly leaping beyond them,
A reminiscence sing.

Once Paumanok,[2]
When the lilac-scent was in the air and Fifth-month grass was growing,
25 Up this seashore in some briers,
Two feather'd guests from Alabama, two together,
And their nest, and four light-green eggs spotted with brown,
And every day the he-bird to and fro near at hand,
And every day the she-bird crouch'd on her nest, silent, with bright eyes,
30 And every day I, a curious boy, never too close, never disturbing them,
Cautiously peering, absorbing, translating.

Shine! shine! shine!
Pour down your warmth, great sun!
While we bask, we two together.

---

1. The Quaker designation for September may
here also suggest the human cycle of fertility
and birth, in contrast with "sterile sands" in
the next line.

2. The Indian name for Long Island.

35   *Two together!*
      Winds blow south, or winds blow north,
      Day come white, or night come black,
      Home, or rivers and mountains from home,
      Singing all time, minding no time,
40   *While we two keep together.*

      Till of a sudden,
      May-be kill'd, unknown to her mate,
      One forenoon the she-bird crouch'd not on the nest,
      Nor return'd that afternoon, nor the next,
45   Nor ever appear'd again.

      And thenceforward all summer in the sound of the sea,
      And at night under the full of the moon in calmer weather,
      Over the hoarse surging of the sea,
      Or flitting from brier to brier by day,
50   I saw, I heard at intervals the remaining one, the he-bird,
      The solitary guest from Alabama.

      Blow! blow! blow!
      Blow up sea-winds along Paumanok's shore;
      I wait and I wait till you blow my mate to me.

55   Yes, when the stars glisten'd,
      All night long on the prong of a moss-scallop'd stake,
      Down almost amid the slapping waves,
      Sat the lone singer wonderful causing tears.

      He call'd on his mate,
60   He pour'd forth the meanings which I of all men know.

      Yes my brother I know,
      The rest might not, but I have treasur'd every note,
      For more than once dimly down to the beach gliding,
      Silent, avoiding the moonbeams, blending myself with the shadows,
65   Recalling now the obscure shapes, the echoes, the sounds and sights after
            their sorts,
      The white arms out in the breakers tirelessly tossing,
      I, with bare feet, a child, the wind wafting my hair,
      Listen'd long and long.

      Listen'd to keep, to sing, now translating the notes,
70   Following you my brother.

      Soothe! soothe! soothe!
      Close on its wave soothes the wave behind,
      And again another behind embracing and lapping, every one close,
      But my love soothes not me, not me.

75   *Low hangs the moon, it rose late,*
      It is lagging—O I think it is heavy with love, with love.

      O madly the sea pushes upon the land,
      With love, with love.

      O night! do I not see my love fluttering out among the breakers?
80   *What is that little black thing I see there in the white?*

      Loud! loud! loud!
      Loud I call to you, my love!

High and clear I shoot my voice over the waves,
Surely you must know who is here, is here,
85 *You must know who I am, my love.*

Low-hanging moon!
What is that dusky spot in your brown yellow?
O it is the shape, the shape of my mate!
O moon do not keep her from me any longer.

90 *Land! land! O land!*
Whichever way I turn, O I think you could give me my mate back again if
       you only would,
For I am almost sure I see her dimly whichever way I look.

O rising stars!
Perhaps the one I want so much will rise, will rise with some of you.

95 *O throat! O trembling throat!*
Sound clearer through the atmosphere!
Pierce the woods, the earth,
Somewhere listening to catch you must be the one I want.

Shake out carols!
100 *Solitary here, the night's carols!*
Carols of lonesome love! death's carols!
Carols under that lagging, yellow, waning moon!
O under that moon where she droops almost down into the sea!
O reckless despairing carols.

105 *But soft! sink low!*
Soft! let me just murmur,
And do you wait a moment you husky-nois'd sea,
For somewhere I believe I heard my mate responding to me,
So faint, I must be still, be still to listen,
110 *But not altogether still, for then she might not come immediately to me.*

Hither my love!
Here I am! here!
With this just-sustain'd note I announce myself to you,
This gentle call is for you my love, for you.

115 *Do not be decoy'd elsewhere,*
That is the whistle of the wind, it is not my voice,
That is the fluttering, the fluttering of the spray,
Those are the shadows of leaves.

O darkness! O in vain!
120 *O I am very sick and sorrowful.*

O brown halo in the sky near the moon, drooping upon the sea!
O troubled reflection in the sea!
O throat! O throbbing heart!
And I singing uselessly, uselessly all the night.

125 *O past! O happy life! O songs of joy!*
In the air, in the woods, over fields,
Loved! loved! loved! loved! loved!
But my mate no more, no more with me!
We two together no more.

130 The aria sinking,
All else continuing, the stars shining,
The winds blowing, the notes of the bird continuous echoing,
With angry moans the fierce old mother incessantly moaning,
On the sands of Paumanok's shore gray and rustling,
135 The yellow half-moon enlarged, sagging down, drooping, the face of the sea
  almost touching,
The boy ecstatic, with his bare feet the waves, with his hair the atmosphere
  dallying,
The love in the heart long pent, now loose, now at last tumultuously bursting,
The aria's meaning, the ears, the soul, swiftly depositing,
The strange tears down the cheeks coursing,
140 The colloquy there, the trio, each uttering,
The undertone, the savage old mother incessantly crying,
To the boy's soul's questions sullenly timing, some drown'd secret hissing,
To the outsetting bard.

Demon or bird! (said the boy's soul,)
145 Is it indeed toward your mate you sing? or is it really to me?
For I, that was a child, my tongue's use sleeping, now I have heard you,
Now in a moment I know what I am for, I awake,
And already a thousand singers, a thousand songs, clearer, louder and more
  sorrowful than yours,
A thousand warbling echoes have started to life within me, never to die.

150 O you singer solitary, singing by yourself, projecting me,
O solitary me listening, never more shall I cease perpetuating you,
Never more shall I escape, never more the reverberations,
Never more the cries of unsatisfied love be absent from me,
Never again leave me to be the peaceful child I was before what there in the
  night,
155 By the sea under the yellow and sagging moon,
The messenger there arous'd, the fire, the sweet hell within,
The unknown want, the destiny of me.

O give me the clew! (it lurks in the night here somewhere,)
O if I am to have so much, let me have more!

160 A word then, (for I will conquer it,)
The word final, superior to all,
Subtle, sent up—what is it?—I listen;
Are you whispering it, and have been all the time, you sea-waves?
Is that it from your liquid rims and wet sands?

165 Whereto answering, the sea,
Delaying not, hurrying not,
Whisper'd me through the night, and very plainly before daybreak,
Lisp'd to me the low and delicious word death,
And again death, death, death, death,
170 Hissing melodious, neither like the bird nor like my arous'd child's heart,
But edging near as privately for me rustling at my feet,
Creeping thence steadily up to my ears and laving me softly all over,
Death, death, death, death, death.

Which I do not forget,
175 But fuse the song of my dusky demon and brother,
That he sang to me in the moonlight on Paumanok's gray beach,
With the thousand responsive songs at random,
My own songs awaked from that hour,
And with them the key, the word up from the waves,

180   The word of the sweetest song and all songs,
       That strong and delicious word which, creeping to my feet,
       (Or like some old crone rocking the cradle, swathed in sweet garments, bend-
             ing aside,)
       The sea whisper'd me.

                                                    1859   1881

The Dalliance of the Eagles

       Skirting the river road, (my forenoon walk, my rest,)
       Skyward in air a sudden muffled sound, the dalliance of the eagles,
       The rushing amorous contact high in space together,
       The clinching interlocking claws, a living, fierce, gyrating wheel,
5   Four beating wings, two beaks, a swirling mass tight grappling,
       In tumbling turning clustering loops, straight downward falling,
       Till o'er the river pois'd, the twain yet one, a moment's lull,
       A motionless still balance in the air, then parting, talons loosing,
       Upward again on slow-firm pinions slanting, their separate diverse flight,
10   She hers, he his, pursuing.

                                                    1880   1881

When Lilacs Last in the Dooryard Bloom'd

                            1
       When lilacs last in the dooryard bloom'd,
       And the great star early droop'd in the western sky in the night,
       I mourn'd, and yet shall mourn with ever-returning spring.

       Ever-returning spring, trinity sure to me you bring,
5   Lilac blooming perennial and drooping star in the west,
       And thought of him I love.
                            2
       O powerful western fallen star!
       O shades of night—O moody, tearful night!
       O great star disappear'd—O the black murk that hides the star!
10   O cruel hands that hold me powerless—O helpless soul of me!
       O harsh surrounding cloud that will not free my soul.
                            3
       In the dooryard fronting an old farm-house near the white-wash'd palings,
       Stands the lilac-bush tall-growing with heart-shaped leaves of rich green,
       With many a pointed blossom rising delicate, with the perfume strong I love,
15   With every leaf a miracle—and from this bush in the dooryard,
       With delicate-color'd blossoms and heart-shaped leaves of rich green,
       A sprig with its flower I break.
                            4
       In the swamp in secluded recesses,
       A shy and hidden bird is warbling a song.

20   Solitary the thrush,
       The hermit withdrawn to himself, avoiding the settlements,
       Sings by himself a song.

       Song of the bleeding throat,
       Death's outlet song of life, (for well dear brother I know,
25   If thou wast not granted to sing thou would'st surely die.)
                            5
       Over the breast of the spring, the land, amid cities,
       Amid lanes and through old woods, where lately the violets peep'd from the
             ground, spotting the gray debris,
       Amid the grass in the fields each side of the lanes, passing the endless grass,
       Passing the yellow-spear'd wheat, every grain from its shroud in the dark-
             brown fields uprisen,

30 Passing the apple-tree blows of white and pink in the orchards,
Carrying a corpse to where it shall rest in the grave,
Night and day journeys a coffin.

6

Coffin that passes through lanes and streets,[3]
Through day and night with the great cloud darkening the land,
35 With the pomp of the inloop'd flags with the cities draped in black,
With the show of the States themselves as of crape-veil'd women standing,
With processions long and winding and the flambeaus of the night,
With the countless torches lit, with the silent sea of faces and the unbared heads,
With the waiting depot, the arriving coffin, and the sombre faces,
40 With dirges through the night, with the thousand voices rising strong and solemn,
With all the mournful voices of the dirges pour'd around the coffin,
The dim-lit churches and the shuddering organs—where amid these you journey,
With the tolling tolling bells' perpetual clang,
Here, coffin that slowly passes,
45 I give you my sprig of lilac.

7

(Nor for you, for one alone,
Blossoms and branches green to coffins all I bring,
For fresh as the morning, thus would I chant a song for you O sane and sacred death.

All over bouquets of roses,
50 O death, I cover you over with roses and early lilies,
But mostly and now the lilac that blooms the first,
Copious I break, I break the sprigs from the bushes,
With loaded arms I come, pouring for you,
For you and the coffins all of you O death.)

8

55 O western orb sailing the heaven,
Now I know what you must have meant as a month since I walk'd,
As I walk'd in silence the transparent shadowy night,
As I saw you had something to tell as you bent to me night after night,
As you droop'd from the sky low down as if to my side, (while the other stars all look'd on,)
60 As we wander'd together the solemn night, (for something I know not what kept me from sleep,)
As the night advanced, and I saw on the rim of the west how full you were of woe,
As I stood on the rising ground in the breeze in the cool transparent night,
As I watch'd where you pass'd and was lost in the netherward black of the night,
As my soul in its trouble dissatisfied sank, as where you sad orb,
65 Concluded, dropt in the night, and was gone.

9

Sing on there in the swamp,
O singer bashful and tender, I hear your notes, I hear your call,
I hear, I come presently, I understand you,
But a moment I linger, for the lustrous star has detain'd me,
70 The star my departing comrade holds and detains me.

10

O how shall I warble myself for the dead one there I loved?
And how shall I deck my song for the large sweet soul that has gone?
And what shall my perfume be for the grave of him I love?
Sea-winds blown from east and west,

---

3. The funeral cortège of Lincoln traveled from Washington to Springfield, Illinois, stopping at cities and towns all along the way for the people to honor the murdered President.

75 Blown from the Eastern sea and blown from the Western sea, till there on
        the prairies meeting,
    These and with these and the breath of my chant,
    I'll perfume the grave of him I love.

                    11
    O what shall I hang on the chamber walls?
    And what shall the pictures be that I hang on the walls,
80 To adorn the burial-house of him I love?

    Pictures of growing spring and farms and homes,
    With the Fourth-month eve at sundown, and the gray smoke lucid and
        bright,
    With floods of the yellow gold of the gorgeous, indolent, sinking sun, burn-
        ing, expanding the air,
    With the fresh sweet herbage under foot, and the pale green leaves of the
        trees prolific,
85 In the distance the flowing glaze, the breast of the river, with a wind-dapple
        here and there,
    With ranging hills on the banks, with many a line against the sky, and
        shadows,
    And the city at hand with dwellings so dense, and stacks of chimneys,
    And all the scenes of life and the workshops, and the workmen homeward
        returning.

                    12
    Lo, body and soul—this land,
90 My own Manhattan with spires, and the sparkling and hurrying tides, and
        the ships,
    The varied and ample land, the South and the North in the light, Ohio's
        shores and flashing Missouri,
    And ever the far-spreading prairies cover'd with grass and corn.

    Lo, the most excellent sun so calm and haughty,
    The violet and purple morn with just-felt breezes,
95 The gentle soft-born measureless light,
    The miracle spreading bathing all, the fulfill'd noon,
    The coming eve delicious, the welcome night and the stars,
    Over my cities shining all, enveloping man and land.

                    13
    Sing on, sing on you gray-brown bird,
100 Sing from the swamps, the recesses, pour your chant from the bushes,
    Limitless out of the dusk, out of the cedars and pines.

    Sing on dearest brother, warble your reedy song,
    Loud human song, with voice of uttermost woe.

    O liquid and free and tender!
105 O wild and loose to my soul—O wondrous singer!
    You only I hear—yet the star holds me, (but will soon depart,)
    Yet the lilac with mastering odor holds me.

                    14
    Now while I sat in the day and look'd forth,
    In the close of the day with its light and the fields of spring, and the farmers
        preparing their crops,
110 In the large unconscious scenery of my land with its lakes and forests,
    In the heavenly aerial beauty, (after the perturb'd winds and the storms,)
    Under the arching heavens of the afternoon swift passing, and the voices of
        children and women.
    The many-moving sea-tides, and I saw the ships how they sail'd,
    And the summer approaching with richness, and the fields all busy with
        labor,
115 And the infinite separate houses, how they all went on, each with its meals
        and minutia of daily usages,

And the streets how their throbbings throbb'd, and the cities pent—lo, then
  and there,
Falling upon them all and among them all, enveloping me with the rest,
Appear'd the cloud, appear'd the long black trail,
And I knew death, its thought, and the sacred knowledge of death.

120 Then with the knowledge of death as walking one side of me,
And the thought of death close-walking the other side of me,
And I in the middle as with companions, and as holding the hands of
  companions,
I fled forth to the hiding receiving night that talks not,
Down to the shores of the water, the path by the swamp in the dimness,
125 To the solemn shadowy cedars and ghostly pines so still.

And the singer so shy to the rest receiv'd me,
The gray-brown bird I know receiv'd us comrades three,
And he sang the carol of death, and a verse for him I love.

From deep secluded recesses,
130 From the fragrant cedars and the ghostly pines so still,
Came the carol of the bird.

And the charm of the carol rapt me,
As I held as if by their hands my comrades in the night,
And the voice of my spirit tallied the song of the bird.

135 *Come lovely and soothing death,*
Undulate round the world, serenely arriving, arriving,
In the day, in the night, to all, to each,
Sooner or later delicate death.

Prais'd be the fathomless universe,
140 *For life and joy, and for objects and knowledge curious,*
And for love, sweet love—but praise! praise! praise!
For the sure-enwinding arms of cool-enfolding death.

Dark mother always gliding near with soft feet,
Have none chanted for thee a chant of fullest welcome?
145 *Then I chant it for thee, I glorify thee above all,*
I bring thee a song that when thou must indeed come, come unfalteringly.

Approach strong deliveress,
When it is so, when thou hast taken them I joyously sing the dead,
Lost in the loving floating ocean of thee,
150 *Laved in the flood of thy bliss O death.*

From me to thee glad serenades,
Dances for thee I propose saluting thee, adornments and feastings for thee,
And the sights of the open landscape and the high-spread sky are fitting,
And life and the fields, and the huge and thoughtful night.

155 *The night in silence under many a star,*
The ocean shore and the husky whispering wave whose voice I know,
And the soul turning to thee O vast and well-veil'd death,
And the body gratefully nestling close to thee.

Over the tree-tops I float thee a song,
160 *Over the rising and sinking waves, over the myriad fields and the prairies*
  wide,
Over the dense-pack'd cities all and the teeming wharves and ways,
I float this carol with joy, with joy to thee O death.

15

To the tally of my soul,
Loud and strong kept up the gray-brown bird,
165   With pure deliberate notes spreading filling the night.

Loud in the pines and cedars dim,
Clear in the freshness moist and the swamp-perfume,
And I with my comrades there in the night.

While my sight that was bound in my eyes unclosed,
170   As to long panoramas of visions.

And I saw askant the armies,
I saw as in noiseless dreams hundreds of battle-flags,
Borne through the smoke of the battles and pierc'd with missiles I saw them,
And carried hither and yon through the smoke, and torn and bloody,
175   And at last but a few shreds left on the staffs, (and all in silence,)
And the staffs all splinter'd and broken.

I saw battle-corpses, myriads of them,
And the white skeletons of young men, I saw them,
I saw the debris and debris of all the slain soldiers of the war,
180   But I saw they were not as was thought,
They themselves were fully at rest, they suffer'd not,
The living remain'd and suffer'd, the mother suffer'd,
And the wife and the child and the musing comrade suffer'd,
And the armies that remain'd suffer'd.

16

185   Passing the visions, passing the night,
Passing, unloosing the hold of my comrades' hands,
Passing the song of the hermit bird and the tallying song of my soul,
Victorious song, death's outlet song, yet varying ever-altering song,
As low and wailing, yet clear the notes, rising and falling, flooding the night,
190   Sadly sinking and fainting, as warning and warning, and yet again bursting
         with joy,
Covering the earth and filling the spread of the heaven,
As that powerful psalm in the night I heard from recesses,
Passing, I leave thee lilac with heart-shaped leaves,
I leave thee there in the door-yard, blooming, returning with spring.

195   I cease from my song for thee,
From my gaze on thee in the west, fronting the west, communing with thee,
O comrade lustrous with silver face in the night.

Yet each to keep and all, retrievements out of the night,
The song, the wondrous chant of the gray-brown bird,
200   And the tallying chant, the echo arous'd in my soul,
With the lustrous and drooping star with the countenance full of woe,
With the holders holding my hand nearing the call of the bird,
Comrades mine and I in the midst, and their memory ever to keep, for the
         dead I loved so well,
For the sweetest, wisest soul of all my days and lands—and this for his dear
         sake,
205   Lilac and star and bird twined with the chant of my soul,
There in the fragrant pines and the cedars dusk and dim.

                                            1865–66   1881

Chanting the Square Deific

1

Chanting the square deific, out of the One advancing, out of the sides,
Out of the old and new, out of the square entirely divine,
Solid, four-sided, (all the sides needed,) from this side Jehovah am I,
Old Brahm I, and I Saturnius am;[4]
5 Not Time affects me—I am Time, old, modern as any,
Unpersuadable, relentless, executing righteous judgments,
As the Earth, the Father, the brown old Kronos,[5] with laws,
Aged beyond computation, yet ever new, ever with those mighty laws rolling,
Relentless I forgive no man—whoever sins dies—I will have that man's life;
10 Therefore let none expect mercy—have the seasons, gravitation, the appointed days, mercy? no more have I,
But as the seasons and gravitation, and as all the appointed days that forgive not,
I dispense from this side judgments inexorable without the least remorse.

2

Consolator most mild, the promis'd one advancing,
With gentle hand extended, the mightier God am I,
15 Foretold by prophets and poets in their most rapt prophecies and poems,
From this side, lo! the Lord Christ gazes—lo! Hermes I—lo! mine is Hercules' face,[6]
All sorrow, labor, suffering, I, tallying it, absorb in myself,
Many times have I been rejected, taunted, put in prison, and crucified, and many times shall be again,
All the world have I given up for my dear brothers' and sisters' sake, for the soul's sake,
20 Wending my way through the homes of men, rich or poor, with the kiss of affection,
For I am affection, I am the cheer-bringing God, with hope and all-enclosing charity,
With indulgent words as to children, with fresh and sane words, mine only,
Young and strong I pass knowing well I am destin'd myself to an early death;
But my charity has no death—my wisdom dies not, neither early nor late,
25 And my sweet love bequeath'd here and elsewhere never dies.

3

Aloof, dissatisfied, plotting revolt,
Comrade of criminals, brother of slaves,
Crafty, despised, a drudge, ignorant,
With sudra[7] face and worn brow, black, but in depths of my heart, proud as any,
30 Lifted now and always against whoever scorning assumes to rule me,
Morose, full of guile, full of reminiscences, brooding, with many wiles,
(Though it was thought I was baffled and dispel'd and my wiles done, but that will never be,)
Defiant, I, Satan, still live, still utter words, in new lands duly appearing, (and old ones also,)
Permanent here from my side, warlike, equal with any, real as any,
35 Nor time nor change shall ever change me or my words.

4

Santa Spirita,[8] breather, life,
Beyond the light, lighter than light,
Beyond the flames of hell, joyous, leaping easily above hell,

---

4. Jehovah is the god of the Jewish religion; Brahma and Saturnius are important deities of the Hindu and Roman pantheons.
5. Ancient Greek god, father of Zeus, who dethroned Kronos. His name, since classical times, has been confused with that of the god *Chronos* (*time* in Greek).

6. Hermes was the messenger and herald of the gods; Hercules was a mortal but the type of the hero in his prodigious labors and deeds, most of which were regarded as signifying the defeat of evil in the world.
7. The Sudra was the lowest of the four Hindu castes; the untouchables.
8. The Holy Spirit.

Beyond Paradise, perfumed solely with mine own perfume,
40 Including all life on earth, touching, including God, including Saviour and
        Satan,
    Ethereal, pervading all, (for without me what were all? what were God?)
    Essence of forms, life of the real identities, permanent, positive, (namely
        the unseen,)
    Life of the great round world, the sun and stars, and of man, I, the general
        soul,
    Here the square finishing, the solid, I the most solid,
45 Breathe my breath also through these songs.
                                                    1865–66   1881

A Noiseless Patient Spider

    A noiseless patient spider,
    I mark'd where on a little promontory it stood isolated,
    Mark'd how to explore the vacant vast surrounding,
    It launch'd forth filament, filament, filament, out of itself,
5   Ever unreeling them, ever tirelessly speeding them.

    And you O my soul where you stand,
    Surrounded, detached, in measureless oceans of space,
    Ceaselessly musing, venturing, throwing, seeking the spheres to connect
        them,
    Till the bridge you will need be form'd, till the ductile anchor hold,
10 Till the gossamer thread you fling catch somewhere, O my soul.
                                                    1868   1881

MATTHEW ARNOLD
(1822–1888)

The Forsaken Merman

    Come, dear children, let us away;
    Down and away below!
    Now my brothers call from the bay,
    Now the great winds shoreward blow,
5   Now the salt tides seaward flow;
    Now the wild white horses play,
    Champ and chafe and toss in the spray.
    Children dear, let us away!
    This way, this way!

10 Call her once before you go—
    Call once yet!
    In a voice that she will know:
    "Margaret! Margaret!"
    Children's voices should be dear
15 (Call once more) to a mother's ear;
    Children's voices, wild with pain—
    Surely she will come again!
    Call her once and come away;
    This way, this way!
20 "Mother dear, we cannot stay!
    The wild white horses foam and fret."
    Margaret! Margaret!

Come, dear children, come away down;
Call no more!
25   One last look at the white-walled town,
And the little gray church on the windy shore;
Then come down!
She will not come though you call all day;
Come away, come away!

30   Children dear, was it yesterday
We heard the sweet bells over the bay?
In the caverns where we lay,
Through the surf and through the swell,
The far-off sound of a silver bell?
35   Sand-strewn caverns, cool and deep,
Where the winds are all asleep;
Where the spent lights quiver and gleam,
Where the salt weed sways in the stream,
Where the sea-beasts, ranged all round,
40   Feed in the ooze of their pasture-ground;
Where the sea-snakes coil and twine,
Dry their mail and bask in the brine;
Where great whales come sailing by,
Sail and sail, with unshut eye,
45   Round the world for ever and aye?
When did music come this way?
Children dear, was it yesterday?

Children dear, was it yesterday
(Call yet once) that she went away?
50   Once she sate with you and me,
On a red gold throne in the heart of the sea,
And the youngest sate on her knee.
She combed its bright hair, and she tended it well,
When down swung the sound of a far-off bell.
55   She sighed, she looked up through the clear green sea;
She said: "I must go, for my kinsfolk pray
In the little gray church on the shore today.
'Twill be Easter-time in the world—ah me!
And I lose my poor soul, Merman! here with thee."
60   I said: "Go up, dear heart, through the waves;
Say thy prayer, and come back to the kind sea-caves!"
She smiled, she went up through the surf in the bay.
Children dear, was it yesterday?

Children dear, were we long alone?
65   "The sea grows stormy, the little ones moan;
Long prayers," I said, "in the world they say;
Come!" I said; and we rose through the surf in the bay.
We went up the beach, by the sandy down
Where the sea-stocks bloom, to the white-walled town;
70   Through the narrow paved streets, where all was still,
To the little gray church on the windy hill.
From the church came a murmur of folk at their prayers,
But we stood without in the cold blowing airs.
We climbed on the graves, on the stones worn with rains,
75   And we gazed up the aisle through the small leaded panes.
She sate by the pillar; we saw her clear:
"Margaret, hist! come quick, we are here!
Dear heart," I said, "we are long alone;
The sea grows stormy, the little ones moan."
80   But, ah, she gave me never a look,
For her eyes were sealed to the holy book!

Loud prays the priest; shut stands the door.
Come away, children, call no more!
Come away, come down, call no more!

85   Down, down, down!
Down to the depths of the sea!
She sits at her wheel in the humming town,
Singing most joyfully.
Hark what she sings: "O joy, O joy,
90   For the humming street, and the child with its toy!
For the priest, and the bell, and the holy well;
For the wheel where I spun,
And the blessed light of the sun!"
And so she sings her fill.
95   Singing most joyfully,
Till the spindle drops from her hand,
And the whizzing wheel stands still.
She steals to the window, and looks at the sand,
And over the sand at the sea;
100   And her eyes are set in a stare;
And anon there breaks a sigh,
And anon there drops a tear,
From a sorrow-clouded eye,
And a heart sorrow-laden,
105   A long, long sigh;
For the cold strange eyes of a little Mermaiden
And the gleam of her golden hair.

Come away, away children;
Come children, come down!
110   The hoarse wind blows coldly;
Lights shine in the town.
She will start from her slumber
When gusts shake the door;
She will hear the winds howling,
115   Will hear the waves roar.
We shall see, while above us
The waves roar and whirl,
A ceiling of amber,
A pavement of pearl.
120   Singing: "Here came a mortal,
But faithless was she!
And alone dwell for ever
The kings of the sea."

But, children, at midnight,
125   When soft the winds blow,
When clear falls the moonlight,
When spring-tides are low;
When sweet airs come seaward
From heaths starred with broom,
130   And high rocks throw mildly
On the blanched sands a gloom;
Up the still, glistening beaches,
Up the creeks we will hie,
Over banks of bright seaweed
135   The ebb-tide leaves dry.
We will gaze, from the sand-hills,
At the white, sleeping town;
At the church on the hill-side—
And then come back down.

140　Singing: "There dwells a loved one,
　　　　But cruel is she!
　　　　She left lonely for ever
　　　　The kings of the sea."

　　　　　　　　　　　　　　　　　　　1849

To Marguerite

　　Yes! in the sea of life enisled,
　　With echoing straits between us thrown,
　　Dotting the shoreless watery wild,
　　We mortal millions live *alone*.
5　The islands feel the enclasping flow,
　　And then their endless bounds they know.

　　But when the moon their hollows lights,
　　And they are swept by balms of spring,
　　And in their glens, on starry nights,
10　The nightingales divinely sing;
　　And lovely notes, from shore to shore,
　　Across the sounds and channels pour—

　　Oh! then a longing like despair
　　Is to their farthest caverns sent;
15　For surely once, they feel, we were
　　Parts of a single continent!
　　Now round us spreads the watery plain—
　　Oh might our marges meet again!

　　Who ordered, that their longing's fire
20　Should be, as soon as kindled, cooled?
　　Who renders vain their deep desire?—
　　A God, a God their severance ruled!
　　And bade betwixt their shores to be
　　The unplumbed, salt, estranging sea.

　　　　　　　　　　　　　　　　　　　1852

A Summer Night

　　In the deserted, moon-blanched street,
　　How lonely rings the echo of my feet!
　　Those windows, which I gaze at, frown,
　　Silent and white, unopening down,
5　Repellent as the world; but see,
　　A break between the housetops shows
　　The moon! and, lost behind her, fading dim
　　Into the dewy dark obscurity
　　Down at the far horizon's rim,
10　Doth a whole tract of heaven disclose!

　　And to my mind the thought
　　Is on a sudden brought
　　Of a past night, and a far different scene.
　　Headlands stood out into the moonlit deep
15　As clearly as at noon;
　　The spring-tide's brimming flow
　　Heaved dazzlingly between;
　　Houses, with long white sweep,
　　Girdled the glistening bay;
20　Behind, through the soft air,
　　The blue haze-cradled mountains spread away,

That night was far more fair—
But the same restless pacings to and fro,
And the same vainly throbbing heart was there,
25   And the same bright, calm moon.

And the calm moonlight seems to say:
Hast thou then still the old unquiet breast,
Which neither deadens into rest,
Nor ever feels the fiery glow
30   *That whirls the spirit from itself away,*
But fluctuates to and fro,
Never by passion quite possessed
And never quite benumbed by the world's sway?
And I, I know not if to pray
35   Still to be what I am, or yield and be
Like all the other men I see.

For most men in a brazen prison live,
Where, in the sun's hot eye,
With heads bent o'er their toil, they languidly
40   Their lives to some unmeaning taskwork give,
Dreaming of nought beyond their prison-wall.
And as, year after year,
Fresh products of their barren labor fall
From their tired hands, and rest
45   Never yet comes more near,
Gloom settles slowly down over their breast;
And while they try to stem
The waves of mournful thought by which they are prest,
Death in their prison reaches them,
50   Unfreed, having seen nothing, still unblest.

And the rest, a few,
Escape their prison and depart
On the wide ocean of life anew.
There the freed prisoner, where'er his heart
55   Listeth, will sail;
Nor doth he know how there prevail,
Despotic on that sea,
Trade-winds which cross it from eternity.
Awhile he holds some false way, undebarred
60   By thwarting signs, and braves
The freshening wind and blackening waves.
And then the tempest strikes him; and between
The lightning-bursts is seen
Only a driving wreck,
65   And the pale master on his spar-strewn deck
With anguished face and flying hair
Grasping the rudder hard,
Still bent to make some port he knows not where,
Still standing for some false, impossible shore.
70   And sterner comes the roar
Of sea and wind, and through the deepening gloom
Fainter and fainter wreck and helmsman loom,
And he too disappears, and comes no more.

Is there no life, but these alone?
75   Madman or slave, must man be one?

Plainness and clearness without shadow of stain!
Clearness divine!
Ye heavens, whose pure dark regions have no sign

Of languor, though so calm, and, though so great,
80   Are yet untroubled and unpassionate;
Who, though so noble, share in the world's toil,
And, though so tasked, keep free from dust and soil!
I will not say that your mild deeps retain
A tinge, it may be, of their silent pain
85   Who have longed deeply once, and longed in vain—
But I will rather say that you remain
A world above man's head, to let him see
How boundless might his soul's horizons be,
How vast, yet of what clear transparency!
90   How it were good to abide there, and breathe free;
How fair a lot to fill
Is left to each man still!

                                                            1852

Thyrsis

A MONODY,[1] TO COMMEMORATE THE AUTHOR'S FRIEND, ARTHUR HUGH
CLOUGH, WHO DIED AT FLORENCE, 1861[2]

How changed is here each spot man makes or fills!
    In the two Hinkseys[3] nothing keeps the same;
        The village street its haunted mansion lacks,
        And from the sign is gone Sibylla's name,[4]
5   And from the roofs the twisted chimney-stacks—
            Are ye too changed, ye hills?
See, 'tis no foot of unfamiliar men
    Tonight from Oxford up your pathway strays!
    Here came I often, often, in old days—
10   Thyrsis and I; we still had Thyrsis then.

Runs it not here, the track by Childsworth Farm,
    Past the high wood, to where the elm-tree crowns
        The hill behind whose ridge the sunset flames?
        The signal-elm, that looks on Ilsley Downs,
15   The Vale, the three lone weirs,° the youthful Thames?   *rivor-dams*
            This winter-eve is warm,
Humid the air! leafless, yet soft as spring,
    The tender purple spray on corpse and briers!
    And that sweet city with her dreaming spires,
20   She needs not June for beauty's heightening,

Lovely all times she lies, lovely tonight!
    Only, methinks, some loss of habit's power
        Befalls me wandering through this upland dim.
        Once passed I blindfold here, at any hour;
25   Now seldom come I, since I came with him.
            That single elm-tree bright
Against the west—I miss it! is it gone?
    We prized it dearly; while it stood, we said,
    Our friend, the Gypsy-Scholar, was not dead;
30   While the tree lived, he in these fields lived on.

---

1. Species of poem in which a single mourner laments.
2. The friendship between Arnold and Clough (1819–61), himself a distinguished poet, had been at its closest while they were at Oxford, and Arnold chooses as the framework for his poem a visit to Oxford—at least in reminiscence—and more specifically to a hill above the town crowned by the signal-elm. The tree had had a particular significance for them, since they connected it with the continuing symbolic presence in the countryside of the Scholar-Gypsy and his lonely faithfulness to an ideal of truth-seeking. (See Arnold's poem *The Scholar-Gypsy* and his note to it, above.) As the name Thyrsis (and later, Corydon) indicates, Arnold is adopting the conventions of the Greek and Latin pastoral elegy for his poem.
3. Two villages (North and South Hinkley) near Oxford.
4. Sibylla Kerr, a tavern-keeper when Arnold and Clough were students.

Too rare, too rare, grow now my visits here,
   But once I knew each field, each flower, each stick;
      And with the country-folk acquaintance made
   By barn in threshing-time, by new-built rick.
35   Here, too, our shepherd-pipes we first assayed.
         Ah me! this many a year
   My pipe is lost, my shepherd's holiday!
      Needs must I lose them, needs with heavy heart
      Into the world and wave of men depart;
40   But Thyrsis of his own will went away.[5]

It irked him to be here, he could not rest.
   He loved each simple joy the country yields,
      He loved his mates; but yet he could not keep,
   For that a shadow loured on the fields,
45   Here with the shepherds and the silly° sheep.   *innocent*
         Some life of men unblest
   He knew, which made him droop; and filled his head.
      He went; his piping took a troubled sound
      Of storms that rage outside our happy ground;
50   He could not wait their passing, he is dead.

So, some tempestuous morn in early June,
   When the year's primal burst of bloom is o'er,
      Before the roses and the longest day—
   When garden-walks and all the grassy floor
55   With blossoms red and white of fallen May
         And chestnut-flowers are strewn—
   So have I heard the cuckoo's parting cry,
      From the wet field, through the vext garden-trees,
      Come with the volleying rain and tossing breeze:
60   *The bloom is gone, and with the bloom go I!*

Too quick despairer, wherefore wilt thou go?
   Soon will the high Midsummer pomps come on,
      Soon will the musk carnations break and swell,
   Soon shall we have gold-dusted snapdragon,
65   Sweet-William with his homely cottage-smell,
         And stocks in fragrant blow;
   Roses that down the alleys shine afar,
      And open, jasmine-muffled lattices,
      And groups under the dreaming garden-trees,
70   And the full moon, and the white evening-star.

He hearkens not! light comer, he is flown!
   What matters it? next year he will return,
      And we shall have him in the sweet spring-days,
   With whitening hedges, and uncrumpling fern,
75   And bluebells trembling by the forest-ways,
         And scent of hay new-mown.
   But Thyrsis never more we swains shall see;
      See him come back, and cut a smoother reed,
      And blow a strain the world at last shall heed—
80   For Time, not Corydon, hath conquered thee!

Alack, for Corydon no rival now!
   But when Sicilian shepherds lost a mate,
      Some good survivor with his flute would go,

---

5. Clough resigned his fellowship at Oxford in 1848, rather than subscribe to the Thirty-nine Articles of the Anglican Church.

Piping a ditty sad for Bion's fate;[6]
85   And cross the unpermitted ferry's flow,[7]
        And relax Pluto's brow,
    And make leap up with joy the beauteous head
      Of Proserpine, among whose crownéd hair
      Are flowers first opened on Sicilian air,
90 And flute his friend, like Orpheus,[8] from the dead.

    O easy access to the hearer's grace
      When Dorian[9] shepherds sang to Proserpine!
        For she herself had trod Sicilian fields,
        She knew the Dorian water's gush divine,
95   She knew each lily white which Enna yields,
          Each rose with blushing face;
      She loved the Dorian pipe, the Dorian strain.
        But ah, of our poor Thames she never heard!
        Her foot the Cumner cowslips never stirred;
100 And we should tease her with our plaint in vain!

    Well! wind-dispersed and vain the words will be,
      Yet, Thyrsis, let me give my grief its hour
        In the old haunt, and find our tree-topped hill!
      Who, if not I, for questing here hath power?
105   I know the wood which hides the daffodil,
          I know the Fyfield tree,
      I know what white, what purple fritillaries°   *flowers*
        The grassy harvest of the river-fields,
        Above by Ensham, down by Sandford, yields,
110 And what sedged brooks are Thames's tributaries;

    I know these slopes; who knows them if not I?
      But many a dingle° on the loved hillside,   *valley*
        With thorns once studded, old, white-blossomed trees,
      Where thick the cowslips grew, and far descried
115   High towered the spikes of purple orchises,
          Hath since our day put by
      The coronals of that forgotten time;[1]
        Down each green bank hath gone the ploughboy's team,
        And only in the hidden brookside gleam
120 Primroses, orphans of the flowery prime.

    Where is the girl, who by the boatman's door,
      Above the locks, above the boating throng,
        Unmoored our skiff when through the Wytham flats,
      Red loosestrife and blond meadow-sweet among
125   And darting swallows and light water-gnats,
          We tracked the shy Thames shore?
      Where are the mowers, who, as the tiny swell
        Of our boat passing heaved the river-grass,
        Stood with suspended scythe to see us pass?
130 They all are gone, and thou art gone as well!

    Yes, thou art gone! and round me too the night
      In ever-nearing circle weaves her shade.
        I see her veil draw soft across the day,

---

6. Greek pastoral poet of the first century B.C. who lived in Sicily and who was mourned in *Lament for Bion,* sometimes ascribed to his pupil Moschus.
7. The ferry across the River Styx to Hades, ruled over by Pluto and his queen, Proserpine, whom he had abducted while she was gathering flowers in the fields near Enna, in Sicily. She spent half of each year in the underworld and half on earth.
8. Orpheus, because of the power and charm of his music, had been permitted to attempt to lead his wife, Eurydice, back from the dead.
9. One of the ancient Greek lyrical modes, characterized by simplicity and nobility.
1. I.e., the flowers that once crowned them.

I feel her slowly chilling breath invade
135   The cheek grown thin, the brown hair sprent° with grey;   *sprinkled*
              I feel her finger light
      Laid pausefully upon life's headlong train;
          The foot less prompt to meet the morning dew,
          The heart less bounding at emotion new,
140   And hope, once crushed, less quick to spring again.

      And long the way appears, which seemed so short
          To the less practiced eye of sanguine youth;
          And high the mountain-tops, in cloudy air,
      The mountain-tops where is the throne of Truth,
145   Tops in life's morning-sun so bright and bare!
              Unbreachable the fort
      Of the long-battered world uplifts its wall;
          And strange and vain the earthly turmoil grows,
          And near and real the charm of thy repose,
150   And night as welcome as a friend would fall.

      But hush! the upland hath a sudden loss
          Of quiet!—Look, adown the dusk hillside,
          A troop of Oxford hunters going home,
      As in old days, jovial and talking, ride!
155   From hunting with the Berkshire hounds they come.
              Quick! let me fly, and cross
      Into yon farther field!—'Tis done; and see,
          Backed by the sunset, which doth glorify
          The orange and pale violet evening-sky,
160   Bare on its lonely ridge, the Tree! the Tree!

      I take the omen! Eve lets down her veil,
          The white fog creeps from bush to bush about,
          The west unflushes, the high stars grow bright,
      And in the scattered farms the lights come out.
165   I cannot reach the signal-tree to-night,
              Yet, happy omen, hail!
      Hear it from thy broad lucent Arno-vale[2]
          (For there thine earth-forgetting eyelids keep
          The morningless and unawakening sleep
170   Under the flowery oleanders pale),

      Hear it, O Thyrsis still our tree is there!
          Ah, vain! These English fields, this upland dim,
          These brambles pale with mist engarlanded,
      That lone, sky-pointing tree, are not for him;
175   To a boon southern country he is fled,
              And now in happier air,
      Wandering with the great Mother's train divine[3]
          (And purer or more subtle soul than thee,
          I trow, the mighty Mother doth not see)
180   Within a folding of the Apennine,[4]

      Thou hearest the immortal chants of old!
          Putting his sickle to the perilous grain
              In the hot cornfield of the Phrygian king,
          For thee the Lityerses-song again

2. Clough is buried in the Protestant cemetery in Florence, through which city the Arno flows.
3. Possibly the devotees of Demeter, the Earth Mother.
4. The Apennines are a mountain range in Italy.

185   Young Daphnis with his silver voice doth sing;[5]
       Sings his Sicilian fold,
    His sheep, his hapless love, his blinded eyes—
    And how a call celestial round him rang,
    And heavenward from the fountain-brink he sprang,
190   And all the marvel of the golden skies.

    There thou art gone, and me thou leavest here
      Sole in these fields! yet will I not despair.
       Despair I will not, while I yet descry
    Neath the mild canopy of English air
195   That lonely tree against the western sky.
       Still, still these slopes, 'tis clear,
    Our Gypsy-Scholar haunts, outliving thee!
      Fields where soft sheep from cages pull the hay,
      Woods with anemonies in flower till May,
200   Know him a wanderer still; then why not me?

    A fugitive and gracious light he seeks,
      Shy to illumine; and I seek it too.
       This does not come with houses or with gold,
    With place, with honor, and a flattering crew;
205   'Tis not in the world's market bought and sold—
       But the smooth-slipping weeks
    Drop by, and leave its seeker still untired;
      Out of the heed of mortals he is gone,
      He wends unfollowed, he must house alone;
210   Yet on he fares, by his own heart inspired.

    Thou too, O Thyrsis, on like quest wast bound;
      Thou wanderest with me for a little hour!
       Men gave thee nothing; but this happy quest,
    If men esteemed thee feeble, gave thee power,
215   If men procured thee trouble, gave thee rest.
       And this rude Cumner ground,
    Its fir-topped Hurst, its farms, its quiet fields,
      Here cam'st thou in thy jocund youthful time,
      Here was thine height of strength, thy golden prime!
220   And still the haunt beloved a virtue yields.

    What though the music of thy rustic flute
      Kept not for long its happy, country tone;
       Lost it too soon, and learnt a stormy note
    Of men contention-tost, of men who groan,
225   Which tasked thy pipe too sore, and tired thy throat—
       It failed, and thou wast mute!
    Yet hadst thou alway visions of our light,
      And long with men of care thou couldst not stay,
      And soon thy foot resumed its wandering way,
230   Left human haunt, and on alone till night.

---

5. "Daphnis, the ideal Sicilian shepherd of Greek pastoral poetry, was said to have followed into Phrygia his mistress Piplea, who had been carried off by robbers, and to have found her in the power of the king of Phrygia, Lityerses. Lityerses used to make strangers try a contest with him in reaping corn, and to put them to death if he overcame them. Hercules arrived in time to save Daphnis, took upon himself the reaping-contest with Lityerses, overcame him, and slew him. The Lityerses-song connected with this tradition was, like the Linus-song, one of the early plaintive strains of Greek popular poetry, and used to be sung by corn-reapers. Other traditions represented Daphnis as beloved by a nymph who exacted from him an oath to love no one else. He fell in love with a princess, and was struck blind by the jealous nymph. Mercury, who was his father, raised him to heaven, and made a fountain spring up in the place from which he ascended. At this fountain the Sicilians offered yearly sacrifices. —See Servius, *Comment. in Virgil. Bucol.*, v.20 and viii.68" [Arnold's note].

Too rare, too rare, grow now my visits here!
  'Mid city-noise, not, as with thee of yore,
    Thyrsis! in reach of sheep-bells is my home.
  —Then through the great town's harsh, heart-wearying roar,
235   Let in thy voice a whisper often come,
      To chase fatigue and fear:
  Why faintest thou? I wandered till I died.
    Roam on! The light we sought is shining still.
    Dost thou ask proof? Our tree yet crowns the hill,
240 *Our Scholar travels yet the loved hillside.*

                                              1866

Dover Beach

The sea is calm tonight.
The tide is full, the moon lies fair
Upon the straits; on the French coast the light
Gleams and is gone; the cliffs of England stand,
5 Glimmering and vast, out in the tranquil bay.
Come to the window, sweet is the night-air!
Only, from the long line of spray
Where the sea meets the moon-blanched land,
Listen! you hear the grating roar
10 Of pebbles which the waves draw back, and fling,
At their return, up the high strand,
Begin, and cease, and then again begin,
With tremulous cadence slow, and bring
The eternal note of sadness in.

15 Sophocles long ago
Heard it on the Aegean, and it brought
Into his mind the turbid ebb and flow
Of human misery;[6] we
Find also in the sound a thought,
20 Hearing it by this distant northern sea.

The Sea of Faith
Was once, too, at the full, and round earth's shore
Lay like the folds of a bright girdle furled.
But now I only hear
25 Its melancholy, long, withdrawing roar,
Retreating, to the breath
Of the night-wind, down the vast edges drear
And naked shingles[7] of the world.

Ah, love, let us be true
30 To one another! for the world, which seems
To lie before us like a land of dreams,
So various, so beautiful, so new,
Hath really neither joy, nor love, nor light,
Nor certitude, nor peace, nor help for pain;
35 And we are here as on a darkling plain
Swept with confused alarms of struggle and flight,
Where ignorant armies clash by night.

                                              1867

6. Compare Sophocles' *Antigone*, lines 583–91.   7. Beaches covered with water-worn small stones and pebbles.

Palladium[8]

Set where the upper streams of Simois flow[9]
Was the Palladium, high 'mid rock and wood;
And Hector was in Ilium,[1] far below,
And fought, and saw it not—but there it stood!

5   It stood, and sun and moonshine rained their light
On the pure columns of its glen-built hall.
Backward and forward rolled the waves of fight
Round Troy—but while this stood, Troy could not fall.

So, in its lovely moonlight, lives the soul.
10 Mountains surround it, and sweet virgin air;
Cold plashing, past it, crystal waters roll;
We visit it by moments, ah, too rare!

We shall renew the battle in the plain
Tomorrow; red with blood will Xanthus[2] be,
15 Hector and Ajax will be there again,
Helen will come upon the wall to see.

Then we shall rust in shade, or shine in strife,
And fluctuate 'twixt blind hopes and blind despairs,
And fancy that we put forth all our life,
20 And never know how with the soul it fares.

Still doth the soul, from its lone fastness high,
Upon our life a ruling effluence send.
And when it fails, fight as we will, we die;
And while it lasts, we cannot wholly end.

1867

DANTE GABRIEL ROSSETTI
(1828–1882)

The Blessed Damozel[1]

The blessed damozel leaned out
   From the gold bar of Heaven;
Her eyes were deeper than the depth
   Of waters stilled at even;
5 She had three lilies in her hand,
   And the stars in her hair were seven.

Her robe, ungirt from clasp to hem,
   No wrought flowers did adorn,
But a white rose of Mary's gift,
10   For service meetly worn;
Her hair that lay along her back
   Was yellow like ripe corn.°   *wheat, grain*

8. The image of the goddess Pallas Athena (or, as perhaps here, the temple in which the image was housed), believed to guarantee the safety of the city which possessed it.
9. In the *Iliad,* a river near Troy (Ilium).
1. Hector, the Trojan hero, son of Priam and Hecuba, whose abduction of the beautiful Helen from her husband Menelaus, brother of the Greek king Agamemnon, had caused the war between Greeks and Trojans. Ajax, second only to Achilles among the Greek heroes, fought in single combat with Hector in the tenth year of the war.
2. In the *Iliad,* the Scamander river (called Xanthus by the gods).
1. Older form of *damsel,* meaning "young unmarried lady," preferred by Romantic and later writers because it avoids the simpler, homelier associations of *damsel.*

Herseemed she scarce had been a day
 One of God's choristers;
15 The wonder was not yet quite gone
 From that still look of hers;
Albeit, to them she left, her day
 Had counted as ten years.

(To one, it is ten years of years.
20   . . . Yet now, and in this place,
Surely she leaned o'er me—her hair
 Fell all about my face. . . .
Nothing: the autumn fall of leaves.
 The whole year sets apace.)

25 It was the rampart of God's house
 That she was standing on;
By God built over the sheer depth
 The which is Space begun;
So high, that looking downward thence
30 She scarce could see the sun.

It lies in Heaven, across the flood
 Of ether, as a bridge.
Beneath, the tides of day and night
 With flame and darkness ridge
35 The void, as low as where this earth
 Spins like a fretful midge.

Around her, lovers, newly met
 In joy no sorrow claims,
Spoke evermore among themselves
40 Their rapturous new names;
And the souls mounting up to God
 Went by her like thin flames.

And still she bowed herself and stooped
 Out of the circling charm;
45 Until her bosom must have made
 The bar she leaned on warm,
And the lilies lay as if asleep
 Along her bended arm.

From the fixed place of Heaven she saw
50 Time like a pulse shake fierce
Through all the worlds. Her gaze still strove
 Within the gulf to pierce
Its path; and now she spoke as when
 The stars sang in their spheres.

55 The sun was gone now; the curled moon
 Was like a little feather
Fluttering far down the gulf; and now
 She spoke through the still weather.
Her voice was like the voice the stars
60 Had when they sang together.

(Ah sweet! Even now, in that bird's song,
 Strove not her accents there,
Fain to be hearkened? When those bells
 Possessed the midday air,
65 Strove not her steps to reach my side
 Down all the echoing stair?)

"I wish that he were come to me,
  For he will come," she said.
"Have I not prayed in Heaven?—on earth,
70   Lord, Lord, has he not prayed?
Are not two prayers a perfect strength?
  And shall I feel afraid?

"When round his head the aureole clings,
  And he is clothed in white,
75 I'll take his hand and go with him
    To the deep wells of light;
We will step down as to a stream,
  And bathe there in God's sight.

"We two will stand beside that shrine,
80   Occult, withheld, untrod,
Whose lamps are stirred continually
  With prayer sent up to God;
And see our old prayers, granted, melt
  Each like a little cloud.

85 "We two will lie i' the shadow of
    That living mystic tree
Within whose secret growth the Dove
  Is sometimes felt to be,
While every leaf that His plumes touch
90   Saith His Name audibly.

"And I myself will teach to him,
  I myself, lying so,
The songs I sing here; which his voice
  Shall pause in, hushed and slow,
95 And find some knowledge at each pause,
  Of some new thing to know."

(Alas! We two, we two, thou say'st!
  Yea, one wast thou with me
That once of old. But shall God lift
100   To endless unity
The soul whose likeness with thy soul
  Was but its love for thee?)

"We two," she said, "will seek the groves
  Where the lady Mary is,
105 With her five handmaidens, whose names
  Are five sweet symphonies,
Cecily, Gertrude, Magdalen,
  Margaret and Rosalys.

"Circlewise sit they, with bound locks
110   And foreheads garlanded;
Into the fine cloth white like flame
  Weaving the golden thread,
To fashion the birth-robes for them
  Who are just born, being dead.

115 "He shall fear, haply, and be dumb:
  Then will I lay my cheek
To his, and tell about our love,
  Not once abashed or weak:
And the dear Mother will approve
120   My pride, and let me speak.

"Herself shall bring us, hand in hand,
    To Him round whom all souls
Kneel, the clear-ranged unnumbered heads
    Bowed with their aureoles:
125 And angels meeting us shall sing
    To their citherns and citoles.[2]

"There will I ask of Christ the Lord
    Thus much for him and me:—
Only to live as once on earth
130   With Love—only to be,
As then awhile, forever now
    Together, I and he."

She gazed and listened and then said,
    Less sad of speech than mild,
135 "All this is when he comes." She ceased.
    The light thrilled towards her, filled
With angels in strong level flight.
    Her eyes prayed, and she smiled.

(I saw her smile.) But soon their path
140   Was vague in distant spheres:
And then she cast her arms along
    The golden barriers,
And laid her face between her hands,
    And wept. (I heard her tears.)

                1846   1850

Sudden Light

I have been here before,
    But when or how I cannot tell:
I know the grass beyond the door,
    The sweet keen smell,
5 The sighing sound, the lights around the shore.

You have been mine before,
    How long ago I may not know:
But just when at that swallow's soar
    Your neck turned so,
10 Some veil did fall—I knew it all of yore.

Has this been thus before?
    And shall not thus time's eddying flight
Still with our lives our love restore
    In death's despite,
15 And day and night yield one delight once more?

                1854   1863

The Woodspurge

The wind flapped loose, the wind was still,
Shaken out dead from tree and hill:
I had walked on at the wind's will—
I sat now, for the wind was still.

5 Between my knees my forehead was—
My lips, drawn in, said not Alas!
My hair was over in the grass,
My naked ears heard the day pass.

---

2. Antique musical instruments: the cithern (17th century), a guitar-like instrument with wire strings; the citole, a stringed instrument dating from the 13th–15th century.

My eyes, wide open, had the run
10 Of some ten weeds to fix upon;
Among those few, out of the sun,
The woodspurge flowered, three cups in one.

From perfect grief there need not be
Wisdom or even memory:
15 One thing then learnt remains to me—
The woodspurge has a cup of three.

1856   1870

From The House of Life

19. *Silent Noon*

Your hands lie open in the long fresh grass—
    The finger-points look through like rosy blooms:
    Your eyes smile peace. The pasture gleams and glooms
'Neath billowing skies that scatter and amass.
5 All round our nest, far as the eye can pass,
    Are golden kingcup-fields with silver edge
    Where the cow-parsley skirts the hawthorn-hedge.
'Tis visible silence, still as the hour-glass.

Deep in the sun-searched growths the dragonfly
10 Hangs like a blue thread loosened from the sky:
    So this winged hour is dropt to us from above.
Oh! clasp we to our hearts, for deathless dower,
This close-companioned inarticulate hour
    When twofold silence was the song of love.

70. *The Hill Summit*

This feast-day of the sun, his altar there
    In the broad west has blazed for vesper-song;
    And I have loitered in the vale too long
And gaze now a belated worshipper.
5 Yet may I not forget that I was 'ware,
    So journeying, of his face at intervals
    Transfigured where the fringed horizon falls,
A fiery bush with coruscating hair.

And now that I have climbed and won this height,
10 I must tread downward through the sloping shade
And travel the bewildered tracks till night.
    Yet for this hour I still may here be stayed
    And see the gold air and the silver fade
And the last bird fly into the last night.

83. *Barren Spring*

Once more the changed year's turning wheel returns:
    And as a girl sails balanced in the wind,
    And now before and now again behind
Stoops as it swoops, with cheek that laughs and burns—
5 So Spring comes merry towards me here, but earns
    No answering smile from me, whose life is twined
    With the dead boughs that winter still must bind,
And whom to-day the Spring no more concerns.

Behold, this crocus is a withering flame;
10 This snowdrop, snow; this apple-blossom's part
    To breed the fruit that breeds the serpent's art.
Nay, for these Spring-flowers, turn thy face from them,
Nor gaze till on the year's last lily-stem
    The white cup shrivels round the golden heart.

91. *Lost on Both Sides*

As when two men have loved a woman well,
    Each hating each, through Love's and Death's deceit;
    Since not for either this stark marriage-sheet
And the long pauses of this wedding-bell;
5 Yet o'er her grave the night and day dispel
    At last their feud forlorn, with cold and heat;
    Nor other than dear friends to death may fleet
The two lives left that most of her can tell:

So separate hopes, which in a soul had wooed
10 The one same Peace, strove with each other long,
    And Peace before their faces perished since:
So through that soul, in restless brotherhood,
    They roam together now, and wind among
    Its bye-streets, knocking at the dusty inns.

97. *A Superscription*

Look in my face; my name is Might-have-been;
    I am also called No-more, Too-late, Farewell;
    Unto thine ear I hold the dead-sea shell
Cast up thy Life's foam-fretted feet between;
5 Unto thine eyes the glass where that is seen
    Which had Life's form and Love's, but by my spell
    Is now a shaken shadow intolerable,
Of ultimate things unuttered the frail screen.

Mark me, how still I am! But should there dart
10 One moment through thy soul the soft surprise
    Of that winged Peace which lulls the breath of sighs,
Then shalt thou see me smile, and turn apart
    Thy visage to mine ambush at thy heart
    Sleepless with cold commemorative eyes.

                       1847–80   1870, 1881

EMILY DICKINSON
(1830–1886)

89

Some things that fly there be—
Birds—Hours—the Bumblebee—
Of these no Elegy.

Some things that stay there be—
5 Grief—Hills—Eternity—
Nor this behooveth me.

There are that resting, rise.
Can I expound the skies?
How still the Riddle lies!

                       1859?   1890

187

How many times these low feet staggered—
Only the soldered mouth can tell—
Try—can you stir the awful rivet—
Try—can you lift the hasps of steel!

5 Stroke the cool forehead—hot so often—
Lift—if you care— the listless hair—
Handle the adamantine° fingers   *rigid, unmovable*
Never a thimble—more—shall wear—

Buzz the dull flies—on the chamber window—
10 Brave—shines the sun through the freckled pane—
Fearless—the cobweb swings from the ceiling—
Indolent Housewife—in Daises—lain!

                              1860?   1890

214

I taste a liquor never brewed—
From Tankards scooped in Pearl—
Not all the Frankfort Berries[1]
Yield such an Alcohol!

5 Inebriate of Air—am I—
And Debauchee of Dew—
Reeling—thro endless summer days—
From inns of Molten Blue—

When "Landlords" turn the drunken Bee
10 Out of the Foxglove's door—
When Butterflies—renounce their "dram"—
I shall but drink the more!

Till Seraphs swing their snowy Hats—
And Saints—to windows run—
15 To see the little Tippler
From Manzanilla[2] come!

                    1860?   1861, 1890

216

Safe in their Alabaster Chambers—
Untouched by Morning
And untouched by Noon—
Sleep the meek members of the Resurrection—
5 Rafter of satin,
And Roof of stone.

Light laughs the breeze
In her Castle above them—
Babbles the Bee in a stolid Ear,
10 Pipe the Sweet Birds in ignorant cadence—
Ah, what sagacity perished here!

                    1859 version   1862

1. Wine grapes from the vicinity of Frankfort and the Rhine in Germany.   2. Name of a sherry wine from the Guadalquivar River area in Spain, and also the name of towns in Trinidad, Mexico, and Panama.

216³

Safe in their Alabaster Chambers—
Untouched by Morning—
And untouched by Noon—
Lie the meek members of the Resurrection—
5   Rafter of Satin—and Roof of Stone!

Grand go the Years—in the Crescent—above them—
Worlds scoop their Arcs—
And Firmaments—row—
Diadems—drop—and Doges—surrender—
10   Soundless as dots—on a Disc of Snow—

                    1861 version   1890

287

A Clock stopped—
Not the Mantel's—
Geneva's farthest skill⁴
Cant put the puppet bowing—
5   That just now dangled still—

An awe came on the Trinket!
The Figures hunched, with pain—
Then quivered out of Decimals—
Into Degreeless Noon—

10   It will not stir for Doctor's—
This Pendulum of snow—
The Shopman importunes it—
While cool—concernless No—

Nods from the Gilded pointers—
15   Nods from the Seconds slim—
Decades of Arrogance between
The Dial life—
And Him—

                    1861?   1896

303

The Soul selects her own Society—
Then—shuts the Door—
To her divine Majority—
Present no more—

5   Unmoved—she notes the Chariots—pausing—
At her low Gate—
Unmoved—an Emperor be kneeling
Upon her Mat—

---

3. This poem has been familiar to readers of Emily Dickinson in a three-stanza version which we now know was never her conception of the poem. Thomas H. Johnson's account of the composition of the poem traces Emily's characteristic trying and re-trying of various articulations of her poetic idea. The 1859 version was sent to Sue Dickinson, Emily's sister-in-law, for advice, and Sue evidently did not like it much. The notes between the two women (they lived in adjoining houses) show Emily's labors over the poem, and her 1861 version was an attempt to meet her own and Sue's exactions. Professor John- son believes Emily Dickinson was never fully satisfied with the poem. It was printed once during her lifetime (1862) in the 1859 version, but when she began her famous correspondence with Thomas W. Higginson, the literary critic and editor, she sent a modified version of the 1861 poem. When Higginson edited Emily Dickinson's poetry for posthumous publica- tion (1890), he combined the two versions, and it is this three-stanza poem that readers had known as Emily's until Johnson's definitive edition of the poems in 1955.
4. Geneva, Switzerland, is traditionally famous for watch-making.

I've known her—from an ample nation—
10 Choose One—
Then—close the Valves of her attention—
Like Stone—

1862?   1890

341

After great pain, a formal feeling comes—
The Nerves sit ceremonious, like Tombs—
The stiff Heart questions was it He, that bore,
And Yesterday, or Centuries before?

5 The Feet, mechanical, go round—
Of Ground, or Air, or Ought—°   *nothing, a void*
A Wooden way
Regardless grown,
A Quartz contentment, like a stone—

10 This is the Hour of Lead—
Remembered, if outlived,
As Freezing persons, recollect the Snow—
First—Chill—then Stupor—then the letting go—

1862?   1929

357

God is a distant—stately Lover—
Woos, as He states us—by His Son—
Verily, a Vicarious Courtship—
"Miles", and "Priscilla", were such an One[5]—

5 But, lest the Soul—like fair "Priscilla"
Choose the Envoy—and spurn the Groom—
Vouches, with hyperbolic archness—
"Miles", and "John Alden" were Synonyme—

1862?   1891, 1929

449

I died for Beauty—but was scarce
Adjusted in the Tomb
When One who died for Truth, was lain
In an adjoining Room—

5 He questioned softly "Why I failed"?
"For Beauty", I replied—
"And I—for Truth—Themself are One—
We Brethren, are", He said—

And so, as Kinsmen, met a Night—
10 We talked between the Rooms—
Until the Moss had reached our lips—
And covered up—our names—

1862?   1890

---

5. Allusion to the story in Longfellow's *Courtship of Miles Standish*, where Miles wishes to court Priscilla Mullins but sends John Alden to speak for him. Priscilla falls in love with John himself.

465

I heard a Fly buzz—when I died—
The Stillness in the Room
Was like the Stillness in the Air—
Between the Heaves of Storm—

5 The Eyes around—had wrung them dry—
And Breaths were gathering firm
For that last Onset—when the King
Be witnessed—in the Room—

I willed my Keepsakes—Signed away
10 What portion of me be
Assignable—and then it was
There interposed a Fly—

With Blue—uncertain stumbling Buzz—
Between the light—and me—
15 And then the Windows failed—and then
I could not see to see—

                              1862?   1896

510

It was not Death, for I stood up,
And all the Dead, lie down—
It was not Night, for all the Bells
Put out their Tongues, for Noon.

5 It was not Frost, for on my Flesh
I felt Siroccos[6]—crawl—
Nor Fire—for just my Marble feet
Could keep a Chancel, cool—

And yet, it tasted, like them all,
10 The Figures I have seen
Set orderly, for Burial,
Reminded me, of mine—

As if my life were shaven,
And fitted to a frame,
15 And could not breathe without a key,
And 'twas like Midnight, some—

When everything that ticked—has stopped—
And Space stares all around—
Or Grisly frosts—first Autumn morns,
20 Repeal the Beating Ground—

But, most, like Chaos—Stopless—cool—
Without a Chance, or Spar—
Or even a Report of Land—
To justify—Despair.

                              1862   1891

---

6. Hot, moist southeasterly winds usually associated with the Libyan desert.

528

Mine—by the Right of the White Election!
Mine—by the Royal Seal!
Mine—by the Sign in the Scarlet prison—
Bars—cannot conceal!

5   Mine—here—in Vision—and in Veto!
Mine—by the Grave's Repeal—
Titled—Confirmed—
Delirious Charter!
Mine—long as Ages steal!

                                          1862?   1890

640

I cannot live with You—
It would be Life—
And Life is over there—
Behind the Shelf

5   The Sexton keeps the Key to—
Putting up
Our Life—His Porcelain—
Like a Cup—

Discarded of the Housewife—
10 Quaint—or Broke—
A newer Sevres[7] pleases—
Old Ones crack—

I could not die—with You—
For One must wait
15 To shut the Other's Gaze down—
You—could not—

And I—Could I stand by
And see You—freeze—
Without my Right of Frost—
20 Death's privilege?

Nor could I rise—with You—
Because Your Face
Would put out Jesus'—
That New Grace

25 Glow plain—and foreign
On my homesick Eye—
Except that You than He
Shone closer by—

They'd judge Us—How—
30 For You—served Heaven—You know,
Or sought to—
I could not—

Because You saturated Sight—
And I had no more Eyes
35 For sordid excellence
As Paradise

7. A fine and expensive French porcelain.

And were You lost, I would be—
Though My Name
Rang loudest
40 On the Heavenly fame—

And were You—saved—
And I—condemned to be
Where You were not—
That self—were Hell to Me—

45 So We must meet apart—
You there—I—here—
With just the Door ajar
That Oceans are—and Prayer—
And that White Sustenance—
50 Despair—

                                        1862?   1890

712

Because I could not stop for Death—
He kindly stopped for me—
The Carriage held but just Ourselves—
And Immortality.

5   We slowly drove—He knew no haste
And I had put away
My labor and my leisure too,
For His Civility—

We passed the School, where Children strove
10 At Recess—in the Ring—
We passed the Fields of Gazing Grain—
We passed the Setting Sun—

Or rather—He passed Us—
The Dews drew quivering and chill—
15 For only Gossamer, my Gown—
My Tippet[8]—only Tulle—

We paused before a House that seemed
A Swelling of the Ground—
The Roof was scarcely visible—
20 The Cornice—in the Ground—

Since then—'tis Centuries—and yet
Feels shorter than the Day
I first surmised the Horses Heads
Were toward Eternity—

                                        1863?   1890

1068

Further in Summer than the Birds
Pathetic from the Grass
A minor Nation celebrates
Its unobtrusive Mass.

---

8. A woman's short cape or cloak.

5 No Ordinance[9] be seen
   So gradual the Grace
   A pensive Custom it becomes
   Enlarging Loneliness.

   Antiquest felt at Noon
10 When August burning low
   Arise this spectral Canticle[1]
   Repose to typify.

   Remit as yet no Grace
   No Furrow on the Glow
15 Yet a Druidic[2] Difference
   Enhances Nature now.

                                    1866?   1891

1232

   The Clover's simple Fame
   Remembered of the Cow—
   Is better than enameled Realms
   Of notability.
5 Renown perceives itself
   And that degrades the Flower—
   The Daisy that has looked behind
   Has compromised its power—

                                    1872?   1945

1463

   A Route of Evanescence
   With a revolving Wheel—
   A Resonance of Emerald—
   A Rush of Cochineal°—   *scarlet*
5 And every Blossom on the Bush
   Adjusts its tumbled Head—
   The mail from Tunis, probably,
   An easy Morning's Ride—

                        1879   1891, 1891

CHRISTINA ROSSETTI
(1830–1894)

Song

   When I am dead, my dearest,
     Sing no sad songs for me;
   Plant thou no roses at my head,
     Nor shady cypress tree:
5 Be the green grass above me
     With showers and dewdrops wet:
   And if thou wilt, remember,
     And if thou wilt, forget.

---

9. A prescribed religious or ceremonial practice, as applied to the sacrament of the Lord's Supper.

1. A hymn or song used by the church in public services.
2. Pertaining to the mysterious religious practices of Celtic priest-magicians.

I shall not see the shadows,
10   I shall not feel the rain;
I shall not hear the nightingale
     Sing on as if in pain:
And dreaming through the twilight
     That doth not rise nor set,
15 Haply I may remember,
     And haply may forget.

1848   1862

Remember

Remember me when I am gone away,
     Gone far away into the silent land;
     When you can no more hold me by the hand,
Nor I half turn to go yet turning stay.
5 Remember me when no more day by day
     You tell me of our future that you planned:
     Only remember me: you understand
It will be late to counsel then or pray.
Yet if you should forget me for a while
10   And afterwards remember, do not grieve:
     For if the darkness and corruption leave
A vestige of the thoughts that once I had,
Better by far you should forget and smile
     Than that you should remember and be sad.

1849   1862

Shut Out

The door was shut. I looked between
     Its iron bars; and saw it lie,
     My garden, mine, beneath the sky,
Pied° with all flowers bedewed and green.   *variegated*

5 From bough to bough the song-birds crossed,
     From flower to flower the moths and bees:
     With all its nests and stately trees
It had been mine, and it was lost.

A shadowless spirit kept the gate,
10   Blank and unchanging like the grave.
     I, peering through, said, "Let me have
Some buds to cheer my outcast state."

He answered not. "Or give me, then,
     But one small twig from shrub or tree;
15   And bid my home remember me
Until I come to it again."

The spirit was silent; but he took
     Mortar and stone to build a wall;
     He left no loophole great or small
20 Through which my straining eyes might look.

So now I sit here quite alone,
     Blinded with tears; nor grieve for that,
     For nought is left worth looking at
Since my delightful land is gone.

25 A violet bed is budding near,
       Wherein a lark has made her nest;
       And good they are, but not the best;
  And dear they are, but not so dear.

                                         1856   1862

Uphill

  Does the road wind uphill all the way?
       Yes, to the very end.
  Will the day's journey take the whole long day?
       From morn to night, my friend.

5 But is there for the night a resting-place?
       A roof for when the slow dark hours begin.
  May not the darkness hide it from my face?
       You cannot miss that inn.

  Shall I meet other wayfarers at night?
10   Those who have gone before.
  Then must I knock, or call when just in sight?
       They will not keep you standing at that door.

  Shall I find comfort, travel-sore and weak?
       Of labor you shall find the sum.
15 Will there be beds for me and all who seek?
       Yea, beds for all who come.

                                         1858   1862

In an Artist's Studio

  One face looks out from all his canvases,
       One selfsame figure sits or walks or leans:
       We found her hidden just behind those screens,
5 That mirror gave back all her loveliness.
  A queen in opal or in ruby dress,
       A nameless girl in freshest summer-greens,
       A saint, an angel—every canvas means
  The same one meaning, neither more nor less.
  He feeds upon her face by day and night,
10   And she with true kind eyes looks back on him,
  Fair as the moon and joyful as the light:
       Not wan with waiting, not with sorrow dim;
  Not as she is, but was when hope shone bright;
       Not as she is, but as she fills his dream.

                                         1856   1896

ALGERNON CHARLES SWINBURNE
(1834–1896)

Chorus from *Atalanta in Calydon*

Before the Beginning of Years

  Before the beginning of years
       There came to the making of man
  Time, with a gift of tears;
       Grief, with a glass that ran;
5 Pleasure, with pain for leaven;
       Summer, with flowers that fell;

Remembrance fallen from heaven,
    And madness risen from hell;
Strength without hands to smite;
10   Love that endures for a breath:
Night, the shadow of light,
    And life, the shadow of death.
And the high gods took in hand
    Fire, and the falling of tears,
15 And a measure of sliding sand
    From under the feet of the years;
And froth and drift of the sea;
    And dust of the laboring earth;
And bodies of things to be
20   In the houses of death and of birth;
And wrought with weeping and laughter,
    And fashioned with loathing and love
With life before and after
    And death beneath and above,
25 For a day and a night and a morrow,
    That his strength might endure for a span
With travail and heavy sorrow,
    The holy spirit of man.
From the winds of the north and the south
30   They gathered as unto strife;
They breathed upon his mouth,
    They filled his body with life;
Eyesight and speech they wrought
    For the veils of the soul therein,
35 A time for labor and thought,
    A time to serve and to sin;
They gave him light in his ways,
    And love, and a space for delight,
And beauty and length of days,
40   And night, and sleep in the night.
His speech is a burning fire;
    With his lips he travaileth;
In his heart is a blind desire,
    In his eyes foreknowledge of death;
45 He weaves, and is clothed with derision;
    Sows, and he shall not reap;
His life is a watch or a vision
    Between a sleep and a sleep.

                        1865

Stage Love

When the game began between them for a jest,
He played king and she played queen to match the best;
Laughter soft as tears, and tears that turned to laughter,
These were things she sought for years and sorrowed after.

5   Pleasure with dry lips, and pain that walks by night;
All the sting and all the stain of long delight;
These were things she knew not of, that knew not of her,
When she played at half a love with half a lover.

Time was chorus, gave them cues to laugh or cry;
10 They would kill, befool, amuse him, let him die;
Set him webs to weave to-day and break to-morrow,
Till he died for good in play, and rose in sorrow.

What the years mean; how time dies and is not slain;
How love grows and laughs and cries and wanes again;
15 These were things she came to know, and take their measure,
When the play was played out so for one man's pleasure.

1866

The Garden of Proserpine[1]

Here, where the world is quiet;
 Here, where all trouble seems
Dead winds' and spent waves' riot
 In doubtful dreams of dreams;
5 I watch the green field growing
For reaping folk and sowing,
For harvest-time and mowing,
 A sleepy world of streams.

I am tired of tears and laughter,
10   And men that laugh and weep;
Of what may come hereafter
 For men that sow to reap:
I am weary of days and hours,
Blown buds of barren flowers,
15 Desires and dreams and powers
 And everything but sleep.

Here life has death for neighbor,
 And far from eye or ear
Wan waves and wet winds labor,
20   Weak ships and spirits steer;
They drive adrift, and whither
They wot not who make thither;
But no such winds blow hither,
 And no such things grow here.

25 No growth of moor or coppice,
 No heather-flower or vine,
But bloomless buds of poppies,
 Green grapes of Proserpine,
Pale beds of blowing rushes
30 Where no leaf blooms or blushes
Save this whereout she crushes
 For dead men deadly wine.

Pale, without name or number,
 In fruitless fields of corn,°   *wheat*
35 They bow themselves and slumber
 All night till light is born;
And like a soul belated,
In hell and heaven unmated,
By cloud and mist abated
40   Comes out of darkness morn.

Though one were strong as seven,
 He too with death shall dwell,
Nor wake with wings in heaven,
 Nor weep for pains in hell;
45 Though one were fair as roses,
His beauty clouds and closes;
And well though love reposes,
 In the end it is not well.

1. Persephone, in Roman mythology Proserpine, the daughter of Zeus and Demeter, had been abducted by Hades (the Roman Pluto), god of the underworld, over which she ruled with him thereafter as his queen.

Pale, beyond porch and portal,
50   Crowned with calm leaves, she stands
Who gathers all things mortal
        With cold immortal hands;
Her languid lips are sweeter
Than love's who fears to greet her
55   To men that mix and meet her
        From many times and lands.

She waits for each and other,
        She waits for all men born;
Forgets the earth her mother,
60   The life of fruits and corn;
And spring and seed and swallow
Take wing for her and follow
Where summer song rings hollow
        And flowers are put to scorn.

65   There go the loves that wither,
        The old loves with wearier wings;
And all dead years draw thither,
        And all disastrous things;
Dead dreams of days forsaken,
70   Blind buds that snows have shaken,
Wild leaves that winds have taken,
        Red strays of ruined springs.

We are not sure of sorrow,
        And joy was never sure;
75   Today will die tomorrow;
        Time stoops to no man's lure;[2]
And love, grown faint and fretful,
With lips but half regretful
Sighs, and with eyes forgetful
80   Weeps that no love endure.

From too much love of living,
        From hope and fear set free,
We thank with brief thanksgiving
        Whatever gods may be
85   That no life lives for ever;
That dead men rise up never;
That even the weariest river
        Winds somewhere safe to sea.

Then star nor sun shall waken,
90   Nor any change of light:
Nor sound of waters shaken,
        Nor any sound or sight:
Nor wintry leaves nor vernal,
Nor days nor things diurnal;
95   Only the sleep eternal
        In an eternal night.

                                                1866

The Sundew

A little marsh-plant, yellow green,
And pricked at lip with tender red.
Tread close, and either way you tread
Some faint black water jets between
5   Lest you should bruise the curious head.

---

2. In falconry, the lure is a device used to recall the hawk to the falconer's wrist.

A live thing maybe; who shall know?
The summer knows and suffers it;
For the cool moss is thick and sweet
Each side, and saves the blossom so
10   That it lives out the long June heat.

The deep scent of the heather burns
About it; breathless though it be,
Bow down and worship; more than we
Is the least flower whose life returns,
15   Least weed renascent in the sea.

We are vexed and cumbered in earth's sight
With wants, with many memories;
These see their mother what she is,
Glad-growing, till August leave more bright
20   The apple-colored cranberries.

Wind blows and bleaches the strong grass,
Blown all one way to shelter it
From trample of stayed kine, with feet
Felt heavier than the moorhen was,
25   Strayed up past patches of wild wheat.

You call it sundew: how it grows,
If with its color it have breath,
If life taste sweet to it, if death
Pain its soft petal, no man knows:
30   Man has no sight or sense that saith.

My sundew, grown of gentle days,
In these green miles the spring begun
Thy growth ere April had half done
With the soft secret of her ways
35   Or June made ready for the sun.

O red-lipped mouth of marsh-flower,
I have a secret halved with thee.
The name that is love's name to me
Thou knowest, and the face of her
40   Who is my festival to see.

The hard sun, as thy petals knew,
Colored the heavy moss-water:
Thou wert not worth green midsummer
Nor fit to live to August blue,
45   O sundew, not remembering her.

                                        1862   1866

A Forsaken Garden

In a coign of the cliff between lowland and highland,
    At the sea-down's edge between windward and lee,
Walled round with rocks as an inland island,
    The ghost of a garden fronts the sea.
5   A girdle of brushwood and thorn encloses
        The steep square slope of the blossomless bed
Where the weeds that grew green from the graves of its roses
                Now lie dead.

The fields fall southward, abrupt and broken,
    To the low last edge of the long lone land.
If a step should sound or a word be spoken,
    Would a ghost not rise at the strange guest's hand?
So long have the grey bare walks lain guestless,
    Through branches and briars if a man make way,
He shall find no life but the sea-wind's, restless
        Night and day.

The dense hard passage is blind and stifled
    That crawls by a track none turn to climb
To the strait waste place that the years have rifled
    Of all but the thorns that are touched not of time.
The thorns he spares when the rose is taken;
    The rocks are left when he wastes the plain.
The wind that wanders, the weeds wind-shaken,
        These remain.

Not a flower to be pressed of the foot that falls not;
    As the heart of a dead man the seed-plots are dry;
From the thicket of thorns whence the nightingale calls not,
    Could she call, there were never a rose to reply.
Over the meadows that blossom and wither
    Rings but the note of a sea-bird's song;
Only the sun and the rain come hither
        All year long.

The sun burns sere° and the rain dishevels   *dry*
    One gaunt bleak blossom of scentless breath.
Only the wind here hovers and revels
    In a round where life seems barren as death.
Here there was laughing of old, there was weeping,
    Haply, of lovers none ever will know,
Whose eyes went seaward a hundred sleeping
        Years ago.

Heart handfast in heart as they stood, "Look thither,"
    Did he whisper? "look forth from the flowers to the sea,
For the foam-flowers endure when the rose-blossoms wither,
    And men that love lightly may die—but we?"
And the same wind sang and the same waves whitened,
    And or ever the garden's last petals were shed,
In the lips that had whispered, the eyes that had lightened,
        Love was dead.

Or they loved their life through, and then went whither?
    And were one to the end—but what end who knows?
Love deep as the sea as a rose must wither,
    As the rose-red seaweed that mocks the rose.
Shall the dead take thought for the dead to love them?
    What love was ever as deep as a grave?
They are loveless now as the grass above them
        Or the wave.

All are at one now, roses and lovers,
    Not known of the cliffs and the fields and the sea.
Not a breath of the time that has been hovers
    In the air now soft with a summer to be.
Not a breath shall there sweeten the seasons heerafter
    Of the flowers or the lovers that laugh now or weep,
When as they that are free now of weeping and laughter
        We shall sleep.

65 Here death may deal not again for ever;
     Here change may come not till all change end.
From the graves they have made they shall rise up never,
     Who have left nought living to ravage and rend.
Earth, stones, and thorns of the wild ground growing,
70   While the sun and the rain live, these shall be;
Till a last wind's breath upon all these blowing
               Roll the sea.

Till the slow sea rise and the sheer cliff crumble,
     Till terrace and meadow the deep gulfs drink,
75 Till the strength of the waves of the high tides humble
     The fields that lessen, the rocks that shrink,
Here now in his triumph where all things falter,
     Stretched out on the spoils that his own hand spread,
As a god self-slain on his own strange altar,
80   Death lies dead.

                                        1876   1878

THOMAS HARDY
(1840–1928)

I Look into My Glass

I look into my glass,
And view my wasting skin,
And say, "Would God it came to pass
My heart had shrunk as thin!"

5 For then, I, undistrest
By hearts grown cold to me,
Could lonely wait my endless rest
With equanimity.

But Time, to make me grieve,
10 Part steals, lets part abide;
And shakes this fragile frame at eve
With throbbings of noontide.

                                                    1898

Drummer Hodge[1]

        1
They throw in drummer Hodge, to rest
        Uncoffined—just as found:
His landmark is a kopje-crest[2]
        That breaks the veldt around;
5 And foreign constellations west
        Each night above his mound.

---

1. The poem presents an incident from the Boer War (1899–1902) and when first published bore the note: "One of the Drummers killed was a native of a village near Casterbridge," i.e., Dorchester, the principal city of the region of southern England to which, in his novels and poems, Hardy gave its medieval name of Wessex.

2. In Afrikaans, the language of the Dutch settlers in South Africa, the crest of a small hill. The veldt (line 4) is open country, unenclosed pasture land; the Karoo (line 9), barren tracts of plateau-land.

2
Young Hodge the Drummer never knew—
        Fresh from his Wessex home—
The meaning of the broad Karoo,
10   The Bush, the dusty loam,
And why uprose to nightly view
        Strange stars amid the gloam.

3
Yet portion of that unknown plain
        Will Hodge forever be;
15 His homely Northern breast and brain
        Grow to some Southern tree,
And strange-eyed constellations reign
        His stars eternally.

                                        1902

A Broken Appointment

                You did not come,
And marching Time drew on, and wore me numb.
Yet less for loss of your dear presence there
Than that I thus found lacking in your make
5 That high compassion which can overbear
Reluctance for pure lovingkindness' sake
Grieved I, when, as the hope-hour stroked its sum,
                You did not come.

                You love not me,
10 And love alone can lend you loyalty;
—I know and knew it. But, unto the store
Of human deeds divine in all but name,
Was it not worth a little hour or more
To add yet this: Once you, a woman, came
15 To soothe a time-torn man; even though it be
                You love not me?

                                        1902

The Self-Unseeing

Here is the ancient floor,
Footworn and hollowed and thin,
Here was the former door
Where the dead feet walked in.

5 She sat here in her chair,
Smiling into the fire;
He who played stood there,
Bowing it higher and higher.

Childlike, I danced in a dream;
10 Blessings emblazoned that day;
Everything glowed with a gleam;
Yet we were looking away!

                                        1902

The Rejected Member's Wife

We shall see her no more
        On the balcony,
Smiling, while hurt, at the roar
        As of surging sea

5   From the stormy sturdy band
              Who have doomed her lord's cause,
       Though she waves her little hand
              As it were applause.

       Here will be candidates yet,
10   And candidates' wives,
       Fervid with zeal to set
              Their ideals on our lives:
       Here will come market-men
              On the market-days,
15   Here will clash now and then
              More such party assays.

       And the balcony will fill
              When such times are renewed,
       And the throng in the street will thrill
20   With today's mettled mood;
       But she will no more stand
              In the sunshine there,
       With that wave of her white-gloved hand,
              And that chestnut hair.

                              January 1906   1909

The Ballad-Singer[3]

Sing, Ballad-singer, raise a hearty tune;
Make me forget that there was ever a one
I walked with in the meek light of the moon
       When the day's work was done.

5   Rhyme, Ballad-rhymer, start a country song;
Make me forget that she whom I loved well
Swore she would love me dearly, love me long,
       Then—what I cannot tell!

Sing, Ballad-singer, from your little book;
10 Make me forget those heartbreaks, achings, fears;
Make me forget her name, her sweet sweet look—
       Make me forget her tears.

                                                1909

The Convergence of the Twain

LINES ON THE LOSS OF THE TITANIC[4]

       1
       In a solitude of the sea
       Deep from human vanity,
And the Pride of Life that planned her, stilly couches she.
       2
       Steel chambers, late the pyres
       Of her salamandrine fires,[5]
Cold currents thrid,° and turn to rhythmic tidal lyres.   *thread*
       3
       Over the mirrors meant
       To glass the opulent
The sea-worm crawls—grotesque, slimed, dumb, indifferent.

---

3. From a sequence of seven poems with the general title *At Casterbridge Fair*.
4. The White Star liner R.M.S. *Titanic* was sunk, with great loss of life, as the result of collision with an iceberg on its maiden voyage from Southampton to New York on April 15, 1912.
5. The ship's fires, which burn though immersed in water, are compared to the salamander, a lizard-like creature which according to fable could live in the midst of fire.

4
10   Jewels in joy designed
        To ravish the sensuous mind
Lie lightless, all their sparkles bleared and black and blind.

5
        Dim moon-eyed fishes near
        Gaze at the gilded gear
15 And query: "What does this vaingloriousness down here?"

6
        Well: while was fashioning
        This creature of cleaving wing,
The Immanent Will that stirs and urges everything

7
        Prepared a sinister mate
20   For her—so gaily great—
A Shape of Ice, for the time far and dissociate.

8
        And as the smart ship grew
        In stature, grace, and hue,
In shadowy silent distance grew the Iceberg too.

9
25   Alien they seemed to be:
        No mortal eye could see
The intimate welding of their later history,

10
        Or sign that they were bent
        By paths coincident
30 On being anon twin halves of one august event,

11
        Till the Spinner of the Years
        Said "Now!" And each one hears,
And consummation comes, and jars two hemispheres.

1912

Channel Firing

That night your great guns, unawares,
Shook all our coffins as we lay,
And broke the chancel window-squares,
We thought it was the Judgment-day

5 And sat upright. While drearisome
Arose the howl of wakened hounds:
The mouse let fall the altar-crumb,
The worms drew back into the mounds,

The glebe cow[6] drooled. Till God called, "No;
10 It's gunnery practice out at sea
Just as before you went below;
The world is as it used to be:

"All nations striving strong to make
Red war yet redder. Mad as hatters
15 They do no more for Christés sake
Than you who are helpless in such matters.

"That this is not the judgment-hour
For some of them's a blessed thing,
For if it were they'd have to scour
20 Hell's floor for so much threatening. . . .

6. Cow pastured on the glebe, a piece of land attached to a vicarage or rectory.

"Ha, ha. It will be warmer when
I blow the trumpet (if indeed
I ever do; for you are men,
And rest eternal sorely need)."

25 So down we lay again. "I wonder,
Will the world ever saner be,"
Said one, "than when He sent us under
In our indifferent century!"

And many a skeleton shook his head.
30 "Instead of preaching forty year,"
My neighbor Parson Thirdly said,
"I wish I had stuck to pipes and beer."

Again the guns disturbed the hour,
Roaring their readiness to avenge,
35 As far inland as Stourton Tower,
And Camelot, and starlit Stonehenge.[7]

April 1914   1914

In Time of "The Breaking of Nations"[8]

1
Only a man harrowing clods
    In a slow silent walk
With an old horse that stumbles and nods
    Half asleep as they stalk.
2
5 Only thin smoke without flame
    From the heaps of couch-grass;
Yet this will go onward the same
    Though Dynasties pass.
3
Yonder a maid and her wight
10   Come whispering by:
War's annals will cloud into night
    Ere their story die.

1915   1916

Afterwards

When the Present has latched its postern° behind my tremulous stay,   *back gate*
    And the May month flaps its glad green leaves like wings,
Delicate-filmed as new-spun silk, will the neighbors say,
    "He was a man who used to notice such things"?

5 If it be in the dusk when, like an eyelid's soundless blink,
    The dewfall-hawk comes crossing the shades to alight
Upon the wind-warped upland thorn, a gazer may think,
    "To him this must have been a familiar sight."

If I pass during some nocturnal blackness, mothy and warm,
10   When the hedgehog travels furtively over the lawn,
One may say, "He strove that such innocent creatures should come to no harm,
    But he could do little for them; and now he is gone."

---

7. "Stourton Tower" is Hardy's name for Stour Head, a small town in Staffordshire, on the river Stour. Camelot was the supposed seat of King Arthur's court, variously thought to have been located in Cornwall or Somerset. Stonehenge is a megalithic structure on Salis-bury Plain, Wiltshire, which dates back to the late Neolithic or early Bronze Age.
8. See Jeremiah li.20: "Thou art my battle ax and weapons of war: for with thee will I break in pieces the nations, and with thee will I destroy kingdoms."

If, when hearing that I have been stilled at last, they stand at the door,
  Watching the full-starred heavens that winter sees,
15 Will this thought rise on those who will meet my face no more,
  "He was one who had an eye for such mysteries"?

And will any say when my bell of quittance is head in the gloom,
  And a crossing breeze cuts a pause in its outrollings,
Till they rise again, as they were a new bell's boom,
20   "He hears it not now, but used to notice such things"?

1917

Jezreel

ON ITS SEIZURE BY THE ENGLISH UNDER ALLENBY, SEPTEMBER 1918[9]

Did they catch as it were in a Vision at shut of the day—
When their cavalry smote through the ancient Esdraelon Plain,
And they crossed where the Tishbite[1] stood forth in his enemy's way—
His gaunt mournful Shade as he bade the King haste off amain?

5 On war-men at this end of time—even on Englishmen's eyes—
Who slay with their arms of new might in the long-ago place,
Flashed he who drove furiously?[2] . . . Ah, did the phantom arise
Of that queen, of that proud Tyrian woman who painted her face?[3]

Faintly marked they the words "Throw her down!" from the night eerily,
10 Specter-spots of the blood of her body on some rotten wall?
And the thin note of pity that came: "A King's daughter is she,"
As they passed where she trodden was once by the chargers' footfall?

Could such be the hauntings of men of today, at the cease
Of pursuit, at the dusk-hour, ere slumber their senses could seal?
15 Enghosted seers, kings—one on horseback who asked "Is it peace?"[4] . . .
Yea, strange things and spectral may men have beheld in Jezreel!

September 24, 1918   1918

The Children and Sir Nameless

Sir Nameless, once of Athelhall, declared:
"These wretched children romping in my park
Trample the herbage till the soil is bared,
And yap and yell from early morn till dark!
5 Go keep them harnessed to their set routines:
Thank God I've none to hasten my decay;
For green remembrance there are better means
Than offspring, who but wish their sires away."

Sir Nameless of that mansion said anon:
10 "To be perpetuate for my mightiness
Sculpture must image me when I am gone."
—He forthwith summoned carvers there express
To shape a figure stretching seven-odd feet
(For he was tall) in alabaster stone,
15 With shield, and crest, and casque, and sword complete:
When done a statelier work was never known.

9. Towards the end of World War I, in the autumn of 1918, General Allenby, commanding the Egyptian Expeditionary Force, won the final victory against the Turks when his cavalry swept through the plain of Esdraelon, called in Hebrew *Emeq Yizre'el*, the plain of Jezreel: the plain lies southeast of Haifa, in northern Israel. In biblical times the city of Jezreel was the location of the palace of Ahab, the wicked king of Israel, and his wife Jezebel.
1. The prophet Elijah (I Kings xvii), implacable enemy of King Ahab (I Kings xvi. 29–34).
2. II Kings ix.20. Jehu was anointed King of Israel by Elisha, Elijah's successor.
3. II Kings ix.30–37.
4. II Kings ix.17.

Three hundred years hied; Church-restorers came,
And, no one of his lineage being traced,
They thought an effigy so large in frame
20 Best fitted for the floor. There it was placed,
Under the seats for schoolchildren. And they
Kicked out his name, and hobnailed off his nose;
And, as they yawn through sermon-time, they say,
"Who was this old stone man beneath our toes?"

1922

No Buyers

A STREET SCENE

A load of brushes and baskets and cradles and chairs
Labors along the street in the rain:
With it a man, a woman, a pony with whiteybrown hairs.
The man foots in front of the horse with a shambling sway
5 At a slower tread than a funeral train,
While to a dirge-like tune he chants his wares,
Swinging a Turk's-head brush (in a drum-major's way
When the bandsmen march and play).

A yard from the back of the man is the whiteybrown pony's nose:
10 He mirrors his master in every item of pace and pose:
He stops when the man stops, without being told,
And seems to be eased by a pause; too plainly he's old,
Indeed, not strength enough shows
To steer the disjointed wagon straight,
15 Which wriggles left and right in a rambling line,
Deflected thus by its own warp and weight,
And pushing the pony with it in each incline.

The woman walks on the pavement verge,
Parallel to the man:
20 She wears an apron white and wide in span,
And carries a like Turk's head, but more in nursing-wise:
Now and then she joins in his dirge,
But as if her thoughts were on distant things.
The rain clams her apron till it clings.
25 So, step by step, they move with their merchandise,
And nobody buys.

1925

ROBERT BRIDGES
(1844–1930)

Long Are the Hours the Sun Is Above

Long are the hours the sun is above,
But when evening comes I go home to my love.

I'm away the daylight hours and more,
Yet she comes not down to open the door.

5 She does not meet me upon the stair,
She sits in my chamber and waits for me there.

As I enter the room she does not move:
I always walk straight up to my love;

And she lets me take my wonted place
10   At her side, and gaze in her dear dear face.

There as I sit, from her head thrown back
Her hair falls straight in a shadow black.

Aching and hot as my tired eyes be,
She is all that I wish to see.

15   And in my wearied and toil-dinned ear,
She says all things that I wish to hear.

Dusky and duskier grows the room,
Yet I see her best in the darker gloom.

When the winter eves are early and cold,
20   The firelight hours are a dream of gold.

And so I sit here night by night,
In rest and enjoyment of love's delight.

But a knock at the door, a step on the stair
Will startle, alas, my love from her chair.

25   If a stranger comes she will not stay:
At the first alarm she is off and away.

And he wonders, my guest, usurping her throne,
That I sit so much by myself alone.

1873

The Windmill

The green corn waving in the dale,
The ripe grass waving on the hill:
I lean across the paddock pale
And gaze upon the giddy mill.

5   Its hurtling sails a mighty sweep
Cut through the air: with rushing sound
Each strikes in fury down the steep,
Rattles, and whirls in chase around.

Besides his sacks the miller stands
10   On high within the open door:
A book and pencil in his hands,
His grist and meal he reckoneth o'er.

His tireless merry slave the wind
Is busy with his work today:
15   From whencesoe'er, he comes to grind;
He hath a will and knows the way.

He gives the creaking sails a spin,
The circling millstones faster flee,
The shuddering timbers groan within,
20   And down the shoot the meal runs free.

The miller giveth him no thanks,
And doth not much his work o'erlook:
He stands beside the sacks, and ranks
The figures in his dusty book.

1890

GERARD MANLEY HOPKINS
(1844–1889)

The Alchemist in the City

My window shows the travelling clouds,
Leaves spent, new seasons, alter'd sky,
The making and the melting crowds:
The whole world passes; I stand by.

5   They do not waste their meted hours,
But men and masters plan and build:
I see the crowning of their towers,
And happy promises fulfill'd.

And I—perhaps if my intent
10   Could count on prediluvian age,[1]
The labours I should then have spent
Might so attain their heritage,

But now before the pot can glow
With not to be discover'd gold,
15   At length the bellows shall not blow,
The furnace shall at last be cold.

Yet it is now too late to heal
The incapable and cumbrous shame
Which makes me when with men I deal
20   More powerless than the blind or lame.

No, I should love the city less
Even than this my thankless lore;
But I desire the wilderness
Or weeded landslips of the shore.

25   I walk my breezy belvedere
To watch the low or levant sun,
I see the city pigeons veer,
I mark the tower swallows run

Between the tower-top and the ground
30   Below me in the bearing air;
Then find in the horizon-round
One spot and hunger to be there.

And then I hate the most that lore
That holds no promise of success;
35   Then sweetest seems the houseless shore,
Then free and kind the wilderness.

Or ancient mounds that cover bones,
Or rocks where rockdoves do repair
And trees of terebinth[2] and stones
40   And silence and a gulf of air.

1. I.e., age as great as the ages attained by men who lived before the Flood (Genesis v). 2. A European tree which yields turpentine.

There on a long and squarèd height
After the sunset I would lie,
And pierce the yellow waxen light
With free long looking, ere I die.

1865   1948

The Habit of Perfection

Elected Silence, sing to me
And beat upon my whorlèd ear,
Pipe me to pastures still and be
The music that I care to hear.

5   Shape nothing, lips; be lovely-dumb:
It is the shut, the curfew sent
From there where all surrenders come
Which only makes you eloquent.

Be shellèd, eyes, with double dark
10 And find the uncreated light:[3]
This ruck and reel which you remark
Coils, keeps, and teases simple sight.

Palate, the hutch of tasty lust,
Desire not to be rinsed with wine:
15 The can° must be so sweet, the crust   *tankard, cup*
So fresh that come in fasts divine!

Nostrils, your careless breath that spend
Upon the stir and keep of pride,
What relish shall the censers[4] send
20 Along the sanctuary side!

O feel-of-primrose hands, O feet
That want the yield of plushy sward,
But you shall walk the golden street
And you unhouse and house the Lord.[5]

25 And, Poverty, be thou the bride
And now the marriage feast begun,
And lily-coloured clothes provide
Your spouse not laboured-at nor spun.[6]

1866   1918

God's Grandeur

The world is charged with the grandeur of God.
　It will flame out, like shining from shook foil;[7]
　It gathers to a greatness, like the ooze of oil
Crushed.[8] Why do men then now not reck his rod?
5 Generations have trod, have trod, have trod;
　And all is seared with trade; bleared, smeared with toil;
　And wears man's smudge and shares man's smell: the soil
Is bare now, nor can foot feel, being shod.

3. W. H. Gardner, in his notes to the poem, explains "uncreated light" as "the *lux increata* of the Schoolmen, the creative energy of God's mind."
4. Vessels in which incense is burned.
5. I.e., the hands will open and close the pyx, the vessel containing the host, the consecrated bread, used in the sacrament.
6. See Matthew vi.28–29: "* * * Consider the lilies of the field, how they grow; they toil not, neither do they spin."

7. In a letter to Robert Bridges (January 4, 1883), Hopkins says: "* * * I mean foil in its sense of leaf or tinsel, and no other word whatever will give the effect I want. Shaken goldfoil gives off broad glares like sheet lightning and also, and this is true of nothing else, owing to its zigzag dints and crossings and network of small many cornered facets, a sort of fork lightning too."
8. I.e., as when olives are crushed for their oil.

And for all this, nature is never spent;
10   There lives the dearest freshness deep down things;
And though the last lights off the black West went
   Oh, morning, at the brown brink eastward, springs—
Because the Holy Ghost over the bent
   World broods with warm breast and with ah! bright wings.

                                        1877   1895

The Windhover[9]

TO CHRIST OUR LORD

I caught this morning morning's minion,° king-   *darling, favorite*
   dom of daylight's dauphin,[1] dapple-dawn-drawn Falcon, in his riding
   Of the rolling level underneath him steady air, and striding
High there, how he rung upon the rein of a wimpling° wing   *rippling*
5   In his ecstasy! then off, off forth on swing,
      As a skate's heel sweeps smooth on a bow-bend: the hurl and gliding
   Rebuffed the big wind. My heart in hiding
Stirred for a bird,—the achieve of, the mastery of the thing!

Brute beauty and valour and act, oh, air, pride, plume, here
   Buckle![2] AND the fire that breaks from thee then, a billion
10 Times told lovelier, more dangerous, O my chevalier![3]

No wonder of it: shéer plód makes plough down sillion°   *furrow*
Shine, and blue-bleak embers, ah my dear,
   Fall, gall themselves, and gash gold-vermilion.

                                        1877   1918

Pied Beauty[4]

Glory be to God for dappled things—
   For skies of couple-colour as a brinded° cow;   *streaked, brindled*
      For rose-moles all in stipple upon trout that swim;
Fresh-firecoal chestnut-falls;[5] finches' wings;
5   Landscape plotted and pieced—fold, fallow and plough;[6]
      And áll trádes, their gear and tackle and trim.
All things counter, original, spare, strange;
   Whatever is fickle, freckled (who knows how?)
      With swift, slow; sweet, sour; adazzle, dim;
10 He fathers-forth whose beauty is past change:
                        Praise him.

                                        1877   1918

Felix Randal

Felix Randal the farrier,° O is he dead then? my duty all ended,   *blacksmith*
Who have watched his mould of man, big-boned and hardy-handsome
Pining, pining, till time when reason rambled in it and some
Fatal four disorders, fleshed there, all contended?

9. "A name for the kestral [a species of small hawk], from its habit of hovering or hanging with its head to the wind" [O.E.D.].
1. The eldest son of the king of France was called the *dauphin*: hence, the word here means heir to a splendid, kingly condition.
2. The word "buckle" brings to a single focus the several elements of line 8, in both their literal sense, as descriptive of a single, sudden movement of the airborne bird, and in their symbolic sense as descriptive of Christ and with further reference to the poet himself and the lesson he draws from his observation. It may be read either as indicative or imperative, and in one or another of its possible meanings: "to fasten," "to join closely," "to equip for battle," "to grapple with, engage," but also "to cause to bend, give way, crumple."
3. Knight, nobleman, champion.
4. Having two or more colors, in patches or blotches.
5. W. H. Gardner cites a note from Hopkins's *Journals*: "Chestnuts as bright as coals or spots of vermilion."
6. The land makes a pattern of varicolored patches by reason of its several uses, as for pasture, or being left fallow for a season, or being plowed and sown.

5 Sickness broke him. Impatient, he cursed at first, but mended
   Being anointed and all; though a heavenlier heart began some
   Months earlier, since I had our sweet reprieve and ransom
   Tendered to him.[7] Ah well, God rest him all road ever he offended![8]

   This seeing the sick endears them to us, us too it endears.
10 My tongue had taught thee comfort, touch had quenched thy tears,
   Thy tears that touched my heart, child, Felix, poor Felix Randal;

   How far from then forethought of, all thy more boisterous years,
   When thou at the random[9] grim forge, powerful amidst peers,
   Didst fettle[1] for the great grey drayhorse his bright and battering sandal!

                                                    1880   1918

Spring and Fall

TO A YOUNG CHILD

   Márgarét, áre you gríeving
   Over Goldengrove unleaving?
   Leáves, líke the things of man, you
   With your fresh thoughts care for, can you?
5 Áh! ás the heart grows older
   It will come to such sights colder
   By and by, nor spare a sigh
   Though worlds of wanwood leafmeal lie;[2]
   And yet you *will* weep and know why.
10 Now no matter, child, the name:
   Sórrow's spríngs áre the same.
   Nor mouth had, no nor mind, expressed
   What heart heard of, ghost° guessed: *spirit, soul*
   It ís the blight man was born for,
15 It is Margaret you mourn for.

                                                    1880   1893

[As Kingfishers Catch Fire, Dragonflies Draw Flame]

   As kingfishers catch fire, dragonflies draw flame;[3]
       As tumbled over rim in roundy wells
       Stones ring; like each tucked° string tells, each hung bell's *touched, plucked*
   Bow swung finds tongue to fling out broad its name;
5 Each mortal thing does one thing and the same:
       Deals out that being indoors each one dwells;[4]
       Selves[5]—goes itself; *myself* it speaks and spells,
   Crying *What I do is me: for that I came.*

   I say more: the just man justices;
10   Kéeps gráce: thát keeps all his goings graces;
   Acts in God's eye what in God's eye he is—
       Chríst. For Christ plays in ten thousand places,
   Lovely in limbs, and lovely in eyes not his
       To the Father through the features of men's faces.

                                                    1882?   1918

7. I.e., since I had a priest visit him to hear his confession and give absolution.
8. I.e., for any way in which he may have offended.
9. Ramshackle, as applied to the forge itself; but also meaning that the man's life as a blacksmith was merely one casual earthly life as opposed to the sure way of Christian salvation.
1. To line or cover with a refractory material; hence, to shoe.
2. "Wanwood": *pale* or *dim*—the groves are pale because of their light-colored autumn foliage, or dim because of the filtered light. "Leafmeal" (a word coined by Hopkins by analogy with *piecemeal*): *leaf by leaf*, or *leaf mold*—in the first sense, the foliage lies about the grove, having fallen leaf by leaf; in the second, foliage gradually decays to leaf mold.
3. I.e., as their bright colors flash in the light.
4. I.e., gives utterance to the essential nature that dwells within ("indoors") each individual being.
5. I.e., gives being to its own individuality.

[No Worst, There Is None. Pitched Past Pitch of Grief]

No worst, there is none. Pitched past pitch of grief,
More pangs will, schooled at forepangs, wilder wring.
Comforter, where, where is your comforting?
Mary, mother of us, where is your relief?
5 My cries heave, herds-long; huddle in a main, a chief-
woe, world-sorrow; on an age-old anvil wince and sing—
Then lull, then leave off. Fury had shrieked 'No ling-
ering! Let me be fell:° force° I must be brief'.   *fierce, deadly/perforce*
O the mind, mind has mountains; cliffs of fall
10 Frightful, sheer, no-man-fathomed. Hold them cheap
May who ne'er hung there. Nor does long our small
Durance deal with that steep or deep. Here! creep,
Wretch, under a comfort serves in a whirlwind: all
Life death does end and each day dies with sleep.

                                   1885   1918

[I Wake and Feel the Fell of Dark, Not Day.]

I wake and feel the fell[6] of dark, not day.
What hours, O what black hoürs we have spent
This night! what sights you, heart, saw; ways you went!
And more must, in yet longer light's delay.

5 With witness I speak this. But where I say
Hours I mean years, mean life. And my lament
Is cries countless, cries like dead letters sent
To dearest him that lives alas! away.

I am gall, I am heartburn. God's most deep decree
10 Bitter would have me taste: my taste was me;
Bones built in me, flesh filled, blood brimmed the curse.

Selfyeast of spirit a dull dough sours. I see
The lost are like this, and their scourge to be
As I am mine, their sweating selves, but worse.

                                   1885   1918

[My Own Heart Let Me More Have Pity On]

My own heart let me more have pity on; let
Me live to my sad self hereafter kind,
Charitable; not live this tormented mind
With this tormented mind tormenting yet.

5 I cast for comfort I can no more get
By groping round my comfortless, than blind
Eyes in their dark can day or thirst can find
Thirst's all-in-all in all a world of wet.[7]

Soul, self; come, poor Jackself,[8] I do advise
10 You, jaded, let be; call off thoughts awhile
Elsewhere; leave comfort root-room;[9] let joy size

---

6. "Fell" is capable of being read in a number of senses: as "the hide or hairy skin of a beast," or, in an obsolete or rare sense, as "gall, bitterness; hence, animosity, rancor" [O.E.D.], or possibly as the adjective *fell*— fierce, savage, cruel—used as a noun.
7. I.e., as shipwrecked persons adrift without drinking water cannot quench their thirst, even though they are surrounded by "wet." The noun *world* is common to all three instances: the speaker's "comfortless" world, the blind man's "dark" world, the "world of wet" in which the shipwrecked are adrift.
8. The humble self—"Jack" used in a pitying, deprecating sense (as in *jack-of-all-trades*).
9. Room for its roots to grow.

At God knows when to God knows what;[1] whose smile
's not wrung,[2] se you; unforeseen times rather—as skies
Betweenpie mountains[3]—lights a lovely mile.

1885   1918

That Nature is a Heraclitean[4] Fire and of the comfort of the Resurrection

Cloud-puffball, torn tufts, tossed pillows | flaunt forth, then
    chevy° on an air-   *race, scamper*
built thoroughfare: heaven-roysterers, in gay-gangs | they throng;
    they glitter in marches.
Down roughcast, down dazzling whitewash, | wherever an elm arches,
Shivelights[5] and shadowtackle[6] in long | lashes lace, lance, and pair.
5 Delightfully the bright wind boisterous | ropes, wrestles, beats earth bare
Of yestertempest's creases; | in pool and rutpeel parches
Squandering ooze to squeezed | dough, crust, dust; stanches, starches
Squadroned masks and manmarks | treadmire toil there
Footfretted in it. Million-fuelèd, | nature's bonfire burns on.
10 But quench her bonniest, dearest | to her, her clearest-selvèd spark
Man, how fast his firedint,[7] | his mark on mind, is gone!
Both are in an unfathomable, all is in an enormous dark
Drowned. O pity and indig | nation! Manshape, that shone
Sheer off, disseveral, a star, | death blots black out; nor mark
15   Is any of him at all so stark
But vastness blurs and time | beats level. Enough! the Resurrection,
A heart's-clarion! Away grief's gasping, | joyless days, dejection.
      Across my foundering deck shone
A beacon, an eternal beam. | Flesh fade, and mortal trash
20 Fall to the residuary worm; | world's wildfire, leave but ash:
      In a flash, at a trumpet crash,
I am at once what Christ is, | since he was what I am, and
This Jack,[8] joke, poor potsherd, | patch, matchwood, immortal diamond,
      Is immortal diamond.

1888   1918

A. E. HOUSMAN
(1859–1936)

Loveliest of Trees, the Cherry Now

Loveliest of trees, the cherry now
Is hung with bloom along the bough,
And stands about the woodland ride
Wearing white for Eastertide.

1. "Size" (line 11): grow, increase in size; "At God knows when": at unpredictable times; "to God knows what": until it reaches an unpredictable condition.
2. Cannot be forced, but must come as it will.
3. "Betweenpie" (a verb of Hopkins's invention [see *Pied Beauty*]): the brightness of skies seen between mountains, which makes a variegated patterning of light and dark.
4. Heraclitus of Ephesus (flourished 500 B.C.) was the founder of an important school of pre-Socratic philosophy who taught that the world had its origin in fire and would end in fire. "He is best known for his doctrine of perpetual change and impermanence in nature * * * ." For him the principle of the universe was "a law of opposites, whose conflicts were controlled by eternal justice and whose contrary tensions produced the apparent stability of being. Fire, the underlying primary substance, is the prototype of the world, which is an 'ever-living fire with measures of it kindling and measures of it going out.' Fire passes by combustion through the fiery waterspout * * * into water and earth; and the reverse process occurs simultaneously, when part of the earth liquefies and passes by evaporation and 'exhalation' as fuel into fire. Thus are constituted a 'way up' and a 'way down,' a two-way process of interchange between the elements, with approximate balance of 'measures.' 'All is perpetual flux and nothing abides.' " [A. J. D. Porteous, in *Chambers's Encyclopedia*].
5. Light in splinters, fragments.
6. Shadows in complicated shapes, as of ship's ropes, tackle, gear.
7. Hopkins's compound, meaning the mark made by the flame of man's spirit, the spirit's power to make its mark.
8. Common mortal like "poor Jackself" in *My Own Heart Let Me More Have Pity On.*

5 Now, of my threescore years and ten,
Twenty will not come again,
And take from seventy springs a score,
It only leaves me fifty more.

And since to look at things in bloom
10 Fifty springs are little room,
About the woodlands I will go
To see the cherry hung with snow.

1896

Reveille

Wake: the silver dusk returning
    Up the beach of darkness brims,
And the ship of sunrise burning
    Strands upon the eastern rims.

5 Wake: the vaulted shadow shatters,
    Trampled to the floor it spanned,
And the tent of night in tatters
    Straws° the sky-pavilioned land.   *strews*

Up, lad, up, 'tis late for lying:
10   Hear the drums of morning play;
Hark, the empty highways crying
    "Who'll beyond the hills away?"

Towns and countries woo together,
    Forelands beacon, belfries call;
15 Never lad that trod on leather
    Lived to feast his heart with all.

Up, lad; thews° that lie and cumber   *limbs*
    Sunlit pallets never thrive;
Morns abed and daylight slumber
20   Were not meant for man alive.

Clay lies still, but blood's a rover;
    Breath's a ware that will not keep.
Up, lad: when the journey's over
    There'll be time enough to sleep.

1896

It Nods and Curtseys and Recovers

It nods and curtseys and recovers
    When the wind blows above,
The nettle on the graves of lovers
    That hanged themselves for love.

5 The nettle nods, the wind blows over,
    The man, he does not move,
The lover of the grave, the lover
    That hanged himself for love.

1896

To an Athlete Dying Young

The time you won your town the race
We chaired you through the market-place;
Man and boy stood cheering by,
And home we brought you shoulder-high.

5 Today, the road all runners come,
Shoulder-high we bring you home,
And set you at your threshold down,
Townsman of a stiller town.

Smart lad, to slip betimes away
10 From fields where glory does not stay
And early though the laurel grows
It withers quicker than the rose.

Eyes the shady night has shut
Cannot see the record cut,
15 And silence sounds no worse than cheers
After earth has stopped the ears:

Now you will not swell the rout
Of lads that wore their honors out,
Runners whom renown outran
20 And the name died before the man.

So set, before its echoes fade,
The fleet foot on the sill of shade,
And hold to the low lintel up
The still-defended challenge-cup.

25 And round that early-laureled head
Will flock to gaze the strengthless dead,
And find unwithered on its curls
The garland briefer than a girl's.

                                                        1896

With Rue My Heart Is Laden

With rue my heart is laden
    For golden friends I had,
For many a rose-lipt maiden
    And many a lightfoot lad.

5 By brooks too broad for leaping
    The lightfoot boys are laid;
The rose-lipt girls are sleeping
    In fields where roses fade.

                                                        1896

"Terence,[1] This Is Stupid Stuff . . ."

"Terence, this is stupid stuff:
You eat your victuals fast enough;
There can't be much amiss, 'tis clear,
To see the rate you drink your beer.
5 But oh, good Lord, the verse you make,
It gives a chap the belly-ache.
The cow, the old cow, she is dead;
It sleeps well, the hornéd head:
We poor lads, 'tis our turn now
10 To hear such tunes as killed the cow.
Pretty friendship 'tis to rhyme
Your friends to death before their time
Moping melancholy mad:
Come, pipe a tune to dance to, lad."

1. Housman had at first planned to call the volume in which this poem appeared *The Poems of Terence Hearsay.*

15   Why, if 'tis dancing you would be,
        There's brisker pipes than poetry.
        Say, for what were hop-yards meant,
        Or why was Burton built on Trent?[2]
        Oh many a peer of England brews
20   Livelier liquor than the Muse,
        And malt does more than Milton can
        To justify God's ways to man.
        Ale, man, ale's the stuff to drink
        For fellows whom it hurts to think:
25   Look into the pewter pot
        To see the world as the world's not.
        And faith, 'tis pleasant till 'tis past:
        The mischief is that 'twill not last.
        Oh I have been to Ludlow[3] fair
30   And left my necktie God knows where,
        And carried halfway home, or near,
        Pints and quarts of Ludlow beer:
        Then the world seemed none so bad,
        And I myself a sterling lad;
35   And down in lovely muck I've lain,
        Happy till I woke again.
        Then I saw the morning sky:
        Heigho, the tale was all a lie;
        The world, it was the old world yet,
40   I was I, my things were wet,
        And nothing now remained to do
        But begin the game anew.

        Therefore, since the world has still
        Much good, but much less good than ill,
45   And while the sun and moon endure
        Luck's a chance, but trouble's sure,
        I'd face it as a wise man would,
        And train for ill and not for good.
        'Tis true, the stuff I bring for sale
50   Is not so brisk a brew as ale:
        Out of a stem that scored the hand
        I wrung it in a weary land.
        But take it: if the smack is sour,
        The better for the embittered hour;
55   It should do good to heart and head
        When your soul is in my soul's stead;
        And I will friend you, if I may,
        In the dark and cloudy day.

        There was a king reigned in the East:
60   There, when kings will sit to feast,
        They get their fill before they think
        With poisoned meat and poisoned drink.
        He gathered all that springs to birth
        From the many-venomed earth;
65   First a little, thence to more,
        He sampled all her killing store;
        And easy, smiling, seasoned sound,
        Sate the king when healths went round.
        They put arsenic in his meat
70   And stared aghast to watch him eat;
        They poured strychnine in his cup

---

2. Burton-on-Trent, a town in Staffordshire   3. A town in Shropshire.
whose principal industry is the brewing of ale.

And shook to see him drink it up:
They shook, they stared as white's their shirt:
Them it was their poison hurt.
75 —I tell the tale that I heard told.
Mithridates, he died old.[4]

1896

Eight O'clock

He stood, and heard the steeple
    Sprinkle the quarters on the morning town.
One, two, three, four, to market-place and people
    It tossed them down.

5 Strapped, noosed, nighing his hour,
    He stood and counted them and cursed his luck;
And then the clock collected in the tower
    Its strength, and struck.

1922

The Oracles[5]

'Tis mute, the word they went to hear on high Dodona mountain
    When winds were in the oakenshaws and all the cauldrons tolled,
And mute's the midland navel-stone beside the singing fountain,
    And echoes list to silence now where gods told lies of old.

5 I took my question to the shrine that has not ceased from speaking,
    The heart within, that tells the truth and tells it twice as plain;
And from the cave of oracles I heard the priestess shrieking
    That she and I should surely die and never live again.

Oh priestess, what you cry is clear, and sound good sense I think it;
10   But let the screaming echoes rest, and froth your mouth no more.
'Tis true there's better booze than brine, but he that drowns must drink it;
    And oh, my lass, the news is news that men have heard before.

The King with half the East at heel is marched from lands of morning;
    Their fighters drink the rivers up, their shafts benight the air.
15 *And he that stands will die for nought, and home there's no returning.*
    The Spartans on the sea-wet rock sat down and combed their hair.[6]

1922

---

4. Mithridates VI, king of Pontus in Asia Minor in the first century B.C., produced in himself an immunity to certain poisons by administering them to himself in small, gradual doses.
5. It was a feature of the Greek religion that the gods could be consulted through their oracles. Questions concerning the future or asking advice in matters of conduct, both political and moral, were presented at the shrine of the oracle, and the answers—usually vague, ambiguous, or incoherent—were interpreted by a priest. The two most famous oracles, both alluded to in Housman's poem, were that of Zeus at Dodona, in Epirus, and that of Apollo at Delphi. At Dodona the answers came from the oak sacred to Zeus, either through the sound of the wind in its leaves or from the sound of a spring which gushed up at its roots; this temple contained a large cauldron, renowned for its echoes. At Delphi, where the answers were given by the Pythia, a divinely inspired priestess who uttered her pronouncements in an incoherent frenzy, there was a stone called the Omphalos, or navel, supposed to be the central point of the earth.

6. Xerxes (the "King," line 13), the leader of the Persian forces who were to defeat the Greeks, including a small body of unyielding Spartans, at the battle of Thermopylae. The details of the last stanza may be referred to Herodotus' account of the battle and the events leading up to it in Book VII of his *History*. The Athenians had twice consulted the oracle at Delphi, but even the predictions of defeat, which "struck fear into their hearts, failed to persuade them to fly from Greece. They had the courage to remain faithful to their land, and await the coming of the foe." Of Xerxes' army, Herodotus asks, "* * * Was there a nation in all Asia which Xerxes did not bring with him against Greece? Or was there a river, except those of unusual size, which sufficed for his troops to drink?" At one point, Xerxes had sent a spy to observe the Greeks; the Spartans, who happened to hold the outer guard, "were seen by the spy, some of them engaged in gymnastic exercises, others combing their long hair," which struck Xerxes as laughable. He "had no means of surmising the truth—namely, that the Spartans were preparing to do or die manfully * * * "

Revolution

West and away the wheels of darkness roll,
  Day's beamy banner up the east is borne,
Specters and fears, the nightmare and her foal,
  Drown in the golden deluge of the morn.

5   But over sea and continent from sight
  Safe to the Indies has the earth conveyed
The vast and moon-eclipsing cone of night,
  Her towering foolscap of eternal shade.

See, in mid heaven the sun is mounted; hark,
10   The belfries tingle to the noonday chime.
'Tis silent, and the subterranean dark
  Has crossed the nadir,[7] and begins to climb.

1922

Diffugere Nives[8]

HORACE: ODES *iv.7*

The snows are fled away, leaves on the shaws
  And grasses in the mead renew their birth,
The river to the river-bed withdraws,
  And altered is the fashion of the earth.

5   The Nymphs and Graces three put off their fear
  And unappareled in the woodland play.
The swift hour and the brief prime of the year
  Say to the soul, *Thou wast not born for aye.*

Thaw follows frost; hard on the heel of spring
10   Treads summer sure to die, for hard on hers
Comes autumn, with his apples scattering;
  Then back to wintertide, when nothing stirs.

But oh, whate'er the sky-led seasons mar,
  Moon upon moon rebuilds it with her beams:
15 Come *we* where Tullus and where Ancus are,
  And good Aeneas, we are dust and dreams.[9]

Torquatus,[1] if the gods in heaven shall add
  The morrow to the day, what tongue has told?
Feast then thy heart, for what thy heart has had
20   The fingers of no heir will ever hold.

When thou descendest once the shades among,
  The stern assize and equal judgment[2] o'er,
Not thy long lineage nor thy golden tongue,
  No, nor thy righteousness, shall friend thee more.

---

7. "The point of the heavens diametrically opposite to the zenith; the point directly under the observer" [O.E.D.].
8. The opening words of the ode by the Roman poet Horace, of which Housman's poem is a translation.
9. Neither the wealth of Tullus Hostilius and Ancus Marcius, legendary third and fourth kings of Rome respectively, nor the traditional piety of Aeneas, Rome's founder, kept them from the end that is the common lot of men.
1. A friend, his exact identity uncertain, to whom Horace also addressed Epistle I.5.
2. The judgment of Minos, son of Zeus and Europa, who after his death was made judge over the dead in Hades.

²⁵ Night holds Hippolytus the pure of stain,
    Diana steads him nothing, he must stay;[3]
And Theseus leaves Pirithöus in the chain
    The love of comrades cannot take away.[4]

1936

Stars, I Have Seen Them Fall

Stars, I have seen them fall,
    But when they drop and die
No star is lost at all
    From all the star-sown sky.
⁵ The toil of all that be
    Helps not the primal fault;
It rains into the sea,
    And still the sea is salt.

1936

Smooth Between Sea and Land

Smooth between sea and land
Is laid the yellow sand,
And here through summer days
The seed of Adam plays.

⁵ Here the child comes to found
His unremaining mound,
And the grown lad to score
Two names upon the shore.

Here, on the level sand,
¹⁰ Between the sea and land,
What shall I build or write
Against the fall of night?

Tell me of runes[5] to grave°   *engrave*
That hold the bursting wave,
¹⁵ Or bastions to design
For longer date than mine.

Shall it be Troy or Rome
I fence against the foam,
Or my own name, to stay
²⁰ When I depart for aye?

Nothing: too near at hand,
Planing the figured sand,
Effacing clean and fast
Cities not built to last
²⁵ And charms devised in vain,
Pours the confounding main.

1936

---

3. Hippolytus, a devotee of the chase and worshipper of Artemis (Diana), renowned for the purity of his life.
4. Pirithöus, Greek mythological king of the Lapiths, hearing of Theseus' exploits of valor and strength, first challenged him and then, convinced of his greatness, swore eternal friendship with him. Theseus went with Pirithöus to the underworld to bring back Persephone; when they were made captive there, Theseus escaped but was unable to free Pirithöus.
5. Written signs or characters having magic powers.

RUDYARD KIPLING
(1865–1936)

Tommy[1]

I went into a public-'ouse to get a pint o' beer,
The publican° 'e up an' sez, "We serve no red-coats here."   *bar-keeper*
The girls be'ind the bar they laughed an' giggled fit to die,
I outs into the street again an' to myself sez I:
5   O it's Tommy this, an' Tommy that, an' "Tommy, go away";
    But it's "Thank you, Mister Atkins," when the band begins to play—
    The band begins to play, my boys, the band begins to play,
    O it's "Thank you, Mister Atkins," when the band begins to play.

I went into a theater as sober as could be,
10 They gave a drunk civilian room, but 'adn't none for me;
They sent me to the gallery or round the music-'alls,[2]
But when it comes to fightin', Lord! they'll shove me in the stalls!
    For it's Tommy this, an' Tommy that, an' "Tommy, wait outside";
    But its "Special train for Atkins" when the trooper's on the tide—
15   The troopship's on the tide, my boys, the troopship's on the tide,
    O it's "Special train for Atkins" when the trooper's on the tide.

Yes, makin' mock o' uniforms that guard you while you sleep
Is cheaper than them uniforms, an' they're starvation cheap;
An' hustlin' drunken soldiers when they're goin' large a bit
20 Is five times better business than paradin' in full kit.
    Then it's Tommy this, an' Tommy that, an' "Tommy, 'ow's yer soul?"
    But it's "Thin red line of 'eroes"[3] when the drums begin to roll—
    The drums begin to roll, my boys, the drums begin to roll,
    O it's "Thin red line of 'eroes" when the drums begin to roll.

25 We aren't no thin red 'eroes, nor we aren't no blackguards too,
But single men in barricks, most remarkable like you;
An' if sometimes our conduck isn't all your fancy paints,
Why, single men in barricks don't grow into plaster saints;
    While it's Tommy this, an' Tommy that, an' "Tommy, fall be'ind,"
30   But it's "Please to walk in front, sir," when there's trouble in the wind—
    There's trouble in the wind, my boys, there's trouble in the wind,
    O it's "Please to walk in front, sir," when there's trouble in the wind.

You talk o' better food for us, an' schools, an' fires, an' all:
We'll wait for extry rations if you treat us rational.
35 Don't mess about the cook-room slops, but prove it to our face
The Widow's Uniform[4] is not the soldier-man's disgrace.
    For it's Tommy this, an' Tommy that, an' "Chuck him out, the brute!"
    But it's "Savior of 'is country" when the guns begin to shoot;
    An' it's Tommy this, an' Tommy that, an' anything you please;
40   An' Tommy ain't a bloomin' fool—you bet that Tommy sees!

           1890

1. Derived from "Thomas Atkins," as the typical name for a soldier in the British army.
2. Cheaper seats in a theater, in the balcony; the best seats, in the orchestra, are the stalls.
3. W. H. Russell, a London *Times* correspondent, had used the phrase "thin red line tipped with steel" to describe the 93rd Highlanders infantry regiment as they stood to meet the advancing Russian cavalry at Balaclava (1854), in the Crimean War.
4. I.e., the queen's uniform. In his poems and stories Kipling occasionally referred to Queen Victoria as "The Widow at Windsor."

Et Dona Ferentes[5]

1896

In extended observation of the ways and works of man,
From the Four-mile Radius[6] roughly to the Plains of Hindustan:
I have drunk with mixed assemblies, seen the racial ruction rise,
And the men of half Creation damning half Creation's eyes.

5   I have watched in their tantrums, all that pentecostal[7] crew,
French, Italian, Arab, Spaniard, Dutch and Greek, and Russ and Jew,
Celt and savage, buff and ochre, cream and yellow, mauve and white,
But it never really mattered till the English grew polite;

Till the men with polished toppers, till the men in long frock-coats,
10   Till the men who do not duel, till the men who war with votes,
Till the breed that take their pleasures as Saint Lawrence took his grid,[8]
Began to "beg your pardon" and—the knowing croupier hid.

Then the bandsmen with their fiddles, and the girls that bring the beer,
Felt the psychological moment, left the lit Casino clear;
15   But the uninstructed alien, from the Teuton to the Gaul,
Was entrapped, once more, my country, by that suave, deceptive drawl.

As it was in ancient Suez or 'neath wilder, milder skies,
I "observe with apprehension" how the racial ructions rise;
And with keener apprehension, if I read the times aright,
20   Hear the old Casino order: "Watch your man, but be polite.

"Keep your temper. Never answer (*that* was why they spat and swore).
Don't hit first, but move together (there's no hurry) to the door.
Back to back, and facing outward while the linguist tells 'em how—
'*Nous sommes allong ar notre batteau, nous ne voulong pas un row.*' "

25   So the hard, pent rage ate inward, till some idiot went too far . . .
"Let 'em have it!" and they had it, and the same was merry war—
Fist, umbrella, cane, decanter, lamp and beer-mug, chair and boot—
Till behind the fleeing legions rose the long, hoarse yell for loot.

Then the oil-cloth with its numbers, like a banner fluttered free;
30   Then the grand piano cantered, on three castors, down the quay;
White, and breathing through their nostrils, silent, systematic, swift—
They removed, effaced, abolished all that man could heave or lift.

Oh, my country, bless the training that from cot to castle runs—
The pitfall of the stranger but the bulwark of thy sons—
35   Measured speech and ordered action, sluggish soul and unperturbed,
Till we wake our Island-Devil—nowise cool for being curbed!

When the heir of all the ages "has the honor to remain,"
When he will not hear an insult, though men make it ne'er so plain,
When his lips are schooled to meekness, when his back is bowed to
          blows—
40   Well the keen *aas-vogels*° know it—well the waiting jackal knows.   *vultures*

---

5. From Virgil's *Aeneid*. II.49, "* * * *timeo Danaos et dona ferentes*" ("I fear the Greeks when they come bearing gifts").
6. In London, "a circle of four miles in all directions from Charing Cross, outside of which cab-fares are higher" [*O.E.D.*].
7. Here, in the sense of "speaking many tongues."
8. According to legend, Saint Lawrence, suffering martyrdom on the gridiron, told his torturers, "Turn me over, I am done on that side."

Build on the flanks of Etna where the sullen smoke-puffs float—
Or bathe in tropic waters where the lean fin dogs the boat—
Cock the gun that is not loaded, cook the frozen dynamite—
But oh, beware my country, when my country grows polite!

1903

The Recall

I am the land of their fathers.
In me the virtue stays.
I will bring back my children,
After certain days.

5 Under their feet in the grasses
My clinging magic runs.
They shall return as strangers.
They shall remain as sons.

Over their heads in the branches
10 Of their new-bought, ancient trees,
I weave an incantation
And draw them to my knees.

Scent of smoke in the evening,
Smell of rain in the night—
15 The hours, the days and the seasons,
Order their souls aright,

Till I make plain the meaning
Of all my thousand years—
Till I fill their hearts with knowledge,
20 While I fill their eyes with tears.

1909

WILLIAM BUTLER YEATS[1]
(1865–1939)

The Lamentation of the Old Pensioner

Although I shelter from the rain
Under a broken tree,
My chair was nearest to the fire
In every company
5 That talked of love or politics,
Ere time transfigured me.

Though lads are making pikes° again   *weapons*
For some conspiracy,
And crazy rascals rage their fill
10 At human tyranny,
My contemplations are of Time
That has transfigured me.

1. In providing footnotes to Yeats's poems, the principle has been (as throughout this anthology) to give necessary background information without entering into interpretation or including biographical information for its own sake. With Yeats, however, the line dividing these areas from each other is not always easy to maintain, since the poems often make direct use of detail from Yeats's life and develop ideas and images that can be fully understood only by reference to other poems of Yeats's or to his prose. Although the notes are sometimes detailed, they are intended to provide a minimum background of essential matter, and to provide it, wherever possible, by citing complementary or explanatory passages from Yeats's own writings.

There's not a woman turns her face
Upon a broken tree,
15   And yet the beauties that I loved
Are in my memory;
I spit into the face of Time
That has transfigured me.

1892

The Magi

Now as at all times I can see in the mind's eye,[2]
In their stiff, painted clothes, the pale unsatisfied ones
Appear and disappear in the blue depth of the sky
With all their ancient faces like rain-beaten stones,
5   And all their helms of silver hovering side by side,
And all their eyes still fixed, hoping to find once more,
Being by Calvary's turbulence[3] unsatisfied,
The uncontrollable mystery on the bestial floor.

1914

Easter 1916[4]

I have met them at close of day
Coming with vivid faces
From counter or desk among gray
Eighteenth-century houses.
5   I have passed with a nod of the head
Or polite meaningless words,
Or have lingered awhile and said
Polite meaningless words,
And thought before I had done
10   Of a mocking tale or a gibe
To please a companion
Around the fire at the club,
Being certain that they and I
But lived where motley is worn:
15   All changed, changed utterly:
A terrible beauty is born.

That woman's days were spent
In ignorant good will,
Her nights in argument
20   Until her voice grew shrill.
What voice more sweet than hers
When, young and beautiful,
She rode to harriers?[5]

2. Yeats describes such a vision at the end of the essay "Symbolism in Painting" (1898): "Every visionary knows that the mind's eye soon comes to see a capricious and variable world, which the will cannot shape or change, though it can call it up and banish it again. I closed my eyes a moment ago, and a company of people in blue robes swept by in a blinding light * * * " In a note to "The Dolls" (1914), he says, "After I had made the poem, I looked up one day into the blue of the sky, and suddenly imagined, as if lost in the blue of the sky, stiff figures in procession. I remembered that they were the habitual image suggested by blue sky, and looking for a second fable called them 'The Magi,' * * * complementary forms of those enraged dolls."
3. "Turbulence" in the sense that, in Yeats's view of history as moving in cycles of roughly two thousand years each, the advent of the Christian era brought with it the destruction of the classical world and classical civilization.
4. An Irish Nationalist uprising had been planned for Easter Sunday 1916, and although the German ship which was bringing munitions had been intercepted by the British, attempts to postpone the uprising failed; it began in Dublin on Easter Monday. "Fifteen hundred men seized key points and an Irish republic was proclaimed from the General Post Office. After the initial surprise prompt British military action was taken, and when over 300 lives had been lost the insurgents were forced to surrender on 29 April * * * The seven signatories of the republican proclamation, including [Pádraic] Pearse and [James] Connolly, and nine others were shot after court martial between 3 and 12 May; 75 were reprieved and over 2000 held prisoners" [From "Ireland: History," by D. B. Quinn, in *Chambers's Encyclopedia*].
5. Countess Constance Georgina Markiewicz, *née* Gore-Booth, about whom Yeats wrote *On a Political Prisoner* and a later poem, *In Memory of Eva Gore-Booth and Con Markiewicz*.

This man had kept a school
25 And rode our wingéd horse;[6]
This other his helper and friend
Was coming into his force;
He might have won fame in the end,
So sensitive his nature seemed,
30 So daring and sweet his thought.
This other man I had dreamed
A drunken, vainglorious lout.[7]
He had done most bitter wrong
To some who are near my heart,
35 Yet I number him in the song;
He, too, has resigned his part
In the casual comedy;
He, too, has been changed in his turn,
Transformed utterly:
40 A terrible beauty is born.

Hearts with one purpose alone
Through summer and winter seem
Enchanted to a stone
To trouble the living stream.
45 The horse that comes from the road,
The rider, the birds that range
From cloud to tumbling cloud,
Minute by minute they change;
A shadow of cloud on the stream
50 Changes minute by minute;
A horse-hoof slides on the brim,
And a horse plashes within it;
The long-legged moor-hens dive,
And hens to moor-cocks call;
55 Minute by minute they live:
The stone's in the midst of all.

Too long a sacrifice
Can make a stone of the heart.
O when may it suffice?
60 That is Heaven's part, our part
To murmur name upon name,
As a mother names her child
When sleep at last has come
On limbs that had run wild.
65 What is it but nightfall?
No, no, not night but death;
Was it needless death after all?
For England may keep faith
For all that is done and said.
70 We know their dream; enough
To know they dreamed and are dead;
And what if excess of love
Bewildered them till they died?
I write it out in a verse—
75 MacDonagh and MacBride
And Connolly and Pearse
Now and in time to be,
Wherever green is worn,
Are changed, changed utterly:
80 A terrible beauty is born.

September 25, 1916   1916

6. Pádraic Pearse, headmaster of St. Enda's School, and a prolific writer of poems, plays, and stories as well as of essays on Irish politics and Gaelic literature. "This other" was Thomas MacDonough, also a schoolteacher.

7. Major John MacBride, who had married Maud Gonne (the woman with whom Yeats had for years been hopelessly in love) in 1903 and separated from her in 1905.

The Wild Swans at Coole[8]

The trees are in their autumn beauty,
The woodland paths are dry,
Under the October twilight the water
Mirrors a still sky;
5 Upon the brimming water among the stones
Are nine-and-fifty swans.

The nineteenth autumn has come upon me
Since I first made my count;[9]
I saw, before I had well finished,
10 All suddenly mount
And scatter wheeling in great broken rings
Upon their clamorous wings.

I have looked upon those brilliant creatures,
And now my heart is sore.
15 All's changed since I, hearing at twilight,
The first time on this shore,
The bell-beat of their wings above my head,
Trod with a lighter tread.

Unwearied still, lover by lover,
20 They paddle in the cold
Companionable streams or climb the air;
Their hearts have not grown old;
Passion or conquest, wander where they will,
Attend upon them still.

25 But now they drift on the still water,
Mysterious, beautiful;
Among what rushes will they build,
By what lake's edge or pool
Delight men's eyes when I awake some day
30 To find they have flown away?

1917

The Scholars

Bald heads forgetful of their sins,
Old, learned, respectable bald heads
Edit and annotate the lines
That young men, tossing on their beds,
5 Rhymed out in love's despair
To flatter beauty's ignorant ear.

All shuffle there; all cough in ink;
All wear the carpet with their shoes;
All think what other people think;
10 All know the man their neighbor knows.
Lord, what would they say
Did their Catullus walk that way?

1917

---

8. Coole Park, the estate in western Ireland   9. Yeats had first visted Coole Park in 1897;
of Lady Augusta Gregory, Yeats's patroness   the poem was written in October 1916.
and friend.

On a Political Prisoner[1]

She that but little patience knew,
From childhood on, had now so much
A gray gull lost its fear and flew
Down to her cell and there alit,
5   And there endured her fingers' touch
And from her fingers ate its bit.

Did she in touching that lone wing
Recall the years before her mind
Became a bitter, an abstract thing,
10   Her thought some popular enmity:
Blind and leader of the blind
Drinking the foul ditch where they lie?

When long ago I saw her ride
Under Ben Bulben[2] to the meet,
15   The beauty of her countryside
With all youth's lonely wildness stirred,
She seemed to have grown clean and sweet
Like any rock-bred, sea-borne bird:

Sea-borne, or balanced on the air
20   When first it sprang out of the nest
Upon some lofty rock to stare
Upon the cloudy canopy,
While under its storm-beaten breast
Cried out the hollows of the sea.

1921

The Second Coming

Turning and turning in the widening gyre[3]
The falcon cannot hear the falconer;
Things fall apart; the center cannot hold;
Mere anarchy is loosed upon the world,
5   The blood-dimmed tide is loosed, and everywhere
The ceremony of innocence is drowned;
The best lack all conviction, while the worst
Are full of passionate intensity.

Surely some revelation is at hand;
10   Surely the Second Coming is at hand;
The Second Coming! Hardly are those words out
When a vast image out of *Spiritus Mundi*[4]
Troubles my sight: somewhere in sands of the desert

1. The Countess Constance Georgina Markie-
wicz, *née* Gore-Booth, who was imprisoned in
Holloway Gaol for her part in the Easter Re-
bellion of 1916.
2. Mountain in County Sligo, in the West of
Ireland, where Yeats spent large parts of his
childhood and youth.
3. The gyre—the cone whose shape is traced
in the falcon's sweep upward and out in widen-
ing circles from the falconer who should con-
trol its flight—involves a reference to the
geometrical figure of the interpenetrating
cones, the "fundamental symbol" Yeats used
to diagram his cyclical view of history. (See
the opening pages of "The Great Wheel," in
A Vision [1937]). He saw the cycle of Greco-
Roman civilization as having been brought
to a close by the advent of Christianity, and
in the violence of his own times—"the growing
murderousness of the world"—he saw signs
that the 2000-year cycle of Christianity was
itself about to end, and to be replaced by a
system anithetical to it.
4. Or *Anima Mundi*, the Great Memory. "Be-
fore the mind's eye, whether in sleep or wak-
ing, came images that one was to discover
presently in some book one had never read,
and after looking in vain for explanation to
the current theory of forgotten personal
memory, I came to believe in a great memory
passing on from generation to generation
* * * Our daily thought was certainly but
the line of foam at the shallow edge of a vast
luminous sea" [*Per Amica Silentia Lunae*,
"Anima Mundi," § ii].

A shape with lion body and the head of a man,[5]
15 A gaze blank and pitiless as the sun,
Is moving its slow thighs, while all about it
Reel shadows of the indignant desert birds.
The darkness drops again; but now I know
That twenty centuries of stony sleep
20 Were vexed to nightmare by a rocking cradle,
And what rough beast, its hour come round at last,
Slouches towards Bethlehem to be born?

                                                                    1921

Leda and the Swan[6]

A sudden blow: the great wings beating still
Above the staggering girl, her thighs caressed
By the dark webs, her nape caught in his bill,
He holds her helpless breast upon his breast.

5 How can those terrified vague fingers push
The feathered glory from her loosening thighs?
And how can body, laid in that white rush,
But feel the strange heart beating where it lies?

A shudder in the loins engenders there
10 The broken wall, the burning roof and tower
And Agamemnon dead.
                            Being so caught up,
So mastered by the brute blood of the air,
Did she put on his knowledge with his power
15 Before the indifferent beak could let her drop?

                                              1923   1924

Sailing to Byzantium[7]

1

That is no country for old men. The young
In one another's arms, birds in the trees
—Those dying generations—at their song,

---

5. In the Introduction to his play *The Resurrection* (in *Wheels and Butterflies,* 1935), Yeats describes the way in which the sphinx image had first manifested itself to him: "Our civilisation was about to reverse itself, or some new civilisation about to be born from all that our age had rejected * * *; because we had worshipped a single god it would worship many * * * Had I begun *On Baile's Strand* or not when I began to imagine, as always at my left side just out of the range of the sight, a brazen winged beast (afterwards described in my poem *The Second Coming*) that I associated with laughing, ecstatic destruction?"
6. Leda, possessed by Zeus in the guise of a swan, gave birth to Helen of Troy and the twins Castor and Pollux. (Leda was also the mother of Clytemnestra, Agamemnon's wife, who murdered him on his return from the war at Troy.) Helen's abduction by Paris from her husband, Menelaus, brother of Agamemnon, was the cause of the Trojan war. Yeats saw Leda as the recipient of an annunciation that would found Greek civilization, as the Annunciation to Mary would found Christianity.
7. Of the ancient city of Byzantium—on the site of modern Istanbul, capital of the Eastern Roman Empire, and the center, especially in the fifth and sixth centuries, of highly developed and characteristic forms of art and architecture—Yeats made a many-faceted symbol, which, since it is a symbol, should not be brought within the limits of too narrowly specific interpretation. Byzantine painting and the mosaics which decorated its churches (Yeats had seen later derivatives of these mosaics in Italy, at Ravenna and elsewhere) were stylized and formal, making no attempt at the full naturalistic rendering of human forms, so that the city and its art can appropriately symbolize a way of life in which art is frankly accepted and proclaimed as artifice. As artifice, as a work of the intellect, this art is not subject to the decay and death which overtake the life of "natural things." But while such an opposition of artifice and nature is central to the poem, there are references to Byzantium in Yeats's prose which suggest the wider range of meaning that the city held for him. In *A Vision*, particularly, he makes of it an exemplar of a civilization which had achieved "Unity of Being": "I think if I could be given a month of Antiquity and leave to spend it where I chose, I would spend it in Byzantium a little before Justinian [who ruled at Byzantium from 527 to 565] opened St. Sophia and closed the Academy of Plato. I think I could find in some little wine-shop some philosophical worker in mosaic who could answer all my questions, the supernatural descending nearer to him than to Plotinus even, for the pride of his delicate skill would make what was an instrument of power to princes and clerics, a murderous madness in the mob, show as a lovely flexible presence like that of a perfect human body * * * I think that in early Byzantium, maybe never before or since in recorded history, religious, aesthetic and practical life were one, that architect and artificers * * * spoke to the multitude and the few alike. The painter, the mosaic worker, the worker in gold and silver, the illuminator of sacred books, were almost impersonal, almost perhaps without the consciousness of individual design, absorbed in their subject-matter and that the vision of a whole people."

The salmon-falls, the mackerel-crowded seas,
5 Fish, flesh, or fowl, commend all summer long
Whatever is begotten, born, and dies.
Caught in that sensual music all neglect
Monuments of unaging intellect.

2

An aged man is but a paltry thing,
10 A tattered coat upon a stick, unless
Soul clap its hands and sing, and louder sing
For every tatter in its mortal dress,
Nor is there singing school but studying
Monuments of its own magnificence;
15 And therefore I have sailed the seas and come
To the holy city of Byzantium.

3

O sages standing in God's holy fire
As in the gold mosaic of a wall,
Come from the holy fire, perne in a gyre,[8]
20 And be the singing-masters of my soul.
Consume my heart away; sick with desire
And fastened to a dying animal
It knows not what it is; and gather me
Into the artifice of eternity.

4

25 Once out of nature I shall never take
My bodily form from any natural thing,
But such a form as Grecian goldsmiths make
Of hammered gold and gold enameling
To keep a drowsy Emperor awake;
30 Or set upon a golden bough to sing
To lords and ladies of Byzantium
Of what is past, or passing, or to come.

                        1927

Among School Children

1

I walk through the long schoolroom questioning;
A kind old nun in a white hood replies;
The children learn to cipher and to sing,
To study reading-books and histories,
5 To cut and sew, be neat in everything
In the best modern way—the children's eyes
In momentary wonder stare upon
A sixty-year-old smiling public man.

2

I dream of a Ledaean body,[9] bent
10 Above a sinking fire, a tale that she
Told of a harsh reproof, or trivial event
That changed some childish day to tragedy—
Told, and it seemed that our two natures blent
Into a sphere from youthful sympathy,
15 Or else, to alter Plato's parable,
Into the yoke and white of the one shell.[10]

8. Out of the noun *pern* (usually *pirn*), a weaver's bobbin, spool, or reel, Yeats makes a verb meaning to move in the spiral pattern taken by thread being unwound from a bobbin or being wound upon it. Here the speaker entreats the sages to descend to him in this manner, to come down into the gyres of history, the cycles of created life, out of their eternity in "the simplicity of fire" where is "all music and all rest." (For "the two realities, the terrestrial and the condition of fire," see *Per Amica Silentia Lunae*, "Anima Mundi," § x.)
9. I.e., the body of a woman the poet has known and loved and who has seemed to him as beautiful as Leda or her daughter, Helen of Troy.
10. In Plato's *Symposium*, one of the speakers, to explain the origin of human love, recounts the legend according to which human beings were originally double their present form until Zeus, fearful of their power, decided to cut them in two, which he did "as men cut sorb-apples in two when they are preparing them for pickling, or as they cut eggs in two with a hair." Since then, "each of us is * * * but the half of a human being, * * * each is forever seeking his missing half."

3

And thinking of that fit of grief or rage
I look upon one child or t'other there
And wonder if she stood so at that age—
20   For even daughters of the swan can share
Something of every paddler's heritage—
And had that color upon cheek or hair,
And thereupon my heart is driven wild:
She stands before me as a living child.

4

25   Her present image floats into the mind—
Did Quattrocento finger[1] fashion it
Hollow of cheek as though it drank the wind
And took a mess of shadows for its meat?
And I though never of Ledaean kind
30   Had pretty plumage once—enough of that,
Better to smile on all that smile, and show
There is a comfortable kind of old scarecrow.

5

What youthful mother, a shape upon her lap
Honey of generation had betrayed,[2]
35   And that must sleep, shriek, struggle to escape
As recollection or the drug decide,
Would think her son, did she but see that shape
With sixty or more winters on its head,
A compensation for the pang of his birth,
40   Or the uncertainty of his setting forth?

6

Plato thought nature but a spume that plays
Upon a ghostly paradigm of things;[3]
Solider Aristotle played the taws
Upon the bottom of a king of kings;[4]
45   World-famous golden-thighed Pythagoras
Fingered upon a fiddle-stick or strings
What a star sang and careless Muses heard:[5]
Old clothes upon old sticks to scare a bird.

7

Both nuns and mothers worship images,
50   But those the candles light are not as those
That animate a mother's reveries,
But keep a marble or a bronze repose.
And yet they too break hearts—O Presences
That passion, piety or affection knows,
55   And that all heavenly glory symbolize—
O self-born mockers of man's enterprise;

8

Labor is blossoming or dancing where
The body is not bruised to pleasure soul,
Nor beauty born out of its own despair,

---

1. I.e., the hand of an Italian artist of the fifteenth century.
2. In a note to the poem, Yeats says: "I have taken the 'honey of generation' from Porphyry's essay on 'The Cave of the Nymphs' but find no warrant in Porphyry for considering it the 'drug' that destroys the 'recollection' of pre-natal freedom * * * " In the essay explaining the symbolism of a passage from the Thirteenth Book of the *Odyssey*, Porphyry (ca. A.D. 232–305) makes such statements as that "the sweetness of honey signifies * * * the same thing as the pleasure arising from copulation," the pleasure "which draws souls downward to generation."
3. In Plato's idealistic philosophy the world of nature, of appearances, that we know is but the copy of a world of ideal, permanently enduring prototypes.

4. The philosophy of Aristotle differed most markedly from that of Plato in that it emphasized the systematic investigation of verifiable phenomena. Aristotle was tutor to the son of King Philip of Macedonia, later Alexander the Great. "Played the taws": whipped.
5. A Greek philosopher (sixth century B.C.), about whom clustered many legends even in his own lifetime, as that he was the incarnation of Apollo, that he had a golden hip- or thigh-bone, and so on. Central to the Pythagorean school of philosophy (along with the doctrine of the transmigration of souls) was the premise that the universe is mathematically regular, which premise had as one of its starting points the Pythagoreans' observations of the exact mathematical relationships underlying musical harmony.

60 Nor blear-eyed wisdom out of midnight oil.
O chestnut-tree, great-rooted blossomer,
Are you the leaf, the blossom or the bole?
O body swayed to music, O brightening glance,
How can we know the dancer from the dance?

1927

At Algeciras[6]—A Meditation Upon Death

The heron-billed pale cattle-birds
That feed on some foul parasite
Of the Moroccan flocks and herds
Cross the narrow straits to light
5 In the rich midnight of the garden trees
Till the dawn break upon those mingled seas.
Often at evening when a boy
Would I carry to a friend—
Hoping more substantial joy
10 Did an older mind commend—
Not such as are in Newton's metaphor,[7]
But actual shells of Rosses' level shore.[8]

Greater glory in the sun,
An evening chill upon the air,
15 Bid imagination run
Much on the Great Questioner;
What He can question, what if questioned I
Can with a fitting confidence reply.

November 1928   1929

Coole Park and Ballylee, 1931[9]

Under my window-ledge the waters race,
Otters below and moor-hens on the top,
Run for a mile undimmed in heaven's face
Then darkening through "dark" Raftery's "cellar" drop,
5 Run underground, rise in a rocky place
In Coole demesne, and there to finish up
Spread to a lake and drop into a hole.[1]
What's water but the generated soul?[2]

Upon the border of that lake's a wood
10 Now all dry sticks under a wintry sun,
And in a copse of beeches there I stood,
For Nature's pulled her tragic buskin[3] on

6. A town in Spain, lying across the Straits of Gibraltar (where Atlantic and Mediterranean waters meet) from Spanish Morocco.
7. " 'I seem to have been only like a boy playing on the seashore and diverting myself in now and then finding a smoother pebble, or a prettier shell, than ordinary, whilst the great ocean of truth lay all undiscovered before me' " [Newton, in Brewster's *Memoirs of the Life, Writings and Discoveries of Sir Isaac Newton*, vol. 2, chapter 27].
8. Rosses Point, on Sligo Bay, in the west of Ireland.
9. Coole Park, near Gort in County Galway, was the estate of Lady Augusta Gregory (ca. 1859–1932), the playwright who had been Yeats's collaborator in his early efforts to found an Irish national theater, and who was his lifelong friend. Thoor (Tower) Ballylee was the half-ruined square castle or tower, once a part of Coole estate, which Yeats had bought in 1917 and put into repair for a dwelling.

1. The nearly-blind Gaelic poet Raftery, in a poem about the beautiful Mary Hynes, had said "there is a strong cellar in Ballylee," and Yeats describes in an early essay how a guide had told him that by this was meant "the great hole where the river sank under ground, and he brought me to a deep pool where an otter hurried away under a grey boulder * * *"
2. In an essay "On the Cave of the Nymphs in the Thirteenth Book of the Odyssey," to which Yeats occasionally refers, the neoplatonist philosopher Porphyry (ca. A.D. 232–305) speaks of souls as "descending into generation" out of their free pre-existent state, and says that the ancients thought such souls had a particular involvement with water, itself related to divinity.
3. The half-boot worn by actors in Greek tragedy.

And all the rant's a mirror of my mood:
At sudden thunder of the mounting swan
15 I turned about and looked where branches break
The glittering reaches of the flooded lake.

Another emblem there! That stormy white
But seems a concentration of the sky;
And, like the soul, it sails into the sight
20 And in the morning's gone, no man knows why;
And is so lovely that it sets to right
What knowledge or its lack had set awry,
So arrogantly pure, a child might think
It can be murdered with a spot of ink.

25 Sound of a stick upon the floor, a sound
From somebody that toils from chair to chair;[4]
Beloved books that famous hands have bound,
Old marble heads, old pictures everywhere;
Great rooms where traveled men and children found
30 Content or joy; a last inheritor
Where none has reigned that lacked a name and fame
Or out of folly into folly came.

A spot whereon the founders lived and died
Seemed once more dear than life; ancestral trees,
35 Or gardens rich in memory glorified
Marriages, alliances and families,
And every bride's ambition satisfied.
Where fashion or mere fantasy decrees
We shift about—all that great glory spent—
40 Like some poor Arab tribesman and his tent.

We were the last romantics—chose for theme
Traditional sanctity and loveliness;
Whatever's written in what poets name
The book of the people; whatever most can bless
45 The mind of man or elevate a rhyme;
But all is changed, that high horse riderless,
Though mounted in that saddle Homer rode
Where the swan drifts upon a darkening flood.

1932

Byzantium[5]

The unpurged images of day recede;
The Emperor's drunken soldiery are abed;
Night resonance recedes, night-walkers' song
After great cathedral gong;
5 A starlit or a moonlit dome disdains[6]
All that man is,
All mere complexities,
The fury and the mire of human veins.

4. This stanza refers to Lady Gregory, living alone in the last year of her life on the estate of which she was "last inheritor," her only son, Major Robert Gregory, having died in the First World War.
5. Under the heading "Subject for a Poem," April 30th," Yeats wrote in his *1930 Diary*: "Describe Byzantium as it is in the system [that is, his system in *A Vision*] towards the end of the first Christian millennium. A walking mummy. Flames at the street corners where the soul is purified, birds of hammered gold singing in the golden trees, in the harbor [dolphins], offering their backs to the wailing dead that they may carry them to Paradise."
6. If the dome is seen as "starlit" at the dark of the moon and as "moonlit" at the full, then these terms may be seen as referring to Phase

1 and Phase 15, respectively, of the twenty-eight phases of the moon in the system of *A Vision*. As Michael Robartes says in *The Phases of the Moon,* "* * * There's no human life at the full or the dark," these being "the superhuman phases," opposite to one another on the Wheel of Being. Phase 1 is the phase of complete objectivity, the soul being "completely absorbed by its supernatural environment," waiting to be formed, in a state of "complete plasticity." Phase 15 is the state of complete subjectivity, when the soul is completely absorbed in an achieved state, "a phase of complete beauty." Thus, the world of "mere complexities," the world in which man is in a state of becoming, is banished from the poem at the beginning, as the "unpurged images of day" have been banished.

Before me floats an image, man or shade,
10 Shade more than man, more image than a shade;
For Hades' bobbin bound in mummy-cloth
May unwind the winding path;[7]
A mouth that has no moisture and no breath
Breathless mouths may summon;[8]
15 I hail the superhuman;
I call it death-in-life and life-in-death.

Miracle, bird or golden handiwork,
More miracle than bird or handiwork,
Planted on the starlit golden bough,
20 Can like the cocks of Hades crow,[9]
Or, by the moon embittered, scorn aloud
In glory of changeless metal
Common bird or petal
And all complexities of mire or blood.

25 At midnight on the Emperor's pavement flit
Flames that no faggot feeds, nor steel has lit,
Nor storm disturbs, flames begotten of flame,
Where blood-begotten spirits come
And all complexities of fury leave,
30 Dying into a dance,
An agony of trance,
An agony of flame that cannot singe a sleeve.

Astraddle on the dolphin's mire and blood,
Spirit after spirit! The smithies break the flood.
35 The golden smithies of the Emperor!
Marbles of the dancing floor
Break bitter furies of complexity,
Those images that yet
Fresh images beget,
That dolphin-torn, that gong-tormented sea.

1930   1932

Lapis Lazuli[1]

(FOR HARRY CLIFTON)

I have heard that hysterical women say
They are sick of the palette and fiddle-bow,
Of poets that are always gay,
For everybody knows or else should know
5 That if nothing drastic is done
Aeroplane and Zeppelin will come out,
Pitch like King Billy[2] bomb-balls in
Until the town lie beaten flat.

7. The soul and/or body of the dead. The comparison to the bobbin or spindle is at first visual, to describe the figure of the dead, wrapped in a winding-sheet or mummy-cloth, but it also emphasizes the idea that the soul may unwind the thread of its fate by retracing its path, returning to the world to serve as guide, instructor, inspiration.
8. The two lines have been read in two different ways, depending on which of the two phrases ("a mouth * * * " or "breathless mouths * * * ") is seen as subject and which as object of "may summon." Taking "breathless mouths" as subject: mouths of the living, breathless with the intensity of the act of invocation, may call up the mouths of the dead to instruct them.
9. A symbol of rebirth and resurrection. In a book on Roman sculpture which Yeats is believed to have known, *Apotheosis and After Life* (1915), Mrs. Arthur Strong says: "* * * The great vogue of the cock on later Roman tombstones is due * * * to the fact that as herald of the sun he becomes by an easy transi-

tion the herald of rebirth and resurrection." In the next sentence she mentions another visual symbol which figures in the poem's last stanza: "The dolphins and marine monsters, another frequent decoration, form a mystic escort of the dead to the Islands of the Blest * * * "
1. A deep-blue semi-precious stone. In a letter dated July 6, 1935, Yeats wrote, "* * * Someone has sent me a present of a great piece [of lapis lazuli] carved by some Chinese sculptor into the semblance of a mountain with temple, trees, paths and an ascetic and pupil about to climb the mountain. Ascetic, pupil, hard stone, eternal theme of the sensual east. The heroic cry in the midst of despair. But no, I am wrong, the east has its solutions always and therefore knows nothing of tragedy. It is we, not the east, that must raise the heroic cry."
2. At the Battle of the Boyne on July 1, 1690, William III, king of England since 1689, had defeated the forces of the deposed king, James II.

All perform their tragic play,
10 There struts Hamlet, there is Lear,
That's Ophelia, that Cordelia;
Yet they, should the last scene be there,
The great stage curtain about to drop,
If worthy their prominent part in the play,
15 Do not break up their lines to weep.
They know that Hamlet and Lear are gay;
Gaiety transfiguring all that dread.
All men have aimed at, found and lost;
Black out; Heaven blazing into the head:
20 Tragedy wrought to its uttermost.
Though Hamlet rambles and Lear rages,
And all the drop-scenes drop at once
Upon a hundred thousand stages,
It cannot grow by an inch or an ounce.

25 On their own feet they came, or on shipboard,
Camelback, horseback, ass-back, mule-back,
Old civilizations put to the sword.
Then they and their wisdom went to rack:
No handiwork of Callimachus,[3]
30 Who handled marble as if it were bronze,
Made draperies that seemed to rise
When sea-wind swept the corner, stands;
His long lamp-chimney shaped like the stem
Of a slender palm, stood but a day;
35 All things fall and are built again,
And those that build them again are gay.

Two Chinamen, behind them a third,
Are carved in lapis lazuli,
Over them flies a long-legged bird,
40 A symbol of longevity;
The third, doubtless a serving-man,
Carries a musical instrument.

Every discoloration of the stone,
Every accidental crack or dent,
45 Seems a water-course or an avalanche,
Or lofty slope where it still snows
Though doubtless plum or cherry-branch
Sweetens the little half-way house
Those Chinamen climb towards, and I
50 Delight to imagine them seated there;
There, on the mountain and the sky,
On all the tragic scene they stare.
One asks for mournful melodies;
Accomplished fingers begin to play.
55 Their eyes mid many wrinkles, their eyes,
Their ancient, glittering eyes, are gay.

1938

3. Greek sculptor of the fifth century B.C., of whom Yeats says in *A Vision* that only one example of his work remains, a marble chair, and goes on to mention "that bronze lamp [in the Erechtheum, a temple of the guardian deities of Athens] shaped like a palm, known to us by a description in Pausanias * * *"

Long-Legged Fly

That civilization may not sink,
Its great battle lost,
Quiet the dog, tether the pony
To a distant post;
5   Our master Caesar is in the tent
Where the maps are spread,
His eyes fixed upon nothing,
A hand under his head.
Like a long-legged fly upon the stream
10 *His mind moves upon silence.*

That the topless towers be burnt
And men recall that face,[4]
Move most gently if move you must
In this lonely place.
15 She thinks, part woman, three parts a child,
That nobody looks; her feet
Practice a tinker shuffle
Picked up on a street.
Like a long-legged fly upon the stream
20 *Her mind moves upon silence.*

That girls at puberty may find
The first Adam in their thought,
Shut the door of the Pope's chapel,[5]
Keep those children out.
25 There on that scaffolding reclines
Michael Angelo.
With no more sound than the mice make
His hand moves to and fro.
Like a long-legged fly upon the stream
30 *His mind moves upon silence.*

1939

The Black Tower

Say that the men of the old black tower,
Though they but feed as the goatherd feeds,
Their money spent, their wine gone sour,
Lack nothing that a soldier needs,
5   That all are oath-bound men:
Those banners come not in.

There in the tomb stand the dead upright,
But winds come up from the shore:
They shake when the winds roar,
10 *Old bones upon the mountain shake.*

Those banners come to bribe or threaten,
Or whisper that a man's a fool
Who, when his own right king's forgotten,
Cares what king sets up his rule.
15 If he died long ago
Why do you dread us so?

---

4. An echo of Marlowe's lines on Helen of Troy in *Dr. Faustus:* "Was this the face that launched a thousand ships, / And burnt the topless towers of Ilium?"

5. On the ceiling of the Sistine Chapel, so called because it was built under Pope Sixtus IV, Michelangelo painted a series of biblical scenes, including the creation of Adam.

There in the tomb drops the faint moonlight,
But wind comes up from the shore:
They shake when the winds roar,
20   *Old bones upon the mountain shake.*

The tower's old cook that must climb and clamber
Catching small birds in the dew of the morn
When we hale men lie stretched in slumber
Swears that he hears the king's great horn.
25   But he's a lying hound:
Stand we on guard oath-bound!

There in the tomb the dark grows blacker,
But wind comes up from the shore:
They shake when the winds roar,
30   *Old bones upon the mountain shake.*

January 21, 1939   1939

Under Ben Bulben[6]

1

Swear by what the sages spoke
Round the Mareotic Lake[7]
That the Witch of Atlas knew,
Spoke and set the cocks a-crow.[8]

5   Swear by those horsemen, by those women
Complexion and form prove superhuman,
That pale, long-visaged company
That air in immortality
Completeness of their passions won;
10   Now they ride the wintry dawn
Where Ben Bulben sets the scene.[9]

Here's the gist of what they mean.

2

Many times man lives and dies
Between his two eternities,
15   That of race and that of soul,
And ancient Ireland knew it all.
Whether man die in his bed
Or the rifle knocks him dead,
A brief parting from those dear
20   Is the worst man has to fear.
Though gravediggers' toil is long,
Sharp their spades, their muscles strong,
They but thrust their buried men
Back in the human mind again.

6. A mountain in County Sligo, in the west of Ireland, which overlooks Drumcliff Church-yard, where Yeats is buried. The last three lines of the poem are carved on his tombstone.
7. Lake Mareotis, a salt lake in northern Egypt, near which the members of the Thebaid, among them St. Anthony (A.D. 251–356) had withdrawn to contemplation. About the The-baid, in his *1930 Diary*, Yeats wrote, "* * * men went on pilgrimage to Saint Anthony that they might learn about their spiritual states, what was about to happen and why it happened, and Saint Anthony would reply neither out of traditional casuistry nor com-mon sense but from spiritual powers."
8. In Shelley's poem *The Witch of Atlas*, the protagonist, a spirit of love, beauty, and freedom, visits Egypt and the Mareotic Lake in the course of her magic journeyings. The knowledge and belief that Yeats describes as common to her and to the sages "set the cocks a-crow" in the sense that, like "the cocks of Hades" and the golden bird in *Byzantium*, they summon to a spiritual rebirth.
9. In another late poem, *Alternative Song for the Severed Head in "The King of the Great Clock Tower,"* Yeats re-introduces some of the Irish mythological or legendary heroes and heroines who figure in his early poems—Cuchulain, Niam, and others—with whom the supernatural riders of these lines may be identified.

3

²⁵ You that Mitchel's prayer have heard,
"Send war in our time, O Lord!"[1]
Know that when all words are said
And a man is fighting mad,
Something drops from eyes long blind,
³⁰ He completes his partial mind,
For an instant stands at ease,
Laughs aloud, his heart at peace.
Even the wisest man grows tense
With some sort of violence
³⁵ Before he can accomplish fate,
Know his work or choose his mate.

4

Poet and sculptor, do the work,
Nor let the modish painter shirk
What his great forefathers did,
⁴⁰ Bring the soul of man to God,
Make him fill the cradles right.

Measurement began our might:[2]
Forms a stark Egyptian thought,
Forms that gentler Phidias wrought.
⁴⁵ Michael Angelo left a proof
On the Sistine Chapel roof,
Where but half-awakened Adam
Can disturb globe-trotting Madam
Till her bowels are in heat,
⁵⁰ Proof that there's a purpose set
Before the secret working mind:
Profane perfection of mankind.

Quattrocento[3] put in paint
On backgrounds for a God or Saint
⁵⁵ Gardens where a soul's at ease;
Where everything that meets the eye,
Flowers and grass and cloudless sky,
Resemble forms that are or seem
When sleepers wake and yet still dream,
⁶⁰ And when it's vanished still declare,
With only bed and bedstead there,
That heavens had opened.
                    Gyres[4] run on;
When that greater dream had gone
⁶⁵ Calvert and Wilson, Blake and Claude,
Prepared a rest for the people of God,
Palmer's phrase, but after that[5]
Confusion fell upon our thought.

1. John Mitchel (1815–75), the Irish patriot, wrote in his *Jail Journal, or Five Years in British Prisons* (published in New York, 1854): "Czar, I bless thee, I kiss the hem of thy garment. I drink to thy health and longevity. Give us war in our time, O Lord" [Quoted by T. R. Henn, *The Lonely Tower*].
2. The achievements of Western civilization—now, according to the poem, being challenged or destroyed—began with the exact mathematical rules which the Egyptians followed in working out the proportions of their sculptured figures—rules which Phidias (line 44), the great Greek sculptor of the fifth century B.C., used, and which have been implicit in the greatest Western art up to the present, when "confusion [falls] upon our thought."
3. The Italian fifteenth century.
4. I.e., the cycles of history.
5. The verse paragraph assembles five artists who had provided Yeats with images and with ideals of what art should be. Claude Lorrain (1600–82), the great French landscape painter, was a central standard for landscape painters up to the early 19th century, including those mentioned here, especially Richard Wilson (1714–82). Edward Calvert (1799–1883) and Samuel Palmer (1805–81), visionaries, landscape painters, and engravers, had found inspiration in many aspects of Blake's life and work.

5

Irish poets, learn your trade,
70   Sing whatever is well made,
Scorn the sort now growing up
All out of shape from toe to top,
Their unremembering hearts and heads
Base-born products of base beds.
75   Sing the peasantry, and then
Hard-riding country gentlemen,
The holiness of monks, and after
Porter-drinkers' randy laughter;
Sing the lords and ladies gay
80   That were beaten into the clay
Through seven heroic centuries;
Cast your mind on other days
That we in coming days may be
Still the indomitable Irishry.

6

85   Under bare Ben Bulben's head
In Drumcliff churchyard Yeats is laid.
An ancestor was rector there
Long years ago, a church stands near,
By the road an ancient cross.
90   No marble, no conventional phrase;
On limestone quarried near the spot
By his command these words are cut:

Cast a cold eye
On life, on death.
95   *Horseman, pass by!*

September 4, 1938   1939

WALTER DE LA MARE
(1867–1900)

The Keys of Morning

While at her bedroom window once,
    Learning her task for school,
Little Louisa lonely sat
    In the morning clear and cool,
5   She slanted her small bead-brown eyes
    Across the empty street,
And saw Death softly watching her
    In the sunshine pale and sweet.

His was a long lean sallow face;
10   He sat with half-shut eyes,
Like an old sailor in a ship
    Becalmed 'neath tropic skies.
Beside him in the dust he had set
    His staff and shady hat;
15   These, peeping small, Louisa saw
    Quite clearly where she sat—
The thinness of his coal-black locks,
    His hands so long and lean
They scarcely seemed to grasp at all
20   The keys that hung between:
Both were of gold, but one was small,
    And with this last did he
Wag in the air, as if to say,
    "Come hither, child, to me!"

25 Louisa laid her lesson book
        On the cold window-sill;
    And in the sleepy sunshine house
        Went softly down, until
    She stood in the half-opened door,
30   And peeped. But strange to say,
    Where Death just now had sunning sat
        Only a shadow lay:
    Just the tall chimney's round-topped cowl,
        And the small sun behind,
35 Had with its shadow in the dust
        Called sleepy Death to mind.
    But most she thought how strange it was
        Two keys that he should bear,
    And that, when beckoning, he should wag
40   The littlest in the air.

                                                    1912

The Moth

Isled in the midnight air,
Musked with the dark's faint bloom,
Out into glooming and secret haunts
        The flame cries, "Come!"

5 Lovely in dye and fan,
A-tremble in shimmering grace,
A moth from her winter swoon
        Uplifts her face:

Stares from her glamorous eyes;
10 Wafts her on plumes like mist;
In ecstasy swirls and sways
        To her strange tryst.

                                                    1921

Goodbye

The last of last words spoken is Goodbye—
The last dismantled flower in the weed-grown hedge,
The last thin rumor of a feeble bell far ringing,
The last blind rat to spurn the mildewed rye.

5 A hardening darkness glasses the haunted eye,
Shines into nothing the watcher's burnt-out candle,
Wreathes into scentless nothing the wasting incense,
Faints in the outer silence the hunting-cry.

Love of its muted music breathes no sigh,
10 Thought in her ivory tower gropes in her spinning,
Toss on in vain the whispering trees of Eden,
Last of all last words spoken is Goodbye.

                                                    1921

Away

There is no sorrow
Time heals never;
No loss, betrayal,
Beyond repair.
5 Balm for the soul, then,
Though grave shall sever
Lover from loved

And all they share;
See, the sweet sun shines,
10   The shower is over,
Flowers preen their beauty,
The day how fair!
Brood not too closely
On love, or duty;
15   Friends long forgotten
May wait you where
Life with death
Brings all to an issue;
None will long mourn for you,
20   Pray for you, miss you,
Your place left vacant,
You not there.

1938

EDWIN ARLINGTON ROBINSON
(1869–1935)

Reuben Bright

Because he was a butcher and thereby
Did earn an honest living (and did right),
I would not have you think that Reuben Bright
Was any more a brute than you or I;
5   For when they told him that his wife must die,
He stared at them, and shook with grief and fright,
And cried like a great baby half that night,
And made the women cry to see him cry.

And after she was dead, and he had paid
10   The singers and the sexton and the rest,
He packed a lot of things that she had made
Most mournfully away in an old chest
Of hers, and put some chopped-up cedar boughs
In with them, and tore down the slaughter-house.

1897

Miniver Cheevy

Miniver Cheevy, child of scorn,
   Grew lean while he assailed the seasons;
He wept that he was ever born,
   And he had reasons.

5   Miniver loved the days of old
   When swords were bright and steeds were prancing;
The vision of a warrior bold
   Would set him dancing.

Miniver sighed for what was not,
10   And dreamed, and rested from his labors;
He dreamed of Thebes and Camelot,
   And Priam's neighbors.[1]

---

1. Thebes was a Greek city, anciently famous in history and legend; Camelot is said to have been the site of King Arthur's court; Priam was king of Troy during the Trojan War.

Miniver mourned the ripe renown
   That made so many a name so fragrant;
15 He mourned Romance, now on the town,
   And Art, a vagrant.

Miniver loved the Medici,[2]
   Albeit he had never seen one;
He would have sinned incessantly
20   Could he have been one.

Miniver cursed the commonplace
   And eyed a khaki suit with loathing;
He missed the medieval grace
   Of iron clothing.

25 Miniver scorned the gold he sought,
   But sore annoyed was he without it;
Miniver thought, and thought, and thought,
   And thought about it.

Miniver Cheevy, born too late,
30   Scratched his head and kept on thinking;
Miniver coughed, and called it fate,
   And kept on drinking.

                            1910

New England

Here where the wind is always north-north-east
And children learn to walk on frozen toes,
Wonder begets an envy of all those
Who boil elsewhere with such a lyric yeast
5 Of love that you will hear them at a feast
Where demons would appeal for some repose,
Still clamoring where the chalice overflows
And crying wildest who have drunk the least.

Passion is here a soilure of the wits,
10 We're told, and Love a cross for them to bear;
Joy shivers in the corner where she knits
And Conscience always has the rocking-chair,
Cheerful as when she tortured into fits
The first cat that was ever killed by Care.

                            1925

STEPHEN CRANE
(1871–1900)

In a Lonely Place

In a lonely place,
I encountered a sage
Who sat, all still,
Regarding a newspaper.
5 He accosted me:
"Sir, what is this?"
Then I saw that I was greater,

---

2. A family of merchant-princes of the Italian Renaissance, rulers of Florence for nearly two centuries; they were known both for cruelty and for their support of learning and art.

Aye, greater than this sage.
I answered him at once:
10   "Old, old man, it is the wisdom of the age."
The sage looked upon me with admiration.

1895

There Was Crimson Clash of War

There was crimson clash of war.
Lands turned black and bare;
Women wept;
Babes ran, wondering.
5   There came one who understood not these things.
He said: "Why is this?"
Whereupon a million strove to answer him.
There was such intricate clamor of tongues,
That still the reason was not.

1895

PAUL LAURENCE DUNBAR
(1872–1906)

Ere Sleep Comes Down to Soothe the Weary Eyes

Ere sleep comes down to soothe the weary eyes,
    Which all the day with ceaseless care have sought
The magic gold which from the seeker flies;
    Ere dreams put on the gown and cap of thought,
5   And make the waking world a world of lies—
    Of lies most palpable, uncouth, forlorn,
That say life's full of aches and tears and sighs—
    Oh, how with more than dreams the soul is torn,
Ere sleep comes down to soothe the weary eyes.

10   Ere sleep comes down to soothe the weary eyes,
    How all the griefs and heartaches we have known
Come up like pois'nous vapors that arise
    From some base witch's caldron, when the crone,
To work some potent spell, her magic plies.
15   The past which held its share of bitter pain,
Whose ghost we prayed that Time might exorcise,
    Comes up, is lived and suffered o'er again,
Ere sleep comes down to soothe the weary eyes.

Ere sleep comes down to soothe the weary eyes,
20   What phantoms fill the dimly lighted room;
What ghostly shades in awe-creating guise
    Are bodied forth within the teeming gloom.
What echoes faint of sad and soul-sick cries,
    And pangs of vague inexplicable pain
25   That pay the spirit's ceaseless enterprise,
    Come thronging through the chambers of the brain,
Ere sleep comes down to soothe the weary eyes.

Ere sleep comes down to soothe the weary eyes,
    Where ranges forth the spirit far and free?
30   Through what strange realms and unfamiliar skies
    Tends her far course to lands of mystery?

To lands unspeakable—beyond surmise,
    Where shapes unknowable to being spring,
Till, faint of wing, the Fancy fails and dies
35   Much wearied with the spirit's journeying,
Ere sleep comes down to soothe the weary eyes.

Ere sleep comes down to soothe the weary eyes,
    How questioneth the soul that other soul—
The inner sense which neither cheats nor lies,
40   But self exposes unto self, a scroll
Full writ with all life's acts unwise or wise,
    In characters indelible and known;
So, trembling with the shock of sad surprise,
    The soul doth view its awful self alone,
45 Ere sleep comes down to soothe the weary eyes.

When sleep comes down to seal the weary eyes,
    The last dear sleep whose soft embrace is balm,
And whom sad sorrow teaches us to prize
    For kissing all our passions into calm,
50 Ah, then, no more we heed the sad world's cries,
    Or seek to probe th' eternal mystery,
Or fret our souls at long-withheld replies,
    At glooms through which our visions cannot see,
When sleep comes down to seal the weary eyes.

1896

When Malindy Sings

G'way an' quit dat noise, Miss Lucy—
    Put dat music book away;
What's de use to keep on tryin'?
    Ef you practise twell you're gray,
5 You cain't sta't no notes a-flyin'
    Lak de ones dat rants and rings
F'om de kitchen to de big woods
    When Malindy sings.

You ain't got de nachel o'gans
10   Fu' to make de soun' come right,
You ain't got de tu'ns an' twistin's
    Fu' to make it sweet an' light.
Tell you one thing now, Miss Lucy,
    An' I'm tellin' you fu' true,
15 When hit comes to raal right singin',
    'T ain't no easy thing to do.

Easy 'nough fu' folks to hollah,
    Lookin' at de lines an' dots,
When dey ain't no one kin sence it,
20   An' de chune comes in, in spots;
But fu' real melojous music,
    Dat jes' strikes yo' hea't and clings,
Jes' you stan' an' listen wif me
    When Malindy sings.

25 Ain't you nevah hyeahd Malindy?
    Blessed soul, tek up de cross!
Look hyeah, ain't you jokin', honey?
    Well, you don't know whut you los'.
Y' ought to hyeah dat gal a-wa'blin',
30   Robins, la'ks, an' all dem things,
Heish dey moufs an' hides dey face.
    When Malindy sings.

Fiddlin' man jes' stop his fiddlin',
　　Lay his fiddle on de she'f;
35 Mockin'-bird quit tryin' to whistle,
　　'Cause he jes' so shamed hisse'f.
Folks a-playin' on de banjo
　　Draps dey fingahs on de strings—
Bless yo' soul—fu'gits to move em,
40　　When Malindy sings.

She jes' spreads huh mouf and hollahs,
　　"Come to Jesus," twell you hyeah
Sinnahs' tremblin' steps and voices
　　Timid-lak a-drawin' neah;
45 Den she tu'ns to "Rock of Ages,"
　　Simply to de cross she clings,
An' you fin' yo' teahs a-drappin'
　　When Malindy sings.

Who dat says dat humble praises
50　　Wif de Master nevah counts?
Heish yo' mouf, I hyeah dat music,
　　Ez hit rises up an' mounts—
Floatin' by de hills an' valleys,
　　Way above dis buryin' sod,
55 Ez hit makes its way in glory
　　To de very gates of God!

Oh, hit's sweetah dan de music
　　Of an edicated band;
An' hit's dearah dan de battle's
60　　Song o' triumph in de lan'.
It seems holier dan evenin'
　　When de solemn chu'ch bell rings,
Ez I sit an' ca'mly listen
　　While Malindy sings.

65 Towsah, stop dat ba'kin', hyeah me!
　　Mandy, mek dat chile keep still;
Don't you hyeah de echoes callin'
　　F'om de valley to de hill?
Let me listen, I can hyeah it,
70　　Th'oo de bresh of angels' wings,
Sof' an' sweet, "Swing Low,
　　Sweet Chariot,"
Ez Malindy sings.

1896

ROBERT FROST
(1874–1963)

The Tuft of Flowers

I went to turn the grass once after one
Who moved it in the dew before the sun.

The dew was gone that made his blade so keen
Before I came to view the levelled scene.

5　I looked for him behind an isle of trees;
I listened for his whetstone on the breeze.

But he had gone his way, the grass all mown,
And I must be, as he had been—alone,

'As all must be,' I said within my heart,
10 'Whether they work together or apart.'

But as I said it, swift there passed me by
On noiseless wing a bewildered butterfly,

Seeking with memories grown dim o'er night
Some resting flower of yesterday's delight.

15 And once I marked his flight go round and round,
As where some flower lay withering on the ground.

And then he flew as far as eye could see,
And then on tremulous wing came back to me.

I thought of questions that have no reply,
20 And would have turned to toss the grass to dry;

But he turned first, and led my eye to look
At a tall tuft of flowers beside a brook,

A leaping tongue of bloom the scythe had spared
Beside a reedy brook the scythe had bared.

25 I left my place to know them by their name,
Finding them butterfly weed when I came.

The mower in the dew had loved them thus,
By leaving them to flourish, not for us,

Nor yet to draw one thought of ours to him,
30 But from sheer morning gladness at the brim.

The butterfly and I had lit upon,
Nevertheless, a message from the dawn,

That made me hear the wakening birds around,
And hear his long scythe whispering to the ground,

35 And feel a spirit kindred to my own;
So that henceforth I worked no more alone;

But glad with him, I worked as with his aid,
And weary, sought at noon with him the shade;

And dreaming, as it were, held brotherly speech
40 With one whose thought I had not hoped to reach.

'Men work together,' I told him from the heart,
'Whether they work together or apart.'

1913

Mending Wall

Something there is that doesn't love a wall,
That sends the frozen-ground-swell under it,
And spills the upper boulders in the sun;
And makes gaps even two can pass abreast.
5 The work of hunters is another thing:

I have come after them and made repair
Where they have left not one stone on a stone,
But they would have the rabbit out of hiding,
To please the yelping dogs. The gaps I mean,
10   No one has seen them made or heard them made,
But at spring mending-time we find them there.
I let my neighbor know beyond the hill;
And on a day we meet to walk the line
And set the wall between us once again.
15   We keep the wall between us as we go.
To each the boulders that have fallen to each.
And some are loaves and some so nearly balls
We have to use a spell to make them balance:
'Stay where you are until our backs are turned!'
20   We wear our fingers rough with handling them.
Oh, just another kind of out-door game,
One on a side. It comes to little more:
There where it is we do not need the wall:
He is all pine and I am apple orchard.
25   My apple trees will never get across
And eat the cones under his pines, I tell him.
He only says, 'Good fences make good neighbors.'
Spring is the mischief in me, and I wonder
If I could put a notion in his head:
30   '*Why* do they make good neighbors? Isn't it
Where there are cows? But here there are no cows.
Before I built a wall I'd ask to know
What I was walling in or walling out,
And to whom I was like to give offense.
35   Something there is that doesn't love a wall,
That wants it down.' I could say 'Elves' to him,
But it's not elves exactly, and I'd rather
He said it for himself. I see him there
Bringing a stone grasped firmly by the top
40   In each hand, like an old-stone savage armed.
He moves in darkness as it seems to me,
Not of woods only and the shade of trees.
He will not go behind his father's saying,
And he likes having thought of it so well
45   He says again, 'Good fences make good neighbors.'

                                                    1914

The Wood-Pile

Out walking in the frozen swamp one gray day,
I paused and said, 'I will turn back from here.
No, I will go on farther—and we shall see.'
The hard snow held me, save where now and then
5   One foot went through. The view was all in lines
Straight up and down of tall slim trees
Too much alike to mark or name a place by
So as to say for certain I was here
Or somewhere else: I was just far from home.
10   A small bird flew before me. He was careful
To put a tree between us when he lighted,
And say no word to tell me who he was
Who was so foolish as to think what *he* thought.
He thought that I was after him for a feather—
15   The white one in his tail; like one who takes
Everything said as personal to himself.
One flight out sideways would have undeceived him.
And then there was a pile of wood for which

I forgot him and let his little fear
20 Carry him off the way I might have gone,
Without so much as wishing him good-night.
He went behind it to make his last stand.
It was a cord of maple, cut and split
And piled—and measured, four by four by eight.
25 And not another like it could I see.
No runner tracks in this year's snow looped near it.
And it was older sure than this year's cutting,
Or even last year's or the year's before.
The wood was gray and the bark warping off it
30 And the pile somewhat sunken. Clematis
Had wound strings round and round it like a bundle.
What held it though on one side was a tree
Still growing, and on one a stake and prop,
These latter about to fall. I thought that only
35 Someone who lived in turning to fresh tasks
Could so forget his handiwork in which
He spent himself, the labor of his axe,
And leave it there far from a useful fireplace
To warm the frozen swamp as best it could
40 With the slow smokeless burning of decay.

1914

The Oven Bird

There is a singer everyone has heard,
Loud, a mid-summer and a mid-wood bird,
Who makes the solid tree trunks sound again.
He says that leaves are old and that for flowers
5 Mid-summer is to spring as one to ten.
He says the early petal-fall is past
When pear and cherry bloom went down in showers
On sunny days a moment overcast;
And comes that other fall we name the fall.
10 He says the highway dust is over all.
The bird would cease and be as other birds
But that he knows in singing not to sing.
The question that he frames in all but words
Is what to make of a diminished thing.

1916

Birches

When I see birches bend to left and right
Across the lines of straighter darker trees,
I like to think some boy's been swinging them.
But swinging doesn't bend them down to stay.
5 Ice-storms do that. Often you must have seen them
Loaded with ice a sunny winter morning
After a rain. They click upon themselves
As the breeze rises, and turn many-colored
As the stir cracks and crazes their enamel.
10 Soon the sun's warmth makes them shed crystal shells
Shattering and avalanching on the snow-crust—
Such heaps of broken glass to sweep away
You'd think the inner dome of heaven had fallen.
They are dragged to the withered bracken by the load,
15 And they seem not to break; though once they are bowed
So low for long, they never right themselves:
You may see their trunks arching in the woods
Years afterwards, trailing their leaves on the ground

Like girls on hands and knees that throw their hair
20 Before them over their heads to dry in the sun.
But I was going to say when Truth broke in
With all her matter-of-fact about the ice-storm
I should prefer to have some boy bend them
As he went out and in to fetch the cows—
25 Some boy too far from town to learn baseball,
Whose only play was what he found himself,
Summer or winter, and could play alone.
One by one he subdued his father's trees
By riding them down over and over again
30 Until he took the stiffness out of them,
And not one but hung limp, not one was left
For him to conquer. He learned all there was
To learn about not launching out too soon
And so not carrying the tree away
35 Clear to the ground. He always kept his poise
To the top branches, climbing carefully
With the same pains you use to fill a cup
Up to the brim, and even above the brim.
Then he flung outward, feet first, with a swish,
40 Kicking his way down through the air to the ground.
So was I once myself a swinger of birches.
And so I dream of going back to be.
It's when I'm weary of considerations,
And life is too much like a pathless wood
45 Where your face burns and tickles with the cobwebs
Broken across it, and one eye is weeping
From a twig's having lashed across it open.
I'd like to get away from earth awhile
And then come back to it and begin over.
50 May no fate willfully misunderstand me
And half grant what I wish and snatch me away
Not to return. Earth's the right place for love:
I don't know where it's likely to go better.
I'd like to go by climbing a birch tree,
55 And climb black branches up a snow-white trunk
Toward heaven, till the tree could bear no more,
But dipped its top and set me down again.
That would be good both going and coming back.
One could do worse than be a swinger of birches.

                                                    1916

The Hill Wife

Loneliness
HER WORD

One ought not to have to care
    So much as you and I
Care when the birds come round the house
    To seem to say good-bye;

5 Or care so much when they come back
    With whatever it is they sing;
The truth being we are as much
    Too glad for the one thing
As we are too sad for the other here—
10   With birds that fill their breasts
But with each other and themselves
    And their built or driven nests.

House Fear

Always—I tell you this they learned—
Always at night when they returned
To the lonely house from far away
To lamps unlighted and fire gone gray,
5 They learned to rattle the lock and key
To give whatever might chance to be
Warning and time to be off in flight:
And preferring the out- to the in-door night,
They learned to leave the house-door wide
10 Until they had lit the lamp inside.

The Smile
HER WORD

I didn't like the way he went away.
That smile! It never came of being gay.
Still he smiled—did you see him?—I was sure!
Perhaps because we gave him only bread
5 And the wretch knew from that that we were poor.
Perhaps because he let us give instead
Of seizing from us as he might have seized.
Perhaps he mocked at us for being wed,
Or being very young (and he was pleased
10 To have a vision of us old and dead).
I wonder how far down the road he's got.
He's watching from the woods as like as not.

The Oft-Repeated Dream

She had no saying dark enough
    For the dark pine that kept
Forever trying the window-latch
    Of the room where they slept.

5 The tireless but ineffectual hands
    That with every futile pass
Made the great tree seem as a little bird
    Before the mystery of glass!

It never had been inside the room,
10   And only one of the two
Was afraid in an oft-repeated dream
    Of what the tree might do.

The Impulse

It was too lonely for her there,
    And too wild,
And since there were but two of them,
    And no child,

5 And work was little in the house,
    She was free,
And followed where he furrowed field,
    Or felled tree.

She rested on a log and tossed
10   The fresh chips,
With a song only to herself
    On her lips.

And once she went to break a bough
   Of black alder.
15 She strayed so far she scarcely heard
   When he called her—

And didn't answer—didn't speak—
   Or return.
She stood, and then she ran and hid
20   In the fern.

He never found her, though he looked
   Everywhere,
And he asked at her mother's house
   Was she there.

25 Sudden and swift and light as that
   The ties gave,
And he learned of finalities
   Besides the grave.

1916

The Aim Was Song

Before man came to blow it right
   The wind once blew itself untaught,
And did its loudest day and night
   In any rough place where it caught.

5 Man came to tell it what was wrong:
   It hadn't found the place to blow;
It blew too hard—the aim was song.
   And listen—how it ought to go!

He took a little in his mouth,
10   And held it long enough for north
To be converted into south,
   And then by measure blew it forth.

By measure. It was word and note,
   The wind the wind had meant to be—
15 A little through the lips and throat.
   The aim was song—the wind could see.

1923

Stopping by Woods on a Snowy Evening

Whose woods these are I think I know
His house is in the village though;
He will not see me stopping here
To watch his woods fill up with snow.

5 My little horse must think it queer
To stop without a farmhouse near
Between the woods and frozen lake
The darkest evening of the year.

He gives his harness bells a shake
10 To ask if there is some mistake.
The only other sound's the sweep
Of easy wind and downy flake.

The woods are lovely, dark and deep.
But I have promises to keep,
15   And miles to go before I sleep,
And miles to go before I sleep.

1923

To Earthward

Love at the lips was touch
As sweet as I could bear;
And once that seemed too much;
I lived on air

5   That crossed me from sweet things,
The flow of—was it musk
From hidden grapevine springs
Down hill at dusk?

I had the swirl and ache
10   From sprays of honeysuckle
That when they're gathered shake
Dew on the knuckle.

I craved strong sweets, but those
Seemed strong when I was young;
15   The petal of the rose
It was that stung.

Now no joy but lacks salt
That is not dashed with pain
And weariness and fault;
20   I crave the stain

Of tears, the aftermark
Of almost too much love,
The sweet of bitter bark
And burning clove.

25   When stiff and sore and scarred
I take away my hand
From leaning on it hard
In grass and sand,

The hurt is not enough:
30   I long for weight and strength
To feel the earth as rough
To all my length.

1923

Spring Pools

These pools that, though in forests, still reflect
The total sky almost without defect,
And like the flowers beside them, chill and shiver,
Will the flowers beside them soon be gone,
5   And yet not out by any brook or river,
But up by roots to bring dark foliage on.
The trees that have it in their pent-up buds
To darken nature and be summer woods—

10 Let them think twice before they use their powers
    To blot out and drink up and sweep away
    These flowery waters and these watery flowers
    From snow that melted only yesterday.

                                                            1928

West-running Brook

'Fred, where is north?'
                        'North? North is there, my love.
The brook runs west.'
                        'West-running Brook then call it.'
(West-running Brook men call it to this day.)
'What does it think it's doing running west
5   When all the other country brooks flow east
To reach the ocean? It must be the brook
Can trust itself to go by contraries
The way I can with you—and you with me—
Because we're—we're—I don't know what we are.
What are we?'
            'Young or new?'
10   'We must be something.
We've said we two. Let's change that to we three.
As you and I are married to each other,
We'll both be married to the brook. We'll build
Our bridge across it, and the bridge shall be
15 Our arm thrown over it asleep beside it.
Look, look, it's waving to us with a wave
To let us know it hears me.'
                            'Why, my dear,
That wave's been standing off this jut of shore—'
(The black stream, catching on a sunken rock,
20 Flung backward on itself in one white wave,
And the white water rode the black forever,
Not gaining but not losing, like a bird
White feathers from the struggle of whose breast
Flecked the dark stream and flecked the darker pool
25 Below the point, and were at last driven wrinkled
In a white scarf against the far shore alders.)
'That wave's been standing off this jut of shore
Ever since rivers, I was going to say,
Were made in heaven. It wasn't waved to us.'

30 'It wasn't, yet it was. If not to you
It was to me—in an annunciation.'

'Oh, if you take it off to lady-land,
As't were the country of the Amazons[1]
We men must see you to the confines of
35 And leave you there, ourselves forbid to enter,—
It is your brook! I have no more to say.'

'Yes, you have, too. Go on. You thought of something.'

'Speaking of contraries, see how the brook
In that white wave runs counter to itself.
40 It is from that in water we were from
Long, long before we were from any creature.
Here we, in our impatience of the steps,
Get back to the beginning of beginnings,
The stream of everything that runs away.

---

1. Legendary female warriors who inhabited a country without men.

45 Some say existence like a Pirouot
And Pirouette, forever in one place,
Stands still and dances, but it runs away,
It seriously, sadly, runs away
To fill the abyss' void with emptiness.
50 It flows beside us in this water brook,
But it flows over us. It flows between us
To separate us for a panic moment.
It flows between us, over us, and *with* us.
And it is time, strength, tone, light, life and love—
55 And even substance lapsing unsubstantial;
The universal cataract of death
That spends to nothingness—and unresisted,
Save by some strange resistance in itself,
Not just a swerving, but a throwing back,
60 As if regret were in it and were sacred.
It has this throwing backward on itself
So that the fall of most of it is always
Raising a little, sending up a little.
Our life runs down in sending up the clock.
65 The brook runs down in sending up our life.
The sun runs down in sending up the brook.
And there is something sending up the sun.
It is this backward motion toward the source,
Against the stream, that most we see ourselves in,
70 The tribute of the current to the source.
It is from this in nature we are from.
It is most us.'
            "Today will be the day
You said so.'
            'No, today will be the day
You said the brook was called West-running Brook.'
75 'Today will be the day of what we both said.'

                                        1928

A Lone Striker

The swinging mill bell changed its rate
To tolling like the count of fate,
And though at that the tardy ran,
One failed to make the closing gate.
5 There was a law of God or man
That on the one who came too late
The gate for half an hour be locked,
His time be lost, his pittance docked.
He stood rebuked and unemployed.
10 The straining mill began to shake.
The mill, though many, many eyed,
Had eyes inscrutably opaque;
So that he couldn't look inside
To see if some forlorn machine
15 Was standing idle for his sake.
(He couldn't hope its heart would break.)
And yet he thought he saw the scene:
The air was full of dust of wool.
A thousand yarns were under pull,
20 But pull so slow, with such a twist,
All day from spool to lesser spool,
It seldom overtaxed their strength;
They safely grew in slender length.
And if one broke by any chance,
25 The spinner saw it at a glance.
The spinner still was there to spin.

That's where the human still came in.
Her deft hand showed with finger rings
Among the harp-like spread of strings.
30 She caught the pieces end to end
And, with a touch that never missed,
Not so much tied as made them blend.
Man's ingenuity was good.
He saw it plainly where he stood,
35 Yet found it easy to resist.

He knew another place, a wood,
And in it, tall as trees, were cliffs;
And if he stood on one of these,
'Twould be among the tops of trees,
40 Their upper branches round him wreathing,
Their breathing mingled with his breathing.
If—if he stood! Enough of ifs!
He knew a path that wanted walking;
He knew a spring that wanted drinking;
45 A thought that wanted further thinking;
A love that wanted re-renewing.
Nor was this just a way of talking
To save him the expense of doing.
With him it boded action, deed.

50 The factory was very fine;
He wished it all the modern speed.
Yet, after all, 'twas not a church.
He never would assume that he'd
Be any institution's need.
55 But he said then and still would say
If there should ever come a day
When industry seemed like to die
Because he left it in the lurch,
Or even merely seemed to pine
60 For want of his approval, why,
Come get him—they knew where to search.

1936

The White-tailed Hornet

The white-tailed hornet lives in a balloon
That floats against the ceiling of the woodshed.
The exit he comes out at like a bullet
Is like the pupil of a pointed gun.
5   And having power to change his aim in flight,
He comes out more unerring than a bullet.
Verse could be written on the certainty
With which he penetrates my best defense
Of whirling hands and arms about the head
10 To stab me in the sneeze-nerve of a nostril.
Such is the instinct of it I allow.
Yet how about the insect certainty
That in the neighborhood of home and children
Is such an execrable judge of motives
15 As not to recognize in me the exception
I like to think I am in everything—
One who would never hang above a bookcase
His Japanese crepe-paper globe for trophy?
He stung me first and stung me afterward.
20 He rolled me off the field head over heels,
And would not listen to my explanations.

That's when I went as visitor to his house.
As visitor at my house he is better.
Hawking for flies about the kitchen door,
25 In at one door perhaps and out another,
Trust him then not to put you in the wrong.
He won't misunderstand your freest movements.
Let him light on your skin unless you mind
So many prickly grappling feet at once.
30 He's after the domesticated fly
To feed his thumping grubs as big as he is.
Here he is at his best, but even here—
I watched him where he swooped, he pounced, he struck;
But what he found he had was just a nailhead.
35 He struck a second time. Another nailhead.
'Those are just nailheads. Those are fastened down.'
Then disconcerted and not unannoyed,
He stooped and struck a little huckleberry
The way a player curls around a football.
40 'Wrong shape, wrong color, and wrong scent,' I said.
The huckleberry rolled him on his head.
At last it was a fly. He shot and missed;
And the fly circled round him in derision.
But for the fly he might have made me think
45 He had been at his poetry, comparing
Nailhead with fly and fly with huckleberry:
How like a fly, how very like a fly.
But the real fly he missed would never do;
The missed fly made me dangerously skeptic.

50 Won't this whole instinct matter bear revision?
Won't almost any theory bear revision?
To err is human, not to, animal.
Or so we pay the compliment to instinct,
Only too liberal of our compliment
55 That really takes away instead of gives.
Our worship, humor, conscientiousness
Went long since to the dogs under the table.
And served us right for having instituted
Downward comparisons. As long on earth
60 As our comparisons were stoutly upward
With gods and angels, we were men at least,
But little lower than the gods and angels.
But once comparisons were yielded downward,
Once we began to see our images
65 Reflected in the mud and even dust,
'Twas disillusion upon disillusion.
We were lost piecemeal to the animals,
Like people thrown out to delay the wolves.
Nothing but fallibility was left us,
70 And this day's work made even that seem doubtful.

The Strong Are Saying Nothing

The soil now gets a rumpling soft and damp,
And small regard to the future of any weed.
The final flat of the hoe's approval stamp
Is reserved for the bed of a few selected seed.

5 There is seldom more than a man to a harrowed piece.
Men work alone, their lots plowed far apart,
One stringing a chain of seed in an open crease,
And another stumbling after a halting cart.

To the fresh and black of the squares of early mould
10 The leafless bloom of a plum is fresh and white;
Though there's more than a doubt if the weather is not too cold
For the bees to come and serve its beauty aright.

Wind goes from farm to farm in wave on wave,
But carries no cry of what is hoped to be.
15 There may be little or much beyond the grave,
But the strong are saying nothing until they see.

1936

Neither Out Far Nor In Deep

The people along the sand
All turn and look one way.
They turn their back on the land.
They look at the sea all day.

5 As long as it takes to pass
A ship keeps raising its hull;
The wetter ground like glass
Reflects a standing gull.

The land may vary more;
10 But wherever the truth may be—
The water comes ashore,
And the people look at the sea.

They cannot look out far.
They cannot look in deep.
15 But when was that ever a bar
To any watch they keep?

1936

Design

I found a dimpled spider, fat and white,
On a white heal-all,[2] holding up a moth
Like a white piece of rigid satin cloth—
Assorted characters of death and blight
5 Mixed ready to begin the morning right,
Like the ingredients of a witches' broth—
A snow-drop spider, a flower like froth,
And dead wings carried like a paper kite.

What had that flower to do with being white,
10 The wayside blue and innocent heal-all?
What brought the kindred spider to that height,
Then steered the white moth thither in the night?
What but design of darkness to appall?—
If design govern in a thing so small.

1936

Never Again Would Birds' Song Be the Same

He would declare and could himself believe
That the birds there in all the garden round
From having heard the daylong voice of Eve
Had added to their own an oversound,
5 Her tone of meaning but without the words.
Admittedly an eloquence so soft
Could only have had an influence on birds

2. One of a variety of plants thought to have curative powers.

When call or laughter carried it aloft.
Be that as may be, she was in their song
10 Moreover her voice upon their voices crossed
Had now persisted in the woods so long
That probably it never would be lost.
Never again would birds' song be the same.
And to do that to birds was why she came.

1942

The Gift Outright

The land was ours before we were the land's.
She was our land more than a hundred years
Before we were her people. She was ours
In Massachusetts, in Virginia,
5 But we were England's, still colonials,
Possessing what we still were unpossessed by,
Possessed by what we now no more possessed.
Something we were withholding made us weak
Until we found it was ourselves
10 We were withholding from our land of living,
And forthwith found salvation in surrender.
Such as we were we gave ourselves outright
(The deed of gift was many deeds of war)
To the land vaguely realizing westward,
15 But still unstoried, artless, unenhanced,
Such as she was, such as she would become.

1942

In Winter in the Woods Alone

In winter in the woods alone
Against the trees I go.
I mark a maple for my own
And lay the maple low.

5 At four o'clock I shoulder axe
And in the afterglow
I link a line of shadowy tracks
Across the tinted snow.

I see for Nature no defeat
10 In one tree's overthrow
Or for myself in my retreat
For yet another blow.

1962

EDWARD THOMAS
(1878–1917)

The Owl

Downhill I came, hungry, and yet not starved;
Cold, yet had heat within me that was proof
Against the North wind; tired, yet so that rest
Had seemed the sweetest thing under a roof.

5 Then at the inn I had food, fire, and rest,
Knowing how hungry, cold, and tired was I.
All of the night was quite barred out except
An owl's cry, a most melancholy cry

Shaken out long and clear upon the hill,
10 No merry note, nor cause of merriment,
But one telling me plain what I escaped
And others could not, that night, as in I went.

And salted was my food, and my repose,
Salted and sobered, too, by the bird's voice
15 Speaking for all who lay under the stars,
Soldiers and poor, unable to rejoice.

                                                            1917

Melancholy

The rain and wind, the rain and wind, raved endlessly.
On me the Summer storm, and fever, and melancholy
Wrought magic, so that if I feared the solitude
Far more I feared all company: too sharp, too rude,
5 Had been the wisest or the dearest human voice.
What I desired I knew not, but whate'er my choice
Vain it must be, I knew. Yet naught did my despair
But sweeten the strange sweetness, while through the wild air
All day long I heard a distant cuckoo calling
10 And, soft as dulcimers, sounds of near water falling,
And, softer, and remote as if in history,
Rumors of what had touched my friends, my foes, or me.

                                                            1917

Lights Out

I have come to the borders of sleep,
The unfathomable deep
Forest where all must lose
Their way, however straight,
5 Or winding, soon or late;
They cannot choose.

Many a road and track
That, since the dawn's first crack,
Up to the forest brink,
10 Deceived the travelers,
Suddenly now blurs,
And in they sink.

Here love ends,
Despair, ambition ends;
15 All pleasure and all trouble,
Although most sweet or bitter,
Here ends in sleep that is sweeter
Than tasks most noble.

There is not any book
20 Or face of dearest look
That I would not turn from now
To go into the unknown
I must enter, and leave, alone,
I know not how.

25 The tall forest towers;
Its cloudy foliage lowers
Ahead, shelf above shelf;
Its silence I hear and obey
That I may lose my way
30 And myself.

                                                            1917

Words

Out of us all
That make rhymes,
Will you choose
Sometimes—
5 As the winds use
A crack in a wall
Or a drain,
Their joy or their pain
To whistle through—
10 Choose me,
You English words?

I know you:
You are light as dreams,
Tough as oak,
15 Precious as gold,
As poppies and corn,
Or an old cloak:
Sweet as our birds
To the ear,
20 As the burnet rose[1]
In the heat
Of Midsummer:
Strange as the races
Of dead and unborn:
25 Strange and sweet
Equally,
And familiar,
To the eye,
As the dearest faces
30 That a man knows,
And as lost homes are:
But though older far
Than oldest yew—
As our hills are, old—
35 Worn new
Again and again:
Young as our streams
After rain:
And as dear
40 As the earth which you prove
That we love.

Make me content
With some sweetness
From Wales
45 Whose nightingales
Have no wings—
From Wiltshire and Kent
And Herefordshire,
And the villages there—
50 From the names, and the things
No less.
Let me sometimes dance
With you,
Or climb

---

1. Or Scotch rose—a low bush densely provided with slender prickles and producing white, pale pink, or yellow flowers.

55   Or stand perchance
     In ecstasy,
     Fixed and free
     In a rhyme,
     As poets do.

                                                                1917

The Dark Forest

Dark is the forest and deep, and overhead
Hang stars like seeds of light
In vain, though not since they were sown was bred
Anything more bright.

5   And evermore mighty multitudes ride
     About, nor enter in;
     Of the other multitudes that dwell inside
     Never yet was one seen.

     The forest foxglove is purple, the marguerite
10   Outside is gold and white,
     Nor can those that pluck either blossom greet
     The others, day or night.

                                                                1918

Good-Night

The skylarks are far behind that sang over the down;
I can hear no more those suburb nightingales;
Thrushes and blackbirds sing in the gardens of the town
In vain: the noise of man, beast, and machine prevails.

5   But the call of children in the unfamiliar streets
     That echo with a familiar twilight echoing,
     Sweet as the voice of nightingale or lark, completes
     A magic of strange welcome, so that I seem a king

     Among man, beast, machine, bird, child, and the ghost
10   That in the echo lives and with the echo dies.
     The friendless town is friendly; homeless, I am not lost;
     Though I know none of these doors, and meet but strangers' eyes.
     Never again, perhaps, after tomorrow, shall
     I see these homely streets, these church windows alight,
15   Not a man or woman or child among them all:
     But it is All Friends' Night, a traveler's good-night.

                                                                1918

The Gypsy

A fortnight before Christmas Gypsies were everywhere:
Vans were drawn up on wastes, women trailed to the fair.
"My gentleman," said one, "you've got a lucky face."
"And you've a luckier," I thought, "if such a grace
5   And impudence in rags are lucky." "Give a penny
     For the poor baby's sake." "Indeed I have not any
     Unless you can give change for a sovereign,[2] my dear."
     "Then just half a pipeful of tobacco can you spare?"
     I gave it. With that much victory she laughed content.
10   I should have given more, but off and away she went

---

2. Formerly, a British gold coin, value one pound, so called because it bore the effigy of the ruler on one face.

With her baby and her pink sham flowers to rejoin
The rest before I could translate to its proper coin
Gratitude for her grace. And I paid nothing then,
As I pay nothing now with the dipping of my pen
15 For her brother's music when he drummed the tambourine
And stamped his feet, which made the workmen passing grin,
While his mouth-organ changed to a rascally Bacchanal dance
"Over the hills and far away." This and his glance
Outlasted all the fair, farmer, and auctioneer,
20 Cheap-jack,° balloon-man, drover with crooked stick, and steer,   *peddler*
Pig, turkey, goose, and duck, Christmas corpses to be.
Not even the kneeling ox had eyes like the Romany.°   *gypsy*
That night he peopled for me the hollow wooded land,
More dark and wild than stormiest heavens, that I searched and scanned
25 Like a ghost new-arrived. The gradations of the dark
Were like an underworld of death, but for the spark
In the Gypsy boy's black eyes as he played and stamped his tune,
"Over the hills and far away," and a crescent moon.

1918

WALLACE STEVENS
(1879–1955)

The Snow Man

One must have a mind of winter
To regard the frost and the boughs
Of the pine-trees crusted with snow;

And have been cold a long time
5 To behold the junipers shagged with ice,
The spruces rough in the distant glitter

Of the January sun; and not to think
Of any misery in the sound of the wind,
In the sound of a few leaves,

10 Which is the sound of the land
Full of the same wind
That is blowing in the same bare place
For the listener, who listens in the snow,
And, nothing himself, beholds
15 Nothing that is not there and the nothing that is.

1923

Sunday Morning

1

Complacencies of the peignoir, and late
Coffee and oranges in a sunny chair,
And the green freedom of a cockatoo
Upon a rug mingle to dissipate
5 The holy hush of ancient sacrifice.
She dreams a little, and she feels the dark
Encroachment of that old catastrophe,
As a calm darkens among water-lights.
The pungent oranges and bright, green wings
10 Seem things in some procession of the dead,
Winding across wide water, without sound.

The day is like wide water, without sound,
Stilled for the passing of her dreaming feet
Over the seas, to silent Palestine,
15   Dominion of the blood and sepulchre.

2

Why should she give her bounty to the dead?
What is divinity if it can come
Only in silent shadows and in dreams?
Shall she not find in comforts of the sun,
20   In pungent fruit and bright, green wings, or else
In any balm or beauty of the earth,
Things to be cherished like the thought of heaven?
Divinity must live within herself:
Passions of rain, or moods in falling snow;
25   Grievings in loneliness, or unsubdued
Elations when the forest blooms; gusty
Emotions on wet roads on autumn nights;
All pleasures and all pains, remembering
The bough of summer and the winter branch.
30   These are the measures destined for her soul.

3

Jove in the clouds had his inhuman birth.
No mother suckled him, no sweet land gave
Large-mannered motions to his mythy mind
He moved among us, as a muttering king,
35   Magnificent, would move among his hinds,°   *shepherds*
Until our blood, commingling, virginal,
With heaven, brought such requital to desire
The very hinds discerned it, in a star.
Shall our blood fail? Or shall it come to be
40   The blood of paradise? And shall the earth
Seem all of paradise that we shall know?
The sky will be much friendlier then than now,
A part of labor and a part of pain,
And next in glory to enduring love,
45   Not this dividing and indifferent blue.

4

She says, "I am content when wakened birds,
Before they fly, test the reality
Of misty fields, by their sweet questionings;
But when the birds are gone, and their warm fields
50   Return no more, where, then, is paradise?"
There is not any haunt of prophecy,
Nor any old chimera of the grave,
Neither the golden underground, nor isle
Melodious, where spirits gat them home,
55   Nor visionary south, nor cloudy palm
Remote on heaven's hill, that has endured
As April's green endures; or will endure
Like her remembrance of awakened birds,
Or her desire for June and evening, tipped
60   By the consummation of the swallow's wings.

5

She says, "But in contentment I still feel
The need of some imperishable bliss."
Death is the mother of beauty; hence from her,
Alone, shall come fulfilment to our dreams
65   And our desires. Although she strews the leaves
Of sure obliteration on our paths,
The path sick sorrow took, the many paths
Where triumph rang its brassy phrase, or love
Whispered a little out of tenderness,

70 She makes the willow shiver in the sun
   For maidens who were wont to sit and gaze
   Upon the grass, relinquished to their feet.
   She causes boys to pile new plums and pears
   On disregarded plate.[1] The maidens taste
75 And stray impassioned in the littering leaves.

6

   Is there no change of death in paradise?
   Does ripe fruit never fall? Or do the boughs
   Hang always heavy in that perfect sky,
   Unchanging, yet so like our perishing earth,
80 With rivers like our own that seek for seas
   They never find, the same receding shores
   That never touch with inarticulate pang?
   Why set the pear upon those river-banks
   Or spice the shores with odors of the plum?
85 Alas, that they should wear our colors there,
   The silken weavings of our afternoons,
   And pick the strings of our insipid lutes!
   Death is the mother of beauty, mystical,
   Within whose burning bosom we devise
90 Our earthly mothers waiting, sleeplessly.

7

   Supple and turbulent, a ring of men
   Shall chant in orgy on a summer morn
   Their boisterous devotion to the sun,
   Not as a god, but as a god might be,
95 Naked among them, like a savage source.
   Their chant shall be a chant of paradise,
   Out of their blood, returning to the sky;
   And in their chant shall enter, voice by voice,
   The windy lake wherein their lord delights,
100 The trees, like serafin,° and echoing hills,   celestial beings
    That choir among themselves long afterward.
    They shall know well the heavenly fellowship
    Of men that perish and of summer morn.
    And whence they came and whither they shall go
105 The dew upon their feet shall manifest.

8

    She hears, upon that water without sound,
    A voice that cries, "The tomb in Palestine
    Is not the porch of spirits lingering.
    It is the grave of Jesus, where he lay."
110 We live in an old chaos of the sun,
    Or old dependency of day and night,
    Or island solitude, unsponsored, free,
    Of that wide water, inescapable.
    Deer walk upon our mountains, and the quail
115 Whistle about us their spontaneous cries;
    Sweet berries ripen in the wilderness;
    And, in the isolation of the sky,
    At evening, casual flocks of pigeons make
    Ambiguous undulations as they sink,
120 Downward to darkness, on extended wings.

                              1915   1923

---

1. "Plate is used in the sense of so-called
family plate. Disregarded refers to the disuse
into which things fall that have been possessed
for a long time. I mean, therefore, that death
releases and renews" [*Letters of Wallace
Stevens,* New York, 1966, pp. 183–184].

The Bird with the Coppery, Keen Claws

Above the forest of the parakeets,
A parakeet of parakeets prevails,
A pip of life amid a mort° of tails.   *great quantity*

(The rudiments of tropics are around,
5 Aloe² of ivory, pear of rusty rind.)
His lids are white because his eyes are blind.

He is not paradise of parakeets,
Of his gold ether, golden alguazil,°   *bailiff, sheriff*
Except because he broods there and is still.

10 Panache³ upon panache, his tails deploy
Upward and outward, in green-vented forms,
His tip a drop of water full of storms.

But though the turbulent tinges undulate
As his pure intellect applies its laws,
15 He moves not on his coppery, keen claws.

He munches a dry shell while he exerts
His will, yet never ceases, perfect cock,
To flare, in the sun-pallor of his rock.

                                                        1923

The Idea of Order at Key West

She sang beyond the genius of the sea.
The water never formed to mind or voice,
Like a body wholly body, fluttering
Its empty sleeves; and yet its mimic motion
5 Made constant cry, caused constantly a cry,
That was not ours although we understood,
Inhuman, of the veritable ocean.

The sea was not a mask. No more was she.
The song and water were not medleyed sound
10 Even if what she sang was what she heard,
Since what she sang was uttered word by word.
It may be that in all her phrases stirred
The grinding water and the gasping wind;
But it was she and not the sea we heard.
15 For she was the maker of the song she sang.
The ever-hooded, tragic-gestured sea
Was merely a place by which she walked to sing.
Whose spirit is this? we said, because we knew
It was the spirit that we sought and knew
20 That we should ask this often as she sang.

If it was only the dark voice of the sea
That rose, or even colored by many waves;
If it was only the outer voice of sky
And cloud, of the sunken coral water-walled,
25 However clear, it would have been deep air,
The heaving speech of air, a summer sound
Repeated in a summer without end
And sound alone. But it was more than that,

---

2. Plants of the lily family.   3. Tuft or plume of feathers.

More even than her voice, and ours, among
30 The meaningless plungings of water and the wind,
    Theatrical distances, bronze shadows heaped
    On high horizons, mountainous atmospheres
    Of sky and sea.
                    It was her voice that made
35 The sky acutest at its vanishing.
    She measured to the hour its solitude.
    She was the single artificer of the world
    In which she sang. And when she sang, the sea,
    Whatever self it had, became the self
40 That was her song, for she was the maker. Then we,
    As we beheld her striding there alone,
    Knew that there never was a world for her
    Except the one she sang and, singing, made.

    Ramon Fernandez,[4] tell me, if you know,
45 Why, when the singing ended and we turned
    Toward the town, tell why the glassy lights,
    The lights in the fishing boats at anchor there,
    As the night descended, tilting in the air,
    Mastered the night and portioned out the sea,
50 Fixing emblazoned zones and fiery poles,
    Arranging, deepening, enchanting night.

    Oh! Blessed rage for order, pale Ramon,
    The maker's rage to order words of the sea,
    Words of the fragrant portals, dimly-starred,
55 And of ourselves and of our origins,
    In ghostlier demarcations, keener sounds.

                                                    1935

Table Talk

    Granted, we die for good.
    Life, then, is largely a thing
    Of happens to like, not should.

    And that, too, granted, why
5   Do I happen to like red bush,
    Gray grass and green-gray sky?

    What else remains? But red,
    Gray, green, why those of all?
    That is not what I said:
10 Not those of all. But those.
    One likes what one happens to like.
    One likes the way red grows.

    It cannot matter at all.
    Happens to like is one
15 Of the ways things happen to fall.

                            ca. 1935   1957

---

4. Stevens pointed out to two of his corre-
spondents that in choosing this name he had
simply combined two common Spanish names
at random, without conscious reference to
Ramon Fernandez the critic: "Ramon Fernan-
dez was not intended to be anyone at all."

A Room on a Garden

O stagnant east-wind, palsied mare,
Giddap! The ruby roses' hair
Must blow.

Behold how order is the end
5   Of everything. The roses bend
As one.

Order, the law of hoes and rakes,
May be perceived in windy quakes
And squalls.

10   The gardener searches earth and sky
The truth in nature to espy
In vain.

He well might find that eager balm
In lilies' stately-statued calm;
15   But then

He well might find it in this fret
Of lilies rusted, rotting, wet
With rain.

ca. 1935   1957

WILLIAM CARLOS WILLIAMS
(1883–1963)

Portrait of a Lady

Your thighs are appletrees
whose blossoms touch the sky.
Which sky? The sky
where Watteau[1] hung a lady's
5   slipper. Your knees
are a southern breeze—or
a gust of snow. Agh! what
sort of man was Fragonard?[2]
—as if that answered
10   anything. Ah, yes—below
the knees, since the tune
drops that way, it is
one of those white summer days,
the tall grass of your ankles
15   flickers upon the shore—
Which shore?—
the sand clings to my lips—
Which shore?
Agh, petals maybe. How
20   should I know?
Which shore? Which shore?
I said petals from an appletree.

1915

---

1. Jean Antoine Watteau (1684–1721), French
painter famous for genre pictures of aristo-
crats in pastoral settings.

2. Jean Honoré Fragonard (1732–1806),
French painter in the rococo style.

Queen-Ann's-Lace

Her body is not so white as
anemone petals nor so smooth—nor
so remote a thing. It is a field
of the wild carrot taking
5 the field by force; the grass
does not raise above it.
Here is no question of whiteness,
white as can be, with a purple mole
at the center of each flower.
10 Each flower is a hand's span
of her whiteness. Wherever
his hand has lain there is
a tiny purple blemish. Each part
is a blossom under his touch
15 to which the fibres of her being
stem one by one, each to its end,
until the whole field is a
white desire, empty, a single stem,
a cluster, flower by flower,
20 a pious wish to whiteness gone over—
or nothing.

1925

The Yachts

contend in a sea which the land partly encloses
shielding them from the too-heavy blows
of an ungoverned ocean which when it chooses

tortures the biggest hulls, the best man knows
5 to pit against its beatings, and sinks them pitilessly.
Mothlike in mists, scintillant in the minute

brilliance of cloudless days, with broad bellying sails
they glide to the wind tossing green water
from their sharp prows while over them the crew crawls

10 ant-like, solicitously grooming them, releasing,
making fast as they turn, lean far over and having
caught the wind again, side by side, head for the mark.

In a well guarded arena of open water surrounded by
lesser and greater craft which, sycophant, lumbering
15 and flittering follow them, they appear youthful, rare

as the light of a happy eye, live with the grace
of all that in the mind is fleckless, free and
naturally to be desired. Now the sea which holds them

is moody, lapping their glossy sides, as if feeling
20 for some slightest flaw but fails completely.
Today no race. Then the wind comes again. The yachts

move, jockeying for a start, the signal is set and they
are off. Now the waves strike at them but they are too
well made, they slip through, though they take in canvas.

25 Arms with hands grasping seek to clutch at the prows.
Bodies thrown recklessly in the way are cut aside.
It is a sea of faces about them in agony, in despair

until the horror of the race dawns staggering the mind,
the whole sea become an entanglement of watery bodies
30   lost to the world bearing what they cannot hold. Broken,

beaten, desolate, reaching from the dead to be taken up
they cry out, failing, failing! their cries rising
in waves still as the skillful yachts pass over.

1935

Fine Work with Pitch and Copper

Now they are resting
in the fleckless light
separately in unison

like the sacks
5   of sifted stone stacked
regularly by twos

about the flat roof
ready after lunch
to be opened and strewn

10   The copper in eight
foot strips has been
beaten lengthwise

down the center at right
angles and lies ready
15   to edge the coping

One still chewing
picks up a copper strip
and runs his eye along it

1936

The Dance

In Breughel's[3] great picture, The Kermess,
the dancers go round, they go round and
around, the squeal and the blare and the
tweedle of bagpipes, a bugle and fiddles
5   tipping their bellies (round as the thick-
sided glasses whose wash they impound)
their hips and their bellies off balance
to turn them. Kicking and rolling about
the Fair Grounds, swinging their butts, those
10   shanks must be sound to bear up under such
rollicking measures, prance as they dance
in Breughel's great picture, The Kermess.

1944

The Ivy Crown

The whole process is a lie,
       unless,
               crowned by excess,
   it break forcefully,
5   one way or another,
               from its confinement—

3. Pieter Breughel (died 1569), Flemish painter of peasant life.

    or find a deeper well.
              Antony and Cleopatra
                    were right;
10   they have shown
              the way. I love you
                    or I do not live
    at all.

    Daffodil time
15   is past. This is
                  summer, summer!
    the heart says,
             and not even the full of it.
                No doubts
20   are permitted—
             though they will come
                and may
    before our time
             overwhelm us.
25   We are only mortal
    but being mortal
             can defy our fate.
              We may
    by an outside chance
30   even win! We do not
                look to see
    jonquils and violets
            come again
                but there are,
35   still,
            the roses!

    Romance has no part in it.
            The business of love is
                cruelty *which,*
40   by our wills,
            we transform
                to live together.
    It has its seasons,
            for and against,
45   whatever the heart
    fumbles in the dark
            to assert
                toward the end of May.
    Just as the nature of briars
50   is to tear flesh,
                I have proceeded
    through them.
            Keep
                the briars out,
55   they say.
            You cannot live
                and keep free of
    briars.

    Children pick flowers.
60   Let them.
                Though having them
    in hand
            they have no further use for them
                but leave them crumpled
65   at the curb's edge.

At our age the imagination
            across the sorry facts
                   lifts us
to make roses
70   stand before thorns.
                  Sure
love is cruel
        and selfish
                and totally obtuse—
75 at least, blinded by the light,
          young love is.
               But we are older,
I to love
        and you to be loved,
80   we have,
no matter how,
        by our wills survived
              to keep
the jeweled prize
85   always
            at our finger tips.
We will it so
        and so it is
           past all accident.

                                        1955

D. H. LAWRENCE
(1885–1930)

Baby Running Barefoot

When the white feet of the baby beat across the grass
The little white feet nod like white flowers in a wind,
They poise and run like puffs of wind that pass
Over water where the weeds are thinned.

5 And the sight of their white playing in the grass
Is winsome as a robin's song, so fluttering;
Or like two butterflies that settle on a glass
Cup for a moment, soft little wing-beats uttering.

And I wish that the baby would tack across here to me
10 Like a wind-shadow running on a pond, so she could stand
With two little bare white feet upon my knee
And I could feel her feet in either hand

Cool as syringa buds in morning hours,
Or firm and silken as young peony flowers.

                                        1916

Piano

Softly, in the dusk, a woman is singing to me;
Taking me back down the vista of years, till I see
A child sitting under the piano, in the boom of the tingling strings
And pressing the small, poised feet of a mother who smiles as she sings.

5 In spite of myself, the insidious mastery of song
Betrays me back, till the heart of me weeps to belong
To the old Sunday evenings at home, with winter outside
And hymns in the cozy parlor, the tinkling piano our guide.

So now it is vain for the singer to burst into clamor
10   With the great black piano appassionato. The glamour
Of childish days is upon me, my manhood is cast
Down in the flood of remembrance, I weep like a child for the past.

1918

Reading a Letter

She sits on the recreation ground
    Under an oak whose yellow buds dot the pale blue sky.
The young grass twinkles in the wind, and the sound
    Of the wind in the knotted buds makes a canopy.

5   So sitting under the knotted canopy
    Of the wind, she is lifted and carried away as in a balloon
Across the insensible void, till she stoops to see
    The sandy desert beneath her, the dreary platoon.

She knows the waste all dry beneath her, in one place
10   Stirring with earth-colored life, ever turning and stirring.
But never the motion has a human face
    Nor sound, only intermittent machinery whirring.

And so again, on the recreation ground
    She alights a stranger, wondering, unused to the scene;
15   Suffering at sight of the children playing around,
    Hurt at the chalk-colored tulips, and the evening-green.

1918

Snake

A snake came to my water-trough
On a hot, hot day, and I in pajamas for the heat,
To drink there.

In the deep, strange-scented shade of the great dark carob-tree
5   I came down the steps with my pitcher
And must wait, must stand and wait, for there he was at the trough before
    me.

He reached down from a fissure in the earth-wall in the gloom
And trailed his yellow-brown slackness soft-bellied down, over the edge of
    the stone trough
And rested his throat upon the stone bottom,
10   And where the water had dripped from the tap, in a small clearness,
He sipped with his straight mouth,
Softly drank through his straight gums, into his slack long body,
Silently.

Someone was before me at my water-trough,
15   And I, like a second comer, waiting.

He lifted his head from his drinking, as cattle do,
And looked at me vaguely, as drinking cattle do,
And flickered his two-forked tongue from his lips, and mused a moment,
And stooped and drank a little more,
20   Being earth-brown, earth-golden from the burning bowels of the earth
On the day of Sicilian July, with Etna smoking.

The voice of my education said to me
He must be killed,
For in Sicily the black, black snakes are innocent, the gold are venomous.

²⁵ And voices in me said, If you were a man
You would take a stick and break him now, and finish him off.

But must I confess how I liked him,
How glad I was he had come like a guest in quiet, to drink at my water-
        trough

And depart peaceful, pacified, and thankless,
³⁰ Into the burning bowels of this earth?

Was it cowardice, that I dared not kill him?
Was it perversity, that I longed to talk to him?
Was it humility, to feel so honored?
I felt so honored.

And yet those voices:
³⁵ *If you were not afraid, you would kill him!*

And truly I was afraid, I was most afraid,
But even so, honored still more
That he should seek my hospitality
From out the dark door of the secret earth.

⁴⁰ He drank enough
And lifted his head, dreamily, as one who has drunken,
And flickered his tongue like a forked night on the air, so black,
Seeming to lick his lips,
And looked around like a god, unseeing, into the air,
⁴⁵ And slowly turned his head,
And slowly, very slowly, as if thrice adream,
Proceeded to draw his slow length curving round
And climb again the broken bank of my wall-face.

And as he put his head into that dreadful hole,
⁵⁰ And as he slowly drew up, snake-easing his shoulders, and entered farther,
A sort of horror, a sort of protest against his withdrawing into that horrid
        black hole,
Deliberately going into the blackness, and slowly drawing himself after,
Overcame me now his back was turned.

I looked round, I put down my pitcher,
⁵⁵ I picked up a clumsy log
And threw it at the water-trough with a clatter.

I think it did not hit him,
But suddenly that part of him that was left behind convulsed in undignified
        haste.
Writhed like lightning, and was gone
⁶⁰ Into the black hole, the earth-lipped fissure in the wall-front,
At which, in the intense still noon, I stared with fascination.

And immediately I regretted it.
I thought how paltry, how vulgar, what a mean act!
I despised myself and the voices of my accursed human education.

⁶⁵ And I thought of the albatross[1]
And I wished he would come back, my snake.

For he seemed to me again like a king,
Like a king in exile, uncrowned in the underworld,
Now due to be crowned again.

1. In Coleridge's *Rime of the Ancient Mariner*.

70 And so, I missed my chance with one of the lords
Of life.
And I have something to expiate;
A pettiness.

Taormina.
1923

Bavarian Gentians

Not every man has gentians in his house
in Soft September, at slow, sad Michaelmas.

Bavarian gentians, big and dark, only dark
darkening the daytime, torch-like with the smoking blueness of Pluto's gloom,
5 ribbed and torch-like, with their blaze of darkness spread blue
down flattening into points, flattened under the sweep of white day
torch-flower of the blue-smoking darkness, Pluto's dark-blue daze,
black lamps from the halls of Dis,[2] burning dark blue,
giving off darkness, blue darkness, as Demeter's pale lamps give off light,
10 lead me then, lead the way.

Reach me a gentian, give me a torch!
let me guide myself with the blue, forked torch of this flower
down the darker and darker stairs, where blue is darkened on blueness
even where Persephone goes, just now, from the frosted September
15 to the sightless realm where darkness is awake upon the dark
and Persephone herself is but a voice
or a darkness invisible enfolded in the deeper dark
of the arms Plutonic, and pierced with the passion of dense gloom,
among the splendor of torches of darkness, shedding darkness on the lost
    bride and her groom.

1932

The Ship of Death[3]

1

Now it is autumn and the falling fruit
and the long journey towards oblivion.

The apples falling like great drops of dew
to bruise themselves an exit from themselves.

5 And it is time to go, to bid farewell
to one's own self, and find an exit
from the fallen self.

2

Have you built your ship of death, O have you?
O build your ship of death, for you will need it.

10 The grim frost is at hand, when the apples will fall
thick, almost thundrous, on the hardened earth.

And death is on the air like a smell of ashes!
Ah! can't you smell it?

---

2. Another Roman name for Pluto (Greek Hades), ruler of the underworld. He had abducted Persephone (Roman Proserpine) the daughter of Demeter (Roman Ceres), goddess of growing vegetation and living nature; Persephone ruled with him as queen of the underworld, but returned to spend six months of each year with her mother in the world above.

3. In *Etruscan Places,* the book which describes his visit to the Etruscan painted tombs in Central Italy, in the spring of 1927, Lawrence mentions that originally, before the tombs were pillaged, there would be found in the last chamber among "the sacred treasures of the dead, the little bronze ship that should bear [the soul of the dead] over to the other world * * * "

And in the bruised body, the frightened soul
15   finds itself shrinking, wincing from the cold
that blows upon it through the orifices.
        3
And can a man his own quietus make
with a bare bodkin?[4]

With daggers, bodkins, bullets, man can make
20   a bruise or break of exit for his life;
but is that a quietus, O tell me, is it quietus?

Surely not so! for how could murder, even self-murder
ever a quietus make?
        4
O let us talk of quiet that we know,
25   that we can know, the deep and lovely quiet
of a strong heart at peace!

How can we this, our own quietus, make?
        5
Build then the ship of death, for you must take
the longest journey, to oblivion.

30   And die the death, the long and painful death
that lies between the old self and the new.

Already our bodies are fallen, bruised, badly bruised,
already our souls are oozing through the exit
of the cruel bruise.

35   Already the dark and endless ocean of the end
is washing in through the breaches of our wounds,
already the flood is upon us.

Oh build your ship of death, your little ark
and furnish it with food, with little cakes, and wine
40   for the dark flight down oblivion.
        6
Piecemeal the body dies, and the timid soul
has her footing washed away, as the dark flood rises.

We are dying, we are dying, we are all of us dying
and nothing will stay the death-flood rising within us
45   and soon it will rise on the world, on the outside world.

We are dying, we are dying, piecemeal our bodies are dying
and our strength leaves us,
and our soul cowers naked in the dark rain over the flood,
cowering in the last branches of the tree of our life.
        7
50   We are dying, we are dying, so all we can do
is now to be willing to die, and to build the ship
of death to carry the soul on the longest journey.

A little ship, with oars and food
and little dishes, and all accoutrements
55   fitting and ready for the departing soul.

Now launch the small ship, now as the body dies
and life departs, launch out, the fragile soul
in the fragile ship of courage, the ark of faith

4. From *Hamlet,* III.i.75–6.

with its store of food and little cooking pans
60 and change of clothes,
upon the flood's black waste
upon the waters of the end
upon the sea of death, where still we sail
darkly, for we cannot steer, and have no port.

65 There is no port, there is nowhere to go
only the deepening blackness darkening still
blacker upon the soundless, ungurgling flood
darkness at one with darkness, up and down
and sideways utterly dark, so there is no direction any more.
70 and the little ship is there; yet she is gone.
She is not seen, for there is nothing to see her by.
She is gone! gone! and yet
somewhere she is there.
Nowhere!
                    8
75 And everything is gone, the body is gone
completely under, gone, entirely gone.
The upper darkness is heavy as the lower,
between them the little ship
is gone
80 she is gone.

It is the end, it is oblivion.
                    9
And yet out of eternity, a thread
separates itself on the blackness,
a horizontal thread
85 that fumes a little with pallor upon the dark.

Is it illusion? or does the pallor fume
A little higher?
Ah wait, wait, for there's the dawn,
the cruel dawn of coming back to life
90 out of oblivion.

Wait, wait, the little ship
drifting, beneath the deathly ashy gray
of a flood-dawn.

Wait, wait! even so, a flush of yellow
95 and strangely, O chilled wan soul, a flush of rose.

A flush of rose, and the whole thing starts again.
                    10
The flood subsides, and the body, like a worn sea-shell
emerges strange and lovely.
And the little ship wings home, faltering and lapsing
100 on the pink flood,
and the frail soul steps out, into her house again
filling the heart with peace.

Swings the heart renewed with peace
even of oblivion.

105 Oh build your ship of death, oh build it!
for you will need it.
For the voyage of oblivion awaits you.

                                            1932

EZRA POUND
(1885–   )

Ballatetta[1]

The light became her grace and dwelt among
Blind eyes and shadows that are formed as men;
Lo, how the light doth melt us into song:

The broken sunlight for a healm° she beareth   *helm*
5 Who hath my heart in jurisdiction.
In wild-wood never fawn nor fallow[2] fareth
So silent light; no gossamer° is spun   *spiderweb*
So delicate as she is, when the sun
Drives the clear emeralds from the bended grasses
10 Lest they should parch too swiftly, where she passes.

1911

Portrait d'Une Femme[3]

Your mind and you are our Sargasso Sea,[4]
London has swept about you this score years
And bright ships left you this or that in fee:
Ideas, old gossip, oddments of all things,
5 Strange spars of knowledge and dimmed wares of price.
Great minds have sought you—lacking someone else.
You have been second always. Tragical?
No. You preferred it to the usual thing:
One dull man, dulling and uxorious,
10 One average mind—with one thought less, each year.
Oh, you are patient, I have seen you sit
Hours, where something might have floated up.
And now you pay one. Yes, you richly pay.
You are a person of some interest, one comes to you
15 And takes strange gain away:
Trophies fished up; some curious suggestion;
Fact that leads nowhere; and a tale or two,
Pregnant with mandrakes,[5] or with something else
That might prove useful and yet never proves,
20 That never fits a corner or shows use,
Or finds its hour upon the loom of days:
The tarnished, gaudy, wonderful old work;
Idols and ambergris[6] and rare inlays,
These are your riches, your great store; and yet
25 For all this sea-hoard of deciduous things,
Strange woods half sodden, and new brighter stuff:
In the slow float of differing light and deep,
No! there is nothing! In the whole and all,
Nothing that's quite your own.
                    Yet this is you.

1912

---

1. "Little ballad." Early Italian poets, such as Guido Cavalcanti or Dante, sometimes apostrophized their poems with this word.
2. Fallow deer, so called from the yellowish-brown color of its coat.
3. Portrait of a Lady.
4. A region of the North Atlantic partially covered with accumulations of floating gulf-weed.
5. A plant, of narcotic properties, and sometimes believed to be aphrodisiac, whose forked root was traditionally thought to resemble the human body.
6. Secretion of the whale, used in perfumery.

The Garden

En robe de parade.[7]
—SAMAIN

Like a skein of loose silk blown against a wall
She walks by the railing of a path in Kensington Gardens,[8]
And she is dying piecemeal
          of a sort of emotional anemia.

5   And round about there is a rabble
Of the filthy, sturdy, unkillable infants of the very poor.
They shall inherit the earth.

In her is the end of breeding.
Her boredom is exquisite and excessive.
10   She would like some one to speak to her,
And is almost afraid that I
          will commit that indiscretion.

                                        1916

The Study in Aesthetics

The very small children in patched clothing,
Being smitten with an unusual wisdom,
Stopped in their play as she passed them
And cried up from their cobbles:

5   *Guarda! Ahi, guarda! ch' è be' a!*[9]

But three years after this
I heard the young Dante, whose last name I do not know—
For there are, in Sirmione,[1] twenty-eight young Dantes
      and thirty-four Catulli;
And there had been a great catch of sardines,
10   And his elders
Were packing them in the great wooden boxes
For the market in Brescia, and he
Leapt about, snatching at the bright fish
And getting in both of their ways;
15   And in vain they commanded him to *sta fermo!*[2]
And when they would not let him arrange
The fish in the boxes
He stroked those which were already arranged,
Murmuring for his own satisfaction
20   This identical phrase:

                    Ch' è be' a.

And at this I was mildly abashed.

                                        1916

---

7. Dressed as for a state occasion." The
phrase is from a poem by the French poet Al-
bert Samain (1858–1900), *The Infanta.*
8. Extensive public gardens in the residential
district west of Hyde Park, London.

9. *"Be'a: bella"* [Pound's note]. Look! Ah,
look! how beautiful she is!
1. Town on Lake Garda, in northern Italy.
2. Stand still!

Ts' ai Chi'h[3]

The petals fall in the fountain,
        the orange-colored rose-leaves,
Their ochre clings to the stone.

1916

In a Station of the Metro

The apparition of these faces in the crowd;
Petals on a wet, black bough.

1916

Black Slippers: Bellotti[4]

At the table beyond us
With her little suede slippers off,
With her white-stocking'd feet
Carefully kept from the floor by a napkin,
5   She converses:

          'Connaissez-vous Ostende?'[5]

The gurgling Italian lady on the other side of the restaurant
Replies with a certain hauteur,
But I await with patience,
10 To see how Celestine will re-enter her slippers.
She re-enters them with a groan.

1916

Simulacra[6]

Why does the horse-faced lady of just the unmentionable age
Walk down Longacre[7] reciting Swinburne to herself, inaudibly?
Why does the small child in the soiled-white imitation fur coat
Crawl in the very black gutter beneath the grape stand?
5   Why does the really handsome young woman approach me in Sackville
        Street[8]
Undeterred by the manifest age of my trappings?

1916

The River-Merchant's Wife: a Letter

While my hair was still cut straight across my forehead
I played about the front gate, pulling flowers.
You came by on bamboo stilts, playing horse,
You walked about my seat, playing with blue plums.
5   And we went on living in the village of Chokan:
Two small people, without dislike or suspicion.

At fourteen I married My Lord you.
I never laughed, being bashful.
Lowering my head, I looked at the wall.
10 Called to, a thousand times, I never looked back.

3. Ts'ai Chi'h, or more usually Ts'ao Chih, is the name of a Chinese poet who lived from 192–232, and Pound's using it as the title of his poem perhaps indicates that in it he is adopting the mode of Ts'ao Chih's "five-character poems," or even translating one of them.
4. Bellotti's was a restaurant in Soho, London.
5. Do you know Ostend?
6. A simulacrum is an image, or an imitation, a sham representation of something.
7. Street in the Covent Garden district of London.
8. Runs into Picadilly, not far from Picadilly Circus.

At fifteen I stopped scowling,
I desired my dust to be mingled with yours
Forever and forever and forever.
Why should I climb the look out?

15 At sixteen you departed,
You went into far Ku-to-yen, by the river of swirling eddies,
And you have been gone five months.
The monkeys make sorrowful noise overhead.

You dragged your feet when you went out.
20 By the gate now, the moss is grown, the different mosses,
Too deep to clear them away!
The leaves fall early this autumn, in wind.
The paired butterflies are already yellow with August
Over the grass in the West garden;
25 They hurt me. I grow older.
If you are coming down through the narrows of the river Kiang,
Please let me know beforehand,
And I will come out to meet you
          As far as Cho-fu-Sa.

                                        By *Rihaku*[9]
                                        1915

MAUBERLEY[1]

"Vacuos exercet aera morsus."[2]

I

Turned from the 'eau-forte
Par Jaquemart[3]
To the strait head
Of Messalina:[4]

5 'His true Penelope
Was Flaubert,'[5]
And his tool
The engraver's.

Firmness,
10 Not the full smile,
His art, but an art
In profile;

9. *Rihaku* is the transcription from the Japanese of the name of one of the greatest of the Chinese poets of the T'ang Dynasty, Li Po (ca. 700–762).
1. The volume entitled *Hugh Selwyn Mauberley*, which Pound published in 1920, consisted of two parts: first, a set of thirteen poems (ending with one called *Envoi* [1919]) descriptive of specific aspects of cultural life in England as Pound had known it in the years up to and including the First World War. The poems emphasize the conflicts between the ideals of the new movement in art and letters, of which he was an instigator, and the time-serving attitudes of entrenched interests. Part II was devoted to *Mauberley*, the sequence of five poems printed here.
2. From Ovid's description (*Metamorphoses* VII) of Cephalus' hunting dog as he pursues a monster that has been plaguing Thebes, almost catching him but not quite: "his jaws move in the void and take bites in the air." Then, as Cephalus watches, he sees that both his dog and the monster have been turned to stone.
3. French painter of watercolors and engraver (1837–80), delicate, refined, a distinguished illustrator of books on gems, porcelains, etc. "Eau-forte": etching.
4. The profligate wife of the Roman emperor Claudius, whose head might have figured on coins from Claudius' reign.
5. French novelist (1821–80), extremely painstaking both in the realism of his observation and in the finish of his style. Lines 5 and 6 are quoted from *Ode pour L'Election de son Sépulchre*, the first poem in the first *Mauberley* sequence. Penelope was Odysseus' faithful wife, to whom he returned.

Colorless
Pier Francesca,[6]
15   Pisanello lacking the skill
To forge Achaia.

II

> *"Qu'est ce qu'ils savent de l'amour, et qu'est ce
> qu'ils peuvent comprendre?*
> *S'ils ne comprennent pas la poésie, s'ils ne
> sentent pas la musique, qu'est ce qu'ils peuvent
> comprendre de cette passion en comparaison avec
> laquelle la rose est grossière et le parfum des
> violettes un tonnerre?"*[7]
>
> —CAID ALI

For three years, diabolus in the scale,[8]
He drank ambrosia,[9]
All passes, ANANGKE[1] prevails,
Came end, at last, to that Arcadia.[2]

5   He had moved amid her phantasmagoria,
Amid her galaxies,
NUKTIS 'AGALMA[3]

.   .   .   .

Drifted . . . drifted precipitate,
10   Asking time to be rid of . . .
Of his bewilderment; to designate
His new found orchid. . . .

To be certain . . . certain . . .
(Amid aerial flowers) . . . time for arrangements—
15   Drifted on
To the final estrangement;

Unable in the supervening blankness
To sift TO AGATHON[4] from the chaff
Until he found his sieve . . .
20   Ultimately, his seismograph:

—Given that is his 'fundamental passion,'
This urge to convey the relation
Of eye-lid and cheek-bone
By verbal manifestations;

25   To present the series
Of curious heads in medallion—

6. Pound may have meant to imply that Piero della Francesca (1410/20–1492) was a "colorless" painter, or he may have meant that the figure his poem describes is to be seen as a Piero who lacks the gift of color. Similarly with the reference to Pisanello, the great 15th-century draftsman and medallist. "To forge Achaia": to produce or represent a civilization like that of ancient Greece.
7. "What do they know about love, and what can they understand?/If they do not understand poetry, if they do not feel music, what can they understand of this passion in comparison with which the rose is crude and the perfume of violets a clap of thunder?" (In *Ezra Pound's Mauberley* [1955], John Espey points out that "Caid Ali" is a pseudonym for Pound himself.)

8. " 'Diabolus in Musica' (Lat., 'the devil in music'). A medieval term in which the tritone (augmented fourth or diminished fifth) was denounced by theorists as an interval to be avoided in composition" [*Grove's Dictionary of Music and Musicians*]. The line repeats the sense of the first line of the first sequence: "For three years, out of key with his time * * * "
9. Nectar and ambrosia formed the nourishment of the gods.
1. Greek for *necessity*.
2. In mythology, a district of Greece celebrated as a place of idyllically simple and peaceful existence.
3. Greek for "glory [or ornament] of the night," i.e., a star or constellation.
4. Greek for "the truly good."

He had passed, inconscient, full gaze,
The wide-branded irides[5]
And botticellian[6] sprays implied
30   In their diastasis;°   *separation, spread*

Which anaesthesis,° noted a year late,   *failure to perceive*
And weighed, revealed his great affect,
(Orchid), mandate
Of Eros,[7] a retrospect.

        . . .
35   Mouths biting empty air,[8]
The still stone dogs,
Caught in metamorphosis, were
Left him as epilogues.

'The Age Demanded'[9]

VIDE POEM II.

For this agility chance found
Him of all men, unfit
As the red-beaked steeds of
The Cytherean[1] for a chain bit.

5   The glow of porcelain
Brought no reforming sense
To his perception
Of the social inconsequence.

Thus, if her color
10   Came against his gaze,
Tempered as if
It were through a perfect glaze[2]

He made no immediate application
Of this to relation of the state
15   To the individual, the month was more temperate
Because this beauty had been.

       The coral isle, the lion-colored sand
       Burst in upon the porcelain revery:
       Impetuous troubling
20   Of his imagery.

Mildness, amid the neo-Nietzschean clatter,[3]
His sense of graduations,
Quite out of place amid
Resistance to current exacerbations,

25   Invitation, mere invitation to perceptivity
Gradually led him to the isolation
Which these presents[4] place
Under a more tolerant, perhaps, examination.

5. Plural of "iris," whether of the eye or the name of the flower.
6. Refers to the 15th-century Italian painter, Botticelli, and probably to one or the other of his best-known paintings, the Primavera (Spring) or the Birth of Venus.
7. God of love.
8. The line translates the epigraph from Ovid.
9. Phrase quoted from the second poem in the first *Mauberley* sequence, which declares that the age demanded from its writers and artists cheap, quickly produced works, giving back its own image.

1. Venus, so called because she was supposed to have risen from the sea near the island of Cythera. Her chariot was drawn by doves.
2. I.e., the glaze on porcelain.
3. The "clatter" composed of events, points of view, philosophies that had sprung from the views of the German philosopher Nietzsche (1844–1900).
4. That is, the examination of Mauberley and his motives which is being undertaken in the present set of poems.

By constant elimination
30   The manifest universe
Yielded an armor
Against utter consternation,

A Minoan undulation,[5]
Seen, we admit, amid ambrosial circumstances
35   Strengthened him against
The discouraging doctrine of chances,

And his desire for survival,
Faint in the most strenuous moods,
Became an Olympian *apathein*[6]
40   In the presence of selected perceptions.

A pale gold, in the aforesaid pattern,
The unexpected palms[7]
Destroying, certainly, the artist's urge,
Left him delighted with the imaginary
45   Audition of the phantasmal sea-surge,

Incapable of the least utterance or composition,
Emendation, conservation of the 'better tradition,'
Refinement of medium, elimination of superfluities,
August attraction or concentration.

50   Nothing, in brief, but maudlin confession,
Irresponse to human aggression,
Amid the precipitation, down-float
Of insubstantial manna,[8]
Lifting the faint susurrus[9]
55   Of his subjective hosannah.

Ultimate affronts to
Human redundancies;

Non-esteem of self-styled 'his betters'
Leading, as he well knew,
60   To his final
Exclusion from the world of letters.

IV

Scattered Moluccas[1]
Not knowing, day to day
The first day's end, in the next noon;
The placid water
5   Unbroken by the Simoon;[2]

Thick foliage
Placid beneath warm suns,
Tawn fore-shores
Washed in the cobalt of oblivions;

---

5. The graceful movements suggested by works of art from ancient Crete.
6. A godlike impassibility (Greek).
7. Palm-trees, to be related to line 17 of the present poem.
8. Miraculous nourishment which God sent to the Israelites in the desert, hence, any sustenance miraculously or surprisingly supplied.
9. Sibilant whispering.
1. Islands scattered over the sea between Celebes and New Guinea.
2. Hot, dry wind.

10 Or through dawn-mist
The gray and rose
Of the juridical[3]
Flamingoes;

A consciousness disjunct,
15 Being but this overblotted
Series
Of intermittences;

Coracle[4] of Pacific voyages,
The unforecasted beach;
20 Then on an oar,
Read this:

'I was
And I no more exist;
Here drifted
25 An hedonist.'

Medallion

Luini[5] in porcelain!
The grand piano
Utters a profane
Protest with her clear soprano.

5 The sleek head emerges
From the gold-yellow frock
As Anadyomene[6] in the opening
Pages of Reinach.

Honey-red, closing the face-oval,
10 A basket-work of braids which seem as if they were
Spun in King Minos'[7] hall
From metal, or intractable amber;

The face-oval beneath the glaze,
Bright in its suave bounding-line, as,
15 Beneath half-watt rays,
The eyes turn topaz.

1920

ROBINSON JEFFERS
(1887–1962)

Shine, Perishing Republic

While this America settles in the mold of its vulgarity, heavily thickening to empire,
And protest, only a bubble in the molten mass, pops and sighs out, and the mass hardens,

I sadly smiling remember that the flower fades to make fruit, the fruit rots to make earth.
Out of the mother; and through the spring exultances, ripeness and decadence; and home to the mother.

3. Judge-like (referring to the pose of the flamingo when standing still.)
4. Small fishing boat, made of hide or oiled cloth on a light frame.
5. Italian painter (ca. 1485–1532).
6. An epithet applied to Venus (literally, "rising from the sea"). Salomon Reinach's *Apollo: an Illustrated History of Art throughout the Ages* illustrates, in its chapters on Greek sculpture, both the Medici Venus and the Venus de Milo.
7. In Greek mythology, king of Crete.

5   You making haste haste on decay: not blameworthy; life is good, be it
        stubbornly long or suddenly
    A mortal splendor: meteors are not needed less than mountains: shine,
        perishing republic.

    But for my children, I would have them keep their distance from the
        thickening center; corruption
    Never has been compulsory, when the cities lie at the monster's feet there
        are left the mountains.

    And boys, be in nothing so moderate as in love of man, a clever servant,
        insufferable master.
10 There is the trap that catches noblest spirits, that caught—they say—God,
        when he walked on earth.

                                                                    1924

Hurt Hawks

                    1
    The broken pillar of the wing jags from the clotted shoulder,
    The wing trails like a banner in defeat,
    No more to use the sky forever but live with famine
    And pain a few days: cat nor coyote
5   Will shorten the week of waiting for death, there is game without talons.
    He stands under the oak-bush and waits
    The lame feet of salvation; at night he remembers freedom
    And flies in a dream, the dawns ruin it.
    He is strong and pain is worse to the strong, incapacity is worse.
10 The curs of the day come and torment him
    At distance, no one but death the redeemer will humble that head,
    The intrepid readiness, the terrible eyes.
    The wild God of the world is sometimes merciful to those
    That ask mercy, not often to the arrogant.
15 You do not know him, you communal people, or you have forgotten him;
    Intemperate and savage, the hawk remembers him;
    Beautiful and wild, the hawks, and men that are dying, remember him.
                    2
    I'd sooner, except the penalties, kill a man than a hawk; but
        the great redtail°   *red-tailed hawk*
    Had nothing left but unable misery
20 From the bone too shattered for mending, the wing that trailed under
        his talons when he moved.
    We had fed him six weeks, I gave him freedom,
    He wandered over the foreland hill and returned in the evening,
        asking for death,
    Not like a beggar, still eyed with the old
    Implacable arrogance. I gave him the lead gift in the twilight. What
        fell was relaxed,
25 Owl-downy, soft feminine feathers; but what
    Soared: the fierce rush: the night-herons by the flooded river cried
        fear at its rising
    Before it was quite unsheathed from reality.

                                                                    1928

MARIANNE MOORE
(1887–   )

No Swan So Fine

"No water so still as the
    dead fountains of Versailles."[1] No swan,
with swart blind look askance
and gondoliering legs,[2] so fine
5   as the chintz china one with fawn-
brown eyes and toothed gold
collar on to show whose bird it was.

Lodged in the Louis Fifteenth
    candelabrum-tree[3] of cockscomb-
10 tinted buttons, dahlias,
sea-urchins, and everlastings,[4]
    it perches on the branching foam
of polished sculptured
flowers—at ease and tall. The king is dead.

                                   1932, 1951

Peter

    Strong and slippery,
built for the midnight grass-party
confronted by four cats, he sleeps his time away—
the detached first claw on the foreleg corresponding
5 to the thumb, retracted to its tip; the small tuft of fronds
or katydid-legs above each eye numbering all units
in each group; the shadbones[5] regularly set about the mouth
to droop or rise in unison like porcupine-quills.
He lets himself be flattened out by gravity,
10 as seaweed is tamed and weakened by the sun,
compelled when extended, to lie stationary.
Sleep is the result of his delusion that one must
do as well as one can for oneself,
sleep—epitome of what is to him the end of life.
15 Demonstrate on him how the lady placed a forked stick
on the innocuous neck-sides of the dangerous southern snake.
One need not try to stir him up; his prune-shaped head
and alligator-eyes are not party to the joke.
Lifted and handled, he may be dangled like an eel
20 or set up on the forearm like a mouse;
his eyes bisected by pupils of a pin's width,
are flickeringly exhibited, then covered up.
May be? I should have said might have been;
when he has been got the better of in a dream—
25 as in a fight with nature or with cats, we all know it.
Profound sleep is not with him a fixed illusion.
Springing about with froglike accuracy, with jerky cries
when taken in hand, he is himself again;

---

1. Famed palace of French kings in the late 17th and early 18th centuries, now a museum.
2. Italian gondoliers paddle from the stern to propel their gondolas.
3. "A pair of Louis XV candelabra with Dresden figures of swans belonging to Lord Balfour" [Moore's note].
4. Plants whose flowers may be dried without losing their form or color; also, the flowers from such plants.
5. Long, very fine bones of the shad fish.

to sit caged by the rungs of a domestic chair
30   would be unprofitable—human. What is the good of hypocrisy?
it is permissible to choose one's employment,
to abandon the nail, or roly-poly,
when it shows signs of being no longer a pleasure,
to score the nearby magazine with a double line of strokes.
35   He can talk but insolently says nothing. What of it?
When one is frank, one's very presence is a compliment.
It is clear that he can see the virtue of naturalness,
that he does not regard the published fact as a surrender.
As for the disposition invariably to affront,
40   an animal with claws should have an opportunity to use them.
The eel-like extension of trunk into tail is not an accident.
To leap, to lengthen out, divide the air, to purloin, to pursue.
To tell the hen: fly over the fence, go in the wrong way
in your perturbation—this is life;
45   to do less would be nothing but dishonesty.

1935

T. S. ELIOT
(1888–1965)

The Love Song of J. Alfred Prufrock

S'io credesse che mia risposta fosse
A persona che mai tornasse al mondo,
Questa fiamma staria senza piu scosse.
Ma perciocche giammai di questo fondo
Non torno vivo alcun, s'i'odo il vero,
Senza tema d'infamia ti rispondo.[1]

Let us go then, you and I,
When the evening is spread out against the sky
Like a patient etherized upon a table;
Let us go, through certain half-deserted streets,
5   The muttering retreats
Of restless nights in one-night cheap hotels
And sawdust restaurants with oyster-shells:
Streets that follow like a tedious argument
Of insidious intent
10   To lead you to an overwhelming question. . .
Oh, do not ask, "What is it?"
Let us go and make our visit.

In the room the women come and go
Talking of Michelangelo.

15   The yellow fog that rubs its back upon the window-panes
The yellow smoke that rubs its muzzle on the window-panes
Licked its tongue into the corners of the evening,
Lingered upon the pools that stand in drains,
Let fall upon its back the soot that falls from chimneys,
20   Slipped by the terrace, made a sudden leap,
And seeing that it was a soft October night,
Curled once about the house, and fell asleep.

---

1. Dante, *Inferno*, XXVII.61–66. These words are spoken by Guido da Montefeltro, whom Dante and Virgil have encountered in the Eighth Chasm, that of the False Counselors, where each spirit is concealed within a flame which moves as the spirit speaks: "If I thought my answer were given/to anyone who would ever return to the world,/this flame would stand still without moving any further./But since never from this abyss/has anyone ever returned alive, if what I hear is true,/without fear of infamy I answer thee."

And indeed there will be time
For the yellow smoke that slides along the street,
25 Rubbing its back upon the window-panes;
There will be time, there will be time
To prepare a face to meet the faces that you meet;
There will be time to murder and create,
And time for all the works and days[2] of hands
30 That lift and drop a question on your plate;
Time for you and time for me,
And time yet for a hundred indecisions,
And for a hundred visions and revisions,
Before the taking of a toast and tea.

35 In the room the women come and go
Talking of Michelangelo.

And indeed there will be time
To wonder, "Do I dare?" and, "Do I dare?"
Time to turn back and descend the stair,
40 With a bald spot in the middle of my hair—
[They will say: "How his hair is growing thin!"]
My morning coat, my collar mounting firmly to the chin,
My necktie rich and modest, but asserted by a simple pin—
[They will say: "But how his arms and legs are thin!"]
45 Do I dare
Disturb the universe?
In a minute there is time
For decisions and revisions which a minute will reverse.

For I have known them all already, known them all:
50 Have known the evenings, mornings, afternoons,
I have measured out my life with coffee spoons;
I know the voices dying with a dying fall
Beneath the music from a farther room.
    So how should I presume?

55 And I have known the eyes already, known them all—
The eyes that fix you in a formulated phrase,
And when I am formulated, sprawling on a pin,
When I am pinned and wriggling on the wall,
Then how should I begin
60 To spit out all the butt-ends of my days and ways?
    And how should I presume?

And I have known the arms already, known them all—
Arms that are braceleted and white and bare
[But in the lamplight, downed with light brown hair!]
65 Is it perfume from a dress
That makes me so digress?
Arms that lie along a table, or wrap about a shawl.
    And should I then presume?
    And how should I begin?
                .   .   .   .   .   .

70 Shall I say, I have gone at dusk through narrow streets
And watched the smoke that rises from the pipes
Of lonely men in shirt-sleeves, leaning out of windows? .   .   .

I should have been a pair of ragged claws
Scuttling across the floors of silent seas.
                .   .   .   .   .   .

---

2. Possibly alludes to the title of a didactic work on the seasonal pursuits of country life,
Works and Days, by the Greek poet Hesiod (eighth century B.C.).

75 And the afternoon, the evening, sleeps so peacefully!
Smoothed by long fingers,
Asleep . . . tired . . . or it malingers,
Stretched on the floor, here beside you and me.
Should I, after tea and cakes and ices,
80 Have the strength to force the moment to its crisis?
But though I have wept and fasted, wept and prayed,
Though I have seen my head [grown slightly bald] brought in upon a
    platter,[3]
I am no prophet—and here's no great matter;
I have seen the moment of my greatness flicker,
85 And I have seen the eternal Footman hold my coat, and snicker,
And in short, I was afraid.

And would it have been worth it, after all,
After the cups, the marmalade, the tea,
Among the porcelain, among some talk of you and me,
90 Would it have been worth while,
To have bitten off the matter with a smile,
To have squeezed the universe into a ball
To roll it toward some overwhelming question,
To say: "I am Lazarus,[4] come from the dead,
95 Come back to tell you all, I shall tell you all"—
If one, settling a pillow by her head,
    Should say: "That is not what I meant at all.
    That is not it, at all."

And would it have been worth it, after all,
100 Would it have been worth while,
After the sunsets and the dooryards and the sprinkled streets,
After the novels, after the teacups, after the skirts that trail along the floor—
And this, and so much more?—
It is impossible to say just what I mean!
105 But as if a magic lantern threw the nerves in patterns on a screen:
Would it have been worth while
If one, settling a pillow or throwing off a shawl,
And turning toward the window, should say:
    "That is not it at all,
110   That is not what I meant, at all."

    . . . . . .

No! I am not Prince Hamlet, nor was meant to be;
Am an attendant lord, one that will do
To swell a progress,[5] start a scene or two,
Advise the prince; no doubt, an easy tool,
115 Deferential, glad to be of use,
Politic, cautious, and meticulous;
Full of high sentence,° but a bit obtuse;   *sententiousness*
At times, indeed, almost ridiculous—
Almost, at times, the Fool.

120 I grow old . . . I grow old . . .
I shall wear the bottoms of my trousers rolled.

Shall I part my hair behind? Do I dare to eat a peach?
I shall wear white flannel trousers, and walk upon the beach.
I have heard the mermaids singing, each to each.

125 I do not think that they will sing to me.

3. See the story of the martyrdom of St. John the Baptist (Matthew xiv.1–12), whose head was presented to Salome on a plate at the order of the tetrarch Herod.
4. See John xi, and xii 1–2.
5. In Elizabethan sense: state journey.

I have seen them riding seaward on the waves
Combing the white hair of the waves blown back
When the wind blows the water white and black.

130   We have lingered in the chambers of the sea
By sea-girls wreathed with seaweed red and brown
Till human voices wake us, and we drown.

1917

Preludes

1

The winter evening settles down
With smell of steaks in passageways.
Six o'clock.
The burnt-out ends of smoky days.
5   And now a gusty shower wraps
The grimy scraps
Of withered leaves about your feet
And newspapers from vacant lots;
The showers beat
10   On broken blinds and chimney-pots,
And at the corner of the street
A lonely cab-horse steams and stamps.
And then the lighting of the lamps.

2

The morning comes to consciousness
15   Of faint stale smells of beer
From the sawdust-trampled street
With all its muddy feet that press
To early coffee-stands.
With the other masquerades
20   That time resumes,
One thinks of all the hands
That are raising dingy shades
In a thousand furnished rooms.

3

You tossed a blanket from the bed,
25   You lay upon your back, and waited;
You dozed, and watched the night revealing
The thousand sordid images
Of which your soul was constituted;
They flickered against the ceiling.
30   And when all the world came back
And the light crept up between the shutters
And you heard the sparrows in the gutters,
You had such a vision of the street
As the street hardly understands;
35   Sitting along the bed's edge, where
You curled the papers from your hair,
Or clasped the yellow soles of feet
In the palms of both soiled hands.

4

His soul stretched tight across the skies
40   That fade behind a city block,
Or trampled by insistent feet
At four and five and six o'clock;
And short square fingers stuffing pipes,
And evening newspapers, and eyes
45   Assured of certain certainties,
The conscience of a blackened street
Impatient to assume the world.

I am moved by fancies that are curled
Around these images, and cling:
50 The notion of some infinitely gentle
Infinitely suffering thing.

Wipe your hand across your mouth, and laugh;
The worlds revolve like ancient women
Gathering fuel in vacant lots.

1917

Gerontion[6]

*Thou hast nor youth nor age
But as it were an after dinner sleep
Dreaming of both.*[7]

Here I am, an old man in a dry month,
Being read to by a boy, waiting for rain.
I was neither at the hot gates[8]
Nor fought in the warm rain
5 Nor knee deep in the salt marsh, heaving a cutlass,
Bitten by flies, fought.
My house is a decayed house,
And the jew squats on the window sill, the owner,
Spawned in some estaminet[9] of Antwerp,
10 Blistered in Brussels, patched and peeled in London.
The goat coughs at night in the field overhead;
Rocks, moss, stonecrop,[1] iron, merds.[2]
The woman keeps the kitchen, makes tea,
Sneezes at evening, poking the peevish gutter.
15   I an old man,
A dull head among windy spaces.

Signs are taken for wonders. "We would see a sign!"
The word within a word, unable to speak a word,[3]
Swaddled with darkness. In the juvescence[4] of the year
20 Came Christ the tiger

In depraved May, dogwood and chestnut, flowering judas,[5]
To be eaten, to be divided, to be drunk
Among whispers; by Mr. Silvero[6]
With caressing hands, at Limoges
25 Who walked all night in the next room;

By Hakagawa, bowing among the Titians;
By Madame de Tornquist, in the dark room
Shifting the candles; Fräulein von Kulp
Who turned in the hall, one hand on the door.
30   Vacant shuttles
Weave the wind. I have no ghosts,
An old man in a drafty house
Under a windy knob.

6. The title is the Greek word γερόντιον, diminutive of γέρων, "old man"; hence, "little old man."
7. Shakespeare, *Measure for Measure* III.i. 32–34.
8. The phrase "hot gates" translates "Thermopylae," the name of the narrow pass into Greece which Leonidas and his Spartans nobly but unsuccessfully defended against the Persians in 480 B.C.
9. Small lower-class tavern or café.
1. A yellow-flowered herb (*Sedum acre*) that grows in rocky places.
2. Dung, excrement.
3. Lines 17 and 18 echo a passage from Bishop Lancelot Andrewes's twelfth Nativity sermon, delivered before the king on Christmas Day 1618. "*Signes* are taken for wonders: *Master we would faine see a Signe* [Matthew xii.38, the words of the scribes and Pharisees to Christ], that is, a miracle. And, in this sense, it is a *Signe*, to wonder at. Indeed, every word (heer) is a wonder: το βρέφος an infant; *Verbum infans*, the Word without a word; the *aeternall Word* not hable to speake a *word* * * *" [Lancelot Andrewes, *Sermons*, ed. G. M. Story, 1967].
4. Similar in meaning to "juvenescence"; regeneration, rejuvenation.
5. A tree whose purple flowers appear before the leaves; its name is thought to derive from the folk-belief that Judas hanged himself from such a tree.
6. Proper names in lines 23–28 and in line 69 are generic or suggestive rather than being the names of actual figures from history or literature.

After such knowledge, what forgiveness? Think now
35 History has many cunning passages, contrived corridors
And issues, deceives with whispering ambitions,
Guides us by vanities. Think now
She gives when our attention is distracted
And what she gives, gives with such supple confusions
40 That the giving famishes the craving. Gives too late
What's not believed in, or if still believed,
In memory only, reconsidered passion. Gives too soon
Into weak hands, what's thought can be dispensed with
Till the refusal propagates a fear. Think
45 Neither fear nor courage saves us. Unnatural vices
Are fathered by our heroism. Virtues
Are forced upon us by our impudent crimes.
These tears are shaken from the wrath-bearing tree.

The tiger springs in the new year. Us he devours.
50   Think at last
We have not reached conclusion, when I
Stiffen in a rented house. Think at last
I have not made this show purposelessly
And it is not by any concitation[7]
55 Of the backward devils
I would meet you upon this honestly.
I that was near your heart was removed therefrom
To lose beauty in terror, terror in inquisition.
I have lost my passion: why should I need to keep it
60 Since what is kept must be adulterated?
I have lost my sight, smell, hearing, taste and touch:
How should I use them for your closer contact?

These with a thousand small deliberations
Protract the profit of their chilled delirium,
65 Excite the membrane, when the sense has cooled,
With pungent sauces, multiply variety
In a wilderness of mirrors. What will the spider do,
Suspend its operations, will the weevil
Delay? De Bailhache, Fresca, Mrs. Cammel, whirled
70 Beyond the circuit of the shuddering Bear[8]
In fractured atoms. Gull against the wind, in the windy straits
Of Belle Isle,[9] or running on the Horn,[1]
White feathers in the snow, the Gulf claims,
And an old man driven by the Trades[2]
75 To a sleepy corner.

Tenants of the house,
Thoughts of a dry brain in a dry season.

1920

7. Stirring up, arousing.
8. Either the Great Bear or the Lesser Bear, constellations of the Northern Hemisphere.
9. The Straits of Belle Isle lie between Newfoundland and Labrador.
1. Cape Horn, at the extreme tip of South America.

2. A trade wind is "a drying wind blowing almost continually in the same course, or *trade*, toward the equator but from an easterly direction" [Webster].

Sweeney Among the Nightingales

ὦμοι, πέπληγμαι καιρίαν πληγὴν ἔσω.³

Apeneck Sweeney spreads his knees
Letting his arms hang down to laugh,
The zebra stripes along his jaw
Swelling to maculate° giraffe.   *spotted*

5   The circles of the stormy moon
Slide westward toward the River Plate,⁴
Death and the Raven⁵ drift above
And Sweeney guards the hornéd gate.⁶

Gloomy Orion⁷ and the Dog
10 Are veiled; and hushed the shrunken seas;
The person in the Spanish cape
Tries to sit on Sweeney's knees

Slips and pulls the table cloth
Overturns a coffee-cup,
15 Reorganized upon the floor
She yawns and draws a stocking up;

The silent man in mocha brown
Sprawls at the window-sill and gapes;
The waiter brings in oranges
20 Bananas figs and hothouse grapes;

The silent vertebrate in brown
Contracts and concentrates, withdraws;
Rachel *née* Rabinovitch
Tears at the grapes with murderous paws;

25 She and the lady in the cape
Are suspect, thought to be in league;
Therefore the man with heavy eyes
Declines the gambit, shows fatigue,

Leaves the room and reappears
30 Outside the window, leaning in,
Branches of wistaria
Circumscribe a golden grin;

The host with someone indistinct
Converses at the door apart,
35 The nightingales are singing near
The Convent of the Sacred Heart,

And sang within the bloody wood
When Agamemnon cried aloud,
And let their liquid siftings fall
40 To stain the stiff dishonored shroud.

1919

3. Aeschylus, *Agamemnon*, line 1343. Agamemnon's cry, heard from inside the palace, as Clytemnestra strikes her first blow: "Oh, I have been struck a direct deadly blow, within!"
4. Río de la Plata, an estuary of the Paraná and Uruguay rivers, between Uruguay and Argentina.
5. The southern constellation Corvus.

6. In Greek legend, dreams came to mortals through two sets of gates: the gates of horn, for dreams which were true, the gates of ivory, for dreams which were untrue.
7. A constellation in which is seen the figure of a hunter, with belt and sword; near it, the dog-star, Sirius, represents the hunter's dog.

Journey of the Magi[8]

'A cold coming we had of it,[9]
Just the worst time of the year
For a journey, and such a long journey:
The ways deep and the weather sharp,
5   The very dead of winter.'
And the camels galled, sore-footed, refractory,
Lying down in the melting snow.
There were times we regretted
The summer palaces on slopes, the terraces,
10 And the silken girls bringing sherbet.
Then the camel men cursing and grumbling
And running away, and wanting their liquor and women,
And the night-fires going out, and the lack of shelters,
And the cities hostile and the towns unfriendly
15 And the villages dirty and charging high prices:
A hard time we had of it.
At the end we preferred to travel all night,
Sleeping in snatches,
With the voices singing in our ears, saying
20 That this was all folly.

Then at dawn we came down to a temperate valley,
Wet, below the snow line, smelling of vegetation;
With a running stream and a water-mill beating the darkness,
And three trees on the low sky,[1]
25 And an old white horse galloped away in the meadow.
Then we came to a tavern with vine-leaves over the lintel,
Six hands at an open door dicing for pieces of silver,
And feet kicking the empty wine-skins.
But there was no information, and so we continued
30 And arrived at evening, not a moment too soon
Finding the place; it was (you may say) satisfactory.

All this was a long time ago, I remember,
And I would do it again, but set down
This set down
35 This: were we led all that way for
Birth or Death? There was a Birth, certainly,
We had evidence and no doubt. I had seen birth and death,
But had thought they were different; this Birth was
Hard and bitter agony for us, like Death, our death.
40 We returned to our places, these Kingdoms,
But no longer at ease here, in the old dispensation,
With an alien people clutching their gods.
I should be glad of another death.

1927

8. The poem recreates the recollections of one of the three Wise Men, or Magi, who, guided by the star, had come to Bethlehem to witness the birth of Christ, as told in Matthew ii.1–2.
9. The first five lines are adapted from the sermon preached at Christmas, 1622, by Bishop Lancelot Andrewes: "Last, we consider the *time* of their coming, the season of the yeare. It was no *summer Progresse*. A cold comming they had of it, at this time of the year; just, the worst time of the yeare, to take a journey, and specially a long journey, in. The waies deep, the weather sharp, the daies short, the sunn farthest off * * * , the very dead of *Winter*."
1. The image prefigures the three crosses of the Crucifixion, as line 27 suggests the Roman soldiers dicing for Christ's robe, as well as the pieces of silver paid to Judas for betraying Christ.

Marina[2]

Quis hic locus, quae regio, quae mundi plaga?[3]

What seas what shores what gray rocks and what islands
What water lapping the bow
And scent of pine and the woodthrush singing through the fog
What images return
5 O my daughter.

Those who sharpen the tooth of the dog, meaning
Death
Those who glitter with the glory of the hummingbird, meaning
Death
10 Those who sit in the stye of contentment, meaning
Death
Those who suffer the ecstasy of the animals, meaning
Death

Are become unsubstantial, reduced by a wind,
15 A breath of pine, and the woodsong fog
By this grace dissolved in place

What is this face, less clear and clearer
The pulse in the arm, less strong and stronger—
Given or lent? more distant than stars and nearer than the eye

20 Whispers and small laughter between leaves and hurrying feet
Under sleep, where all the waters meet.

Bowsprit cracked with ice and paint cracked with heat.
I made this, I have forgotten
And remember.
25 The rigging weak and the canvas rotten
Between one June and another September.
Made this unknowing, half conscious, unknown, my own.
The garboard strake[4] leaks, the seams need caulking.
This form, this face, this life
30 Living to live in a world of time beyond me; let me
Resign my life for this life, my speech for that unspoken,
The awakened, lips parted, the hope, the new ships.

What seas what shores what granite islands towards my timbers
And woodthrush calling through the fog
35 My daughter.

1930

From Landscapes

I. New Hampshire

Children's voices in the orchard
Between the blossom- and the fruit-time:
Golden head, crimson head,
Between the green tip and the root.
5 Black wing, brown wing, hover over;

2. The title is usually taken as referring to Marina in Shapespeare's play *Pericles, Prince of Tyre.* She is the prince's daughter who is lost at sea but recovered; she and her parents, after the further trials which beset them, and which they overcome by piety and virtue, are reunited at the end of the play.
3. In Seneca's tragedy *Hercules Furens* (Hercules Maddened), Juno afflicts Hercules with madness, so that he kills his wife and children. The quoted line (line 1138), "What is this place, what country, what quarter of the world?," is spoken as he comes to himself, when he is still unable to recognize his home or realize that the corpses he sees are his victims.
4. The first line of planking laid upon a ship's keel.

Twenty years and the spring is over;
Today grieves, tomorrow grieves,
Cover me over, light-in-leaves;
Golden head, black wing,
10   Cling, swing,
Spring, sing,
Swing up into the apple-tree.

II. *Virginia*

Red river, red river,
Slow flow heat is silence
No will is still as a river
Still. Will heat move
5   Only through the mocking-bird
Heard once? Still hills
Wait. Cates wait. Purple trees,
White trees, wait, wait,
Delay, decay. Living, living
10   Never moving. Ever moving
Iron thoughts came with me
And go with me:
Red river, river, river.

1934

JOHN CROWE RANSOM
(1888–   )

Bells for John Whiteside's Daughter

There was such speed in her little body,
And such lightness in her footfall,
It is no wonder her brown study
Astonishes us all.

5   Her wars were bruited in our high window.
We looked among orchard trees and beyond
Where she took arms against her shadow,
Or harried unto the pond

The lazy geese, like a snow cloud
10   Dripping their snow on the green grass,
Tricking and stopping, sleepy and proud,
Who cried in goose, Alas,

For the tireless heart within the little
Lady with rod that made them rise
15   From their noon apple-dreams and scuttle
Goose-fashion under the skies!

But now go the bells, and we are ready,
In one house we are sternly stopped
To say we are vexed at her brown study,
20   Lying so primly propped.

1924

Dead Boy

The little cousin is dead, by foul subtraction,
A green bough from Virginia's aged tree,
And none of the county kin like the transaction,
Nor some of the world of outer dark, like me.

5 A boy not beautiful, nor good, nor clever,
   A black cloud full of storms too hot for keeping,
   A sword beneath his mother's heart—yet never
   Woman bewept her babe as this is weeping.

   A pig with a pasty face, so I had said,
10 Squealing for cookies, kinned by poor pretense
   With a noble house. But the little man quite dead,
   I see the forbears' antique lineaments.

   The elder men have strode by the box of death
   To the wide flag porch, and muttering low send round
15 The bruit° of the day. O friendly waste of breath!   *news, report*
   Their hearts are hurt with a deep dynastic wound.

   He was pale and little, the foolish neighbors say;
   The first-fruits, saith the Preacher, the Lord hath taken;
   But this was the old tree's late branch wrenched away,
20 Grieving the sapless limbs, the shorn and shaken.

                                                        1927

CONRAD AIKEN
(1889–   )

The Wedding

   At noon, Tithonus,[1] withered by his singing,
   Climbing the oatstalk with his hairy legs,
   Met gray Arachne,[2] poisoned and shrunk down
   By her own beauty; pride had shriveled both.
5 In the white web—where seven flies hung wrapped—
   She heard his footstep; hurried to him; bound him;
   Enshrouded him in silk; then poisoned him.
   Twice shrieked Tithonus, feebly; then was still.
   Arachne loved him. Did he love Arachne?
10 She watched him with red eyes, venomous sparks,
   And the furred claws outspread . . . "O sweet Tithonus!
   Darling! Be kind, and sing that song again!
   Shake the bright web again with that deep fiddling!
   Are you much poisoned? sleeping? do you dream?
15 Darling Tithonus!"

              And Tithonus, weakly
   Moving one hairy shin against the other
   Within the silken sack, contrived to fiddle
   A little tune, half-hearted: "Shrewd Arachne!
20 Whom pride in beauty withered to this shape
   As pride in singing shriveled me to mine—
   Unwrap me, let me go—and let me limp,
   With what poor strength your venom leaves me, down
   This oatstalk, and away."

1. In Greek legend, Tithonus, a beautiful and
musically gifted youth, at the plea of his
wife, Aurora, goddess of the dawn, to Zeus,
was given eternal life but, unfortunately, with-
out eternal youth. After many years and pro-
gressive aging, Tithonus was turned into a
cicada by the pitying gods.

2. Arachne was a superb weaver who angered
Athena by weaving a better tapestry than the
goddess. Arachne tried to hang herself because
of Athena's anger, but was spared and turned
into a spider.

25   Arachne, angry,
Stung him again, twirling him with rough paws,
The red eyes keen. "What! You would dare to leave me?
Then let you go. But sing that tune again—
So plaintive was it!"

30   And Tithonus faintly
Moved the poor fiddles, which were growing cold,
And sang: "Arachne, goddess envied of gods,
Beauty's eclipse eclipsed by angry beauty,
Have pity, do not ask the withered heart
35 To sing too long for you! My strength goes out,
Too late we meet for love. O be content
With friendship, which the noon sun once may kindle
To give one flash of passion, like a dewdrop,
Before it goes! . . . Be reasonable, Arachne!"

40 Arachne heard the song grow weaker, dwindle
To first a rustle, and then half a rustle,
And last a tick, so small no ear could hear it
Save hers, a spider's ear. And her small heart,
(Rusted away, like his, to a pinch of dust,)
45 Gleamed once, like his, and died. She clasped him tightly
And sunk her fangs in him. Tithonus dead,
She slept awhile, her last sensation gone;
Woke from the nap, forgetting him; and ate him.

1925

CLAUDE McKAY
(1890–1948)

If We Must Die

If we must die, let it not be like hogs
Hunted and penned in an inglorious spot,
While round us bark the mad and hungry dogs,
Making their mock at our accursèd lot.
5 If we must die, O let us nobly die,
So that our precious blood may not be shed
In vain; then even the monsters we defy
Shall be constrained to honor us though dead!
O kinsmen we must meet the common foe!
10 Though far outnumbered let us show us brave,
And for their thousand blows deal one deathblow!
What though before us lies the open grave?
Like men we'll face the murderous, cowardly pack,
Pressed to the wall, dying, but fighting back!

1922

ARCHIBALD MacLEISH
(1892–   )

You, Andrew Marvell[1]

And here face down beneath the sun
And here upon earth's noonward height
To feel the always coming on
The always rising of the night

5   To feel creep up the curving east
The earthy chill of dusk and slow
Upon those under lands the vast
And ever climbing shadow grow

And strange at Ecbatan[2] the trees
10   Take leaf by leaf the evening strange
The flooding dark about their knees
The mountains over Persia change

And now at Kermanshah the gate
Dark empty and the withered grass
15   And through the twilight now the late
Few travelers in the westward pass

And Baghdad darken and the bridge
Across the silent river gone
And through Arabia the edge
20   Of evening widen and steal on

And deepen on Palmyra's street
The wheel rut in the ruined stone
And Lebanon fade out and Crete
High through the clouds and overblown

25   And over Sicily the air
Still flashing with the landward gulls
And loom and slowly disappear
The sails above the shadowy hulls

And Spain go under and the shore
30   Of Africa the gilded sand
And evening vanish and no more
The low pale light across that land

Nor now the long light on the sea
And here face downward in the sun
35   To feel how swift how secretly
The shadow of the night comes on. . . .

1930

---

1. Andrew Marvell (1621–1678) wrote *To His Coy Mistress,* the poem to which MacLeish specifically alludes.
2. The poet's thoughts, following the daily path of the sun, move westward, from Ecbatana, once the capital of Media Magna (part of Persia), on to Kermanshah, Baghdad, Palmyra, Sicily, and so on.

Empire Builders

The Museum Attendant:

This is *The Making of America in Five Panels*:

This is Mister Harriman[3] making America:
Mister-Harriman-is-buying-the-Union-Pacific-at-Seventy:
The Sante Fe is shining on his hair.

5　This is Commodore Vanderbilt[4] making America:
Mister-Vanderbilt-is-eliminating-the short-interest-in-Hudson:
Observe the carving on the rocking chair.

This is J. P. Morgan[5] making America:
(The Tennessee Coal is behind to the left of the Steel Company.)
10　Those in mauve are braces he is wearing.

This is Mister Mellon[6] making America:
Mister-Mellon-is-represented-as-a-symbolic-figure-in-aluminum-
Strewing-bank-stocks-on-a-burnished-stair.

This is the Bruce is the Barton[7] making America:
15　Mister-Barton-is-selling-us-Doctor's-Deliciousest-Dentifrice.
This is he in beige with the canary.

You have just beheld the Makers making America:
This is The Making of America in Five Panels:
America lies to the west-southwest of the switch-tower:
20　There is nothing to see of America but land.

The Original Document under the Panel Paint:

"To Thos. Jefferson Esq. his obd't serv't
M. Lewis: captain: detached:
　　　　　　　Sir:

Having in mind your repeated commands in this matter,
25　And the worst half of it done and the streams mapped,

And we here on the back of this beach beholding the
Other ocean—two years gone and the cold

Breaking with rain for the third spring since St. Louis,
The crows at the fishbones on the frozen dunes,

30　The first cranes going over from south north,
And the river down by a mark of the pole since the morning,

And time near to return, and a ship (Spanish)
Lying in for the salmon: and fearing chance or the

Drought or the Sioux should deprive you of these discoveries—
35　Therefore we send by sea in this writing.

---

3. Edward H. Harriman (1848–1909), American railroad magnate and one of those called "robber barons" in the period.
4. Cornelius Vanderbilt (1794–1872), financier and railroad magnate.
5. J. P. Morgan (1837–1913), banker and financier.
6. Andrew Mellon (1885–1937), financier, one-time Secretary of the Treasury and, like Harriman, Vanderbilt, and Morgan, a man of enormous wealth and power.
7. Bruce Barton (1886–　　), pioneer American advertising executive who made extraordinary use of that profession in his religious writings.

Above the
Platte[8] there were long plains and a clay country:
Rim of the sky far off, grass under it,

Dung for the cook fires by the sulphur licks.
40 After that there were low hills and the sycamores,

And we poled up by the Great Bend in the skiffs:
The honey bees left us after the Osage River.[9]

The wind was west in the evenings, and no dew and the
Morning Star larger and whiter than usual—

45 The winter rattling in the brittle haws.
The second year there was sage and the quail calling.

All that valley is good land by the river:
Three thousand miles and the clay cliffs and

Rue and beargrass by the water banks
50 And many birds and the brant going over and tracks of

Bear, elk, wolves, marten: the buffalo
Numberless so that the cloud of their dust covers them:

The antelope fording the fall creeks, and the mountains and
Grazing lands and the meadow lands and the ground

55 Sweet and open and well-drained.
We advise you to
Settle troops at the forks and to issue licenses:

Many men will have living on these lands.
There is wealth in the earth for them all and the wood standing

60 And wild birds on the water where they sleep.
There is stone in the hills for the towns of a great people . . ."

You have just beheld the Makers Making America:

They screwed her scrawny and gaunt with their seven-year panics:
They bought her back on their mortgages old-whore-cheap:

65 They fattened their bonds at her breasts till the thin blood ran from them.

Men have forgotten how full clear and deep
The Yellowstone moved on the gravel and the grass grew
When the land lay waiting for her westward people!

1933

---

8. A river in Nebraska.   9. The Great Bend and Osage are rivers in Kansas.

E. E. CUMMINGS
(1894–1963)

In Just-   spring

in Just-
spring   when the world is mud-
luscious the little
lame balloonman

5   whistles   far   and wee

and eddieandbill come
running from marbles and
piracies and it's
spring

10   when the world is puddle-wonderful

the queer
old balloonman whistles
far   and   wee
and bettyandisbel come dancing

15   from hop-scotch and jump-rope and

it's
spring
and
        the

20   goat-footed
balloonMan   whistles
far
and
wee

                                    1923

somebody knew Lincoln somebody Xerxes

somebody knew Lincoln somebody Xerxes

this man: a narrow thudding timeshaped face
plus innocuous winking hands, carefully
inhabits number 1 on something street

5   Spring comes
                the lean and definite houses

are troubled. A sharp blue day
fills with peacefully leaping air
the minute mind of the world.
10   The lean and

definite houses are
troubled. in the sunset their chimneys converse
angrily, their
roofs are nervous with the soft furious

15 light, and while fire-escapes and
    roofs and chimneys and while roofs and fire-escapes and
    chimneys and while chimneys and fire-escapes
    and roofs are talking rapidly all together there happens
    Something, and They

20 cease(and
    one by one are turned suddenly and softly
    into irresponsible toys.)
                    when this man with

    the brittle legs winces
25 swiftly out of number 1 someThing
    street and trickles carefully into the park
    sits

    Down.   pigeons circle
    around and around and around the

30 irresponsible toys
    circle wildly in the slow-ly-in creasing fragility
    —. Dogs
    bark
    children
35 play
    -ing
        Are

    in the beautiful nonsense of twilight

    and somebody Napoleon
                                            1923

the Cambridge ladies who live in furnished souls

    the Cambridge ladies who live in furnished souls
    are unbeautiful and have comfortable minds
    (also, with the church's protestant blessings
    daughters, unscented shapeless spirited)
5   they believe in Christ and Longfellow, both dead,
    are invariably interested in so many things—
    at the present writing one still finds
    delighted fingers knitting for the is it Poles?
    perhaps. While permanent faces coyly bandy
10 scandal of Mrs. N and Professor D
    . . . . the Cambridge ladies do not care, above
    Cambridge if sometimes in its box of
    sky lavender and cornerless, the
    moon rattles like a fragment of angry candy
                                            1923

who's most afraid of death? thou

    who's most afraid of death? thou
                            art of him
    utterly afraid, i love of thee
    (beloved) this

5   and truly i would be
    near when his scythe takes crisply the whim
    of thy smoothness. and mark the fainting
    murdered petals. with the caving stem.

But of all most would i be one of them

10 round the hurt heart which do so frailly cling . . . .)
i who am but imperfect in my fear

Or with thy mind against my mind, to hear
nearing our hearts' irrevocable play—
through the mysterious high futile day

15 an enormous stride
                    (and drawing thy mouth toward

my mouth, steer our lost bodies carefully downward)

1925

since feeling is first

25 since feeling is first
who pays any attention
to the syntax of things
will never wholly kiss you;
wholly to be a fool
30 while Spring is in the world

my blood approves,
and kisses are a better fate
than wisdom
lady i swear by all flowers. Don't cry
35 —the best gesture of my brain is less than
your eyelids' flutter which says

we are for each other: then
laugh, leaning back in my arms
for life's not a paragraph

40 And death i think is no parenthesis

1926

my father moved through dooms of love

my father moved through dooms of love
through sames of am through haves of give,
singing each morning out of each night
my father moved through depths of height

5 this motionless forgetful where
turned at his glance to shining here;
that if(so timid air is firm)
under his eyes would stir and squirm

newly as from unburied which
10 floats the first who,his april touch
drove sleeping selves to swarm their fates
woke dreamers to their ghostly roots

and should some why completely weep
my father's fingers brought her sleep:
15 vainly no smallest voice might cry
for he could feel the mountains grow.

Lifting the valleys of the sea
my father moved through griefs of joy;
praising a forehead called the moon
20 singing desire into begin

joy was his song and joy so pure
a heart of star by him could steer
and pure so now and now so yes
the wrists of twilight would rejoice

25 keen as midsummer's keen beyond
conceiving mind of sun will stand,
so strictly(over utmost him
so hugely)stood my father's dream

his flesh was flesh his blood was blood:
30 no hungry man but wished him food;
no cripple wouldn't creep one mile
uphill to only see him smile.

Scorning the pomp of must and shall
my father moved through dooms of feel;
35 his anger was as right as rain
his pity was as green as grain

septembering arms of year extend
less humbly wealth to foe and friend
than he to foolish and to wise
40 offered immeasurable is

proudly and(by octobering flame
beckoned)as earth will downward climb,
so naked for immortal work
his shoulders marched against the dark

45 his sorrow was as true as bread:
no liar looked him in the head;
if every friend became his foe
he'd laugh and build a world with snow.

My father moved through theys of we,
50 singing each new leaf out of each tree
(and every child was sure that spring
danced when she heard my father sing)

then let men kill which cannot share,
let blood and flesh be mud and mire,
55 scheming imagine,passion willed,
freedom a drug that's bought and sold

giving to steal and cruel kind,
a heart to fear,to doubt a mind,
to differ a disease of same,
60 conform the pinnacle of am

though dull were all we taste as bright,
bitter all utterly things sweet,
maggoty minus and dumb death
all we inherit,all bequeath

65 and nothing quite so least as truth
—i say though hate were why men breathe—
because my father lived his soul
love is the whole and more than all

1940

ROBERT GRAVES
(1895–   )

Lost Love

His eyes are quickened so with grief,
He can watch a grass or leaf
Every instant grow; he can
Clearly through a flint wall see,
5   Or watch the startled spirit flee
From the throat of a dead man.
    Across two counties he can hear
And catch your words before you speak.
The woodlouse or the maggot's weak
10 Clamor rings in his sad ear,
And noise so slight it would surpass
Credence—drinking sound of grass,
Worm talk, clashing jaws of moth
Chumbling holes in cloth;
15 The groan of ants who undertake
Gigantic loads for honor's sake
(Their sinews creak, their breath comes thin);
Whir of spiders when they spin,
And minute whispering, mumbling, sighs
20 Of idle grubs and flies.
    This man is quickened so with grief,
He wanders god-like or like thief
Inside and out, below, above,
Without relief seeking lost love.

1919

The Cool Web

Children are dumb to say how hot the day is,
How hot the scent is of the summer rose,
How dreadful the black wastes of evening sky,
How dreadful the tall soldiers drumming by.

5 But we have speech, to chill the angry day,
And speech, to dull the rose's cruel scent.
We spell away the overhanging night,
We spell away the soldiers and the fright.

There's a cool web of language winds us in,
10 Retreat from too much joy or too much fear:
We grow sea-green at last and coldly die
In brininess and volubility.

But if we let our tongues lose self-possession,
Throwing off language and its watery clasp
15 Before our death, instead of when death comes,
Facing the wide glare of the children's day,
Facing the rose, the dark sky and the drums,
We shall go mad no doubt and die that way.

1927

Warning to Children

Children, if you dare to think
Of the greatness, rareness, muchness,
Fewness of this precious only
Endless world in which you say
5   You live, you think of things like this:
Blocks of slate enclosing dappled
Red and green, enclosing tawny
Yellow nets, enclosing white
And black acres of dominoes,
10 Where a neat brown paper parcel
Tempts you to untie the string.
In the parcel a small island,
On the island a large tree,
On the tree a husky fruit.
15 Strip the husk and pare the rind off:
In the kernel you will see
Blocks of slate enclosed by dappled
Red and green, enclosed by tawny
Yellow nets, enclosed by white
20 And black acres of dominoes,
Where the same brown paper parcel—
Children, leave the string alone!
For who dares undo the parcel
Finds himself at once inside it,
25 On the island, in the fruit,
Blocks of slate about his head,
Finds himself enclosed by dappled
Green and red, enclosed by yellow
Tawny nets, enclosed by black
30 And white acres of dominoes,
With the same brown paper parcel
Still unopened on his knee.
And, if he then should dare to think
Of the fewness, muchness, rareness,
35 Greatness of this endless only
Precious world in which he says
He lives—he then unties the string.

1929

The Frog and the Golden Ball

She let her golden ball fall down the well
    And begged a cold frog to retrieve it;
For which she kissed his ugly, gaping mouth—
    Indeed, he could scarce believe it.

5 And seeing him transformed to his princely shape,
    Who had been by hags enchanted,
She knew she could never love another man
    Nor by any fate be daunted.

But what would her royal father and mother say?
10   They had promised her in marriage
To a cousin whose wide kingdom marched with theirs,
    Who rode in a jeweled carriage.

'Our plight, dear heart, would appear past human hope
    To all except you and me: to all
15 Who have never swum as a frog in a dark well
    Or have lost a golden ball.'

'What then shall we do now?' she asked her lover.
    He kissed her again, and said:
'Is magic of love less powerful at your Court
20   Than at this green well-head?'

1965

HART CRANE
(1899–1932)

Praise for an Urn

IN MEMORIAM: ERNEST NELSON

It was a kind and northern face
That mingled in such exile guise
The everlasting eyes of Pierrot[1]
And, of Gargantua,[2] the laughter.

5   His thoughts, delivered to me
From the white coverlet and pillow,
I see now, were inheritances—
Delicate riders of the storm.

The slant moon on the slanting hill
10 Once moved us toward presentiments
Of what the dead keep, living still,
And such assessments of the soul

As, perched in the crematory lobby,
The insistent clock commented on,
15 Touching as well upon our praise
Of glories proper to the time.

Still, having in mind gold hair,
I cannot see that broken brow
And miss the dry sound of bees
20 Stretching across a lucid space.

Scatter these well-meant idioms
Into the smoky spring that fills
The suburbs, where they will be lost.
They are no trophies of the sun.

1926

From The Bridge

Proem: To Brooklyn Bridge

How many dawns, chill from his rippling rest
The seagull's wings shall dip and pivot him,
Shedding white rings of tumult, building high
Over the chained bay waters Liberty—

5   Then, with inviolate curve, forsake our eyes
As apparitional as sails that cross
Some page of figures to be filed away;
—Till elevators drop us from our day . . .

---

1. Traditionally the sad clown with loose white costume, white face, and dark mournful eyes.   2. The gigantic king-hero of Rabelais' *Gargantua* (1535) who inspires hearty laughter.

I think of cinemas, panoramic sleights
10 With multitudes bent toward some flashing scene
Never disclosed, but hastened to again,
Foretold to other eyes on the same screen;

And Thee,[3] across the harbor, silver-paced
As though the sun took step of thee, yet left
15 Some motion ever unspent in thy stride—
Implicitly thy freedom staying thee!

Out of some subway scuttle, cell or loft
A bedlamite° speeds to thy parapets,   *madman*
Tilting there momently, shrill shirt ballooning,
20 A jest falls from the speechless caravan.

Down Wall, from girder into street noon leaks,
A rip-tooth of the sky's acetylene,
All afternoon the cloud-flown derricks turn . . .
Thy cables breathe the North Atlantic still.

25 And obscure as that heaven of the Jews,
Thy guerdon . . . Accolade thou dost bestow
Of anonymity time cannot raise:
Vibrant reprieve and pardon thou dost show.

O harp and altar, of the fury fused,
30 (How could mere toil align thy choiring strings!)
Terrific threshold of the prophet's pledge,
Prayer of pariah, and the lover's cry—

Again the traffic lights that skim thy swift
Unfractioned idiom, immaculate sigh of stars,
35 Beading thy path—condense eternity:
And we have seen night lifted in thine arms.

Under thy shadow by the piers I waited;
Only in darkness is thy shadow clear.
The City's fiery parcels all undone,
40 Already snow submerges an iron year . . .

O Sleepless as the river under thee,
Vaulting the sea, the prairies' dreaming sod,
Unto us lowliest sometime sweep, descend
And of the curveship lend a myth to God.

1930

Royal Palm

Green rustlings, more-than-regal charities
Drift coolly from that tower of whispered light.
Amid the noontide's blazed asperities
I watched the sun's most gracious anchorite

5 Climb up as by communings, year on year
Uneaten of the earth or aught earth holds,
And the gray trunk, that's elephantine, rear
Its frondings sighing in ethereal folds.

Forever fruitless, and beyond that yield
10 Of sweat the jungle presses with hot love
And tendril till our deathward breath is sealed—
It grazes the horizons, launched above

---

3. I.e., Brooklyn Bridge.

Mortality—ascending emerald-bright,
A fountain at salute, a crown in view—
15 Unshackled, casual of its azured height,
As though it soared suchwise through heaven too.

1933

ALLEN TATE
(1899–   )

Ode to the Confederate Dead

Row after row with strict impunity
The headstones yield their names to the element,
The wind whirrs without recollection;
In the riven troughs the splayed leaves
5   Pile up, of nature the casual sacrament
To the seasonal eternity of death;
Then driven by the fierce scrutiny
Of heaven to their election in the vast breath,
They sough the rumor of mortality.

10 Autumn is desolation in the plot
Of a thousand acres where these memories grow
From the inexhaustible bodies that are not
Dead, but feed the grass row after rich row.
Think of the autumns that have come and gone!
15 Ambitious November with the humors of the year,
With a particular zeal for every slab,
Staining the uncomfortable angels that rot
On the slabs, a wing chipped here, an arm there:
The brute curiosity of an angel's stare
20 Turns you, like them, to stone,
Transforms the heaving air
Till plunged to a heavier world below
You shift your sea-space blindly
Heaving, turning like the blind crab.

25   Dazed by the wind, only the wind
The leaves flying, plunge

You know who have waited by the wall
The twilight certainty of an animal,
Those midnight restitutions of the blood
30 You know—the immitigable° pines, the smoky frieze   *unvarying*
Of the sky, the sudden call: you know the rage,
The cold pool left by the mounting flood,
Of muted Zeno and Parmenides.[1]
You who have waited for the angry resolution
35 Of those desires that should be yours tomorrow,
You know the unimportant shrift of death
And praise the vision
And praise the arrogant circumstance
Of those who fall
40 Rank upon rank, hurried beyond decision—
Here by the sagging gate, stopped by the wall.

        Seeing, seeing only the leaves
        Flying, plunge and expire

1. Zeno and Parmenides were Greek philosophers of the Eleatic school who, among other beliefs, held that what is various and changeable, all "development," is a delusive phantom. "To be imagined and to be able to exist are the same thing, and there is no development."

Turn your eyes to the immoderate past,
45   Turn to the inscrutable infantry rising
Demons out of the earth—they will not last.
Stonewall, Stonewall, and the sunken fields of hemp,
Shiloh, Antietam, Malvern Hill, Bull Run.[2]
50   Lost in that orient of the thick and fast
You will curse the setting sun.

          Cursing only the leaves crying
          Like an old man in a storm

You hear the shout, the crazy hemlocks point
55   With troubled fingers to the silence which
Smothers you, a mummy, in time.
                    The hound bitch
Toothless and dying, in a musty cellar
Hears the wind only.

60   Now that the salt of their blood
Stiffens the saltier oblivion of the sea,
Seals the malignant purity of the flood,
What shall we who count our days and bow
Our heads with a commemorial woe
65   In the ribboned coats of grim felicity,
What shall we say of the bones, unclean,
Whose verdurous anonymity will grow?

The ragged arms, the ragged heads and eyes
Lost in these acres of the insane green?
70   The gray lean spiders come, they come and go;
In a tangle of willows without light
The singular screech-owl's tight
Invisible lyric seeds the mind
With the furious murmur of their chivalry.

75   We shall say only the leaves
          Flying, plunge and expire

We shall say only the leaves whispering
In the improbable mist of nightfall
That flies on multiple wing:
80   Night is the beginning and the end
And in between the ends of distraction
Waits mute speculation, the patient curse
That stones the eyes, or like the jaguar leaps
For his own image in a jungle pool, his victim.

85   What shall we say who have knowledge
Carried to the heart? Shall we take the act
To the grave? Shall we, more hopeful, set up the grave
In the house? The ravenous grave?

          Leave now
90   The shut gate and the decomposing wall:
The gentle serpent, green in the mulberry bush,
Riots with his tongue through the hush—
Sentinel of the grave who counts us all!

                                        1928

2. Names of important Civil War battles.

LANGSTON HUGHES
(1902–1967)

The Weary Blues

Droning a drowsy syncopated tune,
Rocking back and forth to a mellow croon,
    I heard a Negro play.
Down on Lenox Avenue[1] the other night
5 By the pale dull pallor of an old gas light
    He did a lazy sway. . . .
    He did a lazy sway. . . .
To the tune o' those Weary Blues.
With his ebony hands on each ivory key
10 He made that poor piano moan with melody.
    O Blues!
Swaying to and fro on his rickety stool
He played that sad raggy tune like a musical fool.
    Sweet Blues!
15 Coming from a black man's soul.
    O Blues!
In a deep song voice with a melancholy tone
I heard that Negro sing, that old piano moan—
    "Ain't got nobody in all this world,
20   Ain't got nobody but ma self.
    I's gwine to quit ma frownin'
    And put ma troubles on the shelf."
Thump, thump, thump, went his foot on the floor.
He played a few chords then he sang some more—
25   "I got the Weary Blues
    And I can't be satisfied.
    Got the Weary Blues
    And can't be satisfied—
    I ain't happy no mo'
30   And I wish that I had died."
And far into the night he crooned that tune.
The stars went out and so did the moon.
The singer stopped playing and went to bed
While the Weary Blues echoed through his head.
35 He slept like a rock or a man that's dead.

                            1926

The Negro Speaks of Rivers

(TO W. E. B. DUBOIS)[2]

I've known rivers:
I've known rivers ancient as the world and older than the
    flow of human blood in human veins.

My soul has grown deep like the rivers.

5 I bathed in the Euphrates when dawns were young.
I built my hut near the Congo and it lulled me to sleep.
I looked upon the Nile and raised the pyramids above it.
I heard the singing of the Mississippi when Abe Lincoln
    went down to New Orleans, and I've seen its muddy
10   bosom turn all golden in the sunset.

1. A main thoroughfare in the heart of Harlem.
2. The American historian, educator, and Negro leader (1868–1963).

I've known rivers:
Ancient, dusky rivers.

My soul has grown deep like the rivers.

1926

Harlem

What happens to a dream deferred?

    Does it dry up
    like a raisin in the sun?
    Or fester like a sore—
5   And then run?
    Does it stink like rotten meat?
    Or crust and sugar over—
    like a syrupy sweet?

    Maybe it just sags
10   like a heavy load.

    Or does it explode?

1951

RICHARD EBERHART
(1904–   )

Maze

I have a tree in my arm,
There are two hounds in my feet,
The earth can do me no harm
And the lake of my eyes is sweet.

5   But a fire has burnt the tree down,
I have no blood for the hounds.
Why has the will made me a crown
For a human mind that has bounds?

Who made the tree? Who made fire?
10   The hounds have gone back to the master.
The earth has killed my desire
That leaped up faster and faster.

It is man did it, man,
Who imagined imagination,
15   And he did what man can,
He uncreated creation.

There is no tree in my arm,
I have no hounds in my feet,
The earth can soothe me and harm,
20   And the lake of my eyes is a cheat.

1937

Sea-Hawk

The six-foot nest of the sea-hawk,
Almost inaccessible,
Surveys from the headland the lonely, the violent waters.

  I have driven him off,
5   Somewhat foolhardily,
And look into the fierce eye of the offspring.

It is an eye of fire,
An eye of icy crystal,
A threat of ancient purity,

10   Power of an immense reserve,
An agate-well of purpose,
Life before man, and maybe after.

How many centuries of sight
In this piercing, inhuman perfection
15   Stretch the gaze off the rocky promontory,

To make the mind exult
At the eye of a sea-hawk,
A blaze of grandeur, permanence of the impersonal.

1957

ROBERT PENN WARREN
(1905–   )

Two Pieces After Suetonius[1]

I. Apology for Domitian[2]

He was not bad, as emperors go, not really—
Not like Tiberius cruel, or poor Nero silly.[3]
The trouble was only that omens said he would die,
So what could he, mortal, do? Not worse, however, than you might, or I.

5   Suppose from long back you had known the very hour—
"Fear the fifth hour"—and yet for all your power
Couldn't strike it out from the day, or the day from the year,
Then wouldn't you have to strike something at least? If you did, would it
seem so queer?

Suppose you were proud of your beauty, but baldness set in?
10   Suppose your good leg were dwindling to spindly and thin?
Wouldn't you, like Domitian, try the classic bed-stunt
To prove immortality on what was propped to bear the imperial brunt?

Suppose you had dreamed a gold hump sprouted out of your back,
And such a prosperous burden oppressed you to breath-lack;
15   Suppose lightning scorched the sheets in your own bedroom;
And from your own statue a storm yanked the name plate and chucked it
into a tomb—

Well, it happened to him. Therefore, there's little surprise
That for hours he'd lock himself up to pull wings from flies.
Fly or man, what odds? He would wander his hall of moonstone,
20   Mirror-bright so he needn't look over his shoulder to see if he was alone.

1. Roman historian in the reign of Vespasian (A.D. 70–79), whose chief work is a history of the first twelve emperors of Rome.
2. Domitian (A.D. 51–96), son of Vespasian, was a Roman emperor of bad reputation: cruel, suspicious, tyrannical, decadent. He is reported to have liked catching flies and piercing them with sharp instruments. He is also said to have been much under the influence of soothsayers and prognosticators.
3. Tiberius, emperor of Rome from A.D. 14 to 37, is remembered as a despot; Nero's (A.D. 37–68) reign as emperor of Rome was marked by his great cruelties and erratic behavior.

Let's stop horsing around—it's not Domitian, it's you
We mean, and the omens are bad, very bad, and it's true
That virtue comes hard in face of the assiduous clock,
And music, at sunset, faint as a dream, is heard from beyond the burdock,

25   And as for Domitian, the first wound finds the groin,
And he claws like a cat, but the blade continues to go in,
And the body is huddled forth meanly, and what ritual
It gets is at night, and from his old nurse, a woman poor, nonpolitical.

II. Tiberius on Capri[4]

1

All is nothing, nothing all:
To tired Tiberius soft sang the sea thus,
Under his cliff-palace wall.
The sea, in soft approach and repulse,
5   Sings thus, and Tiberius,
Sea-sad, stares past the dusking sea-pulse
Yonder, where come,

One now by one, the lights, far off, of Surrentum.[5]
He stares in the blue dusk-fall,
10   For all is nothing, nothing all.

Let darkness up from Asia tower.
On that darkening island behind him *spintriae*[6] now stir.
In grot and scented bower,
They titter, yawn, paint lip, grease thigh,
15   And debate what role each would prefer
When they project for the Emperor's eye
Their expertise
Of his Eastern lusts and complex Egyptian fantasies.
But darkward he stares in that hour,
20   Blank now in totality of power.

2

There once, on that goat island, I,
As dark fell, stood and stared where Europe stank.
Many were soon to die—
From acedia[7] snatched, from depravity, virtue,
25   Or frolic, not knowing the reason, in rank
On rank hurled, or in bed, or in church, or
Dishing up supper,
Or in a dark doorway, loosening the girl's elastic to tup her,
While high in the night sky,
30   The murderous tear dropped from God's eye;

And faintly forefeeling, forefearing, all
That to fulfill our time, and heart, would come,
I stood on the crumbling wall
Of that foul place, and my lungs drew in
35   Scent of dry gorse on the night air of autumn,
And I seized, in dark, a small stone from that ruin,
And I made outcry
At the paradox of powers that would grind us like grain, small and dry.
Dark down, the stone, in its fall,
40   Found the sea: I could do that much, after all.

1960

---

4. The ruins of Tiberius' villa on the island
of Capri, Italy, still stand.
5. Now Sorrento, Italy.

6. Male prostitutes.
7. Sloth, or spiritual laziness.

WILLIAM EMPSON
(1906–   )

To an Old Lady[1]

Ripeness is all; her in her cooling planet
Revere; do not presume to think her wasted.
Project her no projectile, plan nor man it;
Gods cool in turn, by the sun long outlasted.

5   Our earth alone given no name of god
Gives, too, no hold for such a leap to aid her;
Landing, you break some palace and seem odd;
Bees sting their need, the keeper's queen invader.

No, to your telescope; spy out the land;
10 Watch while her ritual is still to see,
Still stand her temples emptying in the sand
Whose waves o'erthrew their crumbled tracery;

Still stand uncalled-on her soul's appanage;[2]
Much social detail whose successor fades,
15 Wit used to run a house and to play bridge,
And tragic fervor, to dismiss her maids.

Years her precession do not throw from gear.
She reads a compass certain of her pole;
Confident, finds no confines on her sphere,
20 Whose failing crops are in her sole control.

Stars how much further from me fill my night.
Strange that she too should be inaccessible,
Who shares my sun. He curtains her from sight,
And but in darkness is she visible.

1935

Legal Fiction[3]

Law makes long spokes of the short stakes of men.
Your well fenced out real estate of mind
No high flat of the nomad citizen
Looks over, or train leaves behind.

5   Your rights extend under and above your claim
Without bound; you own land in heaven and hell;
Your part of earth's surface and mass the same,
Of all cosmos' volume, and all stars as well.

Your rights reach down where all owners meet, in hell's
10 Pointed exclusive conclave, at earth's center
(Your spun farm's root still on that axis dwells);
And up, through galaxies, a growing sector.

1. "First three words from *King Lear. Our earth* without a god's name such as the other planets have is compared to some body of people (absurd to say 'the present generation') without fundamental beliefs as a basis for action. When a hive needs a new queen and the keeper puts one in the bees sometimes kill her. *Her precession* is some customary movement of the planet, meant to suggest the dignity of "procession." The unconfined surface of her sphere is like the universe in being finite but unbounded, but I failed to get that into the line" [Empson's note].
2. Natural attribute or accomplishment.
3. "Legal fiction" as used here means the assumption that ownership of land extends into the earth beneath and into the air above.

You are nomad yet; the lighthouse beam you own
Flashes, like Lucifer,[4] through the firmament.
15 Earth's axis varies; your dark central cone
Wavers a candle's shadow, at the end.

1935

W. H. AUDEN
(1907–   )

Musée des Beaux Arts[1]

About suffering they were never wrong,
The Old Masters: how well they understood
Its human position; how it takes place
While someone else is eating or opening a window or just walking dully along;
5 How, when the aged are reverently, passionately waiting
For the miraculous birth, there always must be
Children who did not specially want it to happen, skating
On a pond at the edge of the wood:
They never forgot
10 That even the dreadful martyrdom must run its course
Anyhow in a corner, some untidy spot
Where the dogs go on with their doggy life and the torturer's horse
Scratches its innocent behind on a tree.

In Breughel's *Icarus*,[2] for instance: how everything turns away
15 Quite leisurely from the disaster; the ploughman may
Have heard the splash, the forsaken cry,
But for him it was not an important failure; the sun shone
As it had to on the white legs disappearing into the green
Water; and the expensive delicate ship that must have seen
20 Something amazing, a boy falling out of the sky,
Had somewhere to get to and sailed calmly on.

1940

Law Like Love

Law, say the gardeners, is the sun,
Law is the one
All gardeners obey
Tomorrow, yesterday, today.

5 Law is the wisdom of the old
The impotent grandfathers feebly scold;
The grandchildren put out a treble tongue,
Law is the senses of the young.

Law, says the priest with a priestly look,
10 Expounding to an unpriestly people,
Law is the words in my priestly book,
Law is my pulpit and my steeple.

4. The morning star.
1. The Museum of Fine Arts in Brussels, where hangs the painting of The Fall of Icarus, by Pieter Brueghel (ca. 1525–69) described in the poem.
2. Daedalus, the greatly skilled Athenian craftsman, constructed for Minos, king of Crete, a labyrinth in which the Minotaur was kept; but Daedalus was himself imprisoned in it with his son Icarus. He made wings of feathers and wax, with which they flew away; but Icarus flew too near the sun, the wax melted, and he fell into the sea.

Law, says the judge as he looks down his nose,
Speaking clearly and most severely,
15 Law is as I've told you before,
Law is as you know I suppose,
Law is but let me explain it once more,
Law is The Law.

Yet law-abiding scholars write;
20 Law is neither wrong nor right,
Law is only crimes
Punished by places and by times,
Law is the clothes men wear
Anytime, anywhere,
25 Law is Goodmorning and Goodnight.

Others say, Law is our Fate;
Others say, Law is our State;
Others say, others say
Law is no more
30 Law has gone away.

And always the loud angry crowd
Very angry and very loud
Law is We,
And always the soft idiot softly Me.

35 If we, dear, know we know no more
Than they about the Law,
If I no more than you
Know what we should and should not do
Except that all agree
40 Gladly or miserably
That the Law is
And that all know this,
If therefore thinking it absurd
To identify Law with some other word,
45 Unlike so many men
I cannot say Law is again,
No more than they can we suppress
The universal wish to guess
Or slip out of our own position
50 Into an unconcerned condition.
Although I can at least confine
Your vanity and mine
To stating timidly
A timid similarity,
55 We shall boast anyway:
Like love I say.

Like love we don't know where or why,
Like love we can't compel or fly,
Like love we often weep,
60 Like love we seldom keep.

1940

Our Bias

The hour-glass whispers to the lion's roar,
The clock-towers tell the gardens day and night,
How many errors Time has patience for,
How wrong they are in being always right.

5   Yet Time, however loud its chimes or deep,
     However fast its falling torrent flows,

     Has never put one lion off his leap
     Nor shaken the assurance of a rose.

     For they, it seems, care only for success:
10   While we choose words according to their sound
     And judge a problem by its awkwardness;

     And time with us was always popular.
     When have we not preferred some going round
     To going straight to where we are?

                                                        1940

As I Walked Out One Evening

     As I walked out one evening,
         Walking down Bristol Street,
     The crowds upon the pavement
         Were fields of harvest wheat.

5   And down by the brimming river
         I heard a lover sing
     Under an arch of the railway:
         "Love has no ending.

     "I'll love you, dear, I'll love you
10   Till China and Africa meet,
     And the river jumps over the mountain
         And the salmon sing in the street,

     "I'll love till the ocean
         Is folded and hung up to dry
15   And the seven stars go squawking
         Like geese about the sky.

     The years shall run like rabbits,
         For in my arms I hold
     The Flower of the Ages,
20   And the first love of the world."

     But all the clocks in the city
         Began to whirr and chime:
     "O let not Time deceive you,
         You cannot conquer Time.

25   "In the burrows of the Nightmare
         Where Justice naked is,
     Time watches from the shadow
         And coughs when you would kiss.

     "In headaches and in worry
30   Vaguely life leaks away,
     And Time will have his fancy
         Tomorrow or today.

     "Into many a green valley
         Drifts the appalling snow;
35   Time breaks the threaded dances
         And the diver's brilliant bow.

"O plunge your hands in water,
    Plunge them in up to the wrist;
Stare, stare in the basin
40   And wonder what you've missed.

"The glacier knocks in the cupboard,
    The desert sighs in the bed,
And the crack in the teacup opens
    A lane to the land of the dead.

45 "Where the beggars raffle the banknotes
    And the Giant is enchanting to Jack,
And the Lily-white Boy is a Roarer,
    And Jill goes down on her back.

"O look, look in the mirror,
50   O look in your distress;
Life remains a blessing
    Although you cannot bless.

"O stand, stand at the window
    As the tears scald and start;
55 You shall love your crooked neighbor
    With your crooked heart."

It was late, late in the evening,
    The lovers they were gone;
The clocks had ceased their chiming,
60   And the deep river ran on.

                                        1940

The Shield of Achilles[3]

    She looked over his shoulder
        For vines and olive trees,
    Marble well-governed cities
        And ships upon untamed seas,
5   But there on the shining metal
        His hands had put instead
    An artificial wilderness
        And a sky like lead.

A plain without a feature, bare and brown,
10   No blade of grass, no sign of neighborhood,
Nothing to eat and nowhere to sit down,
    Yet, congregated on its blankness, stood
    An unintelligible multitude,
A million eyes, a million boots in line,
15 Without expression, waiting for a sign.

---

3. Achilles, the chief Greek hero in the war with Troy, loses his armor when his great friend Patroclus, wearing it, is slain by Hector. While Achilles is mourning the death of his friend, his mother, the goddess Thetis, goes to Olympus to entreat Hephaestos to make new armor for him: both she and Hephaestos pity Achilles because he is fated to die soon and because his life has not been happy. The splendid shield, incorporating gold and silver as well as less precious metals, is described at length in Book XVIII of the *Iliad* (lines 478–608), the scenes depicted on it constituting an epitome of the universe and the lives of men. Hephaestos portrays on it the earth, the heavens, the sea, and the planets; a city in peace (with a wedding and a trial-at-law) and a city at war; scenes from country life, including a harvest feast and a grape-gathering; scenes from animal life and the joyful life of young men and maidens. Around all these scenes, closing them in as the outer border, flows the ocean.

Out of the air a voice without a face
   Proved by statistics that some cause was just
In tones as dry and level as the place:
   No one was cheered and nothing was discussed;
20   Column by column in a cloud of dust
They marched away enduring a belief
Whose logic brought them, somewhere else, to grief.

     She looked over his shoulder
        For ritual pieties,
25   White flower-garlanded heifers,
        Libation and sacrifice,
     But there on the shining metal
        Where the altar should have been,
     She saw by his flickering forge-light
30   Quite another scene.

Barbed wire enclosed an arbitrary spot
   Where bored officials lounged (one cracked a joke)
And sentries sweated for the day was hot:
   A crowd of ordinary decent folk
35   Watched from without and neither moved nor spoke
As three pale figures were led forth and bound
To three posts driven upright in the ground.

The mass and majesty of this world, all
   That carries weight and always weighs the same
40   Lay in the hands of others; they were small
   And could not hope for help and no help came:
   What their foes liked to do was done, their shame
Was all the worst could wish; they lost their pride
And died as men before their bodies died.

45   She looked over his shoulder
        For athletes at their games,
     Men and women in a dance
        Moving their sweet limbs
     Quick, quick, to music,
50   But there on the shining shield
     His hands had set no dancing-floor
        But a weed-choked field.

A ragged urchin, aimless and alone,
   Loitered about that vacancy, a bird
55   Flew up to safety from his well-aimed stone:
   That girls are raped, that two boys knife a third,
   Were axioms to him, who'd never heard
Of any world where promises were kept,
Or one could weep because another wept.

60   The thin-lipped armorer,
        Hephaestos hobbled away,
     Thetis of the shining breasts
        Cried out in dismay
     At what the god had wrought
65   To please her son, the strong
     Iron-hearted man-slaying Achilles
        Who would not live long.

1955

LOUIS MacNEICE
(1907–   )

The Sunlight on the Garden

The sunlight on the garden
Hardens and grows cold,
We cannot cage the minute
Within its nets of gold,
5 When all is told
We cannot beg for pardon.

Our freedom as free lances
Advances towards its end;
The earth compels, upon it
10 Sonnets and birds descend;
And soon, my friend,
We shall have no time for dances.

The sky was good for flying
Defying the church bells
15 And every evil iron
Siren and what it tells:
The earth compels,
We are dying, Egypt, dying[1]

And not expecting pardon,
20 Hardened in heart anew,
But glad to have sat under
Thunder and rain with you,
And grateful too
For sunlight on the garden.

1938

London Rain

The rain of London pimples
The ebony street with white
And the neon-lamps of London
Stain the canals of night
5 And the park becomes a jungle
In the alchemy of night.

My wishes turn to violent
Horses black as coal—
The randy mares of fancy,
10 The stallions of the soul—
Eager to take the fences
That fence about my soul.

Across the countless chimneys
The horses ride and across
15 The country to the channel
Where warning beacons toss,
To a place where God and No-God
Play at pitch and toss.

1. From *Antony and Cleopatra*, IV.xv.41, Antony's speech to Cleopatra, "I am dying, Egypt, dying."

Whichever wins I am happy
20 For God will give me bliss
But No-God will absolve me
From all I do amiss
And I need not suffer conscience
If the world was made amiss.

25 Under God we can reckon
On pardon when we fall
But if we are under No-God
Nothing will matter at all,
Adultery and murder
30 Will count for nothing at all.

So reinforced by logic
As having nothing to lose
My lust goes riding horseback
To ravish where I choose,
35 To burgle all the turrets
Of beauty as I choose.

But now the rain gives over
Its dance upon the town,
Logic and lust together
40 Come dimly tumbling down,
And neither God nor No-God
Is either up or down.

The argument was wilful,
The alternatives untrue,
45 We need no metaphysics
To sanction what we do
Or to muffle us in comfort
From what we did not do.

Whether the living river
50 Began in bog or lake,
The world is what was given,
The world is what we make.
And we only can discover
Life in the life we make.

55 So let the water sizzle
Upon the gleaming slates,
There will be sunshine after
When the rain abates
And rain returning duly
60 When the sun abates.

My wishes now come homeward,
Their gallopings in vain,
Logic and lust are quiet
And again it starts to rain;
65 Falling asleep I listen
To the falling London rain.

1941

THEODORE ROETHKE
(1908–1963)

The Light Comes Brighter

The light comes brighter from the east; the caw
Of restive crows is sharper on the ear.
A walker at the river's edge may hear
A cannon crack announce an early thaw.

5   The sun cuts deep into the heavy drift,
Though still the guarded snow is winter-sealed,
At bridgeheads buckled ice begins to shift,
The river overflows the level field.

Once more the trees assume familiar shapes,
10 As branches loose last vestiges of snow.
The water stored in narrow pools escapes
In rivulets; the cold roots stir below.

Soon field and wood will wear an April look,
The frost be gone, for green is breaking now;
15 The ovenbird will match the vocal brook,
The young fruit swell upon the pear-tree bough.

And soon a branch, part of a hidden scene,
The leafy mind, that long was tightly furled,
Will turn its private substance into green,
20 And young shoots spread upon our inner world.

1941

My Papa's Waltz

The whiskey on your breath
Could make a small boy dizzy;
But I hung on like death:
Such waltzing was not easy.

5   We romped until the pans
Slid from the kitchen shelf;
My mother's countenance
Could not unfrown itself.

The hand that held my wrist
10 Was battered on one knuckle;
At every step you missed
My right ear scraped a buckle.

You beat time on my head
With a palm caked hard by dirt,
15 Then waltzed me off to bed
Still clinging to your shirt.

1948

The Waking

I wake to sleep, and take my waking slow.
I feel my fate in what I cannot fear.
I learn by going where I have to go.

We think by feeling. What is there to know?
5   I hear my being dance from ear to ear.
I wake to sleep, and take my waking slow.

Of those so close beside me, which are you?
God bless the Ground! I shall walk softly there,
And learn by going where I have to go.

10   Light takes the Tree; but who can tell us how?
The lowly worm climbs up a winding stair;
I wake to sleep, and take my waking slow.

Great Nature has another thing to do
To you and me; so take the lively air,
15   And, lovely, learn by going where to go.

This shaking keeps me steady. I should know.
What falls away is always. And is near.
I wake to sleep, and take my waking slow.
I learn by going where I have to go.

1953

The Dream

1

I met her as a blossom on a stem
Before she ever breathed, and in that dream
The mind remembers from a deeper sleep:
Eye learned from eye, cold lip from sensual lip.
5   My dream divided on a point of fire;
Light hardened on the water where we were;
A bird sang low; the moonlight sifted in;
The water rippled, and she rippled on.

2

She came toward me in the flowing air,
10   A shape of change, encircled by its fire
I watched her there, between me and the moon;
The bushes and the stones danced on and on;
I touched her shadow when the light delayed;
I turned my face away, and yet she stayed.
15   A bird sang from the center of a tree;
She loved the wind because the wind loved me.

3

Love is not love until love's vulnerable.
She slowed to sigh, in that long interval.
A small bird flew in circles where we stood;
20   The deer came down, out of the dappled wood.
All who remember, doubt. Who calls that strange?
I tossed a stone, and listened to its plunge.
She knew the grammar of least motion, she
Lent me one virtue, and I live thereby.

4

25   She held her body steady in the wind;
Our shadows met, and slowly swung around;
She turned the field into a glittering sea;
I played in flame and water like a boy

And I swayed out beyond the white seafoam;
30 Like a wet log, I sang within a flame.
In that last while, eternity's confine,
I came to love, I came into my own.

1958

I Knew a Woman

I knew a woman, lovely in her bones,
When small birds sighed, she would sigh back at them;
Ah, when she moved, she moved more ways than one:
The shapes a bright container can contain!
5 Of her choice virtues only gods should speak,
Or English poets who grew up on Greek
(I'd have them sing in chorus, cheek to cheek).

How well her wishes went! She stroked my chin,
She taught me Turn, and Counter-turn, and Stand;[1]
10 She taught me Touch, that undulant white skin;
I nibbled meekly from her proffered hand;
She was the sickle; I, poor I, the rake,
Coming behind her for her pretty sake
(But what prodigious mowing we did make).

15 Love likes a gander, and adores a goose:
Her full lips pursed, the errant note to seize;
She played it quick, she played it light and loose,
My eyes, they dazzled at her flowing knees;
Her several parts could keep a pure repose,
20 Or one hip quiver with a mobile nose
(She moved in circles, and those circles moved).

Let seed be grass, and grass turn into hay:
I'm martyr to a motion not my own;
What's freedom for? To know eternity.
25 I swear she cast a shadow white as stone.
But who would count eternity in days?
These old bones live to learn her wanton ways:
(I measure time by how a body sways).

1958

The Far Field

1
I dream of journeys repeatedly:
Of flying like a bat deep into a narrowing tunnel,
Of driving alone, without luggage, out a long peninsula,
The road lined with snow-laden second growth,
5 A fine dry snow ticking the windshield,
Alternate snow and sleet, no on-coming traffic,
And no lights behind, in the blurred side-mirror,
The road changing from glazed tarface to a rubble of stone,
Ending at last in a hopeless sand-rut,
10 Where the car stalls,
Churning in a snowdrift
Until the headlights darken.
2
At the field's end, in the corner missed by the mower,
Where the turf drops off into a grass-hidden culvert,
15 Haunt of the cat-bird, nesting-place of the field-mouse,
Not too far away from the ever-changing flower-dump,

1. Literary terms, for the three parts of the Pindaric ode.

Among the tin cans, tires, rusted pipes, broken machinery,—
One learned of the eternal;
And in the shrunken face of a dead rat, eaten by rain and ground-beetles
20 (I found it lying among the rubble of an old coal bin)
And the tom-cat, caught near the pheasant-run,
Its entrails strewn over the half-grown flowers,
Blasted to death by the night watchman.

I suffered for birds, for young rabbits caught in the mower,
25 My grief was not excessive.
For to come upon warblers in early May
Was to forget time and death:
How they filled the oriole's elm, a twittering restless cloud, all one morning,
And I watched and watched till my eyes blurred from the bird shapes,—
30 Cape May, Blackburnian, Cerulean—
Moving, elusive as fish, fearless,
Hanging, bunched like young fruit, bending the end branches,
Still for a moment,
Then pitching away in half-flight,
35 Lighter than finches,
While the wrens bickered and sang in the half-green hedgerows,
And the flicker drummed from his dead tree in the chicken-yard.

—Or to lie naked in sand,
In the silted° shallows of a slow river,   *sedimented*
40 Fingering a shell,
Thinking:
Once I was something like this, mindless,
Or perhaps with another mind, less peculiar;
Or to sink down to the hips in a mossy quagmire;[2]
45 Or, with skinny knees, to sit astride a wet log,
Believing:
I'll return again,
As a snake or a raucous bird,
Or, with luck, as a lion.

50 I learned not to fear infinity,
The far field, the windy cliffs of forever,
The dying of time in the white light of tomorrow,
The wheel turning away from itself,
The sprawl of the wave,
55 The on-coming water.
                        3
The river turns on itself,
The tree retreats into its own shadow.
I feel a weightless change, a moving forward
As of water quickening before a narrowing channel
60 When banks converge, and the wide river whitens;
Or when two rivers combine, the blue glacial torrent
And the yellowish-green from the mountainy upland,—
At first a swift rippling between rocks,
Then a long running over flat stones

65 Before descending to the alluvial plain,[3]
To the clay banks, and the wild grapes hanging from the elmtrees.
The slightly trembling water
Dropping a fine yellow silt where the sun stays;
And the crabs bask near the edge,
70 The weedy edge, alive with small snakes and bloodsuckers—
I have come to a still, but not a deep center,

2. Soft, wet land.   3. Sand or soil built up from the deposits of
                                              running water.

A point outside the glittering current;
My eyes stare at the bottom of a river,
At the irregular stones, iridescent sandgrains,
75 My mind moves in more than one place,
In a country half-land, half-water.

I am renewed by death, thought of my death,
The dry scent of a dying garden in September,
The wind fanning the ash of a low fire.
80 What I love is near at hand,
Always, in earth and air.

4

The lost self changes,
Turning toward the sea,
A sea-shape turning around—
85 An old man with his feet before the fire,
In robes of green, in garments of adieu.

A man faced with his own immensity
Wakes all the waves, all their loose wandering fire.
The murmur of the absolute, the why
90 Of being born fails on his naked ears.
His spirit moves like monumental wind
That gentles on a sunny blue plateau.
He is the end of things, the final man.

All finite things reveal infinitude:
95 The mountain with its singular bright shade
Like the blue shine on freshly frozen snow,
The after-light upon ice-burdened pines;
Odor of basswood on a mountain-slope,
A scent beloved of bees;
100 Silence of water above a sunken tree:
The pure serene of memory in one man—
A ripple widening from a single stone
Winding around the waters of the world.

1964

The Meadow Mouse

1

In a shoe box stuffed in an old nylon stocking
Sleeps the baby mouse I found in the meadow,
Where he trembled and shook beneath a stick
Till I caught him up by the tail and brought him in,
5 Cradled in my hand,
A little quaker, the whole body of him trembling,
His absurd whiskers sticking out like a cartoon-mouse,
His feet like small leaves,
Little lizard-feet,
10 Whitish and spread wide when he tride to struggle away,
Wriggling like a minuscule puppy.

Now he's eaten his three kinds of cheese and drunk from his bottle-cap
watering-trough—
So much he just lies in one corner,
15 His tail curled under him, his belly big
As his head; his bat-like ears
Twitching, tilting toward the least sound.

Do I imagine he no longer trembles
When I come close to him?
20 He seems no longer to tremble.

2

But this morning the shoe-box house on the back porch is empty.
Where has he gone, my meadow mouse,
My thumb of a child that nuzzled in my palm?
To run under the hawk's wing,
25   Under the eye of the great owl watching from the elm-tree,
To live by courtesy of the shrike, the snake, the tom-cat.

I think of the nestling fallen into the deep grass,
The turtle gasping in the dusty rubble of the highway,
The paralytic stunned in the tub, and the water rising—
30   All things innocent, hapless, forsaken.

1964

ROBERT HAYDEN
(1913–   )

Mourning Poem for the Queen of Sunday

Lord's lost Him His mockingbird,
His fancy warbler;
Satan sweet-talked her,
four bullets hushed her.
5   Who would have thought
she'd end that way?

Four bullets hushed her. And the world a-clang with evil.
Who's going to make old hardened sinner men tremble now
and the righteous rock?
10   Oh who and oh who will sing Jesus down
to help with struggling and doing without and being colored
all through blue Monday?
Till way next Sunday?

All those angels
15   in their cretonne clouds and finery
the true believer saw
when she rared back her head and sang,
all those angels are surely weeping.
Who would have thought
20   she'd end that way?

Four holes in her heart. The gold works wrecked.
But she looks so natural in her big bronze coffin
among the Broken Hearts and Gates-Ajar,
it's as if any moment she'd lift her head
25   from its pillow of chill gardenias
and turn this quiet into shouting Sunday
and make folks forget what she did on Monday.

Oh, Satan sweet-talked her,
and four bullets hushed her.
30   Lord's lost Him His diva,
His fancy warbler's gone.
Who would have thought,
who would have thought she'd end that way?

1966

RANDALL JARRELL
(1914–1965)

Nestus Gurley

Sometimes waking, sometimes sleeping,
Late in the afternoon, or early
In the morning, I hear on the lawn,
On the walk, on the lawn, the soft quick step,
5   The sound half song, half breath: a note or two
That with a note or two would be a tune.
It is Nestus Gurley.

It is an old
Catch or snatch or tune
10   In the Dorian mode:[1] the mode of the horses
That stand all night in the fields asleep
Or awake, the mode of the cold
Hunter, Orion, wheeling upside-down,
All space and stars, in cater-cornered Heaven.
15   When, somewhere under the east,
The great march begins, with birds and silence;
When, in the day's first triumph, dawn
Rides over the houses, Nestus Gurley
Delivers to me my lot.

20   As the sun sets, I hear my daughter say:
"He has four routes and makes a hundred dollars."
Sometimes he comes with dogs, sometimes with children,
Sometimes with dogs and children.
He collects, today.
25   I hear my daughter say:
"Today Nestus has got on his derby."
And he says, after a little: "It's two-eighty."
"How could it be two-eighty?"
"Because this month there're five Sundays: it's two-eighty."

30   He collects, delivers. Before the first, least star
Is lost in the paling east; at evening
While the soft, side-lit, gold-leafed day
Lingers to see the stars, the boy Nestus
Delivers to me the Morning Star, the Evening Star
35   —Ah no, only the Morning *News*, the Evening *Record*
Of what I have done and what I have not done
Set down and held against me in the Book
Of Death, on paper yellowing
Already, with one morning's sun, one evening's sun.

40   Sometimes I only dream him. He brings then
News of a different morning, a judgment not of men.
The bombers have turned back over the Pole,
Having met a star. . . . I look at that new year
And, waking, think of our Moravian Star
45   Not lit yet, and the pure beeswax candle
With its red flame-proofed paper pompom
Not lit yet, and the sweetened
Bun we brought home from the love-feast, still not eaten,
And the song the children sang: *O Morning Star—*

1. The grave mode in ancient Greek music.

50 And at this hour, to the dew-hushed drums
    Of the morning, Nestus Gurley
    Marches to me over the lawn; and the cat Elfie,
    Furred like a musk-ox, coon-tailed, gold-leaf-eyed,
    Looks at the paper boy without alarm
55 But yawns, and stretches, and walks placidly
    Across the lawn to his ladder, climbs it, and begins to purr.

    I let him in,
    Go out and pick up from the grass the paper hat
    Nestus has folded: this tricorne fit for a Napoleon
60 Of our days and institutions, weaving
    Baskets, being bathed, receiving
    Electric shocks, Rauwolfia.[2] . . . I put it on
    —Ah no, only unfold it.
    There is dawn inside; and I say to no one
65 About—
              it is a note or two
    That with a note or two would—
                          say to no one
    About nothing: "He delivers dawn."

70 When I lie coldly
    —Lie, that is, neither with coldness nor with warmth—
    In the darkness that is not lit by anything,
    In the grave that is not lit by anything
    Except our hope: the hope
75 That is not proofed against anything, but pure
    And shining as the first, least star
    That is lost in the east on the morning of Judgment—
    May I say, recognizing the step
    Or tune or breath. . . .
80   recognizing the breath,
    May I say, "It is Nestus Gurley."

                                                    1960

HENRY REED
(1914–   )

Lessons of the War

TO ALAN MITCHELL

Vixi duellis nuper idoneus
Et militavi non sine gloria[1]

1. Naming of Parts

Today we have naming of parts. Yesterday,
We had daily cleaning. And tomorrow morning,
We shall have what to do after firing. But today,
Today we have naming of parts. Japonica[2]
5 Glistens like coral in all of the neighboring gardens,
            And today we have naming of parts.

---

2. A plant whose substance is sometimes used in the treatment of certain mental disorders.
1. The opening lines of a poem by Horace (III.26), but with Horace's word *"puellis"* (girls) changed to *"duellis"* (war, battles):

"Lately I have lived in the midst of battles, creditably enough,/And have soldiered, not without glory."
2. The flowering quince (*Cydonia japonica*), a shrub with brilliant scarlet flowers.

This is the lower sling swivel. And this
Is the upper sling swivel, whose use you will see,
When you are given your slings. And this is the piling swivel,
10 Which in your case you have not got. The branches
Hold in the gardens their silent, eloquent gestures,
    Which in our case we have not got.

This is the safety-catch, which is always released
With an easy flick of the thumb. And please do not let me
15 See anyone using his finger. You can do it quite easy
If you have any strength in your thumb. The blossoms
Are fragile and motionless, never letting anyone see
    Any of them using their finger.

And this you can see is the bolt. The purpose of this
20 Is to open the breech, as you see. We can slide it
Rapidly backwards and forwards: we call this
Easing the spring. And rapidly backwards and forwards
The early bees are assaulting and fumbling the flowers:
    They call it easing the Spring.

25 They call it easing the Spring: it is perfectly easy
If you have any strength in your thumb: like the bolt,
And the breech, and the cocking-piece, and the point of balance,
Which in our case we have not got; and the almond-blossom
Silent in all of the gardens and the bees going backwards and forwards,
30   For today we have naming of parts.

2. *Judging Distances*

Not only how far away, but the way that you say it
Is very important. Perhaps you may never get
The knack of judging a distance, but at least you know
How to report on a landscape: the central sector,
35 The right of arc and that, which we had last Tuesday,
    And at least you know

That maps are of time, not place, so far as the army
Happens to be concerned—the reason being,
Is one which need not delay us. Again, you know
40 There are three kinds of tree, three only, the fir and the poplar,
And those which have bushy tops to; and lastly
    That things only seem to be things.

A barn is not called a barn, to put it more plainly,
Or a field in the distance, where sheep may be safely grazing.
45 You must never be over-sure. You must say, when reporting:
At five o'clock in the central sector is a dozen
Of what appear to be animals; whatever you do,
    Don't call the bleeders *sheep.*

I am sure that's quite clear; and suppose, for the sake of example,
50 The one at the end, asleep, endeavors to tell us
What he sees over there to the west, and how far away,
After first having come to attention. There to the west,
On the fields of summer the sun and the shadows bestow
    Vestments of purple and gold.

55 The still white dwellings are like a mirage in the heat,
And under the swaying elms a man and a woman
Lie gently together. Which is, perhaps, only to say
That there is a row of houses to the left of arc,
And that under some poplars a pair of what appear to be humans
60   Appear to be loving.

Well that, for an answer, is what we might rightly call
Moderately satisfactory only, the reason being,
Is that two things have been omitted, and those are important.
The human beings, now: in what direction are they,
65   And how far away, would you say? And do not forget
        There may be dead ground in between.

There may be dead ground in between; and I may not have got
The knack of judging a distance; I will only venture
A guess that perhaps between me and the apparent lovers,
70   (Who, incidentally, appear by now to have finished,)
At seven o'clock from the houses, is roughly a distance
        Of about one year and a half.

3. *Unarmed Combat*

In due course of course you will all be issued with
Your proper issue; but until tomorrow,
75   You can hardly be said to need it; and until that time,
We shall have unarmed combat. I shall teach you
The various holds and rolls and throws and breakfalls
        Which you may sometimes meet.

And the various holds and rolls and throws and breakfalls
80   Do not depend on any sort of weapon,
But only on what I might coin a phrase and call
The ever-important question of human balance,
And the ever-important need to be in a strong
        Position at the start.

85   There are many kinds of weakness about the body
Where you would least expect, like the ball of the foot.
But the various holds and rolls and throws and breakfalls
Will always come in useful. And never be frightened
To tackle from behind: it may not be clean to do so,
90   But this is global war.

So give them all you have, and always give them
As good as you get; it will always get you somewhere.
(You may not know it, but you can tie a Jerry[3]
Up without rope; it is one of the things I shall teach you.)
95   Nothing will matter if only you are ready for him.
        The readiness is all.

The readiness is all. How can I help but feel
I have been here before? But somehow then,
I was the tied-up one. How to get out
100   Was always then my problem. And even if I had
A piece of rope I was always the sort of person
        Who threw the rope aside.

And in my time I have given them all I had,
Which was never as good as I got, and it got me nowhere.
105   And the various holds and rolls and throws and breakfalls
Somehow or other I always seemed to put
In the wrong place. And as for war, my wars
        Were global from the start.

Perhaps I was never in a strong position,
110   Or the ball of my foot got hurt, or I had some weakness
Where I had least expected. But I think I see your point.
While awaiting a proper issue, we must learn the lesson
Of the ever-important question of human balance.
        It is courage that counts.

3. World War II slang for "German."

115 Things may be the same again; and we must fight
Not in the hope of winning but rather of keeping
Something alive: so that when we meet our end,
It may be said that we tackled wherever we could,
That battle-fit we lived, and though defeated,
120   Not without glory fought.

1946

DYLAN THOMAS
(1914–1953)

The Force That
Through the Green Fuse
Drives the Flower

The force that through the green fuse drives the flower
Drives my green age; that blasts the roots of trees
Is my destroyer.
And I am dumb to tell the crooked rose
5   My youth is bent by the same wintry fever.

The force that drives the water through the rocks
Drives my red blood; that dries the mouthing streams
Turns mine to wax.
And I am dumb to mouth unto my veins
10   How at the mountain spring the same mouth sucks.

The hand that whirls the water in the pool
Stirs the quicksand; that ropes the blowing wind
Hauls my shroud sail.
And I am dumb to tell the hanging man
15   How of my clay is made the hangman's lime.

The lips of time leech to the fountain head;
Love drips and gathers, but the fallen blood
Shall calm her sores.
And I am dumb to tell a weather's wind
20   How time has ticked a heaven round the stars.

And I am dumb to tell the lover's tomb
How at my sheet goes the same crooked worm.

1934

A Process in the Weather of the Heart

A process in the weather of the heart
Turns damp to dry; the golden shot
Storms in the freezing tomb.
A weather in the quarter of the veins
5   Turns night to day; blood in their suns
Lights up the living worm.

A process in the eye forwarns
The bones of blindness; and the womb
Drives in a death as life leaks out.

10   A darkness in the weather of the eye
Is half its light; the fathomed sea
Breaks on unangled land.
The seed that makes a forest of the loin
Forks half its fruit; and half drops down,
15   Slow in a sleeping wind.

A weather in the flesh and bone
Is damp and dry; the quick and dead
Move like two ghosts before the eye.

A process in the weather of the world
20   Turns ghost to ghost; each mothered child
Sits in their double shade.
A process blows the moon into the sun,
Pulls down the shabby curtains of the skin;
And the heart gives up its dead.

1934

The Hunchback in the Park

The hunchback in the park
A solitary mister
Propped between trees and water
From the opening of the garden lock
5   That lets the trees and water enter
Until the Sunday somber bell at dark[1]

Eating bread from a newspaper
Drinking water from the chained cup
That the children filled with gravel
10   In the fountain basin where I sailed my ship
Slept at night in a dog kennel
But nobody chained him up.

Like the park birds he came early
Like the water he sat down
15   And Mister they called Hey mister
The truant boys from the town
Running when he had heard them clearly
On out of sound

Past lake and rockery
20   Laughing when he shook his paper
Hunchbacked in mockery
Through the loud zoo of the willow groves
Dodging the park keeper
With his stick that picked up leaves.

25   And the old dog sleeper
Alone between nurses and swans
While the boys among willows
Made the tigers jump out of their eyes
To roar on the rockery stones
30   And the groves were blue with sailors

Made all day until bell time
A woman figure without fault
Straight as a young elm
Straight and tall from his crooked bones
35   That she might stand in the night
After the locks and chains

All night in the unmade park
After the railings and shrubberies

1. The bell that warns visitors that the park gates are about to be closed for the night.

The birds the grass the trees the lake
40   And the wild boys innocent as strawberries
Had followed the hunchback
To his kennel in the dark.

                                              1942

Poem in October

          It was my thirtieth year to heaven
Woke to my hearing from harbor and neighbor wood
          And the mussel pooled and the heron
                    Priested shore
5   The morning beckon
With water praying and call of seagull and rook
And the knock of sailing boats on the net webbed wall
                    Myself to set foot
                    That second
10   In the still sleeping town and set forth.

          My birthday began with the water-
Birds and the birds of the winged trees flying my name
          Above the farms and the white horses
                    And I rose
15   In rainy autumn
And walked abroad in a shower of all my days.
High tide and the heron dived when I took the road
                    Over the border
                    And the gates
20   Of the town closed as the town awoke.

          A springful of larks in a rolling
Cloud and the roadside bushes brimming with whistling
          Blackbirds and the sun of October
                    Summery
25   On the hill's shoulder,
Here were fond climates and sweet singers suddenly
Come in the morning where I wandered and listened
                    To the rain wringing
                    Wind blow cold
30   In the wood faraway under me.

          Pale rain over the dwindling harbor
And over the sea wet church the size of a snail
          With its horns through mist and the castle
                    Brown as owls
35   But all the gardens
Of spring and summer were blooming in the tall tales
Beyond the border and under the lark full cloud.
                    There could I marvel
                    My birthday
40   Away but the weather turned around.

          It turned away from the blithe country
And down the other air and the blue altered sky
          Streamed again a wonder of summer
                    With apples
45   Pears and red currants
And I saw in the turning so clearly a child's
Forgotten mornings when he walked with his mother
                    Through the parables
                    Of sun light
50   And the legends of the green chapels

And the twice told fields of infancy
That his tears burned my cheeks and his heart moved in mine.
These were the woods the river and sea
Where a boy
55   In the listening
Summertime of the dead whispered the truth of his joy
To the trees and the stones and the fish in the tide.
And the mystery
Sang alive
60   Still in the water and singingbirds.

And there could I marvel my birthday
Away but the weather turned around. And the true
Joy of the long dead child sang burning
In the sun.
65   It was my thirtieth
Year to heaven stood there then in the summer noon
Though the town below lay leaved with October blood.
O may my heart's truth
Still be sung
70   On this high hill in a year's turning.

1946

The Conversation of Prayer

The conversation of prayers about to be said
By the child going to bed and the man on the stairs
Who climbs to his dying love in her high room,
The one not caring to whom in his sleep he will move
5   And the other full of tears that she will be dead,

Turns in the dark on the sound they know will arise
Into the answering skies from the green ground,
From the man on the stairs and the child by his bed.
The sound about to be said in the two prayers
10   For the sleep in a safe land and the love who dies

Will be the same grief flying. Whom shall they calm?
Shall the child sleep unharmed or the man be crying?
The conversation of prayers about to be said
Turns on the quick and the dead, and the man on the stairs
15   Tonight shall find no dying but alive and warm

In the fire of his care his love in the high room.
And the child not caring to whom he climbs his prayer
Shall drown in a grief as deep as his true grave,
And mark the dark eyed wave, through the eyes of sleep,
20   Dragging him up the stairs to one who lies dead.

1946

Fern Hill

Now as I was young and easy under the apple boughs
About the lilting house and happy as the grass was green,
The night above the dingle starry,
Time let me hail and climb
5   Golden in the heydays of his eyes,
And honored among wagons I was prince of the apple towns
And once below a time I lordly had the trees and leaves
Trail with daisies and barley
Down the rivers of the windfall light.

10 And as I was green and carefree, famous among the barns
    About the happy yard and singing as the farm was home,
        In the sun that is young once only,
            Time let me play and be
            Golden in the mercy of his means,
15 And green and golden I was huntsman and herdsman, the calves
    Sang to my horn, the foxes on the hills barked clear and cold,
            And the sabbath rang slowly
        In the pebbles of the holy streams.

    All the sun long it was running, it was lovely, the hay
20 Fields high as the house, the tunes from the chimneys, it was air
            And playing, lovely and watery
                And fire green as grass.
            And nightly under the simple stars
    As I rode to sleep the owls were bearing the farm away,
25 All the moon long I heard, blessed among stables, the night-jars
            Flying with the ricks, and the horses
                Flashing into the dark.

    And then to awake, and the farm, like a wanderer white
    With the dew, come back, the cock on his shoulder: it was all
30   Shining, it was Adam and maiden,
            The sky gathered again
        And the sun grew round that very day.
    So it must have been after the birth of the simple light
    In the first, spinning place, the spellbound horses walking warm
35   Out of the whinnying green stable
            On to the fields of praise.

    And honored among foxes and pheasants by the gay house
    Under the new made clouds and happy as the heart was long,
            In the sun born over and over,
40   I ran my heedless ways,
            My wishes raced through the house high hay
    And nothing I cared, at my sky blue trades, that time allows
    In all his tuneful turning so few and such morning songs
            Before the children green and golden
45   Follow him out of grace,

    Nothing I cared, in the lamb white days, that time would take me
    Up to the swallow thronged loft by the shadow of my hand,
            In the moon that is always rising,
                Nor that riding to sleep
50   I should hear him fly with the high fields
    And wake to the farm forever fled from the childless land.
    Oh as I as young and easy in the mercy of his means,
            Time held me green and dying
        Though I sang in my chains like the sea.

                                            1946

GWENDOLYN BROOKS
(1915–   )

my dreams, my works, must wait till after hell

I hold my honey and I store my bread
In little jars and cabinets of my will.
I label clearly, and each latch and lid
I bid, Be firm till I return from hell.
5   I am very hungry. I am incomplete.
And none can tell when I may dine again.
No man can give me any word but Wait,
The puny light. I keep eyes pointed in;
Hoping that, when the devil days of my hurt
10   Drag out to their last dregs and I resume
On such legs as are left me, in such heart
As I can manage, remember to go home,
My taste will not have turned insensitive
To honey and bread old purity could love.

1945

Medgar Evers[1]

FOR CHARLES EVERS

The man whose height his fear improved he
arranged to fear no further. The raw
intoxicated time was time for better birth or
a final death.

5   Old styles, old tempos, all the engagement of
the day—the sedate, the regulated fray—
the antique light, the Moral rose, old gusts,
tight whistlings from the past, the mothballs
in the Love at last our man forswore.

10   Medgar Evers annoyed confetti and assorted
brands of businessmen's eyes.

The shows came down: to maxims and surprise.
And palsy.

Roaring no rapt arise-ye to the dead, he
15   leaned across tomorrow. People said that
he was holding clean globes in his hands.

1968

ROBERT LOWELL
(1917–   )

The Crucifix

How dry time screaks in its fat axle-grease,
As spare November strikes us through the ice
And the Leviathan breaks water in the rice
Fields, at the poles, at the hot gates to Greece;
5   It's time: the old unmastered lion roars

1. Negro civil rights leader in Mississippi, murdered in 1963.

And ramps like a mad dog outside the doors,
Snapping at gobbets in my thumbless hand.
The seaways lurch through Sodom's knees of sand
Tomorrow. We are sinking. 'Run, rat, run,"
10 The prophets thunder, and I run upon
My father, Adam. Adam, if our land
Become the desolation of a hand
That shakes the Temple back to clay, how can
War ever change my old into new man?
15 Get out from under my feet, old man. Let me pass;
On Ninth Street, through the Hallowe'en's soaped glass,
I picked at an old bone on two crossed sticks
And found, to *Via et Vita et Veritas*[1]
A stray dog's signpost is a crucifix.

1946

The Quaker Graveyard in Nantucket

(FOR WARREN WINSLOW, DEAD AT SEA)

*Let man have dominion over the fishes of the
sea and the fowls of the air and the beasts and the
whole earth, and every creeping creature that
moveth upon the earth.*[2]

1

A brackish reach of shoal off Madaket[3]
The sea was still breaking violently and night
Had steamed into our North Atlantic Fleet,
When the drowned sailor clutched the drag-net. Light
5 Flashed from his matted head and marble feet,
He grappled at the net
With the coiled, hurdling muscles of his thighs:
The corpse was bloodless, a botch of reds and whites,
Its open, staring eyes
10 Were lusterless dead-lights
Or cabin-windows on a stranded hulk
Heavy with sand.[4] We weight the body, close
Its eyes and heave it seaward whence it came,
Where the heel-headed dogfish barks its nose
15 On Ahab's[5] void and forehead; and the name
Is blocked in yellow chalk.
Sailors, who pitch this portent at the sea
Where dreadnaughts shall confess
Its hell-bent deity,
20 When you are powerless
To sand-bag this Atlantic bulwark, faced
By the earth-shaker, green, unwearied, chaste
In his steel scales: ask for no Orphean lute
To pluck life back.[6] The guns of the steeled fleet
25 Recoil and then repeat
The hoarse salute.

1. The Latin phrase of the Vulgate is translated thus in the Authorized Version (John xiv.6): "Jesus saith unto him, I am the way, the truth, and the life: no man cometh unto the Father, but by me."
2. Genesis i.26.
3. Name of a small settlement, and a bay, on Nantucket Island, Massachusetts.
4. Lines 1–12 are based on the opening chapter of Thoreau's *Cape Cod*.
5. Captain Ahab, who is protagonist of Herman Melville's *Moby Dick* (1851) and a
recurring presence in this sequence of poems, sailed from Nantucket on the *Pequod* in pursuit of the white whale.
6. Orpheus went to the underworld to recover his wife Eurydice and so charmed its queen, Persephone, by his playing on the lyre that she allowed him to lead Eurydice up from Hades, on condition that he not look back before the end of the journey: he did look back, and Eurydice vanished forever. The "earth-shaker" is Poseidon, god of the sea.

2

Whenever winds are moving and their breath
Heaves at the roped-in bulwarks of this pier,
The terns and sea-gulls tremble at your death
30   In these home waters. Sailor, can you hear
The Pequod's sea wings, beating landward, fall
Headlong and break on our Atlantic wall
Off 'Sconset,[7] where the yawing S-boats° splash   *sailboats*
The bellbuoy, with ballooning spinnakers,
35   As the entangled, screeching mainsheet clears
The blocks: off Madaket, where lubbers lash
The heavy surf and throw their long lead squids
For blue-fish? Sea-gulls blink their heavy lids
Seaward. The winds' wings beat upon the stones,
40   Cousin, and scream for you and the claws rush
At the sea's throat and wring it in the slush
Of this old Quaker graveyard where the bones
Cry out in the long night for the hurt beast
Bobbing by Ahab's whaleboats in the East.

3

45   All you recovered from Poseidon died
With you, my cousin, and the harrowed brine
Is fruitless on the blue beard of the god,
Stretching beyond us to the castles in Spain,
Nantucket's westward haven. To Cape Cod
50   Guns, cradled on the tide,
Blast the eelgrass about a waterclock
Of bilge and backwash, roil the salt and sand
Lashing earth's scaffold, rock
Our warships in the hand
55   Of the great God, where time's contrition blues
Whatever it was these Quaker sailors lost

In the mad scramble of their lives. They died
When time was open-eyed,
Wooden and childish; only bones abide
60   There, in the nowhere, where their boats were tossed
Sky-high, where mariners had fabled news
Of IS, the whited monster. What it costs
Them is their secret. In the sperm-whale's slick
I see the Quakers drown and hear their cry:
65   "If God himself had not been on our side,
If God himself had not been on our side,
When the Atlantic rose against us, why,
Then it had swallowed us up quick."

4

This is the end of the whaleroad and the whale
70   Who spewed Nantucket bones on the thrashed swell
And stirred the troubled waters to whirlpools
To send the Pequod packing off to hell:
This is the end of them, three-quarters fools,
Snatching at straws to sail
75   Seaward and seaward on the turntail whale,
Spouting out blood and water as it rolls,
Sick as a dog to these Atlantic shoals:
Clamavimus, O depths.[8] Let the sea-gulls wail

For water, for the deep where the high tide
80   Mutters to its hurt self, mutters and ebbs.
Waves wallow in their wash, go out and out,

7. Siasconset, a town on Nantucket.   "Out of the depths have I cried unto thee,
8. "We have cried * * * ": Psalms cxxx.1—   O Lord."

Leave only the death-rattle of the crabs,
The beach increasing, its enormous snout
Sucking the ocean's side.
85 This is the end of running on the waves;
We are poured out like water. Who will dance
The mast-lashed master of Leviathans
Up from this field of Quakers in their unstoned graves?

5

When the whale's viscera go and the roll
90 Of its corruption overruns this world
Beyond tree-swept Nantucket and Wood's Hole[9]
And Martha's Vineyard, Sailor, will your sword
Whistle and fall and sink into the fat?
In the great ash-pit of Jehoshaphat[1]
95 The bones cry for the blood of the white whale,
The fat flukes arch and whack about its ears,
The death-lance churns into the sanctuary, tears
The gun-blue swingle, heaving like a flail,
And hacks the coiling life out: it works and drags
100 And rips the sperm-whale's midriff into rags,
Gobbets of blubber spill to wind and weather,
Sailor, and gulls go round the stoven timbers
Where the morning stars sing out together
And thunder shakes the white surf and dismembers
105 The red flag hammered in the mast-head.[2] Hide,
Our steel, Jonas Messias,[3] in Thy side.

6. Our Lady of Walsingham[4]

There once the penitents took off their shoes
And then walked barefoot the remaining mile;
And the small trees, a stream and hedgerows file
110 Slowly along the munching English lane,
Like cows to the old shine, until you lose
Track of your dragging pain.
The stream flows down under the druid tree,
Shiloah's whirlpools gurgle and make glad
115 The castle of God. Sailor, you were glad
And whistled Sion[5] by that stream. But see:

9. Harbor and township in southern Massachusetts, north of the island of Martha's Vineyard, which lies to the west of Nantucket.
1. Identified by some commentators as an image for the Day of Judgment, when the world will end in fire.
2. As was the flag in the concluding chapter of *Moby Dick.*
3. For the juxtaposition of Jonah with the Messiah, see the words of Jesus in Matthew xii.39–41, and especially: "For as Jonas was three days and three nights in the whale's belly; so shall the Son of man be three days and three nights in the heart of the earth" [See Robert Lowell, *Poesie 1943–1952,* ed. Rolando Anzilotti, p. 86].
4. Walsingham is a small town in Norfolk, England; a shrine to the Virgin Mary, built in the 11th century, was an object of pilgrimage until it was destroyed in the Reformation. Lowell points out in a prefatory note to *Lord Weary's Castle* that " 'Our Lady of Walsingham' is an adaptation of several paragraphs from E. I. Watkin's *Catholic Art and Culture"* which describe the present Roman Catholic shrine. The passage is in part as follows: "Now once again pilgrims visit her image erected in a mediaeval chapel, where, it is said, they took off their shoes to walk barefoot the remaining mile to the shrine. * * * The road to the chapel is a quiet country lane shaded with trees, and lined on one side by a hedgerow. On the other, a stream flows down beneath the trees, the water symbol of the Holy Spirit, 'the waters of Shiloah that go softly,' the 'flow of the river making glad the city of God.' Within the chapel, an attractive example of Decorated achitecture, near an altar of mediaeval fashion, is seated Our Lady's image. It is too small for its canopy, and is not superficially beautiful. 'Non est species neque decor,' there is no comeliness of charm in that expressionless face with heavy eyelids. But let us look carefully, and allow the image, as every work of art should be allowed, to speak to us in its own language. We become aware of an inner beauty more impressive than outward grace. That expressionless countenance expresses what is beyond expression. It is the countenance of one whose spirit dwells in a region beyond emotion and thought, the centre of which mystical writers speak. Mary is beyond joy and sorrow. For her spirit is in God, and she knows as He knows, receiving His knowledge. No longer the Mother of Sorrows nor yet of the human joy of the crib, she understands the secret counsel of God to whose accomplishment Calvary and Bethlehem alike ministered. Therefore her peace, the central peace of God, is beyond the changes of earthly experience. And the inscrutability of that illegible countenance is the inscrutability of the Divine Will made known to her."
5. Sion, or Zion, was a hill in Jerusalem, the residence of King David and his successors: the heavenly city.

Our Lady, too small for her canopy,
Sits near the altar. There's no comeliness
At all or charm in that expressionless
120 Face with its heavy eyelids. As before,
This face, for centuries a memory,
Non est species, neque decor,
Expressionless, expresses God: it goes
Past castled Sion. She knows what God knows,
125 Not Calvary's Cross nor crib at Bethlehem
Now, and the world shall come to Walsingham.

                    7
The empty winds are creaking and the oak
Splatters and splatters on the cenotaph,[6]
The boughs are trembling and a gaff°   *spar*
130 Bobs on the untimely stroke
Of the greased wash exploding on a shoal-bell
In the old mouth of the Atlantic. It's well;
Atlantic, you are fouled with the blue sailors,
Sea-monsters, upward angel, downward fish:[7]
135 Unmarried and corroding, spare of flesh
Mart once of supercilious, wing'd clippers,
Atlantic, where your bell-trap guts its spoil
You could cut the brackish winds with a knife
Here in Nantucket, and cast up the time
140 When the Lord God formed man from the sea's slime
And breathed into his face the breath of life,
And blue-lung'd combers lumbered to the kill.
The Lord survives the rainbow of His will.[8]

After the Surprising Conversions[9]

September twenty-second, Sir: today
I answer. In the latter part of May,
Hard on ou Lord's Ascension, it began
To be more sensible.° A gentleman   *evident*
5 Of more than common understanding, strict
In morals, pious in behavior, kicked

6. An empty tomb, or monument erected to the dead but not containing their remains; often for those lost at sea.
7. From Milton, *Paradise Lost,* I.462–63: "Dagon his name, sea monster, upward man/ And downward fish * * * "
8. See Genesis ix.11–17, especially "I do set my bow in the cloud, and it shall be for a token of a covenant between me and the earth."
9. The poem takes its departure from an account by Jonathan Edwards (1703–58) of a resurgence of religious enthusiasm that took place in and around Northampton, Massachusetts, during several months of 1734–35. Edwards's *Narrative of Surprising Conversions,* in the form of a letter to the Rev. Dr. Colman of Boston, dated Nov. 6, 1736, traces the revival from its beginnings through its decline. One passage towards the end of the letter (see *The Works of President Edwards,* New York, 1851, III, 69–72) figures prominently in the poem:
    "In the latter part of May, it began to be very sensible that the Spirit of God was gradually withdrawing from us, and after this time Satan seemed to be more let loose, and raged in a dreadful manner. The first instance wherein it appeared, was a person's putting an end to his life by cutting his throat. He was a gentleman of more than common understanding, of strict morals, religious in his behavior, and a useful, honorable person in the town; but was of a family that are exceeding prone to melancholy, and his mother was killed with it. He had, from the beginning of this extraordinary time, been exceedingly con-

cerned about the state of his soul, and there were some things in his experience, that appeared very hopefully, but he durst entertain no hope concerning his own good estate. Towards the latter end of his time, he grew much discouraged, and melancholy grew amain upon him, till he was wholly overpowered by it, and was, in great measure, past a capacity of receiving advice, or being reasoned with to any purpose: the devil took the advantage, and drove him into despairing thoughts. He was kept awake nights meditating upon terror, so that he had scarce any sleep at all, for a long time together. And it was observable at last, that he was scarcely well capable of managing his ordinary business, and was judged delirious by the coroner's inquest. The news of this extraordinarily affected the minds of people here, and struck them as it were with astonishment. After this, multitudes in this and other towns seemed to have it strongly suggested to them, and pressed upon them, to do as this person had done. And many that seemed to be under no melancholy, some pious persons, that had no special darkness or doubts about the goodness of their state, nor were under any special trouble or concern of mind about any thing spiritual or temporal, yet had it urged upon them, as if somebody had spoken to them, *Cut your own throat, now is a good opportunity.* Now! Now! So that they were obliged to fight with all their might to resist it, and yet no reason suggested to them why they should do it." Elsewhere, Edwards identified the man as his uncle, Joseph Hawley, who cut his throat on June 1, 1735.

Against our goad. A man of some renown,
An useful, honored person in the town,
He came of melancholy parents; prone
To secret spells, for years they kept alone—
His uncle, I believe, was killed of it:
Good people, but of too much or little wit.
I preached one Sabbath on a text from Kings;
He showed concernment for his soul. Some things
In his experience were hopeful. He
Would sit and watch the wind knocking a tree
And praise this countryside our Lord has made.
Once when a poor man's heifer died, he laid
A shilling on the doorsill; though a thirst
For loving shook him like a snake, he durst
Not entertain much hope of his estate
In heaven. Once we saw him sitting late
Behind his attic window by a light
That guttered on his Bible; through that night
He meditated terror, and he seemed
Beyond advice or reason, for he dreamed
That he was called to trumpet Judgment Day
To Concord. In the latter part of May
He cut his throat. And though the coroner
Judged him delirious, soon a noisome° stir   *noxious, disgusting*
Palsied our village. At Jehovah's nod
Satan seemed more let loose amongst us: God
Abandoned us to Satan, and he pressed
Us hard, until we thought we could not rest
Till we had done with life. Content was gone.
All the good work was quashed. We were undone.
The breath of God had carried out a planned
And sensible withdrawal from this land;
The multitude, once unconcerned with doubt,
Once neither callous, curious nor devout,
Jumped at broad noon, as though some peddler groaned
At it in its familiar twang: "My friend,
Cut your own throat. Cut your own throat. Now! Now!"
September twenty-second, Sir, the bough
Cracks with the unpicked apples, and at dawn
The small-mouth bass breaks water, gorged with spawn.

1946

In the Cage

The lifers file into the hall,
According to their houses—twos
Of laundered denim. On the wall
A colored fairy tinkles blues
And titters by the balustrade;
Canaries beat their bars and scream.
We come from tunnels where the spade
Pick-axe and hod for plaster steam
In mud and insulation. Here
The Bible-twisting Israelite[1]
Fasts for his Harlem. It is night,
And it is vanity, and age
Blackens the heart of Adam. Fear,
The yellow chirper, beaks its cage.

1946

---

1. Member of a Negro religious cult.

For George Santayana[2]

1863–1952

In the heydays of 'forty-five,
bus-loads of souvenir-deranged
G.I.'s and officer-professors of philosophy
came crashing through your cell,
5   puzzled to find you still alive,
free-thinking Catholic infidel,
stray spirit, who'd found
the Church too good to be believed.
Later I used to dawdle
10   past Circus and Mithraic Temple
to *Santo Stefano* grown paper-thin
like you from waiting. . . .
There at the monastery hospital,
you wished those geese-girl sisters wouldn't bother
15   their heads and yours by praying for your soul:
"There is no God and Mary is His Mother."

Lying outside the consecrated ground
forever now, you smile
like Ser Brunetto running for the green
20   cloth at Verona—not like one
who loses, but like one who'd won. . . .[3]
as if your long pursuit of Socrates'
demon, man-slaying Alcibiades,[4]
the demon of philosophy, at last had changed
25   those fleeting virgins into friendly laurel trees
at *Santo Stefano Rotondo*, when you died
near ninety,
still unbelieving, unconfessed and unreceived,
true to your boyish shyness of the Bride.
Old trooper, I see your child's red crayon pass,
30   bleeding deletions on the galleys° you hold   *galley proofs*
under your throbbing magnifying glass,
that worn arena, where the whirling sand
and broken-hearted lions lick your hand
refined by bile as yellow as a lump of gold.

1959

The Lesson

No longer to lie reading *Tess of the d'Urbervilles*,
while the high, mysterious squirrels
rain small green branches on our sleep!

All that landscape, one likes to think it died
5   or slept with us, that we ourselves died
or slept then in the age and second of our habitation.

The green leaf cushions the same dry footprint,
or the child's boat luffs[5] in the same dry chop,[6]
and we are where we were. We were!

---

2. The Spanish-born Harvard philosopher, George Santayana, spent the last years of his life, from October 1944, at the Blue Sisters' Nursing Home, next door to the old round church of Santo Stefano Rotondo, on the Monte Celio, in Rome. During the last months of the Second World War, in 1944 and 1945, he was much visited by Allied soldiers and airmen.
3. See Dante, *Inferno*, XV.121–24, where Dante describes Brunetto Latini, as he takes leave of him, in these terms.
4. Athenian statesman and general (ca. 451–404 B.C.); reading a book about Alexander the Great, in 1950, Santayana calls him "one of my favourite heroes, a *good* one, to balance a *bad* one like Alcibiades * * * "
5. Sails into the wind.
6. Choppiness of waves.

10 Perhaps the trees stopped growing in summer amnesia;
their day that gave them veins is rooted down—
and the nights? They are for sleeping now as then.

Ah the light lights the window of my young night,
and you never turn off the light,
15 while the books lie in the library, and go on reading.

The barberry berry sticks on the small hedge,
cold slits the same crease in the finger,
the same thorn hurts. The leaf repeats the lesson.

1964

The Public Garden[7]

Burnished, burned-out, still burning as the year
you lead me to our stamping ground.
The city and its cruising cars surround
the Public Garden. All's alive—
5 the children crowding home from school at five,
punting a football in the bricky air,
the sailors and their pick-ups under trees
with Latin labels. And the jaded flock
of swanboats paddles to its dock.
10 The park is drying.
Dead leaves thicken to a ball
inside the basin of a fountain, where
the heads of four stone lions stare
and suck on empty fawcets. Night
15 deepens. From the arched bridge, we see
the shedding park-bound mallards, how they keep
circling and diving in the lanternlight,
searching for something hidden in the muck.
And now the moon, earth's friend, that cared so much
20 for us, and cared so little, comes again—
always a stranger! As we walk,
it lies like chalk
over the waters. Everything's aground.
Remember summer? Bubbles filled
25 the fountain, and we splashed. We drowned
in Eden, while Jehovah's grass-green lyre
was rustling all about us in the leaves
that gurgled by us, turning upside down . . .
The fountain's failing waters flash around
30 the garden. Nothing catches fire.

1964

The Neo-Classical Urn

I rub my head and find a turtle shell
stuck on a pole,
each hair electrical
with charges, and the juice alive
5 with ferment. Bubbles drive
the motor, always purposeful . . .
Poor head!
How its skinny shell once hummed,
as I sprinted down the colonnade

7. A small park next to the Common in Boston, Massachusetts, containing flower-beds, walks, greensward, and a pond on which, during the summer, open pleasure-boats decorated with large artificial swans, circulate.

10 of bleaching pines, cylindrical
clipped trunks without a twig between them. Rest!
I could not rest. At full run on the curve,
I left the caste stone statue of a nymph,
her soaring armpits and her one bare breast,
15 gray from the rain and graying in the shade,
as on, on, in sun, the pathway now a dyke,
I swerved between two water bogs,
two seines of moss, and stooped to snatch
the painted turtles on dead logs.

20 In that season of joy,
my turtle catch
was thirty-three,
dropped splashing in our garden urn,
like money in the bank,
25 the plop and splash
of turtle on turtle,
fed raw gobs of hash . . .

Oh neo-classical white urn, Oh nymph,
Oh lute! The boy was pitiless who strummed
30 their elegy,
for as the month wore on,
the turtles rose,
and popped up dead on the stale scummed
surface—limp wrinkled heads and legs withdrawn
35 in pain. What pain? A turtle's nothing. No
grace, no cerebration, less free will
than the mosquito I must kill—
nothings! Turtles! I rub my skull,
that turtle shell,
40 and breathe their dying smell,
still watch their crippled last survivors pass,
and hobble humpbacked through the grizzled grass.

1964

For the Union Dead[8]

"Relinquunt Omnia Servare Rem Publicam."

The old South Boston Aquarium stands
in a Sahara of snow now. Its broken windows are boarded.
The bronze weathervane cod has lost half its scales.
The airy tanks are dry.

5 Once my nose crawled like a snail on the glass;
my hand tingled
to burst the bubbles
drifting from the noses of the cowed, compliant fish.

My hand draws back. I often sigh still
10 for the dark downward and vegetating kingdom
of the fish and reptile. One morning last March,
I pressed against the new barbed and galvanized

8. At the edge of Boston Common, across from the Massachusetts State House, stands a monument to Colonel Robert Gould Shaw (1837–63) and the Negro troops of the 54th Massachusetts regiment whom he was leading in the assault on Fort Wagner, South Carolina, when he was killed on July 18, 1863. The memorial, by Augustus St. Gaudens, representing Shaw in equestrian high-relief, with his troops, was dedicated in 1897. In the upper right it bears the motto of the Society of the Cincinnati (slightly altered in the epigraph to Lowell's poem), *"Omnia relinquit servare rempublicam,"* "He leaves all else to serve the republic."

fence on the Boston Common. Behind their cage,
yellow dinosaur steamshovels were grunting
15 as they cropped up tons of mush and gass
to gouge their underworld garage.

Parking spaces luxuriate like civic
sandpiles in the heart of Boston.
A girdle of orange, Puritan-pumpkin colored girders
20 braces the tingling Statehouse,

shaking over the excavations, as it faces Colonel Shaw
and his bell-cheeked Negro infantry
on St. Gaudens' shaking Civil War relief,
propped by a plank splint against the garage's earthquake.

25 Two months after marching through Boston,
half the regiment was dead;
at the dedication,
William James could almost hear the bronze Negroes breathe.

Their monument sticks like a fishbone
30 in the city's throat.
Its Colonel is as lean
as a compass-needle.

He has an angry wrenlike vigilance,
a greyhound's gentle tautness;
35 he seems to wince at pleasure,
and suffocate for privacy.

He is out of bounds now. He rejoices in man's lovely,
peculiar power to choose life and die—
when he leads his black soldiers to death,
40 he cannot bend his back.

On a thousand small town New England greens,
the old white church holds their air
of sparse, sincere rebellion; frayed flags
quilt the graveyards of the Grand Army of the Republic

45 The stone statues of the abstract Union Soldier
grow slimmer and younger each year—
wasp-waisted, they doze over muskets
and muse through their sideburns . . .

Shaw's father wanted no monument
50 except the ditch,
where his son's body was thrown
and lost with his "niggers."

The ditch is nearer.
There are no statutes for the last war here;
on Boylston Street, a commerical photograph
55 shows Hiroshima boiling

over a Mosler Safe, the "Rock of Ages"
that survived the blast. Space is nearer.
When I crouch to my television set,
the drained faces of Negro school-children rise like balloons.

60 Colonel Shaw
is riding on his bubble,
he waits
for the blesséd break.

The Aquarium is gone. Everywhere,
65   giant finned cars nose forward like fish;
a savage servility
slides by on grease.

1964

Harvard

1

Beauty-sleep for the writer, and the beauty,
both fighting off muscular cramps, the same fatigue.
Lying in bed, letting the bright, white morning
rise to mid-heaven though a gag of snow,
5   through high school, through college, through the last vacation—
I've slept so late here, snow has stubbled my throat;
students in their hundreds rise from the beehive,
swarm-mates; they have clocks and instincts, make
classes. In the high sky, a parochial school,
10   the top floors looking like the Place des Vosges—[9]
a silk stocking, blown thin as smog, coils in a twig-fork,
dangling a wire coathanger, rapier-bright—
a long shot for a hard cold day . . . wind lifting
the stocking like the lecherous, lost leg.

2

15   Each hour the stocking thins, the hanger dulls;
cold makes the thin green copper cupola
greener over the defoliated playground;
clouds lie in cotton wads on the Dutch sky,
death to the superhuman, worse for the human.
20   My mind can't hold the focus for a minute.
A sentence? A paragraph? The best tale
stales to homework. Flash-visions; as if I saw
the dark of the moon on the white of my eye;
and now, her Absent-present . . . black fishnet legs,
25   curve of the hourglass standing by the shower,
shut, verbalizing lips, her finger pointing;
no clean slate! And who will sit out the sermon?
The clean blade is too sharp, the old poisons.

3

The gluttony of eating out alone
30   here in Cambridge, where anyone can be no one,
and the people we'd flee at dinner parties change
to the mysterious, the beautiful . . .
on display on my small table, overwhite,
overobserved, ignored . . . the moment tries
35   my soul grown seasick on cold solitude—
the swimmer has chickened short of Labrador;
yet everyone who is seated is a lay,
or Paul Claudel.[1] He's near me now, declaiming:
"*L'Académie Groton, eh, c'est une école admirable*,"[2]
40   soaring from hobbled English to a basic French,
a vocabulary poorer than Racine's,
no word unknown, no syntax understood.

4

Inching along the bayfront on the icepools,
sea and shipping cut out by the banks of cars,
45   and our relationship advancing or
declining to private jokes, and chaff and lust. . . .

9. A square in Paris, noted for its 16th- and
17th-century architecture.
1. French writer and diplomat (1868–1955).

2. "Groton Academy, well, it's an admirable
school."

Our leeway came so seldom, fell so short,
overwatched by some artist's skylight in the city,
or some suburban frame-house basement window,
50   angular, night-bluish, blear-eyed, spinsterish—
still this is something, something we can both
take hold of willingly, go smash on, if we will:
all flesh is grass, and like the flower in the field;
no! lips, breasts, eyes, hands, lips, hair;
55   as the overworked central heating bangs the frame,
as a milkhorse, time gone, would crash the morning milkcan.

1969

ROBERT DUNCAN
(1919–   )

My Mother Would Be a Falconress

My mother would be a falconress,
And I, her gay falcon treading her wrist,
would fly to bring back
from the blue of the sky to her, bleeding, a prize,
5   where I dream in my little hood with many bells
jangling when I'd turn my head.

My mother would be a falconress,
and she sends me as far as her will goes.
She lets me ride to the end of her curb
10   where I fall back in anguish.
I dread that she will cast me away,
for I fall, I mis-take, I fail in her mission.

She would bring down the little birds.
And I would bring down the little birds.
15   When will she let me bring down the little birds,
pierced from their flight with their necks broken,
their heads like flowers limp from the stem?

I tread my mother's wrist and would draw blood.
Behind the little hood my eyes are hooded.
20   I have gone back into my hooded silence,
talking to myself and dropping off to sleep.

For she has muffled my dreams in the hood she has made me,
sewn round with bells, jangling when I move.
She rides with her little falcon upon her wrist.
25   She uses a barb that brings me to cower.
She sends me abroad to try my wings
and I come back to her. I would bring down
the little birds to her
I may not tear into, I must bring back perfectly.

30   I tear at her wrist with my beak to draw blood,
and her eye holds me, anguisht, terrifying.
She draws a limit to my flight.
Never beyond my sight, she says.
She trains me to fetch and to limit myself in fetching.
35   She rewards me with meat for my dinner.
But I must never eat what she sends me to bring her.

Yet it would have been beautiful, if she would have carried me,
always, in a little hood with the bells ringing,
at her wrist, and her riding
40   to the great falcon hunt, and me
flying up to the curb of my heart from her heart
to bring down the skylark from the blue to her feet,
straining, and then released for the flight.

My mother would be a falconress,
45   and I her gerfalcon,° raised at her will,   *large falcon*
from her wrist sent flying, as if I were her own
pride, as if her pride
knew no limits, as if her mind
sought in me flight beyond the horizon.

50   Ah, but high, high in the air I flew.
And far, far beyond the curb of her will,
were the blue hills where the falcons nest.
And then I saw west to the dying sun—
it seemd my human soul went down in flames.

55   I tore at her wrist, at the hold she had for me,
until the blood ran hot and I heard her cry out,
far, far beyond the curb of her will

to horizons of stars beyond the ringing hills of the world where
        the falcons nest
I saw, and I tore at her wrist with my savage beak.
60   I flew, as if sight flew from the anguish in her eye beyond her sight,
sent from my striking loose, from the cruel strike at her wrist,
striking out from the blood to be free of her.

My mother would be a falconress,
and even now, years after this,
65   when the wounds I left her had surely heald,
and the woman is dead,
her fierce eyes closed, and if her heart
were broken, it is stilld

I would be a falcon and go free.
70   I tread her wrist and wear the hood,
talking to myself, and would draw blood.

1968

LAWRENCE FERLINGHETTI
(1919–   )

The Pennycandystore Beyond the El[1]

The pennycandystore beyond the El
is where I first
            fell in love
                        with unreality
5   Jellybeans glowed in the semi-gloom
of that september afternoon
A cat upon the counter moved among
                        the licorice sticks
            and tootsie rolls
10   and Oh Boy Gum

1. The Elevated Railway.

Outside the leaves were falling as they died

A wind had blown away the sun

A girl ran in
Her hair was rainy
15   Her breasts were breathless in the little room

Outside the leaves were falling
                and they cried
                        Too soon! too soon!

                                                    1958

Dog

The dog trots freely in the street
and sees reality
and the things he sees
are bigger than himself
5   and the things he sees
are his reality
Drunks in doorways
Moons on trees
The dog trots freely thru the street
10   and the things he sees
are smaller than himself
Fish on newsprint
Ants in holes
Chickens in Chinatown windows
15   their heads a block away
The dog trots freely in the street
and the things he smells
smell something like himself
The dog trots freely in the street
20   past puddles and babies
cats and cigars
poolrooms and policemen
He doesn't hate cops
He merely has no use for them
25   and he goes past them
and past the dead cows hung up whole
in front of the San Francisco Meat Market
He would rather eat a tender cow
than a tough policeman
30   though either might do
And he goes past the Romeo Ravioli Factory
and past Coit's Tower
and past Congressman Doyle
He's afraid of Coit's Tower
35   but he's not afraid of Congressman Doyle
although what he hears is very discouraging
very depressing
very absurd
to a sad young dog like himself
40   to a serious dog like himself
But he has his own free world to live in
His own fleas to eat
He will not be muzzled
Congressman Doyle is just another
45   fire hydrant
to him
The dog trots freely in the street

and has his own dog's life to live
and to think about
50 and to reflect upon
touching and tasting and testing everything
investigating everything
without benefit of perjury
a real realist
55 with a real tale to tell
and a real tail to tell it with
a real live
                    barking
                              democratic dog
60 engaged in real
                          free enterprise
with something to say
                          about ontology
something to say
65   about reality
                              and how to see it
                                      and how to hear it
with his head cocked sideways
                                  at streetcorners
70 as if he is just about to have
                              his picture taken
                                      for Victor Records
                          listening for
                                  His Master's Voice
75   and looking
                              like a living questionmark
                                          into the
                                      great gramaphone
                                      of puzzling existence
80   with its wondrous hollow horn
                          which always seems
                          just about to spout forth
                                          some Victorious answer
                                          to everything

                                                                  1958

HOWARD NEMEROV
(1920–   )

Angel and Stone

In the world are millions and millions of men, and each man,
With a few exceptions, believes himself to be at the center,
A small number of his more or less necessary planets careering
Around him in an orderly manner, some morning stars singing together,
5 More distant galaxies shining like dust in any stray sunbeam
Of his attention. Since this is true not of one man or of two,
But of ever so many, it is hard to imagine what life must be like.
But if you drop a stone into a pool, and observe the ripples
Moving in circles successively out to the edges of the pool and then
10 Reflecting back and passing through the ones which continue to come
Out of the center over the sunken stone, you observe it is pleasing.
And if you drop two stones it will still be pleasing, because now
The angular intersections of the two sets form a more complicated
Pattern, a kind of reticulation regular and of simple origins.
15 But if you throw a handful of sand into the water, it is confusion,
Not because the same laws have ceased to obtain, but only because

The limits of your vision in time and number forbid you to discriminate
Such fine, quick, myriad events as the angels and archangels, thrones
And dominations, principalities and powers, are delegated to witness
20 And declare the glory of before the Lord of everything that is.
Of these great beings and mirrors of being, little at present is known,
And of the manner of their perceiving not much more. We imagine them
As benign, as pensively smiling and somewhat coldly smiling, but
They may not be as we imagine them. Among them there are some who count
25 The grassblades and the grains of sand by one and one and one
And number the raindrops and memorize the eccentricities of snowflakes.
One of the greater ones reckons and records the tides of time,
Distinguishing the dynasties of mountains, races, cities,
As they rise, flower and fall, to whom an age is as a wave,
30 A nation the spray thrown from its crest; and one, being charged
With all the crossing moments, the comings-together and drivings-apart,
Reads in the chromatin[3] its cryptic scripture as the cell divides;
And one is the watcher over chance events and the guardian of disorder
According to the law of the square root of n, so that a certain number
35 Of angels or molecules shall fall in irrelevance and be retrograde.
So do they go, those shining creatures, counting without confusion
And holding in their slow immeasurable gaze all the transactions
Of all the particles, item by atom, while the pyramids stand still
In the desert and the deermouse huddles in his hole and the rain falls
40 Piercing the skin of the pool with water in water and making a million
And a million designs to be pleasingly latticed and laced and interfused
And mirrored to the Lord of everything that is by one and one and one.

1960

RICHARD WILBUR
(1921–   )

Objects

Meridians are a net
Which catches nothing; that sea-scampering bird
The gull, though shores lapse every side from sight, can yet
Sense him to land, but Hanno[1] had not heard

5   Hesperidean song,[2]
Had he not gone by watchful periploi:[3]
Chalk rocks, and isles like beasts, and mountain stains along
The water-hem, calmed him at last nearby

The clear high hidden chant
10 Blown from the spellbound coast, where under drifts
Of sunlight, under plated leaves, they guard the plant
By praising it. Among the wedding gifts

Of Herë, were a set
Of golden McIntoshes, from the Greek
15 Imagination. Guard and gild what's common, and forget
Uses and prices and names; have objects speak.

---

3. The part of a cell nucleus that stains intensely with basic dyes and is regarded as containing the physical basis of heredity.
1. Carthaginian navigator who led an expedition down the west coast of Africa in the fifth century B.C.

2. The Hesperides were sweet-voiced nymphs who guarded the golden apples ("McIntoshes") given by Ge to Hera for her marriage to Zeus (see lines 12–14).
3. Plural of *periplus,* a voyage or trip around an island or a coast.

There's classic and there's quaint,
And then there is that devout intransitive eye
Of Pieter de Hooch:[4] see feinting from his plot of paint
20   The trench of light on boards, the much-mended dry

Courtyard wall of brick,
And sun submerged in beer, and streaming in glasses,
The weave of a sleeve, the careful and undulant tile. A quick
Change of the eye and all this calmly passes

25   Into a day, into magic.
For is there any end to true textures, to true
Integuments; do they ever desist from tacit, tragic
Fading away? Oh maculate, cracked, askew,

Gay-pocked and potsherd world
30   I voyage, where in every tangible tree
I see afloat among the leaves, all calm and curled,
The Cheshire smile[5] which sets me fearfully free.

                                                    1947

Still, Citizen Sparrow

Still, citizen sparrow, this vulture which you call
Unnatural, let him but lumber again to air
Over the rotten office, let him bear
The carrion ballast up, and at the tall

5   Tip of the sky lie cruising. Then you'll see
That no more beautiful bird is in heaven's height,
No wider more placid wings, no watchfuller flight
He shoulders nature there, the frightfully free,

The naked-headed one. Pardon him, you
10   Who dart in the orchard aisles, for it is he
Devours death, mocks mutability,
Has heart to make an end, keeps nature new.

Thinking of Noah, childheart, try to forget
How for so many bedlam hours his saw
15   Soured the song of birds with its wheezy gnaw,
And the slam of his hammer all the day beset

The people's ears. Forget that he could bear
To see the towns like coral under the keel,
And the fields so dismal deep. Try rather to feel
20   How high and weary it was, on the waters where

He rocked his only world, and everyone's.
Forgive the hero, you who would have died
Gladly with all you knew; he rode that tide
To Ararat; all men are Noah's sons.

                                                    1950

4. Pieter de Hooch (1629–ca. 1677), Dutch   5. In *Alice in Wonderland,* when the Cheshire
genre painter.   cat disappeared, its smile lingered.

PHILIP LARKIN
(1922–   )

Lines on a Young Lady's Photograph Album

At last you yielded up the album, which,
Once open, sent me distracted. All your ages
Matt and glossy on the thick black pages!
Too much confectionary, too rich:
5 I choke on such nutritious images.

My swivel eye hungers from pose to pose—
In pigtails, clutching a reluctant cat;
Or furred yourself, a sweet girl-graduate;
Or lifting a heavy-headed rose
10 Beneath a trellis, or in a trilby hat

(Faintly disturbing, that, in several ways)—
From every side you strike at my control,
Not least through these disquieting chaps who loll
At ease about your earlier days:
15 Not quite your class, I'd say, dear, on the whole.

But o, photography! as no art is,
Faithful and disappointing! that records
Dull days as dull, and hold-it smiles as frauds,
And will not censor blemishes
20 Like washing-lines, and Hall's-Distemper boards,

But shows the cat as disinclined, and shades
A chin as doubled when it is, what grace
Your candor thus confers upon her face!
How overwhelmingly persuades
25 That this is a real girl in a real place,

In every sense empirically true!
Or is it just *the past?* Those flowers, that gate,
These misty parks and motors,° locerate   *automobiles*
Simply by being over; you
30 Contract my heart by looking out of date.

Yes, true; but in the end, surely, we cry
Not only at exclusion, but because
It leaves us free to cry. We know *what was*
Won't call on us to justify
35 Our grief, however hard we yowl across

The gap from eye to page. So I am left
To mourn (without a chance of consequence)
You, balanced on a bike against a fence;
To wonder if you'd spot the theft
40 Of this one of you bathing; to condense,

In short, a past that no one now can share,
No matter whose your future; calm and dry,
It holds you like a heaven, and you lie
Unvariably lovely there,
45 Smaller and clearer as the years go by.

1955

Church Going

Once I am sure there's nothing going on
I step inside, letting the door thud shut.
Another church: matting, seats, and stone,
And little books; sprawlings of flowers, cut
5   For Sunday, brownish now; some brass and stuff
Up at the holy end; the small neat organ;
And a tense, musty, unignorable silence,
Brewed God knows how long. Hatless, I take off
My cycle-clips in awkward reverance,

10   Move forward, run my hand around the font.
From where I stand, the roof looks almost new—
Cleaned, or restored? Somone would know: I don't.
Mounting the lectern, I peruse a few
Hectoring large-scale verses, and pronounce
15   "Here endeth" much more loudly than I'd meant.
The echoes snigger briefly. Back at the door
I sign the book, donate an Irish sixpence,
Reflect the place was not worth stopping for.

Yet stop I did: in fact I often do,
20   And always end much at a loss like this,
Wondering what to look for; wondering, too,
When churches fall completely out of use
What we shall turn them into, if we shall keep
25   A few cathedrals chronically on show,
Their parchment, plate and pyx[1] in locked cases,
And let the rest rent-free to rain and sheep.
Shall we avoid them as unlucky places?

Or, after dark, will dubious women come
30   To make their children touch a particular stone;
Pick simples° for a cancer; or on some   herbs
Advised night see walking a dead one?
Power of some sort or other will go on
In games, in riddles, seemingly at random;
35   But superstition, like belief, must die,
And what remains when disbelief has gone?
Grass, weedy pavement, brambles, buttress, sky,

A shape less recognizable each week,
A purpose more obscure. I wonder who
40   Will be the last, the very last, to seek
This place for what it was; one of the crew
That tap and jot and know what rood-lofts were?
Some ruin-bibber, randy for antique,
Or Christmas-addict, counting on a whiff
45   Of gown-and-bands and organ-pipes and myrrh?
Or will he be my representative,

Bored, uninformed, knowing the ghostly silt
Dispersed, yet tending to this cross of ground
Through suburb scrub because it held unspilt
50   So long and equably what since is found
Only in separation—marriage, and birth,
And death, and thoughts of these—for whom was built
This special shell? For, though I've no idea
What this accoutred frowsty barn is worth,
55   It pleases me to stand in silence here;

1. The vessel in which the Host is kept.

A serious house on serious earth it is,
In whose blent air all our compulsions meet,
Are recognized, and robed as destinies.
And that much never can be obsolete,
60 Since someone will forever be surprising
A hunger in himself to be more serious,
And gravitating with it to this ground,
Which, he once heard, was proper to grow wise in,
If only that so many dead lie round.

1955

JAMES DICKEY
(1923–   )

Between Two Prisoners

I would not wish to sit
In my shape bound together with wire,
Wedged into a child's sprained desk
In the schoolhouse under the palm tree.
5 Only those who did could have done it.

One bled from a cut on his temple,
And sat with his tousled head bowed,
His wound for him painfully thinking.
A belief in words grew upon them
10 That the unbound, who walk, cannot know.

The guard at the window leaned close
In a movement he took from the palm tree,
To hear, in a foreign tongue,
All things which cannot be said.
15 In the splintering clapboard room

They rested the sides of their faces
On the tops of the desks as they talked.
Because of the presence of children
In the deep signs carved in the desk tops,
20 Signs on the empty blackboard

Began, like a rain, to appear.
In the luminous chalks of all colors,
Green face, yellow breast, white sails
Whose wing feathers made the wall burn
25 Like a waterfall seen in a fever,

An angel came boldly to light
From his hands casting green, ragged bolts
Each having the shape of a palm leaf.
Also traced upon darkness in chalk
30 Was the guard at the rear window leaning

Through the red, vital strokes of his tears.
Behind him, men lying with swords
As with women, heard themselves sing,
And woke, then, terribly knowing
35 That they were a death squad, singing

In its sleep, in the middle of a war.
A wind sprang out of the tree.
The guard awoke by the window,
And found he had talked to himself
40 All night, in two voices, of Heaven.

He stood in the sunlit playground
Where the quiet boys knelt together
In their bloodletting trusses of wire,
And saw their mussed, severed heads
45 Make the ground jump up like a dog.

I watched the small guard be hanged
A year later, to the day,
In a closed horse stall in Manila.[1]
No one knows what language he spoke
50 As his face changed into all colors,

And gave off his red, promised tears,
Or if he learned blindly to read
A child's deep, hacked hieroglyphics
Which can call up an angel from nothing,
55 Or what was said for an instant, there,

In the tied, scribbled dark, between him
And a figure drawn hugely in chalk,
Speaking words that can never be spoken
Except in a foreign tongue,
60 In the end, at the end of a war.

1962

Buckdancer's Choice

So I would hear out those lungs,
The air split into nine levels,
Some gift of tongues of the whistler

In the invalid's bed: my mother,
5 Warbling all day to herself
The thousand variations of one song;

It is called Buckdancer's Choice.
For years, they have all been dying
Out, the classic buck-and-wing[2] men

10 Of traveling minstrel shows;
With them also an old woman
Was dying of breathless angina,[3]

Yet still found breath enough
To whistle up in my head
15 A sight like a one-man band,

Freed black, with cymbals at heel,
An ex-slave who thrivingly danced
To the ring of his own clashing light

Through the thousand variations of one song
20 All day to my mother's prone music,
The invalid's warbler's note,

1. The capture of Manila by the Japanese in early 1942 was a major setback for the United States in World War II. The Japanese occupation lasted until the Americans liberated the city in February 1945.
2. A dance associated with American minstrel shows, and similar to a clog dance. The dancer's feet (sometimes he beats his own rhythm on a tambourine) make movements like wings.
3. A respiratory disease usually related to heart ailments.

While I crept close to the wall
Sock-footed, to hear the sounds alter,
Her tongue like a mockingbird's break

25 Through stratum after stratum of a tone
Proclaiming what choices there are
For the last dancers of their kind,

For ill women and for all slaves
Of death, and children enchanted at walls
30 With a brass-beating glow underfoot,

Not dancing but nearly risen
Through barnlike, theaterlike houses
On the wings of the buck and wing.

1965

DENISE LEVERTOV
(1923–   )

Triple Feature

Innocent decision: to enjoy.
And the pathos
of hopefulness, of his solicitude:

—he in mended serape,
5 she having plaited carefully
magenta ribbons into her hair,
the baby a round half-hidden shape
slung in her rebozo,° and the young son steadfastly   *shawl*
gripping a fold of her skirt,
10 pale and severe under a
handed-down sombrero—

              all regarding
the stills with full attention, preparing
to pay and go in—
15 to worlds of shadow-violence, half-
familiar, warm with popcorn, icy
with strange motives, barbarous splendors!

1959

From the Roof

This wild night, gathering the washing as if it were flowers
          animal vines twisting over the line and
          slapping my face lightly, soundless merriment
          in the gesticulations of shirtsleeves,
5 I recall out of my joy a night of misery

walking in the dark and the wind over broken earth,
          halfmade foundations and unfinished
          drainage trenches and the spaced-out
                    circles of glaring light
10   marking streets that were to be,
walking with you but so far from you,

and now alone in October's
first decision towards winter, so close to you—
        my arms full of playful rebellious linen, a freighter
15   going down-river two blocks away, outward bound,
        the green wolf-eyes of the Harborside Terminal
            glittering on the Jersey shore,
and a train somewhere under ground bringing you towards me
to our new living-place from which we can see

20 a river and its traffic (the Hudson and the
hidden river, who can say which it is we see, we see
something of both. Or who can say
the crippled broom-vendor yesterday, who passed
just as we needed a new broom, was not
25 one of the Hidden Ones?)
        Crates of fruit are unloading
        across the street on the cobbles,
        and a brazier flaring
        to warm the men and burn trash. He wished us
30 luck when we bought the broom. But not luck
brought us here. By design

clear air and cold wind polish
the river lights, by design
we are to live now in a new place.

                              1961

The Victors

In June the bush we call
alder was heavy, listless,
its leaves studded with galls,

growing wherever we didn't
5 want it. We cut it
savagely, hunted it from the pasture, chopped it

away from the edge of the wood.
In July, still everywhere, it appeared
wearing green berries.

10 Anyway it must go. It takes
the light and air and the good of the earth
from flowers and young trees.

But now in August
its berries are red. Do the birds
15 eat them?   Swinging

clusters of red, the hedges are full of them,
red-currant red, a graceful
ornament or a merry smile.

                              1964

October

Certain branches cut
certain leaves fallen
the grapes
        cooked and put up
5 for winter

mountains without one
shrug of cloud
no feint of blurred
wind-willow leaf-light

10   their chins up
in blue of the eastern sky
their red cloaks
wrapped tight to the bone

1964

LOUIS SIMPSON
(1923–   )

The True Weather for Women

Young women in their April moodiness
Complain of showers, for they cannot go
Swimming, or to the courts to play tennis.
But if they suffer from a gentle blow,
5   What will the storm, the terror of saints, do?
If April presses their green tenderness
How will they stand the full weight of the snow?

Now they are killing time, with darts and chess,
And others dancing to the radio,
10   And some for kisses take a turn to guess
At names, and laugh at tales of love also.
Jenny, in her hot tub, repaints a toe,
Admiring her perfect nakedness
While thunders crack and summer lightnings glow.

15   There is one date that they will keep, although
They have been often late to come to men,
For death hits all such deer with his long bow
And drags them by the neck into his den,
And there eternally they may complain
20   And tap and gesture in a frantic show
And look at summer through a window-pane.

Wind up the pulse with poppy, sleep them so!
Their selfishness will always entertain,
And even death will seem small weather woe
25   When love is all their sun and all their rain.
The clock will never strike, adjusted then
To their sweet drowsings, and they will not know
How punctual death is, or else how slow.

1955

A Woman Too Well Remembered

Having put on new fashions, she demands
New friends. She trades her beauty and her humor
In anybody's eyes. If diamonds
Were dark, they'd sparkle so. Her aura is
5   The glance of scandal and the speed of rumor.

One day, as I recall, when we conversed
In kisses, it amused her to transmit
"What hath God wrought!"—the message that was first
Sent under the Atlantic.[1] Nonsense, yet
10   It pleases me sometimes to think of it.

Noli me tangere[2] was not her sign.
Her pilgrim trembled with the softest awe.
She was the only daughter of a line
That sleeps in poetry and silences.
15   She might have sat upon the Sphinx's paw.

Then is she simply false, and falsely fair?
(The promise she would break she never made)
I cannot say, but truly can compare,
For when the stars move like a steady fire
20   I think of her, and other faces fade.

1955

KENNETH KOCH
(1925–   )

Permanently

One day the Nouns were clustered in the street.
An Adjective walked by, with her dark beauty.
The Nouns were struck, moved, changed.
The next day a Verb drove up, and created the Sentence.

5   Each Sentence says one thing—for example, "Although it was a dark rainy day
     when the Adjective walked by, I shall remember the pure and sweet
     expression on her face until the day I perish from the green, effective
     earth."
Or, "Will you please close the window, Andrew?"
Or, for example, "Thank you, the pink pot of flowers on the window sill has
     changed color recently to a light yellow, due to the heat from the boiler
     factory which exists nearby."

In the springtime the Sentences and the Nouns lay silently on the grass.
A lonely Conjunction here and there would call, "And! But!"
10   But the Adjective did not emerge.

As the adjective is lost in the sentence,
So I am lost in your eyes, ears, nose, and throat—
You have enchanted me with a single kiss
Which can never be undone
15   Until the destruction of language.

1962

You Were Wearing

You were wearing your Edgar Allan Poe printed cotton blouse.
In each divided up square of the blouse was a picture of Edgar Allan Poe.
Your hair was blonde and you were cute. You asked me, "Do most boys think
     that most girls are bad?"

1. By Samuel F. B. Morse (1791–1872), in-
ventor of the telegraph and Morse code, whose
first message on the first telegraph between
Washington and Baltimore in 1844 was "What
hath God wrought!"
2. "Touch me not."

I smelled the mould of your seaside resort hotel bedroom on your hair held
in place by a John Greenleaf Whittier clip.
5 "No," I said, "it's girls who think that boys are bad." Then we read
Snowbound together
And ran around in an attic, so that a little of the blue enamel was scraped off
my George Washington, Father of His Country, shoes.

Mother was walking in the living room, her Strauss Waltzes comb in her hair.
We waited for a time and then joined her, only to be served tea in cups
painted with pictures of Herman Melville
As well as with illustrations from his book *Moby Dick* and from his novella,
Benito Cereno.
10 Father came in wearing his Dick Tracy necktie: "How about a drink,
everyone?"
I said, "Let's go outside a while." Then we went onto the porch and sat on
the Abraham Lincoln swing.
You sat on the eyes, mouth, and beard part, and I sat on the knees.
In the yard across the street we saw a snowman holding a garbage can lid
smashed into a likeness of the mad English king, George the Third.

1962

ALLEN GINSBERG
(1926–   )

To Aunt Rose

Aunt Rose—now—might I see you
with your thin face and buck tooth smile and pain
of rheumatism—and a long black heavy shoe
for your bony left leg
5 limping down the long hall in Newark on the running carpet
past the black grand piano
in the day room
where the parties were
and I sang Spanish loyalist songs
10 in a high squeaky voice
(hysterical) the committee listening
while you limped around the room
collected the money—
Aunt Honey, Uncle Sam, a stranger with a cloth arm
15 in his pocket
and huge young bald head
of Abraham Lincoln Brigade[1]

—your long sad face
your tears of sexual frustration
20 (what smothered sobs and bony hips
under the pillows of Osborne Terrace)
—the time I stood on the toilet seat naked
and you powdered my thighs with Calomine
against the poison ivy—my tender
25 and shamed first black curled hairs
what were you thinking in secret heart then
knowing me a man already—
and I an ignorant girl of family silence on the thin pedestal
of my legs in the bathroom—Museum of Newark.
30 Aunt Rose
Hitler is dead, Hitler is in Eternity; Hitler is with
Tamburlane and Emily Brontë

1. A group of American volunteers, led by Martin Wolff, in the Spanish Civil War of the 1930's.

Though I see you walking still, a ghost on Osborne Terrace
      down the long dark hall to the front door
35   limping a little with a pinched smile
          in what must have been a silken
            flower dress
  welcoming my father, the Poet, on his visit to Newark
      —see you arriving in the living room
40   dancing on your crippled leg
        and clapping hands his book
          had been accepted by Liveright

Hitler is dead and Liveright's gone out of business
The Attic of the Past and *Everlasting Minute* are out of print
45   Uncle Harry sold his last silk stocking
      Claire quit interpretive dancing school
        Buba[2] sits a wrinkled monument in Old
          Ladies Home blinking at new babies

last time I saw you was the hospital
50   pale skull protruding under ashen skin
          blue veined unconscious girl
            in an oxygen tent
     the war in Spain has ended long ago
        Aunt Rose

                          Paris 1958   1961

JAMES MERRILL
(1926–   )

Kite Poem

"One is reminded of a certain person,"
Continued the parson, setting back in his chair
With a glass of port, "who sought to emulate
The sport of birds (it was something of a chore)
5 By climbing up on a kite. They found his coat
Two counties away; the man himself was missing."

His daughters tittered: it was meant to be a lesson
To them—they had been caught kissing, or some such nonsense,
The night before, under the crescent moon.
10 So, finishing his pheasant, their father began
This thirty-minute discourse, ending with
A story improbable from the start. He paused for breath,

Having shown but a few of the dangers. However, the wind
Blew out the candles and the moon wrought changes
15 Which the daughters felt along their stockings. Then,
Thus persuaded, they fled to their young men
Waiting in the sweet night by the raspberry bed,
And kissed and kissed, as though to escape on a kite.

                                    1954

---

2. Yiddish for "Grandmother."

W. D. SNODGRASS
(1926–   )

Papageno[1]

FOR JANICE

Far in the woods my stealthy flute
Had jailed all gaudy feathered birds
And brought their songs back true to life;
Equipped with lime and quick salt, fruit
5   And fifty linking nets of works
I went to whistle up a wife.

My mouth was padlocked for a liar.
Losing what old hands never seek
To snare in their most cunning art,
10   I starved till my rib cage was wire
Under a towel. I could not speak
To hush this chattering, blue heart.

I beat about dead bushes where
No song starts and my cages stand
15   Bare in the crafty breath of you.
Night's lady, spreading your dark hair,
Come take this rare bird into hand;
In that deft cage, he might sing true.

1959

Heart's Needle: 5

Winter again and it is snowing;
Although you are still three,
You are already growing
Strange to me.

5   You chatter about new playmates, sing
Strange songs; you do not know
Hey ding-a-ding-a-ding
Or where I go

Or when I sang for bedtime, *Fox*
10   *Went out on a chilly night*,
Before I went for walks
And did not write;

You never mind the squalls and storms
That are renewed long since;
15   Outside, the thick snow swarms
Into my prints

And swirls out by warehouses, sealed,
Dark cowbarns, huddled, still,
Beyond to the blank field,
20   The fox's hill

---

1. The bird-catcher in Mozart's *Magic Flute;* he is usually dressed as a bird. His wife is Papagen.

Where he backtracks and sees the paw,
Gnawed off, he cannot feel;
Conceded to the jaw
Of toothed, blue steel.

                                                                    1959

W. S. MERWIN
(1927–   )

My Friends

My friends without shields walk on the target

It is late the windows are breaking

My friends without shoes leave
What they love
5   Grief moves among them as a fire among
Its bells
My friends without clocks turn
On the dial they turn
They part

10 My friends with names like gloves set out
Bare handed as they have lived
And nobody knows them
It is they that lay the wreaths at the milestones it is their
Cups that are found at the wells
15 And are then chained up

My friends without feet sit by the wall
Nodding to the lame orchestra
Brotherhood it says on the decorations
My friend without eyes sits in the rain smiling
20 With a nest of salt in his hand

My friends without fathers or houses hear
Doors opening in the darkness
Whose halls announce
Behold the smoke has come home

25 My friends and I have in common
The present a wax bell in a wax belfry
This message telling of
Metals this
Hunger for the sake of hunger this owl in the heart
30 And these hands one
For asking one for applause

My friends with nothing leave it behind
In a box
My friends without keys go out from the jails it is night
35 They take the same road they miss
Each other they invent the same banner in the dark
They ask their way only of sentries too proud to breathe

At dawn the stars on their flag will vanish

The water will turn up their footprints and the day will rise
40 Like a monument to my
Friends the forgotten

                                                                    1963

THOM GUNN
(1929–   )

On the Move

'Man, you gotta Go.'

The blue jay scuffling in the bushes follows
Some hidden purpose, and the gust of birds
That spurts across the field, the wheeling swallows,
Have nested in the trees and undergrowth.
5   Seeking their instinct, or their poise, or both,
One moves with an uncertain violence
Under the dust thrown by a baffled sense
Or the dull thunder of approximate words.

On motorcycles, up the road, they come:
10   Small, black, as flies hanging in heat, the Boys,
Until the distance throws them forth, their hum
Bulges to thunder held by calf and thigh.
In goggles, donned impersonality,
In gleaming jackets trophied with the dust,
15   They strap in doubt—by hiding it, robust—
And almost hear a meaning in their noise.

Exact conclusion of their hardiness
Has no shape yet, but from known whereabouts
They ride, direction where the tires press.
20   They scare a flight of birds across the field:
Much that is natural, to the will must yield.
Men manufacture both machine and soul,
And use what they imperfectly control
To dare a future from the taken routes.

25   It is a part solution, after all.
One is not necessarily discord
On earth; or damned because, half animal,
One lacks direct instinct, because one wakes
Afloat on movement that divides and breaks.
30   One joins the movement in a valueless world,
Choosing it, till, both hurler and the hurled,
One moves as well, always toward, toward.

A minute holds them, who have come to go:
The self-defined, astride the created will
35   They burst away; the towns they travel through
Are home for neither bird nor holiness,
For birds and saints complete their purposes.
At worse, one is in motion; and at best,
Reaching no absolute, in which to rest,
40   One is always nearer by not keeping still.

California   1957

ADRIENNE RICH
(1929–   )

Double Monologue

To live illusionless, in the abandoned mine-
   shaft of doubt, and still
mime illusions for others? A puzzle
   for the maker who has thought
5   once too often too coldly.

Since I was more than a child
   trying on a thousand faces
I have wanted one thing: to know
   simply as I know my name
10   at any given moment, where I stand.

How much expense of time and skill
   which might have set itself
to angelic fabrications! All merely
   to chart one needle in the haymow?
15   Find yourself and you find the world?

Solemn presumption! Mighty Object
   no one but itself has missed,
what's lost, if you stay lost? Someone
   ignorantly loves you—will that serve?
20   Shrug that off, and presto!—

the needle drowns in the haydust.
   Think of the whole haystack—
a composition so fortuitous
   it only looks monumental.
25   There's always a straw twitching somewhere.

Wait out the long chance, and
   your needle too could get nudged up
to the apex of that bristling calm.
   Rusted, possibly. You might not want
30   to swear it was the Object, after all.

Time wears us old utopians.
   I now no longer think
"truth" is the most beautiful of words.
   Today when I see "truthful"
35   written somewhere, it flares

like a white orchid in wet woods,
   rare and grief-delighting, up from the page.
Sometimes, unwittingly even,
   we have been truthful.
40   In a random universe, what more

exact and starry consolation?
   Don't think I think
facts serve better than ignorant love.
   Both serve, and still
45   our need mocks our gear.

1960   1962

Face to Face

Never to be lonely like that—
the Early American figure on the beach
in black coat and knee-breeches
scanning the didactic storm in privacy,

5   never to hear the prairie wolves
in their lunar hilarity
circling one's little all, one's claim
to be Law and Prophets

for all that lawlessness,
10   never to whet the appetite
weeks early, for a face, a hand
longed-for and dreaded—

How people used to meet!
starved, intense, the old
15   Christmas gifts saved up till spring,
and the old plain words,

and each with his God-given secret,
spelled out through months of snow and silence,
burning under the bleached scalp; behind dry lips
20   a loaded gun.

1965   1966

Ghazals[1]

7/16/68:ii

When they mow the fields, I see the world reformed
as if by snow, or fire, or physical desire.

First snow. Death of the city. Ghosts in the air.
Your shade among the shadows, interviewing the mist.

5   The mail came every day, but letters were missing;
by this I knew things were not what they ought to be.

The trees in the long park blurring back
into Olmstead's[2] original dream-work.

The impartial scholar writes me from under house arrest.
10   I hope you are rotting in hell, Montaigne[3] you bastard.

7/23/68

When your sperm enters me, it is altered;
when my thought absorbs yours, a world begins.

If the mind of the teacher is not in love with the mind of the student,
he is simply practising rape, and deserves at best our pity.

1. "This poem began to be written after I read Aijaz Ahmad's literal English versions of the work of the Urdu poet Mirza Ghalib, 1797–1869. While the structure and metrics used by Ghalib are much stricter than mine, I have adhered to his use of a minimum five couplets to a *ghazal*, each couplet being autonomous and independent of the others. The continuity and unity flow from the associations and images playing back and forth among the couplets in any single *ghazal*. I have left the ghazals dated as I wrote them" [Rich's note].
2. Frederick L. Olmsted (1822–1903) became superintendent of New York's Central Park in 1857 and turned it into America's first planned city park.
3. Michel E. de Montaigne (1533–95), French essayist and Renaissance gentleman of highly intellectual and skeptical, but humane, temper.

5 To live outside the law! Or, barely within it,
   a twig on boiling waters, enclosed inside a bubble.

   Our words are jammed in an electronic jungle;
   sometimes, though, they rise and wheel croaking above the treetops.

   An open window; thick summer night; electric fences trilling.
10 What are you doing here at the edge of the death-camps, Vivaldi?[4]

7/24/68:ii

   The friend I can trust is the one who will let me have my death.
   The rest are actors who want me to stay and further the plot.

   At the drive-in movie, above the PanaVision,
   beyond the projector beams, you project yourself, great Star.

5 The eye that used to watch us is dead, but open.
   Sometimes I still have a sense of being followed.

   How long will we be waiting for the police?
   How long must I wonder which of my friends would hide me?

   Driving at night I feel the Milky Way
10 streaming above me like the graph of a cry.

7/26/68:ii

   A dead mosquito, flattened against a door;
   his image could survive our comings and our goings.

   LeRoi! Eldridge![5] listen to us, we are ghosts
   condemned to haunt the cities where you want to be at home.

5 The white children turn black on the negative.
   The summer clouds blacken inside the camera-skull.

   Every mistake that can be made, we are prepared to make;
   anything less would fall short of the reality we're dreaming.

   Someone has always been desperate, now it's our turn—
10 we who were free to weep for Othello and laugh at Caliban.

   I have learned to smell a *conservateur* a mile away:
   they carry illustrated catalogues of all that there is to lose.

                                                                1969

TED HUGHES
(1930–   )

November

The month of the drowned dog. After long rain the land
Was sodden as the bed of an ancient lake,
Treed with iron and birdless. In the sunk lane
The ditch—a seep silent all summer—

---

4. Antonio Vivaldi (1678?–1741), Venetian composer in the baroque mode.

5. LeRoi Jones and Eldridge Cleaver, contemporary Afro-American writers and political radicals.

5   Made brown foam with a big voice: that, and my boots
    On the lane's scrubbed stones, in the gulleyed leaves,
    Against the hill's hanging silence;
    Mist silvering the droplets on the bare thorns

    Slower than the change of daylight.
10 In a let of the ditch a tramp was bundled asleep:
    Face tucked down into beard, drawn in
    Under its hair like a hedgehog's. I took him for dead,

    But his stillness separated from the death
    Of the rotting grass and the ground. A wind chilled,
15 And a fresh comfort tightened through him,
    Each hand stuffed deeper into the other sleeve.

    His ankles, bound with sacking and hairy band,
    Rubbed each other, resettling. The wind hardened;
    A puff shook a glittering from the thorns,
20 And again the rains' dragging gray columns

    Smudged the farms. In a moment
    The fields were jumping and smoking; the thorns
    Quivered, riddled with the glassy verticals.
    I stayed on under the welding cold

25 Watching the tramp's face glisten and the drops on his coat
    Flash and darken. I thought what strong trust
    Slept in him—as the trickling furrows slept,
    And the thorn-roots in their grip on darkness;

    And the buried stones, taking the weight of winter;
30 The hill where the hare crouched with clenched teeth.
    Rain plastered the land till it was shining
    Like hammered lead, and I ran, and in the rushing wood

    Shuttered by a black oak leaned.
    The keeper's gibbet* had owls and hawks   *gallows*
35 By the neck, weasels, a gang of cats, crows:
    Some, stiff, weightless, twirled like dry bark bits

    In the drilling rain. Some still had their shape,
    Had their pride with it; hung, chins on chests,
    Patient to outwait these worst days that beat
40 Their crowns bare and dripped from their feet.

                                                               1960

SYLVIA PLATH
(1932–1963)

Point Shirley

    From Water-Tower Hill to the brick prison
    The shingle booms, bickering under
    The sea's collapse.
    Snowcakes break and welter. This year
5   The gritted wave leaps
    The seawall and drops onto a bier
    Of quahog chips,
    Leaving a salty mash of ice to whiten

In my grandmother's sand yard. She is dead,
10 Whose laundry snapped and froze here, who
Kept house against
What the sluttish, rutted sea could do.
Squall waves once danced
Ship timbers in through the cellar window;
15 A thresh-tailed, lanced
Shark littered in the geranium bed—

Such collusion of mulish elements
She wore her broom straws to the nub.
Twenty years out
20 Of her hand, the house still hugs in each drab
Stucco socket
The purple egg-stones: from Great Head's knob
To the filled-in Gut
The sea in its cold gizzard ground those rounds.

25 Nobody wintering now behind
The planked-up windows where she set
Her wheat loaves
And apple cakes to cool. What is it
Survives, grieves
30 So, over this battered, obstinate spit
Of gravel? The waves'
Spewed relics clicker masses in the wind,

Gray waves the stub-necked eiders ride.
A labor of love, and that labor lost.
35 Steadily the sea
East at Point Shirley. She died blessed,
And I come by
Bones, bones only, pawed and tossed,
A dog-faced sea.
40 The sun sinks under Boston, bloody red.

I would get from these dry-papped stones
The milk your love instilled in them.
The black ducks dive.
And though your graciousness might stream,
45 And I contrive,
Grandmother, stones are nothing of home
To that spumiest dove.
Against both bar and tower the black sea runs.

1960

LeROI JONES
(1934–   )

In Memory of Radio

Who has ever stopped to think of the divinity of Lamont Cranston?[1]
(Only Jack Kerouac, that I know of: & me.
The rest of you probably had on WCBS and Kate Smith,
Or something equally unattractive.)

5   What can I say?
It is better to have loved and lost
Than to put linoleum in your living rooms?

---

1. The hero of the radio serial "The Shadow." The poem refers to prominent characters and personalities that Jones would have heard on radio as a boy. Jack Kerouac (1922–1969) was a novelist of the "Beat Generation."

Am I a sage or something?
Mandrake's hypnotic gesture of the week?
10 (Remember, I do not have the healing powers of Oral Roberts . . .
I cannot, like F. J. Sheen, tell you how to get saved *& rich!*
I cannot even order you to gaschamber satori like Hitler or Goody Knight

& Love is an evil word.
15 Turn it backwards/see, what I mean?
An evol word. & besides
Who understands it?
I certainly wouldn't like to go out on that kind of limb.

Saturday mornings we listened to *Red Lantern* & his undersea folk.
20 At 11, *Let's Pretend*/& we did/& I, the poet, still do, Thank God!

What was it he used to say (after the transformation, when he was safe
& invisible & the unbelievers couldn't throw stones?) "Heh, heh, heh,
Who knows what evil lurks in the hearts of men? The Shadow knows."

O, yes he does
25 O, yes he does.
An evil word it is,
This Love.

1961

The New Sheriff

There is something
in me so cruel, so
silent. It hesitates
to sit on the grass
5 with the young white
                    virgins
of my time. The blood-
letter, clothed in what
it is. Elemental essence,
10 animal grace, not that, but
a rude stink of color
huger, more vast, than
this city suffocating. Red
street. Waters noise
15 in the ear, inside
the hard bone
of the brain. Inside
the soft white meat
of the feelings. Inside
20 your flat white stomach
I move my tongue

1961

ISHMAEL REED
(1938–   )

I Am A Cowboy In The Boat Of Ra[1]

"The devil must be forced to reveal any such physical evil (potions, charms, fetishes,
etc.) still outside the body and these must be burned." —RITUALE ROMANUM, *pub-
lished 1947, endorsed by the coat of arms and introduction letter from Francis Cardinal
Spellman*

I am a cowboy in the boat of Ra,
sidewinders in the saloons of fools
bit my forehead   like   O
the untrustworthiness of Egyptologists
5   Who do not know their trips. Who was that
dog-faced man? they asked, the day I rode
from town.

School marms with halitosis cannot see
the Nefertiti fake chipped on the run by slick
10 germans, the hawk behind Sonny Rollins' head or
the ritual beard of his axe; a longhorn winding
its bells thru the Field of Reeds.

I am a cowboy in the boat of Ra. I bedded
down with Isis, Lady of the Boogaloo, dove
15 down deep in her horny, stuck up her Wells-Far-ago
in daring midday get away. "Start grabbing the
blue," i said from top of my double crown.

I am a cowboy in the boat of Ra. Ezzard Charles
of the Chisholm Trail. Took up the bass but they
20 blew off my thumb. Alchemist in ringmanship but a
sucker for the right cross.

I am a cowboy in the boat of Ra. Vamoosed from
the temple i bide my time. The price on the wanted
poster was a-going down, outlaw alias copped my stance
25 and moody greenhorns were making me dance; while my mouth's
shooting iron got its chambers jammed.

I am a cowboy in the boat of Ra. Boning-up in
the ol West i bide my time. You should see
me pick off these tin cans whippersnappers. I
30 write the motown long plays for the comeback of
Osiris. Make them up when stars stare at sleeping
steer out here near the campfire. Women arrive
on the backs of goats and throw themselves on
my Bowie.

35 I am a cowboy in the boat of Ra. Lord of the lash,
the Loup Garou Kid. Half breed son of Pisces and
Aquarius. I hold the souls of men in my pot. I do
the dirty boogie with scorpions. I make the bulls
keep still and was the first swinger to grape the taste.

1. Ra was the chief deity of ancient Egypt, the sun-god, the creator, protector of men and
vanquisher of evil.

40 I am a cowboy in his boat. Pope Joan of the
    Ptah Ra. C/mere a minute willya doll?
    Be a good girl and
    Bring me my Buffalo horn of black powder
    Bring me my headdress of black feathers
45 Bring me my bones of Ju-Ju snake
    Go get my eyelids of red paint.
    Hand me my shadow
    I'm going into town after Set[2]

    I am a cowboy in the boat of Ra
50 look out Set   here i come Set
    to get Set   to sunset Set
    to unseat Set   to Set down Set
                    usurper of the Royal couch
                    imposter RAdio of Moses' bush
55   party pooper O hater of dance
                    vampire outlaw of the milky way

                                        1969

---

2. Ancient Egyptian god, usually represented as a composite of various animals, and associated with the desert and oases, a counterpart to his brother Osiris, god of vegetation. Sometimes he is the personification of evil, sometimes the vigorous protector of the sun-god's boat.

Prosody

Commentary*

Prosody is the scientific study of those formal patterns of sound, like **meter** and **rhyme**, to which poems are systematically accommodated. The term refers, by extension, to irregular phonetic systems of rhythm devised by certain poets.

PROSODY BASED ON NATIVE CADENCES

The oldest recorded English poetry was void of rhyme, and of meter as we are familiar with it, and relied instead on a system of **alliteration** and accentual balance. A fragment of medieval verse, modernized in language but with the alliteration and phrasing intact, reads,

> And you *lovely ladies*, || with your *long fingers*,
> Who would have *silk* and *satin* || to *sew* on oc*ca*sion
> *Cha*subles for *chap*lains || to the *church's hon*or,
> *Wives* and *wi*dows too, || *wool* and *flax* spin.
>   (Italics added)

When stanzaic lyrics came into the literature, with end-rhyme partly displacing alliteration and partly existing alongside it, the cadences in them were often various and free. The exquisite first stanza of one medieval lyric (p. 22) would naturally be read,

> Ĭ síng ŏf ă máydĕn
>   Thăt ĭs mákĕlĕss;
> Kíng ŏf állĕ kíngĕs
>   Tŏ hér sŏn shĕ chés.

The stresses falling two by two and the answering alliteration of *mayden, makeless*; *King, kinges*; and (more remotely) *sing, son* suggest the old prosody, while the rhyme, the stanzaic arrangement, and the competing rhythm clearly apparent in the third line acknowledge new influences. (The present anthology, with its extensive representation of medieval poetry, will enable the reader who proceeds chronologically to acquaint himself early with the variety of which English prosody is capable.)

The freedom claimed in these early centuries was sought again, sometimes in a doctrinaire spirit, by romantic poets, rebelling against a regularity of which their medieval predecessors had been simply unaware. A fertile inventor of his own rhythms was the mid-nineteenth-century American Walt Whitman, who composed lines such as

> Oút of the crádle éndlessly rócking,
> Oút of the mócking-bird's thróat, the músical shúttle,
> Oút of the Nínth-month mídnight,
> Óver the stérile sánds and the fíelds beyónd where the chíld
>   léaving his béd wánder'd alóne, báreheaded, bárefoot,
> (*Out of the Cradle Endlessly Rocking*, lines 1–4, p. 376).

Such freedom is congenial to English poetry because our language falls naturally into phrases, like "Out of the cradle || endlessly rocking," which can be either balanced against each other or strung together in loosely rhythmic sequences. Modern poets who have adopted free rhythms have

---

* **Boldface** type denotes a glossary entry.

occasionally (like Gerard Manley Hopkins) remembered Old English poetry and often (like Theodore Roethke) fallen into cadences recalling Whitman's.

SYLLABIC METER

The principal conventions of English prosody nevertheless remain the traditional meters, of which students are very often apprised in high school or before. These meters, deriving from cultural borrowings, are not altogether natural to English and must be mastered anew, with some degree of difficulty, by each generation of readers. One sign that they are hard to accommodate in English is the long period of uncertainty in the early and middle sixteenth century when poets like Thomas Wyatt hesitated between a new regularity and the freer accentuation of the medieval past. The hesitation is apparent, for example, in Wyatt's *They Flee from Me* (p. 54).

The basis for conventional English metrics, ever since late-medieval and Renaissance poets began to imitate French and Italian models, has been the line of a fixed number of syllables. But such lines do not of themselves approach self-sufficiency in English, as they do in the poetry of the Romance languages. The English ear cannot count syllables unless they are differentiated according to some regular system. The preceding sentence, which happens to contain thirty syllables, is divisible into three parts:

> The English ear cannot count syllables
> Unless they are differentiated
> According to some regular system.

But only by adding up on his fingers can the reader tell that ten syllables have elapsed in each of these lines.

In practice, the syllabic lines of English poetry are divided into units called **feet**. These are groups of two or three syllables of which one is accented and the remainder unaccented. Four different feet, two of them disyllabic and two trisyllabic, are the constituent units of significant numbers of English poems.

SYLLABIC FEET

The first and most common of these is the iambic foot or iamb, which consists of an unaccented syllable followed by an accented. Four successive iambs yield Thomas Wyatt's line,

> Fŏrgét | nŏt yét | thĕ tríed | ĭntént.
> (*Forget Not Yet*, line 1, p. 55)

The other disyllabic foot, the trochaic foot or trochee, consists of an accented syllable followed by an unaccented. It is the unit of Robert Burns's line

> Hád wĕ | névĕr | lóved săe | kíndlў, . . .

Sequences, whether of iambic feet or trochaic, are heard as a continuous alternation of accented syllables and unaccented. And one soon loses his sense of whether iambs or trochees are the constituent units, just as he loses his sense of whether a regularly ticking clock is saying *tic-toc* or *toc-tic*. Iambic and trochaic lines are not, in fact, necessarily distinguishable from each other except in the first foot and the last. In Ben Jonson's lines

> Quéen ănd húntrĕss, cháste ănd fáir,
> Nŏw thĕ sún ĭs láid tŏ sléep,

the meter may be defined either as iambic with an initial unaccented sylla ble suppressed or as trochaic with a final unaccented syllable suppressed.

The concepts of the iamb and the trochee are nevertheless useful for description and analysis. One can reasonably argue, for example, that the first of Ben Jonson's lines above is predominantly trochaic because the trochaic word *huntress* acts decisively on the phrasing, whereas the second line is heard rather as iambic because the successive grammatical units "the sún | is laíd | to sleép" form iambs.

The more common of the two trisyllabic feet is the anapest, in which two unaccented syllables are followed by an accented, as in Byron's line

With the déw | on his brów | and the rúst | on his mail.
(*The Destruction of Sennacherib*, line 18, p. 281)

The **dactyl**, finally, is an accented syllable followed by two unaccented. A dactylic meter of six feet—a literary reminiscence of the meter of Homer and Virgil—is found in Longfellow's *Evangeline*, one line of which reads

Black were her | eyes as the | berry that | grows on the | thorn by the | wayside.

Anapests and dactyls, like iambs and trochees, become indistinguishable in a sustained sequence, though sequences of the trisyllabic feet are indicated, very naturally, by accents falling on every third syllable rather than on every second. Such sequences can absorb some disyllabic feet without losing their essential character. In the following lines from Swinburne, a dactylic norm is subsumed into a generally anapestic-dactylic progression, which absorbs occasional iambs as it goes:

Sweet is the treading of wine, and sweet the feet of the dove;
But a goodlier gift is thine than foam of the grapes or love.

Even in poetry which is within the pale of traditional prosody, the differentiation of meters is seen to be partly an abstract exercise. The English language resists accommodation to feet of a fixed number of syllables.

The meters of the anapestic-dactylic family can lilt very pleasantly, as familiar poems like *Lochinvar* and *Paul Revere's Ride* attest. Their rollicking quality tends to disqualify them as a serious medium, however. Those English poems to which we unequivocally ascribe high seriousness are almost all in iambic meter.

VARIATIONS WITHIN A FOOT

Although an iamb is accurately definable as an unaccented syllable followed by an accented, the phenomenon of accentuation is less simple than that easy definition implies. A single long word, like *disestablishmentarian*, can contain wholly unaccented syllables and syllables with any one of three different degrees of positive stress. Accents supplying semantic emphasis ("But Jack is *tall*er than Jill") introduce a further diversity. A succession of iambic feet, therefore, is seldom in practice a series of closely similar entities. We demand of it only that the even syllables show some increment of accentuation, great or small, over the syllables adjoining them.

Something of the diversity of the iamb is apparent even in so regular a poem as Gray's *Elegy Written in a Country Churchyard:*

The curfew tolls the knell of parting day,
The lowing herd wind slowly o'er the lea,
(lines 1–2, p. 208).

In the first line the increment of accent distinguishing the even syllables is both considerable and constant. In the second line, however, the word *wind* resists being sunk into an unaccented position, and *o'er,* though in strong position, is rather weakly stressed. The meter of the last three feet, "wind slow | ly o'er | the lea," is hence less than decisive. Such lines, detracting from regularity but enhancing variety, are made possible by the several degrees of accentuation in the English language.

When one accents a syllable, moreover, he not only utters it somewhat loudly; he raises it in pitch and tends to lengthen it. Any one of these characteristics, or any combination of them, can be used to signal a metrical accent. By a flexible use of all these resources together, a poet can preserve all but the most mechanical metrical exercises from an undue sameness.

He can, in particular, make two or more sound patterns concurrently audible. He need not choose between free, organic rhythms and a conventional meter; he can have both at once.

In the concluding line of a familiar Shakespeare sonnet, for example, there is a decently regular iambic beat:

> To love that well which thou must leave ere long.
> (73 ["That time of year thou mayst in me behold"], p. 80)

Yet the sense of the line, as patterns of alliteration and syntax direct us to it, seems concentrated in three consecutive monosyllables near the beginning of the line and three at the end: *love that well . . . leave ere long.* The reader can here perhaps raise the triad *love that well* in pitch while letting the stress fulfill the metrical demand: "to love that well." What one does with the triad *leave ere long* is complicated by its position at the end of the sentence, but he should still acknowledge it as part of a balanced scheme as well as of a sequence of iambs. Perhaps he can lengthen all three words significantly: leave ere long. But it is impossible to attain a satisfactory reading by recipe. Ideally, one builds the metrical principle into his consciousness, rather as the accomplished pianist builds in the principle of the metronome, and diversifies it by ear as he goes along.

SUBSTITUTIONS FOR FEET IN A LINE

Thus far it has been tacitly assumed that every line embodies, however variously, the precise accentual pattern which the meter requires. But there are also some transfers of accent within iambic lines which have become nearly as conventional as the iambic meter itself. Chief among these is the initial trochee in place of an iamb, as in Shakespeare's line

> Age cannot wither her, nor custom stale. . . .

It is permissible as well to resume on a trochee, in lieu of an iamb, after a caesura in the line. Ben Jonson included this line in a sequence of iambics:

> All that I am in arts, || all that I know.

Another common variation involves the transfer to the third syllable of the accent belonging to the second syllable, as in Dryden's line,

> And the long glories of majestic Rome.

This pattern was often used by Dryden, Pope, and their contemporaries to lend finality to the last line of a verse paragraph.

The substitutions described will sometimes be admitted elsewhere than in the initial feet. Poets both old and new have claimed the license of departing from metrical norms here and there whenever they could gain an

intelligible end thereby. Shakespeare, wanting to break into sudden expostu-
lation, began a sonnet with the highly irregular line,

Lét me nót tŏ thē marriăge ŏf trúe minds
(116, p. 81).

Milton, who would introduce a wailful repetition into the first line of an
elegy, began his *Lycidas*,

Yĕt once móre, Ŏ yĕ laurĕls, ănd once móre
(p. 130).

And Gerard Manley Hopkins, who would affirm by various metrical expedi-
ents the immanence of God in Nature, ventured a sonnet chiefly iambic but
incorporating also features of alliterative verse:

The world is chárged with the grandeur of Gód.
It will flame oút, like shining from shóok foíl;
(*God's Grandeur*, lines 1–2, p. 426).

METER AS A GUIDE TO INTERPRETATION

One can discover, or perhaps invent, relationships between the readings
given and a regular meter. In the Milton line, the iambic norm suggests that
we modify the reading "*once more . . . and once more*" in the direction
of "*once* more . . . and once *more*," enhancing its interest and possibly
its lamentable quality. In Hopkins's second line, an iambic undertone pro-
poses that the in-dwelling grandeur will not only "*flame out*," but that it
"*will flame out*," *is intent* on flaming out.

Where no such particular effects are assignable, the pull exerted on the
language by the metrical standard still keeps it tense and renders it fitter
for exalted and impassioned utterance. To dispense with any such norm is,
as Robert Frost once wrote, like playing tennis without a net. It is congenial
to the temper of a libertarian age to dwell on the freedoms which even the
strictest of meters admit. The cardinal fact about meters is that they remain,
in their way, binding.

QUANTITATIVE METER

Before leaving the topic of meters, we should perhaps take note of a
confusion in the terminology, and occasionally the understanding, of English
metrics, due to a too-literal application of the principles of Latin and Greek
prosody. For over three centuries poets and critics received long instruction
in the classical literatures before they approached English poetry in any
formal way. Inevitably, they introduced into English poetry and criticism
some largely alien concepts, chief among them being that of quantity.

To grasp this idea, one must envisage a language in which simple dura-
tion of utterance distinguishes some vowel sounds from others. There are
vestiges of this distinction in English: in most dialects, *bomb* is so set apart
from *balm*, for example, and *have* from the verb *halve*. When the verse
conventions of classical poetry were settled upon, the difference between
long quantity (*balm* and *halve*) and short quantity (*bomb* and *have*)
entered as largely into determinations of meaning as the distinction between
accent and want of accent does in English today, and it served quite as
dependably as a basis for meters. Greek and Latin poets founded upon it
feet like the one interestingly called the *dactyl* (from the Greek word for
finger), which was made up of a long syllable followed by two short and
was represented by the symbol — ◡ ◡. A **spondee**, made up of two long syl-
lables marked — —, was equivalent to a dactyl in quantity and could

substitute for it. For metrical purposes, all syllables terminating in consonant clusters (*hulks* as opposed to *hut*), as well as all syllables containing long vowels, counted as long.

The dactyl, we note, has given its name to a trisyllabic· English foot. The names of the other meters hitherto defined are also genetically Greek. The breve (˘), the classical symbol for short quantity, has been borrowed to designate the unaccented position in English poetry, and some texts still use the macron (−), the symbol for long quantity, to designate the accented position. The general fact is that we have borrowed classical terms and symbols quite freely, merely substituting (where necessary) accentuation for long quantity and want of it for short quantity.

In poetic practice, quantitative measures are neither well-suited to the English language nor entirely ill-suited. There are indeed, in English, syllables of longer duration and of shorter. Yet we are conscious of no sharp, clear distinction between these, because our ears are not attuned to quantity as a regular determinant of meaning. One unequivocally successful classical imitation is Thomas Campion's *Rose-cheeked Laura* (p. 91). A predominance of long vowels in accented syllables—a carry-over of quantitative principles into English poetry—enhances the musical quality of lines like Thomas Carew's

> Ask me no more where Jove bestows,
> When June is past, the fading rose;
> (*A Song*, lines 1–2, p. 127).

This anthology further contains English imitations of **Sapphic** and **Alcaic** strophes (identified in the Glossary) which, though considerably strained, are more than mere *tours de force*.

⇥⇥⇥⇤⇤⇤

The conventions other than meter are by no means unimportant. The ear and the voice need tutelage in the convention of rhyme, especially, so that it may contribute to order rather than to mere sameness. Diversity of inflection will preserve rhyme-words from the uniform and deadly dying fall which they receive in a naive reading. It is principally meter, however, which requires special discussion. Reflecting on the alien character of the syllabic line and the difficulty which children of nature have in hearing iambs, one is grateful that no one told William Shakespeare he was laboring under a crippling disadvantage. One perceives by the same tokens, happily, that students who still have trouble reading English poems in the traditional meters are not somehow depraved, but only require additional informed practice.

ALEXANDER W. ALLISON

Glossary*

ACCENT: Metrical accent is the regularly recurring stress or beat of measured poetry, the emphasis which falls on one syllable of a **foot** and defines the **meter** by its placement within the foot.

ALCAIC STROPHE: A stanza named for the Greek poet Alcaeus. A scheme for it, which ignores permissible **quantitative** variants but includes the conventionally overlaid pattern of stresses, is

$$- \mid \acute{-} \cup \mid \acute{-} - \parallel \acute{-} \cup \cup \mid \acute{-} \cup \mid \acute{-}$$
$$- \mid \acute{-} \cup \mid \acute{-} - \parallel \acute{-} \cup \cup \mid \acute{-} \cup \mid \acute{-}$$
$$- \mid \acute{-} \cup \mid \acute{-} - \mid \acute{-} \cup \mid \acute{-} \cup$$
$$\acute{-} \cup \cup \mid \acute{-} \cup \cup \mid \acute{-} \cup \mid \acute{-} \cup$$

Tennyson imitated this strophe in his ode *Milton* (p. 352). Robert Frost was influenced by the meter of the first two lines in his *The Strong Are Saying Nothing*. See Commentary, "Quantitative Meter."

ALEXANDRINE: A twelve-syllable line; in English always a line of six iambic feet. It forms the last line of the **Spenserian stanza** and is an occasional variant for the second line of the **Heroic couplet.**

ALLITERATION: The close repetition of initial sounds: *from stem to stern.* Loosely, any close phonetic recurrence: *immemorial elms.*

ALLITERATIVE VERSE: A verse form distinguished by regular recurrence of the initial sounds of stressed syllables within the line. The alliteration lights, typically, on two principal words in the first half-line and one in the second half-line. For illustration, see Commentary, "Prosody Based on Native Cadences."

ANACRUSIS: The prefixing of an unstressed syllable or syllables to a line of which they form no metrical part:

> Sport that wrinkled Care derides,
> And Laughter holding both his sides.

ANAPEST: A metrical foot made up of two unaccented syllables followed by an accented. See Commentary, "Syllabic Feet."

ANTISTROPHE: The second of two corresponding metrical divisions; in Greek choral recitation, the response to the strophe. See **ode.**

ASSONANCE: Similarity of sounds; particularly, as distinguished from **rhyme,** the similarity of like vowels followed by unlike consonants: *cat, map; holy, story.*

BALLAD STANZA: A four-line stanza of which the first and third lines are iambic tetrameter and the second and fourth lines are iambic trimeter, the second and fourth lines rhyming. The meter of the ballad stanza, called also common meter, is often varied in practice, as witness medieval folk ballads (pp. 32–53), and literary ballads like Coleridge's *Rime of the Ancient Mariner.*

BALLADE: A poem commonly of three eight-line stanzas with all stanzas following the rhyme-scheme *ababbcbc,* concluded by a four-line **envoy** rhyming *bcbc.* Chaucer wrote ballades, as did some late-nineteenth-century poets.

BLANK VERSE: Unrhymed iambic pentameter. The meter of Shakespeare's plays, Milton's *Paradise Lost* and Wordsworth's *Prelude.*

---

* Cross-references are in **boldface** type.

BURDEN: The refrain of a song, as (typically) of a **carol**. The burden of a familiar Christmas carol is

> Hark! the herald angels sing
> Glory to the newborn King!

In musical performance a burden is usually sung through once before the first stanza. In this text, therefore, as in most others, it is printed in that position.

CADENCE: A rhythm or unit of rhythmic progression; distinguished from Meter as not necessarily regular. Walt Whitman wrote in cadences rather than in meters.

CAESURA: Normally, in English poetry, a break occurring in the middle of a line of five or more feet. Represented by the symbol ||:

> To err is human, || to forgive, divine.

Sometimes used for any break within the line. In classical prosody, caesuras occurred whenever a word ended within a foot.

CAROL: A song or hymn of joy; now usually a Christmas song with a burden. Example: *The Corpus Christi Carol* (p. 28).

CATALEXIS: The dropping of one or two unaccented syllables from the end of a line—necessarily, in practice, a trochaic line or a dactylic. The first of the following lines represents a normal trochaic tetrameter; the second is the same meter with catalexis:

> Dúst thŏu | árt tŏ | dúst rĕ | túrnĕst
> Wás nŏt | spókĕn | óf thĕ | sóul.

Normal lines, like the first line above, are sometimes distinguished as *acatalectic* (*not* catalectic).

CLOSED COUPLET: A **couplet** self-contained in syntax and sense.

COMMON METER: The meter of the **ballad stanza.**

COUPLET: Two successive lines of the same meter and length, usually rhyming with each other. Couplets sometimes constitute two-line stanzas.

DACTYL: A metrical foot made up of an accented syllable followed by two unaccented. See Commentary, "Syllabic Feet."

DIMETER: A verse line of two feet.

DISTICH: A **couplet.**

DOUBLE RHYME: **Feminine rhyme.** See **rhyme.**

ELISION: The omission of a syllable or the running together of two syllables to form one: ne'er, th'eternal, as happy as I.

END-RHYME: Rhyme occurring at the ends of poetic lines.

END-STOP: The conclusion of a line, a couplet, or (occasionally) a longer metrical unit, with a period or other clear pause.

ENJAMBMENT: The running of one line into another. Lines not enjambed are **end-stopped.**

ENVOY (*Envoi*): A stanza, usually of four or five lines, concluding a **ballade**, a **sestina,** or some other such form; normally interlaced with the foregoing stanzas by its rhyme-scheme.

EPODE: The third division of the Pindaric ode, contrasting metrically with the strophe and antistrophe. See **ode.**

EYE-RHYME: Words or terminal syllables spelled alike but pronounced differently: *some, home.*

FEMININE ENDING: A final unstressed syllable appended to an iambic or anapestic line:

> To be | or nót | to bé, | thát ĭs | the quéstiŏn.

FEMININE RHYME: A double or disyllabic rhyme: *nation, station.* See **rhyme.**

FOOT: A group of two or three syllables constituting the unit of a metrical line. Normally, in English, an **iamb, trochee, anapest** or **dactyl.**

FOURTEENER: A line of fourteen syllables and seven iambic feet. A pair of fourteeners is often resolvable into **common meter.**

FREE VERSE: Verse without a regular metrical pattern.

HEROIC COUPLET: An iambic pentameter couplet, usually end-stopped and often containing interior patterns of balance. Called Heroic because, for a century after the Restoration (1660), it was the accustomed form for English translations of classical epics (called heroic poems) and for native mock-heroic verse.

HEXAMETER: A verse line of six feet.

IAMB: A metrical foot made up of an unaccented syllable followed by an accented. See Commentary.

ICTUS: The metrical **accent,** or some other rhythmic beat.

INTERNAL RHYME: Rhyme occurring within the line of verse:

> And all is *seared* with trade; *bleared, smeared* with toil.
> (Gerard Manley Hopkins, *God's Grandeur,* line 6, p. 426)

ITALIAN SONNET: See **sonnet.**

LEONINE RHYME: A scheme in which the word preceding the caesura rhymes with the last word of the line:

> I bring fresh *showers* || for the thirsting *flowers,*
> (Percy Bysshe Shelley, *The Cloud* [p. 290], line 1. Italics added).

MADRIGAL: A brief lyric, averaging eight or ten lines, suitable for part singing. Popular in Elizabethan England. Example: Fletcher's *Take, O, Take Those Lips Away.*

MEASURE: Meter.

METER: The pattern of arrangement in poetic lines having a regularly measurable phonetic structure. The traditional meters are identified by (1) the names of the constituent feet, as **iambic, trochaic, anapestic, dactylic;** and (2) the number of feet per line, as **trimeter, tetrameter, pentameter.** Examples: iambic pentameter, trochaic tetrameter.

MONOMETER: A verse line of one foot.

OCTAVE: An eight line stanza (as of the **ballade**) or self-sufficient part of a stanza (like the first division of the Italian **sonnet**).

OCTOSYLLABIC: Containing eight syllables; a variant designation for iambic tetrameter. Octosyllabic couplets are very frequent: Marlowe's *The Passionate Shepherd to His Love* (p. 79), Marvell's *To His Coy Mistress* (p. 152); Swift's verse narratives.

ODE: An exalted lyric which enlarges upon a serious theme. The regular or Pindaric ode, a legacy of Greek choral song, is divided into sections, each with a **strophe,** a metrically identical **antistrophe,** and a contrasting epode. (These three parts may, in English odes, be called the turn, the counterturn, and the stand.) The irregular ode (like Wordsworth's *Intimations of Immortality* [p. 250]) reproduces the internal elaborateness of the Pindaric strophe but dispenses with regular strophic recurrence. The Horatian ode (of which Keats's *Ode to a Nightingale* [p. 317] is a somewhat distant derivative) employs a uniform stanza throughout.

OTTAVA RIMA: A stanza of eight iambic pentameter lines rhyming *abababcc.* The medium of Italian heroic romance, it is used lyrically by William Butler Yeats in *Among School Children* (p. 445).

PENTAMETER: A verse line of five feet.

PROSODY: The scientific study of those formal patterns of sound, like meter

and rhyme, to which poems are systematically accommodated; compre-
hending by extension such irregular phonetic systems as the cadences of
Walt Whitman and the **"sprung rhythm"** of Gerard Manley Hopkins.

PYRRHIC FOOT: A foot of two unaccented syllables; bearing the name of a
quantitative foot of two short syllables. Example: the third foot of

The slĭngs | ănd ắr | rŏws ŏf | oŭtrá | geŏus fórtune.

QUANTITATIVE METER: A metrical system based on a division of syllables
into those of long duration and those of short. See Commentary, section
entitled "Quantitative Meter."

QUATRAIN: A four-line stanza or division of a stanza. Still used also in its
original sense, a four-line poem.

REFRAIN: A line or phrase of regular recurrence, appended typically to the
several stanzas of a stanzaic poem. Refrains may be the same throughout,
or similar but with progressive variations. They may also repeat the last
line or phrase of each successive stanza. A vestige of choral response,
they attach most naturally to songs. Compare **burden.**

RHYME: A concurrence of terminal sounds, usually those at the ends of lines
(End-rhyme). Masculine rhymes, which are the rule, coincide in the
vowel, and in the final consonant(s) if any, of stressed terminal syllables:
strife, life; com*pel, bell* (see **feminine rhyme**). Triple rhymes add yet
another unstressed syllable: *glorious,* vic*torious.* Imperfect rhymes (vari-
ously called slant rhymes, off-rhymes, or half-rhymes) usually entail, in
the rhyming syllables, either identical vowels or identical terminal con-
sonants, but not both: *hats, pets; ice, prize; fear, four.*

RHYTHM: A regular or at least clearly progressive sequence of sound pat-
terns, as distinguished by recurrence of beat or stress; normally, in poetry,
the verbal embodiment of an abstract metrical norm. It is a comprehensive
term: there are both prose rhythms (or **cadences**) and poetic rhythms
(or **meters**).

RHYME ROYAL: A seven-line iambic pentameter stanza rhyming *ababbcc.*
Wyatt's *They Flee From Me* is a (metrically loose) example.

RONDEL: A fourteen-line poem rhyming *abbaabababbaab.* The medial lines
(seven and eight) and the final lines (thirteen and fourteen) repeat lines
one and two. Charles d' Orléans employed the form.

RUN-ON: Enjambed; see **enjambment.**

SAPPHIC STROPHE: A stanza named for the Greek poetess Sappho. A scheme
for it, which ignores permissible **quantitative** variants but includes the
conventionally overlaid pattern of stresses, is

$$\bar{\cup} \;|\; \acute{-} - \;|\; \acute{-} \;\|\; \cup \cup \;|\; \acute{-} \cup \;|\; \acute{-} \cup$$
$$\bar{\cup} \;|\; \acute{-} - \;|\; \acute{-} \;\|\; \cup \cup \;|\; \acute{-} \cup \;|\; \acute{-} \cup$$
$$\bar{\cup} \;|\; \acute{-} - \;|\; \acute{-} \;\|\; \cup \cup \;|\; \acute{-} \cup \;|\; \acute{-} \cup$$
$$\acute{-} \cup \cup \;|\; \acute{-} \cup$$

Isaac Watts imitated this strophe in *The Day of Judgment* (p. 180),
and Algernon Swinburne in *Sapphics.*

SCANSION: The analysis of poetic lines to determine the meter, the variations
upon it, and the deviations from it. (See Commentary, "Variations Within
a Foot" and "Substitutions for Feet in a Line.")

SEPTET: A seven-line stanza, like that of **rhyme royal.**

SESTET: The last six lines of an Italian sonnet (see **sonnet**); occasionally
some other six-line division of a poem.

SESTINA: A poem of six six-line stanzas with a three-line **envoy.** The lines of
the several stanzas employ, in a regular permutation, the same six terminal

words: each stanza after the first picks up successively the terminal words of lines 6, 1, 5, 2, 4, and 3 of the stanza before it. The envoy incorporates all six terminal words. Sir Philip Sidney's *Ye Goatherd Gods* is a double sestina (see poem and title note, p. 73).

SKELTONICS: Loosely rhythmic lines of two or three accents each, rhyming on the same word for as many as six lines together. Exemplified by their inventor, John Skelton (pp. 30–31).

SONNET: A fourteen-line lyric poem, almost always iambic pentameter, the form of which was first borrowed from Italy and which is still, in the variant clearly acknowledging that origin, called the Italian or Petrarchan sonnet. Italian sonnets are divided into an **octave** rhyming *abbaabba,* and a **sestet** rhyming *cdecde, cdcdcd,* or more or less as the poet pleases. Donne, Milton, and Wordsworth wrote Italian sonnets. The English or Shakespearean sonnet is divided into three **quatrains** and a **couplet,** which together rhyme *ababcdcdefefgg.* Spenser interlocked the rhymes of his quatrains: *ababbcbccdcd.* Gerard Manley Hopkins and others varied the sonnet form.

SPENSERIAN STANZA: A nine-line stanza, comprising eight lines of iambic pentameter and a final **Alexandrine,** and rhyming *ababbcbcc.* Invented by Edmund Spenser for his *Faerie Queene;* used also by Keats in *The Eve of St. Agnes* (p. 309).

SPONDEE: A foot of two accented syllables; bearing the name of the **quantitative** foot of two long syllables. (See Commentary, "Quantitative Meter.") Milton introduced a spondee into the fourth foot of the following line to suggest a clot of density in primordial chaos:

O'er bóg | or steep, | through strait, | rough, dense, | or rare, . . .

SPRUNG RHYTHM: A metrical system named and discussed by Gerard Manley Hopkins, and in part exemplified by his poetry, in which a foot consists of an accented syllable followed by a varying number of unaccented syllables, but in which all feet take up the same time interval.

STANZA: A group of lines conformed to a regular and typical scheme, usually of both meter and rhyme. It is the unit of larger poetic structures. Examples: *ottava rima,* the Spenserian stanza.

STROPHE: A **stanza** or, in verse not regularly stanzaic, a section of a poem accomplishing a clearly defined metrical movement. In Greek choral recitation, it is the first of two metrically identical divisions. See ode.

TERCET: A three-line stanza (or division of a stanza) in which all lines rhyme either with each other or with the lines of an adjoining tercet. **Sestets** rhyming *cdecde* contain two tercets.

TERZA RIMA: A three-line stanza concatenated with adjoining stanzas according to the formula *aba, bcb, cdc,* and so forth. The stanza of Dante's *Divine Comedy,* it was employed by Shelley in his *Ode to the West Wind* p. 288).

TETRAMETER: A verse line of four feet.

TRIMETER: A verse line of three feet.

TROCHEE: A metrical foot made up of an accented syllable followed by an unaccented. See Commentary.

VERSE: Metrical composition, or poetry in its metrical aspect; sometimes implying that the other functions of poetry are absent. More broadly, a line of poetry, with implicit reference to its meter. In popular hymnody, and erroneously in **prosody,** it is used as a synonym for **stanza.**

Index

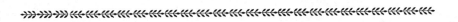

Index